TOURISM
Principles and Practice

Second Edition

CHRIS COOPER, JOHN FLETCHER,
DAVID GILBERT AND STEPHEN WANHILL
EDITED BY REBECCA SHEPHERD

LONGMAN

Addison Wesley Longman Limited
Edinburgh Gate
Harlow, Essex CM20 2JE, England
and Associated Companies throughout the world.

Published in the United States of America
by Addison Wesley Longman Publishing, New York

First published 1993
Reprinted 1993, 1995, 1996
Second Edition 1998

ISBN 0 582 31273-6

British Library Cataloguing-in-Publication Data

A catalogue record for this book is
available from the British Library.

Set by 35 in 9.5/12pt Garamond
Produced by Addison Wesley Longman Singapore (Pte) Ltd.,
Printed in Singapore

TOURISM
Principles and Practice

Contents

PART THREE *The tourism industry* 221

PART FOUR *Marketing for tourism*   *339*

PART FIVE *The future of tourism*   417

PART SIX *Major Case Studies*   465

List of Figures

List of Tables

List of Case Studies

List of Boxes

About the authors and contributors

Authors

Professor Chris Cooper received his doctorate from University College London on the geography of tourism on small islands. Since then he has worked in marketing planning and research for both tour operator and retail companies. He worked at the University of Surrey in the tourism group before helping to establish the International Centre for Tourism and Hospitality Research at Bournemouth University where he is Director of Research.

He has been instrumental in shaping a range of tourism publications. For example, he conceived, launched and edited *Progress in Tourism Recreation and Hospitality Management* which has become a quarterly, fully refereed international journal – *Progress in Tourism and Hospitality Research*. In addition, Chris Cooper has co-written *The Geography of Travel and Tourism* and a number of other books and journal papers in the field. He works closely with the World Tourism Organization and has worked in many countries.

Professor John Fletcher is Professor of Tourism and Head of the International Centre of Tourism and Hospitality Research at Bournemouth University. His academic career started at the University College of North Wales, Bangor, where he received his doctorate in economics and was Director of the Institute of Economic Research. He was leader of the tourism group at the University of Surrey before moving to Bournemouth University in 1996 to head the International Centre.

His research experience includes the development of interactive software for tourism impact and forecasting modes. He has undertaken numerous tourism impact and development studies in the Caribbean, the South Pacific, the Indian Ocean and throughout Europe. He works closely with the World Tourism Organization and is on the editorial board of leading academic journals.

Dr David Gilbert is Reader in Tourism Marketing and Course Tutor for the Diploma/MSc course in Tourism Marketing at the University of Surrey. Alongside his academic duties, he has worked with several organisations and consultancies on project work. He also has over eight years operational experience in tourism for the private sector, having worked as Product Manager and as Marketing Manager for Rank Leisure. He has organised and run courses in tourism and hospitality marketing in many overseas countries. He also set up the Thomas Cook Research Centre at the University of Surrey.

Professor Stephen Wanhill is Travelbag Professor of Tourism at the School of Service Industries, Bournemouth University and Head of Tourism Research at the Research Centre of Bornholm, Denmark, where he is involved in a multi-annual programme, funded by the Danish Social Science Foundation, researching tourism in the peripheral areas of Europe. His experience as a practitioner and as an academic in the field of tourism spans more than 25 years and he has previously held professorial posts at the University of Surrey and the University of Wales, Cardiff. He has been a parliamentary Specialist Adviser on tourism to the UK House of Commons and a Board Member of the Wales Tourist Board. His research interests lie in the area of tourism development and he has published on development policy, tourism projects, investment incentives and the impact of tourism. He is editor of *Tourism Economics* and has collaborated with Chris Cooper to edit *Tourism Development: Environmental and Community Issues.*

Editor

Rebecca Shepherd worked as a marketing consultant in the UK and Australia before joining the Department of Management Studies for Tourism and Hospitality at the University of Surrey as Course Development Officer for Tourism and Hospitality Education in 1990. Subsequently, she became Lecturer in Tourism at the University of Surrey. She is currently working as an independent researcher.

Contributors

Professor Tom Baum is Professor of International Hospitality Management in the Scottish Hotel School, University of Strathclyde where he is also Director of Research. Formerly, Professor Baum was Professor of International Hotel and Tourism Management at the University of Buckingham where he founded the undergraduate and postgraduate programmes in hospitality and tourism.

Professor Baum's research interests are centred in human resource management in tourism and hospitality and small island/peripheral tourism and he has published extensively in these areas.

Dr Dimitrios Buhalis is Senior Lecturer in Tourism at the Department of Tourism, University of Westminster and Adjunct Professor at the Institut de Management Hotelier International (Cornell University-Ecole Superieure des Sciences Economiques et Commerciales ESSEC) in Paris. He graduated in Business Administration from the University of the Aegean in Greece and gained his MSc and PhD in Tourism Management and Marketing from the University of Surrey.

Dr Buhalis is a consultant for the World Tourism Organization, Assistant Editor for *Progress in Tourism and Hospitality Research* and a Chairman of the Association of Tourism Teachers and Trainers and Executive Committee member of the International Federation of Information Technology and Tourism. He was the Scientific part Chairman for the ENTER '98 and '99 conferences on IT and Tourism.

John Latham is Professor of Business Analysis and Dean at Southampton Business School, having previously worked at the University of Surrey and Bournemouth University. His research interests are in the areas of the analysis of tourism demand, tourism statistics and market research methodology.

John Westlake is Director of Continuing Education and Development at the International Centre for Tourism and Hospitality Research, Bournemouth University. He is a planner and geographer by background and previously worked in central govenment in a research capacity. He has acted as consultant on training activities in many countries.

Preface

Welcome to the 2nd edition of *Tourism: Principles and Practice*. As an extended and updated version of the 1st edition which was published by Pitman in 1993, we hope you will find the revisions and additions that we have incorporated informative and stimulating.

This book retains many of the key philosophies that made the 1st edition so successful and this latest edition has also been written to provide the basic framework for higher level tourism courses. It offers readers the fundamental and underlying principles with which to approach the study of tourism, contributing a complete framework that effectively integrates theory and practice.

While the basic format of this book resembles the presentation of the 1st edition, we have refined and improved all subject areas, added substantial additional material in several new chapters and conceived some important features to enhance this edition further. Specifically, we have aimed to make the book more comprehensive in its coverage and more reader-orientated in its approach by introducing a host of innovations to differentiate it from other textbooks. The most notable new features for the 2nd edition of *Tourism: Principles and Practice* are:

- The introduction of **Chapter Learning Objectives** at the beginning of every chapter to orientate the reader and to focus his or her mind in respect of the key concepts that underpin each chapter in the book.

- The inclusion of **Chapter Discussion Questions** at the end of each chapter which relate back to the Chapter Learning Objectives identified at the outset. These are designed to draw out key contemporary issues and to encourage the reader to apply the theoretical content of the chapter to industry practice.

- The identification of key texts and articles in **Recommended Further Reading** which provide an opportunity for guided specialised investigation where core concepts are reviewed in more detail and from which the user may derive a deeper understanding.

- The incorporation of six complete and comprehensive **Major Case Studies**, including discussion points, where we have taken advantage of our experience in the field of research to provide real-life case studies and problems pertinent to the content of this book. In addition, the case studies will provide students and teachers alike with a framework for the discussion of important issues and an appropriate perspective from which solutions may be drawn. The case studies have been selected to demonstrate the complexity of tourism by simultaneously integrating two or more key areas of study, offering readers the opportunity to apply theoretical knowledge to a practical situation.

- The provision of new and updated **mini-cases** which have been designed to illustrate key points and give readers a framework of application. The mini-cases reflect the issues that are facing all subsectors of the tourism industry as we approach the next millennium.

- The commissioning of four new chapters which have been included in response to feedback from the 1st edition. In order to provide users of this textbook with an exhaustive overview of all aspects of tourism, these new chapters are headed:
  - The socio-cultural impact of tourism;
  - The environmental impact of tourism;
  - Tourism and development planning; and
  - Information technology.

In addition, we have also reviewed, revised and extensively updated all existing chapters which have been retained from the 1st edition. This has been undertaken to ensure the 2nd edition continues to meet fully the needs of those studying and teaching tourism and continues to reflect the changing face of an industry and field of study which is dynamic and exciting.

Textbook structure

Leiper's model of the tourism system, presented in the chapter entitled 'An introduction to tourism', provides the basic format for the book which has been structured around five key headings:

- Part 1   Tourism demand;
- Part 2   The tourism destination;
- Part 3   The tourism industry;
- Part 4   Marketing for tourism; and
- Part 5   The future of tourism.

An additional section, Part 6, has also been added to accommodate the Major Case Studies.

Part 1

Part 1 of the book examines all aspects of tourism demand in detail. We review the various concepts of demand, examine models of consumer behaviour and the decision-making process as it relates to tourism, look at factors that will influence demand for tourism at individual and global levels and analyse the techniques and approaches used to analyse demand.

Part 2

Part 2 focuses on the supply elements of the tourism system. In particular, we are concerned with the tourism destination which is, after all, the focal point of tourism demand and the point at which tourism activity is concentrated.

The impacts of tourism are also heavily concentrated at the destination and Part 2 will investigate and review both the obvious economic impacts and the more subtle environmental and socio-cultural impacts which evolve over time. Part 2 will also demonstrate the role and importance of tourism planning in minimising impacts of tourism and developing strategies to ensure sustainable evolution.

Part 3

In Part 3, we turn our attention to the tourism industry and governmental organisations that influence and support tourism demand and supply. We demonstrate the global and local policy frameworks for tourism and the role fulfilled by both the public and private sectors in respect of all aspects of tourism.

Part 4

Part 4 deals with marketing for tourism and its importance as the tourism market matures and growth rates for tourism decline. We highlight the importance of effective marketing in tourism, an industry where loyalty in the distribution chain and to individual companies is notoriously low and where, quite often, the marketing effort of companies is concentrated towards intermediaries and carriers rather than potential travellers.

Part 5

Part 5 highlights issues pertinent to the future of tourism. This section incorporates two chapters: information technology and the future of tourism. Part 5 is instrumental in consolidating the strands and themes discussed in Parts 1–4 and presenting them in a format that demonstrates the likely future development of all aspects of the tourism system. A wide range of influences are reviewed and assessed, together with an evaluation of impacts on tourism and tourists.

Part 6

Part 6 is one of the key improvements inserted for the 2nd edition. It contains six major case studies which encapsulate many of the key issues and challenges facing the tourism industry for the future. One of the primary objectives of these case studies is to tie together the various strands and elements of tourism which have been analysed in the book. In any text the subject matter has to be broken down in a structured way, but for a subject such as tourism it is important to understand how these various elements are linked; indeed tourism is very much more than the sum of its constituent parts. The case studies are therefore designed to provide a meaningful interpretation of the complex relationship between the various parts of the tourism system. In utilising Part 6, students will develop an understanding of the interactivity that characterises the tourism system and a greater appreciation of its dynamism.

Overview

The philosophy behind this book remains the same as the 1st edition: namely to provide a comprehensive text which can be used for both teaching and learning about tourism. Since the 1st edition, a large number of the authors have moved institution and set up the International Centre for Tourism and Hospitality Research at Bournemouth

University, on the south coast of England. The approach of the book is mirrored in the teaching at both Bournemouth and Surrey University where tourism specialists teach and advise students from Masters degrees to PhD level.

From her base in Miami, Rebecca Shepherd has done an excellent job in managing this wayward group of authors and in ensuring consistency throughout the text. Her diligence has ensured the book has a greater level of internal consistency than otherwise would have been the case.

As the publisher, Ian Little has been a delight to work with and, as evidenced by the format and style of the latest edition, has significantly raised the production quality of the book since the 1st edition.

Finally, we must thank the many people who have wittingly or unwittingly helped in the writing of this book, especially Mrs Cooper senior for her patient typing of the various sections and Matt Sampson for providing some of the photographs for the front cover.

Chris Cooper
John Fletcher
David Gilbert
Stephen Wanhill

Abbreviations

AA	Automobile Association
AAA	American Automobile Association
ABTA	Association of British Travel Agents
APC	Annual physical capacity
APEX	Advanced purchase excursion fare
ARC	Airlines Reporting Corporation
ASEAN	Association of South East Asian Nations
ASTA	American Society of Travel Agents
BA	British Airways
BTA	British Tourist Authority
BWCA	Boundary Waters Canoe Area
CAPI	Computer-assisted personal interviewing
CPGI	Country potential generation index
CRO	Central reservations office
CRS	Computer reservation system
CSF	Community support framework
CTO	Caribbean Tourism Organisation
CVB	Convention and visitor bureau
DICIRMS	Destination integrated computer information reservation management systems
DMO	Destination management/marketing organisation
DMS	Destination management system
EAGGF	European Agricultural Guidance and Guarantee Fund Guidance System
EAP	East Asia and the Pacific
EC	European Community
ECSC	European Coal and Steel Community
EDI	Electronic data exchange
EEA	European Economic Area

EFTA	European Free Trade Association
EIA	Environmental impact assessment
EIB	European Investment Bank
EPS model	Extended problem solving model
ERDF	European Regional Development Fund
ESF	European Social Fund
ETB	English Tourist Board
ETC	European Travel Commission
EU	European Union
FBF	Family brand performance
FFP	Frequent flyer programme
FIFG	Financial Instrument for Fisheries Guidance
FIT	Fully-inclusive tour
FTE	Full-time equivalent
GDS	Global distribution system
GDP	Gross domestic product
GNP	Gross national product
HFS	Hospitality franchise system
IATA	International Air Transport Association
ICAO	International Civil Aviation Organisation
IDD	International direct dial
ILG	International Leisure Group
IMF	International Monetary Fund
IPEX	Instant purchase fares
IPS	International passenger survey
ISIC	International Standard Industrial Classification
IT	Information technology
ITN	Internet Travel Network
LAC	Limits to acceptable change
LPS models	Limited problem-solving models
MA	Moving average
MIS	Management information system
NAFTA	North American Free Trade Association
NGO	Non-Governmental Organisation
NITB	Northern Ireland Tourist Board
NTO	National tourist office
OAS	Organization of American States
OECD	Organization for Economic Co-operation and Development
OPEC	Organisation of Petroleum Exporting Countries
PATA	Pacific Asia Travel Association
PBF	Product brand performance

PMS	Property management system
PNR	Passenger name records
PR	Public relations
PRC	Peoples' Republic of China
RBD	Recreational business district
RM	Relationship marketing
RVs	Recreational vehicles
SAS	Scandinavian Airline System
SBU	Strategic business unit
SCH	Scotland's Commended Hotels
SIC	Standard industrial classification
SICTA	Standard industrial classification of activities
SIS	Strategic information system
SIT	System of information technologies
SMART	Specific, measurable, achievable, realistic, time limits
SME	Small and medium-sized enterprise
SPC	Sustained physical capacity
SPD	Single programming document
STB	Scottish Tourist Board
STEP	Social, technological, economic and political factors
SWOT	Strengths, weaknesses, opportunities and threats
TALC	Tourist area life cycle
TAT	Tourist Authority of Thailand
TCSP	Tourism Council for the South Pacific
TDC	Tourist Development Corporation
THISCO	The Hotel Industry Switch Company
TIC	Tourist information centre
TIP	Tourist information point
TOMM	Tourism optimum management model
TOP	Thomson open-line programme
TQM	Total quality management
TGV	Train de Grande Vitesse
UN	United Nations
UNDP	United Nations Development Programme
UNEP	United Nations Environment Programme
UNSTAT	United Nations Statistical Commission
USTTA	United States Travel and Tourism Association
UKTS	United Kingdom Tourism Survey
VALS	Values and lifestyles
VFR	Visiting friends and relatives
VOC	Visitor orientation centre
VR	Virtual reality
WestLB	Westdeutsche Landesbank
WTB	Wales Tourist Board

WTO	World Tourism Organization
WTTC	World Travel and Tourism Council
WWW	World Wide Web
YHA	Youth Hostel Association
YM/WCA	Young Men's/Women's Christian Association

An introduction
to tourism

Introduction

In this chapter, we introduce the concept of a tourism system and outline its role in offering a way of thinking about tourism and providing a framework of knowledge for students approaching the subject of tourism. In addition, we use this chapter to demonstrate the scale and significance of tourism.

At the same time, we outline some of the commonly held myths that surround tourism and identify some of the issues that are inherent both in the subject area and in the study of tourism. In particular, we emphasise the variety and scope of tourism as an activity and highlight the fact that all elements of the tourism system are interlinked, despite the fact that they have to be artificially isolated for teaching and learning purposes. Finally, we consider the difficulties involved in attempting to define tourism and provide some ideas as to how definitions are evolving.

Chapter learning objectives

In this chapter, we focus on the terminology and definitions that underpin the study of tourism to provide the reader with:

- a basic understanding of the 'real' nature of tourism activity and a knowledge of the myths that surround tourism today;

- a comprehension of the problems associated with the academic and practical study of tourism;

- an appreciation of the individual elements which, when combined, comprise the tourism system; and

- a knowledge of basic supply-side and demand-side definitions of tourism and the associated difficulties and issues.

Tourism myths and realities

In a world of change, one constant in the last quarter of the twentieth century has been the sustained growth of tourism both as an activity and an industry. By the mid-1990s, the World Travel and Tourism Council (WTTC) estimated that tourism was the world's largest industry (WTTC, 1996):

● Tourism directly and indirectly generates and supports 204 million jobs. This is equivalent to more than 10% of the world's workforce and is forecast to rise to over 11% of global manpower in the early years of the next millennium.

● Tourism is responsible for over 10% of global gross domestic product (GDP), a figure that is forecast to rise to over 11% early in the twenty-first century.

It is clear that tourism is a major force in the economy of the world, an activity of global importance and significance. This fact was acknowledged by President Clinton when he convened the White House Tourism Conference in 1995. Yet a combination of the 'youth' of the tourism industry – international mass tourism is at best only 30 years old – with the pace of growth in demand has given tourism a Cinderella-like existence. This has created a variety of issues for the sector.

Firstly, as well as demonstrating sustained growth, tourism has been remarkable in its resistance to adverse economic and political conditions. Inevitably, however, growth is slowing as the market matures and, as the nature of the tourist and his/her demands changes, the sector will need to be creative in supplying products to satisfy the 'new tourist'.

Secondly, international organisations support tourism for its contribution to world peace, the benefits of the intermingling of peoples and cultures, the economic advantages that can ensue, and the fact that tourism is a relatively 'clean' industry. But an increasingly important issue is the negative image of tourism as a despoiler of destinations, a harbinger of adverse social change and even the employment and monetary gains of tourism are seen to be illusory in many destinations. A critical issue for the successful future of tourism will be for all involved to demonstrate that the sector is responsible and worthy of acceptance as a global activity. The WTTC has been an influential lobbyist in this regard. As the representative body of the major companies in the tourism sector, it has led an active campaign to promote the need for the industry to take responsibility for its actions.

Finally, in many respects general perceptions of tourism are misplaced. Tourism is surrounded by a number of myths which have contributed unrealistically to its glamorous image. These are demonstrated in Table 1.

Table 1: Myths and realities of tourism

Myth	The majority of tourism in the world is international.
Reality	Tourism in the world is predominantly domestic (people travelling in their own country). Domestic tourism accounts for about 80% of tourist trips.
Myth	Most tourism journeys in the world are by air as tourists jet-set from country to country.
Reality	The majority of trips are by surface transport (mainly the car).
Myth	Tourism is only about leisure holidays.
Reality	Tourism includes all types of purpose of visit including business, conference and education.
Myth	Employment in tourism means substantial travel and the chance to learn languages.
Reality	Most employment in tourism is in the hospitality sector and involves little travel.

The subject of tourism

In historical terms, tourism activity is a relatively new development and only recently has it been considered worthy of serious business endeavour or academic study. However, the tourism industry is of sufficient economic importance and its impact upon economies, environments and societies is significant enough for the subject of tourism to deserve academic consideration. There is no doubt in our minds that tourism is a subject area or domain of study, but that at the moment it lacks the level of theoretical underpinning that would allow it to become a discipline. Nevertheless the popularity of tourism as a subject, and the recognition of its importance by governments, has accelerated the study of tourism. Tourism as a subject is showing signs of early maturity with a growing academic community, increasing numbers of both journals and textbooks which are becoming specialised rather than all-embracing, and a number of professional societies both internationally and within individual countries. All of these indicators point to the increasing professionalism of the tourism sector.

As an area of study, tourism is still relatively young and this creates a range of issues for all of us involved in teaching, researching and studying the subject:

- The subject area itself is bedeviled by conceptual weakness and fuzziness. We are therefore faced with many questions that would be taken as common ground in other subjects (such as finding a way through the maze of terminology – green, alternative, responsible, sustainable, eco!). There is even no real agreement over definitions of tourism or just what constitutes the tourism industry – the WTTC, for example, tells us that tourism is the largest industry in the world, but this statement is open to question simply because we have no common agreement as to what comprises the tourism sector. All of these issues result in a basic lack of rigour and focus.

- The subject encompasses a number of diverse industrial sectors and academic subjects, raising the question for those studying tourism as to whether or not tourism is, in fact, too diverse and chaotic to merit separate consideration as a subject or economic sector. We would argue, of course, that it should warrant a subject and sector in its own right, but that there is a need for a disciplined approach to help alleviate potential sources of confusion for students. It is therefore important in this respect to provide a framework within which to locate these subject approaches and industries.

- As if these problems were not sufficient, tourism also suffers from a particularly weak set of data sources – in terms of both comparability and quality.

- Traditional approaches have tended to operationalise and reduce tourism to a set of activities or economic transactions while more recent authors have been critical of this 'reductionism', stressing instead post-modern frameworks which analyse the significance and meaning of tourism to individuals.

- Finally, tourism does suffer from an image problem in academic circles. Indeed, many are attracted to it as an exciting, vibrant subject and an applied area of economic activity – which we believe that it is. But to be successful, tourism demands very high standards of professionalism, knowledge and application from everyone involved. This is sometimes felt to be in contrast to the image of jet-setting, palm-fringed beaches and a leisure activity.

A tourism system

In response to the issues identified above, we feel that is important at the outset to provide an organising framework for the study of tourism. There are many ways to do this. Individual disciplines, for example, view the activity of tourism as an application of their own ideas and concepts, and an approach from geography, economics or whatever could be adopted. An alternative is to take a multidisciplinary, or even an interdisciplinary, approach. Figure 1 shows one such attempt to integrate a variety of subjects and disciplines and to focus upon tourism.

However, in a book of this nature it is impossible to cover the complete range of approaches to tourism. Instead, as an organising framework, we have adopted the model suggested by Leiper in 1979 and updated in 1990 (Figure 2). As Figure 2 shows, Leiper's

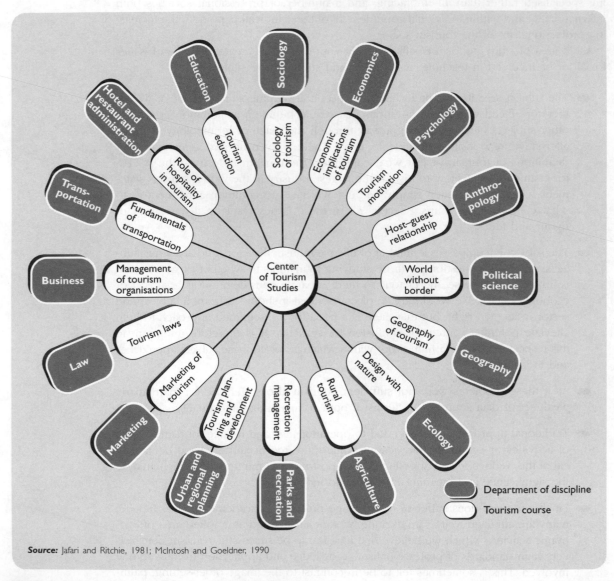

Source: Jafari and Ritchie, 1981; McIntosh and Goeldner, 1990

Figure 1: Study of tourism and choice of discipline and approach

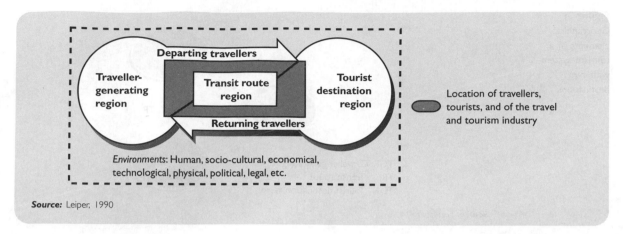

Source: Leiper, 1990

Figure 2: Basic tourism system

model neatly takes into account many of the issues identified above by considering the activity of tourists, allowing industry sectors to be located and providing the geographical element which is inherent to all travel.

There are three basic elements of Leiper's model:

1. **Tourists**. The tourist is the actor in this system. Tourism, after all, is a very human experience, enjoyed, anticipated and remembered by many as some of the most important times of their lives. Defining the tourist and attempting to produce classifications of tourists form the latter section of this chapter.

2. **Geographical elements**. Leiper outlines three geographical elements in his model:
   (a) Traveller-generating region;
   (b) Tourist destination region; and
   (c) Transit route region.

   The traveller-generating region represents the generating market for tourism and, in a sense, provides the 'push' to stimulate and motivate travel. It is from here that the tourist searches for information, makes the booking and departs.

   In many respects, the tourist destination region represents the 'sharp end' of tourism. At the destination, the full impact of tourism is felt and planning and management strategies are implemented. The destination too is the *raison d'etre* for tourism, with a range of special places distinguished from the everyday by their cultural, historic or natural significance (Rojek and Urry, 1997). The 'pull' to visit destinations energises the whole tourism system and creates demand for travel in the generating region. It is therefore at the destination: 'where the most noticeable and dramatic consequences of the system occur' (Leiper, 1990, p. 23).

   The transit route region does not simply represent the short period of travel to reach the destination, but also includes the intermediate places which may be visited *en route*: 'There is always an interval in a trip when the traveller feels they have left their home region but have not yet arrived . . . [where] they choose to visit' (Leiper, 1990, p. 22).

3. **Tourism Industry**. The third element of Leiper's model is the tourism industry, which we can think of as the range of businesses and organisations involved in delivering the tourism product. The model allows the location of the various industrial sectors to be identified. For example, travel agents and tour operators are mostly found in the traveller-generating region, attractions and the hospitality industry are

Figure 3:
Geographical
elements in a
tourism system
with two
destinations

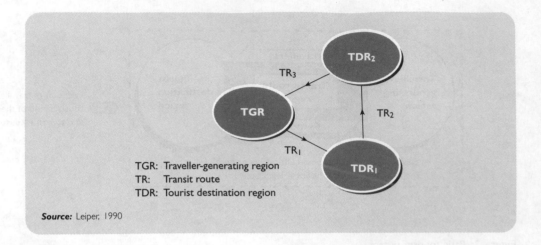

TGR: Traveller-generating region
TR: Transit route
TDR: Tourist destination region

Source: Leiper, 1990

found in the destination region, and the transport sector is largely represented in the transit route region.

Each of the elements of Leiper's tourism system interacts, not only to deliver the tourism product, but also in terms of transactions and impacts, and of course, the differing contexts within which tourism occurs (Figure 3). The fact that tourism is also an industry of contrasts is illustrated by examining two major elements of Leiper's model. Demand for tourism in the generating region is inherently volatile, seasonal and irrational. Yet this demand is satisfied by a destination region where supply is fragmented, and inflexible – surely a possible recipe for the financial instability of tourism!

The major advantages of Leiper's model are its general applicability and simplicity which provide a useful 'way of thinking' about tourism. Indeed, each of the alternative models that we have considered tend to reveal Leiper's basic elements when they are dissected. There are also other advantages of this approach:

● It has the ability to incorporate interdisciplinary approaches to tourism because it is not rooted in any particular subject or discipline but instead provides a framework within which disciplinary approaches can be located.

● It is possible to use the model at any scale or level of generalisation – from a local resort to the international industry.

● The model is infinitely flexible and will allow the incorporation of different forms of tourism, while at the same time demonstrating their common elements. For example heritage or eco-tourism can be analysed using the model (see Case Study 1). Here, we can see that say, eco-tourism does not require a completely new approach, but simply an analysis of each of the particular characteristics of each of the elements of the eco-tourism system.

● Finally, the model demonstrates the highly important principle of tourism studies that all the elements of tourism are related and interact – in essence we are studying a system of customers and suppliers who demand and supply the tourism product and services. Naturally, in any textbook or course, the elements of tourism have to be separated and examined individually, but in reality all are linked and the realisation of their interrelationships provides a true understanding of tourism.

Case Study 1 Characteristics of elements of the eco-tourism system

Generating region

Demand for eco-tourism:

- is purposeful;
- is poorly documented;
- desires first-hand experience/contact with nature/culture;
- has the motive to study, admire and/or enjoy nature/culture;
- is tempered by the need to consume tourism responsibly;
- can be segmented in many ways including by level of commitment, level of physical effort, motives;
- comes from those who are more likely to be well-educated, have a higher income and be slightly older than the average tourist.

Destination region

Destinations for eco-tourism:

- are relatively natural areas which are undisturbed and/or uncontaminated;
- have attractions of scenery, flora, fauna and/or indigenous culture;
- allow eco-tourism to deliver economic and conservation benefits to the local people;
- develop eco-tourism with a view to conserving/enhancing/maintaining the natural/cultural system;
- apply integrated planning and management techniques;
- apply environmental impact and auditing procedures to all elements of the tourism destination (such as accommodation, facilities);
- encourage local ownership of facilities.

Transit zone

Transport for eco-tourism

- should be of low impact to the environment in terms of noise, emissions, congestion, fuel consumption and waste;
- should monitor emissions, environmental impact, etc.;
- should promote the conservation ethic;
- should be used as a management tool;
- should encourage use of public transport;
- should encourage the use of locally owned transport companies.

Definitions of tourism

We can see from Leiper's model that tourism can be thought of as a whole range of individuals, businesses, organisations and places which combine in some way to deliver a travel experience. Tourism is a multidimensional, multifaceted activity, which touches many lives and many different economic activities. Not surprisingly tourism has therefore proved difficult to define – the word 'tourist' first appeared in the English language in the early 1800s, yet almost two centuries later we still cannot agree on a definition. In some senses, this is a reflection of the complexity of tourism, but it is also indicative of its immaturity as a field of study. It is difficult to find an underpinning coherence of approach in defining tourism, aside from the need to characterise the 'otherness' of tourism from similar activities such as migration. Instead, definitions have been created to cater for particular needs and situations. Yet, it is vital to attempt definitions of tourism, not only to provide a sense of credibility and ownership for those involved, but also for the practical considerations of both measurement and legislation.

Definitions of tourism can be thought of as either:

- demand-side definitions; or
- supply-side definitions.

Tourism definitions are unusual in that they have been driven more by demand-side than supply-side considerations. Some writers find this surprising: 'Defining tourism in terms of the motivations or other characteristics of travellers would be like trying to define the health-care professions by describing a sick person' (Smith, 1989, p. 33). The 1990s have seen considerable progress in the development and consensus of definitions. This was stimulated by the World Tourism Organization's (WTO) 1991 International Conference on Travel and Tourism Statistics – a conference called to tidy up definitions, terminology and measurement issues. The recommendations of this conference were adopted by the United Nations Statistical Commission (UNSTAT) and published as 'Recommendations on Tourism Statistics' (WTO and UNSTAT, 1994).

Demand-side definitions of tourism

Demand-side definitions have evolved by firstly attempting to encapsulate the idea of tourism into 'conceptual' definitions and secondly through the development of 'technical' definitions for measurement and legal purposes.

From a conceptual point of view, we can think of tourism as: 'The activities of persons travelling to and staying in places outside their usual environment for not more than one consecutive year for leisure, business and other purposes' (WTO and UNSTAT, 1994). While this is not a strict technical definition, it does convey the essential nature of tourism, i.e.:

- Tourism arises out of a movement of people to, and their stay in, various places, or destinations.
- There are two elements in tourism – the journey to the destination and the stay (including activities) at the destination.
- The journey and stay take place outside the usual environment or normal place of residence and work so that tourism gives rise to activities that are distinct from the resident and working populations of the places through which they travel and stay.

- The movement to destinations is temporary and short term in character – the intention is to return within a few days, weeks or months.

- Destinations are visited for purposes other than taking up permanent residence or employment in the places visited.

From a 'technical' point of view, attempts to define tourism have been led by the need to isolate tourism trips from other forms of travel for statistical purposes. These 'technical' definitions demand that an activity has to pass certain 'tests' before it counts as tourism. Such tests include the following:

- Minimum length of stay – one night (visitors who do not stay overnight are termed same day visitors or excursionists).

- Maximum length of stay – one year.

- Strict purpose of visit categories.

- A distance consideration is sometimes included on the grounds of delineating the term 'usual environment' – the WTO recommendation is 160 kilometres.

Supply-side definitions of tourism

As with demand-side definitions there are two basic approaches to defining the tourism sector – the conceptual, or descriptive, and the technical. From a conceptual point of view, Leiper suggests: 'The tourist industry consists of all those firms, organisations and facilities which are intended to serve the specific needs and wants of tourists' (1979, p. 400).

A major problem concerning 'technical' supply-side definitions is the fact that there is a spectrum of tourism businesses, from those who are wholly serving tourists to those who also serve local residents and other markets. One approach to the problem is to classify businesses into two types:

- Tier 1: businesses that would not be able to survive without tourism.

- Tier 2: businesses that could survive without tourism, but in a diminished form (Figure 4).

This approach is consistent with other industrial sectors, and allows the size of the tourism industry to be gauged using standard industrial classifications (SICs) – an important development as there is no SIC for tourism (Smith, 1989). The WTO has taken this further by developing a Standard International Classification of Tourism Activities (SICTA). The SICTA also adopts the idea of part involvement with tourism or total dedication to tourism (see Table 2).

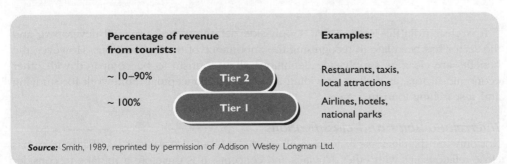

Percentage of revenue from tourists:

Examples:

~ 10–90%   Tier 2   Restaurants, taxis, local attractions

~ 100%   Tier 1   Airlines, hotels, national parks

Source: Smith, 1989, reprinted by permission of Addison Wesley Longman Ltd.

Figure 4: Supply-side definition of the tourism industry

Table 2: WTO supply-side definition of tourism (International Standard Industrial Classification, ISIC)

ISIC divisions	Business activity[a]	Example
Construction	T	Hotels, recreational facilities, transport facilities, resort residence.
Wholesale and retail	P	Motor vehicles sales, sales of motor vehicle fuels, retail food sales, retail sales of textiles.
	T	Retail sales of travel accessories, souvenir sales, etc.
Hotels and restaurants	P	Fast food restaurants, food.
	T	Hotels, camping sites.
Transport, storage and communications	P	Transport via railways, chauffeured vehicles, inland water transport.
	T	Interurban rail, airlines, special rail tour service, long-distance bus services, cruise ships.
Financial intermediation	P	Exchange of currencies, life insurance, credit cards.
	T	Travel insurance.
Real estate, renting and business activities	P	Buying or selling of leased property, letting or owning of leased property.
	T	Rental of ski equipment, letting of owned tourism property.
Public administration	P	Translation services, customs administration, fishing regulation, foreign affairs, border guards.
	T	Tourism administration, information bureaux, visa issuance, regulation of private transport.
Education	P	Adult education, driving schools, flying schools, boating instruction.
	T	Hotel schools, tourism education programmes, recreation and park service schools, tourist instruction.
Other community	P	Swimming, scuba instruction, flying instruction, boating instruction, motion picture entertainment.
	T	Visitor bureaux, travel clubs, travel unions.
Extra-territorial organisations	P	OECD, World Bank, IMF, ASEAN.
	T	International tourism bodies.

[a] P = part involvement with tourism; T = totally dedicated to tourism.
Source: WTO (1994).

It is clear from this section that supply-side definitions are less well developed, and the sector has been late in recognising the importance of these definitions. However, the benefits are clear, as supply-side definitions allow tourism to be compared with other economic sectors, as well as providing an important conceptual framework for studying and researching tourism.

Interrelationships and classifications

Not only are the elements of tourism all interlinked, but also we can see that tourism has close relationships with other activities and concepts. It is therefore a mistake to consider

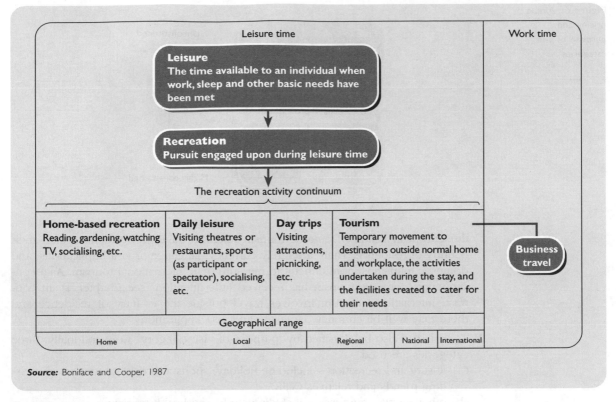

Source: Boniface and Cooper, 1987

Figure 5: Leisure, recreation and tourism

tourism in isolation from these other related activities. For example, most tourism through-out the world is a leisure activity and it is important to locate tourism in the spectrum of leisure activities.

Although the Latin translation of leisure literally means 'to be free', defining leisure is, if anything, more problematic than defining tourism. In essence, leisure can be thought of as a combined measure of time and attitude of mind to create periods of time when other obligations are at a minimum. Recreation can be thought of as the pursuits engaged in during leisure time and an activity spectrum can be identified with, at one end of the scale, recreation around the home, through to tourism where an overnight stay is involved (Figure 5).

Although same-day visits or excursions are a common recreational activity, for tourism to occur, leisure time has to be blocked together to allow a stay away from home. Traditionally, these blocks of leisure time were taken as paid holiday entitlement, though innovations such as flexi-time and three day weekends have also facilitated tourism.

Tourists

While all-embracing definitions of tourism and a tourist are desirable, in practice tourists represent a heterogeneous, not a homogeneous, group with different personalities, demo-graphics and experiences. We can classify tourists in two basic ways which relate to the nature of their trip:

1. A basic distinction can be made between domestic and international tourists, although this distinction is blurring in many parts of the world (for example, in

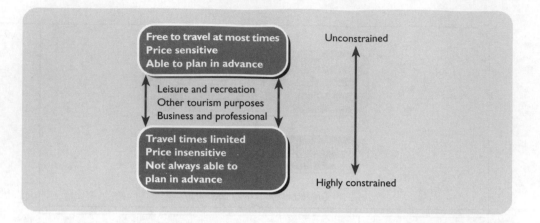

Figure 6: Airline pricing and purpose of visit categories

the European Union). Domestic tourism refers to travel by residents within their country of residence. There are rarely currency, language or visa implications, and domestic tourism is more difficult to measure than international tourism. As a consequence, domestic tourism has received little attention (see Chapter 4). In contrast, international tourism involves travel outside the country of residence and there may well be currency, language and visa implications.

2. Tourists can also be classified by 'purpose of visit category'. Conventionally, three categories are used:
   (a) leisure and recreation – including holiday, sports and cultural tourism and visiting friends and relatives (VFR);
   (b) other tourism purposes – including study and health tourism;
   (c) business and professional – including meetings, conferences, missions, incentive and business tourism.

Not only are these categories used for statistical purposes, they are also useful for the marketing of tourism. Consider, for example, Figure 6 where we demonstrate the flexibility of travel for each of the categories from the point of view of airline fare pricing and validity.

There are many other ways to classify tourists (see for example Table 3). These range from their lifestyles and personalities, to their perception of risk and familiarity and postmodern interpretations of consumers and commodities. However, one approach with increasing relevance to contemporary tourism is to classify tourists according to their level and type of interaction with the destination. Classifications of tourists that adopt this approach commonly place mass tourism at one extreme and some form of alternative, small-scale tourism at the other with a variety of classes in between. It is then argued that mass tourism has a major impact upon the destination because of the sheer scale of the industry and the nature of the consumer. On the other hand, small-scale, alternative types of tourism are said to have a much reduced impact upon the destination, not only because of the type of consumer involved but also because they will shun the travel trade and stay in local pensions or with families. In this case, it is argued, the impact of tourism is less disruptive than for mass tourism. Unfortunately:

some commentators have oversimplified the complex relationship between the consumption and development of tourism resources. This is particularly true of the so-called 'alternative' tourism movement which is lauded by some as a solution to the ills of mass tourism. Indeed, the tenor of much of the writing

Table 3: Suggested socio-economic characteristics for tourism analysis

Levels of measurement

Socio-economic variable

1. Age	Collect by single years. It may be convenient to summarise by age cohorts.
2. Sex	Male/female. Age–sex cohorts may also be useful.
3. Education	Given the diversity of educational systems in North America, a basic four-part classification may be most useful: elementary, secondary, post-secondary non-university and university. It may be useful in other circumstances to distinguish between completion of secondary or post-secondary programmes and partial work (drop-out before completion).
4. Occupational status	Categories can include employed full-time, employed part-time, retired (some reference to former occupation may be desired), homemaker, student, unemployed. If employed, refer the respondent to the next question, 'occupation'.
5. Occupation	This is best determined through an open-ended question. Responses can be summarized according to the *Occupation Classification Manual* or other comparable national statistical coding system such as the *Canadian Classification and Dictionary of Occupations*. These codes refer to the type of industry in which the traveller is employed.
6. Annual income	This is an especially sensitive subject; some of the concern over reporting income can be reduced by using income categories. The specific categories should be based on those used in the most recent national census. Household income is often the most relevant measure of income, although the respondent's income may be useful in special circumstances.

7. Family composition	This can be an especially important variable if the purpose of study includes some analysis of the effect of travel party composition on travel behaviour. One possible classification is:
	Single individual living alone
	Husband–wife family
	   No children under 18 years
	   No children at home or no children at all
	   Adult children or other adult relatives living at home
	   With children under 18 years
	   With no other adult relatives
	   With other relatives
	Single-parent families
	   Male head
	   Female head
	All other families

8. Party composition	This is closely related to the previous variable for many travelling parties. Levels include:
	   One person alone
	   One family with children
	   Two families with children
	   Organised group
	   One couple
	   Two or more couples
	   Group of friends (unorganised group)
	   Other

Table 3 (cont.)

	Levels of measurement

Trip variable

1. Season or trip period

Calendar quarters:
  January to March
  April to June
  July to September
  October to December
If the trip overlaps two or more quarters, the following convention is often used: for household surveys, use the quarter in which the trip ends; for exits or re-entry surveys, use the date of the survey.
It is sometimes desirable to distinguish weekend trips from other trips.

2. Trip duration

Both days and nights are used as the unit of measurement. The number of nights is usually one less than the number of days; a three-day weekend lasts 'two nights'. The actual number of days or nights up to one week is often collected. Periods longer than one week are often measured as ranges, e.g. 8–15 days (or 7–13 nights).

3. Trip distance

This should be based, in part, on the threshold distance required for definition of a trip. Narrow ranges for lowest levels are desirable to permit aggregating or exclusion of data so that comparisons can be made between surveys using different distance thresholds. A possible classification would be:
  25–49 miles
  50–99 miles
  100–499 miles
  500–999 miles
1000–1499 miles
More than 1500 miles (2400 km)
Metric conversion is usually necessary for international comparisons; however, international travel is normally not measured by distance.

4. Purpose of trip

Very simple classifications are used, such as business versus pleasure. This dichotomy is normally inadequate for analytical purposes and is too simplistic to represent the purposes of many trips. More precise classifications would include:
  Conventions or other business meetings
  Buying, selling, installation, or other business
  Recreation/vacation
  Touring/sightseeing
  Attending cultural/sporting events
  Participating in cultural/sporting events
  Visiting friends or relatives
  Other family or personal matters
  Shopping
  Study tour
  Health/rest
  Many trips involve more than one purpose, so it may be useful to specify 'primary' purpose.

5. Mode of transportation

Private automobile
Rental automobile
Bus/motor coach

Table 3 (cont.)

Levels of measurement
Train
Scheduled airline
Chartered airline
Private aeroplane
Boat/ship (additional categories for ferries, cruise ships, private boats may be added as necessary)
Some trips involve multiple modes, such as a combination of scheduled airline and rental car. These combinations may be specified or a primary mode may be requested.

	Levels of measurement
6. Expenditures	Transportation (broken down by mode, if desired)
	Accommodation (including camping fees, but not park entrance fees)
	Food and beverages (restaurant meals may be separated from food purchased at a store)
	Convention or registration fees
	Admission fees and other entertainment, including park admissions, licence fees for hunting and fishing
	Souvenirs
	Other purchase
7. Type of accommodation	Hotels and inns
	Motels and motor inns
	Resorts
	Campgrounds
	Hostels
	Commercial cottages
	Institutional camps
	Private cottages
	Bed and breakfast/tourist home
	Homes of friends or relatives
	Other
	Additional classifications could be based on size of accommodation, price, public versus private ownership, function (e.g. fishing camp, ski resort), type of location, e.g. airport strip; downtown), availability of liquor, and so on.

Source: Tourism Research Planning Committee of the Federal–Provincial Conference on Tourism, 1975; Smith (1989).

about alternative tourism is that any alternative tourism scheme is good whilst all mass tourism is bad. There is, of course, a case for alternative tourism, but only as another form of tourism in the spectrum. It can never be an alternative to mass tourism, nor can it solve all the problems of tourism. (Archer and Cooper, 1994)

These issues, and the fallacy of lauding 'alternative' tourism as a literal alternative to mass tourism, come into clear focus when examined against the frameworks of analysis developed in this book. For example, only by matching appropriate types of visitor to particular types of destination will truly sustainable development be achieved.

Conclusion

Mass tourism, as an activity, remains relatively youthful and while it has experienced unprecedented growth rates in the past three decades, the study of tourism inevitably lacks the maturity of other subject areas and disciplines. This lack of maturity is manifested in many ways, not least the lack of agreement as to what actually constitutes tourism activity on both the demand- and supply-sides. Nevertheless, the economic importance of tourism has guaranteed increased governmental and international attention and accompanying this has been a growing recognition of the significance and importance of tourism and the need to be able to define and measure all aspects of it.

Thus, this introduction provides the basic underpinning framework for the remainder of this book, offering contemporary views on important tourism-related definitions and acquainting the reader with the fundamentals of the dynamics of the tourism system.

Chapter discussion questions

1. Why is it both necessary and artificial to divide up the tourism system into individual elements?

2. Why is tourism so difficult to define and what are the implications of these difficulties for the measurement of tourism?

3. How do the concepts of leisure, recreation and tourism relate to each other?

4. Why is it important to study tourism?

Recommended further reading

- Gilbert, D. C. (1990) 'Conceptual issues in the meaning of tourism', pp. 4–27 in *Progress in Tourism, Recreation and Hospitality Management*, Vol. 1, Cooper, C., Belhaven, London.
- Leiper, N. (1990) *Tourism Systems*, Massey University Department of Management Systems Occasional Paper 2, Auckland, New Zealand.
- Smith, S. L. J. (1989) *Tourism Analysis*, Longman, Harlow.
- WTO and UNSTAT (1994) *Recommendations on Tourism Statistics*, WTO, Madrid; and UN, New York.

Bibliography

- Archer, B. H. A. and Cooper, C. P. (1994) 'The positive and negative aspects of tourism', pp. 73–91 in *Global Tourism: The Next Decade*, Theobold, W. F. (ed.), Butterworth-Heinemann, Oxford.
- Boniface, B. and Cooper, C. (1987) *The Geography of Travel and Tourism*, Heinemann, London.
- Burkart, A. and Medlik, S. (1974) *Tourism Past Present and Future*, Heinemann, London.
- Butler, R. (1990) 'Alternative tourism: pious hope or Trojan horse?', *Journal of Travel Research*, (Winter) pp. 40–5.

● Cooper, C. (1989) Editorial preface in *Progress in Tourism, Recreation and Hospitality Management*, Vol. I, Belhaven, London.

● Gilbert, D. C. (1990) 'Conceptual issues in the meaning of tourism', pp. 4–27 in *Progress in Tourism, Recreation and Hospitality Management*, Vol. I, Cooper, C., Belhaven, London.

● Hvengaard, G. T. (1994) 'Eco-tourism: a status report and conceptual framework', *Journal of Tourism Studies*, **5**(2), 24–35.

● Jafari, J. and Ritchie, J. R. B. (1981) 'Towards a framework for tourism education', *Annals of Tourism Research*, **8**(1), 13–34.

● Leiper, N. (1979) 'The framework of tourism', *Annals of Tourism Research*, **6**(4), pp. 390–407.

● Leiper, N. (1990) *Tourism Systems*, Massey University Department of Management Systems Occasional Paper 2, Auckland, New Zealand.

● Mathieson, A. and Wall, G. (1982) *Tourism: Economic, Physical and Social Impacts*, Longman, London.

● McIntosh, R. W. and Goeldner, C. R. (1990) *Tourism: Principles, Practices, Philosophies*, Wiley, New York.

● McIntosh, R. W., Goeldner, C. R. and Ritchie, J. R. B. (1995) *Tourism: Principles, Practices and Philosophies*, 2nd edn, Wiley, Chichester.

● Rojek, C. and Urry, J. (1997) *Touring Cultures – Transformations of Travel Theory*, Routledge, London.

● Smith, S. L. J. (1988) 'Defining tourism: a supply side view', *Annals of Tourism Research*, **15**(2), 179–90.

● Smith, S. L. J. (1989) *Tourism Analysis: A Handbook*, Longman, Harlow.

● WTO (1991) *International Conference on Travel and Tourism Statistics*, WTO, Madrid.

● WTTC (1996) *Progress and Priorities 1996*, World Travel and Tourism Council, Brussels.

● WTO and UNSTAT (1994) *Recommendations on Tourism Statistics*, WTO, Madrid; and United Nations, New York.

Tourism demand

Introduction

While the history of tourism may be traced back many thousands of years to the Ancient Greeks and Romans, it is only relatively recently, with the advent of mass tourism, that international activity has become so prevalent in the developed world. The rapid expansion of leisure travel from the 1960s onwards continues to influence all aspects of the tourism system today.

The level of demand for tourism is predicted to reach unprecedented levels over the next two decades, providing the tourism industry and all those involved in its production and consumption with major challenges. New problems requiring new solutions are constantly arising and predicted changes in all aspects of the tourism system will inevitably influence its future direction. The tourism industry is a complex and dynamic system where the constituent elements change constantly and often unpredictably. It is with this in mind that we have approached this textbook, offering a framework for the study of tourism which is simple and yet complete.

Part 1 is concerned primarily with the analysis of demand for tourism. However, as an important prerequisite to this, the previous chapter, 'An introduction to tourism', identified and explained Leiper's model of the tourism system. This model provides the structure and framework for our textbook. In addition to dispelling some of the commonly held misconceptions that are currently associated with tourism and its study, 'An introduction to tourism' also incorporated the spectrum of definitions that are required to form the basis of analysis for subsequent sections and chapters.

Part 1 itself – which incorporates four chapters – is concerned with the aspect of Leiper's model which deals with the traveller-generating region, an area of study fundamental to the analysis of tourism.

Chapter 1 provides the basic definitions of tourism demand, demonstrating components of demand that, when combined, constitute total demand for tourism. Included here is the category of 'no demand', i.e. those individuals who may wish to travel but are unable for reasons ranging from lack of money to fear of travel.

In Chapter 1, we also introduce the concepts of demand schedules and elasticity to illustrate the relationship between tourism demand and identified variables such as price and income. From these demand schedules, we can demonstrate that tourism is, indeed, a luxury activity that is enjoyed by relatively few. This raises the issue of barriers to travel and brings to the fore the notion of 'social tourism' which is a mechanism utilised to remove barriers to travel for underprivileged groups in society.

In Chapters 2 and 3, we discuss the nature of the variables that influence the consumption of tourism. Chapter 2, entitled 'Consumer behaviour and tourism demand', reviews the decision-making process as it relates to tourism. Specifically, we concentrate on the stages through which an individual might go prior to the purchase of a tourism product and the critical role of motivation in this process. In addition, we consider the importance of family influence and destination image on travel purchasing behaviour. To complete this chapter, we review those determinants of demand, such as income, employment, education, race and gender, that may affect an individual's ability and desire to participate in tourism activity.

In Chapter 3, the focus shifts from the individual to aggregated 'Models and patterns of tourism demand'. Models of consumer behaviour in tourism such as those developed by Schmoll and Moscardo *et al.* are all considered in detail. We also evaluate those factors that, at a global level, influence the patterns of demand for tourism, such as demographic, political, economic and technological trends.

In Chapter 4, we turn our attention to the measurement of domestic and international tourism, providing a comprehensive discussion of why measurement is so critical and what is measured in respect of tourism demand. In addition, we stress the enormous difficulties that are encountered in measuring tourism demand and identify issues that are fundamental in respect of this. We conclude this chapter by reviewing the research process and evaluating the methodological approaches available to investigate tourism demand.

Overview

In respect of demand for tourism, therefore, we are able to identify a number of key issues:

- **Measurement**. The measurement of tourism demand is extremely problematic and susceptible to statistical inaccuracies as a result of the difficulties in identifying and accurately researching aspects of tourists' behaviour.

- **Concentration of demand**. Demand for tourism is heavily concentrated in the industrialised regions of the world where the determinants of demand, at both an individual and an aggregated level, encourage participation. Thus, there remains a 'no demand' category in respect of tourism demand and despite commonly held misconceptions to the contrary, this category makes up a significant percentage of the population of the developed regions, where travel is expensive, as well the developing areas of the world.

- **Tourism demand is unpredictable and volatile**. Demand for tourism is heavily influenced, at least in the short term, by external events. Thus, while the overall level of demand for tourism is resistant to influences such as war and instability, individual tourist destinations are not.

Clearly, therefore, the nature of tourism demand is difficult to identify and measure and this represents, perhaps, the most resounding conclusion pertaining to Part 1. Nevertheless, it is possible to make general conclusions about demand for tourism, its volume and its direction as long as we are aware of the statistical weaknesses.

We know, for example, that tourism demand will continue to grow and that newly industrialising areas of the world, such as East Asia and the Pacific, will become important generators and receivers of tourism although activity will continue to remain concentrated in North America and Europe. Thus, demand for tourism is dynamic and while the overall level of demand may continue to rise, albeit at a slower rate, individual destinations will inevitably be subject to the whims of changing taste and patterns of demand. This leads on to Part 2 of this book which focuses on the destination and the implications of tourism upon an area, region or locality. While demand for tourism may be defined as representing the tourist's desire to travel to new places and to escape the routine of home, i.e. the 'push' factor, it is the role of the destination to provide the 'pull' factor by offering a product to accommodate the host of motivations which may be displayed by the tourist.

Part 3 deals with all the elements of the tourism industry and investigates the processes by which tourism demand is realised. Part 4 will review the central role of marketing in tourism and the importance of communicating a destination's tourism product to its potential market(s), while Part 5 will focus on the probable trends that will shape the future of tourism.

It is important to stress that, as you read this book, you should bear in mind that distinguishing individual elements of the whole system is introducing a somewhat artificial distinction and that tourism, as an area of study, must be viewed in its entirety for an accurate and complete understanding to be realised. For ease of study, we have divided up the whole into smaller, more manageable component parts, but it is the synergistic relationship between these individual elements, as demonstrated in the Major Case Studies in Part 6, that will provide a true comprehension of tourism activity and study.

Chapter One

Concepts, definitions and indicators of tourism demand

Introduction

By introducing the concepts and definitions that underpin the study and activity of tourism, we are offering the reader a model of the tourism system as a way of thinking about tourism and providing a framework for students approaching the subject. Thus, this chapter may be used as a perspective for the remainder of the material in this book.

There are many difficulties associated with the study of tourism, not least the issue of definition. Without a consensus on what actually constitutes the activity of tourism, it would, for example, be impossible to measure tourism activity and to discuss destination-based concepts such as carrying capacity. During the course of this chapter, we review the problems and issues that are derived from attempting to define tourism demand.

Chapter learning objectives

The underlying chapter learning objective for Chapter 1 is to encourage an understanding of the basic concepts and definitions pertaining to tourism demand. By the end of this chapter, readers should:

- understand the concept of tourism demand and be able to identify the basic components of tourism demand which, when combined, constitute total demand;
- appreciate the importance of indicators of demand such as propensity to travel and be aware of the way in which these indicators may be calculated; and
- comprehend the purpose of demand schedules and be familiar enough with them to interpret the information they provide.

Overview

We can identify a number of official proclamations which affirm every individual's right to demand tourism. As far back as 1948 the United Nations (UN) stated in its Universal Declaration of Human Rights that: 'everyone has the right to rest and leisure including . . . periodic holidays with pay'. By 1980 the Manila declaration on world tourism declared the ultimate aim of tourism to be: 'the improvement of the quality of life and the creation of better living conditions for all peoples' (WTO, 1980). With this statement we can see the emphasis changing from the earlier 'right' of everyone to demand tourism, to statements of the 'quality of demand' and the 'form' of demand and/or experience. This observation is supported by declarations in the 1990s which state that if individuals demand tourism, they must take responsibility for the environment and host societies: 'tourists share responsibility for conservation of the environment and cultural heritage' (Osaka Tourism Declaration, WTO, 1994).

Yet as we approach and enter the new millennium, it is still true that only a very small percentage of the world's total population engages in international tourism and although a considerably greater number participate in domestic travel, tourism remains an unobtainable luxury for many.

Definitions of tourism demand

Definitions of demand vary according to the subject perspective of the author. For example, economists consider demand to be the schedule of the amount of any product or service that people are willing and able to buy at each specific price in a set of possible prices during a specified period of time. In contrast, psychologists view demand from the perspective of motivation and behaviour. Geographers, on the other hand, define tourist demand as: 'the total number of persons who travel, or wish to travel, to use tourist facilities and services at places away from their places of work and residence' (Mathieson and Wall, 1982).

Each approach is useful. The economic approach introduces the idea of elasticity – which describes the relationship between demand and price, or other variables. The geographer's definition implies a wide range of influences, in addition to price, as determinants of demand and includes not only those who actually participate in tourism, but also those who wish to, but for some reason do not. On the other hand, the psychologist scratches underneath the skin of the tourist to examine the interaction of personality, environment and demand for tourism.

Concepts of tourism demand

The notion that some individuals may harbour a demand for tourism but are unable to realise that demand suggests that demand for tourism consists of a number of components. We can identify three basic components that make up the total demand for tourism:

1. **Effective** or **actual demand** is the actual number of participants in tourism or those who are travelling, i.e. *de facto* tourists. This is the component of demand most commonly and easily measured and the bulk of tourism statistics refer to effective demand.

2. **Suppressed demand** is made up of that section of the population who do not travel for some reason.

Two elements of suppressed demand can be distinguished. Firstly, **potential demand** refers to those who will travel at some future date if they experience a change in their circumstances. For example, their purchasing power may increase, or they may receive more paid holiday entitlement, and they therefore have the potential to move into the effective demand category.

Deferred demand is a demand postponed because of a problem in the supply environment, such as a lack of capacity in accommodation, weather conditions or maybe terrorist activity. Again this implies that when the supply conditions are more favourable, those in the deferred demand category will convert to effective demand at some future date.

3. Finally, there will always be those who simply do not wish to travel or are unable to travel, constituting a category of **no demand**.

We can also consider other ways in which demand for tourism may be viewed. For example, **substitution of demand** refers to the case when demand for one activity (say a self-catering holiday) is substituted by another (staying in serviced accommodation). A similar concept is **redirection of demand** where the geographical location of demand is changed – say a trip to Spain is redirected to Greece because of over-booking of accommodation. Finally the opening of new tourism supply – say a resort, attraction or accommodation – will:

- redirect demand from similar facilities in the area;
- substitute demand from other facilities; and
- generate new demand.

Economists refer to the first two of these as the 'displacement effect' – in other words, demand from other facilities is displaced to the new one and no extra demand is generated. This can be a problem in tourism and is an important consideration when appraising the worth of new tourism projects.

Indicators of tourism demand

Travel propensity

One of the most useful indicators of effective demand in any particular population is **travel propensity**. This measure simply considers the penetration of tourism trips in a population. There are two forms of travel propensity:

1. **Net travel propensity** refers to the percentage of the population that takes at least one tourism trip in a given period of time. In other words it is a measure of the penetration of travel among 'individuals' in the population. The suppressed and no demand components will therefore ensure that net travel propensity never approaches 100% and a figure of 70% or 80% is likely to be the maximum for developed Western economies.

2. **Gross travel propensity** gives the total number of tourism trips taken as a percentage of the population. This is a measure of the penetration of 'trips', not individual travellers. Clearly then, as second and third holidays increase in importance, so gross travel propensity becomes more relevant. Gross travel propensity can exceed 100% and often approaches 200% in some Western European countries where those participating in tourism may take more than one trip away from home per annum.

Box 1.1 Calculation of travel propensity and travel frequency

Out of a population of 10 million inhabitants:

3.0 million inhabitants take one trip of one night or more	i.e.	$3 \times 1 = 3.0$ m trips
1.5 million inhabitants take two trips of one night or more	i.e.	$1.5 \times 2 = 3.0$ m trips
0.4 million inhabitants take three trips of one night or more	i.e.	$0.4 \times 3 = 1.2$ m trips
0.2 million inhabitants take four trips of one night or more	i.e.	$0.2 \times 4 = 0.8$ m trips
5.1 million inhabitants take at least one trip		8.0 m trips

Therefore:

$$\text{Net travel propensity} = \frac{\text{Number of population taking at least one trip}}{\text{Total population}} \times 100 = \frac{5.1}{10} \times 100 = 51\%$$

$$\text{Gross travel propensity} = \frac{\text{Number of total trips}}{\text{Total population}} \times 100 = \frac{8}{10} \times 100 = 80\%$$

$$\text{Travel frequency} = \frac{\text{Gross travel propensity}}{\text{Net travel propensity}} = \frac{80\%}{51\%} = 1.57$$

A further refinement to the above calculations is to assess the capability of a country to generate trips. This involves three stages. Firstly, the number of trips originating in the country is divided by the total number of trips taken in the world. This gives an index of the ability of each country to generate travellers. Secondly, the population of the country is divided by the total population of the world, thus ranking each country by relative importance in relation to world population. By dividing the result of the first stage by the result of the second the 'country potential generation index' (CPGI) is produced.

$$\text{CPGI} = \frac{N_e/N_w}{P_e/P_w}$$

where N_e = number of trips generated by country
N_w = number of trips generated in world
P_e = population of country
P_w = population of world

An index of 1.0 indicates an average generation capability. Countries with an index greater than unity are generating more tourists than expected by their population. Countries with an index below 1.0 generate fewer trips than average.

Source: Boniface and Cooper (1987), adapted from Burkart and Medlik (1975), pp. 53–60.

Simply dividing gross travel propensity by net will give the *travel frequency*, in other words, the average number of trips taken by those participating in tourism during the period in question (see Box 1.1).

Demand schedules

In economic terms, a demand schedule refers to the quantities of a product that an individual wishes to purchase at different prices at a given point in time. Generally, the form of this relationship between price and quantity purchased is an inverse one, i.e. the higher

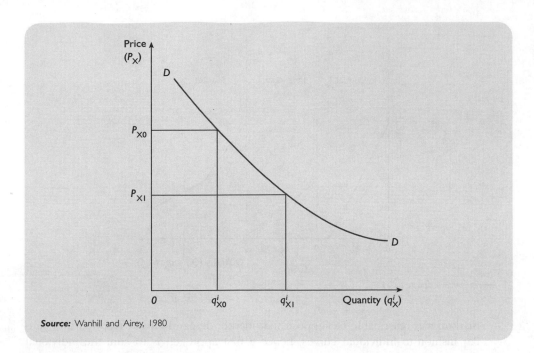

Source: Wanhill and Airey, 1980

the price of the product, the lower is the demand; the lower the price, the greater is the demand. This is shown in Figure 1.1.

It is normal to characterise the demand curve *DD* in Figure 1.1 by an appropriate measure which expresses the responsiveness of quantity to changes in price. Such a measure is termed the 'elasticity of demand' for product X with respect to its own price P_x. The own price elasticity of demand (ei) measures the ratio of the percentage change in quantity to the percentage change in price, i.e.

$$ei = \frac{\% \text{ change in quantity}}{\% \text{ change in price}}$$

It is conventional to consider ei in its absolute or positive value, thus we refer to an own price elasticity of demand as 1.0, 2.0, 3.0, etc., and not −1.0, −2.0 or −3.0. The critical value of ei is 1.0; for goods that have an own price elasticity greater than 1, demand is said to be elastic. Products exhibiting this property are goods that are normally viewed as luxury items – overseas holidays or dining out. When a good has an own price elasticity of demand of less than 1 it is classed as a necessity. For necessities, quantity adjustments respond sluggishly to price changes – food is classed as a necessity.

So far we have examined both individual consumer demand for a product and also single variables such as price. However, in truth the world is more complex than this and we need to extend the concept of demand schedules in two ways:

1. There are several factors other than price that affect a consumer's demand for a tourism product. These include prices of other goods, an individual's income and social tastes and habits. Economists find that it is not practical to consider variations in all the components at one time so they assume all components are constant except the one in question.

2. Tourism is not only concerned with individuals but also responses of the market to variations in the factors affecting demand. Since individual tourists make up the

Figure 1.2:
Derivation of a
market demand
curve

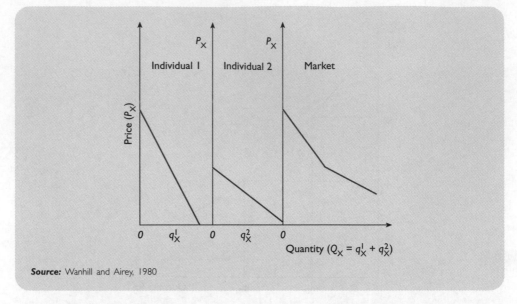

Source: Wanhill and Airey, 1980

market, it is reasonable to suppose that market demand curves respond in a similar fashion to individual curves, hence a first approach is to sum the individual demand schedules to arrive at the market schedule. This is illustrated in Figure 1.2 which supposes that there are only two individuals in the market. The market demand schedule is derived from the horizontal summation of the two individual curves. We can see that the market curve has a distinct 'kink' where the two individual curves join: this arises because the market is assumed to consist of only two persons. As the number in the market increases so any kinks are ironed out and a more or less smooth curve results.

Conclusion

While it is crucial for the effective planning and management of tourism, the measurement of tourism demand is extremely problematic (as explored in Chapter 4). However, despite the difficulties, it is critical that demand for tourism is measured and the basis for this measurement is the underlying definitions and concepts identified and discussed in this chapter. This chapter, therefore, provides important prerequisite information for the subsequent study of tourism demand and the remainder of the tourism system.

Chapter discussion questions

1. Identify factors that might account for individuals in the 'no demand' category.

2. Taking statistics from a country of your choice, calculate the net travel propensity, gross travel propensity and travel frequency.

3. Consider how the market and individual demand curves for tourism might differ from other commodities.

Recommended further reading

- Boniface, B. G. and Cooper, C. P. (1994) *The Geography of Travel and Tourism*, Butterworth-Heinemann, Oxford.
- Burkart, A. J. and Medlik, S. (eds) (1975) *The Management of Tourism*, Heinemann, London.
- McIntosh, R. W., Goeldner, C. R. and Ritchie, J. R. B. (1995) *Tourism Principles, Practices, Philosophies*, Wiley, New York.
- Mathieson, A. and Wall, G. (1982) *Tourism: Economic Physical and Social Impacts*, Longman, London.
- Mill, R. C. (1990) *Tourism: The International Business*, Prentice Hall, Englewood Cliffs, NJ.
- Mill, R. C. and Morrison, A. (1985) *The Tourism System*, Prentice Hall, Englewood Cliffs, NJ.

Bibliography

- Boniface, B. and Cooper, C. (1987) *The Geography of Travel and Tourism*, Heinemann, London.
- Boniface, B. G. and Cooper, C. P. (1994) *The Geography of Travel and Tourism*, 2nd edn, Butterworth-Heinemann, Oxford.
- Burkart, J. and Medlik, S. (eds) (1975) *The Management of Tourism*, Heinemann, London.
- Chadwick, R. A. (1994) 'Concepts, measurement and definitions used in travel and tourism research', pp. 65–80 in *Handbook of Travel, Tourism and Hospitality Research*, Ritchie, J. R. B. and Goeldner, C. R. (eds), Wiley, New York.
- Chubb, M. and Chubb, H. R. (1981) *One Third of Our Time*, Wiley, New York.
- Holloway, C. (1994) *The Business of Tourism*, Addison Wesley Longman, Harlow.
- Lavery, P. (1971) (ed.) *Recreational Geography*, David and Charles, Newton Abbott.
- McIntosh, R. W., Goeldner, C. R. and Ritchie, J. R. B. (1995) *Tourism Principles, Practices, Philosophies*, Wiley, New York.
- Mathieson, A. and Wall, G. (1982) *Tourism: Economic Physical and Social Impacts*, Longman, London.
- Mill, R. C. (1990) *Tourism: The International Business*, Prentice Hall, Englewood Cliffs, NJ.
- Mill, R. C. and Morrison, A. (1985) *The Tourism System*, Prentice Hall, Englewood Cliffs, NJ.
- Pearce, D. (1987) *Tourism Today*, Longman, Harlow.
- Pearce, D. (1989) *Tourist Development*, Longman, Harlow.
- Wanhill, S. R. C. and Airey, D. W. (1980) 'Demand for accommodation', pp. 23–44 in *Managerial Economics for Hotel Operation*, Kotas, R. (ed.), Surrey University Press, Guildford.
- WTO (1980) *The Manila Declaration on World Tourism*, WTO, Madrid.
- WTO (1994) *The Osaka Declaration*, WTO, Madrid.

Chapter Two

Consumer behaviour and tourism demand

Introduction

In this section we provide an overview of the consumer decision-making process in tourism. This represents tourism demand at the personal level to complement the broader, world view provided in Chapter 3.

There is no doubt that an understanding of consumer decision processes is essential if we are to understand and predict demand for tourism. Demand for tourism at the individual level can be treated as a consumption process that is influenced by a number of factors which may be a combination of needs and desires, availability of time and money, or images, perceptions and attitude. Thus, we consider the main concepts and theories relating to motivation, needs, roles, images and determinants of demand. Finally, we review the major literature debates surrounding these concepts in an attempt to explain how these factors influence individual behaviour in tourism.

Chapter learning objectives

This chapter deals with the factors and influences which, when combined, will influence a consumer's demand for tourism. By reading this chapter, the reader will:

- understand the theory of motivation and be able to assess the importance of motivation in the demand for different tourism purchases;
- appreciate the way the roles and psychographics of tourists are linked to specific forms of tourism and tourist needs;
- know about the models developed to demonstrate the linkages and dynamics of consumer behaviour and tourism demand; and
- be familiar with the determinants of demand which, at an individual level, are likely to affect propensity to travel.

The individual decision-making process

At the personal level it is clear that the factors influencing demand for tourism are closely linked to models of consumer behaviour. No two individuals are alike and differences in attitudes, perceptions, images and motivation have an important influence on travel decisions. It is important to note that:

- attitudes depend on an individual's perception of the world;
- perceptions are mental impressions of, say, a place or travel company and are determined by many factors which include childhood, family, and work experiences, education, books, television programmes and films and promotional images. Perception involves the encoding of information by individuals and influences attitudes and behaviour towards products but does not explain by itself, or when combined with attitudes, why people want to travel;
- travel motivators do explain why people want to travel and they are the inner urges that initiate travel demand; and
- images are sets of beliefs, ideas and impressions relating to products and destinations.

The fundamentals of consumer behaviour and tourism

It is important to realise that the management of tourism will be ineffective without an understanding of the way in which tourism consumers make decisions and act in relation to the consumption of tourism products. While the term 'consumer' would seem to indicate a single concept of demand, the reality is that there is a whole diversity of consumer behaviour with decisions being made for a range of reasons. We need to study a tourist's consumer behaviour to be aware of:

- the needs, purchase motives and decision process associated with the consumption of tourism;
- the impact of the different effects of various promotional tactics;
- the possible perception of risk for tourism purchases;
- the different market segments based upon purchase behaviour; and
- how managers can improve their chance of marketing success.

Many variables will influence the way consumption patterns differ. Patterns will change based upon the different products available and the way individuals have learnt to purchase tourism products. The variations are complex and therefore it is more practical to deal with general behavioural principles. These are often dealt with in a framework that includes the disciplines of psychology, sociology and economics. Figure 2.1 provides a simplification of some of the main influences affecting the consumer as decision maker. These are discussed within this chapter.

We can view the tourism consumer decision process as a system made up of four basic elements:

1. **Energisers of demand**. These are the forces of motivation that lead a tourist to decide to visit an attraction or go on a holiday.
2. **Effectors of demand**. The consumer will have developed ideas of a destination, product or organisation by a process of learning, attitudes and associations from promotional messages and information. This will affect the consumer's image and knowledge of a tourism product thus serving to heighten or dampen the various energisers that lead to consumer action.

Figure 2.1:
Consumer
decision-making
framework

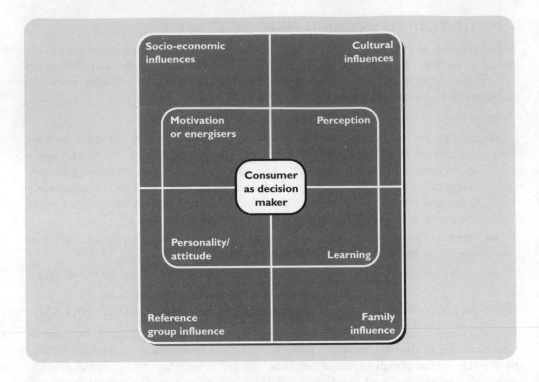

3. **Roles and the decision-making process**. The important role is that of the family member who is normally involved in the different stages of the purchase process and the final resolution of decisions about when, where and how the group will consume the tourism product.

4. **Determinants of demand**. In addition, the consumer decision-making process for tourism is underpinned by the determinants of demand. Even though motivation may exist, demand is filtered, constrained or channelled due to economic (e.g. discretionary income), sociological (reference groups, cultural values) or psychological factors (perception of risk, personality, attitudes).

Energisers and effectors of demand

Motivation

The classic dictionary definition of motivation is derived from the word 'motivate' which is to cause a person to act in a certain way, or to stimulate interest. We can also refer to the word 'motive' which is concerned with initiating movement or inducing a person to act. As would be expected, many texts associated with tourism utilise the concept of motivation as a major influence upon consumer behaviour.

Maslow's hierarchy model

Maslow's hierarchy of needs (Figure 2.2) is probably the best known theory of motivation, perhaps because of its simplicity and intuitive attraction. The theory of motivation proposed by Maslow is in the form of a ranking, or hierarchy, of the arrangements of individual needs. The early humanistic values of Maslow seem to have led him to

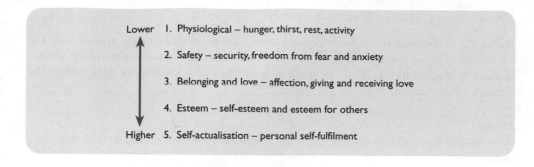

create a model where self-actualisation is valued as the level 'man' should aspire to. He argued that if none of the needs in the hierarchy was satisfied, then the lowest needs, the physiological ones, would dominate behaviour. If these were satisfied, however, they would no longer motivate and the individual would be motivated by the next level in the hierarchy.

Maslow identified two motivational types, which can be greatly simplified as:

● deficiency or tension-reducing motives;

● inductive or arousal-seeking motives.

Maslow maintained that his theory of motivation is holistic and dynamic and can be applied to both work and non-work spheres of life. He treats his levels of need as universal and innate, yet of such instinctual weakness that they can be modified, accelerated or inhibited by the environment. He also stated that while all the needs are innate, only those behaviours that satisfy physiological needs are unlearned. Although a great deal of tourism demand theory has been built upon Maslow's approach there are a number of questions that Maslow does not answer:

● It is not clear from his work why he selected five basic needs.

● Why are the needs ranked as they are?

● How could he justify his model when he did not carry out clinical observation or experiment?

● Why did he never try to expand the original set of motives?

Tourism authors have borrowed extensively from Maslow, simply because he has provided a convenient set of containers that can be relatively easily labelled. The notion that a comprehensive coverage of human needs can be organised into an understandable hierarchical framework is of obvious benefit to tourism theorists.

Within Maslow's model, human activity is wired into predetermined, understandable and predictable aspects of action. This is very much in the behaviourist tradition of psychology as opposed to the cognitive approach which stresses the concepts of irrationality and unpredictability of behaviour. However, Maslow's theory does allow for humans to transcend the mere embodiment of biological needs that sets them apart from other species.

To some extent the popularity of Maslow's theory can be understood in moral terms. It suggests that, given the right circumstances, people will grow out of their concern for the materialistic aspects of life and become more interested in 'higher' things.

The study of motivation in tourism

The study of motivation has been derived from a range of disciplinary areas which has led to a diversity of approach in tourism – an observation that holds true for many aspects of tourism studied in this book. In tourism, a number of authors have approached the concept of motivation.

Dann

Dann (1981) has pointed out that there are seven elements within the overall approach to motivation:

1. Travel is a response to what is lacking yet desired. This approach suggests that tourists are motivated by the desire to experience phenomena that are different from those available in their home environment.

2. Destination pull in response to motivational push. This distinguishes between the motivation of the individual tourist in terms of the level of desire (push) and the pull of the destination or attraction.

3. Motivation as fantasy. This is a subset of the first two factors and suggests that tourists travel in order to undertake behaviour that may not be culturally sanctioned in their home setting.

4. Motivation as classified purpose. A broad category which invokes the main purposes of a trip as a motivator for travel. Purposes may include visiting friends and relatives, enjoying leisure activities, or study.

5. Motivational typologies. This approach is internally divided into:
   (a) behavioural typologies such as the motivators 'sunlust' (search for a better set of amenities than are available at home) and 'wanderlust' (curiosity to experience the strange and unfamiliar) as proposed by Gray (1970); and
   (b) typologies that focus on dimensions of the tourist role.

6. Motivation and tourist experiences. This approach is characterised by the debate regarding the authenticity of tourist experiences and depends upon beliefs about types of tourist experience.

7. Motivation as auto-definition and meaning. This suggests that the way in which tourists define their situations will provide a greater understanding of tourist motivation than simply observing their behaviour.

Dann suggests that these seven identified approaches demonstrate a 'definitional fuzziness' which, if not clarified, may make it difficult to discover 'whether or not individual tourism researchers are studying the same phenomenon'.

McIntosh, Goeldner and Ritchie

McIntosh, Goeldner and Ritchie (1995) utilise four categories of motivation:

1. **Physical motivators:** those related to refreshment of body and mind, health purposes, sport and pleasure. This group of motivators are seen to be linked to those activities which will reduce tension.

2. **Cultural motivators:** those identified by the desire to see and know more about other cultures, to find out about the natives of a country, their lifestyle, music, art, folklore, dance, etc.

3. **Interpersonal motivators:** this group includes a desire to meet new people, visit friends or relatives, and to seek new and different experiences. Travel is an escape from routine relationships with friends or neighbours or the home environment or it is used for spiritual reasons.

4. **Status and prestige motivators:** these include a desire for continuation of education (i.e. personal development, ego enhancement and sensual indulgence). Such motivators are seen to be concerned with the desire for recognition and attention from others, in order to boost the personal ego. This category also includes personal development in relation to the pursuit of hobbies and education.

As with most of the authors dealing with motivation, no scientific basis is claimed for the categories nor is any indication given of the proportion of tourists who would exhibit one type of motivation rather than another. As would be expected, the concept of motivation as a major determinant of tourism behaviour is widely used by tourism authors.

Plog

Plog (1974) developed a theory within which the US population could be classified as a series of interrelated psychographic types.

These types range from two extremes:

1. 'Psychocentric' which is derived from psyche or self-centred where an individual centres thoughts or concerns on the small problem areas of life. These individuals tend to be conservative in their travel patterns, preferring 'safe' destinations and often taking many return trips.

2. 'Allocentric', where the derivision of the root 'allo' means 'varied in form'. These individuals are adventurous and motivated to travel/discover new destinations. They rarely return to the same place twice.

The majority of the population fall in between these extremes in an area which Plog terms 'mid-centric'. Plog also found that those who were at the lower end of income scales were more likely to be psychocentric types whereas at the upper income band there was more of a likelihood of being allocentric. In a later study it was observed that middle-income groups exhibited only a small positive correlation with psychographic types. This created problems because there were a number of psychographic types who could not, through income constraint, choose the type of holiday they preferred even if they were motivated towards it.

While Plog's theory is a useful way of thinking about tourists, it is more difficult to apply it. Tourists will travel with different motivations on different occasions. A second holiday or short-break weekend may be in a nearby, psychocentric destination whereas the main holiday may be in an allocentric destination. Smith (1990) tested Plog's model, utilising evidence from seven different countries. He concluded that his own results did not support Plog's original model of an association between personality types and destination preferences. Smith questioned the applicability of the model to countries other than the USA. In answer to Smith, Plog questioned the validity of Smith's methodology. Regardless of this defence, further controlled empirical studies will be required in order to ensure Plog's theory can be justified as a central pillar within tourism theory.

While very few studies are based upon research, the motivators in Figure 2.3 were identified by research of a sample based upon a quota sample matched to the British Tourist Authority profile for overseas travel from the UK. The response involved individuals providing evidence of a cluster of motives, each of which is important as a determinant of demand.

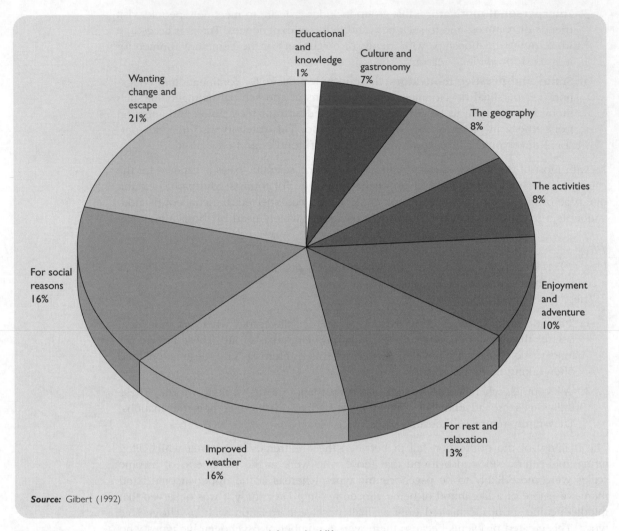

Figure 2.3: The range of motivators for overseas travel from the UK

A summary of the concept of motivation

We can see that the dimensions of the concept of motivation in the context of travel are difficult to map. In summary they can be seen to include:

- the idea that travel is initially need-related and that this manifests itself in terms of wants and the strength of motivation or 'push', as the energiser of action;

- motivation is grounded in sociological and psychological aspects of acquired norms, attitudes, culture, perceptions, etc., leading to person-specific forms of motivation; and

- the image of a destination created through various communication channels will influence motivation and subsequently affect the type of travel undertaken.

Although the motivation literature is still immature in tourism, there is no doubt that motivation is an essential concept in the explanation of tourist demand. However, we should remember that although motivation can be stimulated and activated in relation to the 'want' to travel, 'needs' themselves cannot be created. Needs are dependent on the human element through the psychology and circumstances of the individual. There is also the whole question of what types of motivation may be innate in us all (curiosity, need for physical contact) and what types are learned because they are judged as valuable or positive (status, achievement).

Roles and the decision-making process in tourism

Tourist typologies

Tourists can be characterised into different typologies or roles which exercise motivation as an energising force linked to personal needs. Utilising this approach, roles can be studied in relation to goal-orientated forms of behaviour or holiday choice activity. Therefore some understanding of tourist roles may provide us with a deeper understanding of the choice process of different consumer segments.

The majority of authors who have identified tourist roles have concentrated on the assessment of the social and environmental impact of tourism or the nature of the tourist experience. Any definition or interpretation of tourist roles, such as those of motivation, varies according to the analytical framework used by the individual author. The initial ideas of role developed from the work of sociological theorists such as Goffman (1959), who suggested that individuals behave differently in different situations in order to sustain impressions associated with those situations. As actors have different front and back-stage performances, participants in any activity vary their behaviour according to the nature and context of that activity. Consequently individual roles can be identified and managed according to social circumstances. Whereas tourists may vary considerably, we can discern a pattern of roles from the literature. Theoretical studies focusing on the sociological aspects of tourism role were developed in the 1970s through the work of Cohen (1972, 1974, 1984), MacCannell (1976) and Smith (1990).

The interaction of personality attributes such as attitude, perceptions and motivation allow different types of tourist role to be identified. One classification by Cohen is particularly useful and this is presented in Figure 2.4. He uses a classification based on the theory that tourism combines the curiosity to seek out new experiences with the need for the security of familiar reminders of home. Cohen proposes a continuum of possible combinations of novelty and familiarity and, by breaking up the continuum into typical combinations of these two ingredients, a fourfold classification of tourists is produced.

While destinations may be enjoyed as novel, most tourists prefer to explore them from a familiar base. The degree of familiarity of this base underlies Cohen's typology in which the author identifies four tourist roles: organised mass tourist, individual mass tourist, explorer and drifter (see Figure 2.4). Cohen described the first two roles as institutionalised and the latter types as non-institutionalised. Cohen was interested in classifying groups in order to understand not demand, but the effects or impact of institutionalised forms of tourism which he found to be authenticity issues, standardisation of destinations, festivals and the development of facilities. He also identified the impact of non-institutionalised forms of tourism upon the destination which he found acts as a 'spearhead for mass tourism' as well as having a 'demonstration effect' on the lower socio-economic groups of the host community.

Cohen's typology assists in formulating operational approaches to tourism research and forms a framework for management practice. Although it is not complete and cannot be applied to all tourists at all times, it does afford a way of organising and understanding tourist activity.

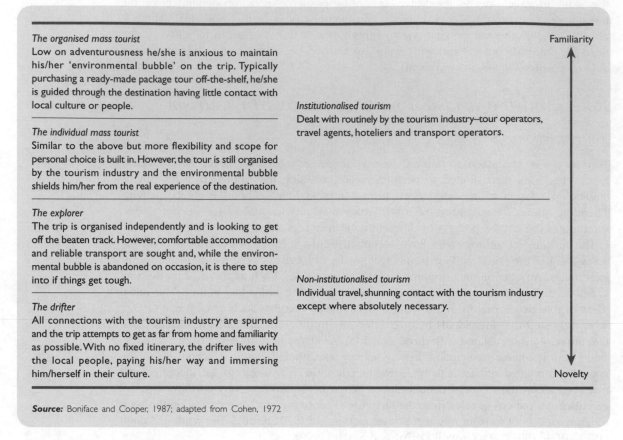

The organised mass tourist
Low on adventurousness he/she is anxious to maintain his/her 'environmental bubble' on the trip. Typically purchasing a ready-made package tour off-the-shelf, he/she is guided through the destination having little contact with local culture or people.

The individual mass tourist
Similar to the above but more flexibility and scope for personal choice is built in. However, the tour is still organised by the tourism industry and the environmental bubble shields him/her from the real experience of the destination.

The explorer
The trip is organised independently and is looking to get off the beaten track. However, comfortable accommodation and reliable transport are sought and, while the environmental bubble is abandoned on occasion, it is there to step into if things get tough.

The drifter
All connections with the tourism industry are spurned and the trip attempts to get as far from home and familiarity as possible. With no fixed itinerary, the drifter lives with the local people, paying his/her way and immersing him/herself in their culture.

Institutionalised tourism
Dealt with routinely by the tourism industry–tour operators, travel agents, hoteliers and transport operators.

Non-institutionalised tourism
Individual travel, shunning contact with the tourism industry except where absolutely necessary.

Familiarity

Novelty

Source: Boniface and Cooper, 1987; adapted from Cohen, 1972

Figure 2.4: Cohen's classification of tourists

Role and family influence

As the fundamental social unit of group formation in society, the influence of a family on tourism demand is extremely important. A family often acts as the purchasing unit which may be supplying the needs of perhaps two or more generations. In addition, it socialises children to adopt particular forms of purchasing and acts as a wider reference group. Given the importance of family behaviour in the purchase of leisure products, we may want to question the preponderance of literature which treats consumer behaviour as an individual model of action.

Each member of a family fulfils a special role within the group. He or she may act as husband/father, wife/mother, son/brother and daughter/sister. Family decision making assigns roles to specific members of the family and decision making may be shared, or made by one person. One member of the family may be the facilitator, while information may be gathered by another. The family acts as a composite buying unit with the different role patterns leading to particular forms of tourism product purchasing.

The importance of image

An individual's awareness of the world is made up of experiences, learning, emotions and perceptions, or, more accurately, the cognitive evaluation of such experiences, learning, emotions and perceptions. Such awareness can be described as knowledge producing a specific image of the world. This image is critically important to an individual's preference, motivation and behaviour towards tourist products and destinations, as it will provide a 'pull' effect resulting in different demand schedules.

There are various kinds of definitions adopted to describe the word 'image' in different fields. For example, the WTO gives its definitions as follows:

- the artificial imitation of the apparent form of an object;

- form resemblance, identity (e.g. art and design);

- ideas, conceptions held individually or collectively of the destination.

Following the work of Gunn (1972), the WTO suggests that the tourist image is only one aspect of a destination's general image, with the two being closely interrelated. Nobody is likely to visit a destination for tourism if for one reason or another he or she dislikes it. Conversely, a tourist discovery may lead to a knowledge of other aspects of an economic, political or cultural nature of that destination. The WTO further adds that the presentation of a destination image must allow for the fact that it is generally a matter not of creating an image from nothing but of transforming an existing image.

Tourist behaviour both of individuals and groups depends upon their image of immediate situations and the world. The notion of image is closely related to behaviour and attitudes. Attitudes and behaviour become established on the basis of a person's derived image and are not easily changed unless new information or experience is gained.

The holiday image

Mayo (1973) examined regional images and regional travel behaviour. Among other things he indicated that the image of a destination area is a critical factor when choosing a destination. Mayo further concluded that, whether or not an image is in fact a true representation of what any given region has to offer the tourist, what is important is the image that exists in the mind of the vacationer.

The tourist may possess a variety of images in connection with travel. These include the image he or she has formed of the destination, of the term 'holiday' itself, of the mode of transport he or she wishes to utilise, of the tour operator/wholesaler or travel agency and of his or her own self-image. For example, it is probable that the term 'holiday' evokes different images for different people. However, it is likely that similar images of a particular holiday experience are held by people within the same segment of society and who have experienced a similar lifestyle or education.

Gunn (1972) identifies two levels of image. Viewed in terms of a country or destination, the 'organic' image is the sum of all information that has not been deliberately directed by advertising or promotion of a country or destination; this information comes from television coverage, radio reports, geography books, history books, what other people have said about the area, newspapers and magazines or even via the Internet. An imaginary picture is built up which is the result of all this information. The individual, following Gestalt psychology, attempts to make sense of it by forming a pattern or a picture of what he or she imagines the area to be like.

The second level of image is the 'induced' image. This is formed by deliberate portrayal and promotion by various organisations involved with tourism.

It is important to distinguish between these two levels since the induced image is controllable while it is more difficult to influence the organic image. Equally, the source of information is a significant influence upon a consumer's perception of its value.

We can identify four stages in the development and establishment of a holiday image:

1. The first is a vague, fantasy type of image created from advertising, education and word of mouth and is formed before the subject has thought seriously about taking a holiday. This belief may be that people engage in taking holidays as a desirable activity.

2. The second stage is when a decision is made to take a holiday and then choices must be made regarding time, destination and type of holiday. This is when the holiday image is modified, clarified and extended. On completion of the holiday plans, the anticipatory image is crystallised.

3. The third stage is the holiday experience itself, which modifies, corrects or removes elements of the image that prove to be invalid and reinforces those that are found to be correct.

4. The fourth stage is the after-image, the recollection of the holiday which may induce feelings of nostalgia, regret or fantasy. This is the stage that will mould an individual's holiday concepts and attitudes and will promote a new sequence of holiday images influencing future holiday decisions.

Determinants of demand for tourism

Although an individual may be motivated to travel, the ability to do so will depend on a number of factors related to both the individual and the supply environment. These factors can be termed determinants of demand and represent the 'parameters of possibility' for the individual. For example, a certain level of discretionary income is required to allow participation in tourism, and this income, and indeed the type of participation, will be influenced by such factors as job type, life-cycle stage, mobility, level of educational attainment and personality. Even within the developed world, many are unable to participate in tourism for some reason.

Once a decision to travel has been taken, the ability to undertake the trip, and the nature of that trip will be determined by a wide range of interrelated factors. These can be broadly divided into two groups.

1. The first group of factors can be termed **lifestyle**, and includes income, employment, holiday entitlement, educational attainment and mobility.

2. A second group can be termed **life cycle** where the age and domestic circumstances of an individual affect both the amount and type of tourism demanded.

Naturally, these factors are interrelated and complementary. In a Western society, a high-status job is normally associated with an individual in middle age with a high-income, above-average holiday entitlement, education and mobility.

Lifestyle determinants of demand for tourism

Income and employment

Income and employment are closely linked and exert important influences upon both the level and the nature of tourism demanded by an individual. Tourism is an expensive activity that demands a certain threshold of income before participation is possible. Gross income gives little indication of the money available to spend on tourism – rather, it is discretionary income that provides the best indicator; that is, the income left over when tax, housing and the basics of life have been accounted for. Clearly, two households with the same gross incomes may have very different discretionary incomes, although discretionary income is difficult to measure.

The relationship between income and tourism is a complex one. For example, certain tourism activities are highly sensitive to income – additional holidays and expensive pursuits such as skiing holidays are a particular case in point. The relationship is also characterised by the fact that, at the extremes of the income spectrum, tourism demand is strongly affected, whereas in the middle of the spectrum it is much more difficult to discern a clear relationship. For example, a very low discretionary income markedly depresses travel propensity. As discretionary income rises, the ability to partake of tourism is associated with the purchase of leisure-orientated goods, until, with a high discretionary income, travel may reach a peak and then level off as the demands of a high-status job, and possibly frequent business trips, reduce the ability and desire to travel for pleasure.

A fundamental distinction is between those in employment and those unemployed. The impact of unemployment on the volume of tourism demand is obvious, but the nature of demand is also changed by employment uncertainty. This encourages later booking of trips, more domestic holidays and shorter lengths of stay, and switches demand away from commercial accommodation to VFR, therefore leading to lower spending levels.

The nature of employment not only influences travel propensity by determining income and holiday entitlement, but it also has an effect upon the type of holiday demanded, as the mechanism of peer and reference group pressure is felt.

Paid holiday entitlement

The increase in leisure time experienced by most individuals in the developed world since 1950 is well documented. However, the relationship between an individual's total time budget, leisure time and paid holiday entitlement is complex. A number of surveys suggest that, in a developed Western economy, individuals have anything from 35 to 50 hours free time a week at their disposal. This free time is greater for males, the young and single adults. Of this free time some two-thirds is spent around the home. However, to enable tourism, leisure time has to be blocked into two or more days to allow a stay away from home. While this obviously is the case with paid holiday entitlement, patterns of leisure time have changed over the past 20 years to allow three-day weekends, flexi-time and longer periods of absence for those in employment.

A variety of holiday arrangements now exists world-wide, with most nations having a number of one-day national holidays, as well as annual paid holiday entitlement by law or collective agreements. Individual levels of paid-holiday entitlement would seem to be an obvious determinant of travel propensity, but in fact the relationship is not straightforward and, rather like the income variable, it is clearer at the extremes. For example, low levels of entitlement do act as a real constraint upon the ability to travel, while a high entitlement encourages travel. This is in part due to the interrelationship between entitlement and factors such as job status, income and mobility. As levels of entitlement increase, the cost of tourism may mean that more of this entitlement will be spent at home.

Paid holiday entitlement tends to be more generous in developed economies and less so in the developing world. The pattern of entitlement is also responsible in part for the seasonality of tourism in some destinations simply because some of the entitlement has to be taken in the summer months. To an extent, this is historical and is rooted in the holiday patterns of manufacturing industries. It does, however, have an impact upon the nature of demand for tourism. In some countries, notably France, staggering of holiday entitlement has been attempted to alleviate seasonality.

Box 2.1   The VALS lifestyle categories

The 'Values and Lifestyles' segmentation has been researched by commercial companies and used as a market segmentation technique in the USA. It was not designed for tourism but does shed insights on tourism behaviour. It attempts to combine demographic variables with people's needs, attitudes and wants. The lifestyle classification is as follows.

Need-driven groups

Here needs are greater than choice as individuals are poor or disadvantaged in some way. There are two lifestyle types:

- **Survivor lifestyle** – the most disadvantaged groups who are removed from the mainstream of society.
- **Sustainer lifestyle** – a group who are struggling, but hopeful that circumstances will change.

Outer-directed groups

These groups are concerned as to how they appear to others and so live and behave according to other people's perceptions. There are three lifestyle types:

- **Belongers lifestyle** – a conservative, comfortable and conventional group.
- **Emulator lifestyle** – not so satisfied, status conscious, competitive and ambitious and often young.
- **Achiever lifestyle** – a successful, happy and hard-working group, middle-aged, prosperous, self-assured, the leaders of society.

Inner-directed groups

Lifestyles more to do with inner satisfaction than concern with other people's views. There are four lifestyle types:

- **I-am-me lifestyle** – Very young, impulsive and confused, and fiercely individual.
- **Experiential lifestyle** – Youthful, seeking experience, oriented to inner growth, artistic.
- **Societally conscious lifestyle** – A mission-oriented group, adopting, say, environmental concerns. They are mature and successful.
- **Self-directed lifestyle** – A group who see emotional rewards as important. They are not motivated by external views of them, or by materialistic rewards.

Combined outer- and inner-directed groups

- **Integrated lifestyle** – This lifestyle group are mature, self-assured and aware.

In terms of tourism, societally conscious groups will seek a holiday trip that offers value for money, is relaxing and provides good scenery, all within a 'safe' setting. The food and the people are more important than the accommodation. Increasingly they will look for 'environmentally sound' destinations.

On the other hand, achievers will show a different pattern of demand, typically flying to their destination, travelling on business and staying in hotels.

Source: adapted from Shih (1986).

Education and mobility

Level of educational attainment is an important determinant of travel propensity as education broadens horizons and stimulates the desire to travel. Also, the better educated the individual, the higher the awareness of travel opportunities, and susceptibility to information, media, advertising and sales promotion.

Personal mobility also has an important influence on travel propensity, especially with regard to domestic holidays. The car is the dominant recreational tool for both international and domestic tourism. It provides door-to-door freedom, can carry tourism equipment (such as tents or boats) and has all-round vision for viewing. Ownership of a car stimulates travel for pleasure in all but recessionary times.

Race and gender

Race and gender are two critical determinants of tourism demand, but the relationships are not clearly understood. Most surveys of participation in tourism suggest that it is whites and males who have the highest levels of effective demand for tourism. However, changes in society are acting to complicate this rather simplistic view. For example, in Japan, 'office ladies' are important consumers of travel.

Clearly for the purposes of analysing each variable, we have to separate them, but it must be remembered that they all are complementary and interrelated. Indeed this is such that some writers have attempted to analyse tourism or leisure lifestyles by performing multivariate analysis on the determinants of tourism demand and then trying to group individuals into particular categories. To date these analyses have met with limited success. Even where they have been commercially adopted as market segments it is difficult to correlate them with other variables such as media habits. This is depicted in Box 2.1.

However, leisure or tourism lifestyles are considerations when viewing the important role of fashion and style in holiday choice. Tourism demand has always been susceptible to fashion and can be influenced perhaps more readily than demand for some other goods by marketing and promotional activity.

Life-cycle determinants of demand for tourism

The propensity to travel, and indeed the type of tourism experience demanded, is closely related to an individual's age. Although the conventional measurement is chronological age, 'domestic age' better discriminates between types of tourist demand and levels of travel propensity. Domestic age refers to the stage in the life cycle reached by an individual, and different stages are characterised by distinctive holiday demand and levels of travel propensity.

The concept of life cycle helps us to understand how situation-specific life-stage conditions exert a great influence on consumer behaviour. For example, the majority of recreational tourism in the USA is made up from the family market. The cycle is not just a progression by phase or age but represents likely fluctuations in disposable income and changes in social responsibilities (see Box 2.2). For example, the bachelor stage represents an individual living away from home with few responsibilities but with the need for affiliation with others and the likelihood of purchases of leisure and entertainment, personal care items and clothes. Wells and Gubar (1966) have conceptualised the life cycle of families in the USA, from the bachelor to solitary survivor stage, as follows:

1. Bachelor stage; young single people not living at home.
2. Newly married couples; young, no children.

Box 2.2 Domestic age and tourism demand

Childhood

At this stage decisions are taken for the individual in terms of holiday taking although of course, children do have a significant influence upon their parents' decisions. By the age of 10 or 11 some children take organised holidays with school or youth groups. These are usually domestic with self-catering arrangements.

Adolescence/young adult

At this stage the preoccupation is for independence, socialising and a search for identity. Typically, holidays independent of parents begin at around 15 years, constrained by lack of finance but compensated by having few other commitments, no shortage of free time, and a curiosity for new places and experiences. This group has a high propensity to travel, mainly on budget holidays using surface transport and self-catering accommodation. Here the preoccupation is simply to 'get away' – the destination is unimportant.

Marriage

Marriage represents the first 'crisis' in terms of unscrambling the preoccupations, interests and activities of an individual. Preoccupations turn to establishment and lifetime investments. Before the arrival of children young couples often have a high income and few other ties, giving them a high travel propensity, frequently overseas. The arrival of children represents the second 'crisis' which coupled with the responsibility of a home may mean that constraints of time and finance depress travel propensity. Holidays become more organisational than geographical with domestic tourism, self-catering accommodation, and visiting friends and relatives becoming increasingly common.

Empty nest stage

As children grow up, reach the adolescence stage and begin to travel independently, constraints of time and finance are lifted from parents and their travel propensity increases. This is often a time for long-haul travel – the cruise market typically comprises this group.

Old age

The emergence of early retirement at 50 or 55 years is creating an active and mobile group in the population of many countries who will demand both domestic and international travel. In later retirement, lack of finance, infirmity and often the loss of a partner act to offset the increase in free time experienced by this group. Holidays become more hotel-based and travel propensity decreases.

3. Full nest I; young married couples with dependent children.
4. Full nest II; married couples with dependent children over 6 years old.
5. Full nest III; married couples with dependent children.
6. Empty nest; older married couples with no children living with them. Head of household in labour force.

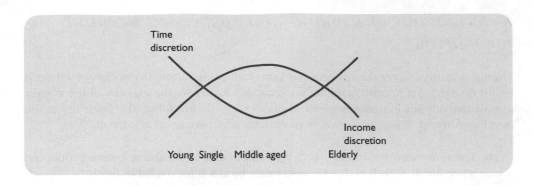

7. As above but head of household is retired.

8. Solitary survivor; older single people in the labour force.

9. As above but retired.

The distinctive pattern of demand found at each stage in the life cycle comes about for a number of reasons. At each stage in the life cycle individuals can be thought of as having:

- preoccupations – which are the mental absorptions arising from motivations;

- interests – which are feelings of what an individual would like to do, or represent the awareness of an idea or opportunity; and

- activities – which are the actions of an individual.

Each stage in the life cycle is characterised by particular combinations of these three factors. For example, in adolescence the preoccupation is with socialising and finding independence while in married adulthood the preoccupations are more with establishment and social institutions. As an individual progresses through life the combinations of the factors, and the nature of the factors themselves, change. At certain 'crisis' points the whole combination is 'unfrozen' and completely reformed. An example here would be having children. At this point in an individual's life, previous constraints and influences upon holiday taking are totally changed as holidays become more organisational and less geographical. The life-cycle framework can also be linked to lifestyle variables to provide a multidimensional analysis. In married middle age, for example, holiday entitlement, income and mobility are often at a maximum and this is reflected in the level of holiday taking (see Figure 2.5). Equally, companies such as Disney and McDonald's utilise the concept to win children as customers at an early age in order to retain them into later life. With the decline in birthrates in the developed world it is important to create hotel, activity and restaurant products that will socialise children to want to take certain types of activity holidays so as to encourage demand at a later stage in their life.

The explanatory framework provided by the domestic life-cycle approach is a powerful one. It has implications for the supply of facilities, for the analysis of market needs of particular population groups (for example, the large numbers of elderly people which some Western countries will have by the end of the century) and has clearly been used as a basis for market segmentation by tour operators and wholesalers. However, the life cycle as outlined in this chapter is only appropriate for developed Western economies and even here it is a generalisation as it does not consider, for example, one-parent families, divorcees or other ethnic groups living within Western economies.

Determinants of demand and suppressed demand for tourism

Throughout this chapter the concern has been to identify factors that influence effective tourist demand. Yet tourism is still an unobtainable luxury for the majority of the world's population, not just in undeveloped and developing countries, but also for many in the developed world. There are a variety of reasons why people do not travel:

● Travel is expensive and demands a certain threshold of income before people can enter the market. It competes with other products for available funds.

● Lack of time is a problem for some individuals who cannot allocate sufficient blocks of time to stay away from home. This may be for business or family reasons.

● Physical limitations (such as ill health) are a significant reason for many people not travelling. In particular heart disease and mental/physical handicap act as a major constraint on travel.

● Family circumstances such as those who are single parents or have to care for elderly relatives may prevent travel.

● Government restrictions such as currency controls and visas may act as a real barrier to travel (both inbound and outbound) for some countries.

● Lack of interest/fear are real barriers for some individuals.

It is not uncommon for people to experience a combination of two or more of these barriers. For example, a one-parent family may find lack of income and time will combine with family circumstances to prevent tourism travel. Obviously it is just these groups who would most benefit from a holiday and tourism planners are increasingly concerned to identify these barriers and devise programmes to encourage non-participants to travel. Perhaps the best known example of this is the social tourism movement which is concerned with facilitating the participation in travel by people with some form of handicap or disadvantage, and the measures used to encourage this participation.

Conclusion

Tourism marketing will become more effective if it develops a fuller understanding of what influences the tourist's consumer behaviour. This requires an appreciation of the way consumers behave and the way they recognise specific needs for travel, search for and evaluate information, make purchases and then evaluate what has been consumed as part of the tourism experience. This involves the need to understand some of the approaches to how motivation may function, the roles we adopt as tourists and how sociological changes will affect demand. The understanding of the consumer is enhanced by the incorporation of the different variables into simplified models. Although these need improvement, they act as a guide to current thinking of how tourism demand may function.

Chapter discussion questions

1. Consider tourist typologies that predominate at a tourist destination with which you are familiar.

2. Review the major determinants of demand at an individual level and assess their relative importance.

3. Consider the factors that might motivate a tourist to travel to a range of different destinations.

Recommended further reading

- Gilbert, D. C. (1991) 'An examination of the consumer decision process related to tourism', pp. 78–105 in *Progress in Tourism Recreation and Hospitality Management*, Vol. III, Cooper, C. (ed.), Belhaven, London.
- Goodall, B. (1991) 'Understanding holiday choice', pp. 58–77 in *Progress in Tourism Recreation and Hospitality Management*, Vol. III, Cooper. C. (ed.), Belhaven, London.
- Johnson, P. and Thomas, B. (eds) (1992) *Choice and Demand in Tourism*, Mansell, London.
- Pearce, D. (1987) *Tourism Today*, Longman, Harlow.
- Pearce, P. L. (1982) *The Social Psychology of Tourist Behaviour*, Pergamon Press, Oxford.

Bibliography

- Ajzen, I. and Fishbein, M. (1975) *Attitude Intention and Behaviour: An Introduction to Theory and Research*, Addison Wesley, Reading, MA.
- Ajzen, I. and Fishbein, M. (1980) *Understanding Attitudes and Predicting Social Behaviour*, Prentice Hall, Englewood Cliffs, NJ.
- Assael, H. (1987) *Consumer Behaviour and Marketing Action*, Kent, Boston.
- Boniface, B. and Cooper, C. (1987) *The Geography of Travel and Tourism*, Heinemann, London.
- Chubb, M. and Chubb, H. R. (1981) *One Third of Our Time*, Wiley, New York.
- Cohen, E. (1972) 'Towards a sociology of international tourism', *Social Research*, **39**(1), 164–82.
- Cohen, E. (1974) 'Who is a tourist? A conceptual clarification', *Sociological Review*, **22**(4), 527–55.
- Cohen, E. (1984) 'The sociology of tourism, approaches, issues findings', *Annual Review of Sociology*, 1984, 373–92.
- Crompton, J. (1979) 'Why people go on pleasure vacation', *Annals of Tourism Research* **6**(4), 408–24.
- Dann, G. M. S. (1981) 'Tourist motivation: an appraisal', *Annals of Tourism Research*, **8**(2), 187–219.
- Engel, J. F., Blackwell, R. D. and Miniard, P. (1986) *Consumer Behaviour*, Dryden Press, New York.
- Gilbert, D. C. (1991) 'An examination of the consumer decision process related to tourism', pp. 78–105 in *Progress in Tourism Recreation and Hospitality Management*, Vol. III, Cooper, C. (ed.), Belhaven, London.
- Gilbert, D. C. (1992) A study of the factors of consumer behaviour related to overseas holidays from the UK. Unpublished PhD Thesis, University of Surrey, Guildford.

- Goffman, E. (1959) *The Presentation of Self in Everyday Life*, Pelican, Middlesex.
- Goodall, B. (1991) 'Understanding holiday choice', pp. 58–77 in *Progress in Tourism Recreation and Hospitality Management*, Vol. III, Cooper, C. (ed.), Belhaven, London.
- Gray, H. P. (1970) *International Travel – International Trade*, Heath Lexington Books, Lexington.
- Gunn, C. (1972) *Vacationscape – Designing Tourist Regions*, University of Texas Press, Austin, TX.
- Howard, J. A. and Seth, J. N. (1969) *The Theory of Buyer Behaviour*, Wiley, New York.
- Jenkins, R. (1978), 'Family vacation decision making', *Journal of Travel Research*, **17**(4) Spring, 2–7.
- Johnson, P. and Thomas, B. (eds) (1992) *Choice and Demand in Tourism*, Mansell, London.
- Krippendorf, J. (1987) *The Holidaymakers*, Heinemann, London.
- MacCannell, D. (1976) *The Tourist, A New Theory of the Leisure Class*, Macmillan, London.
- McIntosh, R. W., Goeldner, C. R. and Ritchie, J. R. B. (1995) *Tourism Principles, Practices, Philosophies*, Wiley, New York.
- Maslow, A. H. (1943) 'A theory of human motivation', *Psychological Review*, **50**, 370–96.
- Maslow, A. H. (1954) *Motivation and Personality*, Harper and Row, New York.
- Maslow, A. H. (1965) *Eupsychian Management*, Irwin, Homewood, IL.
- Maslow, A. H. (1968) *Toward a Psychology of Being*, 2nd edn, Van Nostrand Reinhold, New York.
- Maslow, A. H. (1970) *Motivation and Personality*, 2nd edn, Harper and Row, New York.
- Mathieson, A. and Wall, G. (1982) *Tourism: Economic, Physical and Social Impacts*, Longman, London.
- Mayo, E. (1973) 'Regional images and regional travel consumer behaviour', pp. 211–18 in *TTRA Conference Proceedings*, Idaho.
- Mayo, E. and Jarvis, L. (1981) *The Psychology of Leisure Travel*, CBI Publishing Co., Boston, MA.
- Mazanec, J. A. (1995) 'Consumer behaviour', pp. 273–85 in *Tourism Marketing and Management Handbook*, Student edn, Witt, S. F. and Moutinho, L. (eds), Prentice Hall, Hemel Hempstead.
- Mill, R. C. and Morrison, A. (1985) *The Tourism System*, Prentice Hall, Englewood Cliffs, NJ.
- Mills, A. S. (1985) 'Participation motivations for outdoor recreation: a test of Maslow's theory', *Journal of Leisure Research*, **17**(3), 184–99.
- Nicosia, F. M. (1966) *Consumer Decision Processes: Marketing and Advertising Implications*, Prentice Hall, Englewood Cliffs, NJ.
- Olsen, D. and McCubbin, H. (1983) *Families, What Makes Them Work?*, Sage, Beverley Hills, CA.
- Parker, S. (1983) *Leisure and Work*, Allen and Unwin, Hemel Hempstead.
- Pearce, D. (1987) *Tourism Today*, Longman, Harlow.
- Pearce, D. (1989) *Tourist Development*, Longman, Harlow.
- Pearce, P. L. (1982) *The Social Psychology of Tourist Behaviour*, Pergamon Press, Oxford.
- Plog, S. C. (1974) 'Why destination areas rise and fall in popularity', *Cornell Hotel and Restaurant Quarterly*, **14**(4) (Feb), 55–8.
- Plog, S. C. (1990) 'A carpenter's tools, an answer to Stephen L. J. Smith's review of psychocentrism/allocentrism', *Journal of Travel Research*, **28**(4), Spring, 43–5.
- Rapoport, R. and Rapoport, R. N. (1975) *Leisure and the Family Life Cycle*, Routledge Kegan Paul, London.
- Schmoll, G. A. (1977) *Tourism Promotion*, Tourism International Press, London.

- Sheth, J. (1984) 'A theory of family buying decisions', in *Models of Buyer Behaviour*, J. N. Sheth (ed.), Harper and Row, New York.
- Shih, D. (1986) 'VALS as a tool of tourism market research', *Journal of Travel Research*, Spring, 2–11.
- Smith, S. L. J. (1990) 'A test of Plog's allocentric/psychocentric model: evidence from seven nations', *Journal of Travel Research*, **28**(4), Spring, 40–43.
- Smith, V. (1977) *Hosts and Guests*, University of Pennsylvania Press, Philadelphia, PA.
- Um, S. and Crompton, J. L. (1990) 'Attitude determinants in tourism destination choice', *Annals of Tourism Research*, **17**(3), 432–48.
- Wahab, S. (1975) *Tourism Management*, Tourism International Press, London.
- Wahab, S., Crampon, L. J. and Rothfield, L. M. (1976) *Tourism Marketing*, Tourism International Press, London.
- Wells, W. and Gubar, G. (1966) Life cycle concepts in marketing research', *Journal of Marketing Research*, Nov., 355–63.
- WTO (1979) *Tourist Images*, WTO, Madrid.

Chapter Three

Models and patterns of tourism demand

Introduction

So far we have provided a description of the various factors influencing both effective and suppressed tourism demand at an individual level. These influences can be summarised as attitudes, perceptions, image, roles, motivations and determinants. A number of researchers have attempted to draw together these influences and to structure them in the form of models. We can identify a range of such models but they basically fall into two categories:

1. Models of consumer behaviour.
2. Quantitative models.

These two categories of models are applied at different levels of generalisation – models of consumer behaviour are naturally focused at the individual scale and quantitative models tend to be focused at the aggregate level.

Chapter learning objectives

The purpose of this chapter is to introduce and discuss the buyer decision process as it relates to tourism by reviewing a number of key consumer behaviour models before we turn our attention to the quantitative models of tourism demand. We draw together the chapter by reviewing the major trends in the patterns of demand for tourism from historic and regional perspectives. Thus, the chapter learning objectives may be defined as providing the reader with:

■ an understanding of the buying decision process as it relates to tourism and the differences between this process for low-involvement products and high-involvement purchases such as tourism;

■ a knowledge of some of the key models that seek to explain the decision-making process for the purchase of tourism products;

■ a worked example to illustrate the forecasting process in tourism; and

■ an appreciation and explanation of the key historic and regional patterns of demand for tourism.

Models of consumer behaviour in tourism

One approach to understanding tourism demand is to identify and evaluate the broader theories of consumer behaviour linked to purchasing behaviour. This is far from simplistic for we are faced with a proliferation of research within a subject area that has displayed significant growth and diversity.

We can identify three phases that characterise the development of consumer behaviour theory:

1. The Early Empiricist Phase covered the years between 1930 and the late 1940s and was dominated by empirical commercial research. This research was characterised by attempts in industry to identify the effects of distribution, advertising and promotion decisions. The basis for these models came mainly from economic theories relating to the company.

2. The Motivational Research Phase in the 1950s was an age where stress was placed on Freudian and drive-related concepts. There was a greater emphasis placed upon in-depth interviews, focus groups, thematic apperception tests and other projective techniques. Activity was directed at uncovering 'real' motives for action which were perceived to lie in the deeper recesses of the consumer's mind. Much of the theory was based around the idea of there being instinctual needs which reside in the 'id' and are governed by the 'ego' which acts to balance unrestrained instincts and social constraints. The 'super ego' in turn was seen to embody values but to limit action on the basis of moral constraint. The major problem was the focus on unconscious needs which are by definition extremely difficult to prove empirically. Furthermore, they do not always translate into effective marketing strategies.

3. The Formative Phase of the 1960s can be seen as the formative years of consumer behaviour modelling. The first general consumer behaviour textbook became available in 1968 (Engel, Kollat and Blackwell) and other influential books such as Howard and Sheth (1969) followed soon after. During the formative phase, models of behaviour proved useful as a means of organising disparate knowledge of social action. The major theorists developed 'Grand Models' of consumer behaviour which have been subsequently utilised or transformed by authors interested in the tourism choice process.

These grand models can be found to share several commonalities:

- They all exhibit consumer behaviour as a decision process. This is integral to the model.
- They provide a comprehensive model focusing mainly on the behaviour of the individual consumer.
- They share the belief that behaviour is rational and hence can, in principle, be explained.
- They view buying behaviour as purposive, with the consumer as an active information seeker, both of information stored internally and of information available in the external environment. Thus, the search and evaluation of information is a key component of the decision process.
- They believe that consumers limit the amount of information taken in, and move over time from general notions to more specific criteria and preference for alternatives.

● All the 'grand models' include a notion of feedback, that is, outcomes from purchases will affect future purchases.

● The models envisage consumer behaviour as multi-stage triggered by the individual's expectation that a product will satisfy their needs.

The buying decision process in tourism

We subscribe to the approach of agreeing that consumer behaviour is purposeful and goal-orientated. This places an emphasis on the free choice of an individual in the process of their consumption decisions:

> *Generally speaking, human beings are usually quite rational and make systematic use of the information available to them. We do not subscribe to the view that human social behaviour is controlled by unconscious motives or overpowering desires, rather people consider the implications of their actions before they decide to engage or not engage in a given behaviour. (Ajzen and Fishbein, 1975, 1980)*

Figure 3.1 demonstrates that consumer behaviour is normally conceived as a process of stages. As part of this approach the decision to travel is the involvement of some or all of the following stages. The starting point is where a need is recognised and the individual is energised into becoming a potential customer. The stages can be thought of as:

● need arousal;

● recognition of the need – the prerequisite stage;

Figure 3.1:
Model of
consumer
behaviour

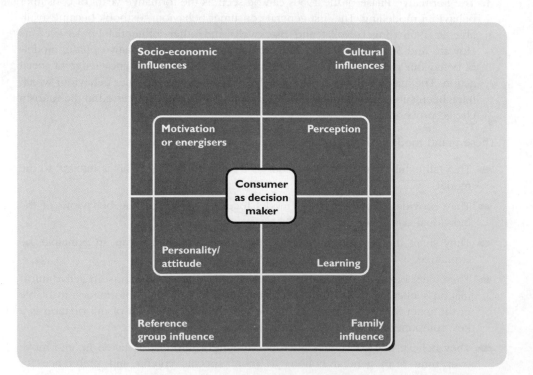

- level of involvement – amount of time and effort invested in the decision process, e.g. degree of search for information;

- identification of alternatives – brands that initially come to mind when considering a purchase are referred to as the evoked set. However, friends, shop assistants, merchandise, leaflets, advertisements, etc. may provide a consideration step;

- evaluation of alternatives – comparisons are made of the salient attributes based upon criteria of the potential purchaser;

- decision – choice made;

- purchase action; and

- post-purchase behaviour – the feelings an individual experiences after the purchase. Quite often with important purchases, such as overseas travel, the purchaser will doubt the wisdom of their choice and have a need for reassurance to what is known as dissonance or disequilibrium. This psychological state is reduced by the means of guarantees or telephone help lines to deal with queries. It is also reduced by the welcome of someone on their return from their trip or experience.

Engel, Blackwell and Miniard (1986) classified models according to the degree of search or problem-solving behaviour by the consumer:

- Limited problem-solving models (LPS models) are applicable to repeat or mundane purchases with a low level of consumer involvement. Apart from short trips near to home these are not applicable to tourism.

- Extended problem-solving models (EPS models) apply to purchases associated with high levels of perceived risk and involvement, and where the information search and evaluation of alternatives plays an important part in the purchasing decision. Models of tourist behaviour fall into this category.

Given the high cost, risk factor and involvement of a tourism purchase, a number of models of consumer behaviour which seek to explain low involvement purchase behaviour are less relevant and therefore not considered here. The following are models are all examples of EPS models.

Wahab, Crampon and Rothfield

One of the first attempts to provide some understanding of tourism purchase behaviour is to be found in the work of Wahab, Crampon and Rothfield (1976). These authors presented the consumer as purposeful and conceptualised his or her buying behaviour in terms of the uniqueness of the buying decision:

- no tangible return on investment;

- considerable expenditure in relation to earned income;

- purchase is not spontaneous or capricious; and

- expenditure involves saving and preplanning

They presented a model of the decision-making process based upon the preceding 'grand models' of consumer behaviour and having the stages outlined in Figure 3.2.

Figure 3.2: The Wahab, Crampon and Rothfield model of consumer behaviour

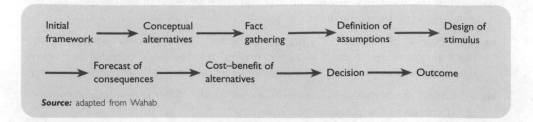

Initial framework → Conceptual alternatives → Fact gathering → Definition of assumptions → Design of stimulus

→ Forecast of consequences → Cost–benefit of alternatives → Decision → Outcome

Source: adapted from Wahab

Schmoll

Schmoll (1977) argued that creating a model of the travel decision process was not just a theoretical exercise, for its value could be found in its aid to travel decision making. His model was based on the Howard–Sheth (1969) and Nicosia (1966) models of consumer behaviour. See Figure 3.3.

Schmoll's model is built upon motivations, desires, needs and expectations as personal and social determinants of travel behaviour. These are influenced by travel stimuli, the traveller's confidence, destination image, previous experience and cost and time constraints. The model has four fields, each of which exerts some influence over the final decision; according to Schmoll (1977), 'The eventual decision (choice of a destination, travel time, type of accommodation, type of travel arrangements, etc.), is in fact the result of a distinct process involving several successive stages or fields.'

- **Field 1:** Travel stimuli. This comprises external stimuli in the form of promotional communication, personal and trade recommendations.

- **Field 2:** Personal and social determinants. These determine customer goals in the form of travel needs and desires, expectations and the objective and subjective risks thought to be connected with travel.

- **Field 3:** External variables. These involve the prospective traveller's confidence in the service provider, destination image, learnt experience and cost and time constraints.

- **Field 4:** This consists of related characteristics of the destination or service that have a bearing on the decision and its outcome.

The model (with the exception of some changes which incorporate the word travel in the headings and the location of previous experience in field 3) has been borrowed directly from the 'grand models' already discussed. In Schmoll's model there is no feedback loop and no input to attitude and values and therefore it is difficult for us to regard the model as dynamic. However, Schmoll does highlight many of the attributes of travel decision-making which, while not unique in themselves, do influence tourism demand. We can include here decisions regarding choice of a mix of services which make up the product: high financial outlay, destination image, the level of risk and uncertainty, necessity to plan ahead and difficulty of acquiring completeness of information.

Schmoll, while highlighting some of the characteristics associated with the problem-solving activity of travel, simply reiterates the determinants of cognitive decision-making processes. Within Schmoll's work we are introduced again to the importance of image which plays a significant part in the demand process.

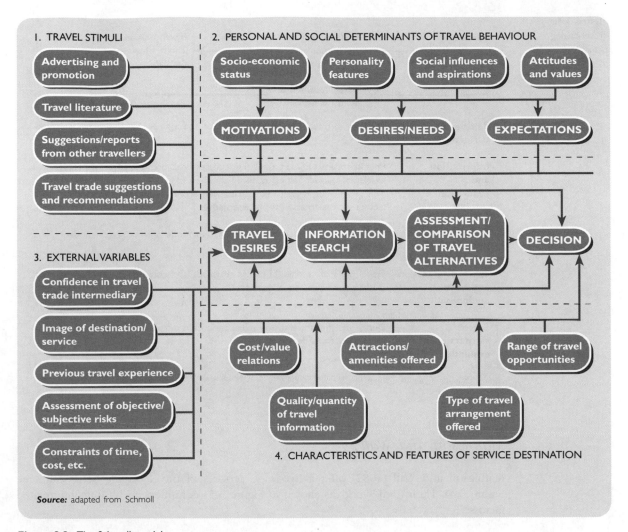

Figure 3.3: The Schmoll model

Mayo and Jarvis

Mayo and Jarvis (1981) have also borrowed from the grand theorist models. They have taken the basic Howard–Sheth three-level decision-making approach where problem solving is seen as extensive, limited or routinised.

Mayo and Jarvis follow the earlier theories by describing extensive decision making (destination purchase for them) as being characterised as having a perceived need for an information search phase and needing a longer decision-making period. The search for, and evaluation of, information is presented as a main component of the decision-making process whereby the consumer moves from general notions to more specific criteria and preferences for alternatives.

Mayo and Jarvis argue that travel is a special form of consumption behaviour involving an intangible, heterogeneous purchase of an experiential product, yet they then fail to develop an activity-based theory.

Figure 3.4:
Travel-buying
behaviour

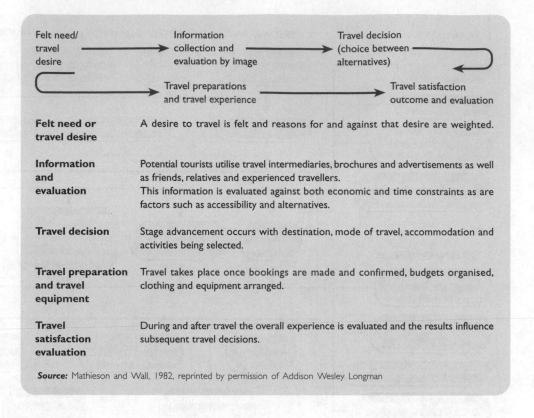

Felt need or travel desire	A desire to travel is felt and reasons for and against that desire are weighted.
Information and evaluation	Potential tourists utilise travel intermediaries, brochures and advertisements as well as friends, relatives and experienced travellers. This information is evaluated against both economic and time constraints as are factors such as accessibility and alternatives.
Travel decision	Stage advancement occurs with destination, mode of travel, accommodation and activities being selected.
Travel preparation and travel equipment	Travel takes place once bookings are made and confirmed, budgets organised, clothing and equipment arranged.
Travel satisfaction evaluation	During and after travel the overall experience is evaluated and the results influence subsequent travel decisions.

Source: Mathieson and Wall, 1982, reprinted by permission of Addison Wesley Longman

Mathieson and Wall

Mathieson and Wall (1982) offer a five-stage process of travel buying behaviour (see Figure 3.4). Their framework (as shown in Figure 3.5) is influenced by four interrelated factors:

1. Tourist profile (age, education, income attitudes, previous experience and motivations).

2. Travel awareness (image of a destination's facilities and services which are based upon the credibility of the source).

3. Destination resources and characteristics (attractions and features of a destination).

4. Trip features (distance, trip duration and perceived risk of the area visited).

In addition, Mathieson and Wall recognise that a holiday is a service product with the characteristics of intangibility, perishability and heterogeneity, which in one way or another affect the consumer's decision making. However, apart from pointing out that consumption and evaluation will occur simultaneously, the basis of their model relies on the previously reviewed grand models. This is not to say that the model reflects the depth of insight of these models; on the contrary it only incorporates the idea of the consumer being purposive in actively seeking information and the importance of external factors. The model omits important aspects of perception, memory, personality and information-

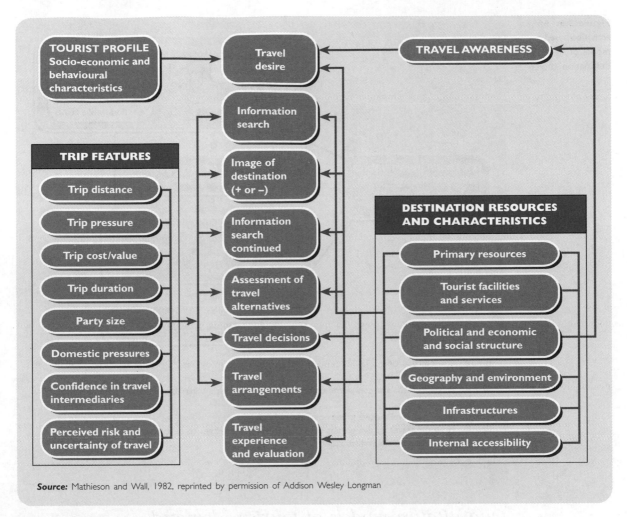

Source: Mathieson and Wall, 1982, reprinted by permission of Addison Wesley Longman

Figure 3.5: The Mathieson and Wall model

processing, which is the basis of the traditional models. The model they provide focuses more on a product-based perspective rather than that of a consumer behaviourist.

Moscardo et al.

Moscardo *et al.* (1996) have provided a different approach to consumer behaviour by stressing the importance of activities as a critical link between travel and destination choice. They argue that motives provide travellers with expectations for activities, and destinations are seen as offering these activities. Figure 3.6 demonstrates this approach as an activities model of destination choice. In this model, Moscardo *et al.* have provided a useful practical outlet for the use of these models by marketers. They argue that activity based traveller segments can be linked to destination activities through product development and communication strategies.

Figure 3.6: An activities-based model of destination choice

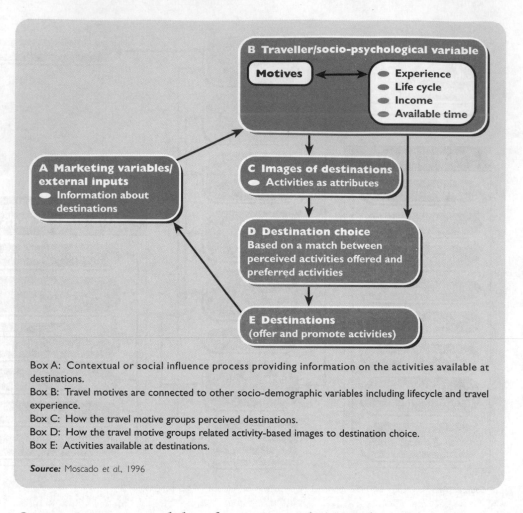

Box A: Contextual or social influence process providing information on the activities available at destinations.

Box B: Travel motives are connected to other socio-demographic variables including lifecycle and travel experience.

Box C: How the travel motive groups perceived destinations.

Box D: How the travel motive groups related activity-based images to destination choice.

Box E: Activities available at destinations.

Source: Moscado et al., 1996

Quantitative models of tourism demand

There are numerous quantitative approaches to analysing patterns of demand, ranging from the simplistic to the highly technical. At the complex end of the spectrum is econometric modelling, using multiple regression. A mathematical relationship is sought that establishes demand as a function of influencing variables (such as income of populations in the generating markets, price of the tourism product and time). However, for most managers who work within tourism such an approach is neither possible nor beneficial. It is far more important to be able to undertake relatively simple analyses in order to interpret demand data, and to highlight trends.

Forecasting

A major use of the analysis of demand is to provide estimates of future values.

Worked Example *Table 3.1 shows the (artificial) quarterly demand for trips on the Smithson ferry over a five-year period. It is required to construct a model for this demand, and to produce forecasts for the following year. Even a cursory glance at the data shows us that demand is highly seasonal. Quarter 3 is the peak season of the year. By considering any of the four quarters over*

Table 3.1:
Demand
(thousands of
passengers)

Year	Quarter			
	Q1	Q2	Q3	Q4
1	63	103	331	74
2	75	118	355	75
3	83	118	410	83
4	92	130	444	99
5	79	135	477	103

the five-year period, there is clear evidence of upward movement, so at this stage it is expected that the analysis will identify an increasing trend. It can be noted even at this stage that demand in year 5 quarter 1 is not in line with the previous values for the same quarter, and hence is unusual.

The aim is to construct a multiplicative model for the demand D; that is

$$D = T*S*R$$

where T is the trend value for that quarter, S is the seasonal index for that quarter, and R is the random or unpredictable element.

The first stage is to compute a four-quarter moving average. For each four consecutive values in the series, their average is calculated and is set against the middle of that time period. For example, take the four consecutive values starting with year 4 quarter 2; these values are 130, 444, 99, 79. Their average is 188 and this is set against the middle of the time period. Note that since the four values taken cover all quarters of the year, their average is 'de-seasonalised' (Table 3.1).

The four-quarter moving averages are now centred as shown in Table 3.2, so as to correspond with the given quarterly time periods. For example the first two four-quarter moving averages 142.75 and 145.75 are averaged to give 144 (to the nearest whole number). In this way each consecutive pair is converted to a centred moving average.

A table showing seasonal indexes can now be produced. The centred moving averages, having been constructed using all seasons of the year, are divided (one by one) by the demand figures of Table 3.1 to produce a seasonality factor for each period of time. The answers are normally multiplied by 100 to give a percentage. So, for example, using Tables 3.1 and 3.2, the seasonality factor for year 1 quarter 3 is equal to

$$\frac{331}{144} \times 100 = 230\%$$

The average of the seasonal factors for each quarter is calculated and shown at the foot of Table 3.3. These four values are the seasonal indexes of demand.

Using standard simple regression analysis based on the centred moving averages of Table 3.2, trend values can be calculated for any time period. The regression line has the equation:

$$trend = 133.3 + 3.67*t$$

Table 3.2: Demand (thousands of passengers)

Year	Q1		Q2		Q3		Q4	
				Quarter				
1 Original series	63		103		331		74	
4-quarter m.a.				142.75		145.75		149.5
Centred m.a.					144		148	
2 Original series	75		118		355		75	
4-quarter m.a.		155.5		155.75		157.75		157.75
Centred m.a.	153		156		157		158	
3 Original series	83		118		410		83	
4-quarter m.a.		171.5		173.5		175.75		178.75
Centred m.a.	165		173		175		177	
4 Original series	92		130		444		99	
4-quarter m.a.		187.25		191.25		188		189.25
Centred m.a.	183		189		190		189	
5 Original series	79		135		477		103	
4-quarter m.a.		197.5		198.5				
Centred m.a.	194		198					

m.a. = moving average.

Table 3.3: Seasonal index of demand

Year	Q1	Q2	Q3	Q4
		Quarter		
1			230	50
2	49	76	226	47
3	50	68	234	47
4	50	69	234	52
5	41	68		
Average (seasonal index)	48	70	231	49

where t = *1, 2, 3, . . . is time starting with the value 1 at year 1 quarter 1, the value 2 at year 1 quarter 2, and so on. Incidentally, regression output gives a correlation coefficient of 0.99 indicating an excellent straight line fit to the centred moving averages. Substituting* t = *1, 2, . . . , 20 into the equation for the regression line, and taking trend values to the nearest whole number, leads to Table 3.4.*

Since the original demand data is to be modelled by the product T*S*R, *dividing the values by the corresponding trend value and then by the appropriate seasonal index from the base of Table 3.3, produces for each period of time the random element R. For example, for year 1, quarter 1, it is calculated as*

$$\frac{63/48\%}{137} = 95.8$$

| Year | Quarter | | | |
	Q1	Q2	Q3	Q4
1	137	140	144	148
2	152	155	159	163
3	166	170	174	177
4	181	185	188	192
5	196	199	203	207

Table 3.4: Trend (thousands of passengers)

| Year | Quarter | | | |
	Q1	Q2	Q3	Q4
1	96	105	100	102
2	103	109	97	94
3	104	99	102	96
4	106	100	102	105
5	84	97	102	102

Table 3.5: Residual index of demand (%)

Table 3.5 represents a complete table of values of R, given to the nearest whole number. These values represent the extent to which demand is made up of the trend identified, combined with the seasonal index. Where the value of R is close to 100%, the random or unpredictable element is negligible in its effect. Only in the case of year 5 quarter 1 is there a sizeable effect on demand due to R. Demand in this quarter could not have been predicted (by this model) because of some random event (which would in practice probably be known).

Quarter 1	101 000
Quarter 2	150 000
Quarter 3	504 000
Quarter 4	108 000

Table 3.6: Forecasts of demand for year 6

In order to use the model of demand established to forecast future demand, it is simply a matter of forming for any particular future time period the product of the trend value for that period (found using the regression line equation), and the appropriate seasonal index from the base of Table 3.3. This method is only suitable for short-term forecasting.

Taking into account that passenger numbers throughout have been in thousands, the forecasts of demand for year 6 are as shown in Table 3.6.

In this section we have described the main components of tourism demand that can be identified, and that can be isolated if required. Aspects of demand introduced here can be developed into formal and often complex models. However, it has to be recognised that even the most complete of analyses of a pattern of tourism demand provides a model that will vary from the true demand by some degree. All series contain elements of the irregular, random or unpredictable. These can take the form of sudden price changes, epidemics, floods, unseasonal weather or even wars.

Analysing patterns of demand over time

An analysis of tourism demand in the long term requires an examination of trends. A recommended first step in the search for a trend within demand data is to sketch a graph showing demand over time. It may be possible to describe the movement simply. The four diagrams in Figure 3.7 provide simple illustrations of patterns of demand over a

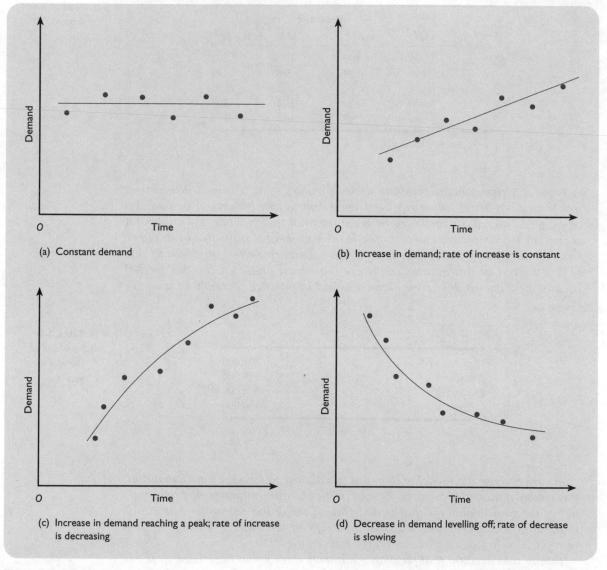

(a) Constant demand

(b) Increase in demand; rate of increase is constant

(c) Increase in demand reaching a peak; rate of increase is decreasing

(d) Decrease in demand levelling off; rate of decrease is slowing

Figure 3.7: Regular patterns of demand

period of time. The continuous lines drawn are suggested models which 'fit' the given demand values and which may then be used to describe the demand and, if required, to project future demand by extrapolation.

The process of formally fitting a line or curve to data to produce a model of demand is called trend curve analysis. In many cases, this can be done 'by eye', without employing statistical methods. Should the importance of the analysis require a more formal and rigorous approach, then standard regression analysis can be employed to find a curve of best fit. Software packages, such as spreadsheet or statistics, will perform what were once tiresome calculations and even inexpensive electronic calculators often have the facility to produce regression output. In this way, and using transformations of variables, a wide range of demand patterns can be analysed.

Macro determinants of demand and propensity to travel

We have examined in detail the influences upon, and models of, tourism demand. This section focuses upon how these influences manifest themselves in terms of patterns of demand in both space and time. It is difficult to generalise about the determinants of demand. There is, for example, a particular problem in terms of linking different levels of generalisation. At one level (and in Chapter 2) we have already considered the individual's consumer behaviour with reference to tourism and analysed the various influences upon his or her behaviour. In this section we consider the aggregate of these individual decisions in terms of the travel propensity of regions or countries. For example, those countries with a high level of economic development and a stable, urbanised population are major generators of tourism demand. The political regime of a country is also relevant here. We can predict then that, despite declarations to the contrary, effective demand for tourism will be highly concentrated among the affluent, industrialised nations. For much of the rest of the world, and indeed many disadvantaged groups in industrialised nations, participation in tourism remains an unobtainable luxury.

We also focus on patterns of demand for international tourism, and provide a brief historical account of the rapid build-up of international tourism demand since the Second World War. We show that rates of growth have not been constant, but have tended to decrease with time, and that growth has not been spread evenly across all parts of the world. Over the second half of the twentieth century, we can see that tourism globally has shown itself to be resilient against major forces that act against travel – individual destinations are, of course, not immune in the same way. Demand is heavily concentrated in Western Europe and North America. In particular we can note the emergence of many countries in the East Asia and Pacific region as receivers and generators of international tourism.

In Chapter 1, we identified travel propensity as a useful measure of demand in a particular population. Broadly, travel propensity for a particular population will increase with characteristics such as:

- income;
- level of urbanisation;
- education levels; and
- mobility levels (such as car ownership).

However, it will decrease with characteristics such as:

- large household size; and
- increasing age.

At the aggregate level the relationship between travel propensity and the characteristics of a population is not straightforward. In particular we must remember that the variables identified above are all related. A high travel propensity would be expected for a developed Western economy with a high degree of urbanisation, high incomes, small household sizes and high levels of mobility. Conversely, low travel propensities would be expected for rural societies with large family sizes and low incomes.

There are also a number of factors that will determine the propensity of a population to travel to particular destinations. We have already examined in detail the importance of destination 'image', and here the difficult issue of measuring promotional spend by a destination in creating the image needs to be considered. In addition, other relevant factors include economic distance, cultural distance and the relative cost of living at the destination. Economic distance, for example, relates to the time and cost of reaching a destination. Although the idea of 'friction of distance' can be used here, in practice distance alone is not the only consideration. For example, it is ironic that international destinations are often closer in economic distance terms than many domestic destinations. (It is easier, and often cheaper, for a traveller to reach the Spanish Costas from London, than it is to reach the Scottish island of Skye.) Cultural distance refers to the difference in culture between the origin area and the destination. For more adventurous travellers this acts to attract rather than to deter a visit. Costs at a destination are not an absolute quantity but have to be considered relative to the value of the traveller's own currency. This is graphically demonstrated by the ebb and flow of traffic across the Atlantic dependent upon whether the dollar or European currencies are the strongest. Perception of price is also an important consideration – Switzerland is perceived by many as an expensive destination but in fact prices have fallen in recent years *vis-à-vis* many European currencies. However, measurement of such variables can be problematic.

Step analysis

When individual purchasing patterns and the influences upon them are aggregated to the national level it is possible to gain a clearer view as to the influences upon global patterns of demand for tourism. This is known as performing a STEP analysis – analysing the impact of:

S   social factors;

T   technological factors;

E   economic factors; and

P   political factors.

Social factors

Levels of population growth, its development, distribution and density affect travel propensity. Population growth and development can be closely linked to the stages of economic growth of a society by considering the **demographic transition** where population growth and development is seen in terms of four connected phases (Box 3.1).

Population density has a less important influence on travel propensity than has the distribution of population between urban and rural areas. Densely populated rural nations may have low travel propensities owing to the level of economic development and the simple fact that the population is mainly dependent upon subsistence agriculture and

Box 3.1 The demographic transition and tourism

The high stationary phase

This corresponds to many undeveloped countries with high birth and death rates, keeping the population at a fluctuating, but low level.

The early expanding phase

Here high birth rates continue, but there is a fall in death rates due to improved health, sanitation and social stability. This leads to a population expansion characterised by young, large families. Countries in this phase are often unable to provide for their growing populations and are gradually becoming poorer. Clearly, tourism is a luxury that cannot be afforded, although some nations are developing an inbound tourism industry to earn foreign exchange.

The late expanding phase

In this phase, a fall in the birth rate is rooted in the growth of an industrial society and birth control technology. Most developing countries fit into the early expanding and late expanding phases with a transition to the late expanding phase paralleling the drive to maturity.

The low stationary phase

This phase corresponds to the high mass consumption stage of economic development. Here, birth and death rates have stabilised at a low level.

has neither the time nor the income to devote to tourism. In contrast, densely populated urban areas normally indicate a developed economy with consumer purchasing power, giving rise to high travel propensity and the urge to escape from the urban environment.

The distribution of population within a nation also affects patterns, rather than strict levels, of tourist demand. Where population is concentrated into one part of the country, tourism demand is distorted. This asymmetrical distribution of population is well illustrated by the USA where two-thirds of the population live in the eastern third of the country. The consequent east to west pattern of tourist focus (and permanent migrants) has placed pressure on the recreation and tourist resources of the western states.

Social changes since the Second World War in the developed world have changed travel demand patterns. Most of these countries are experiencing a slowing of the birth rate, with some having projections of population decline. This, combined with extensions in life expectancy, has created an ageing population.

The older generation in the 'third age' or 'grey panther' group is often made up of those who did not pay into pension schemes and consequently whose pension and benefits barely keep up with inflation. These groups and the unemployed are likely to adapt their lifestyle to basic activities and seek cheap travel activities. Other better off older people are able to travel outside the main season and offer the ideal target market for season extension.

Technological factors

There is no doubt that technology has been a major enabling factor in terms of converting suppressed demand into effective demand. This is particularly the case in terms of transport technology where the development of the jet engine in the late 1950s gave aircraft both speed and range and stimulated the variety of tourism products available in the international market to meet pent-up demand for international travel. Developments in aircraft technology have continued but so has the level of refinement and access to the motor car. Similarly, the development of information technology is a critical enabling factor in terms of tourism demand (see Chapter 20). Generally, technology acts to increase access to tourism by lowering the cost or by making the product more accessible. Examples here include developments in 'recreational technology' such as windsurfers, durable outdoor clothing, heli-skiing and heli-hiking, and off-road recreational vehicles.

Economic factors

A society's level of economic development is a major determinant of the magnitude of tourist demand because the economy influences so many critical, and interrelated, factors. One approach is to consider a simple division of world economies into the affluent 'North', where the countries are major generators and recipients of both international and domestic tourism, and the poorer 'South'. In the latter, some countries are becoming generators of international tourism but mostly tourism is domestic, often supplemented by an inbound international flow of tourists. In fact, the economic development of nations can be divided into a number of stages, as outlined in Table 3.7.

As a society moves towards the high mass consumption stage in Table 3.7 a number of important processes occur. The balance of employment changes from work in the primary sector (agriculture, fishing, forestry) to work in the secondary sector (manufacturing goods) and the tertiary sector (services such as tourism). As this process unfolds, an affluent society usually emerges and the percentage of the population who are economically active increases from less than a third in the developing world to half or more in the high mass consumption stage. With progression to the drive to maturity, discretionary incomes increase and create demand for consumer goods and leisure pursuits such as tourism.

Other developments are closely linked to the changing nature of employment. The population is healthier and has time for recreation and tourism (and has paid holiday entitlement). Improving educational standards and media channels boosts awareness of tourism opportunities, and transportation and mobility rise in line with these changes. Institutions respond to this increased demand by developing a range of leisure products and services. These developments occur in conjunction with each other until, at the high mass consumption stage, all the economic indicators encourage high levels of travel propensity. Clearly, tourism is a result of industrialisation and, quite simply, the more highly developed an economy, the greater the levels of tourist demand.

As more countries reach the drive to maturity or high mass consumption stage, so the volume of trade and foreign investment increases and business travel develops. Business travel is sensitive to economic activity, and although it could be argued that increasingly sophisticated communication systems may render business travel unnecessary, there is no evidence of this to date. Indeed, the very development of global markets and the constant need for face-to-face contact should ensure a continuing demand for business travel.

Table 3.7: Economic development and tourism

Economic stage	Some characteristics	Examples
Traditional society Long-established land-owning aristocracy, traditional customs, majority employed in agriculture. Very low output per capita, impossible to improve without changing system. Poor health levels, high poverty levels.	**The undeveloped world** Economic and social conditions deny most forms of tourism except perhaps domestic VFR.	Parts of Africa, parts of southern Asia.
Preconditions for take-off Innovation of ideas from outside the system. Leaders recognise the desirability of change. **Take-off** Leaders in favour of change gain power and alter production methods and economic structure. Manufacturing and services expand.	**The developing world** From the take-off stage, economic and social conditions allow increasing amounts of domestic tourism (mainly VFR). International tourism is also possible in the drive to maturity. Inbound tourism is often encouraged as a foreign exchange earner.	Parts of South and Central America;[a] parts of the Middle East,[a] Asia and Africa.
Drive to maturity[b] Industrialisation continues in all economic sectors with a switch from heavy manufacturing to sophisticated and diversified products.		Mexico; parts of South America.
High mass consumption Economy now at full potential, producing large numbers of consumer goods and services. New emphasis on satisfying cultural needs.	**The developed world** Major generators of international and domestic tourism.	North America; Western Europe; Japan; Australia; New Zealand.

[a] Countries that are members of the Organization of Petroleum Exporting Countries (OPEC) are a notable exception in these regions.
[b] Centrally planned economies merit a special classification, although most are at the drive to maturity stage.
Source: Boniface and Cooper (1987), adapted from Rostow (1959).

Political factors

Politics affect travel propensities in a variety of ways. For example, the degree of government involvement in promoting and providing facilities for tourism depends upon the political complexion of the government. Governments that support the free market try to create an environment in which the tourism industries can flourish, rather than the administration being directly involved in tourism itself. Socialist administrations, on the other hand, encourage the involvement of the government in tourism and, through 'social tourism', often provide opportunities for the 'disadvantaged' to participate in tourism.

Governments in times of economic problems may control levels of propensity for travel overseas by limiting the amount of foreign currency that can be taken out of a country or demanding a monetary bond to be left in the country while the resident is overseas. Government restrictions on travel also include visa and passport controls as well as taxes on travel. Generally, however, these controls are not totally effective and, of course, they can be evaded.

We can also identify inadvertent political influences – for example, a government with an economy suffering high inflation may find that inbound travel is discouraged. In a more general sense, unstable political regimes (where civil disorder or war is prevalent) may forbid non-essential travel, and inbound tourism will be adversely affected.

Patterns of demand for tourism

Patterns of demand: the historic trend

Since the Second World War, there has been rapid growth world-wide in international tourism (see Table 3.8 and Figure 3.8). After the war increasing proportions of the populations of the industrialised nations were in possession of both the time (in the form of paid leave from employment) and the money (owing to increased disposable incomes) to engage in international travel. Supply to meet this increased demand for leisure tourism in particular was developed mainly in the form of the standard, mass package tour. This was made possible by the arrival of the jet aircraft in 1958, and by cheap oil. Further, international travel was boosted by a substantial increase in business travel.

Table 3.8:
International tourism trends: arrivals and receipts world-wide, 1950–95

	Arrivals (thousands)	Receipts[a] (US\$ million)
1950	25 282	2 100
1960	69 296	6 867
1970	159 690	17 900
1980	284 841	102 372
1981	288 848	104 309
1982	286 780	98 634
1983	284 173	98 395
1984	312 434	109 832
1985	321 240	116 158
1986	330 746	140 019
1987	356 640	171 319
1988	381 824	197 692
1989	415 376	211 366
1990	454 800	255 000
1991	463 100	267 519
1992	502 900	305 021
1993	512 200	307 371
1994	531 400	355 780
1995	567 000[b]	372 000[b]

[a] Excludes international fare receipts.
[b] Estimate.
Source: WTO.

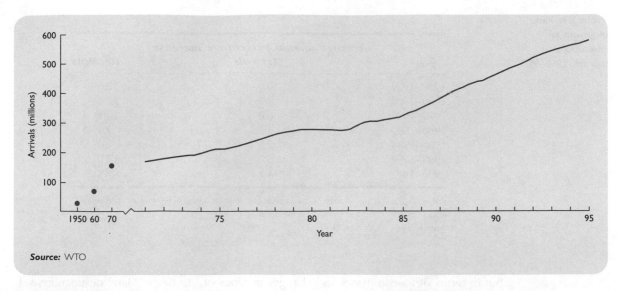

Source: WTO

Figure 3.8: International travel arrivals, 1950–90

Over this period, international tourism has shown itself on a world-wide scale to be robust, showing resilience against such factors as terrorism and political unrest in many parts of the world, world-wide economic recession and fluctuating exchange rates. Generally, at times of economic growth, demand for travel has increased; on the other hand, during times of recession, demand has either remained constant or has soon recovered. This global experience of almost uninterrupted growth is not, though, equally shared by all destinations. For example, tourists tend to stay away from destinations that they rightly or wrongly perceive to be unsafe – this has clearly affected tourism to the Middle East and North Africa. Other destinations might suffer because they are simply no longer fashionable.

Industrialised and developing countries have become all too aware of the potential of incoming tourism as an invisible export to support the current account of their balance of payments. In the 1990s, tourism accounts for up to 10% of world trade in goods and services, and can be considered to be one of the world's top three industries, along with oil and motor vehicles. Every day, well over one million people take an international trip.

The 1980s

As the market has matured, the average annual growth rate has tended to decrease. During the period up to 1980, international arrivals doubled every ten years or so. In contrast, the 1980s experienced a slowing of average annual growth rates to a little over 4%. Growth in the latter half of the decade was in fact more in line with that of the previous two decades and followed the slow growth of the early 1980s.

We can explain such unevenness of tourism demand by a number of major factors and events. The decade opened with economic recession which acted to dampen international travel, and volume did not really recover until 1984. The years 1984 and 1985 were in fact record years with European destinations doing particularly well. However, the accident at the nuclear power plant in Chernobyl, in the then Soviet Union, combined with terrorist activity, the Libyan bombing incident and the weakening of the US dollar against other major currencies, all conspired to contribute to the depressing of demand for tourism. As a result, international travel was severely affected. The effect was not so much in terms of total numbers, which were up on the previous year anyway,

Table 3.9: Rates of growth of international tourism, 1950–95

	Average annual percentage increase	
	Arrivals	*Receipts*
1950–1959	10.6	12.6
1960–1969	8.7	10.0
1970–1979	6.0	19.1
1980–1989	4.5	9.5
1980–1984	2.5	2.6
1985–1989	6.7	17.0
1990–1995	4.1	7.5

The average percentage increase is calculated as the constant annual percentage increase which would result in the overall change over the specified period.
Source: based on WTO data

but in terms of tourism flows and changes in types of trip taken. Many destinations suffered badly, whereas others gained. The second half of the decade saw a return to some sort of normality, both in terms of growth rates and in terms of types of trip taken.

International tourist arrivals grew at an average rate of 4.5% during the 1980s, made up of 2.5% in the first half and 6.7% in the second (WTO, 1994); see Table 3.9. These figures could be regarded as average growth world-wide and therefore conceal considerable variation in performance by region, continent, country or even different destinations within the same country. Some countries (such as Turkey, Hong Kong, Australia, Thailand, China and Portugal) successfully encouraged rapid growth; others experienced either no growth (Ireland) or decreases (Sri Lanka and Lebanon) in visitor numbers.

The 1990s

The 1990s opened with the Gulf War and further economic recession, leading to great uncertainty for international tourism. In the short term, the build-up to the Gulf War, the war itself and the aftermath led initially to the virtual cessation of travel to the Gulf, the eastern Mediterranean and North Africa. It not only depressed international tourism further afield, but also the economic recession experienced by the majority of industrialised countries was aggravated by it. The lessons of earlier years were that international tourism would recover and develop with new products, destinations and generating markets and indeed this has been the case, with tourism responding well to the growth in economic and social conditions and little or no slow down has been seen in international tourism flows in the 1990s. In particular the decade has been characterised by the growth of overseas travel by residents of developing countries and the acceleration of multiple, but short-haul, trips from travellers in industrialised countries.

Patterns of demand: the regional dimension

Table 3.10 shows over the 45-year period 1950 to 1995 the changes in the share of international tourism world-wide of the different regions. Regional shares have to be viewed in the context of a greatly changing total, and so even a constant share represents substantial growth.

Europe and, to a lesser extent, the Americas have for some time dominated the international travel scene in terms of numbers of arrivals and receipts. More specifically, it is

Table 3.10:
Regional share of
international
tourism, 1950–95

	1950 (%)	1960 (%)	1970 (%)	1980 (%)	1990 (%)	1995 (%)
(a) Share of arrivals						
Europe	66.5	72.5	70.5	68.4	63.5	59.5
Americas	29.6	24.1	23.0	18.9	18.8	19.7
East Asia/Pacific	0.8	1.0	3.0	7.0	11.4	14.7
Africa	2.1	1.1	1.5	2.5	3.4	3.3
Middle East	0.9	1.0	1.4	2.4	2.1	1.9
South Asia	0.2	0.3	0.6	0.8	0.7	0.7
(b) Share of receipts						
Europe	41.3	56.8	62.0	59.3	54.4	51.0
Americas	50.5	35.7	26.8	24.9	26.1	25.6
East Asia/Pacific	1.4	2.8	6.2	7.3	14.4	18.6
Africa	4.2	2.6	2.2	2.7	1.9	1.8
Middle East	2.3	1.5	2.3	4.3	2.5	1.7
South Asia	0.3	0.5	0.6	1.5	0.8	0.8

Columns do not necessarily add up to 100% because of rounding.
Source: based on WTO data

Western Europe and North America that have given rise to a high level of geographical concentration of movement. In 1990, Europe accounted for well over half of all international tourist arrivals, with the European Community (EC) alone hosting 40% of the total.

We can identify a number of factors that explain the leading position held by Europe:

- Large segments of the populations receive relatively high incomes, resulting in high levels of disposable income.

- Paid leave from work is normal in European countries.

- High proportions of the populations of, for example, Germany, France and the UK attach very high priority to the annual foreign holiday and are reluctant to let it go even in times of recession.

- There is a wealth of both artificial and natural attractions.

- Demand for foreign travel is satisfied by a large tourist industry and the necessary infrastructure.

- International travel need not involve great distances, owing to the number of relatively small countries.

A number of these factors are equally applicable to North America. However, the sheer size of the USA and Canada means that the majority of their populations prefer to take domestic trips. Nevertheless, there are substantial numbers of North Americans who do engage in foreign travel each year, not merely within their own continent but also in long-haul trips.

The shares of Europe and the Americas have fluctuated somewhat over the years, with some evidence of a decline in terms of both numbers of arrivals and tourism receipts. The clearest trend though has been the emergence of countries of the East Asia and

Box 3.2   Characteristics of generating markets

A specific country's market normally has the following features:

- It includes at least one of the four top generators of international tourism world-wide – Germany, the USA, Japan and the UK.
- It includes neighbouring states, since the distance and cost involved are relatively small.
- It includes countries further afield if, as is the case between the USA and Western Europe, air travel is available and at a cost within the reach of large segments of the population.
- It depends on the size of the population of generating states and their propensity to travel.
- It depends on ease of movement across borders.
- It depends on the real and perceived price of trips to the destination.
- It depends on the attractiveness of the destination.
- It depends on the social, cultural and historic links between countries.
- It depends on marketing activity and an appropriate supply in terms of transport, accommodation, etc.

Pacific (EAP) region as both receivers and generators of international tourism. The EAP share of arrivals world-wide was only 1% in 1960, but grew to 3% in 1970, 7% in 1980 and 11% in 1990. The increasing share is of an expanding market. This represents remarkable growth in a highly competitive environment. Examples of countries in the EAP which have been part of this success are Hong Kong, Singapore, Thailand, Australia, Korea and Indonesia.

We can see that the shares of international tourism of Africa, Middle East and South Asia have throughout the period 1950 to 1990 been small, though with a high level of fluctuation. As regions, they are not able to compete with Europe, the Americas and the EAP either in terms of generating or receiving large numbers of international tourists. The reasons for this are mainly economic. Destination countries within these regions can compete for specific markets from the major generating countries. Many, though, have been vulnerable to the effects of unrest and war, not necessarily in their own countries but near enough for them to be perceived as dangerous places to visit. In general, their incoming international tourism has suffered when business conditions have been depressed in the traditional tourism generating countries. Box 3.2 illustrates some typical characteristics of generating countries.

Patterns of demand: seasonality

We know that within most patterns of demand in tourism, there are regular fluctuations due solely to the time of year. This phenomenon is called seasonality. It is often the result of changes in climate over the calendar year. Thus a destination that is essentially attractive because of its beaches and hot summers is likely to have a highly seasonal demand. The same applies to demand for holidays at a ski resort that has snow for only part of the year. There are though other influencing factors, such as the timing of school and work holidays, or regular special events held at a destination.

As tourism is a service industry, it is not possible to stockpile the product – a hotel room that is unsold on a particular night, an unsold seat on a flight or an unsold theatre ticket all have an economic value of zero. Seasonality of demand therefore causes major problems for the tourist industry. It can result in only seasonal employment for employees, and the under-use or even closing down of facilities at certain times of the year. It can also result in an over-stretching by some destinations and businesses at times of peak activity, to compensate for low demand off-season. This leads to overcrowding, over-bookings, high prices and ultimately to customer dissatisfaction and a worsening reputation.

Responses to seasonality in order to reduce it vary. Typically they involve attempts to create or shift demand to the shoulder or trough months, either through setting price differentials or through the introduction or enhancement of all-year facilities. Marketing may be targeted at groups that have the time and resources to travel at any time of the year, notably the elderly.

In an analysis of monthly demand data, note is often taken of the number of days in the month. Even with identical daily demand in January and February, one would expect their monthly demand figures to differ by about 10%. There can be substantially different levels in demand for the tourism product on different days of the same week, depending on the precise business or activity involved. Hotels often experience differences in room bookings at weekends compared with weekdays. This is particularly the case where a hotel is able to fill with businesspeople during the week at high rates, and achieves at best only reasonable occupancy at weekends through special offers. In some parts of the world, Sundays are often 'dead' nights for large, city-centre hotels. Attractions or recreation sites often attract more visitors at weekends than on weekdays.

Certain destinations receive tourists on certain days of a month as determined by passenger transport schedules. This can affect tourism businesses and needs to be taken into account when comparing sales in the same month of successive years – there may, for example, be four Saturdays in August one year, and five the next.

Our normal calendar can also affect the way demand data are analysed. This is particularly the case for Easter, which occurs in different weeks of successive years and can be in March or April. Thus comparing monthly figures year on year for these two months can be misleading, particularly if Easter is a period of high demand. Other national holidays may cause problems for the business analyst, since demand is affected considerably. The comparison of a week's business with that of the corresponding week of the previous year would take account of the dates of bank holidays, etc.

Like any business activity, tourism is subject to and part of general economic cycles. Also regular events such as festivals, games or exhibitions cause cycles in tourism movement.

Conclusion

Models of consumer behaviour in tourism remain at a relatively early stage of their development and significant levels of research are still required to clarify what are, effectively, subjective psychological influences upon buying processes in tourism. Nevertheless, it is crucial that the inadequacies of these models do not prohibit their use since they offer an important input into quantitative models of forecasting which are required for planning and management in the tourism industry.

Quantitative models are also critical in predicting flows and patterns of demand, in addition to numerical estimations of probable future tourism activity. Difficulties associated with forecasting and the models utilised are exacerbated ▷

Conclusion continued

by the fact that demand for tourism at the aggregated world level is characterised by uncertainty and a vulnerability to events that are uncontrollable. Although rates of growth for demand are slowing, it is predicted that levels of demand will reach unprecedented levels into the next millennium.

Demand remains – and is anticipated to remain – concentrated in the affluent, industrialised nations of the world where the determinants of demand at an individual level outlined in Chapter 2, such as income and paid holiday entitlement, predominate. However, emergent nations in the EAP region, where economic power is becoming increasingly focused, are expected to become major generators and receivers of tourism.

Chapter discussion questions

1. Review the process you went through in the purchase decision process for the last holiday you took.

2. What factors differentiate a high-involvement purchase, such as tourism, from a low-involvement purchase?

3. Taking a country or region of your choice, look at the patterns of demand for tourism and explain them in respect of social, technological, economic and political factors.

4. How might the motivational 'push' of the tourist (e.g. sunlust vs wanderlust) affect the buying decision process for tourism? Identify the elements of the process which are likely to predominate for those motivated by sunlust and wanderlust.

5. Do you think the tourism industry takes full advantage of what is known about the buying decision process in tourism in respect of marketing?

Recommended further reading

- Archer, B. H. (1994) 'Trends in international tourism', pp. 93–8 in *Tourism Marketing and Management Handbook*, 2nd edn, Witt, S. F. and Moutinho, L. (eds), Prentice Hall, Hemel Hempstead.
- Archer, B. H. (1994) 'Demand forecasting and estimation', pp. 86–92 in *Handbook of Travel, Tourism and Hospitality Research*, Ritchie, J. R. B. and Goeldner, C. R. (eds), Wiley, New York.
- Mill, R. C. and Morrison, A. (1985) *The Tourism System*, Prentice Hall, Englewood Cliffs, NJ.
- WTO (1994) *Global Tourism Forecasts to the Year 2000 and beyond*, WTO, Madrid.

Bibliography

- Ajzen, I. and Fishbein, M. (1980) *Understanding Attitudes and Predicting Social Behaviour*, Prentice Hall, Englewood Cliffs, NJ.

● Ajzen, I. and Fishbein, M. (1975) *Attitude Intention and Behaviour: An Introduction to Theory and Research*, Addison Wesley, Reading, MA.

● Allcock, J. B. (1989) 'Seasonality', pp. 387–92 in *Tourism Marketing and Management Handbook*, Witt, S. F. and Moutinho, L. (eds), Prentice Hall, Hemel Hempstead.

● Archer, B. H. (1994) 'Trends in international tourism', pp. 93–8 in *Tourism Marketing and Management Handbook*, 2nd edn, Witt S. F. and Moutinho, L. (eds), Prentice Hall, Hemel Hempstead.

● Archer, B. H. (1994) 'Demand forecasting and estimation', pp. 86–92 in *Handbook of Travel, Tourism and Hospitality Research*, Ritchie, J. R. B. and Goeldner, C. R. (eds), Wiley, New York.

● Assael, H. (1987) *Consumer Behaviour and Marketing Action*, Kent, Boston MA.

● Boniface, B. and Cooper, C. (1987) *The Geography of Travel and Tourism*, Heinemann, London.

● Chubb, M. and Chubb, H. R. (1981) *One Third of Our Time*, Wiley, New York.

● Crompton, J. (1979) 'Why people go on pleasure vacation', *Annals of Tourism Research* **6**(4), 408–24.

● Dann, G. M. S. (1981) 'Tourist motivation: an appraisal', *Annals of Tourism Research*, **8**(2), 187–219.

● Engel, J. F., Kollat, D. J. and Blackwell, R. P. (1968) *Consumer Behaviour*, Holt, Reinehart and Wilson, New York.

● Engel, J. F., Blackwell, R. D. and Miniard, P. (1986) *Consumer Behaviour*, Dryden Press, New York.

● Gilbert, D. C. (1991) 'An examination of the consumer decision process related to tourism', pp. 78–105 in *Progress in Tourism Recreation and Hospitality Management*, Vol. III, Cooper, C. (ed.), Belhaven, London.

● Goffman, E. (1959) *The Presentation of Self in Everyday Life*, Pelican, Middlesex.

● Goodall, B. (1991) 'Understanding holiday choice', pp. 58–77 in *Progress in Tourism Recreation and Hospitality Management*, Vol. III, Cooper, C. (ed.), Belhaven, London.

● Howard, J. A. and Sheth, J. N. (1969) *The Theory of Buyer Behaviour*, Wiley, New York.

● Jenkins, R. (1978) 'Family vacation decision making', *Journal of Travel Research*, **17**(4) Spring, 2–7.

● Johnson, P. and Thomas, B. (eds) (1992) *Choice and Demand in Tourism*, Mansell, London.

● Latham, J. (1992) 'International tourism flows', *Progress in Tourism and Hospitality Research*, **1**(1), 63–71.

● Latham, J. and Fletcher, J. (annual) 'Databank', *Tourism Economics*.

● McIntosh, R. W., Goeldner, C. R. and Ritchie, J. R. B. (1995) *Tourism Principles, Practices, Philosophies*, Wiley, New York.

● Mathieson, A. and Wall, G. (1982) *Tourism: Economic Physical and Social Impacts*, Longman, London.

● Mazanec, J. A. (1995) 'Consumer behaviour', pp. 273–85 in *Tourism and Marketing and Management Handbook*, student edn, Witt, S. F. and Moutinho, L. (eds), Prentice Hall, Hemel Hempstead.

● Mayo, E. and Jarvis, L. (1981) *The Psychology of Leisure Travel*, CBI Publishing, Boston, MA.

● Mill, R. C. and Morrison, A. (1985) *The Tourism System*, Prentice Hall, Englewood Cliffs, NJ.

● Moscardo, G., Morrison, A. M., Pearce, P. L., Lang, C. T. and O'Leary, J. (1996) 'Understanding vacation destination choice through travel motivation and activities', *Journal of Vacation Marketing*, **2**(2), 109–22.

● Nicosia, F. M. (1966) *Consumer Decision Processes: Marketing and Advertising Implications*, Prentice Hall, Englewood Cliffs, NJ.
● Olsen, D. and McCubbin, H. (1983) *Families, What Makes Them Work?*, Sage, Beverley Hills, CA.
● Organization for Economic Co-operation and Development, annual, *Tourism Policy and International Tourism in OECD Member Countries*, OECD, Paris.
● Pearce, D. (1987) *Tourism Today*, Longman, Harlow.
● Pearce, D. (1989) *Tourist Development*, Longman, Harlow.
● Pearce, P. L. (1982) *The Social Psychology of Tourist Behaviour*, Pergamon Press, Oxford.
● Rapoport, R. and Rapoport, R. N. (1975) *Leisure and the Family Life Cycle*, Routledge & Kegan Paul, London.
● Rostow, W. W. (1959) *The Stages of Economic Growth*, Cambridge University Press, Cambridge.
● Schmoll, G. A. (1977) *Tourism Promotion*, Tourism International Press, London.
● Sheth, J. (1974) 'A theory of family buying decisions', in *Models of Buyer Behaviour*, Sheth, J. N. (ed.), Harper and Row, New York.
● Wahab, S., Crampon, L. J., and Rothfield, L. M. (1976) *Tourism Marketing*, Tourism International Press, London.
● Wanhill, S. R. C. and Aircy, D. W. (1980) 'Demand for accommodation', pp. 24 and 29 in *Managerial Economics for Hotel Operation*, Kotas, R. (ed.), Surrey University Press, London.
● Witt, S. F. and Martin, C. A. (1989) 'Demand forecasting in tourism and recreation', pp. 4–32 in *Progress in Tourism, Recreation and Hospitality Management*, Vol. 1, Cooper, C. P. (ed.), Belhaven, London.
● Witt, S. F. and Witt, C. A. (1992) *Modelling and Forecasting Demand in Tourism*, Academic Press, New York.
● Witt, S. F., Brooke, M. Z. and Buckley, P. J. (1991) *The Management of International Tourism*, Unwin Hyman, London.
● WTO (1991) *Impact of the Gulf Crisis on International Tourism* (special report), WTO, Madrid.
● WTO (1994) *Global Tourism Forecasts to the Year 2000 and beyond*, WTO, Madrid.
● WTO (annual) *Yearbook of Tourism Statistics*, WTO, Madrid.
● WTO (annual) *Compendium of Tourism Statistics*, WTO, Madrid.
● WTO (three issues per year) *Travel and Tourism Barometer*, WTO, Madrid.

Chapter Four

Measuring demand for tourism

Introduction

The measurement of demand for tourism is a relatively recent activity. It is difficult to find estimates of international tourism demand relating to the period before the Second World War. Since then, however, measurement has gradually been taken more seriously, and statistics of international tourism demand between 1950 and 1995 were provided in Chapter 3.

The development of methods world-wide to provide reasonably reliable estimates of domestic tourism has been a relatively slow process mainly because it is often given low priority, since there is no obvious or direct effect on a country's balance of payments. Also, since it involves no crossing of international boundaries, the monitoring of travel within a country is inherently more difficult.

In this chapter we initially describe and critically appraise the measurement of demand for both international and domestic tourism. We treat these separately for convenience, although it is recognised that international and domestic movements may be considered essentially the same activity. Certainly they have much in common. We consider why tourism demand is measured, what definitions are used and which statistics are normally compiled. We include a description of methods commonly used and an indication of their strengths and weaknesses.

Closely linked to the measurement of demand is the concept of collecting market intelligence. In tourism, this often means using secondary data (for example, data produced by national or regional government bodies), combined with primary data through market surveys. In the latter part of this chapter we provide a practical guide to market research for the tourism industry, and in particular market surveys. The possible benefits of research to an organisation are outlined. The various stages of research are also explained, from the agreement of research purpose and objectives, through research design, data collection and analysis, to the reporting of the research. We give emphasis to the importance of a manager making use of findings and feeding them into the decision-making process.

Chapter learning objectives

In this chapter, we review the key issues associated with the measurement of tourism demand, providing the reader with:

▪▪ an understanding of the reasons why we measure both international and domestic demand for tourism;

▪▪ a review of what is measured in respect of tourism activity;

▪▪ an appreciation of the difficulties of researching tourism markets and why tourism statistics must be interpreted with caution; and

▪▪ a discussion of the research process and how it might best be implemented in tourism.

Demand for international tourism

Why measure international tourism?

National governments are generally extremely keen to monitor and attach measures to the movement of people into and out of their countries. This is for a variety of reasons, many of which have nothing whatsoever to do with tourism, such as security, health and immigration control. The measurement of tourism movement, however, has increasingly been seen as important because of the effects of tourism activity on a country's balance of payments.

The balance of payments is a country's financial accounts. There are movements of monies into and out of these accounts. Any standard economics text will provide a detailed and proper explanation of the various components. An obvious way in which tourism has an impact on the balance of payments is through the spending of international tourists. We can identify two aspects here:

1. Residents of country X, who travel abroad, spend money abroad. This has a negative effect on the balance of payments of country X (and positive effects on the balance of payments of countries visited). With regard to the movement of money, this can be thought of as an import as far as X is concerned. It is referred to as an invisible import since there is no associated tangible good (such as a car or refrigerator).

2. Residents of a foreign country, who are incoming tourists to country X, spend money in X. This has a positive effect on the balance of payments of X (and corresponding negative effects on the balance of payments of the country of origin of the tourist). As far as X is concerned, the direction of the spending is such that it is considered to be an invisible export.

The two components described above combine to form what is known as the travel account for a country. A positive travel account means that spending by incoming tourists exceeds spending abroad by outgoing tourists, and the combined effect will be of benefit to the balance of payments. Many commentators argue that any comparison of the two types of spending is unfair, since they reflect different activities.

The above analysis does not take into account fares paid to international passenger transport carriers and the various secondary effects of tourist spending. In Part 2 of this book we consider the impacts of tourism in detail, including a comprehensive review of the economic impacts.

We can see, then, that governments are keen to measure the movement of international tourism, but particularly incoming tourism because of its economic benefits. There are, however, a number of other important reasons:

- Official records can be built up and trends in movements can be monitored over a period of time. This means, for example, that the effectiveness of the marketing arm of government can be monitored, or that any particular promotional campaign which attempts to attract visitors from a particular country can be assessed.

- In general, information about the origins of visitors, their trip and attitudes can be used for a variety of purposes in marketing or planning. This is true also for tourism organisations at regional and local levels, provided that data collected at international level can be disaggregated and still be reliable.

In addition, some commercial organisations, although a minority, can and do make use of international tourism statistics. An incoming tour operator or wholesaler, for example, needs to be aware of current trends in order that programmes can be adjusted accordingly. Similarly, international and national hotel chains monitor changes in demand as part of their intelligence activity.

Some definitions

In collecting any information on the movement of travellers, it is essential to decide who is to be included. Everyone would agree that a family on holiday should count in the figures, but what about a businessperson, or the crew of a passenger liner, or even a member of the armed forces on duty in a foreign land? See Figure 4.1 for the answers! We can identify a number of principles that should govern the formation of a terminology:

- Definitions should be unambiguous and easy to understand.
- Definitions should normally be consistent with established usage of the words concerned.
- Definitions should, as far as is reasonably possible, facilitate measurement.

There is a major difficulty concerning the word 'tourism' itself. The normal and everyday use of the word relates to pleasure travel, but it would certainly exclude business travel. This is unfortunately not in line with what has become accepted as standard in the tourism literature. It is standard practice to include, as tourists, not only people who travel for pleasure but also those who travel for the purposes of business, visiting friends and relatives, or even shopping. The reasons concern the use that is made of tourism statistics. After all, passenger transport carriers would wish for such a broad range of travellers to be included; a large number of hoteliers are interested in business travel because of the business it generates for them, and so on.

The definitions we give here are those that have become accepted. Figure 4.1 shows the breakdown of all travellers who cross international frontiers into those who are to be included in tourism statistics (to be called 'visitors') and those who are not. The decision as to whom to include is based on the purpose of visit. Visitors are divided according to whether or not there is an overnight stay in the country: if there is, then the visitor is deemed to be a tourist; otherwise he or she is a same-day visitor (previously called an excursionist). In summary, for the purposes of classifying international travellers:

- A visitor is a traveller who is included in tourism statistics, based on his or her purpose of visit, which includes holidays, visiting friends and relatives, and business. A fuller list is shown in Figure 4.1.

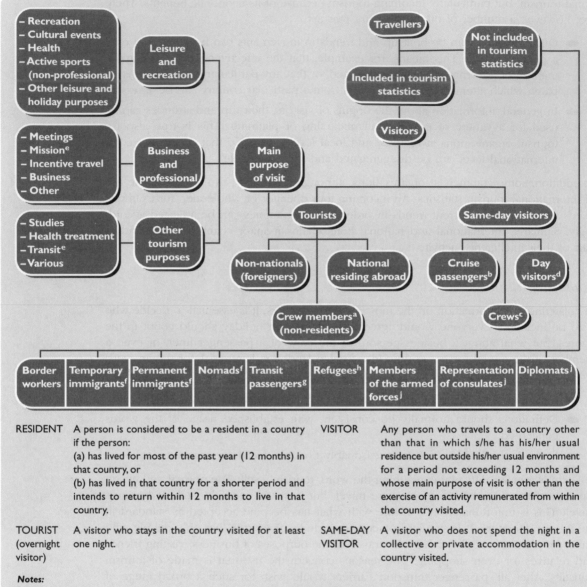

RESIDENT A person is considered to be a resident in a country if the person:
(a) has lived for most of the past year (12 months) in that country, or
(b) has lived in that country for a shorter period and intends to return within 12 months to live in that country.

VISITOR Any person who travels to a country other than that in which s/he has his/her usual residence but outside his/her usual environment for a period not exceeding 12 months and whose main purpose of visit is other than the exercise of an activity remunerated from within the country visited.

TOURIST (overnight visitor) A visitor who stays in the country visited for at least one night.

SAME-DAY VISITOR A visitor who does not spend the night in a collective or private accommodation in the country visited.

Notes:

a Foreign air or ship crews docked or in lay over and who use the accommodation establishments of the country visited.

b Persons who arrive in a country aboard cruise ships (as defined by the International Maritime Organization, 1965) and who spend the night aboard ship even when disembarking for one or more day visits.

c Crews who are not residents of the country visited and who stay in the country for the day.

d Visitors who arrive and leave the same day for leisure and recreation, business and professional or other tourism purposes including transit day visitors *en route* to or from their destination countries.

e Overnight visitors *en route* from their destination countries.

f As defined by the United Nations in the *Recommendations on Statistics of International Migration*, 1980.

g Who do not leave the transit area of the airport or the port, including transfer between airports or ports.

h As defined by the United Nations High Commissioner for Refugees, 1967.

j When they travel from their country of origin to the duty station and vice versa (including household servants and dependants and dependants accompanying or joining them).

Source: WTO

Figure 4.1: Classification of international visitors

- A tourist is a visitor who spends at least one night in the country visited.

- A same-day visitor is a visitor who does not spend the night in a collective or private accommodation in the country visited. So, for example, those returning to ship or train to sleep are considered as same-day visitors.

What is measured?

The measurement of demand normally includes statistics of volume, value and profiles, as we describe in some detail below. In addition, during the collection of such data from visitors, questions are also often asked that relate to visitor opinions and attitudes.

Volume statistics

The total number of international tourist arrivals to a country and the total number of international tourist departures from that country are key measures of demand. It can be seen that such measures are actually of trips. They are not counts of individuals since, for example, a businessman who makes 20 visits to a country will be counted 20 times. However, the numbers of trips and of individuals are related by the equation:

number of trips = number of individuals × average number of trips taken per individual

Estimates for any two of the variables in this equation will therefore provide an estimate for the third. The equation is general in the sense that it can be applied to any group of tourists. For example, the number of trips made in total by Japanese tourists to Ruritania in the year 2000 will be equal to the product of the number of individuals involved and the average number of trips they make to Ruritania.

A serious weakness in using international tourism arrivals, as far as most tourism suppliers are concerned, is that the length of stay is not taken into account. The length of stay is important for accommodation establishments, beach managers, retail outlets and so on, although not of course for passenger termini. A better measure of volume for many purposes is therefore total tourist nights. This also acts as a measure of likely impact on a tourist destination. It can be defined as follows:

total tourist nights = number of tourist trips × average length of stay (nights stayed)

Value (expenditure) statistics

Total visitor expenditure is a simple measure of the economic value of foreign visitors to a country. It normally includes spending within a host country, and excludes fare payments made to international passenger carriers for travel into and out of that country. Similarly, the expenditure of outgoing tourists while abroad is a measure of the economic cost to a country due to its nationals travelling abroad. International tourism expenditure can typically be classified under the headings of accommodation, food and drink, entertainment, shopping and travel within the host country. For the purposes of comparison between countries, value statistics are often converted to US dollars.

Visitor profile statistics

Profile statistics are made up of statistics relating to the visitor and those of the visit. Table 4.1 shows information typically collected.

Table 4.1:
Visitor profile
statistics

The visitor	*The visit*
Age	Origin and destination
Sex	Mode of transport
Group type (e.g. alone, family)	Purpose of visit
Nationality or country of residence	Length of stay
Occupation	Accommodation used
Income	Activities engaged in
	Places visited
	Tour or independently organised

Measurement methods used

Tourism statistics relating to international tourism are normally estimates rather than exact values. The reasons for this mainly centre on the fact that monitoring and measuring what are at times complex movements of people are not easy and are subject to error. We can most easily understand this when contemplating how to obtain detailed profile or expenditure information about tourists. Even the controls at international boundaries and currency controls do not normally work to provide accurate information.

Volume statistics are often obtained using counting procedures at entry and exit points to a country (see Case Study 4.1), or (for inbound tourism) sometimes through the use of registration forms at accommodation establishments. They can be supplemented by summaries of records kept by international passenger carriers, and by surveys of households, such as a national travel survey which will elicit information on foreign (outgoing) as well as domestic tourism. Research at tourist destinations also provides some information on the movement of international visitors to a country.

Case Study 4.1   The UK international passenger survey (IPS)

The UK has one single survey, the International Passenger Survey (IPS), which measures both incoming and outgoing tourism flows. It started in 1961 and then covered major routes only. It now covers all ports of entry/exit.

The survey is based on a stratified sample of passengers entering and leaving the country, sampling being carried out separately for air and sea. Grossing up procedures are used to provide estimates, e.g. of numbers of visitors from the USA, or total spend by visitors from Japan. Statistics resulting from the IPS are published quarterly in *Business Monitor MQ6*.

The aims of the IPS can be summarised as follows:

- to collect data for the UK balance of payments travel account, which acts to compare expenditure by overseas visitors to the UK with expenditure overseas by visitors from the UK;

- to provide detailed information on foreign visitors to the UK, and on outgoing visitors travelling abroad;

- to provide data on international migration;

- to provide information on routes used by passengers as an aid to aviation and shipping authorities.

Source: adapted from *Business Monitor MQ6*

Procedures used at entry and exit points have normally been determined on the basis of administrative control and other reasons not specifically related to tourism. Tourism statistics are thus a by-product of the process rather than its main aim. Nevertheless, there are many countries that do make counts and collect information at frontiers for tourism-related purposes. Clearly islands (such as Great Britain or those of the West Indies) have an advantage in this respect, since there are likely to be fewer entry/exit points anyway. A major problem with counting using accommodation establishments alone is that they give only partial coverage. No estimates would be possible for those staying with friends or relatives, for example.

Expenditure statistics are notoriously difficult to collect. We can derive them using foreign currency estimates from banks, or from suppliers of tourism services and facilities. These methods are cumbersome and normally not satisfactory. Increasingly, therefore, information is collected directly from the tourists themselves, through sample surveys of foreign tourists as they leave the country, and from nationals as they return from a foreign trip.

Demand for domestic tourism

Why measure domestic tourism?

World-wide, relatively few people enjoy the opportunity to travel to and within countries other than their own. By far the most common form of travel is that by residents of a country within that country. The reasons for this are investigated in Chapters 2 and 3. International travel, although given high priority by segments of the populations of industrialised nations, is still very much a minority activity. As a very rough guide, we estimate that expenditure world-wide on domestic tourism may be worth up to ten times that on international tourism.

The WTO reported in 1984 that 'there are relatively few countries that collect domestic travel and tourism statistics', and the situation has not changed significantly since then. Much more information is available on international tourism. Why is this?

First of all, international travel involves, by definition, the crossing of a frontier. It is therefore easier to observe and monitor. Domestic tourism involves movement internally and is therefore more difficult to research. Countries that make use solely of registration forms at hotels miss out all aspects of domestic tourism that involve staying at supplementary accommodation establishments or with friends or relatives. A number of countries do not even try to measure domestic demand because it is considered unimportant owing to the nature of their own domestic tourism. For example, in many developing countries very little domestic movement involves staying in serviced accommodation, and so it does not compete with demand from international visitors. The benefits of collecting information always has to be set against its costs, particularly in a developing country where resources may be severely limited.

On the other hand, within the major international tourism-receiving countries of North America and Western Europe, domestic demand and international demand often compete with and complement each other. We can see this clearly in hotel lobbies, on beaches, in restaurants, at attractions and so on. So in countries such as the USA, Canada and the UK, the measurement of domestic tourism is important.

Use is made of domestic tourism statistics in a variety of ways:

● To measure the contribution of tourism to the overall economy. Although it is impossible to assess accurately, estimates can be produced that measure the effect of tourism on a country's gross domestic product.

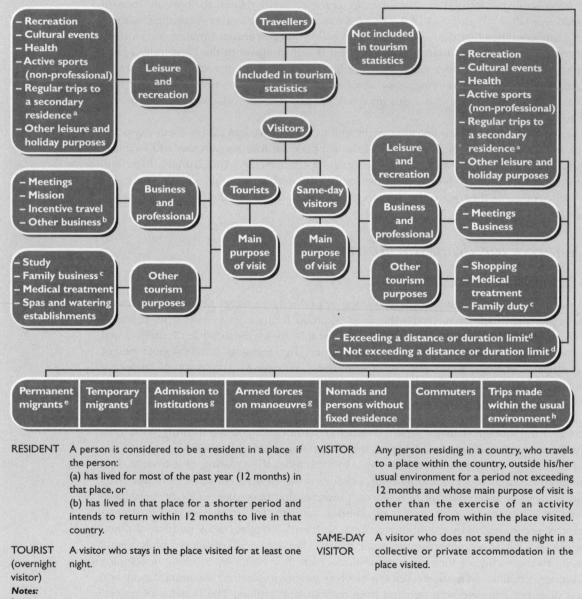

RESIDENT A person is considered to be a resident in a place if the person:
(a) has lived for most of the past year (12 months) in that place, or
(b) has lived in that place for a shorter period and intends to return within 12 months to live in that country.

TOURIST A visitor who stays in the place visited for at least one night.
(overnight visitor)

VISITOR Any person residing in a country, who travels to a place within the country, outside his/her usual environment for a period not exceeding 12 months and whose main purpose of visit is other than the exercise of an activity remunerated from within the place visited.

SAME-DAY A visitor who does not spend the night in a collective or private accommodation in the place visited.
VISITOR

Notes:

[a] Weekly trips to the place of second residence (whether owned, inhabited free of charge or rented) should be classified separately under leisure and recreation.

[b] Persons undertaking frequent trips within the country, e.g. crew members, drivers, tourist guides, salespeople, itinerant sellers, inspectors, artists, sportspeople.

[c] Attending funerals, visiting sick relatives, etc.

[d] Minimum distance and duration of minimum absence and duration of journey may be required for a person to qualify as a same-day visitor.

[e] For a period of more than 6 months, or the minimum time necessary to establish a new residence, including dependants.

[f] For a period of less than 12 months with the purpose of exercising an activity remunerated from within the place of destination, including dependants.

[g] Admission to a hospital, prison and other institutions.

[h] Trips of a routine character, part of a regular business schedule or frequent visits to a place for whatever reason.

Source: WTO

Figure 4.2: Classification of internal visitors

- For promotion and marketing policies. Many countries promote themselves strongly as destinations to their own residents – in this sense, they compete with foreign destinations for their own tourists' spending.

- To assist area development policies. This can involve attempting to ensure a high quality of environment in the main tourism areas, as well as developing other areas to relieve congestion.

- To aid social policies. A statistical knowledge of holiday-taking habits by nationals is required, for example, for providing aid to the underprivileged, perhaps in the form of subsidies for socially orientated sites.

In addition to the above, local and regional tourism organisations and individual businesses make use of domestic tourism statistics as an aid to decision making.

Definitions of visitors vary country by country. When detailed accuracy is important it is advisable to check against the original source. Figure 4.2 gives definitions and classifications of internal (domestic) visitors as recommended by the WTO.

What is measured?

The measurement of domestic tourism demand covers similar areas to that of international demand: volume, value and visitor profile statistics. These can be presented for the country as a whole, but they are often more useful if they can be broken down to provide reliable information for specific destination areas. It is common for individual destinations to conduct their own research, and to complement their findings with the general data of a national study.

Measurement methods used

Statistics of domestic tourism are just like those of international tourism in that they are estimates, normally representing informed guesses and subject to different levels of error. Although some countries base them on returns from accommodation establishments, this does not provide proper coverage. It is increasingly common to collect information from the visitors themselves. This is normally done through sample surveys, and can take different forms, as follows.

Household surveys

Household surveys are based on a knowledge of the resident population, and provide a balanced view of domestic tourism for pleasure or business purposes. A structured sample of households is constructed and interviewers are employed to collect information using a questionnaire. Questions normally relate to past behaviour, covering trips already made, although studies of intentions are sometimes undertaken. Domestic tourism surveys, national travel surveys and holiday travel surveys (the latter excluding business travel) can all be based on household surveys. They also provide, as a matter of course, information on foreign travel by residents and also information on those who do not travel.

En route surveys

En route surveys are surveys of travellers during the course of their journey. Strategic points are selected to stop or approach people, who are then either interviewed or given a questionnaire or other documentation to complete in their own time for return by post.

Case Study 4.2   The United Kingdom Tourism Survey (UKTS)

Background

Prior to 1989 the four UK national tourist boards obtained estimates of domestic tourism volume and value from other surveys. The UKTS came about, following reviews of statistical needs by and among the boards, as a result of a requirement for better data: better in the sense of being compatible over the UK as a whole, of covering aspects of tourism not covered by the earlier surveys, and of deriving from larger, and hence more statistically robust, samples.

Objectives

The objective of UKTS is firstly to provide measurements of tourism by residents of the UK, in terms of both volume (trips taken, nights spent away from home) and value (expenditure on those trips and nights). Secondly, it is to collect details of the trips taken and of the people taking them. These objectives extend to:

- tourism by residents of any age;
- tourism for any purpose;
- tourism in the sense of trips away from home which last for one night or more up to a maximum of 60 nights;
- tourism to any destination in any country of the world, using any accommodation type.

Method

Each month, continuously, interviews are conducted face-to-face in the homes of a fresh representative sample of UK adults aged 15 or more. The sample used is a two-stage stratified probability sample, leading to named persons for interview. Up to four recalls are made at different times and on different days of the week: no substitutes are used in the sample. By this method, approximately 70 000 interviews are conducted each year in the course of fieldwork.

The questionnaire asks, each calendar month, about trips taken away from home that began in the month prior to interview, and the month before that. The two-month memory period is adopted to obtain the most cost-effective use of the interviews, while minimising the risk of poor reporting due to failing memory.

From 1994 onwards, the survey adopted 'CAPI' (Computer Assisted Personal Interviewing). It is considered that this change in method has led to improvements in respondents' accuracy of recall of trips taken, and in the interviewers' recording of those trips at interview.

Publication of findings

Findings are published annually.

Source: adapted from *The UK Tourist*, published jointly by the English Tourist Board, Northern Ireland Tourist Board, Scottish Tourist Board and Wales Tourist Board.

A major problem with this type of work is that the representativeness of the sample can be in doubt because of incomplete knowledge of traffic movement within a country.

Destination surveys

Surveys are often conducted at popular tourist destinations or in areas where there are high levels of tourist activity. They typically take the form of personal interviews by teams of interviewers. The information provided leads to estimates of the volume and value of tourism to the destination, of profiles of visitors and of their visits. Questions are also asked to elicit opinions about the destination and associated attitudes. It is difficult in this type of work to ensure that the sample of visitors is representative, though efforts are made to ensure a spread across appropriate days and weeks, and that interviews are conducted at a wide range of sites.

Surveys of suppliers

Surveys of the suppliers of tourism services are sometimes undertaken in order to gain information on occupancy rates, visitor numbers, etc. Accommodation occupancy surveys are in fact common world-wide. In North America, airlines have been required through the Civil Aeronautics Board (in the USA) and the Canadian Transport Commission to produce origin and destination data.

Using tourism statistics

Some words of caution

According to the WTO, international tourist arrivals in 1996 numbered 594 million, an increase of 30% on levels of demand in 1991. In 1996, receipts from world tourism amounted to US$423 billion, an increase of more than 50% in five years. It is not so much the size of these figures that is so impressive, but the fact that anybody should know the value of tourism, the level of tourism demand or be able to work these figures out. In this chapter, we have detailed methods for measuring tourism demand and it is important to bear them in mind when interpreting the results.

Collecting tourism statistics is time consuming and complex. In some countries it is taken very seriously, to the extent that attempts are made to assess the size of potential errors. It is then possible not merely to provide a point estimate (that is, a single value) of, say, tourist numbers, but to give lower and upper bounds within which the true value is thought to lie. Some countries review their data collection procedures with a view to minimising errors subject to an acceptable cost. However, not all countries attach the same importance to tourism statistics in general, and to certain measures in particular. For example, the expenditure of incoming tourists normally has high priority attached to it, because of its positive contribution to the balance of payments. On the other hand, the number and spending of tourists who are visiting friends and relatives may be underestimated in countries in which measurement is through serviced accommodation establishments.

It is not surprising, then, that the interpretation of tourism data is fraught with danger. Key points to bear in mind are the following:

● Tourism statistics are normally estimates, often derived from sample surveys. As such, they are liable to various forms of error, many of which are impossible to quantify.

- For measurements which result from sample surveys, in general the smaller the sample size, the greater is the probable error.
- Even though the sample size for data relating to a region or country may give rise to acceptable levels of error, analysis of a subset of the data pertaining to a smaller area or region may not be feasible owing to the much reduced sample size.
- Sample size is not everything! The true random sampling of tourists who are, by their very nature, on the move is not normally possible. A sample has to be formally and carefully constructed.
- Where methodology in collecting data changes (even when it is for the better), it is dangerous to compare results.
- There are serious problems involved in attempting either to compare or to combine figures collected by different countries or organisations.

The final point arises because there is not only considerable variation in the methods employed by different countries, but also variation in the measures adopted. A notable example is that some countries count tourist arrivals (at least one night spent in the country visited), whereas others prefer to count visitor arrivals (this includes excursionists, i.e. those who do not stay overnight).

Interpreting tourism statistics

What then are we to make of the fact that we are told that international tourist arrivals in 1996 world-wide numbered 594 million? This total is certainly arrived at by grossing figures submitted to the WTO by governments or national bodies throughout the world. Each component value is subject to different levels of error, arising from different methodologies. It is clear, therefore, that the quoted figure is an estimate, and it is difficult to say how accurate it might be.

The points made above apply more generally than to total international tourist arrivals world-wide. They apply equally to many other situations in which data relating to tourists are collected: at resorts, attractions, passenger termini and so on. However, exact values are normally not what is important and, bearing in mind the shortcomings, we can see that tourism statistics often represent the best estimates available and also provide a guide as to true magnitudes. As a result, they have the following benefits:

- They often provide valuable trend data, where information is produced over a number of time periods.
- They contribute towards a database which may influence decision making, particularly in the areas of marketing, and planning and development.
- They enable the effects of decisions or changes to be monitored.
- They enable current data to be viewed in context.
- They provide a means of making forecasts.

Researching tourism markets: the value of research

Many managers and organisations in the tourism industry attach great value to research, using it to place themselves in a strong competitive position. Sound market intelligence is gained from a variety of formal and informal methods, and bridges the gap between the provider of the product or service and the consumer. Decisions such as those concerning product development and marketing activity can be based on research findings.

Moreover, research can be used to highlight specific problems, and even to demonstrate to customers a caring attitude to customers.

We can see that marketing intelligence and marketing research in tourism can therefore:

- provide information for decision making;
- keep an organisation in touch with its market;
- identify new markets;
- monitor the performance of certain aspects of a business;
- draw attention to specific problems;
- monitor customer reaction to a service or facility;
- reduce waste; and
- demonstrate a caring attitude to the customer.

However, research is viewed with suspicion by others. It can be seen as an unnecessary cost, taking up valuable resources that could be used in a better way. There may just not be the time for it, given the high level of pressure under which many people work. Others may see research as an essentially academic activity with no real value for the business. In any case, some organisations are able to 'feed off' the research conducted and published by others with greater market share, or to make use of the findings and advice of national and regional tourist offices.

The potential benefits of research vary considerably by type of organisation and by size. Major airlines and international hotel chains, for example, collect and analyse data as an aid to making decisions. Individual hotels and attractions often conduct surveys of guests and visitors to gain profile information, opinions and satisfaction ratings. A small restaurant owner or retailer is unlikely to engage in formal research. All businesses monitor sales, however, and all good managers have an instinct for changes in the market-place.

The research process

There is no standard way of approaching research. However, it is instructive to model the research process using the flow diagram shown in Figure 4.3, bearing in mind that stages shown often overlap in time rather than following the precise sequence implied. Some organisations generate research through a planning or marketing department that is able to identify research needs. The reporting of the outcomes can then be fed back into the department concerned for action, and an information base built up. Most organisations, however, generate *ad hoc* projects if and when the need arises.

Research can be undertaken 'in house' by an organisation using its own resources, or an external agency may be employed. In either case, the same principles apply and the process is essentially the same. There are numerous reputable organisations – such as advertising agencies, market research agencies, consultants, academic institutions – that offer their services, and that either specialise in research or are experienced in research as part of their activity. A common practice when commissioning research is for the sponsor to issue a detailed brief. Following discussions, external agencies usually submit research proposals, often in competition, the successful one gaining a contract to undertake the research.

The principles we cover in the rest of this chapter are valid not only for research within the tourism industry, but also for students of tourism in a more academic setting. Research projects at all levels of study will benefit from the structure imposed by Figure 4.3.

Figure 4.3: The
research process

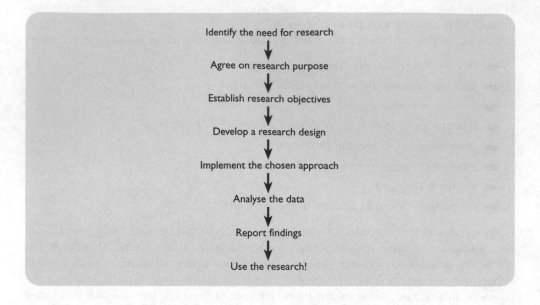

Identify the need for research

↓

Agree on research purpose

↓

Establish research objectives

↓

Develop a research design

↓

Implement the chosen approach

↓

Analyse the data

↓

Report findings

↓

Use the research!

Agreeing the purpose and setting objectives

Research based on a clear picture of its purpose is likely to lead to findings that will be of benefit. The overall purpose should be agreed by the major parties concerned. This is particularly important for the many public-sector projects in tourism that have to satisfy or are steered by representatives from a wide range of interested organisations.

The purpose is satisfied through the attainment of the research objectives set. The objectives should always be formally stated, and again agreed. This not only avoids later misunderstanding, but also gives a focus to the research. It is possible to match findings later with the objectives set in order to assess the success of the research.

Case Study 4.3 Research objectives from a survey of educational visits to the National Maritime Museum

The objectives of the survey were as follows:

● To elicit the profile of educational groups visiting the museum in terms of age, geographical location, sector of school and size of school group.

● To elicit the profile of visits by educational groups in terms of number of visits made, whether schools were on a day trip or staying in London, any publicity or event prompting the visit, and the mode of travel.

● A final objective related to the schools' use and opinions of the museum as an educational resource. The survey aimed to discover the level of use of the educational service and also to obtain schools' opinions of the service and the museum and to identify areas in which the service may be improved.

Source: Reproduced by permission of the National Maritime Museum.

Research design

A research design is a detailed description or plan; it can be used to guide the implementation of the research. The most significant decision involved in design concerns the approach to be taken. For example:

● What reliance is to be placed on secondary sources?

● Should a sample survey or group discussions be used?

● Which survey technique should be used – personal interviews, telephone interviews or postal survey?

Primary or secondary data?

Secondary data are those that have already been collected, possibly by some other individual or organisation and for some other purpose. In any country the most prolific source is government. Although its data are normally too general in nature to be of practical benefit, they often provide good background information. The same applies to data provided by other national and local bodies such as tourist offices. Before engaging in what may prove to be expensive primary data collection (that is, your own), it is worth a researcher identifying and assessing possible sources of information that could supplement primary data or even remove the need for it. There is no point in collecting information that already exists in an accessible form.

In particular, a tourism enterprise's own records are particularly valuable. Data can be taken from sales invoices, booking forms, general accounts, operating data, internal reports and so on. Many organisations have built up databases over a period of time, and these can form the basis of research data. Nevertheless, there are times when it is necessary to collect primary data, even though it is normal to supplement this with secondary data.

Methods of collecting primary data

In tourism, the most common method by far is the sample survey, either of visitors themselves or of businesses. The three main types of survey are personal interview, telephone interview and postal survey. The choice as to which to use depends on the nature of the research concerned, and takes account of the advantages and disadvantages of each method.

Visitor surveys at attractions are often based on personal interviews using questionnaires at or near exit points. Telephone interviewing has become increasingly popular. It can be used in its own right or as part of an overall strategy. For example, an occupancy survey may involve contact by telephone, followed by a personal visit and the delivery of self-administered questionnaires. Postal questionnaires are often used when the manager does not have direct access to the user, or as a follow-up such as when a holiday is sold, using customer addresses. It is also possible to hand out questionnaires for self-completion: for example, on a return holiday flight or return coach journey. There is also scope in tourism for the use of observation methods – in monitoring the popularity of displays or exhibits, or the movement of visitors at open-air sites.

It is possible to make use of modern computer technology in the collection of primary data. This can not only lead to improvements in accuracy (see Case Study 4.2 on page 86), but also remove the need for data input at a later stage.

In a detailed study of attitudes or perceptions, it is probable that a qualitative approach will be taken in order to achieve greater insight and understanding. This might involve

Case Study 4.4 Comparing data collection procedures

Personal interview

Advantages:

- Initial interest can be aroused.
- Complex questioning is possible.
- Visual aids and showcards can be used.
- Flexible.
- Shows a caring attitude.
- Visitors are usually happy to cooperate.

Disadvantages:

- Time consuming.
- Administratively difficult.
- Costly.

Telephone interview

Advantages:

- Close supervision and control is possible.
- Access is easy, call-backs are possible.
- Response rates are usually good.
- Many interviews are possible in a given time period.

Disadvantages:

- Visual aids and complex tasks are not possible.
- Only verbal communication is possible.
- Interview is short (people hang up).

Postal surveys

Advantages:

- Low cost.
- No intermediary, so answers are reliable.
- Superior for sensitive questions (confidentiality must be stressed).

Disadvantages:

- Many variables are not controlled, since there is no interviewer.
- Mailing list is needed.
- Response rates are low.
- Bias due to non-response.
- Detailed or long questionnaires reduce response.

Source: adapted from Cooper and Latham (1990).

in-depth interviews or discussions with individuals, say with successful managers to analyse their decision-making processes. It can also involve the formation of discussion groups of between six and ten people, led by an experienced discussant. In this case the interaction between people can stimulate and encourage ideas, or draw out factors such as those that affect holiday choice.

Designing questionnaires

Questionnaires are by far the most common type of form used for primary data collection in tourism. They are difficult to construct, though much easier to criticise, and it is certainly sensible for a researcher to pass round his or her attempts to colleagues for suggested changes. Final versions are usually very different from early drafts. It is important to bear in mind the objectives of the research when constructing a questionnaire, as they give focus to it. The temptation to include questions not relevant to the study, but for interest's sake, should normally be resisted. Their inclusion can lead to a respondent tiring or losing interest, and put at risk answers to more important questions.

The steps involved in the design of a questionnaire are as follows:

1. Plan what to measure, based on the objectives of the research.
2. Formulate the questions.
3. Decide on the layout and order of questions.
4. Pilot test the questionnaire.
5. Correct problems that arise and retest if necessary.

Here are some general guidelines for constructing or assessing the likely effectiveness of a questionnaire:

- Questions should follow a logical order; the questionnaire should flow.
- There should be a simple introduction and early questions should be straightforward.
- Language used should be appropriate to the respondent.
- Questions should be unambiguous.
- Avoid bias within a question, i.e. a question that suggests that a particular answer is acceptable.
- Do not tax the memory of the respondent.
- Instructions on the form (to interviewer or, in the case of self-completion, the respondent) should be highlighted.
- The questionnaire should be as short as possible.
- The form should be attractive, well laid out and easy to follow.

Sampling

Normally research in tourism seeks to gain information on a large number of people (or sometimes businesses). The term 'population', or 'universe', is used to describe all those under consideration. Examples of populations are all holidaymakers at a resort, all business people using hotels in a city, all users of a leisure complex, or all visitors to an attraction.

For populations that are relatively small, say the 17 coach operators who use a particular stop, it is possible to undertake a census. However, populations are usually large and it is not practical or cost-effective to contact every single member. Instead a sample survey is undertaken. The way in which a sample is constructed is a key element in the research process, since the sample must mirror the population from which it is taken. Then findings based on the sample will be valid for the population as a whole. The technicalities of sampling and the validity of making inferences about populations are complex, and are covered in texts on statistics and research methods.

There are a variety of sampling methods in use. The most common is what might be considered a 'loose' approach, where interviewers are given target numbers of interviews to achieve and are asked to contact a representative spread of people by age and sex. This almost certainly leads to a biased sample. At attractions and passenger termini, it is possible to take the selection of respondent away from the interviewer through the use of 'tighter' procedures such as systematic sampling (say, every twentieth person to pass an exit point).

It is difficult to construct with confidence a representative sample of visitors at a tourist destination such as a resort, or within large recreation areas. This is because visitors are scattered over large areas and their movement is complex. It is normal to take account of the time of year (sample more heavily in the peak months) and to conduct interviews where tourists are likely to frequent (attractions, accommodation establishments, shopping centres, places of interest for destinations, popular sites for recreation areas).

Data analysis

Data from questionnaire returns or other data sheets can be input into computer files for analysis. The use of an appropriate software package speeds up the process and ensures accuracy within the analysis. The scope of analysis is also increased, because the relationships between variables can be examined in depth.

The first stage is often merely establishing counts or frequencies of response. These are often best expressed as percentages. Thus, 40% of visitors are in family groups, 80% arrive by car and so on. This is followed by the 'cross-tabulation' of variables, in which responses to one question are matched with responses to another. An example of output from this form of analysis is: 30% of holiday visitors to the hotel were dissatisfied with the leisure facilities, compared with only 5% of business visitors.

The use of counts and cross-tabulations is sufficient for the majority of studies. More detailed forms of analysis make use of higher-level statistics, and are common in project work undertaken by students registered for higher degrees.

The reporting of research

An essential part of the research process is the final report. This is often accompanied by a formal presentation of findings. The level, method and timing of the reporting should be discussed and agreed at an early stage. Case Study 4.5 gives pointers on report writing.

Research results may well confirm what the manager already believed, and thus provide him or her with hard evidence to make his or her case to others. They can also lead to some surprises and to changes that were not anticipated.

It is a waste of resources to commission research and then not consider the findings. Provided that the research purpose is clear from the beginning and that the objectives set were appropriate to it, the relevance to decision making should be clear. The research report then represents an objective view, relevant to the needs of the organisation.

Case Study 4.5 Towards effective reports: pointers on writing research reports

Presentation

- Reports should be actionable.

- Findings and recommendations should be linked to objectives set.

- There should be a clear summary of findings and recommendations – it is normal for these to appear at the beginning.

- Language should be appropriate and clearly expressed. The main body of the report should be able to be understood by a non-technical manager. Appendices of technical detail should be included if relevant.

Content

- Background information may be included.

- Research methodology should be included.

- Copies of forms (e.g. blank questionnaire) and letters used in the research should be included, normally as appendices.

- Details of analysis and tables should be clear and easy to understand.

- Diagrams may be used in addition to or instead of tables in order to enhance interpretation.

- Information should be full and complete.

- Appendices should be used for technical or other information that would otherwise detract from the reading of the report

Source: Cooper and Latham (1990).

Conclusion

The activity of tourism is prolific – in terms of both volume and revenue generated – and yet its measurement remains problematic at best and wholly inadequate at worst. Since many countries continue to derive their tourism statistics as a by-product of data gained for other, non-tourism-related, research, statistics for international and domestic tourism must be interpreted and utilised with caution and sensitivity.

Despite the difficulties, however, the measurement of incoming and outgoing tourism is crucial for economic and commercial reasons. In addition, the measurement of tourism activity, and an associated understanding of tourist motivations and profiles provides a wealth of information for the planning, management and marketing of tourism at the destination and an appreciation of consumer behaviour in tourism.

Chapter discussion questions

1. Consider how you might approach the researching of tourism activity at a specific destination, reviewing the types of information you need to elicit from tourists and the methodology you might employ.

2. What might be some of the key problems in comparing tourism statistics from different areas and regions of the world?

3. Why should tourism statistics be interpreted with caution?

4. Do you think there is a role for key international bodies such as the WTO to be more involved in the collection of tourism statistics? How might this involvement be manifested and where might the emphasis lie?

Recommended further reading

● Mill, R. C. and Morrison, A. (1985) *The Tourism System*, Prentice Hall, Englewood Cliffs, NJ.
● Brent, R. J. R. and Goeldner, C. R. (eds) (1994) *A Handbook for Managers and Researchers*, Wiley, New York.
● WTO (annual) *Yearbook of Tourism Statistics*, WTO, Madrid.
● WTO (annual) *Compendium of Tourism Statistics*, WTO, Madrid.
● WTO (three issues per year) *Travel and Tourism Barometer*, WTO, Madrid.

Bibliography

● Bar-On, R. R. (1996) 'Databank: definitions and classifications', *Tourism Economics*, **2**(4), 369–73.
● British Tourist Authority/English Tourist Board (quarterly) *Tourist Intelligence Quarterly*, BTA/ETB, London.
● Cooper, C. P. and Latham, J. (1990) 'A layman's guide to market research for the tourist industry', in *Insights*, English Tourist Board, London.
● Hussey, J. and Hussey, R. (1997) *Business Research*, MacMillan Business, Chippenham.
● Latham, J. (1989) 'The statistical measurement of tourism', in *Progress in Tourism, Recreation and Hospitality Management*, Vol. 1, Cooper, C. P. (ed.), Belhaven, London.
● Organization for Economic Co-operation and Development (annual) *Tourism Policy and International Tourism in OECD Member Countries*, OECD, Paris.
● UNSTAT (1994) *Recommendations on Tourism Statistics*, UN Statistical Office, New York with WTO, Madrid.
● WTO (1984) *Domestic Tourism Statistics*, WTO, Madrid.
● WTO (1995a) *Concepts, Definitions and Classifications for Tourism Statistics* (technical manual), WTO, Madrid.
● WTO (1995b) *Collection and Compilation of Tourism Statistics* (technical manual), WTO, Madrid.
● WTO (1995c) *Collection of Domestic Tourism Statistics* (technical manual), WTO, Madrid.
● WTO (annual) *Yearbook of Tourism Statistics*, WTO, Madrid.

Chapter author: Professor John Latham

PART TWO

The tourism destination

Introduction

In Part 1, we concentrated on reviewing all aspects of demand for tourism, providing a comprehensive overview of models and patterns of demand and those factors which underpin propensity to travel. In Leiper's model (outlined in detail in 'An introduction to tourism'), the second key area is the tourist destination region.

As the recipient of tourism, the destination is a key element of the tourism system and provides the focal point for tourism activity and the study of tourism. While our evaluation of demand demonstrated the motivational, or 'push', factors that instigate and influence tourism demand, the destination, and the quality and mix of attractions, infrastructure and superstructure on offer, provide the 'pull' factors.

Representing the sharp end of tourism activity, the issues and problems faced by the destination are unique. Since tourism is consumed where it is produced, the destination comes under intense scrutiny and pressure from a wide range of sources, providing many challenges for all those involved in tourism in the public and private sectors.

Being the 'pull' factor in the tourism equation, the destination is frequently inherently attractive and sensitive. For example, tourists are attracted to beaches, coastlines, mountainous zones and parks, all of which are fragile in nature and susceptible to over-use and irreversible damage. Hence, by definition, the destination will inevitably be vulnerable to undesirable change as a result of the influx of large numbers of visitors, concentrated spatially and temporally.

The impacts of tourism, therefore, are heavily concentrated at the destination. These impacts may range from obvious economic impacts such as inflated land values, to more discreet socio-cultural and environmental impacts which evolve over a period of time and which subtly encroach to alter the fabric of the host community and the environmental context of the destination.

Many areas in the world have already succumbed to the negative impacts of tourism. They have suffered irreversible damage and, consequently, they have been usurped by new destinations. Increasingly, areas wishing to maintain and enhance a strong tourism product are developing integrated tourism planning and management systems, focusing on the control and co-ordination of tourism development and activity. The implementation of professional planning and management in respect of tourism protects the destination from economic over-dependence on tourism in an industry where demand is notoriously fickle and where supply is physically fixed. In addition, planning and management is also crucial in protecting resource integrity and conserving the destination, environmentally and socially, in its original form.

Recently, an increased sensitivity to environmental issues within the populations of the developed world, coupled with the pragmatism of the tourism industry, have been instrumental in moving tourism towards finding new solutions and techniques to alleviate adverse destinational impacts. While many remain unconvinced by the response of the industry, arguing the motivation for this shift is profit-based and not remotely altruistic, the tourism industry is at least making an attempt to go 'green'.

Thus, Part 2 deals with important issues that are contemporary and current. To review and discuss these issues, and the theoretical concepts that underpin them, Part 2 comprises six chapters. We begin by providing an overview of the patterns and characteristics of the supply of tourism. Although the tourism literature highlights many case studies of tourism destinations, there are few writers who attempt to generalise and draw out the common characteristics of tourism supply as we have done in Chapter 5. Destinations are not static and we use this chapter to consider the notion of the destination life cycle which demonstrates the typical evolution of a destination. The underlying principle is that tourism usage must be strategically controlled and limited in the long term in order that the resource is sustained for the use and enjoyment of future generations. By discussing the concept of carrying capacity in relation to sustainability, we are emphasising the importance of identifying and implementing limits to numbers to ensure resource integrity is not compromised.

Having provided a theoretical framework, we then go on to identify and discuss the impacts of tourism on the indigenous economy, environment and people. We dedicate a chapter to each set of impacts – economic, environmental and socio-cultural – although it should be emphasised that it is impossible to comprehend one set of impacts without some reference to the others. We also raise key issues relating to the measurement of tourism impacts. In the past, economic impacts have provided the focus for measurement and assessment, not only because these impacts are more easily measurable and the data available, but also because the sponsors of the research felt that the findings would highlight the positive benefits of tourism spending and employment.

However, more recently, the focus has shifted and negative socio-cultural and environmental impacts of tourism have been highlighted. Unfortunately, techniques of impact assessment in these areas are less sophisticated than those that have been developed to measure economic impacts of tourism activity. This is due partly to the complexity of measuring social and environmental impacts. Not only is it difficult to take into account the full range of impacts, for example, on an ecosystem, but the data relating to the position prior to the intervention of tourism activity are frequently lacking. Moreover, it is sometimes difficult to determine the true extent of tourism's involvement in, say, social change at the destination, when set in the context of other variables which may also provide impetus for change, such as the mass media. In many cases, tourism may simply have become a scapegoat.

Nevertheless, while all tourism activity will inevitably have impacts at the destination, comprehensive planning and management strategies fulfil an important role in alleviating undesirable and excessive change by establishing a carrying capacity, or level of activity, which may be sustained by the resource. Thus, we provide a comprehensive review of the planning process in Chapter 10.

In Part 2, therefore, a number of general trends and issues emerge:

● The notion of sustainable development and carrying capacity will become increasingly important to the management of destinations.

● The measurement of tourism's environmental and socio-cultural impacts is not yet as developed as that of its economic impacts. However, this situation is slowly being addressed.

● New, more robust types of destination are now being developed which will take pressure away from the more fragile and unique ecosystems of the world.

● The planning and management of destinations will become more professional.

● Tourism developers will no longer be able to abandon resorts that have gone into decline; rather they will need to develop strategies that are devised to rejuvenate such destinations.

As with other elements of the tourism system, the destination cannot be fully understood without reference to demand, marketing and the tourism industry, and vice versa. Demand for tourism very often shapes the nature of development at a destination, while the cohesion and professionalism of the industry, and in particular the transportation system and the public sector, can make or break the destination. The marketing activities of public sector agencies such as convention bureaux are well known, but the issues surrounding the marketing of tourist destinations are only now being debated in the light of implications for host communities.

Chapter Five

The destination

Introduction

The richness and variety of destinations around the world have contributed to the success of the tourism sector since 1945. The industry is characterised not only by *change* but also by rapid *growth*. Inevitably this has placed destinations under pressure as demand exceeds supply. Interwoven with this trend is the changing nature of consumers which is placing increased demands upon the destination. The **new tourist** is no longer satisfied with a passive experience, but is seeking instead authenticity at destinations with a view to understanding the indigenous culture, history and environment and, indeed, how local people live and work. We have to understand and appreciate these trends if we are to plan and manage destinations successfully to satisfy the demands of the new tourist, while at the same time ensuring that the destinations themselves are sustainable.

In this chapter we introduce the characteristics of tourism destinations and outline the key issues involved. You will see that, in order to understand destinations, consideration has to be given to the differing environmental, social and economic contexts around the world within which tourism destinations exist. Destinations represent an amalgam, or mix, of attractions and support facilities which demonstrate a number of common features. These include the fact that destinations are cultural appraisals, they are perishable because tourism is consumed where it is produced, destinations involve multiple use of tourism with other uses and to be successful the components of the amalgam need to be of equivalent quality.

We also introduce the idea of destination stakeholders – all those individuals and groups who have a vested interest in tourism at the destination. Planning and management is one mechanism for drawing these stakeholders together and ensuring that the destination develops strategically. Clearly it is in everyone's interests for the destination to deliver a quality experience and product, and in this regard, careful planning and management is essential to ensure a tourism industry based on sustainable principles. We contend that central to the issue of sustainability is the concept of taking a long-term strategic view and clearly understanding the concept of carrying capacity. An important idea here is that of a destination evolving over time and continuing to do so, in order to provide a future range of destinations where technology, authenticity and professionalism will dominate.

Chapter learning objectives

The tourism destination is a crucial element of the tourism system and central to our understanding of its dynamics. We would, therefore, identify the following learning objectives for this chapter and suggest the reader should, by the end of this chapter:

◼◼ understand the destination as a focal point of tourism activity and comprehend the process of evolution that a destination may provide;

◼◼ appreciate the role of planning to maintain and enhance the destination and the importance of the concept of carrying capacity;

◼◼ be able to identify the individual features and components of the tourism composite and the contribution of each to the overall destination product; and

◼◼ be aware of the notion of sustainable tourism and the possible strategies which may be implemented to achieve it.

The destination as a focus for tourism

The supply of tourism demonstrates a complex pattern across the world because it is located in diverse environments and in differing economic and social contexts. The supply of tourism is also continually expanding as the **pleasure periphery** reaches ever more distant and remote locations.

We can think of a destination as *the focus of facilities and services designed to meet the needs of the tourist*. The tourist destination, however defined geographically, provides a convenient focus for the examination of the tourist movement and its impact and significance. Indeed, the destination brings together all aspects of tourism – demand, transportation, supply and marketing – in a useful framework. It represents the third element of Leiper's tourism system, but in many respects the most important one because destinations, and their images, attract tourists, motivate the visit and therefore energise the whole tourism system. We can therefore see that the destination is where the most significant and dramatic elements of tourism occur and where the inbound tourism industry is located: that is, where the attractions and all the other support facilities needed by the visitor are found.

As the demand for tourism has increased, pressure from the growing number of visitors – often concentrated into a short season – has degraded some destinations. In response, planning and management strategies have been implemented in the busier or more fragile destinations; indeed, planning and management are the key to ensuring that existing tourist destinations and resources are more effective in meeting demand. In this respect, the operation of major tourist destinations is increasingly co-ordinated by a destination marketing/management organisation (DMO) or a convention and visitor bureau (CVB).

Common features of tourist destinations

While destinations are very varied, we can identify certain common features of most destinations:

● Destinations are amalgams.
● Destinations are cultural appraisals.

● Destinations are inseparable: that is, tourism is produced where it is consumed.

● Destinations are used not just by tourists but also by many other groups.

Amalgams

Most destinations comprise a core of the following components, which can be characterised as the four As:

● Attractions.

● Amenities – accommodation, food and beverage outlets, entertainment, retailing and other services.

● Access – local transport, transport terminals.

● Ancillary services, in the form of local organisations.

Of course, each of these components has to be in place before tourism can be supported – accommodation alone, for example, will rarely suffice (except perhaps in the case of major luxury hotels such as the Raffles Hotel in Singapore, or the Savoy in London). The mix of facilities and services at a destination is therefore known as an amalgam – the complete mix has to be present for it to work and the complete tourism experience to be delivered.

This amalgamation of the components of a destination comes together in many different ways, and in many different cultural, economic and environmental contexts to create the range of destinations available. These include coastal resorts, mountain resorts, historic towns and cities, festivals and events, single purpose-built destinations – such as Disneyland Paris – and conference/meeting complexes for business travellers.

The very fact that the destination is an amalgam has a number of implications. In particular, it is important that the quality of each component of the destination and the delivery of the tourism service at these components is reasonably uniform: a poor restaurant or hotel bedroom can detract from an otherwise satisfactory vacation. This complementarity of destination components is difficult to control by destination managers given the fragmented nature of enterprises in tourism. Integration of enterprises by larger organisations (tour operators owning hotels and transport carriers) is one means of such control, but for public-sector tourist boards the problem is a critical one.

Cultural appraisals

Visitors have to consider a destination to be attractive and worth the investment of time and money to visit. Because of this we can think of destinations as cultural appraisals. For example, Victorian tourists visited English abattoirs and the sewers of Paris since they felt that they were worthy of a visit. In the nineteenth century, too, the perception of mountains changed from fearsome places to attractive landscapes, which then became popular tourist destinations. An example of this idea from the 1990s is the desire of tourists to visit hostile environments such as Antarctica. As tastes and fashion change, so they are reflected in the tourist destinations that we patronise. This means that, while new opportunities are always available, there is also a constant threat to established destinations which may go out of fashion. It is, therefore, vital to maintain the difference between the destination and the home environment through good design and management, and to avoid the development of uniform tourism landscapes.

Inseparability

Tourism is consumed where it is produced – visitors have to be physically present at the destination to experience tourism – imagine how this would impact upon Detroit if every one who bought a Ford car had to drive it in Detroit! Because tourism, by its very nature, is attracted to the unique and the fragile parts of the world, destinations are vulnerable to tourist pressure and may suffer alteration. This is exacerbated by the fact that visitor pressure is often concentrated seasonally in time and at specific popular locations.

Like all services, the destination is perishable in the sense that, if it is not used, it is lost – the availability of beds, restaurant seats and attraction tickets cannot be stored in the off-season for sale in the peak. Seasonality is a major problem for many destinations, prejudicing profitability and rendering them inefficient in terms of their use of the capital assets. This is because most elements of a destination have a high ratio of fixed to variable costs and therefore, for a highly seasonal destination, the peak (of, say, three or four months) has to make the majority contribution to fixed costs, which are chargeable for 12 months of the year. For example, for many tourist destinations anything up to 80% of total costs are in physical plant, and construction involves long lead times. Of course, destinations with a year-round season (such as the Caribbean) have a considerable advantage in this respect. There is therefore an imperative to ensure that market volume and characteristics are accurately forecast before construction begins.

Multiple use

Destination amenities serve residents and workers throughout the year, but at some, or all, times of the year, there are temporary users of these amenities – day visitors or tourists – who are away from their normal place of residence and work. The multiple use of destinations means that it is possible to classify enterprises according to whether they depend upon tourism only, residents only or a mix of the two. In fact, only the purpose-built destinations (such as theme parks) are in existence purely to serve the tourist. Most destinations share tourism with other uses; indeed, tourists are often the most recent and least respected users. For example, tourism at the coast is shared with other uses such as power generation and fishing, while tourism in rural areas is shared with nature conservation, agriculture and forestry. Tourism may become a source of conflict in such shared destinations, with open antagonism displayed between tourists and other users.

Solutions to this problem involve the careful integration of tourism activities in a variety of ways:

- Phasing tourism uses in time.
- Zoning tourism uses in space (see Case Study 5.1).
- Management schemes to reduce tension and conflict by intervening in problem situations.
- Involving all stakeholders and understanding their differing needs.
- Community-driven tourism planning to ensure that tourism develops in harmony with community wishes.
- Publicity campaigns to inform local residents.
- Information campaigns and codes of conduct targeted at the tourist.

Case Study 5.1 Psychological carrying capacity: the Boundary Waters Canoe Area, USA

A number of studies have examined the idea of different tourists having differing capacity *thresholds*, basically by attempting to zone a destination into differing *activity complexes* to match more closely the needs of users and therefore reduce impacts. One of the best examples is the zoning of the Boundary Waters Canoe Area (BWCA) on the US/Canadian border.

The BWCA is an area of forest, lakes and streams, formally designated as semi-wilderness because some logging and motorised use is permitted. The main use of wilderness areas in North America is for high-quality recreation.

In the early 1960s, Lucas (1964) surveyed users of the BWCA to establish their perceptions of wilderness in general and the BWCA in particular. He found different perceptions between canoeists and those using motorised boats. Motorboat users viewed the wilderness area as very much larger than the canoeists, and tolerated roads and high levels of recreational use.

The implications of these differing perceptions of the same destination are outlined by Lucas:

> The differences [in perception] between these wilderness [users] may provide a key to increasing the capacity of the area in order to provide high-quality recreation. The highest priority use by established policy is wilderness canoeing. The canoeists' wilderness is easily destroyed by heavy use, especially [motor] boat use. The [motor] boaters value wilderness much less highly and fishing more highly, accept heavy use, and are usually in their wilderness before they reach the areas used by the canoeists, or the canoeists' wilderness. It would seem that the canoeists' satisfaction could be raised, or kept high as visitors increase, without reducing the motor-boaters' satisfaction by concentrating new access points, campgrounds, and resort or cabin site leases, and managing the fishing intensively in the bank of forests and lakes away from Boundary Waters Canoe Area but inside the wilderness for most boaters. (p. 410)

In other words, by accepting the differing views of wilderness and zoning an area for canoeists and one for motorboats, the integrity of supply is maintained and both groups of users are satisfied.

Components of the destination amalgam

Before introducing the components of a destination and demonstrating their place in the destination amalgam, we must make the major distinction between attractions and support services. Attractions generate the visit to a destination, while the other support services and facilities are also essential for tourism at the destination, but would not exist without attractions. A particular focus of these components is the resort, which we can define as 'a place that attracts large numbers of tourists and that tourism endows with special characteristics, so that revenue produced by tourism plays an important role in its existence'.

Attractions

As we have just observed, it is the attractions of a destination – whether they be artificial features, natural features or events – that provide the initial motivation to visit. Traditionally, attractions have been a neglected sector of the tourist industry owing to their variety and fragmented ownership pattern. However, the sector is now demonstrating maturity with increased professionalism in the management of attractions. This includes a closer match between the market and supply of attractions through:

- the adoption of marketing philosophy;
- better training for attractions' personnel;
- greater involvement of technology in the development of a wide range of exciting new types of attraction; and
- renewed focus upon and professional management of mega-events, which are emerging as an important sector in their own right.

Alongside this more enlightened management approach, the attraction's industry is forming professional bodies and seeking representation in wider tourist industry circles.

Amenities

A range of amenities, support facilities and services are required by a tourist at a destination. We can characterise this sector as having a low level of concentration of ownership – indeed, these enterprises are often operated by small and medium-sized enterprises (SMEs). On the one hand, this is an advantage because it means that tourist expenditure flows quickly into the local economy. On the other hand, however, SMEs are both fragmented and lack a coherent lobby. Often, too, they lack the investment capability to upgrade and the management/marketing expertise which is demanded by the tourism market-place.

The provision of amenities demonstrates the multi-sectoral nature of tourism supply and the interdependence of the various sectors. For example, the supply of many facilities and services at a resort depends on the number of bed spaces available; that is, the number of tourists who will visit. For example, provision of around 1000 beds will support up to six basic retail outlets, while 4000 beds will support specialist outlets such as hairdressers. Similar ratios can be calculated for restaurants, car parking, entertainment, swimming pools, etc.

Accommodation, food and beverage

The accommodation/food and beverage sector of the destination not only provides physical shelter and sustenance, but also creates the general feeling of welcome and a lasting impression of the local cuisine and produce. Traditionally dominated by SMEs, the accommodation sector usually offers a mix of type of establishment, and it is important for destinations to adapt and change this mix to meet market aspirations. In some resorts, for example, there is a movement towards flexible forms of accommodation, such as apartments and time-share, and away from more traditional serviced (hotels, self-catering apartments, etc.) or in the private informal sector (second homes, caravans, etc.) which is a large, though neglected, part of the accommodation industry (which is dealt with in detail in Chapter 15).

Retailing and other services

There is an increasing range of facilities and services available to a tourist as the size of destination increases. These include retailing, security services and other functions, such as hairdressing, banks, exchange bureaux and insurance. These services tend to locate close to the main attractions of a destination, often creating an identifiable recreational business district.

Access

Clearly the development and maintenance of efficient transport links to the generating markets are essential for the success of destinations. Indeed, there are examples of destinations where transport has made, or broken, the tourist industry. Small islands, for example, are dependent upon their carriers to provide market access, while destinations such as Spain and Mexico are ideally situated to take advantage of international tourism from Europe and North America respectively. In international terms, developing countries have particular problems attracting a share of the market because they are generally distant from the generating markets.

Catchment areas will also vary for destinations according to their drawing power. Tightly drawn geographical catchments will characterise smaller resorts without a particular attraction. For example, the Isle of Man is a domestic British resort catering mainly for markets in northern England and southern Scotland. However, major destinations, such as the theme parks of Orlando, or the Taj Mahal, can draw upon an international catchment.

We can therefore see that physical and market access to the destination are important, but so is the provision of services such as car rental and local transport, in order to service excursion circuits and provide transfers to accommodation at the destination. An increasingly creative approach to transportation at the destination adds to the quality of the tourist experience, and there are many examples of innovative transport provision in this respect, which include:

- scenic drives;
- park and ride schemes;
- shuttle buses for walkers;
- cycle ways;
- explorer buses.

Ancillary services

Most major destinations provide ancillary services to both the consumer and the industry through a local tourist board. These services include marketing, development and coordination activities. The organisation may be in the public sector, may be a public/private sector cooperative, or in some cases, may exist totally within the private sector. Such organisations are often linked to regional and national tourist boards and provide the framework within which tourism operates at the destination (see Chapter 11).

The main services normally provided by the local organisation are as follows:

- Promotion of the destination.
- Coordination and control of development.
- Provision of an information/reservation service to the trade and the public.
- Advice to and coordination of local businesses.
- Provision of certain facilities (catering, sports, etc.).
- Provision of destination leadership.

Infrastructure and superstructure

We can consider infrastructure and superstructure as alternative ways of looking at the components of a destination. **Infrastructure** represents all forms of construction above or below ground needed by an inhabited area, with extensive communication with the outside world as a basis for tourism activity in the area. Adequate infrastructure is essential for destination areas and is mainly in the form of transportation (road, railway, airport, car-parks), utilities (electricity, water, communications) and other services (health care and security). It is normally shared by residents and visitors alike. There are examples where lack of adequate infrastructure prevents growth of tourism (such as restricted water supplies on the Kenyan Mombassa coast). Infrastructure does not normally generate income and is treated as a public investment in most tourist developments. Seasonality is a major problem for infrastructural development and most construction is planned to meet a percentage of peak load rather than peak.

Whereas infrastructure tends to be provided by the public sector, **superstructure** is normally a private-sector activity, as it is the profit-generating element of the destination. It includes accommodation, built attractions and retailing and other services. We should remember, however, that in many countries the public sector is active in providing financial incentives (grants, loans, tax holidays) for private sector tourism investment (see Major Case Study 4).

Although the norm is for the public sector to provide infrastructure as a prerequisite for private sector development of the superstructure, in many cases combinations of public and private sector finance are used to develop destinations.

Sustainable tourism destinations

Clearly the components of the tourist destination can be effective only if careful planning and management deliver a sustainable tourism product, and in so doing ensure that one or more of the components does not *surge* ahead of the others. In the last quarter of the twentieth century we have reassessed the real contribution of tourism as sustainability has become the organising concept. The Brundtland Report (World Commission on Environment and Development, 1987) defines sustainability simply as 'meeting the needs of the present without compromising the ability of future generations to meet their own needs'.

There are a number of forces that promote sustainable tourism:

- Consumer pressure: for example, in the form of vacation decisions being taken on the basis of environmental considerations.
- Public authority planning guidelines: not simply in the case of regulating development, but also in the form of encouraging good environmental practice through awards and endorsement.
- Movements towards environmental impact assessment and environmental auditing: major tourist developments such as the Channel Tunnel are subject to impact assessment, and tourism companies (such as Disney) carry out environmental audits of their operation.

There are also other, primarily economic, forces resisting the adoption of sustainable tourism. In particular, these include the following:

- The economic imperative of the tourist industry and developers, which may put return on investment and profit before longer-term considerations.
- Some regions and developing countries where the need for foreign exchange and employment is felt to outweigh environmental considerations.

The WTTC has provided guidelines for sustainable tourism (Box 5.1). We can see that the concept of sustainability demands a long-term view of tourism and ensures that consumption of tourism does not exceed the ability of a host destination to provide for

Box 5.1 World Travel and Tourism Council Principles for sustainable tourism development

The framework for sustainable development to be established by the travel and tourism industry should be based on the Rio Declaration on Environment and Development, from which the following guiding principles flow:

- Travel and tourism should assist people in leading healthy and productive lives in harmony with nature.
- Travel and tourism should contribute to the conservation, protection and restoration of the Earth's ecosystem.
- Travel and tourism should be based upon sustainable patterns of production and consumption.
- Nations should cooperate to promote an open economic system, in which international trade and travel and tourism services can take place on a sustainable basis.
- Travel and tourism, peace, development and environmental protection are interdependent.
- Protectionism in trade and travel and tourism services should be halted or reversed.
- Environmental protection should constitute and integral part of the tourism development process.
- Tourism development issues should be handled with the participation of concerned citizens, with planning decisions being adopted at local level.
- Nations shall warn one another of natural disasters that could affect tourists or tourist areas.
- Travel and tourism should use its capacity to create employment for women and indigenous peoples to the fullest extent.
- Tourism development should recognise and support the identity, culture and interests of indigenous peoples.
- International laws protecting the environment should be respected by the travel and tourism industry.

Source: WTTC/WTO (1995).

future tourists. In other words, it represents a trade-off between present and future needs. In the past, sustainabililty has been low priority compared with the short-term drive for profitability and growth, but with pressure growing for a more responsible tourism industry, it is difficult to see how such short-term views on consumption can continue. To understand how to deliver sustainable tourism destinations we need to consider two key concepts:

1. carrying capacity;
2. long-term (strategic) planning.

Carrying capacity

Central to the concept of sustainability is the idea of carrying capacity. Quite simply, the carrying capacity of a site, resort or even a region refers to its ability to absorb tourism use without deteriorating. In other words, capacity intervenes in the relationship between the tourist and tourist resource, or destination. The concept of carrying capacity, like sustainabililty, has its roots in resource management, but it is particularly important now

Case Study 5.2   Types of carrying capacity

Physical

This relates to the amount of suitable land available for facilities, and also includes the finite capacity of the facilities (such as car-parking spaces, covers in restaurants, or bed spaces in accommodation). It is the most straightforward of all capacity measures, and can be used for planning and management control (by, say, limiting car-parking spaces at sensitive sites).

Psychological

The psychological (or perceptual) capacity of a site is exceeded when a visitor's experience is significantly impaired. Of course, some people are crowd tolerant and enjoy busy places, while others shun them. Psychological capacity is therefore a very individual concept and difficult to influence by management and planning, although landscaping can be used to reduce the impression of crowding.

Biological

The biological capacity of a site is exceeded when environmental damage or disturbance is unacceptable. This can relate to both flora and fauna, for example, at picnic sites, along paths, or in dune eco-systems. More research has examined the capacity thresholds of vegetation than has looked at the tolerance of animals or birds to tourism (at say whale-watching locations). It is also important to consider the total ecosystem rather than individual elements.

Social

The concept of social carrying capacity is derived from ideas of community-based tourism planning and sustainability. It attempts to define levels of development which are acceptable to the host community residents and businesses and may use techniques that attempt to gauge residents' threshold limits to acceptable change (LAC).

in a situation where finite destination resources are under growing pressure from users (see Case Study 5.2).

Mathieson and Wall (1982, p. 21) define carrying capacity as 'the maximum number of people who can use a site without an unacceptable alteration in the physical environment and without an unacceptable decline in the quality of experience gained by visitors'.

The main problem with carrying capacity is that the concept is easy to grasp but very difficult to put into practice because carrying capacity is a management decision. Managers of the tourist destination, as well as the tourists themselves, decide what is *unacceptable* and when the *quality of experience* has declined. Indeed, any destination can be managed to a high or low capacity, a level that is determined as much by management as by the innate characteristics of the resource, culture and so on.

Strategic planning

Perhaps the central issue here is the gradual shift from short-term to longer-term thinking and planning at the destination. It is no longer acceptable for the industry to exploit and use up destinations and then move on, as has happened, for example, in some coastal areas of Spain. This changing perspective away from the short term has led to a realisation of the importance of taking a strategic approach to both markets and destination management. It is possible to devise appropriate strategies for destinations at each stage of their life cycle such that the destination formula is constantly reviewed and adjusted in order to achieve sustainable tourism at each stage. This long-term perspective provides control and responsibility to prevent the destination exceeding capacity and the inevitable decline in visitation that follows. In other words, what is involved is the crafting of a strategic vision for a destination. The stages of strategic planning are outlined in Box 5.2.

The defining characteristics of the strategic planning approach are:

- the adoption of a long-term perspective;
- the development of a holistic and integrated plan which controls the process of change through the formation of goals; and

Box 5.2 The stages of strategic planning for destinations

Situation analysis/environmental scanning

Situation analysis or place audit involves producing a platform of information relating to the current situation of the destination and then sorting it into a strengths, weaknesses, opportunities and threats (SWOT) analysis. This is an important stage in any strategic plan. An appraisal is made of the destination's competitive position through a series of audits of the various elements of the tourism product and its delivery, as well as a scan of the external environment.

Objectives and goals

The database provided in the first stage allows the identification of key issues from which objectives and goals can be distilled. These objectives and goals provide a direction to the planning process. It is normal for destinations to include objectives and goals relating to both marketing and development and for time frames and responsibilities to be attached. At this stage, parameters to be used to judge the success or otherwise in meeting the objectives will also be identified. For tourist destinations it is common to find that the role of the public sector results in a 'top down' approach to objectives and goals. This is not only because the public sector has the overview to be able to determine objectives, but also it tends to be an inherently political process of resource allocation and conflict resolution. This contrasts with the process in companies, where this stage tends to permeate all levels of the organisation.

Strategy formulation

This stage involves the identification of a business portfolio for the destination through a process of decisions relating to which markets and products should receive more or less emphasis. Here, the objectives act as a guide. This stage recognises the fact that destinations can be thought of as an amalgam of different products appealing to different market segments at each stage of their development. A useful guide to appropriate strategies is to consider both the competitive strength of the destination and also the stage it has reached in the life cycle.

▷

Box 5.2 continued

Marketing, positioning and mix

This stage can be broken down into a series of operations, beginning with the identification of target markets followed by the development of product positioning as a means of differentiating the destination from the competition. The position in the market is communicated through manipulation of the marketing mix with objectives and targets for each market segment and product.

Implementation and monitoring

It is in this final stage where many of the problems of adopting strategic planning at tourist destinations are seen. The implementation process involves deciphering the strategy, assigning roles and responsibilities and putting into place a monitoring system. Clearly there is an organisational issue here and the configuration of tourism agencies at the destination is a critical factor in the success or otherwise of the plan's implementation. Organisations may require changes in the structure of say, the local authority, and the technical capability of its staff. Finally, there is a need for measurement, feedback and control systems to ensure that the plan continues to be implemented through management support systems. It is at this point that the information gathering stage can be transformed into an ongoing monitoring exercise for tourist destinations. Failure of strategies generally occurs on implementation. Typically this can be due to lack of political commitment, local disagreement, political intervention, lack of gearing between tactical and strategic planning, and poorly conceived situation analysis.

Source: adapted from Heath and Wall (1992) and Cooper (1996).

- a formalised decision process focused on the deployment of resources which commit the destination to a future course of action.

In terms of the adoption of sustainable tourism principles, the benefits of the strategic approach to the destination are clear:

- The process of goal setting provides a common sense of ownership and direction for the myriad stakeholders, while at the same time sharpening the guiding objectives of the destination.

- The coherence provided by the approach provides a framework for joint initiatives between the commercial and public sectors and demands the clear identification of roles and responsibilities.

- Finally, the approach delivers a range of performance indicators against which the destination's performance can be judged.

However, the introduction of a longer-term strategic planning perspective by tourist destinations is problematic. Simply, the adoption of strategic planning at the destination is not as straightforward as in a commercial organisation where responsibilities and reporting lines are well defined:

- As we have seen destinations comprise a constantly shifting mosaic of stakeholders and value systems (see Case Study 5.3). Each of these groups has a different view of the role and future of tourism at the destination and therefore the adoption of strategies becomes a political process of conflict resolution and consensus, all set within a local legislative context and where power brokers have a disproportionate influence.

Case Study 5.3   Destination stakeholders

Tourism destinations comprise a mosaic of different groups that we can term **stakeholders**. A truly sustainable destination will recognise that it must satisfy all of its stakeholders in the long term. This can be achieved by a strategic planning approach which balances a **marketing orientation** focused on tourists, with a **planning orientation** focused on the needs of local people. In every destination there are several stakeholders which have a wide range of both compatible and conflicting interests.

● **Indigenous people** are the most important stakeholders as they live and work at the destination and provide the local resources to visitors. It is therefore important to consider issues of social carrying capacity here, to involve the local community in decision-taking and to ensure that tourism does not bring unacceptable impacts upon the local people and their home.

● **Tourists** are looking for a satisfying experience, through properly segmented and developed products. They seek a high quality of service and a well-managed and organised destination.

● **The tourism industry** is to a large extent responsible for the existing development of tourism and seeks an adequate return on investment. The industry can be thought of as polarising between global and niche players. The global players tend to be multinational, well-resourced with capital, expertise and power. Often they have limited interest and commitment to destinations. Niche players are traditionally small, family-based enterprises lacking capital, expertise, qualified human resources and influence at the destination.

● **The public sector** sees tourism as a means to increase incomes, stimulate regional development and generate employment. The public sector is an important stakeholder, often taking a leadership or coordinating role.

● There is also a range of **other stakeholders** which includes pressure groups, chambers of commerce and other power brokers within the local, regional or national community.

● The influence of this political process should not be underestimated. Politics influences those who are responsible for the planning process, and lack of political support commonly leads to the failure, or non-implementation, of plans.

● In addition, the tourist sector at destinations is characterised by fragmentation and a dominance of small businesses, which often trade seasonally. This has led to a lack of management expertise at destinations, a divergence of aims between the commercial and public sectors and a short-term planning horizon which in part is driven by public sector, twelve-monthly budgeting cycles, but also by the tactical operating horizon of small businesses.

● At the same time, the stage of the destination in the life cycle also influences the acceptability of a destination-wide marketing exercise. In the early stages of the life cycle, for example, success often obscures the long-term view, while in the later stages, particularly when a destination is in decline, opposition to long-term planning exercises may be rationalised on the basis of cost.

● Finally, the performance indicators adopted in such exercises can be controversial since tourist volume is the traditional, and politically acceptable, measure of success in many destinations. From the point of view of sustainability such measures are more likely to be the less tangible ones of environmental and social impacts.

Destination evolution

There is no doubt that the evolution of tourism has been closely linked to the evolution of destinations, and, in particular, resorts. The evolution of resorts has been driven by transport developments. Most are now touring centres rather than destinations in their own right, and in response touring circuits and clusters of attractions have developed. At the same time, markets also develop and change, and resorts have had to respond to this in terms of their tourist facilities and services. A more formalised representation of these ideas is expressed by the **tourist area life cycle** (TALC) (see Figure 5.1). This states that destinations go through a cycle of evolution similar to the life cycle of a product (where sales grow as the product evolves through the stages of launch, development, maturity and decline). Simply, numbers of visitors replace sales of a product (Box 5.3). Obviously, the shape of the TALC curve will vary, but for each destination it will be dependent upon factors such as:

- the rate of development;
- access;
- government policy;
- market trends; and
- competing destinations.

Each of these factors can delay or accelerate progress through the various stages. Indeed, development can be arrested at any stage in the cycle, and only tourist developments promising considerable financial returns will mature to experience all stages of the cycle. In turn, the length of each stage, and of the cycle itself, is variable. At one extreme, instant resorts such as Cancun (Mexico) or time-share developments move almost immediately to growth; at the other extreme, well-established resorts such as Scarborough (England) have taken three centuries to move from exploration to rejuvenation.

We can see that one particular benefit of the tourist area life cycle is as a framework for understanding how destinations and their markets evolve. The shape of the curve varies depending upon supply-side factors such as:

- investment;
- capacity constraints;

Figure 5.1:
Hypothetical tourist area life cycle

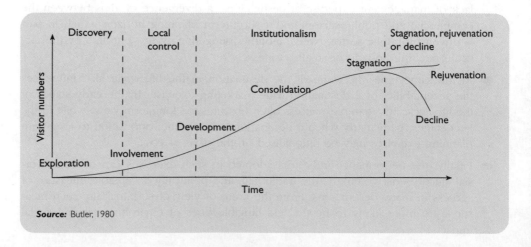

Source: Butler, 1980

Box 5.3 The tourist area life cycle

Exploration

Here the resort is visited by a small volume of explorer-type tourists who tend to shun institutionalised travel. The natural attractions, scale and culture of the resort are the main draw, but volumes are constrained by lack of access and facilities. At this stage the attraction of the resort is that it remains as yet unchanged by tourism and contact with local people will be high. Parts of Latin America and the Canadian Arctic are examples here.

Involvement

At the involvement stage, local communities have to decide whether they wish to encourage tourism, and if so, the type and scale of tourism they prefer. Local initiatives will begin to provide for visitors and advertise the resort which may lead to an increased and regular volume of visitors. A tourist season and market area emerge and pressures may be placed on the public sector to provide infrastructure and institute controls. At this point it is important to establish appropriate organisation and decision-making processes for tourism. Here, involvement of the local community should ensure locally determined capacity limits are adhered to and that sustainable principles are introduced. The smaller, less-developed Pacific and Caribbean islands are examples here, as are countries such as Yemen.

Development

By the development stage, large numbers of visitors are attracted, at peak periods perhaps equalling or exceeding the number of local inhabitants. By this stage, the organisation of tourism may change as control passes out of local hands and companies from outside the area move in to provide products and facilities. These enterprises may have differing aims and time scales from those of the local community in terms of sustainable development. It is therefore at this stage that problems can occur if local decision-taking structures are weak. Control in the public sector can also be affected as regional and national planning may become necessary in part to ameliorate problems, but also to market to the international tourist-generating areas, as visitors become more dependent upon travel arrangements booked through the trade. This is a critical stage as these facilities, and the changing nature of tourism, can alter the very nature of the resort and quality may decline through problems of over-use and deterioration of facilities. Parts of Mexico and the North African coast exemplify this stage.

Consolidation

In the later stages of the cycle, the rate of increase of visitors declines though total numbers are still increasing and exceed permanent residents. The resort is now a fully fledged part of the tourism industry with an identifiable recreational business district (RBD). Many Caribbean and Mediterranean destinations are examples here.

Stagnation

At stagnation, peak tourist volumes have now been reached and the destination is no longer fashionable, relying upon repeat visits from more conservative travellers. Business use of the resort's extensive facilities is also sought, but generally major promotional and development efforts are ▷

Box 5.3 continued

needed to maintain the number of visits. Resorts in this stage often have environmental, social and economic problems and find that competition for visits is fierce and coming from a number of well-entrenched, mature resorts. A number of Spanish resorts (such as the Costa Brava) exemplify this stage.

Decline

Visitors are now being lost to newer resorts and a smaller geographical catchment for day trips and weekend visits is common. However, resorts should not await decline as inevitable but should look to revitalise visits by seeking new markets, re-positioning the resort, or finding new uses for facilities.

Rejuvenation

Destination managers may decide to *rejuvenate* or *re-launch* the destination by looking at new markets or developing the product. Introduction of new types of facility such as casinos is a common response. Here a destination should seek to protect its traditional markets, while also seeking new markets and products such as business, conference or special interest tourism. This helps to stabilise visitation, may combat seasonality, and reduces dependence on declining market segments.

Rejuvenation strategies are difficult to implement as managers are dealing with the built fabric of tourist destinations rather than with a consumer product. Indeed, it is at this stage that the analogy of a product life cycle and the destination cycle breaks down, simply because tourism is so closely woven into the very way of life of resorts and supports jobs, services and carriers. The classic examples of this stage are Atlantic City, USA; Scheveningen, Netherlands; and a number of Spanish destinations – Benidorm and Majorcan resorts – and Welsh destinations – Rhyll and Llanduduno.

Source: adapted from Butler (1980) and Cooper (1997).

● tourist impacts; and

● planning responses.

Indeed, it could be argued that an understanding of the cycle aids the development of community-based and sustainable tourism strategies at the involvement stage. To implement such approaches in later stages may be inappropriate. In other words, tourist destinations are dynamic, with changing provision of facilities and access matched by an evolving market in both quantitative and qualitative terms, as successive waves of different numbers and types of tourists with distinctive preferences, motivations and desires populate the resort at each stage of the life cycle.

It is as a conceptual framework that the TALC is best utilised, although other writers have suggested that it can be used to guide strategic planning at destinations, or as a forecasting tool. There are significant problems with these approaches:

● The difficulty of identifying stages and turning points.

● The difficulty of obtaining long runs of visitor arrivals data from which to assemble the curve.

● The danger of planners responding to (possible false) warning signs, which may be influenced anyway by management intervention.

● The danger of a tailor-made strategy for each stage.

- The level of aggregation is open to many interpretations. After all, there will be a life cycle for a hotel, a resort and a region – as well as differing curves for each market segment.

The TALC has many critics, in part drawn by its very simplicity and apparent deterministic approach. Some argue that, far from being an independent guide for decisions, the TALC is determined by the strategic decisions of management and is heavily dependent on external influences. However, as a framework within which to view the development of destinations, albeit with hindsight, and as a way of thinking about the interrelationship of destination and market evolution, it provides many useful insights.

Future developments

In the future, the competitive advantage of destinations will not be based simply upon their intrinsic attractions, but as much upon the management of the destinations, and their ability to accommodate the new tourism in terms of human resources, technology and the adoption of sustainable principles. The tourist destination of the future will be influenced by a variety of factors, but technology and the demands of the new tourist will be dominant. Technology permeates destination development in many ways – from hotel communication systems and ensuring energy efficiency, through global distribution systems (GDS), to computer-generated imagery and the use of virtual reality at attractions. Add to this a consumer of tourism who is discerning, experienced and probably computer literate, and the stage is set for a range of new tourist destinations to be developed, and for the more effective management of existing destinations. There is no doubt that these new destinations will need to be better planned and managed, and show more concern and responsibility for their environment and host community, than did their earlier counterparts.

Middleton (1992) observes two opposing tendencies in destination development for the future. First, there is the development of purpose-built, enclosed and closely controlled environments or enclaves (such as large-scale theme parks), self-contained, all-inclusive resorts or cruise ships where the emphasis is on escape from everyday life to immersion in a safe, high-quality fantasy environment. This development will be accelerated by GDS which, combined with a more knowledgeable tourist market, will see the emergence of a growing number of independent travellers and a changing role for intermediaries in the tourism distribution chain. Suppliers will attune their products more closely to the desires of their customers in enclaves which will be promoted as a market-orientated alternative to the real, and increasingly fragile, resource-based, non-reproducible attractions of natural, historic or cultural destinations. In addition, these environments will reflect our leisure lifestyles with entertainment and retail tie-ins.

Second, Middleton observes a trend towards *authentic* or *sensitive* travel experiences, where management inputs are minimal and the tourist (or traveller) controls the experience, shunning contact with the travel trade and enjoying unsulllied authentic contact with landscapes and/or cultures.

In fact, the trend towards authentic travel experiences is potentially more damaging than enclave tourism (where contacts with local cultures and environments are controlled and made routine). Destinations are responding to this threat in a variety of ways. Resource-based destinations are adopting sophisticated planning, management and interpretive techniques to provide both a welcome and a rich experience for the tourist, while at the same time ensuring protection of the resource itself. It is felt that, once tourists understand why a destination is significant, they will want to protect it. Good planning and management of the destination lie at the root of providing the new tourist with a high-quality experience, and it may be that tourists will have to accept increasingly restricted viewing times at popular sites, higher prices and even replicas of the real thing. Case Study 5.4 demonstrates an important new approach to destination management.

Case Study 5.4   Kangaroo Island

There are many views about how much and what type of tourism is good for a destination. A system known as the **Tourism Optimisation Management Model** (TOMM) has been developed by a firm of consultants to provide a mechanism to monitor and manage tourism activity in natural areas.

The TOMM approach represents a new way of thinking about destination management and we believe that it is significant because it ties together the best of good practice in destination management with that of business – such as benchmarking. Although TOMM has been developed for Kangaroo Island, South Australia, the approach is also transferable to other tourism destinations.

TOMM monitors tourism and its impacts to assist in decision-taking at the destination. Figure A shows the main stages of TOMM.

Figure A

Main stages
Confirm desired outcomes, parameters and methodology for the study.
Establish a draft set of desirable conditions for tourism on Kangaroo Island (economic, social, environmental and visitor experience).
Investigate indicators that could be measured to suggest the status of the optimal conditions.
Generate a set of tourism scenarios that could be faced on Kangaroo Island in the near future.
Investigate how the indicators could be measured in a simple, reliable and cost-effective manner.
Decide on a select group of optimal conditions. Decide on a select group of indicators. Decide on a select group of monitoring methods.
Combine the optimal conditions, indicators and monitoring methods into a table that becomes the basis for the draft model.
Commence development of Implementation Plan.
Identify missing information and assumptions that will need to be made until the information becomes available.
Identify the benchmark status for each indicator (how close Kangaroo island is to its optimal conditions).
Refine the model by testing it using the scenarios already developed.
Produce a working version of the model.
Launch the model within a consultation draft report.
Refine the model. Produce Final Report.

We can identify three main components:

1. **Context analysis** identifies the current nature of community values, the tourism product, tourism growth, opportunities and positioning. It also identifies alternative scenarios for the future of tourism. The information is used to define the optimal conditions which tourism should create.
2. **A monitoring programme** measures how close the current situation is to the optimal conditions.
3. **A management response system** identifies problem areas and the actions necessary to address them.

Figure B

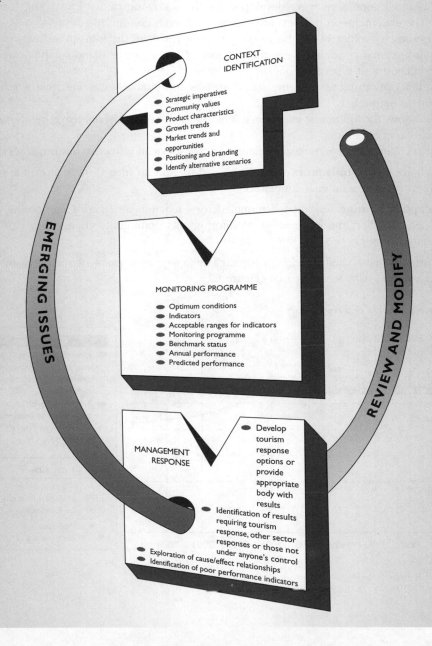

CONTEXT IDENTIFICATION

- Strategic imperatives
- Community values
- Product characteristics
- Growth trends
- Market trends and opportunities
- Positioning and branding
- Identify alternative scenarios

EMERGING ISSUES

REVIEW AND MODIFY

MONITORING PROGRAMME

- Optimum conditions
- Indicators
- Acceptable ranges for indicators
- Monitoring programme
- Benchmark status
- Annual performance
- Predicted performance

MANAGEMENT RESPONSE

- Develop tourism response options or provide appropriate body with results
- Identification of results requiring tourism response, other sector responses or those not under anyone's control
- Exploration of cause/effect relationships
- Identification of poor performance indicators

Case Study 5.4 continued

Figure B shows how these components are rolled into an operational plan. TOMM's innovative approach blends contemporary management techniques with tourism, but delivers and develops them in consultation with all the destination stakeholders. The particular contribution of TOMM to our understanding of destinations is through its concept of optimal conditions, indicators, acceptable range and benchmarks.

1. An **optimal condition** is defined as: a desirable yet realistic status for a sustainable future. Optimal conditions have to be comprehensive, measurable and easily recognised. For Kangaroo Island optimal conditions were developed for the following dimensions using local consultations. (The statements in brackets are examples of each condition):
   (a) economic conditions (e.g. the growth of employment in the tourism industry is consistent);
   (b) environmental conditions (e.g. the majority of visits to the island's natural areas occur in designated visitor service zones);
   (c) market opportunities (e.g. the island attracts the cultural/environmental segments of the tourism market);
   (d) conditions for the tourist experience (e.g. the majority of visitors leave highly satisfied with their experience); and
   (e) socio-cultural conditions (e.g. residents feel that they can influence tourism-related decisions).
2. For each condition, **indicators** were developed to gain an idea of how close the tourism sector was to achieving optimal conditions.
3. An **acceptable range** was then determined for each indicator and a monitoring programme developed to collect the information. Monitoring was dominantly via a visitor exit survey and an operator survey.
4. **Benchmarks** were then developed for each indicator as a point of reference against which new monitoring data are compared (Figure C).

Figure C Fictitious example of a report chart

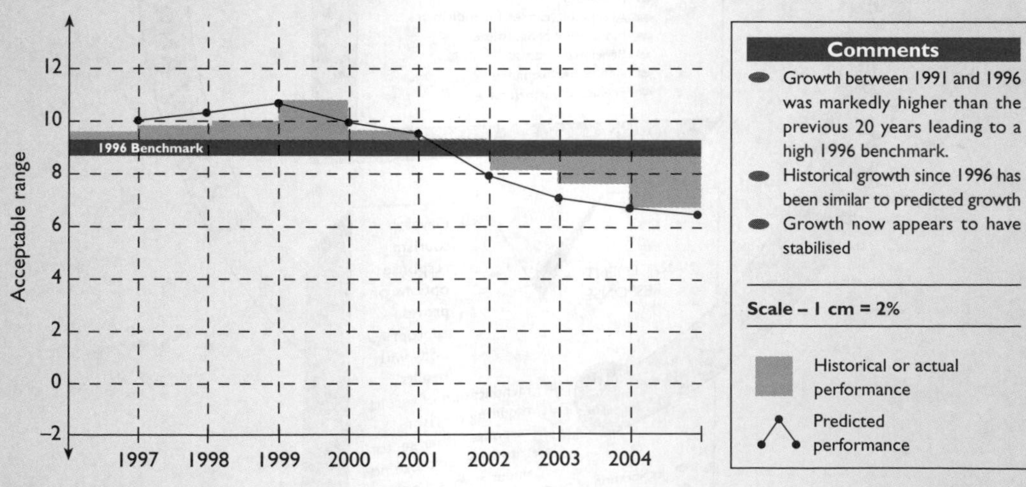
Acceptable range
12
10
8
6
4
2
0
–2
1996 Benchmark
1997
1998
1999
2000
2001
2002
2003
2004
Comments
Growth between 1991 and 1996 was markedly higher than the previous 20 years leading to a high 1996 benchmark.
Historical growth since 1996 has been similar to predicted growth
Growth now appears to have stabilised
Scale – 1 cm = 2%
Historical or actual performance
Predicted performance

Source: Manidis Roberts Consultants (1996)

Throughout all of these developments enhanced professionalism will become evident as the tourism sector collectively attempts to deliver a quality experience at the destination, while at the same time protecting the integrity of the resource itself.

Conclusion

The tourism destination is a crucial element of the tourism system. Not only does it provide a focal point for tourism activity but it also represents the 'pull' factor for the tourist. The type of tourist attracted to a destination will be determined by the quality and mix of attractions, superstructure and infrastructure present and, consequently, the role of planning and management of the whole tourism product at the destination is crucial for target markets to be attracted and for a satisfactory tourism experience to be achieved.

With this in mind, we now turn our attention to some of the probable impacts of unplanned or poorly managed tourism activity at the destination which predominantly fall under the three headings of economic impacts, environmental impacts and socio-cultural impacts. We then complete this part by evaluating the importance of planning in the alleviation of negative impacts at the destinations.

Chapter discussion questions

1. What are the implications for the overall tourism product if all the elements that make up the composite are of unequal quality cost and quality?

2. Can you identify the key trends in destination planning and development?

3. Assess the applicability of the tourism area life cycle on the basis of your own experience.

4. Why is the concept of carrying capacity so crucial to a destination and what are the likely implications if carrying capacity is exceeded?

Recommended further reading

- Murphy, P. E. (1985) *Tourism: A Community Approach*, Methuen, London.
- Pearce, D. (1989) *Tourist Development*, Longman, London.
- Pigram, J. (1983) *Outdoor Recreation and Resource Management*, Croom Helm, New York.
- Shaw, G. and Williams, A. M. (1994) *Critical Issues In Tourism: A Geographical Perspective*, Blackwell, Oxford.

Bibliography

- Ashworth, G. (1984) *Recreation and Tourism*, Bell and Hyman, London.
- Boniface, B. and Cooper, C. (1994) *The Geography of Travel and Tourism*, Butterworth-Heinemann, Oxford.
- Burton, R. (1991) *Travel Geography*, Pitman, London.

- Butler, R. W. (1980) 'The concept of a tourist area cycle of evolution', *Canadian Geographer*, **24**, 5–12.
- Chubb, M. and Chubb, H. R. (1981) *One Third of Our Time*, Wiley, New York.
- Cooper, C. (1996) 'Strategic planning for sustainable tourism: the case of offshore islands of the UK', *Journal of Sustainable Tourism*, **3**(4), 1–19.
- Cooper, C. (1997) 'The environmental consequences of declining destinations', *Progress in Tourism and Hospitality Management*, **2**(3), 337–43.
- Coppock, J. T. and Duffield, D. B. (1975) *Recreation and the Countryside*, Macmillan, London.
- Craig Smith, S. (1994) *Learning to Live with Tourism*, Pitman, Melbourne.
- English Tourist Board (1991) *Tourism and the Environment, Maintaining the Balance*, ETB, London.
- Goodall, B. (1992) 'Environmental auditing for tourism', in *Progress in Tourism and Recreation and Hospitality Management*, vol. 4, Cooper, C. (ed.), Belhaven, London.
- Heath, E. and Wall, G. (1992) *Marketing Tourism Destinations*, Wiley, New York.
- Hewison, R. (1987) *The Heritage Industry*, Methuen, London.
- Hunter, C. and Green, H. (1995) *Tourism and the Environment: A Sustainable Relationship*, Routledge, London.
- Inskeep, E. (1991) *Tourism Planning*, Van Nostrand Reinhold, New York.
- Leiper, N. (1979) 'The framework of tourism', *Annals of Tourism Research*, **6**(4), 390–407.
- Lucas, R. C. (1964) 'Wilderness perception and use: the example of the Boundary Waters Canoe Area', *Natural Resources Journal*, January, 394–411.
- McIntosh, R. W., Ritchie, J. R. B. and Goeldner, C. R. (1996) *Tourism: Principles, Practices and Philosophies*, Wiley, New York.
- Mandis Roberts Consultants (1996) *Developing A Tourism Optimisation Model (TOMM): A Model To Monitor and Manage Tourism on Kangaroo Island, South Australia*, MRC, Surry Hills, New South Wales.
- Mathieson, A. and Wall, G. (1982) *Tourism: Economic, Physical and Social Impacts*, Longman, Harlow.
- Medlik, S. (ed.) (1991) *Managing Tourism*, Heinemann, Oxford.
- Mercer, I. (1980) *In Pursuit of Leisure*, Sorret, Melbourne.
- Middleton, V. T. C. (1992) *Marketing in Travel and Tourism*, 2nd edn, Butterworth-Heinemann, Oxford.
- Mill, R. and Morrison, A. (1992) *The Tourism System*, Prentice Hall, Englewood Cliffs, NJ.
- Patmore, J. A. (1972) *Land and Leisure*, Penguin, Harmondsworth.
- Patmore, J. A. (1983) *Recreation and Resources*, Blackwell, Oxford.
- Pearce, D. (1987) *Tourism Today*, Longman, London.
- Pearce, D. (1992) *Tourism Organisations*, Longman, London.
- Pearce, D. and Butler, R. (1995) *Change in Tourism: People, Places, Processes*, Routledge, London.
- Poon, A. (1989) 'Competitive strategies for a new tourism', in *Progress in Tourism Recreation and Hospitality Management*, Cooper, C. (ed.), Belhaven, London.
- Smith, S. L. J. (1983) *Recreation Geography*, Longman, London.
- Smith, S. L. J. (1988) 'Defining tourism: A supply side view', *Annals of Tourism Research*, **15**(2), 179–90.
- Smith, V. L. and Eddington, W. (1992) *Tourism Alternatives*, University of Pennsylvania Press, Philadelphia, PA.

- Swarbrooke, J. (1995) *The Development and Management of Tourist Attractions*, Butterworth-Heinemann, Oxford.
- Turner, L. and Ash, J. (1975) *The Golden Hordes: International Tourism and the Pleasure Periphery*, Constable, London.
- World Commission on Environment and Development (1987) *Our Common Future*, Brundtland Report, Oxford University Press, New York.
- WTTC/WTO (1995) *Agenda 21 for the Travel and Tourism Industry*, WTTC, London.

Chapter Six

The economic impact of tourism

Introduction

This chapter examines both the positive and the negative economic impacts of tourism. In the same way that the literature tends to exaggerate the negative impacts of tourism upon host societies and environments, so the positive impact of tourism upon economies is often over-stated. An integral part of this chapter is the critical assessment of the methods of measuring economic impact drawing, particularly, on the application of multiplier analysis. All the multiplier models that are outlined in this chapter provide information that is valuable to policy makers and planners. It should also be noted that, within known limitations, multiplier analyses provide powerful and valuable tools for estimating and analysing the economic impact of tourism and comparing the performance of tourism with that of alternative industries.

Chapter learning objectives

This chapter focuses on the economic impacts of tourism and is aimed to provide students with

- an understanding of the economic contribution of tourism locally, nationally and internationally;

- an appreciation of the positive and negative economic impacts of tourism activity; and

- a general knowledge of the strategies that may be implemented to measure the economic impacts of tourism and the weaknesses associated with these technologies.

Overview

In spite of the many altruistic and well-meaning reasons sometimes put forward to support the case for tourism development (such as those put forward in the Manila Declaration; WTO, 1980), it is the economic advantages that provide the main driving force for tourism development. Tourist expenditure is as 'real' as any other form of consumption and international tourist expenditure can be seen as an invisible export from the host country, whereas domestic tourism can be seen as an 'export' between the local regions and, in some instances, an import substitute for the national economy. The former is easier to measure than the latter because it involves custom/immigration procedures and currency exchange, which are measured by central banks and often included in national accounts. However, tourist expenditure can only be accurately estimated by undertaking specific visitor expenditure surveys which can be time consuming and costly. Some countries attempt to estimate the level and patterns of tourist spending from Central Bank statistics, while others try to economise by collecting tourist expenditure data at infrequent intervals (say, every five years). In order to use economic impact analyses for the purpose of tourism planning and development strategies it is important to have reliable flows of expenditure data. Therefore, visitor expenditure data should be collected by exit surveys each year, or at least every other year.

During the past few decades many economies have experienced growth in their service sectors, even when the more traditional agricultural and manufacturing sectors have been subject to stagnation or decline. Tourism is a service-based industry and, as such, has been partly responsible for this service sector growth. In developing countries, the service sector is responsible for around 40% of GDP while in developed or industrialised economies it is responsible for more than 65% of GDP. In spite of its economic importance, the service sector has been sadly neglected in the myopic economic textbooks, which have continued to concentrate on the more traditional manufacturing industries. The dearth of material on service-based industries in the major textbooks can be, in part, explained (if not excused) by the lack of available and comparable statistics for service-based sectors. But in general it is tradition that has dictated the content of such books rather than pragmatism. Nevertheless, the latter half of the 1980s saw a growing interest in the operation and performance of service industries. In 1986, it was observed that, because of the strength of intersectoral linkages, the service sector generally performs a more important function in the process of development than that suggested merely by looking at the service sector's contribution to a country's GDP. In the mid-1990s, the international world is dominated by the service industries. From 1992 to 1994 the growth of tourism receipts was far in excess of the growth of other commercial services. In 1996 tourism receipts grew almost twice as fast as international trade in commodities and more than twice as fast as other commercial services, being responsible for 8% of the world total of the former and 35% of the latter.

Tourism, as a major element of the service economy, has, for some time, been applauded for its sustained and rapid growth. However, not even its most ardent supporters would have forecast just how well it has been able to stand up to the pressures of global economic recession, even recessions that have severely damaged many of the world's major industries. The world has staggered from recession to recession over the past decade and even the mighty giants of industry (such as IBM) have been forced to rationalise their activities. In spite of this, tourism activity has not only been able to maintain its presence, but in many areas it has continued to grow.

Although the purpose of this chapter is to examine the economic impact of tourism, it is useful to examine the economic significance of tourism to a number of countries, most notably the prime generators and/or recipients of international tourists. The economic significance of tourism is determined not only by the level of tourism activity that is taking place, but also by the type and nature of the economy being considered. For instance, the economic significance of tourism activity to a developing country may well be measured in terms of its ability to generate an inflow of foreign exchange or to provide a means for creating greater price flexibility in its export industries, whereas, for a developed or industrialised economy, the researcher may be looking at tourism's ability to assist diversification strategies and to combat regional imbalances.

The significance of tourism may be assessed in terms of the proportion of total global visitors attributable to individual countries, for here one can assess the relative importance of single countries in determining the volume of world travel. On the other hand, the significance of tourism may be examined with respect to the importance of tourist activity to the economy of each destination. This chapter examines both aspects in order to establish how some countries are extremely important as tourist generators and how other countries are highly dependent upon such tourism activity.

Tourist-generating/receiving countries

The selection of countries for inclusion in tables of top generating and top recipient countries is at best difficult and at worst arbitrary. However, the seven countries selected for inclusion in Tables 6.1 and 6.2 (France, Germany, Italy, Spain, the UK, Japan and the USA) have been included because they are among either the top five tourist-generating countries with respect to tourist expenditure and/or the top five countries with respect to tourism receipts.

Table 6.1 shows the principal tourist-generating countries, with respect to their level of tourist expenditure, over the time period from 1986 to 1995. It can be seen that, over the years covered by the table, the proportion of the world's total tourist expenditure attributable to the top five generating countries has fluctuated around the 50% level, with a peak of just over 54% in 1988. Some countries, such as Japan, have increased their tourist expenditure over this period by a factor of more than 5. Japan displaced the UK as the third highest tourism spender in 1988, whereas countries such as the USA failed to double the total value of their tourist expenditure over this period. Of particular inter-

Table 6.1:
Principal tourist-generating countries 1986–95: expenditure (in US$bn)

Country	1986	1987	1988	1989	1990	1991	1992	1993	1994	1995
Germany	18.3	23.6	25.0	23.6	29.5	31.0	36.6	37.5	44.3	50.7
United States	26.0	29.2	33.1	33.4	37.4	35.3	39.9	41.3	43.8	45.9
Japan	7.2	10.8	18.7	22.5	24.9	24.0	26.8	26.9	30.7	37.0
United Kingdom	8.9	11.9	14.6	15.3	19.1	17.6	19.9	17.4	22.2	24.7
France	6.5	8.6	9.7	10.0	12.4	12.3	13.9	12.8	13.8	16.3
Top 5 countries	66.9	84.1	101.1	104.8	123.3	120.2	137.1	135.9	154.8	174.6
Rest of world	59.1	72.2	85.1	93.8	119.9	122.9	140.6	134.2	154.6	182.3
World total	125.0	156.3	186.2	198.6	243.2	243.1	277.7	270.1	309.4	356.9
Top 5 as % of world total	53.5	53.8	54.3	52.8	50.7	49.5	49.4	50.3	50.0	48.9

Source: derived from WTO figures (1988, 1992, 1997).

Table 6.2: Principal destinations in terms of tourism receipts 1986–96: tourism receipts (US$bn)

Country	1986	1987	1988	1989	1990	1991	1992	1993	1994	1995	1996
United States	20.4	23.5	28.9	36.3	43.0	48.4	53.9	56.5	58.4	61.1	64.3
Spain	12.1	14.8	16.7	16.2	18.6	19.0	22.2	19.4	21.5	25.3	28.4
Italy	9.9	12.2	12.4	11.9	20.0	18.4	21.5	20.5	23.8	27.5	27.4
France	9.7	12.0	13.8	16.2	20.2	21.4	25.1	23.4	24.7	27.5	28.2
United Kingdom	8.2	10.2	11.0	11.4	14.9	13.1	13.9	13.5	15.2	19.1	19.7
Top 5 countries	60.3	72.7	82.8	92.0	116.7	120.3	136.6	133.3	143.6	160.5	168.0
Rest of world	77.3	94.1	114.9	123.6	144.4	147.3	167.5	172.5	207.6	232.6	254.7
World total	137.6	166.8	197.7	215.6	261.1	267.6	304.1	305.8	351.2	393.1	422.7
Top 5 as % of world total	43.8	43.6	41.9	42.7	44.7	45.0	44.9	43.6	40.9	40.8	39.7

Source: derived from figures in WTO (1988, 1992, 1997).

est is the fact that the USA and Germany have vied for the position of number 1 tourist generator, with the USA leading the challenge during the 1980s but with Germany recovering throughout the 1990s to be ranked highest spender in 1994 and 1995.

Table 6.2 shows the top five countries in terms of tourism receipts. The proportion of total global tourist receipts attributable to the top five countries has fluctuated around the lower half of the 40% range, with peaks of around 45% at the turn of the decade but falling to 40% by 1996. The USA has improved its position relative to the other top recipient countries, by increasing its receipts more than threefold over the ten-year period. In 1986 the USA was responsible for 14.8% of the world total tourism receipts; in 1996 this figure had risen to 15.3%.

A fact that becomes clear from examining Tables 6.1 and 6.2 is that there is a high degree of correlation between the top tourist-generating countries and the top tourist expenditure recipients. That is, tourism does not appear to perform a great role as a global redistributor of income in the same way that is claimed for regional redistribution. This is particularly true if the relationship between developed and developing countries is considered. It is the developed and industrialised countries that number among both the top generators of tourist expenditure and the top recipients.

The division between the performance of developed and developing countries is of additional significance when it is considered that, on average through the latter half of the 1980s, the developed countries were responsible for 70% of all world exports and received over 72% of all tourism receipts, which contrasts with the developing countries which were responsible for 20% of all world exports and received only 25% of all tourist receipts. The outstanding exports and tourism receipts were accounted for by the non-market economies of that decade.

Dependence upon tourism

Table 6.3 provides another way of examining the economic significance of tourism for countries by looking at dependence on tourism receipts relative to total export earnings and gross national product (GNP) for 1995. It can be seen that among these developed

Table 6.3:
Tourism receipts expressed as a percentage of total export earnings and gross national product, 1995

Country	Tourism receipts (US$m) (1)	Export earnings (US$m) (2)	(1) as a % of (2)	GNP (US$bn) (3)	(1) as a % of (3)
Spain	25 701	91 533	28.1	532 347	4.8
France	27 527	286 852	9.6	1 451 051	1.9
Italy	27 451	231 260	11.9	1 088 085	2.5
United Kingdom	19 073	242 036	7.9	1 094 734	1.7
United States	61 137	584 743	10.5	7 100 007	0.9
Germany	16 221	508 404	3.2	2 252 343	0.7
Japan	3 226	443 265	0.7	4 963 587	0.1

Source: derived from WTO figures (1997).

economies, tourism receipts as a percentage of total export earnings ranges from the relatively unimportant 0.7% for Japan to the quite dependent 28.1% experienced by Spain. Confirming this is the percentage of GNP attributable to tourism receipts which shows that only 0.1% of Japan's GNP is attributable to tourist receipts but this figure rises to 4.8% for Spain.

Two major problems that exist when making international comparisons of tourism expenditure and receipts is that the data are generally expressed in current prices and are standardised in US dollars. The problems created by this form of presentation is that (1) it does not take into account the effects of inflation and (2) movements in the value of the dollar exchange rate (which have been both frequent and dramatic over the past decade) will manifest as changes in the local value of tourist receipts and expenditure. In an attempt to circumvent some of these problems, Figure 6.1 shows an index of tourism receipts in real prices from 1983 to 1990, using 1982 as the base year (1982 = 100).

Figure 6.1 shows a contrast of events for countries such as Japan and Spain. In the former, real tourism receipts have increased consistently and rapidly since 1986. However,

Figure 6.1:
Index of tourist receipts in real prices (1992 = 100)

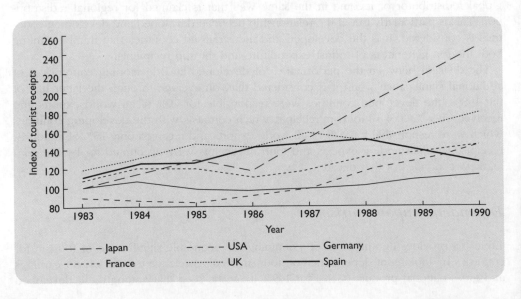

Table 6.4:
Tourism balance
sheet, 1988–1990
(US$m)

	1991	1992	1993	1994	1995
Africa					
Receipts	5 009	6 023	6 133	6 511	6 980
Expenditure	4 498	4 433	4 613	4 378	4 928
Balance[a]	511	1 590	1 520	2 133	2 052
Europe					
Receipts	143 098	163 722	160 470	178 751	207 351
Expenditure	127 400	148 874	141 445	165 195	198 154
Balance[a]	15 698	13 848	19 025	13 556	9 197
Americas					
Receipts	77 683	85 524	97 151	95 104	100 225
Expenditure	61 112	65 666	68 306	71 522	72 847
Balance[a]	16 571	19 858	22 845	23 582	27 378
East Asia/Pacific					
Receipts	40 203	47 278	52 411	62 198	73 411
Expenditure	45 083	53 035	54 575	61 888	73 947
Balance[a]	−4 880	−5 757	−2 164	310	−536
Middle East					
Receipts	4 280	5 400	4 832	5 437	7 285
Expenditure	3 867	3 768	3 975	4 478	4 916
Balance[a]	413	1 632	857	959	2 369
South Asia					
Receipts	2 411	2 838	2 793	3 178	3 646
Expenditure	1 985	2 571	2 315	1 924	2 041
Balance[a]	426	267	478	1 254	1 605

[a] Minus sign indicates a deficit. Owing to rounding of figures, balances may not always equal the difference between receipts and expenditure.
Source: WTO (1997).

in Spain real tourism receipts peaked in 1988 and they have fallen quite dramatically since then. Other countries, such as Germany, have maintained the real value of their tourism receipts over the period whereas France and the UK have managed to achieve some real gain despite some marked fluctuations throughout the period. The USA began the period poorly with a slight decline being recorded between 1983 and 1985; however, since that time there has been sustained and increasing rates of growth and the USA started the 1990s with a strong growth rate.

Table 6.4 takes the analysis one step further and examines the relationship between tourism receipts and expenditures in order to establish the net effect of travel on selected regions of the world. For the period 1991 to 1995, Europe has been in the healthy position of having a positive balance on its travel account but the size of the positive balance has fluctuated considerably and in 1995 it was less than half of the balance enjoyed in 1993. This does, of course, disguise the fact that within Europe some countries performed well in this respect while others did not. The travel trade surplus in Europe fell from US$15 698 million in 1991 to US$9197 million in 1995. With the exception of the EAP region, which was generally recording a negative travel balance over this time period, all of the global regions experienced a growth in their travel balance.

The generation of economic impacts by tourist spending

Tourists spend their money on a wide variety of goods and services. They purchase accommodation, food and beverage, transport, communications, entertainment services, goods from retail outlets and tour/travel services just to name a few. This money may be seen as an injection of demand into the host economy, i.e. demand that would otherwise not be present. However, the value of tourist expenditure represents only a partial picture of the economic impact. The full assessment of economic impact must take into account other aspects such as:

● indirect and induced effects;
● leakages of expenditure out of the local economy;
● displacement and opportunity costs.

Direct, indirect and induced economic effects

Tourist expenditure has a 'cascading' effect throughout the host economy. It begins with tourists spending money in 'front-line' tourist establishments, such as hotels, restaurants and taxis, and then permeates throughout the rest of the economy. It can be examined by assessing the impact at three different levels – the direct, indirect and induced levels.

The direct level of impact is the value of tourist expenditure *less* the value of imports necessary to supply those 'front-line' goods and services. Thus, the direct impact is likely to be less than the value of tourist expenditure except in the rare case where a local economy can provide all of the tourist's wants from its own productive sectors.

The establishments that directly receive the tourist expenditure also need to purchase goods and services from other sectors within the local economy, e.g. hotels will purchase the services of builders, accountants, banks, food and beverage suppliers, electricity and water, etc. Furthermore, the suppliers to these 'front-line' establishments will also need to purchase goods and services from other establishments within the local economy and so the process continues. The generation of economic activity brought about by these subsequent rounds of expenditure is known as the **indirect effect**. The indirect effect will not involve all of the monies spent by tourists during the direct effect since some of that money will leak out of circulation through imports, savings and taxation.

Finally, during the direct and indirect rounds of expenditure, income will accrue to local residents in the form of wages, salaries, distributed profit, rent and interest. This addition to local income will, in part, be re-spent in the local economy on goods and services and this will generate yet further rounds of economic activity.

It is only when all three levels of impact (direct *plus* indirect *plus* induced) are estimated that the full positive economic impact of tourism expenditure is fully assessed. However, there can be negative aspects to the economic impact of tourist expenditure.

Negative economic impacts

The production of tourist goods and services requires the commitment of resources that could otherwise be used for alternative purposes. For instance, the development of a tourism resort may involve the migration of labour from rural to urban areas which brings with it economic implications for both the rural and urban areas – the former losing a productive unit of labour whereas the latter implying additional infrastructure pressure for health, education and other public services. If labour is not in abundance then meeting the tourists' demands may involve the transfer of labour from one industry (such as agriculture or fishing) to tourism industries, involving an opportunity cost that is often ignored in the estimation of tourism's economic impact. Furthermore, if there is a shortage of skilled labour then there may be a need to import labour from other countries which will result in additional economic leakages as income earned from this imported labour may, in part, be repatriated.

Similarly, the use of capital resources (which are often scarce) in the development of tourism-related establishments precludes their use for other forms of economic development. To gain a true picture of the economic impact of tourism it is necessary to take into account the opportunity costs of using scarce resources for tourism development as opposed to alternative uses.

Where tourism development substitutes one form of expenditure and economic activity for another, this is known as the **displacement effect**. The displacement effect should be taken into account when the economic impact of tourism is being estimated. Displacement can take place when tourism development is undertaken at the expense of another industry and is generally referred to as the opportunity cost of the development. However, it is more commonly referred to when a new tourism project is seen to take away custom from an existing facility. For instance, if a destination finds that its all-inclusive hotels are running at high occupancy levels and returning a reasonable yield on the investment, the construction of an additional all-inclusive hotel may simply reduce the occupancy levels of the existing establishments. This means that the destination may find that its overall tourism activity has not increased by as much as the new business from the development. This is displacement.

The measurement of economic impact

The measurement of the economic impact of tourism is far more involved than calculating the level of tourist expenditure. Indeed, estimates of the economic impact of tourism based on tourist expenditure or receipts can be not only inaccurate, but also very misleading. Before examining how the economic impact is measured, it is necessary to look at the different aspects of the economy that are affected by tourism expenditure.

To begin with, a difference can be drawn between the economic impact associated with tourist expenditure and that associated with the development of tourism. The former refers to the ongoing effects of, and changes in, tourist expenditure, whereas the latter is concerned with the impact of the construction and finance of tourism-related facilities. The difference between these two aspects of impact is important because they require different methodological approaches. The calculation of the economic impact of tourist expenditure is achieved by using multiplier analysis and the estimation of the economic impact of tourism development projects is achieved by resorting to project appraisal techniques such as cost–benefit analysis.

Measuring the economic impact of tourist expenditure

At a national level the WTO publishes annual tourist statistics for countries throughout the world. These statistics include figures relating to tourist expenditure, but it would not be correct to assume that these figures reflect the economic impact of tourist expenditure. These figures relate to how much tourists spend in a destination. They take no account of how much of that sum leaks straight out of the economy (paying for imported goods and services to satisfy tourist needs) or how much additional impact is experienced through the 'knock on' effects of this tourist spending.

At a subnational level the availability of tourist expenditure data is far more sparse. Some countries, such as the UK, undertake visitor expenditure surveys (e.g. International Passenger Survey (IPS) and United Kingdom Tourist Survey (UKTS)) which allow expenditure estimates to be made at the regional level. However, it is often necessary to undertake specific tourist expenditure surveys to establish the tourist spend in particular areas.

In order to translate tourist expenditure data into economic impact information the appropriate multiplier values have to be calculated. The term **multiplier** is one of the most quoted economic concepts in the study of tourism. Multiplier values may be used for a variety of purposes and are often used as the basis for public sector decision making.

The multiplier concept

The concept of the multiplier is based upon the recognition that sales for one firm require purchases from other firms within the local economy, i.e. the industrial sectors of an economy are interdependent. This means that firms purchase not only primary inputs such as labour and imports, but also intermediate goods and services produced by other establishments within the local economy. Therefore, a change in the level of final demand for one sector's output will not only affect the industry that produces that final good/service but also other sectors that supply goods/services to that sector and the sectors that act as suppliers to those sectors as well.

Because firms in the local economy are dependent upon other firms for their supplies, any change in tourist expenditure will bring about a change in the economy's level of production, household income, employment, government revenue and foreign exchange flows (where applicable). These changes may be greater than, equal to or less than the value of the change in tourist expenditure that brought them about. The term tourist multiplier refers to the ratio of two changes – the change in one of the key economic variables such as output (income, employment or government revenue) to the change in tourist expenditure.

Therefore, there will be some value by which the initial change in tourist expenditure must be multiplied in order to estimate the total change in output – this is known as the output multiplier. In the same way, there will be a value that, when multiplied by the change in tourist expenditure, will estimate the total change in household income – this is known as the income multiplier. The reason why the initial change in tourist spending must be subject to a multiplier effect can be seen from Figure 6.2.

Figure 6.2 shows that the tourist expenditure goes, initially, to the front-line tourist establishments that provide the tourists with their goods and services. This money will be respent by the firms that receive it. A proportion of the money will leak directly out of the economy in the form of imports. These imports may be in the form of food and beverage that the tourist eats but are not provided locally, or in respect of services provided to the establishment by individuals or firms located outside the economy being analysed. The money paid to persons outside the economy cannot have any further role in generating economic activity within the local economy and, thus, the value of tourist expenditure that actually circulates in the local economy is immediately reduced. The remaining sum of money will be used to purchase locally produced goods and services, labour and entrepreneurial skills (wages, salaries and profits) and to meet government taxes, licences and fees. These effects are all known as the **direct effects**.

We can see from Figure 6.2 that money will flow from the tourism-related establishments to other local businesses. This money will also be re-spent, some of it leaking out as imports, some of it leaking out of circulation as savings and some going to the

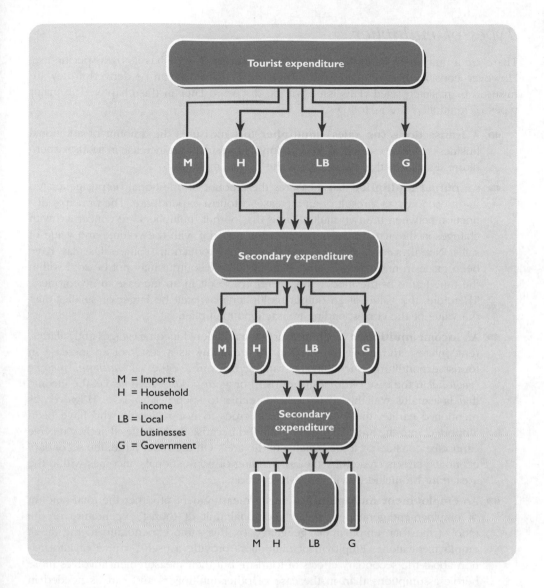

M = Imports
H = Household income
LB = Local businesses
G = Government

government. The remainder will be spent on labour and entrepreneurial skills and purchases from other businesses for goods and services. The businesses which receive money in payment for their goods/services will also make purchases locally, import goods and services and pay government taxes. These effects are known as the **indirect effects**.

During each round of expenditure, some proportion of money accrues to local residents in the form of income (wages, salaries and profits). Some of this money will be saved (by either households or businesses) and will cease to circulate in the economy, i.e. a leakage. The income that accrues to local households and is not saved will be re-spent. Some of it will leak out of the system as imports and some of it will go to the government as tax. The remainder will be respent as household consumption. This spending of income accrued as a result of the initial tourist expenditure will generate further rounds of economic activity – this effect is known as the **induced effect**.

The value of any tourism multiplier is meaningless unless it is qualified by both the methodology used to estimate it, and the type of multiplier involved.

Types of multiplier

There are a number of multipliers in regular use and each type has its own specific use. However, considerable confusion and misleading conclusions can be derived if they are misused or misinterpreted. This issue will be discussed later in this chapter. The major types of multipliers are as follows:

- A **transactions (or sales) multiplier** that measures the amount of additional business revenue created in an economy as a result of an increase in tourist expenditure. Similar to this in concept is the output multiplier.

- An **output multiplier** that measures the amount of additional output generated in an economy as a result of an increase in tourist expenditure. The principal distinction between the two multipliers is that output multipliers are concerned with changes in the actual levels of production and not with the volume and value of sales. Not all sales will be related to current production (some sales may have been made from inventories and some productive output may not be sold within the time frame of the model and, therefore, result in an increase in inventories). Therefore, the value of an output multiplier may well be larger or smaller than the value of the corresponding transactions multiplier.

- An **income multiplier** which measures the additional income (wages and salaries, rent, interest and profits) created in the economy as a result of an increase in tourist expenditure. Such income can be measured either as *national income* (*regional* in the case of domestic tourism) or as *disposable income*, i.e. the income that is actually available to households either to spend or to save. However, as mentioned earlier, the income, which accrues to non-nationals who have been 'imported' into the area, should be excluded because the incomes that they receive cannot be considered to be benefits to the area. On the other hand, the secondary economic effects created by the re-spending of non-nationals' incomes within the area *must* be included within the calculations.

- An **employment multiplier** which is a measurement of either the total amount of employment generated by an additional unit of tourist expenditure or the ratio of the total employment generated by this same expenditure to the direct employment alone. Employment multipliers provide a useful source of information about the secondary effects of tourism, but their measurement involves more heroic assumptions than in the case of other multipliers and care is needed in their interpretation.

- A **government revenue multiplier** that measures the impact on government revenue, from all sources, associated with an increase of tourist expenditure. This multiplier may be expressed in gross terms, that is the gross increase in government revenue as a result of an increase in tourist spending, or in net terms when the increase in government revenue is reduced by the increase in government expenditures associated with the increase in tourist activity.

Since the different types of multiplier are calculated using the same database they are closely interrelated. However, the concepts involved in each of the above multipliers are very different as are the magnitudes of each of the different multipliers calculated for the same economy. Some examples of these multiplier values are shown later in this chapter. Given the number of different multiplier concepts that are available it is not surprising to find that there has been some confusion over their interpretation. This confusion has

Box 6.1   Multiplier analysis using base theory

One early and interesting application of the technique by R. R. Nathan and Associates (1966) was used to calculate the short-run employment effects created by tourism expenditure in each of 375 counties and independent cities of Appalachia. The final model used took the form:

$$\frac{E}{E_{rx2}} = \frac{1}{1 - E_{rc}/E_r} \tag{1}$$

where E_r is total local employment, E_{rc} is local employment servicing local consumer demand and E_{rx2} is the direct change in employment created by a change in tourism expenditure.

Nathan Associates developed the multiplier model further, to measure long-term effects, by incorporating investment activity. This model took the form

$$\frac{E_r}{E_{rx2}} = \frac{1 + i_2}{1 - E_{rc}/E_r} \tag{2}$$

where i_2 is a statistically estimated parameter (the value of which lies between 0 and 1) which relates the change in investment to the change in tourism activity.

This model is far too simplistic to be accurate in calculating tourism multiplier values.

been compounded by the fact that there are also a variety of methods that may be used to calculate each of the above multipliers.

Methodological approaches

There are four major techniques that have been employed to measure the value of the tourist multiplier:

- base theory;
- Keynesian multiplier;
- *ad hoc*; and
- input–output.

Base theory models

The basic assumption underlying base theory models is that there exists a stable relationship between each of the export sectors and the local sectors of an economy, so that changes in the level of tourist expenditure will create predictable and measurable changes in the level of activity in local sectors. An example of this approach is given in Box 6.1. Base theory multipliers are normally over-simplified formulations and are now rarely used.

Keynesian multiplier models

These multipliers are designed to measure the income created in an economy by an additional unit of tourist expenditure. The simplest formulation of the multiplier (k) is shown in equation (6.1):

$$k = \frac{1}{1 - c + m} \tag{6.1}$$

where 1 is the additional unit of tourism expenditure and leakages are the proportion of this expenditure which goes into savings $(1 - c)$ and imports (m).

i.e. $k = \dfrac{1}{\text{leakages}}$

To develop this model into a long-term formulation, which takes investment into account, is shown in equation (6.2):

$$k = \frac{1}{1 - c + m - i} \tag{6.2}$$

where i is the marginal propensity to invest.

Similarly the effects of the re-spending of money accruing to the public sector can be built into the model, and this is shown in equation (6.3):

$$k = \frac{1}{1 - c + m - i - g} \tag{6.3}$$

where g is the marginal propensity of the public sector to spend.

A typical Keynesian short-term multiplier model is shown in equation (6.4). The derivation of this model is given in Archer (1976).

$$k = \frac{1 - L}{1 - c(1 - t_i)(1 - t_d - b) + m} \tag{6.4}$$

where, L = first round leakages out of the economy;
  t_i = the marginal rate of indirect taxation;
  t_d = the marginal rate of taxation and other deductions;
  b = the marginal rate of transfer payments.

The difference in the value of the multiplier created by applying exactly the same data to the short-term models shown in equations (6.1) and (6.4) highlight the dangers of relying on a model whose structure is too simplistic. For example, if we let $L = 0.5$, $c = 0.9$, $m = 0.7$, $t_i = 0.16$, $t_d = 0.2$ and $b = 0.2$ and calculate the income multipliers using first, the model shown in equation (6.1) and then again, using the more developed model shown in equation (6.4), the results are:

$$\frac{1}{1 - c + m} = \frac{1}{1 - 0.9 + 0.7} = 1.25$$

and

$$\frac{1 - L}{1 - c(1 - t_i)(1 - t_d - b) + m} = \frac{1 - 0.5}{1 - 0.9(1 - 0.16)(1 - 0.2 - 0.2) + 0.7}$$
$$= 0.40$$

The two multiplier values derived from the same database are very different and would result in very different policy implications. However, even the more developed model shown in equation (6.4) is far too simplistic and is unable to measure variations in the form and magnitude of sectoral linkages and leakages out of the destination's economy during each round of transactions. Even the most complex and comprehensive Keynesian models developed for some studies are unable to provide the level of detail that is required for policy making and planning. One practical solution is to use *ad hoc* models.

Ad hoc *models*

These models, although similar in principle to the Keynesian approach discussed above, are constructed specifically for each particular study. The simplest form of *ad hoc* model, using matrix algebra, is shown in equation (6.5):

$$A * \frac{1}{1 - BC} \tag{6.5}$$

where A = the proportion of additional tourist expenditure remaining in the economy after first round leakages, i.e. A equals the $(1 - L)$ expression in the Keynesian model;

B = the propensity of local people to consume in the local economy;

C = the proportion of expenditure by local people that accrues as income in the local economy.

The *ad hoc* model shown in equation (6.5) is too simplistic for serious application but more advanced models have been developed and used widely to calculate tourist multipliers to estimate the effect of tourist expenditure on income, public sector revenue, employment and imports. One such model, developed in the early 1970s (Archer and Owen, 1971) is:

$$\sum_{j=1}^{N} \sum_{i=1}^{n} Q_j K_{ij} V_i \frac{1}{1 - c \sum_{i=1}^{n} X_i Z_i V_i} \tag{6.6}$$

where j = each category of tourist, $j = 1$ to N;

i = each type of business establishment, $i = 1$ to n;

Q_j = the proportion of total tourist expenditure spent by the jth type of tourist;

K_{ij} = the proportion of expenditure by the ith type of tourist in the jth category of business;

V_i = the direct and indirect income generated by unit of expenditure by the ith type of business;

X_i = the pattern of consumption, i.e. the proportion of total consumer expenditure by the residents of the area in the ith type of business;

Z_i = the proportion of X_i which takes place within the study area; and

c = the marginal propensity to consume.

The multiplicand equation (6.6) measures the direct and indirect effects of tourist expenditure while the multiplier measures the induced effects. In order to trace the flows of expenditure through successive rounds, separate equations are estimated for a range of V_i values. Examples of these are provided in the literature (see, for example, Archer and Owen, 1971).

Multiplier studies using *ad hoc* models are commonly used and examples can be found in the USA, the UK, South Pacific islands, Caribbean and elsewhere. More recent models have achieved even greater levels of disaggregation, even down to the levels of individual establishments.

Although models of this type can produce a large quantity of detailed and accurate information for policy-making and planning purposes, they are unable to provide the

Figure 6.3:
Basic input–output transactions table

SALES TO	INTERMEDIATE DEMAND Productive sectors					FINAL DEMAND Final demand sectors				TOTAL OUTPUT
PURCHASES FROM	Industry 1	2	3	4	....m	H	I	G	E	
Productive sectors										
Industry 1	X_{11}	X_{12}	X_{13}	X_{14}	....X_{1m}	C_1	I_1	G_1	E_1	X_1
Industry 2	X_{21}	X_{22}	X_{23}	X_{24}	....X_{2m}	C_2	I_2	G_2	E_2	X_2
Industry 3	X_{31}	X_{32}	X_{33}	X_{34}	....X_{3m}	C_3	I_3	G_3	E_3	X_3
Industry 4	X_{41}	X_{42}	X_{43}	X_{44}	....X_{4m}	C_4	I_4	G_4	E_4	X_4
...	.	.	.	.	....	.	.	.	.	.
...	.	.	.	.	....	.	.	.	.	.
Industry m	X_{m1}	X_{m2}	X_{m3}	X_{m4}	....X_{mm}	C_m	I_m	G_m	E_m	X_m
Primary inputs										
Wages and salaries	W_1	W_2	W_3	W_4	....W_m	W_C	W_I	W_G	W_E	W
Profits/ dividends	P_1	P_2	P_3	P_4	....P_m	P_C	P_I	P_G	P_E	P
Taxes	T_1	T_2	T_3	T_4	....T_m	T_C	T_I	T_G	T_E	T
Imports	M_1	M_2	M_3	M_4	....M_m	M_C	M_I	M_G	M_E	M
Total inputs	X_1	X_2	X_3	X_4	....X_m	C	I	G	E	X

where:
X = Output
C = Consumption (households)
I = Investment (private)
G = Government expenditure

E = Exports
M = Imports
W = Wages and salaries
P = Profits and dividends
I = Taxes

Final demand sectors:
H = Household consumption sector
I = Investment expenditure sector
G = Government expenditure sector
E = Exports sectors

wealth of data yielded by the final methodological approach to be discussed, input–output analysis.

Input–output analysis

The input–output model approach, unlike the alternative methods discussed above, presents a general equilibrium, rather than the partial equilibrium approach used in *ad hoc* models, to studying economic impacts.

Input–output analysis begins with the construction of a table, similar to a table of national/regional accounts, which shows the economy of the destination in matrix form. Each sector of the economy is shown in each column as a purchaser of goods and services from other sectors in the economy, and in each row as a seller of output to each of the other sectors. The structure of an input–output table is shown in Figure 6.3. The table may be subdivided into three major quadrants. First, the inter-industry matrix (located in the top left-hand quadrant) details the sales and purchases that take place among the various sectors of the economy (e.g. X_{11}, X_{12}, X_{13}, etc., are the sales of sector 1 to all other sectors within the economy, whereas X_{11}, X_{21}, X_{31}, X_{41}, etc., represent the purchases of sector 1 from all other sectors within the economy). Secondly, the bottom left-hand quadrant shows each sector's purchases of primary inputs (such as payments to labour, W, profits, P, taxes, T and imported goods and services, M. Thirdly, the right-hand quadrant shows the sales made by each sector to each source of final demand.

The simplest formulation is shown in equations (6.7) and (6.8) where, for ease of explanation, all forms of final demand are represented by a column vector ($\mathbf{Y}$).

$$\mathbf{X} = \mathbf{AX} + \mathbf{Y} \tag{6.7}$$
$$\mathbf{X} - \mathbf{AX} = \mathbf{Y}$$
$$(\mathbf{I} - \mathbf{A})\mathbf{X} = \mathbf{Y}$$
$$\mathbf{X} = (\mathbf{I} - \mathbf{A})^{-1}\mathbf{Y}$$
$$\Delta\mathbf{X} = (\mathbf{I} - \mathbf{A})^{-1}\Delta\mathbf{Y} \tag{6.8}$$

where $\mathbf{X}$ = a vector of the total sales of each sector of the economy, i.e. $[x_1 + x_2 + x_3 + x_4]$,

$\mathbf{A}$ = a matrix of the interindustrial transactions within the economy;

$\mathbf{Y}$ = a vector of final demand sales; and

$\mathbf{I}$ = an identity matrix (equivalent to 1 in simple algebra).

Δ = a change in a variable

A change in the level of final demand ($\mathbf{Y}$) will create an increase in the level of activity within the economy which manifests itself as changes in the output and sales of each sector. Further submodels are required to calculate the effects on business revenue, public sector revenue, imports, employment and income. The model shown in equation (6.8) is still too simplistic for practical application and must be developed further.

For instance, in the simplified model discussed above, the imports of the economy are shown as a single row vector. However, the robust and flexible framework of input–output models allows the researcher to incorporate a matrix of import functions in order to draw distinctions between competitive and non-competitive imports. This is an extremely useful distinction because competitive imports are, by their very nature, far less predictable than non-competitive imports.

Incorporating an import function matrix which examines the trade-off between domestic production and competitive imports results in equation (6.8) being revised as follows:

$$\Delta\mathbf{X} = (\mathbf{I} - \mathbf{K}^*\mathbf{A})^{-1}\,\Delta\mathbf{Y} \tag{6.9}$$

where $\mathbf{K}^*$ = a matrix where the diagonal values reflects the level of competitive imports associated with each sector which, when applied to the $\mathbf{A}$ matrix, reduces the domestic component of output by the required amount.

In this manner, changes in primary inputs ($\Delta\mathbf{P}$) created by a change in tourist expenditure ($\Delta\mathbf{T}$) will be given by

$$\Delta\mathbf{P} = \mathbf{B}(\mathbf{I} - \mathbf{K}^*\mathbf{A})^{-1}\,\Delta\mathbf{T} \tag{6.10}$$

where $\mathbf{B}$ = an $m \times n$ matrix of primary inputs.

Furthermore, the input–output model can be developed in order to provide information with respect to changes in employment levels brought about by changes in tourism expenditure. Let $\Delta\mathbf{L}$ represent the change in employment and $\mathbf{E}$ be an $m \times n$ matrix of employment coefficients. The model will now take the form shown in equation (6.11):

$$\Delta\mathbf{L} = \mathbf{E}(\mathbf{I} - \mathbf{K}^*\mathbf{A})^{-1}\,\Delta\mathbf{T} \tag{6.11}$$

Using this procedure, the labour usages of each productive sector can be incorporated on either a skill or educational requirement basis and this will allow the multiplier model to provide human resource planning information. Thus, multiplier models can provide information which will inform the future training needs for the destination.

In general, the input–output model can be as comprehensive as data, time and resources allow. Notwithstanding the fact that input–output analysis has been subject to criticism because of its general approach and the aggregation of firms into 'whole industries', the sectors of the model can be disaggregated to achieve the highest level of detail – even down to the level of individual establishments.

Weaknesses and limitations of multiplier models

Each of the multiplier model approaches outlined above contains several inherent problems that must be overcome for practical applications.

Data deficiencies

Secondary data (published and unpublished data) are rarely adequate to meet the requirements of the more demanding and advanced models. This means that researchers need to spend considerable time, effort and money collecting data for multiplier purposes.

Other data difficulties arise out of the nature of tourism itself as a multiproduct industry directly affecting a large number of sectors in an economy. Tourist expenditure is spread across several sectors of an economy and accurate surveys of visitor expenditure are required in order to obtain an acceptable breakdown of this expenditure into its various components, e.g. accommodation, meals, beverages, transportation and shopping.

Furthermore, problems often arise when attempting to integrate this visitor expenditure into the categories disaggregated in the input–output table. Rarely are pre-existing input–output tables produced in a form sufficiently disaggregated to accept the detailed data derived from visitor expenditure surveys. In such cases, either the tourist expenditure data have to be compressed to fit the sectors already identified in the input–output table with a consequent loss in the accuracy of the results or else much time and effort has to be expended on disaggregating the existing input–output table.

If, however, an input–output (or alternative model) is constructed especially for the study, then the matrix can be arranged in a form which fits the tourist expenditure pattern and the data can be fed directly into the model.

Restrictive assumptions and operational limitations

Many of the weaknesses of multiplier analysis arise out of the restrictive assumptions that are made in during the construction of the model. However, research is progressively removing the worst of these assumptions.

Supply constraints

Supply constraints can inhibit the ability of an economy to supply the quantity and quality of goods and services required to provide for an increase in tourism expenditure. If capacity is inadequate to meet the additional demand and if insufficient factors of production, especially labour, are available, then additional tourism expenditure creates inflation and additional goods and services may have to be imported. Thus the size of the multiplier, if measured by an appropriate model, will fall.

Most multiplier models are static in nature but can be made dynamic. Static models assume:

- that production and consumption functions are linear and that the intersectoral expenditure patterns are stable;
- that all sectors are able to meet any additional demands for their output; and
- that relative prices remain constant.

The first of these assumptions is that any additional tourism expenditure that occurs will generate the same impact on the economy as an equivalent amount of previous tourism expenditure. Thus, any additional production in the economy is assumed to require purchases of inputs in the same proportions and from the same sources as previously. Similarly, any consequential increase in consumer demand is assumed to have exactly the same effect upon the economy as previous consumer expenditure. With respect to the stability of the production functions, tourism, being a labour-intensive personal service, tends to be associated with fairly stable production functions. Thus, the use of average technical coefficients and the assumption of linear homogeneity in production tends not to be a serious drawback when using input–output analysis to study service-based economies.

Dynamic models have been constructed to remove some of these constraints but the increase in data requirements tends to be prohibitive.

Some examples of multiplier values

The magnitude of multiplier values will vary under different circumstances because it is dependent upon the nature of an area's economy and upon the extent to which the various sectors of the economy are linked in their trading patterns.

A large number of tourism multiplier studies have been carried out over the past three decades. Table 6.5 shows the value of tourism output multipliers ranging from 1.16 in a regional economy within the UK, to 3.198 for the national economy of Turkey. The range of output multipliers of states within the USA spans from 1.58 in Sullivan County, Pennsylvania, to 2.17 in Door County, Wisconsin, and examples in the UK include the city of Edinburgh at 1.51 and a value of 1.16 for Gwynedd, North Wales.

For policy-making and planning purposes, income multipliers are the most useful because they provide information about national income rather than merely business output or turnover. Table 6.6 shows multiplier values for a number of countries. Although the income multiplier values are listed in order of magnitude, care must be taken when comparing multiplier values between countries. First, the analyses were undertaken over different time periods and, even though multiplier values are not subject to drastic changes even over two decades, they do tend to increase as economies develop and improve their sectoral linkages. Secondly, and more importantly, not all the multipliers shown in these tables have been calculated using the same methodology and this can make a significant difference to the value. For instance, input–output models, because

Table 6.5: Tourism output multipliers for selected destinations

Country or region	Tourism output multiplier
Turkey	2.34–3.20
Door County, Wisconsin, USA	2.17
Clinton County, Pennsylvania, USA	1.98
Grand County, Colorado, USA	1.94
Walworth County, Wisconsin, USA	1.87
Sullivan County, Pennsylvania, USA	1.58
Edinburgh, Scotland, UK	1.51
Barbados	1.41
Gwynedd, Wales, UK	1.16

Source: compiled by the authors from published articles and unpublished reports to governments.

Table 6.6:
Tourism income multipliers for selected destinations

Country or region	Income multiplier
United Kingdom	1.73
Republic of Ireland	1.72
Sri Lanka	1.59
Jamaica	1.27
Egypt	1.23
Dominican Republic	1.20
Cyprus	1.14
Northern Ireland	1.10
Bermuda	1.09
Fiji	1.07
Seychelles	1.03
Malta	1.00
Mauritius	0.97
Antigua	0.88
Missouri State, USA	0.88
Hong Kong	0.87
Philippines	0.82
The Bahamas	0.79
Walworth County, USA	0.78
Malta	0.68
Gibraltar	0.66
Western Samoa	0.66
Cayman Islands	0.65
Iceland	0.64
Barbados	0.60
Grand County, USA	0.60
British Virgin Islands	0.58
Door County, USA	0.55
Solomon Islands	0.52
Republic of Palau	0.51
Victoria Metropolitan Area, Canada	0.50
Sullivan County, USA	0.44
Carlisle, UK	0.40
Edinburgh, UK	0.35
East Anglia, UK	0.34

Source: compiled by the author from published articles and unpublished government reports.

they are based upon a general equilibrium approach, tend to yield significantly higher multiplier values than *ad hoc* models and, depending upon the level of comprehensiveness and detail achieved in the *ad hoc* models, this difference may be as high as 30%.

It is also noticeable from Table 6.6 that the size of the income multiplier values tends to be correlated with the size of the economy. In general, the larger the economy, the higher will be the multiplier value, although there will obviously be some exceptions to this. The reason for this correlation is that larger economies tend to have a more developed economic structure which means that they have stronger intersectoral linkages and lower propensities to import in order to meet the demands of tourists and the tourist industry.

In addition to calculating the levels of output, income, employment and government revenue generated by additional units of tourist expenditure, multiplier analysis provides

Tourist expenditure (+)		1000.0
Import requirements (−)		
Direct	120.8	
Indirect	115.3	236.1
Net effect on balance of payments		763.9
Induced imports (−)	326.3	326.3
Net impact after induced effects		437.6

Note: Impact figures include F$53.0 repatriated income.
Source: TCSP (1992).

Table 6.7: The impact of F$1000 tourist expenditure on Fiji's balance of payments

valuable information concerning its impact on a country's net foreign exchange flows. Table 6.7 provides an example of the type of information that can be derived from such analysis. Using the national economy of Fiji as an example, Table 6.7 shows that, for each additional F$1000 tourist expenditure, F$120.8 dollars immediately leaks out of the economy as imports necessary to meet the tourists' demand. A further F$115.3 then leaks out of the economy as imports required throughout the Fiji economy in order to support this additional level of tourist activity, leaving a net inflow of foreign exchange equivalent to F$763.9. Therefore, for each additional F$1000 dollars of tourist expenditure Fiji's foreign exchange account benefits by F$763.9.

However, the resulting increase in income levels in Fiji will generate further imports as a portion of this additional income is re-spent. Some of this re-spending of income will be on goods and services that are produced by firms and individuals located outside Fiji's national boundaries, resulting in an increase in imports of F$326.3 thus leaving a net inflow of foreign exchange of F$437.6.

Great care must be exercised in the interpretation of employment multipliers. The data used for their measurement and the assumptions underlying the model constructions are more heroic than for other types of multiplier. The two major problems relate to the fact that:

- in the majority of studies employment is assumed to have a linear relationship with either income or output, whereas the available evidence suggests that this relationship is non-linear; and

- multiplier models assume that employment in each sector is working at full capacity, so that to meet any increase in demand will require additional employment. In practice, this is unlikely to be true and increases (or decreases) in the level of tourist expenditure will not generate a corresponding increase (or decrease) in the number of people employed.

In consequence, tourism employment multipliers should be interpreted as only an *indication* of the number of full-time job opportunities created by changes in tourist expenditure. Whether or not these job opportunities will materialise depends upon a number of factors, most notably the extent to which the existing labour force in each sector is fully utilised, and the degree to which labour is able to transfer between different occupations and between different sectors of the economy.

Table 6.8 shows the employment multipliers for several countries and regions. We can see that these employment multipliers are of a different magnitude from those relating

Table 6.8:
Tourism
employment
multipliers for
selected
destinations

Country or region	Employment multiplier
Bermuda	0.000 044
Jamaica	0.000 128
Malta	0.000 159
Fiji	0.000 079
Edinburgh, UK	0.000 037

Table 6.9:
Standardised
employment
multipliers for
selected
destinations

Country	Employment multiplier
Jamaica	4.61
Mauritius	3.76
Bermuda	3.02
Gibraltar	2.62
Solomon Islands	2.58
Malta	1.99
Western Samoa	1.96
Republic of Palau	1.67

to either output or income. This reflects the need for considerably larger amounts of tourist spending to generate one new full-time equivalent job opportunity.

Unlike the income and output multipliers, it is not possible to compare employment multipliers between different destinations when they are presented in this form. This is because the above figures show the number of full-time equivalent job opportunities created by one unit of tourist expenditure where that unit is expressed in the local currency. Thus, differences in the unit value of local currencies will provide employment multipliers of different magnitudes. A more sensible way of making international comparisons of employment multipliers is to express them as a ratio of total employment generated to direct employment. Examples of this latter type of employment multiplier are shown in Table 6.9.

Table 6.9 shows that in Jamaica, for every new full-time employee directly employed as a result of an increase in tourist expenditure, a further 4.61 full-time equivalent job opportunities are created throughout the Jamaican economy. Again, we can see that the more developed the tourism economy, the larger the employment multiplier. Comparison between Tables 11.8 and 11.9 shows that Malta which records the highest multiplier value when expressed per unit of tourist expenditure does not rank as highly when expressed in the ratio form. This is because of the differences in real value of the local currency per unit.

Finally, Table 6.10 shows a variety of indicators that may be used as the basis for decision making, including tourist income multipliers, receipts, tourist density (as measured by the ratio of arrivals to the host population) and tourism economic dependence (as measured by the contribution of tourism (at the direct level) to GNP). The range of tourist density values and tourism dependence ratios is large. For instance, Bermuda has the highest tourist density factor with a ratio of 7.11, whereas Antigua shows the greatest dependence given that tourism receipts account for over 58% of GNP.

Table 6.10:
Tourist income
multiplier[2],
tourist density
and tourism
dependence,
selected island
economies, 1990

Country	Income multiplier	Tourism receipts (US$m)	GNP (US$m)	Tourist density[3] (tourist/ population)	Tourism dependence[4] (receipts/ GNP)
Sri Lanka	1.59	75	6 448	0.02	1.2
Jamaica	1.27	407	2 090	0.35	19.5
Dominica	1.20	9*	90*	0.56	9.7
Cyprus	1.14	497	2 821	2.22	17.6
Bermuda	1.09	357*	1 030*	7.11	34.7
Seychelles	1.03	40**	146	1.55	27.4
Malta	1.00	149*	1 190*	2.46	12.5
Mauritius	0.96	89	1 188	0.27	7.5
Antigua	0.88	114	195	2.59	58.5
Hong Kong	0.87	2 211	36 664	7.02	6.0
Philippines	0.82	647	30 800	0.02	2.1
Bahamas	0.78	870*	1 670	6.17	52.1
Fiji	1.07	169	1 190	0.37	14.2
Western Samoa	0.66	7*	110*	0.29	6.4

Notes:

1 The data other than the multipliers relate to the year 1990, except where marked * for 1985 or ** for 1984.

2 The tourist income multipliers were not all calculated by the same techniques, nor do they all relate to the same year.

3 Tourist density would be better measured in terms of tourist-nights divided by resident population. Unfortunately, the source data were insufficient to use this method.

4 Tourist dependence is measured here as tourist receipts divided by GNP (and is expressed as a percentage). It should be remembered, however, that GNP includes net tourist receipts – that is, receipts minus expenditure – and the values in the final column of this table should be used only as a measure of dependence upon tourism. They do not indicate tourism's contribution to GNP.

('Tourist' means 'international tourist'.)

The policy implications of multiplier analysis

Tourism multipliers measure the present economic performance of the tourism industry and the short-term economic effects of a change in the level or pattern of tourism expenditure. They are particularly suitable for studying the impact of tourist expenditure on business turnover, incomes, employment, public sector revenue and the balance of payments.

In the 1970s some economists argued strongly in favour of rejecting multiplier analysis as an appropriate technique for studying impact on the grounds that these models yield 'no useful guideline to policy-makers as regards the merits of tourism compared with alternatives' (Bryden, 1973, p. 217), yet a number of writers have shown that this is precisely the type of information which multiplier analysis can provide in a short-term context. For example, Diamond (1976) used an input–output model of the Turkish economy to measure sectoral output multipliers (for tourism and other sectors) in relation to four policy objectives that reflected Turkish planning priorities. His work demonstrated that multiplier analysis deals effectively with problems associated with short-term resource allocation.

However, resource allocation is not the primary use of multiplier analysis. The technique is most frequently used to examine short-term economic impacts where policy objectives other than the efficiency of resource allocation are considered important. A detailed input–output model, for example, yields valuable information about the structure of an economy, the degree to which sectors within the economy are dependent upon each other, the existence of possible supply constraints and the relative capital and labour intensities of each sector.

Detailed multiplier models are suitable for:

- analysing the national or regional effects of public or private sector investment in tourism projects;
- simulating the economic impact, sector by sector, of any proposed tourism developments; and
- examining the relative magnitudes of the impacts made by different types of tourism and by tourism compared with other sectors of the economy.

For instance, a tourism input–output study of Jamaica examined the economic impact of tourism expenditure by purpose of visit, winter or summer visit, first and repeat visit in order to determine which tourists generated the highest level of income, employment and government revenue per unit of expenditure. This type of information can be used to target future marketing in order to maximise the desired benefits derived from tourism activity.

Conclusion

The economic impact of tourism on a host economy is generally positive but also carries with it some negative aspects. The literature is biased towards the positive aspects of economic impacts. It is important to establish how significant tourism spending is to an economy because this allows policy makers and planners to determine dependency and to develop strategies for the future. Of particular note is the fact that tourism spending tends to take place between the richer, industrialised countries rather than between industrialised and non-industrialised countries.

There have been a variety of attempts to develop models in order to estimate the economic impact of tourism but only the *ad hoc* models and input–output are accurate and of any policy use. The input–output method provides the most comprehensive picture of tourism's economic impacts and also information that is useful to the tourism development planners. However, input–output models are also the most expensive type of impact model. The input–output methodology provides income, employment and government revenue multipliers as well as demonstrating the import requirements per unit of tourist spending. All of these different forms of economic impacts can be estimated at the direct, direct plus indirect and direct plus indirect plus induced levels of impact. This information has been successfully used to target market segments in order to enhance the economic benefits associated with tourist spending. Recent developments in the estimation of tourism impact analyses includes the combining of economic, environmental and social impact models with forecasting techniques in order to provide a comprehensive planning tool. There are weaknesses associated with economic impact models but most of these can be alleviated by the adoption of various procedures.

Chapter discussion questions

1. What factors determine the magnitude of the economic impact of tourism on a given destination?
2. What methods can be used to estimate the economic impacts of tourism and what are their relative merits and weaknesses?
3. What policy implications can be drawn from multiplier analyses?
4. Are multiplier study results only useful for short-term planning?

Recommended further reading

● Archer, B. H. and Fletcher, J. E. (1990) *Multiplier Analysis*, Les Cahier du Tourisme, Series C, No. 130, April.
● Fletcher, J. E. and Archer, B. H. (1990) 'The development and application of multiplier analysis', in *Progress in Tourism, Recreation and Hospitality Management*, Vol. 3, Cooper, C. (ed.), Belhaven, London.
● Mathieson, A. and Wall, G. (1989) *Tourism: Economic, Physical and Social Aspects*, Longman, Harlow.

Bibliography

● Archer, B. H. (1976) 'The anatomy of a multiplier', *Regional Studies*, **10**, 71–7.
● Archer, B. H. (1982) 'The value of multipliers and their policy implications', *Tourism Management*, **3**(2), 236–41.
● Archer, B. H. (1985) 'Tourism in Mauritius: an economic impact study with marketing implications', *Tourism Management*, **6**(1), 50–4.
● Archer, B. H. (1986) 'The secondary economic effects of tourism in developing countries', in *Planning for Tourism and Tourism in Developing Countries*, PTRC, London.
● Archer, B. H. (1989) 'Tourism and island economies', in *Progress in Tourism, Recreation and Hospitality Management*, Cooper, C. (ed.), Vol. 1, Belhaven, London.
● Archer, B. H. (1989) *The Bermudian Economy: An Impact Study*, Ministry of Finance, Government of Bermuda.
● Archer, B. H. and Fletcher, J. E. (1989) 'The tourist multiplier', *Teoros*, **7**(3), 6–9.
● Archer, B. H. and Fletcher, J. E. (1990) *Multiplier Analysis*, Les Cahiers du Tourisme, Series C, No. 130, April.
● Archer, B. H. and Owen, C. (1971) 'Towards a tourist regional multiplier', *Regional Studies*, **5**, 289–94.
● Bryden, J. M. (1973) *Tourism and Development: A Case Study in the Commonwealth Caribbean*, Cambridge University Press, Cambridge.
● Curry, S. and Weiss, J. (1993) *Project Analysis in Developing Countries*, Macmillan Press, Basingstoke.
● Diamond, J. (1976) 'Tourism and development policy: a quantitative appraisal', *Bulletin of Economic Research*, **28**(1), 36–50.
● Fletcher, J. E. (1985) (unpublished) *The Economic Impact of International Tourism on the National Economy of Jamaica*, report to Government of Jamaica, USAID/UNDP/WTO.
● Fletcher, J. E. (1989) 'Input–output analysis and tourism impact studies', *Annals of Tourism Research*, **16**(4), 541–56.

● Fletcher, J. E. and Archer, B. H. (1991) 'The development and application of multiplier analysis', pp. 28–47 in *Progress in Tourism, Recreation and Hospitality Management*, Vol. 3, Coopen, C. (ed.), Belhaven, London.
● Fletcher, J. E. and Snee, H. R. (1985) 'The service industries and input–output analysis', *Service Industries Review*, **2**(1), 51–79.
● Kottke, M. (1988) 'Estimating tourism impacts', *Annals of Tourism Research*, **15**(1), 122–33.
● Leontief, W. (1966) *Input–Output Economics*, Oxford University Press, New York.
● Milne, S. S. (1987) 'Differential multipliers', *Annals of Tourism Research*, **14**(4), 499–515.
● Nathan, R. R. and Associates (1966) *Recreation as an Industry*, a report prepared for the Appalachian Regional Commission, Washington, DC.
● O'Connor, E. and Henry, E. W. (1975) *Input–Output Analysis and its Applications*, Griffin's Statistical Monographs, No. 36, Charles Griffin & Co., London.
● OECD (1992) *National Accounts*, OECD, Paris.
● Sinclair, M. T. and Sutcliffe, C. M. S. (1978) 'The first round of the Keynesian income multiplier', *Scottish Journal of Political Economy*, **25**(2), 177–86.
● Sinclair, M. T. and Sutcliffe, C. M. S. (1982) 'Keynesian income multipliers with first and second round effects: an application to tourist expenditure', *Oxford Bulletin of Economics and Statistics*, **44**(4), 321–38.
● TCSP (1992) *The Economic Impact of International Tourism on the National Economy of Fiji*, a report published by the Tourism Council for the South Pacific, Suva, Fiji.
● Wanhill, S. R. C. (1988) 'Tourism multipliers under capacity constraints', *Service Industries Journal*, **8**(1), 136–42.
● WTO (1980) *Manila Declaration on World Tourism*, WTO, Madrid.
● WTO (1980) *Tourism and Employment: Enhancing the Status of Tourism Professions*, WTO, Madrid.
● WTO (1988) *Yearbook of Tourism Statistics*, WTO, Madrid.
● WTO (1992) *Yearbook of Tourism Statistics*, WTO, Madrid.
● WTO (1997) *Yearbook of Tourism Statistics*, WTO, Madrid.

Chapter Seven

The environmental impact of tourism

Introduction

Any form of industrial development will bring with it impacts upon the physical environment in which it takes place. In view of the fact that tourists have to visit the place of production in order to consume the output, it is inevitable that tourism activity will be associated with environmental impacts. The identification of the need to follow an environmentally compatible pattern of tourism development is now well into its second decade but little has been achieved in ensuring that future developments are environmentally compatible. At the end of the 1970s the OECD set out a framework for the study of environmental stress created by tourism activities. This framework highlighted four main categories of stressor activities including permanent environmental restructuring (major construction works such as highways, airports and resorts); waste product generation (biological and non-biological waste which can damage fish production, create health hazards and detract from the attractiveness of a destination); direct environmental stress caused by tourist activities (destruction of coral reefs, vegetation, dunes, etc. by the presence and activities of tourists); effects on the population dynamics (migration, increased urban densities accompanied by declining populations in other rural areas).

In 1992, the United Nations Conference on the Environment and Development, held in Rio de Janeiro, added further impetus to a debate that was growing stale and a new maxim emerged where 'Only whatever can be sustained by nature and society in the long term is permissible'. This new impetus was given the title Agenda 21 to reflect the fact that it was a policy statement aimed at taking the world into the twenty-first century. What made Agenda 21 significant was the fact that it represented the first occasion when a comprehensive programme of environmental actions was agreed to be adopted by 182 governments. The Agenda is based around a framework of themes that are aimed at providing an overall strategy to transform global activity onto a more sustainable course. The matters addressed within Agenda 21 are not solely environmental because they include aspects such as human development and the redressing of the imbalance between rich and poor nations. However, many of the matters discussed and the strategies recommended are environmentally based.

In spite of its elegance and simplicity, the adoption of this maxim requires enforcement that is thus far beyond the reach of most legislative frameworks and none of the recommendations made in Agenda 21 were legally binding to the 182 nations that approved its adoption. Furthermore, the implementation of this maxim requires that those charged with the construction of the necessary legislative framework be fully informed of the environmental repercussions of productive and consumptive activities. To date this is not the case. The literature on the social and environmental impacts of tourism is often biased, painting highly negative pictures of tourism with respect to its associated social and environmental impacts. In this chapter we examine the nature of environmental impacts, how they can be identified and measured and how this information can be integrated into the tourism planning process.

Chapter learning objectives

The objectives of this chapter are to provide students with:

▪▪▪ an understanding of the physical impacts of tourism on the environment, both direct and indirect, positive and negative;

▪▪▪ a review of strategies and techniques that may be implemented to measure and quantify the impacts of tourism on the environment such as environmental impacts assessment;

▪▪▪ an appreciation of the difficulties of assessing environmental impacts; and

▪▪▪ real-life examples to encourage the application of theory to practice.

Environmental impact

The environment, whether it is natural or artificial, is the most fundamental ingredient of the tourism product. However, as soon as tourism activity takes place, the environment is inevitably changed or modified either to facilitate tourism or during the tourism process. Environmental preservation and improvement programmes are now an integral part of many development strategies and such considerations are treated with much greater respect than they were during the first half of this century. A brief literature search shows that relatively little research has been undertaken in analysing tourism's impact on the environment. The empirical studies that have taken place have been very specific – such as the impact of tourism on the wildlife of Africa, the pollution of water in the Mediterranean or studies of particular coastal areas and mountains. But the diverse areas studied, the varying methods used to undertake those studies and the wide range of tourism activities involved makes it difficult to bring these findings together in order to assemble a comprehensive framework within which to work.

In order to study the physical impact of tourism it is necessary to establish:

● the physical impacts created by tourism activity as opposed to other activities;

● what conditions were like before tourism activity took place in order to derive a baseline from which comparisons can be made;

● an inventory of flora and fauna, together with some unambiguous index of tolerance levels to the types of impact created by different sorts of tourism activity;

- what indirect and induced levels of environmental impact are associated with tourism activity.

The environmental impacts associated with tourism development can also be considered in terms of their direct, indirect and induced effects. The impacts can be positive or negative. It is not possible to develop tourism without incurring environmental impacts, but it is possible, with correct planning, to manage tourism development in order to minimise the negative impacts while encouraging the positive impacts.

On the positive side, the direct environmental impacts associated with tourism include:

- the preservation/restoration of ancient monuments, sites and historic buildings, such as the Great Wall of China (PRC), the Pyramids (Egypt), the Taj Mahal (India), Stonehenge and Warwick Castle (UK);

- the creation of national parks and wildlife parks, such as Yellowstone Park (USA), the Amboseli National Park and the Maasai Mara National Reserve (Kenya), Las Canadas (Tenerife), the Pittier National Park (Venezuela), Fjord Land National Park (New Zealand);

- protection of reefs and beaches, the Great Barrier Reef (Australia), Grand Anse (Grenada); and

- the maintenance of forests such as the New Forest (UK), Colo I Suva (Fiji).

Conservation and preservation may be rated highly from the point of view of researchers, or even the tourists. However, if such actions are not considered to be of importance from the hosts' point of view, it may be questionable as to whether they can be considered to be positive environmental impacts. When evaluating the net worth of preservation and conservation activities the opportunity costs associated with such activities must also be taken into account. African wildlife parks, for example, may limit the grazing lands of nomadic tribes and certainly constrain food production capability.

On the negative side, tourism may have direct environmental impacts on the quality of water, air and noise levels. Sewage disposal into water will add to pollution problems, as will the use of powered boats on inland waterways and sheltered seas. Increased usage of the internal combustion engine for tourist transport, oil burning to provide the power for hotel's air conditioning and refrigeration units all add to the diminution of air quality. Noise levels may be dramatically increased in urban areas through nightclubs and other forms of entertainment as well as by increased road, rail and air traffic.

Physical deterioration of both natural and built environments can have serious consequences:

- Hunting and fishing have obvious impacts on the wildlife environment.
- Sand dunes can be damaged and eroded by over-use.
- Vegetation can be destroyed by walkers.
- Camp fires may destroy forests.
- Ancient monuments may be disfigured and damaged by graffiti, eroded or literally taken away by tourists (the Byzantine Fort in Paphos, Cyprus, being a World Heritage Site subject to pilfering).
- The construction of tourism superstructure utilises real estate and may detract from the aesthetics.
- The improper disposal of litter can detract from the aesthetic quality of the environment and harm wildlife.

Examples of direct negative environmental impacts include:

- the erosion of paths to the Pyramids by camels used to transport tourists;
- the construction of the North Wales freeway to provide greater access to the Snowdonia Mountain Range (UK);
- the dynamiting of Balaclava Bay (Mauritius) to provide a beach for tourist use;
- the littering of Base Camp on Mount Everest by tourists who also erode the pathway to this site.

The building of high-rise hotels on beach frontages is an environmental impact of tourism that achieves headline status. This kind of obvious environmental rape is now less common than it was during the rapid growth periods of the 1960s and 1970s. In a number of countries, particularly island economies, the issue of land availability is often high on the agenda of planning meetings. Regulations have been introduced to restrict beachfront developments to a height no greater than that of the palm trees (as for example in Mauritius), or restrict development to a certain distance back from the beach (as in some parts of India).

It is also important to note that many environmental factors are interdependent – often in ways that are not yet fully understood. Damage to coral reefs will reduce the local diversity and population of fish and other creatures that may feed off the coral. This, in turn, may reduce the numbers of birds that feed on the fish and so on. In order to determine the full impact of environmental changes accurately, the ecological system and the way in which it responds to environmental stress must be understood.

Environmental impact assessment

There are no generally accepted models for environmental impact assessment (EIA). In many environmentally sensitive tourism destinations there are few legislative acts and even fewer agencies empowered to safeguard the environment with respect to tourism development (as in the South Pacific; see Box 7.1). However, the absence of legislation to support environmental planning should not deter tourism planners from undertaking their own environmental impact assessment on proposed developments. Environmental protection is so much easier and less costly than environmental correction even when such remedial action is possible.

It is important to understand the motivation that underlies a particular environmental impact assessment before an appropriate methodology is selected. For instance, an EIA may be undertaken in order to determine a development's impact upon a specific ecol-

Box 7.1   Environmental protection in the South Pacific

In the South Pacific, for example, Papua New Guinea is the only member of the Tourism Council for the South Pacific (TCSP) which currently has legislation that covers environmental impact assessment (Environmental Planning Act, 1978). This statute allows the Minister to require potential developers to produce an environmental impact statement when any development project is associated with foreseeable major environmental impacts is proposed. However, even in Papua New Guinea the legislation has not been as effective as its proponents would have wished because the requirement to produce an environmental impact statement is at the discretion of the Minister and is not compulsory, nor is there any requirement for approval of the environmental plan prior to project implementation.

ogy or even upon a single 'rare' species. This type of assessment may not require the evaluation of the environmental impacts in monetary terms. However, other EIAs may be instigated for the express purpose of determining the financial implications of environmental correction in order to reflect accurately the net economic returns of tourism activity or in an attempt to retrieve some of these costs from the industry. Furthermore, EIAs may be required in order to compare alternative developments in order to allocate resources in a manner that maximises the economic benefits of development while minimising the negative environmental impacts. In this case there is a need to take a general equilibrium approach which enables the researcher to compare and contrast development options not only between various tourism strategies but also between different industrial structures.

Finally, EIAs may be required simply to raise the profile of environmental issues. That is, future developments should not be evaluated solely in economic terms but in a more holistic manner that includes the effects upon the local environment. This approach allows the democratic processes of development choice to be fully informed. It also highlights the fact that environmental impacts and environmental audits should become a way of life for business organisations as well as governments and individuals.

Once the environmental consequences of our actions are recognised this information can be incorporated at every decision-making level to ensure the effective use of the planet's finite resources. Environmental awareness during the production and consumption processes may also bring long-term economic and social benefits. For instance, the effective use of scarce resources, particularly energy-related resources, can result in lower marginal costs of production. On the other hand, the careless or reckless use of resources during either the production or consumption processes can add to social resentment of tourism development. This may hinder future development and will certainly detract from the effective use of resources.

In spite of the fact that there is no single accepted framework for conducting EIAs, the true scope of environmental impacts should not be underestimated. Most forms of industrial development impact upon land use, energy consumption and other direct forms of physical impacts. However, to assess the overall environmental impact it is necessary to take into account the consequential impacts occasioned by the direct productive activity. In the same way that the economic impacts associated with tourism development can be direct and indirect, the same must be said for environmental impacts. If tourism activity requires the production of output from a diverse range of industries, including those that do not supply tourist goods and services directly, then the environmental impact associated with the output and production processes of these supporting industries should also be included in the overall evaluation. For example, if the level of tourism increases, and this causes hotels to increase their purchases from the building and construction industry, then the environmental damage created by that increased building and construction must also be included. This is also true with respect to the effects of the quarries that supply the builders and the transport system that facilitates it!

In some areas attempts have been made to construct tourism/environment balance sheets to assess the net effect of tourism development with respect to the environment. One such approach for Scotland concluded that tourism is an important sector of the Scottish economy and that, although there are widespread environmental impacts associated with tourism activity, they were only regarded as being serious in a few specific locations and that careful management could overcome these problems (Box 7.2). The Department of Employment, in the UK, set up a Task Force to examine the relationship between tourism and the environment in England (1991) and the report published under this same title supported the major views expressed by the Scottish Tourism Co-ordinating Group.

Box 7.2   Scottish Tourism Co-ordinating Group environmental balance sheet for Scotland, 1992

This report found that the specific beneficial effects of tourism activity on the physical environment included:

- environmental improvement schemes to create more attractive areas for visitors, including urban regeneration, reclamation projects and conservation schemes;
- the adaptation and restoration of redundant buildings for tourism and visitor use;
- increased provision of recreation and sporting facilities for use by both locals and visitors;
- the restoration of historic buildings and ancient sites;
- improved infrastructure, including roads, car-parks, footpaths and transport services;
- the generation and encouragement of sympathetic design and an appreciation of environmental quality in the development process.

The environmental costs associated with tourism development were perceived to be:

- volume pressure – deterioration of footpaths, disturbance to wildlife, damage to vegetation, damage to areas of wilderness and the loss of peace and quiet;
- traffic pressure – generally incurred at specific locations, includes traffic bottlenecks, parking problems, slow-moving vehicles (caravans) on main routes and the pollution caused by increased traffic;
- visual pressure – some tourism facilities detract from the aesthetic quality because of poor siting, design or inadequate screening. Examples of such facilities include caravan sites and ski centres;
- waste pressure – the increased number of visitors to Scotland has resulted in increasing untidiness and endangers wildlife through inadequate or thoughtless disposal of litter;
- user conflict pressure – wherever there are scarce natural resources there will be user conflict. For example, the growing interest in activities such as bird watching, walking, climbing and photography quickly result in pressure on the facilities available and detract from user satisfaction. More obviously, there is the conflict that exists between the competing use of resources, e.g. jet-skiing and power boating using water also used by anglers or general water-based recreation.

The EIA process

It is important to identify environmental impacts associated with tourism development at an early stage because:

- it is easier to avoid environmental damage by either modifying or rejecting developments than it is to rectify environmental damage once a project has been implemented;
- projects that rely heavily upon areas of outstanding beauty may become non-viable if such developments degrade the environment.

There are a variety of methods that may be used for EIA including checklists and network systems, but generally the EIA is a process that enables researchers to predict the environmental consequence associated with any proposed development project. To draw up a checklist of environmental impacts it is necessary to establish what potential impacts can occur as a result of tourism activity (see Box 7.3). In spite of the apparent comprehensiveness of this checklist it is clear from the examples shown in parentheses throughout Box 7.3 that the primary focus is confined to direct tourism activities and development. This is an inadequate approach because the indirect consequences must also be assessed. It is also important that environmental resources should be utilised efficiently. This means not only that should they be effectively used within the tourism industry but that this effectiveness should also be evaluated in relative terms in comparison with alternative economic development strategies. Only then can fully informed and sound rational planning decisions be made.

Once the potential impacts have been considered a checklist consisting of the fundamental elements at risk can be assembled. This checklist can then be used to form the basis of an evaluation matrix which will assess the impact of proposed developments on

Box 7.3 Green's checklist of the environmental impacts caused by tourism

The natural environment

(a) Changes in floral and faunal species composition
- Disruption of breeding habits
- Killing of animals through hunting
- Killing of animals in order to supply goods for the souvenir trade
- Inward or outward migration of animals
- Destruction of vegetation through the gathering of wood or plants
- Change in extent and/or nature of vegetation cover through clearance or planting to accommodate tourism facilities
- Creation of a wildlife reserve/sanctuary

(b) Pollution
- Water pollution through discharges of sewage, spillage of oil/petrol
- Air pollution from vehicle emissions
- Noise pollution from tourist transportation and activities

(c) Erosion
- Compaction of soils causing increased surface run-off and erosion
- Change in risk of occurrence of land slips/slides
- Change in risk of avalanche occurrence
- Damage to geological features (e.g. tors, caves)
- Damage to river banks

(d) Natural resources
- Depletion of ground and surface water supplies
- Depletion of fossil fuels to generate energy for tourist activity
- Change in risk of occurrence of fire

(e) Visual impact
- Facilities (e.g. buildings, chairlifts, car parks)
- Litter

Box 7.3 continued

The built environment

(a) Urban environment
  - Land taken out of primary production
  - Change of hydrological patterns

(b) Visual impact
  - Growth of the built-up area
  - New architectural styles
  - People and belongings

(c) Infrastructure
  - Overload of infrastructure (roads, railways, car-parking, electricity grid, communications systems, waste disposal, and water supply)
  - Provision of new infrastructure
  - Environmental management to adapt areas for tourist use (e.g. sea walls, land reclamation)

(d) Urban form
  - Changes in residential, retail or industrial land uses (move from houses to hotels/boarding houses)
  - Changes to the urban fabric (e.g. roads, pavements)
  - Emergence of contrasts between urban areas developed for the tourist population and those for the host population

(e) Restoration
  - Re-use of disused buildings
  - Restoration and preservation of historic buildings and sites
  - Restoration of derelict buildings as second homes

(f) Competition
  - Possible decline of tourist attractions or regions because of the opening of other attractions or a change in tourist habits and preferences

Source: Reprinted from *Annals of Tourism Research*, vol. 17, Green *et al.*, 'Applications of the Delphi technique in tourism', pp. 270–9 (1990) with permission from Elsevier Science.

each of the fundamental elements according to whether the development will have no impact, minor impacts, moderate impacts or major impacts.

An EIA will examine:

  - environmental auditing procedures;
  - limitations to natural resources;
  - environmental problems and conflicts that may affect project viability;
  - possible detrimental effects to people, flora and fauna, soil, water, air, peace and quiet, landscapes, cultural sites, etc. that are either within the proposed project area or will be affected by it.

Figure 7.1 sets out a typical process which an environmental impact assessment would adopt. A proposed development is put forward by a developer and this is initially assessed using the destination's environmental policy document as a performance indicator. Following this initial evaluation the proposal moves forward to site selection and undergoes a

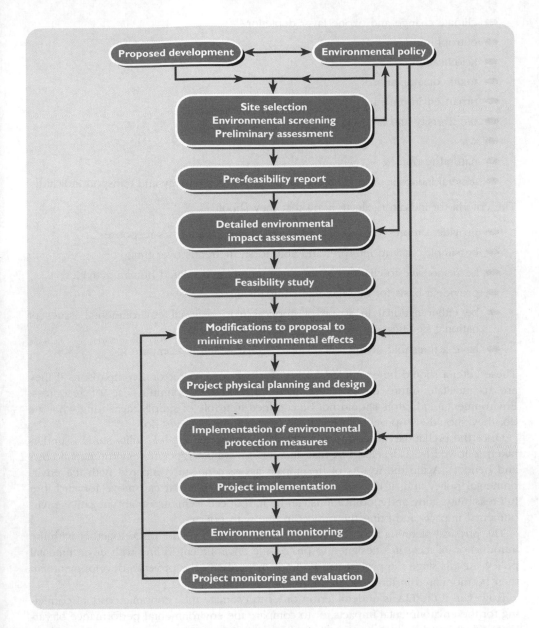

Figure 7.1: The environmental impact assessment process

preliminary environmental impact assessment. This assessment can then be compared in more detail with the environmental performance indicators identified in the policy legislation/regulations in order to investigate potential conflicts.

Environmental indicators

There is a wide range of environmental indicators that can be used. However, few countries have instigated data collection procedures to monitor these environmental variables. The OECD (1994) has listed general environmental indicators subdivided into the following categories:

- climate change and ozone layer depletion;
- eutrophication;
- acidification;
- toxic contamination;
- urban environmental quality;
- biodiversity and landscapes;
- waste;
- natural resources;
- general indicators, including economic, population, energy and transport indicators.

The criteria for indicator selection are that they should:

- provide a representative picture of conditions or society's response;
- be simple, easy to interpret and able to show trends over time;
- be responsive to changes in the environment and related human activities;
- provide a basis for international comparisons;
- be either national in scope or applicable to regional environmental issues of national significance;
- have a threshold or reference value against which to compare it.

These criteria should be expanded further to allow for intersectoral comparisons if they are to facilitate future development planning and the optimum use of resources. Environmental indicators should not be confined to a role of simply measuring what we do, they should also provide information as to what we *should* do.

Once the preliminary assessment has been completed, a pre-feasibility study is undertaken followed by a detailed EIA that attempts to evaluate specific environmental costs and benefits. Again the results of the impact assessment are compared with the environmental policy and, if no serious conflicts arise, the proposal can move forward to a full feasibility study and modifications can be introduced to minimise any negative environmental impacts and bring the project in line with policy.

The physical planning and design of the project can then take place together with the introduction of measures designed to protect the environment in line with environmental policy. At this stage the project can be implemented and the project's development can then be monitored in terms of its future environmental impact.

However, if the EIA is undertaken in order to estimate the economic costs of correcting for the environmental impacts, or to compare the environmental performance of various industries, the above approach requires some modification. A novel approach to EIA has been undertaken by researchers from Bournemouth University (UK) in a study undertaken for Mauritius (OECD, 1994; Fletcher, J. *et al.*, 1996). The essence of the impact model in this instance is its use as a planning tool. The integration of economic, environmental and social impacts is essential if tourism strategies and choices are to be well informed and steps taken to prevent tourism development exceeding the carrying capacity of the destination (see Chapter 5). The Mauritius model utilises the economic linkage information acquired during the input–output analysis (see Chapter 6) to provide the framework for estimating the indirect and induced environmental impacts associated with an industry's output level. The model relies only upon quantifiable environmental indicators in order to maintain objectivity. Planners are then able to select environmental variables from a selection of indicators. Once selected, the direct, indirect and induced environmental consequences of production in each industry can be assessed. By utilising the economic linkage information to trace the consequential environmental effects of production, the model provides a uniform framework for comparing not only different types of tourism activity but also developments in alternative industries. The confinement to measurable environmental indicators provides a platform for at least national comparisons, and at best international comparisons. Because of the reliance on quantifiable variables the financial implications of production and consumption can also be estimated. Finally, because the model that is constructed is an interactive computer-based model, it is ideal for facilitating the environmental auditing process required of developments well into the new millennium.

Environmental auditing

Unlike EIAs, which, with the exception of the Mauritius example referred to above, are primarily impact studies of particular events or developments, environmental auditing represents a *modus operandi*, an ongoing process of monitoring and evaluation. The major differences between EIAs and environmental auditing are:

- environmental audits are generally voluntary in nature while EIAs tend to be written into the legislature and required as part of the planning approval process;

- environmental audits are part of an ongoing process – even a sense of attitude – rather than the one-off EIA studies;

- environmental audits are concerned with performance and focus on how well a process is functioning. In this sense the environmental audit should become part of the organisational structure of private and public sector bodies alike.

However, one of these distinguishing features, the voluntary nature of environmental auditing, is also its Achilles' heel. Without the necessary legislation and regulation required to enforce the implementation and quality of environmental auditing, it is unlikely to be an effective environmental protector. Also, because tourism is a fragmented industry with no clear boundaries, the environmental auditing needs to be economy-wide rather than solely aimed at tourism establishments. There is also an argument that common standards of environmental audits and performance indicators should be adopted on a universal basis because of the dangers of conflict if different industries pursue different environmental goals. All of these factors point to a single conclusion, namely, that environmental auditing is a macro- rather than micro-issue and that the distinction between EIAs and environmental auditing is becoming narrower. A more satisfactory solution is to adopt the general equilibrium EIA approach which encompasses all industrial output and consumption and facilitates the identification of consequential as well as direct impacts. In this way the EIA model can be a subset of the environmental audit process and be used to generate relative performance indicators that will act as benchmarks for each of the productive sectors within the economy. Legislation could then be drafted in such a way as to reward businesses that perform better than their industry average, thereby rewarding best practice.

Where environmental legislation and regulations are in force, then environmental auditing should be used to ensure that these legal and planning requirements are fulfilled. Where there are no legal or regulatory requirements, then environmental auditing should still be implemented in order to secure the long-term benefits associated with the effectiveness of appropriate development.

The environmental auditing process involves three distinct aspects:

1. An assessment of the system, how it functions and the implications of its operation.
2. A rigorous testing of the system to see how its performance compares with some optimal ideal or benchmark performance.
3. The certification of the results from the above comparisons.

Environmental auditing can take place at establishment and corporate levels for national and multinational businesses. However, with the recognition by many countries that the public sector has a vested interest in the development of tourism, environmental auditing should not only be incorporated into the legislature for private sector businesses, it should also be part of the operational remit of public sector divisions and departments. The adoption of environmental auditing can effect good use of resources as well as help create a good marketing image.

Box 7.4 Public announcement for the new Sydney Airport

Second Sydney Airport
p r o p o s a l

The Commonwealth Government is assessing Badgerys Creek and the Holsworthy Military Area as potential sites for the Second Sydney Airport. An Environmental Impact Statement is being prepared to consider the impact of these proposals. Preliminary information is available on:

- **Flight Paths** information prepared by Airplan
- **Master Plans**
- **Road and Rail Access to the Sites**
- **Assessing the Impact of Noise**
- **Air Traffic Forecasts** information prepared by Commonwealth Department of Transport and Regional Development;

to assist you to understand these proposals. When the Draft EIS has been completed it will be released for public comment.

Come to a preliminary information session prior to the release of the Draft EIS

Helensburgh
Helensburgh Community Centre
Walker Street, Helensburgh
Tuesday 22 July, 6.00 pm - 9.30 pm

Penrith
Penrith Civic Centre
High Street, Penirch
Saturday 26 July, 10.00 am - 2.30 pm

Telephone Information Line: 1800 818 017

HOW TO FIND OUT MORE

- **Fax the Community Access Centre on (02) 9600 9741**
- **Look up the internet at http://www.magnet.com.au/2sydair and e-mail us at 2sydair@magnet.com.au**

Source: Advertisement from *The Sun Herald*, 6 July, 1997, p. 9.

Finally, neither the public nor the private sector owns the environment. It is important that all of the stakeholders should be consulted when there are any proposals to implement development policies that will impinge or detract from the environmental store. These consultations can take many forms but should be undertaken well in advance of any implementation to allow proper time to consider and evaluate opposition and alternative strategies. Box 7.4 demonstrates how such consultative procedures can be organised. In this exhibit the proposal for a second airport in Sydney, Australia, is under consideration and the public is being informed of the preparation of an EIA. It is commendable to note that the public is invited to attend preliminary information seminars prior to the release of the draft environmental impact assessment report.

Having transgressed through the 'cautionary platform' of tourism research, the major thrust of experienced researchers is now one of acceptance. That is, there is an acceptance that destinations should not have the ideological stances of 'puritan' researchers imposed upon them. Indeed, destinations should have sovereignty over their own economic and environmental destiny providing that destiny does not impinge upon the destiny of others. Thus, if it is decided that tourism is an appropriate catalyst for economic development, it should not be suffocated under a barrage of concern for environmental conservation. Where tourism researchers can best help these destinations is to provide the framework for environmental auditing so that development may move forward in an optimal manner.

Environmental impact actions

In addition to the development of viable and acceptable environmental impact assessment models, there have been a number of environmental initiatives undertaken in order to enhance the net effects of tourist activities. For instance the Tourism Division of the European Commission (DG XXIII) funded a number of projects related to tourism and the environment in Europe as a direct consequence of Agenda 21. These projects range from the sewage and waste disposal problems created by youth tourism in the eastern cantons of Belgium, through the more widely applicable case studies relating to coastal zone management in seven European states to the more specialised analysis of golf tourism and its ecological implications.

The EU documentation referred to above defines sustainable tourism as follows:

> *A development will be understood to constitute sustainable tourism development where it takes into account not only aspects in visitor source countries, but the form of outward journey, on the one hand, along with the interests of visitors and residents in a region to be defined. Activities at the destination need to be based on nature's capacity to absorb, whereby consumption of all resources should be as sparing as possible. The objective of such a tourism policy is the lasting fulfilment of the ecological, economic and socio-cultural functions, judged on whatever criteria, and whilst preserving a balance between endogenous and exogenous claims to exploit it. (Lorch and Bausch, 1995, p. 9)*

The above definition is not easily accessible and is so vague that it offers little in the way of benchmarking to guide tourism planners. The same document goes on to set out six rules which should be followed in order to develop environmentally sound tourism:

1. The fulfilment of a need shall only be permissible provided that it does not render satisfaction of the same need impossible for ensuing generations.

2. In otherwise identical circumstances, a course of action where there is only a low probability that it will result in a specific evil is to be preferred to another more likely to do so.

3. In otherwise identical circumstances, of evils that are unavoidable, the lesser one is to be preferred to the greater, and the one of lesser duration to the one lasting longer.

4. In the event of conflict, in otherwise identical circumstances, a decision should be taken in favour of many people, rather than the few.

5. A course of action serving a morally good objective is ethically only justified when the negative side effects involved can be reduced to a minimum.

   A course of action designed to serve a morally good objective is ethically only justifiable provided that the evil arising as a side effect is less than the evils that would result from refraining action.

6. The rate of consumption of self-replenishing resources may not exceed their rate of regeneration.

   The rate of consumption of finite resources may not exceed the rate of increase of self-generating raw material resources.

   The rate of pollution emissions must not exceed the environment's capacity for absorbing these.

Clearly, although these rules are commendable, one could question whether any form of industrial production could be continued if it had to abide by such constraints.

The WTO produced a tourism and environmental publication in 1992 that illustrated 'An integrated approach to resort development' (Inskeep and Kallenberger, 1992) by referring to six case studies. These case studies covered a wide variety of resorts in Indonesia, the Republic of Korea, Mexico, Dominican Republic, Turkey and the Canary Islands of Spain.

In spite of the range of countries included in the case studies some general conclusions and recommendations could be noted. One major conclusion was that serious environmental problems can be prevented by the adoption of sound planning and development. The recommendations made by the authors encompassed not only the physical needs of integrated planning such as adequate infrastructure, the implementation of appropriate design standards and the need to integrate the resort planning exercise into the local or regional planning process, but also the organisational structures and training of human resources.

A survey undertaken by the United Nations Environment Programme (UNEP) revealed that more than 100 codes of conduct exist for national tourism organisations, the industry and tourists. For instance, environmental codes of conduct have been adopted by the Tourism Industry Association of Canada and the American Society of Travel Agents as well as by national bodies such as the English Tourist Board (ETB) and international organisations such as the WTTC. The WTTC has also been actively engaged in promoting environmentally sound development with the implementation, in 1994, of its Green Globe programme. This programme is designed to heighten the environmental awareness and improve the environmental management skills of the travel and tourism industry.

While some countries have attempted to create an economic framework that will encourage best practice from an environmental point of view, and examples of these can be found in the national parklands of New Zealand and the Great Barrier Reef Marine

Park of Australia, others have attempted to produce comprehensive environmental guidelines for developers. The WTO, UNEP and the EU have all published guidelines for the development of tourism in protected areas such as national parks.

Finally, some players within the private sector have been notable in their attempts to drive home greater environmental awareness and the pursuit of best practice. Large private sector businesses have adopted environmental management systems which contain four distinct elements:

1. An environmental review – base line impact studies that produce environmental inventories of the businesses activities and functions.

2. An environmental policy – a publicly stated set of identifiable and achievable objectives.

3. The design of an implementation and environmental system – setting out the mechanisms by which the objectives will be pursued.

4. An environmental audit – which can be used to measure the business's actual performance against its declared objectives.

Airlines such as KLM Royal Dutch Airlines and British Airways have been active in a number of ways. The former has been trying to increase the use of public transport by its employees and its customers and the latter has developed a series of environmental awareness events for managers, the creation of the Tourism for Tomorrow Awards programme and the adoption of energy-saving technology for its own activities. American Airlines developed a programme to standardise the approval procedures for chemical products in an attempt to reduce its purchases of environmentally harmful products, and ferry companies, such as P & O European Ferries, developed a cost-effective and environmentally friendly means of disposing of hazardous wastes.

Walt Disney has been effective in forming a committee to evaluate the ways in which freshwater conservation measures can be combined with wastewater reuse and it has also provided its employees with the means to dispose of their personal hazardous wastes such as oils and other household chemicals safely. The European operations of Center Parcs are noted for their car-free resorts which provide a more healthy environment for guests and while the Maya Mountain Tours Company of Belize provides teaching facilities for students and researchers into environmental ethics, the Grecotel hotel chain ensures that all of its staff are trained in environmental issues.

There are also dangers embodied in the growing awareness of environmental issues. With imperfect information the tourist can easily be misled into believing that specific tourist products are environmentally sound. This may encourage tourists to purchase tour operators' packages that are anything but environmentally friendly. Box 7.5 provides an all too common case study of how members of the industry can use the environmental bandwagon to further its profiteering potential while not embracing the environmental codes of conduct.

Finally, it is only the largest of private sector businesses that normally have the expertise and resources to implement their own environmental management systems. Given the fact that the tourism industry is dominated by SMEs, the full impact of environmental management systems will be relatively minor.

Box 7.5 Ecotourism in Thailand

ECOTOURISM

Close-to-nature jungle safaris, scuba diving on pristine coral reefs, wilderness trekking to hilltribe villages ... With no system of regulation in place, anyone can call themselves an 'ecotourism' business and the money comes rolling in. But many tour operators have a strange idea of what being green means.

A boat run by a self-proclaimed 'ecotourism' company is heading toward a pristine coral reef in the Andaman Sea. Once at the destination, the boat drops anchor in the open sea, instantly destroying a myriad of rich coral and the homes of many marine animals.

So much for Thai-style ecotourism. To counter environmentally destructive mass tourism, the Tourism Authority of Thailand (TAT) launched the concept of ecotourism here three years ago, but tour companies seem to have their own idea of what being green is.

Targeting the young and adventurous, companies advertise their jungle treks, diving trips and other 'close-to-nature' expeditions as ecotourism. With no real concern for the environment, the surging popularity of nature tourism means an accelerated invasion of pristine areas and, as a result, more ecological degradation.

Ideally, ecotourism is environmentally-friendly and sustainable tourism which also benefits the local communities.

But in fact, many ecotourism ventures all over the country are destroying the very ecosystems they claim to protect.

With poor planning and on benefits for the locals, ecotourism often ends up providing little beside social tension and environmental degradation while leaving tourists feeling dissatisfied and cheated.

Such problems have led to the fledgling ecotourism industry coming under heavy fire as mere hype and sheer hypocrisy.

Pradech Phayakvichien, TAT's deputy governor of planning and development, said ecotourism in Thailand needs time to mature.

'We're in the transition period. We need more networking and cooperation between concerned agencies such as government, non-government organisations, business operators, tourists and local communities in order to fulfil the objectives of ecotourism,' he said.

One of the main factors in ecotourism's failure, he said, is the lack of participation by local communities due to poor management skills and weak bargaining power against the tourism industry.

'They also lack information, expertise and money to manage the tourism business in their areas,' he said, adding that the government must intervene by giving financial assistance and expert advice to community ecotourism operations.

At present, many communities are struggling with drastic social and environmental change resulting from the reckless behaviour of tourists and tour companies.

A case in point is the Umphang Wildlife Sanctuary where TAT launched its pilot ecotourism project a few years ago despite the fact that the sanctuary, by law, does not allow human intrusion.

The project encouraged a large influx of trekkers and tourists far beyond the area's capacity. The sanctuary is now facing severe degradation.

Like mass tourism, mass jungle trekking fattens the wallets of tour operators while hurting

Box 7.5 continued

the ecosystem and the hilltribe people's source of livelihood.

The ecotourism plague has spread far and wide to most other pristine areas in the country.

'No matter what you call it, mass or ecotourism, it makes no difference to us local villagers because we never benefit from it anyway,' said Meeya Hawa, a villager in Jao Mai, a small Muslim fishing village in Trang province.

'Some of us may be hired as cheap labour in resorts or restaurants. But nothing more,' she said, adding that the environmental damage far outweighs the economic gains.

This quiet Muslim fishing village is located on beautiful Hat Yao beach and is a gateway to many virgin islands. Although the villagers see a large number of tourists passing through every year, they have no stake in tourism money.

'When the tourists come, they stay at comfortable resort hotels and ignore our small huts. They go to the islands by the resort's boat and eat at the resort's restaurant. And they throw garbage into the sea which we have worked so hard to preserve,' she said.

Only a handful of tourists stay in the villagers' homes, travel in their boats, or eat the indigenous food they cook.

What she wants, she said, is the kind of tourism which is run and managed by the community for the community.

Instead of letting individual villagers provide tourism services with the money going into personal pockets, Meeya said the environment will be more effectively protected if tourism is a community effort.

'Many villagers are selfish and are doing their business without concern for the environment. Such tourism is short-lived and hurts the community as a whole.'

MEEYA HAWA
A Jao Mai villager and conservation activist

Community effort, she said, will also give the villagers more bargaining power against tour companies.

While TAT still has no concrete measures in place to support community-run ecotourism, it acknowledges the role of non-governmental organisations (NGOs) in strengthening local community groups, a crucial condition for ecotourism success.

For instance, the Thai Volunteers Service is working with the villagers at Chao Mai in Trang to develop community tourism which is environmentally-friendly.

'They are on the right track although they lack marketing experience, which we have. If TAT and NGOs and the communities can work together, we can create tourism which benefits both the villagers and nature,' commented TAT's Pradech.

Kiriwong, a strong and tightly-knit community at the foot of Khao Luang Mountain in Nakhon Si Thammarat, is a good example of community-based ecotourism.

Apart from being the gateway to Kao Luang, the highest mountain in the South, the village's century-old forest orchards also attract a large number of visitors.

While rural Thailand lacks social security schemes, Kiriwong has a long history of community welfare funds and committed village groups. This community consciousness comes in handy when the village decides to regulate tourism activities in the wake of increasing numbers of tourists and environmental threats.

They set up Kiriwong Ecotourism Club under its Tambon Administrative Council to draw up rules and regulations for tourists to prevent environmental degradation.

Nipat Boonpet, the club secretary, said Kiriwong has limited the number of mountain trekkers to only 30 a month. Each trekker pays about 3000 baht for a four-day trek which covers food, accommodation, luggage carriers, sightseeing, contact fees, and a donation to the community.

'The Khao Luang mountain is like the roof of our houses. We have to safeguard it, otherwise it might collapse which would mean big trouble for us,' he said.

Box 7.5 continued

All profits go back to Kiriwong's community welfare funds.

Kiriwong's income from its ecotourism business is secondary since the community lives primarily on their forest orchards.

'We keep our tourism business small because we want to avoid the mistakes of other tourist spots,' said Nipat. 'We're often tempted though, because tourism is easy money. But we have to constantly ask ourselves if we want to lose our roots or have our families break down by opening up our community too much and too soon.'

Not all tourists are happy with Kiriwong's arrangement though. The fee, they say, is too high, thus making nature trips to Khao Luang unaffordable to students with no income.

The mountain, they add, belongs to everyone and the Kiriwong villagers have no right to claim ownership and to charge people.

Flooded by complaints, Kanittha Ponoum, director of TAT's Nakhon Si Thammarat office, said Kiriwong 'misinterprets its role' and should lower the fee and give preferential treatment to students as a compromise.

Although Kiriwong is considering a new fee structure, it insists that charges are essential to limit the number of tourists to a level within nature's carrying capacity.

'Tourists only think of costs in terms of what they pay for food, travelling and accommodation. Nature for them is free. It is not,' said Nipat of Kiriwong.

According to Pradech, tourists also must change their behaviour for ecotourism to succeed. Although TAT is stepping up its domestic ecotourism campaign, Pradech said Thai tourists in general lack environmental concern for the places they visit.

The number of tourists has increased every year. This means more pressure on nature and local communities.

Short of a real revolution in environmental awareness among tour operators and tourists alike, ecotourism will remain just another hyped-up marketing strategy while short-sighted tourist businesses continue to erode the natural environment on which they depend.

Source: article taken from the *Bangkok Post*, Saturday 10 May 1997.

Conclusion

Environmental impacts are not unique to tourism and tourism receives a disproportional share of criticism for its negative environmental impacts. Environmental impacts manifest themselves at the direct, indirect and induced levels and all three levels of impact should be taken into account during the process of assessment. The methods of assessment available to researchers have been developed in a piecemeal fashion, limiting their usefulness for generalisations. However, the adoption of a matrix approach, utilising input–output modelling structures, provides the most promising outlook for a universally acceptable framework for the study of such impacts. International agencies, through statements such as Agenda 21, have declared their intentions to develop an environment-friendly approach to policy making. Similarly, national governments are responding to the pressures from these international bodies as well as from their own populations, to move towards a more environmentally friendly development path. Finally, the private sector (at least as represented by the larger businesses) is responding to pressures by implementing environmental management systems.

There is an overwhelming need to bring some credibility to the study of environmental impacts and this can be achieved by focusing upon the objective environmental indicators, such as those listed by the OECD, rather than subjective data sets that may only have local relevance.

Chapter discussion questions

1. The environment is an element of the tourism product that is not priced within a market system and, as such, will always be over-exploited. Discuss.

2. When assessing the environmental impact of any sector of production all environmental consequences of that production should be examined not simply the direct effects. Discuss.

3. Is it possible to draw general conclusions from the analysis of environmental impacts?

4. What are the processes involved in implementing an environmental management system and what are the weaknesses of such a system?

Recommended further reading

- Briguglio, L. (ed.) (1995) *Sustainable Tourism*, Cassell, London.
- Mathieson, A. and Wall, G. (1989) *Tourism: Economic, Physical and Social Aspects*, Longman, Harlow.
- Murphy, P. E. (1991) *Tourism: A Community Approach*, Methuen, London.

Bibliography

- Fletcher, J. *et al.* (1996) 'The economic and environmental impacts of tourism in Mauritius', unpublished report to Mauritius Airways and the Government of Mauritius.
- Burnett, G. W. and Conover, R. (1989) 'The efficacy of Africa's national parks: an evaluation of Julius Nyere's Arusha Manifesto of 1961', *Society and Natural Resources*, **2**, 251–60.
- Cohen, E. (1978) 'The impact of tourism on the physical environment', *Annals of Tourism Research*, **5**(2), 215–37.
- de Kadt, E. (1979) (ed.) *Tourism: Passport to Development?*, Oxford University Press, New York.
- Getz, D. (1986) 'Models in tourism planning', *Tourism Management*, **7**(1), 21–32.
- Green, D. H., Hunter, C. J. and Moore, B. (1990) 'Applications of the Delphi technique in tourism', *Annals of Tourism Research*, **17**, 270–9.
- Inskeep, E. (1991) *Tourism Planning: An Integrated and Sustainable Development Approach*, Van Nostrand Reinhold, New York.
- Inskeep, E. and Kallenberger, M. (1992) *An Integrated Approach to Resort Development: six case studies*, WTO, Madrid.
- Lorch, J. and Bausch, T. (1995) Sustainable tourism in Europe. In *Tourism and the Environment in Europe*, EU, Brussels.
- Mathieson, A. and Wall, G. (1982) *Tourism: Economic, Physical and Social Impacts*, Longman, Harlow.
- OECD (1994) *Environmental Indicators*, OECD core set, and Paris.
- Welford, R. and Gouldson, A. (1993) *Environmental Management and Business Strategy*, Pitman, London.

Chapter Eight

The socio-cultural impact of tourism

Introduction

Tourism is a product that relies totally upon simultaneous production and consumption. In effect, if the tourists do not visit a destination then there are no measurable outputs of the industry's activities. There is a wide range of service industries in the world, but there is often no need for the consumer to visit the place of production in order to consume the product. Examples of such service industries include banking, finance and insurance services as well as media and communications. However, tourism is a personal service and, as such, can only be consumed by the tourist visiting the destination. The implication of this for the destination's population is that it will come into contact with an alien population during the production process. This contact can be beneficial or detrimental to the host population depending upon the difference in cultures and the nature of the contact. Much of the literature on social impacts is biased in that it focuses attention upon the detrimental impact of tourism on the host population. Similarly, little attention has been paid to the fact that there can also be socio-cultural impacts on the tourist population, which can again be either positive or negative. In reality socio-cultural impacts tend to contain a mixture of both positive and negative strands and these impacts affect both hosts and guests.

The aim of this chapter is to outline the nature of the socio-cultural impacts, to examine those contacts that are positive and those that may be deemed to be negative. In order to do this it is important to include an examination of the process of tourism development because the speed and nature of development can be a major influence on the magnitude and direction of socio-cultural changes. The chapter will also investigate the causal factors for socio-cultural impacts, suggest possible methods for measurement and outline some policy implications.

The nature of socio-cultural impacts of tourism

The socio-cultural impact of tourism is manifested through an enormous range of aspects from the arts and crafts through to the fundamental behaviour of individuals and collective groups. The impacts can be positive, such as the case where tourism preserves or even resurrects the craft skills of the population or the enhancement of cultural exchange between two distinct populations. The impacts can also be negative, such as the commercialisation and bastardisation of arts and crafts and the commercialisation of ceremonies/rituals of the host population. The impacts can also detract from cultural exchange by presenting a limited and distorted view of one of the populations.

A factor often overlooked by researchers is the socio-cultural impact of tourism on the visitor population. For instance, the growth of UK tourists visiting Spain throughout the 1960s and 1970s resulted in culinary and beverage changes in the UK (paella and Rioja wine being two Spanish products that benefited from this exchange). Visitors to Australia would often find it hard to resist adopting the beach-based lifestyle and the barbecue when they return home. There is evidence of socio-cultural impacts, ranging from the clothes we wear, the food we eat and our general lifestyles and attitudes, which can all be influenced by places we visit.

There is a tradition of viewing the socio-cultural impacts as a combined effect because of the difficulty in distinguishing between sociological and cultural impacts. This distinction is also somewhat artificial given the fact that sociological and cultural effects overlap to a large extent. There is also a tradition of examining the socio-cultural impacts of tourism purely in terms of the contact that takes place between the host and visiting populations: this is a very limited approach. The true socio-cultural impact of tourism is far reaching and encompasses direct and indirect effects in a manner similar to the economic impacts. Again, some of these consequential impacts may be beneficial while others may be seen as detrimental. These matters will be explored in greater detail below.

Approaches to the study of socio-cultural impacts of tourism

There are a variety of ways in which we can examine the relationships between tourism development and socio-cultural and socio-economic changes. The development of the tourist product is inextricably linked to the contribution that tourism development can make to general economic development. In fact, the relationship between tourism development and general economic development can be studied under the heading of dependency or core–periphery theory, which relates to the enrichment of metropolitan areas at the expense of underdeveloped peripheral areas. Studies of dependency theory often cite examples of the Caribbean and the South Pacific to highlight not only the economic and political dependence resulting from tourism activity, but also the socio-cultural dependence.

The development of the tourism product will, to some extent, be determined by the type of tourism activity that takes place. This, in turn will be partly determined by the nature of the destination and the socio-economic characteristics of the tourists. Similarly, the magnitude and direction of the economic and sociological impact of tourism on the host population will be partly determined by the type of tourism product.

The impact brought about by the interaction of hosts and tourists is a well-documented phenomenon, and the findings of researchers, such as Smith (1989) in her book on the anthropology of tourism have rapidly gained acceptance in the academic world. The categorisation of tourists into 'typologies' is now accepted as an orthodox tool in the study of socio-cultural impacts.

The typology of tourists

Typology is a method of sociological investigation that seeks, in this instance, to classify tourists according to a particular phenomenon, usually motivations or behaviour. A simple example of a typology which has implications for the development of the tourism product is shown in Table 8.1:

- Package tourists – usually demand Western amenities, are associated with rapid growth rates and often lead to the restructuring of the local economy.
- Independent tourists – usually fit in better with the local environment and social structure, are associated with relatively slow growth rates and often lead to local ownership.

A more detailed typology, such as the one devised by Valene Smith, relates the type of tourist to volume and adaptation levels.

Table 8.1:
Typology of tourism: frequency of types of tourist and their adaptations to local norms

Types of tourist	Number of tourists	Adaptation to local norms
Explorer	Very limited	Accepts fully
Élite	Rarely seen	Adapts fully
Off-beat	Uncommon but seen	Adapts well
Unusual	Occasional	Adapts somewhat
Incipient mass	Steady flow	Seeks Western amenities
Mass	Continuous flow	Expects Western amenities
Charter	Massive arrivals	Demands Western amenities

Source: Smith (1989).

Before examining the different approaches that can be used to study the socio-cultural impacts of tourism it is important to consider some fundamental matters relating to these impacts that are often ignored by researchers. In spite of the fact that some researchers regard socio-cultural change as one of the evils of tourism development, any form of economic development will, by definition, carry with it implications for the social structure and cultural aspects of the host population. This is true for both international and domestic tourism development. To condemn tourism development because it will inevitably bring with it socio-economic change is tantamount to consigning a destination to a cultural museum. This choice can only come from the host population and not from external researchers who become too embroiled in the sociological resources that are used in the tourist transactions. Furthermore, to criticise researchers for forecasting future growth levels of tourism and manpower requirements on the grounds that such forecasts ignore the fact that these employees are members of families is to deny the whole essence of sound tourism planning. Successful tourism development can only be achieved by undertaking rigorous quantitative and qualitative research.

The speed and concentration of tourism development are also important influences on the magnitude and direction of social impacts and must be taken into account when attempting to attribute the cause of socio-cultural impacts. The nature of the tourism development process and its impact on the host population can be categorised into a variety of subsets and the analyses of each of these subsets can shed additional light on the type and source of impacts attributable to tourism development.

With respect to the speed of development a broad analytical approach would suggest that if tourism develops rapidly, the accompanying change to the economy would create a new power structure. In contrast, slow tourism development tends to be associated with small, locally-owned developments with less change to the power structure.

The tourism development process

Although tourism development can take place in a wide variety of forms, a typical development scenario considers the tourism product as it grows from infancy to maturity and looks something like this:

- A few tourists 'discover' an area or destination.
- In response to this discovery, local entrepreneurs provide new or special facilities to accommodate the growing number of visitors and service their needs. More importantly, they provide the means to attract more visitors in the future.
- The public sector provides new or improved infrastructure to cater for the inflow of visitors.
- Finally, institutionalised or mass tourism is developed, which is commonly resort-based and sold as a package. It is based upon large-volume production techniques in order to exploit economies of large-scale production in marketing, accommodation and transport, such as high payload factors for aircraft.

Many regional and national tourism development plans have attempted to short-cut the above tourism evolution cycle by aiming for the final stage of mass tourism straight away, but few destinations can make this leap without first securing outside capital and expertise and incurring severe social stress.

Unfortunately, there is no single coherent body of knowledge or theory which comprehensively explains tourism development. Evidence, such as it is, is rather piecemeal and comes from a number of disparate case studies. Furthermore, the situation is compounded by the fact that different disciplines approach the subject matter in different ways, and although many aspects of the studies may overlap, it is difficult to tie the different conclusions together into a single body of thought.

The different approaches may be categorised under the following headings:

- psychological;
- sociological;
- socio-economic.

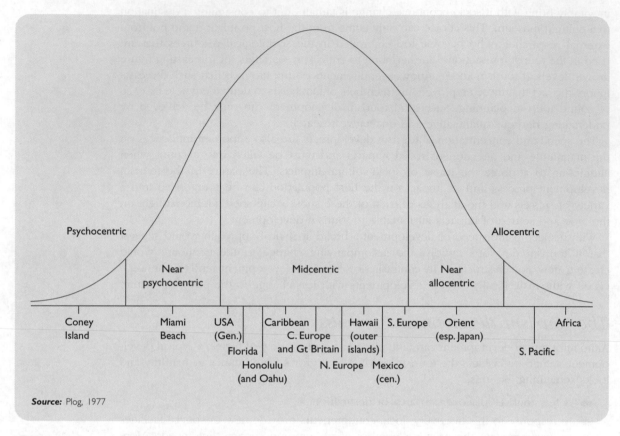

Figure 8.1: Psychographic positions of destinations

The psychological basis of tourism development

In Chapter 2 we introduced Stanley Plog's (1977) approach to a typology of tourists and in this chapter we have reiterated how useful such typologies can be in the study of socio-cultural impacts. Plog devised his classification in terms of psychographic analysis, and in this way attempted to explain why resort destinations appear to follow a pattern that causes them to rise through a period of development and then fall into a period of decline. He saw a continuum of market segments with two diametrically opposed groups occupying either pole (see Figure 8.1).

Plog's theory suggests that the tourist segments can be divided into different psychographic traits, i.e. allocentrics, near allocentrics, midcentrics, near psychocentrics and psychocentrics. The polar extremes of these groups can be described as exhibiting the following characteristics:

- **Allocentrics** seek cultural and environmental differences from their norm, belong to the higher income groups, are adventurous and require very little in the way of tourism plant.
- **Psychocentrics** seek familiar surroundings, belong to the lower income groups, are unadventurous and demand a high level of tourism plant.

According to Plog's framework, a resort may typically begin by attracting a small number of allocentrics (trendsetters), similar to Smith's explorers, but will soon develop in order to attract larger numbers of visitors. Using Plog's terminology this development will move the resort into and through the near-allocentrics and then into the mid-centrics. During this process the allocentrics will be alienated and they will move on to look for new destinations to 'discover'.

Resorts that have a strong competitive advantage, in terms of climate, location or top-quality tourism plant, such as DisneyLand, may continue to thrive in the mid-centric market. However, many resorts will tend to lose favour (perhaps because they are considered by tourists to be too commercialised) and continue their drift towards the psychocentric markets by offering lower tariffs, more comprehensive packaging and more scheduling of activities – the complete 'no-surprise vacation'.

Contrary to original thoughts concerning Plog's theory, this process of rise and decline is not immutable. Such a process may have seemed inevitable for many resorts in the past but, once decision makers realise that limited tourism development can be an attractive means of growth, they may develop tourism plant that is compatible with the environment and the indigenous characteristics of a region, and target them at the 'desired' market segments. Alternatively, recognition of the importance of quality tourism plant can allow destinations to maintain a mid-centric position in the market continuum.

The sociological basis of tourism development

The sociological basis of tourism development can be sub-divided into (a) the social phenomenon of tourism and (b) the socio-economic basis underlying tourism development.

Several factors of the modern world can be identified as the seeds from which international tourism has grown into an inescapable social phenomenon:

- Population growth.
- Increasing urbanisation and the overwhelming pressures of urban life which create the desire to escape.
- Growth in communications and information technology, creating awareness and stimulating interest.
- Changes in mobility and accessibility, brought about largely by the growth of air transport and private motor car ownership.
- Increased leisure time and longer periods of vacation, together with rising real incomes in the wake of sustained economic growth.
- Increases in world trade for business tourism.

When examining the factors that are associated with tourism development it is interesting to note that they can also be categorised according to whether they are *push* factors or *pull* factors. By this we mean that some factors generate a desire to escape (*push*) such as urbanisation, overcrowding, pollution or even tedium, whereas other factors such as specific events (Olympics) or climate and natural phenomenon generate a magnetism that attracts tourists (*pull*). There are a number of factors that will influence the attitude of people towards tourism at both domestic and international levels. These include the following:

- **Age**. The age of the tourist will, within certain boundaries, influence the type of tourism activity pursued. For instance, there is likely to be less demand from the elderly for trekking and mountaineering vacations than from other age groups. Similarly, the greatest demand for tourist destinations with a hectic nightlife is likely to be from the 18–35-year-old age group. Of course there are always exceptions to these rules!

- **Education**. There is a tendency to associate the more adventurous and independent vacations with the more educated portion of the population. These would include Plog's allocentrics as well as Smith's explorers and élite travellers.

- **Income levels**. Income levels have an obvious influence on the decision of people to travel, the location to which they travel, the nature of the activities undertaken while away and the mode(s) of transport utilised.

- **Socio-economic background**. The previous experiences of people will play an important role in determining the type of holiday they will consume in future time periods. For instance, children from the higher socio-economic groups, who are accustomed to frequent trips abroad, are likely to continue this pattern throughout adulthood.

In addition to the socio-economic characteristics of the tourists, the tourism development process, together with its implications for socio-cultural impacts, should be examined. This approach encompasses all three approaches discussed so far – the psychological basis for tourism development, the sociological basis and the socio-economic basis for tourism development. In general there is a *direct* socio-cultural impact which occurs as a result of the contact between the host population and the visitors. De Kadt (1979) suggests that there are three broad categories of such contact:

1. When the tourists buy goods and services from the hosts.
2. When the hosts and tourists share a facility such as the beach, a train or bus, a restaurant or bar, etc.
3. When tourists and hosts come together for the prime purpose of cultural exchange.

The first two of these types of contact are associated with the majority of the negative aspects of social contact, whereas the third type of contact is generally considered to be positive in nature. To draw comparisons between this work of de Kadt and the typology based research of Smith, it is evident that the explorer/adventurer tourist is most likely to take part in the latter, positive type of interaction – providing a favourable association between this type of tourist and their socio-cultural impacts. However, the mass and charter tourist is more likely to be predominantly concerned with the first two types of contact, thereby making their presence generally unfavourable from a socio-cultural impact point of view. A crude conclusion can be drawn from this somewhat simplistic approach – the negative types of interaction are by far the most common and the positive types of contact are relatively rare.

The 'demonstration effect' is also an aspect of the *direct* socio-cultural impact of tourism. Tourists influence the behaviour of the host population by their example. This is an area where tourism development is at a distinct disadvantage when compared with the use of alternative industries as a means to economic development. Tourism is a product that requires simultaneous production and consumption. Although international tourism may be seen as an export industry, in the same way as, say, oil or automobiles, it has the disadvantage that the consumer must visit the place of production (the factory) in order to consume it. This means that tourism will bring with it the physical presence of tourists and this will stimulate changes in the behaviour and attire of the host population.

It is not even necessary for tourists to come into direct contact with members of the host population for the demonstration effect to take place. Those members of the host population who are influenced by the behaviour of the tourists are likely to influence other members of their community by their changed attitudes and behaviour. This can be classified as an *indirect* socio-cultural impact. Moreover, if tourism development is successful, new employment opportunities created by the increased activity will be the harbinger of social change in the same way that any form of economic development will change the consumption habits, the location and the behaviour of the local population. These changes will be stimulated further by the introduction of new or enhanced forms of communications, transport and infrastructure primarily provided for tourism development. These latter factors may also be considered to be *indirect* socio-cultural impacts but this time they are associated with many types of economic development, not just tourism. However, the diversity of productive sectors associated directly and indirectly with the tourism industry is such that these types of socio-cultural impacts will probably be more widely spread as a result of tourism development than any other industry.

As an economy grows and develops there will probably be an increase in income levels and the proportion of the population involved in the monetised sector. This will alter the consumption patterns of the local population. Such changes, if they include consumer durables such as television, videos and radio, will expose the local population to a greater range of wants and, in so doing, speed up the process of social change. These effects, because they are a result of increased income levels and consumer spending, may be seen as being *induced* socio-cultural impacts. This latter type of socio-cultural impact will also be evident irrespective of the type of economic catalyst that generated the development and is not uniquely attributable to tourism development.

The magnitude of the direct socio-cultural impact associated with tourism development will also be determined by the extent of the difference in socio-cultural characteristics between hosts and guests. Inskeep (1991) suggests that these differences include:

- basic value and logic system;
- religious beliefs;
- traditions;
- customs;
- lifestyles;
- behavioural patterns;
- dress codes;
- sense of time budgeting;
- attitudes towards strangers.

To add further complexity to our understanding of the problems, the speed of development and change will have an important role in determining the magnitude of the socio-cultural changes because time allows for the process of adaptation. Compounding the issue further is the fact that the tourists' cultures when abroad (it is probable that the tourists will represent several different cultures) are different from the tourists' cultures at home. In other words, tourists often take on different attitudes and adopt different codes of behaviour when they are on vacation and away from their normal environment.

As discussed earlier, the socio-cultural impacts associated with tourism can be either positive or negative. One of the positive impacts highlighted by de Kadt was the exchange of cultural information, ideas and beliefs. But tourism can also help to stimulate interest in, and conserve aspects of, the host's cultural heritage. This is a significant positive socio-cultural impact and extends over ancient monuments, historic sites, arts, crafts and cultural ceremonies and rituals. If tourists appreciate the cultural heritage of a destination, that appreciation can stimulate the hosts' pride in their heritage and foster local crafts, traditions and customs.

The negative socio-cultural impacts are sometimes the result of *direct* contact and the demonstration effect and these can distort the traditional crafts and customs into shorter, commercialised events that offer the host community little in the way of rich cultural experience. Negative socio-cultural impacts can also be generated if the tourism development is not managed properly and the full economic potential of that development is not realised. For instance, foreign employment in tourism-related jobs and foreign investment in tourism projects both add to the local resentment of tourism development. The exclusion of hosts from certain tourist facilities (such as private beaches, casinos and transport services) will further increase the pressure of resentment and may create conflict between the host population and the tourists.

As with any form of economic development, the new income-earning opportunities created by tourism development are unlikely to be evenly distributed across the destination. This may give rise to some members of the host community feeling resentful and antagonistic towards tourism development. Tourism destinations such as Jamaica in the Caribbean have experienced social problems because tourism development was confined to the north and western coast, although more recently attempts have been made to redress this imbalance. In tourism's favour, it is generally developed in areas where there is little in the way of competing industries (particularly manufacturing); therefore it helps provide employment opportunities in areas where they may be most needed. The creation of job opportunities with higher wage rates than those paid by the more traditional industries of fishing and agriculture can create social pressures between hosts who occupy these posts and their families and peers who do not.

A major problem can also occur because of a real (and sometimes only apparent) difference in wealth between the tourists and their hosts. It is true that there are occasions when the tourists are generally much wealthier than the hosts with whom they come into contact. However, this difference may be exacerbated by the fact that tourists exhibit spending patterns and behaviour that is very different from their norm, simply because they are on vacation. The normal spending habits of tourists is not information readily available to the average host. Furthermore, the difference in wealth between tourist and host may not be as severe a problem as initially perceived given the fact that the vast majority of international tourism takes place between industrialised countries and not between industrialised and developing countries.

When attempting to measure the level of irritation generated by tourist–host contact, Doxey (1976) drew up the following index:

1. **The level of euphoria** – the initial thrill and enthusiasm that comes along with tourism development results in the fact that the tourist is made welcome.

2. **The level of apathy** – once tourism development is under way and the consequential expansion has taken place, the tourist is taken for granted and is now only seen as a source of profit-taking. What contact is made between host and guest is done so on a commercial and formal footing.

3. **The level of irritation** – as the industry approaches saturation point, the hosts can no longer cope with the number of tourists without the provision of additional facilities.

4. **The level of antagonism** – the tourist is now seen as the harbinger of all ills, hosts are openly antagonistic towards tourists and tourists are regarded as being there to be exploited.

5. **The final level** – during the above process of 'development' the host population has forgotten that all they once regarded as being special was exactly the same

thing that attracted the tourist, but in the rush to develop tourism circumstances have changed. The social impact has been comprehensive and complete and the tourists will move to different destinations.

Some specific socio-cultural impacts of tourism

Sex

The fact that tourists will travel abroad to enjoy uninhibited casual sexual encounters is not a new phenomenon. The early European tourists were to some extent motivated by the liberal attitude towards sex in some of the Third World countries they visited. More recently a major tourism market has grown up around sex tourism and destinations such as Thailand, The Gambia and some of the Central European countries have actively marketed the sexual content of their products. The proliferation of AIDS has done much to dampen the rapid growth of this element of the tourism industry but it is still a significant part of the market. It is questionable whether tourism created the social disruption associated with the sex trade or whether the sex trade has stimulated the tourism market. But, as with all forms of prostitution, it is impossible to be conclusive as to the rights and wrongs of either party. Certainly the growth of paedophile activity is one element of the tourist industry that is outlawed in many of the tourist-generating countries and can only be pursued under the guise of international tourism.

The development of tourism using specific sexual activities as its main catalyst is likely to be short-lived in the current world of AIDS and other sexually transmitted diseases. However, many tourists from industrialised countries may expect to relax their sexual morals during a vacation and this can lead to a thin line being drawn between destinations that are primarily trading on sex and those that offer an environment wherein tourists can relax their sexual morals.

Crime

The link between tourism and crime is hard to establish. Many writers, such as Mathieson and Wall (1982), have suggested the link but find it hard to establish whether crime increases simply because of the increased population density or whether it is more specifically associated with tourism. Clearly the presence of large numbers of tourists provides a source for illegal activities including drugs trafficking, robbery and violence. Florida has been subject to international press coverage because of acts of violent crimes against tourists. Other destinations have suffered similar press coverage. Tourists are sometimes obvious victims of crime where they are clearly identifiable by language or colour and can be expected to be carrying significant sums of money with them.

Tourism is often the catalyst for the growth of gaming activities and a number of destinations have used casino developments as a means to attracting tourist spending. Unless properly monitored and controlled, such developments can induce social behaviour that is detrimental to social cohesion.

Health

The problem of AIDS has already been mentioned. However, there are other less newsworthy diseases that can be transmitted when people from different communities interact. Although often not fatal, these illnesses can cause social and economic stress to the host population who may have less immunity to the diseases than the tourist population.

Where tourism growth is rapid and unplanned there can be infrastructure failures that lead to health hazards.

Other aspects

Following the lead of Cohen (1988) it is possible to categorise the key themes that characterise the interface between culture and tourism:

- **Commoditisation** – where the demands of tourism lead to the mutation and sometimes destruction of the meaning of cultural performances and events.
- **Staged authenticity** – where 'pseudo events' are presented to satisfy tourists' needs for new (simulated) experiences.
- **Alien tourist experiences** – which examines the apparent inability to enjoy meaningful cultural experiences without travelling to different environments.

Commoditisation

Commoditisation is a long-standing criticism relating to tourism's effect on culture and art. Crafts, ceremonies and rituals are often driven into an exploitation stance, abbreviated, made more colourful, more dramatic and spectacular in order to capture the attention and imagination of an audience that often does not possess the underlying knowledge/experience that would make the unadapted version appealing. Countless examples can and have been cited, from the sale of concrete carvings of Bob Marley in Jamaica, the '*Bula Fiji*' carved wooden knives and clubs, to the Polynesian dances of Western Samoa and the limbo dancers of the Caribbean. Where culture becomes a commodity for financial transactions it is difficult to be objective. Although it is true that the demands of people from alien cultures who are operating on a very tight and sometimes fixed time budget are very different to the local demands, it is sometimes this foreign demand that enriches and/or preserves decaying and dying skills and performances.

Staged authenticity

With growing public awareness regarding cultural and ethnic differences there has been increasing demand for tourism products that offer cultural authenticity. That is, environments where the tourists can 'get behind the scenes' to meet and observe the real people. Although, in the Plog sense, this may be considered a great leap forward in perception and understanding by volume tourists and a movement back from the psychocentric scale of the tourist market, it can also be regarded as being a signal for impending cultural devastation for some destinations. This represents the social impact dilemma of post-1980 tourism development.

In order to differentiate their product from other tourism products on the market destinations have highlighted environmental, climatic and cultural differences. In this last instance, they are using their cultural heritage as a promotional device to attract increasing numbers of tourists. Although this may be considered to be a positive step in achieving greater awareness concerning cultural differences and, perhaps, a greater empathy between tourist and host, it also exposes a deeper layer of the sociological structure and thereby risks of further 'contamination'.

However, there are ways of differentiating the tourism product, providing tourists with sufficient cultural exposure to satisfy their demands while preserving the true cultural identity of the host population. One such way is the use of staged authenticity whereby the host population provides a more realistic performance of cultural heritage than existed before, but still ensures that the tourists do not manage to penetrate behind the stage curtains. Figure 8.2 demonstrates the concept and dangers of staged authenticity.

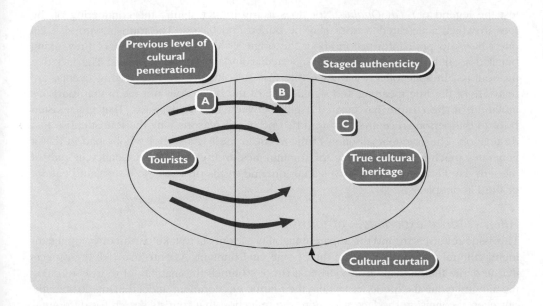

In Figure 8.2 the arena is divided into three distinct areas:

A – the previous level of tourist penetration into the host culture;

B – the new level of cultural penetration that is considered to be authentic by the tourist but is, in fact, staged authenticity;

C – the true cultural heritage of the host society that maintains its integrity by keeping tourists on the other side of the firewall curtain.

Although effective in the short term, this approach to cultural impact containment can lead to increasing levels of penetration when the firewall curtains are continually retreating in order to provide greater tourist experiences and diversity within a competitive market. Even if the social firewall does not retreat there is a danger that some of the tourists will manage to penetrate beyond the curtain. Eventually there will be nowhere for the host population to maintain the integrity of their culture. There is an additional danger in the form of a *gradual* cultural impact. The very act of staging the authenticity of the culture can blur the true boundaries of the local heritage and, in so doing, distort the cultural heritage that is being maintained behind the firewall curtain.

It has also been argued that the *so-called* authenticity of culture is a fleeting moment in the development calendar. Culture is a dynamic living concept and changes continually in order to capture and embrace the needs of society in the present time period. From this point of view culture continually runs through a process of being invented and re-invented and that, in this sense, all of culture can be defined as staged authenticity.

An example of the dynamics of cultural performances can be seen in the Fijian firewalkers. Like the limbo dancers of the Caribbean, the firewalkers of Fiji are, today, almost exclusively found in cultural centres or hotels. In fact, they can be found wherever tourists are willing to exchange money for the privilege of watching these ancient customs that are packaged and transformed into dinner-side entertainment.

The Fijians who perform the ritual known as *Vilavilairevo* (which translates literally into 'jumping into the oven') accept that the walking across the heated stones of a *lovo* (earth oven) is now a commercial event. It is rarely performed as sign of respect for powerful and important visitors and never as a commemorative ritual to celebrate (and test the legend of) *Tui Qualita*. Nor does it any longer signify the conquering of the *lovo* in which a defeated warrior may be buried and baked. The tourists who visit Fiji often have no prior information about the origin of this particular form of firewalking but it does little to detract from the spectacular and impressive displays. The fact that the tourists, in spite of any narrative that may accompany the firewalking events, are unaware of the true meaning and significance of the ritual does not mean that tourism's mutation of the custom has created a gulf between host and visitor. That gulf existed prior to the performance and may well be one of the reasons why the tourist chose that destination. The commercialisation of the event in itself is also not wholly bad in that it generates much-needed currency for communities and, given its redundancy as part of modern day Fijian culture preserves a custom and instils pride in the history and culture of the Fiji people.

Alien cultural experiences of tourists

This issue revolves around the apparent inability of tourists to take part in or enjoy meaningful cultural experiences within their home environment. As with many of the aspects that underlie the motivation of tourists, it is not so much the inability of tourists to enjoy meaningful cultural experiences within their home environment, indeed many do so without even recognising the fact, it is more the reflection that tourists search for different – *or alien* – experiences. The desire to experience different climatic experiences (sun, rain or snow) and different environmental experiences (deserts, rainforests, cities or rolling green fields) are willingly accepted. Therefore, it is not an absurd proposition to suggest that tourists may actively seek out cultural experiences that are deliberately different from their norm – indeed such motivation is becoming an increasingly important aspect of late twentieth century tourism.

Methods of measuring the socio-cultural impact of tourism

Data collection

The socio-cultural factors influenced by tourist activities are, in general, the most difficult ones to measure and quantify. Whereas the economic and many of the environmental indicators do lend themselves to objective measurement, the socio-cultural impacts are often highly qualitative and subjective in nature. The nature of socio-cultural impacts can range from those impacts that are obvious and measurable, such as the outbreak of particular types of disease and/or infections, to those that are hard to identify and measure such as changes in customs and codes of conduct. On the other hand, there are those impacts that may be identifiable, such as increased crime rates, drug abuse and prostitution, but are difficult to attribute to tourism rather than to other factors of influence (such as media intrusion).

There is a wide range of data sources that may be utilised in order to examine the social impact of tourism. It is important to recognise that some of these data may not be exclusively related to tourism activity. Where causes of variable changes are multivariate then deeper analysis must be undertaken in order to filter out other influences. Complete filtering is unlikely to be possible.

Data collection sources can be categorised into primary and secondary. Primary data can be collected by undertaking household and visitor surveys. This method of data collection is time consuming and costly. It is also sometimes difficult to maintain the

Indicators (changes in)	Primary data		Secondary data	
	Survey	*Observe*	*Data*	*Media*
Crime rates/levels	X		X	X
Prostitution		X	X	X
Drug abuse	X		X	X
Promiscuity	X	X	X	X
Gambling	X		X	X
Family relationships	X		X	X
Social values	X	X	X	X
Creative expressions	X	X		X
Traditional ceremonies	X	X		X
Safety levels	X		X	
Health	X		X	
Community organisations	X		X	X
Collective lifestyles	X	X		X
Economic independence	X		X	X
Population dispersion	X		X	
Cultural commercialisation	X	X	X	X
Host/tourist hostility	X		X	X
Demonstration effects	X	X		
Economic and social dualism	X		X	X
Psychological stress	X		X	X
Living standards	X		X	X

appropriate level of objectivity and the resident awareness questionnaires require very careful construction if they are to provide data that are both unbiased and in a form that is user-friendly. Other forms of primary data collection include the interviewing of focus groups, key informants, Delphi analyses and participant observation. Table 8.2 distinguishes between interview/questionnaire/Delphi approaches and those that use observation techniques.

There are a variety of secondary sources for gathering information with respect to socio-cultural impacts. These include criminal activity statistics, notification of infectious diseases statistics, employment and unemployment data, newspaper reports/articles and other media coverage. Some of these data are quantitative in nature whereas others are quite subjective and care must be taken in the interpretation. Table 8.2 distinguishes between those data that are collected, assimilated and tabulated for other purposes, and information (largely qualitative) that can be gleaned from scanning past and present newspaper cuttings, television and radio news and documentary programmes and other media forms of covering current affairs.

The two fundamental means of assessing socio-cultural impacts in a destination are by surveying both tourists and local residents. There are several factors that should be taken into account when undertaking a local resident survey.

Firstly, it is important, as with all sampling procedures, to obtain a representative sample of the population. This may seem obvious, but several social impact studies have relied entirely upon random sampling of the immediate population (those directly in the vicinity of the tourist facilities). In order to gauge the true impact and its level of penetration it is important that the survey population is seen as being wider than this.

Secondly, it is important to establish whether or not the respondent correctly identifies who is a tourist. The misperception as to what constitutes a tourist can render local resident surveys misleading. Thirdly, in areas subject to seasonality, it is also important to undertake the survey at different times of the year. Quite often a good indicator of the magnitude of the social impact of tourism is how quickly the levels of awareness, resentment and other characteristics decline once the peak season recedes. Where there is a significant level of decline shortly after the peak season one can assume that the impacts, although severe during the peak period, are not too deeply embedded in the local population. Where remedial action is required in visitor management flows or infrastructural investment, there is every chance that these actions will be successful. If the levels of resentment continue to run high during the off-peak periods then there is a distinct possibility that any remedial action will need to be fundamental even to the point of reducing the peak levels of tourism flows.

In order to complement the work that has already been undertaken in the field of economic and environmental impacts and to provide a common framework for the analysis of socio-cultural impacts, researchers at Bournemouth University have attempted to embed the process of socio-cultural impacts within the economic and environmental model structure. The inclusion of socio-cultural impacts within such a model allows for the direct, indirect and induced impacts to be considered as well as providing a vehicle for the study of social and cultural changes as a result of other (non-tourism-related) factors.

At this point in time the number of socio-cultural variables that can be included at such a detailed and quantifiable level are limited but include indicators such as:

- the ratio of tourists to host population;
- the number of contacts between hosts and guests for transactions;
- the number of contacts between hosts and guests while sharing facilities;
- the number of contacts between hosts and guests for socio-cultural purposes;
- differences between host and guest age distributions;
- percentage of local population coming into contact with tourists;
- percentage of population working in tourism-related industries weighted by indirect and induced employment;
- tourist/host clustering;
- nature of tourism.

The above data should be collected and analysed at relatively frequent intervals. Some of these data are readily available in most countries and systems can be put into place to show those ratios on a weekly or monthly basis. Others are more difficult to acquire and may only be available at discrete time intervals.

Conclusion

This chapter has examined the nature and determinants of the socio-cultural impacts associated with tourism development. In so doing, the nature of the tourism development process has been explored and the influence of socio-economic factors in driving the development of tourism. The typological studies undertaken by researchers such as Smith and Plog have provided a framework which facilitates the further development of socio-cultural impact methodologies but, it was ▷

Conclusion continued

noted, this framework is severely limited by the nature of the variables used. The development of tourism can have specific implications for incidents of crime and health, as well as influencing the individual and collective lifestyles of the local population. However, it is also important to recognise the fact that tourists can also transmit socio-cultural impacts back to the populations of the originating countries.

The problems associated with measuring either the desirability of preserving the cultural heritage of a destination or determining how this is influenced by the presence of tourists make it a difficult area of research. The staged authenticity approach to tourism development can provide a firewall in order to maintain the integrity of the local cultural heritage. However, staged authenticity can also act as a catalyst for further cultural penetration and act as the 'thin end of the wedge' for further intrusion.

There are data available that can be used to analyse the magnitude and direction of socio-cultural impacts and these were examined in order to suggest a framework for an integrated tourism impact model.

Chapter discussion questions

1. It is not the *absolute* characteristics of the tourists that determine the degree of socio-cultural impact on a destination, it is the *relative* difference between the profiles of the tourists and those of the local population that is important. Discuss.

2. Examine the significance of tourism typology studies as a means to studying the determination of socio-cultural impacts.

3. Are the socio-cultural impacts associated with tourism development necessarily negative?

4. What key variables can be used to measure the magnitude, scope and direction of socio-cultural impacts? Outline the weaknesses and strengths of these variables.

Recommended further reading

- Krippendorf, J. (1987) *The Holiday Makers – Understanding the Impact of Leisure and Travel*, Heinemann, London.
- Mathieson, A. and Wall, G. (1982) *Tourism: Economic, Physical and Social Impacts*, Longman, Harlow.
- Smith, V. L. and Eadington, W. R. (eds) (1995) *Tourism Alternatives: Potential Problems in the Development of Tourism*, University of Pennsylvania Press, Philadelphia, PA.

Bibliography

- Cohen, E. (1988) 'Authenticity and commoditization in tourism', *Annals of Tourism Research*, **15**, 371–86
- De Kadt, E. (ed.) (1979) *Tourism: Passport to Development?*, Oxford University Press, New York.

186

- Doxey, G. V. (1976) 'When enough's enough: the natives are restless in Old Niagara', *Heritage Canada*, **2**(2), 26–7.
- Inskeep, E. (1991) *Tourism Planning: an Integrated and Sustainable Development Approach*, Van Nostrand Reinhold, New York.
- Jafari, J. (1987) 'Tourism models: the sociocultural aspects', *Tourism Management*, **8**(2), 151–9.
- Mathieson, A. and Wall, G. (1982) *Tourism: Economic, Physical and Social Impacts*, Longman, Harlow.
- Murphy, P. E. (1985) *Tourism: A Community Approach*, Methuen, New York.
- Plogg, S. C. (1977) 'Why destination areas rise and fall in popularity', in *Domestic and International Tourism*, Kelly, E. M. (ed.), Institute of Certified Travel Agents, Wellesley, MA.
- Smith, V. L. (1989) *Hosts and Guests: The Anthropology of Tourism*, 2nd edn, University of Pennsylvania Press, Philadelphia, PA.
- Stymeist, D. H. (1996) 'Transformation of Vilavilairevo in Tourism', *Annals of Tourism Research*, **23**(1).

Chapter Nine

Carrying capacity

Introduction

In this chapter we examine the central concept of carrying capacity and the complex issues surrounding its determination. The various notions of carrying capacity are explored together with their implications for tourism development and tourism development planning. The notion of carrying capacity is founded upon each of the economic, environmental and socio-cultural impacts discussed in the previous chapters. Therefore, this chapter builds upon that knowledge and develops the links between measurement, impacts and carrying capacity.

Chapter learning objectives

By the end of the chapter, readers should:

- understand the centrality of the concept of carrying capacity in relation to the identification and measurement of all impacts of tourism;
- appreciate the different types of carrying capacity and the problems associated with quantifying levels of use that do not exceed carrying capacity; and
- comprehend the factors that will influence carrying capacity.

Carrying capacity

The fact that tourism activity has an impact on the social, cultural, environmental and economic aspects of a destination brings with it certain implications. To begin with, if it is assumed that these impacts are positively correlated with the volume of tourist arrivals, it may be realistic to assume that there are certain thresholds beyond which additional tourists will not be tolerated or accepted. Exceeding these thresholds is likely to affect every facet of tourism development. For instance, exceeding

- physical thresholds will limit the volume of tourist flows and expose tourists to safety hazards;
- environmental thresholds will also limit the tourist flows by creating secondary problems, such as health hazards, or detract from the attractiveness of a destination;

- social and cultural thresholds will generate resentment and antagonism towards tourists from the host population;
- tourist flow thresholds will affect the satisfaction levels of tourists and cause them to search elsewhere for a better product;
- economic thresholds will result in misallocation of resources and factors of production.

These threshold limits should not be confused with the notion of carrying capacity; they are best seen as 'saturation limits'. The difference between the two concepts lies in the fact that the former is embedded in the notion of sustainability whereas the latter refers to situations where the growth of tourism is no longer sustainable and will decline or change.

Scientists from a wide range of specialist fields have attempted, with varying degrees of success, to provide a working definition of carrying capacity. For instance, ecologists might define carrying capacity as 'the population of an identified species which can be supported throughout the foreseeable future, within a defined habitat, without causing permanent damage to the ecosystem upon which it is ultimately dependent'. If this type of definition is transferred to the human species some modifications must be made unless it is applied to the planet as a whole. That is, the territorial boundaries are not unique or limiting in terms of the ability of the species' population to survive. What happens within one territorial boundary may well influence the long-term viability of the species in others.

With respect to tourism, one approach is to adopt Hardin's (1991) formulation of human impact and simply transfer it to tourism such as that set out below:

tourism's impact = tourist population × tourist impact, per capita

However, this is not sufficient and such a definition fails to reflect the variety of influences relating to the nature of the tourist activity, the vulnerability of the destination, technological change and so on.

Carrying capacity, for the purpose of this book, can be defined as 'the maximum number of people who can use a site without an unacceptable alteration in the physical environment and without an unacceptable decline in the quality of experience gained by visitors' (Mathieson and Wall, 1982).

Note that the term 'tourist presence' is used as opposed to the more simple notion of tourist numbers. This is because it is necessary, when attempting to identify the levels of carrying capacity, to weight the absolute numbers of tourist arrivals to take account of a number of factors:

- The average length of stay.
- The characteristics of the tourists and hosts.
- The geographical concentration of tourists.
- The degree of seasonality.
- The types of tourism activity.
- The accessibility of specific sites.
- The level of infrastructure use and its spare capacity.
- The extent of spare capacity amongst the various productive sectors of the economy.

Case Study 9.1 Carrying capacity for ecotourism in Hawaii

In the Ecotourism Policy Recommendations for Hawaii, carrying capacity was used to refer to the limits beyond which a resource is over-used. While acknowledging the difficulties associated with finding objective quantitative measurements to determine the capacities, the report chose to define carrying capacity qualitatively, using the following illustrations:

- **Ecological/biophysical carrying capacity**, which relates to the natural environment, is 'the level of visitation beyond which unacceptable ecological impacts will occur, whether from the tourists or the amenities they require'.

  [The report goes on to suggest that capacity is attained when the number of visitors and characteristics of visitor use start to affect the wildlife and degrade the ecosystem. Examples of this capacity being reached are cited as the disruption of mating habits and soil erosion, whereas we would argue that such disruption and erosion are indicators that the capacity has been exceeded.]

- **Socio-cultural carrying capacity**, which relates primarily to the impact on the host population and its culture, 'refers to the maximum use of any site without causing negative effects on the resources, or exerting adverse impact upon society, economy and culture of the area'.

  [Here the report refers to the subjective nature of socio-cultural impacts and how difficult it is to provide objective measures for emotions, feelings and attitudes of both tourists and hosts.]

- **Aesthetic/facility carrying capacity**, which relates to the visitor experience, is 'the level beyond which visitor satisfaction drops unacceptably from overcrowding.'

  [This refers to the fact that tourist satisfaction rates can fall quite markedly if too many visitors are present, or if the overcrowding and over-commercialisation become intolerable to the tourist.]

Source: Ecotourism Opportunities for Hawaii's Visitor Industry, School of Travel Industry Management (TIM), University of Hawaii, Manoa.

Case Study 9.1 clearly shows that there are difficulties involved in taking the definitions used in Hawaii and making them into operational targets. They are qualitative and, as such, do not lend themselves easily to measurement. More, importantly, the word capacity seems to have been used to define the point when damage is occurring. For damage to occur then the true capacity level has been exceeded. Finally, another aspect rarely touched upon in the literature is the fact that different tourists interact with each other in different ways. For example, destinations in the Caribbean, such as St Lucia, draw their tourists from a variety of countries, but the majority come from the US market and a significant number come from European countries. The problem here is the fact that the Caribbean is a relatively inexpensive destination for the American market which is close by, whereas it is a relatively expensive destination for the European market, because of the high cost of transport involved in the package. This means that European tourists are more likely to be of a higher socio-economic grouping than their American counterparts. This problematic mix can shorten the tourist satisfaction ratings quite significantly, suggesting that, from the tourists' point of view, carrying capacity may be as much influenced by the mix of tourists as by the volume of tourists.

When attempting to determine or identify carrying capacity, it is essential that tourism presence is measured in some unambiguous manner. One possibility is to discuss carrying capacity in terms of *tourism units* where a tourism unit is a standardised concept based upon tourist numbers weighted by some composite factor derived from the above influencing elements. In this way each destination is likely to have different carrying capacity levels. However, the derivation of some standardised unit is difficult. For example, there are problems to be encountered if the number of day visitors is to be incorporated into the overall tourist numbers. This is because day visitors tend to be associated with different levels of impacts per hour per tourist from those of their staying counterparts. The shorter the stay of tourists the more pressing will be the sense of time budgeting and the higher will be the level of expenditure per unit of time.

Another issue that is raised concerns the term 'acceptable' which is used continually in terms of carrying capacity definitions. The question is to whom should a change be acceptable or unacceptable? If, as in the case of social impacts, the host population is the body that should consider the acceptability of developments, how is this reflected in policies? In a perfectly democratic political system then we could argue that the residents would be able to register their views on proposed developments. However, such perfect democracy may be hard to find? Furthermore, much tourism development is driven by the private sector who may take a much narrower perspective of the issues surrounding development.

The issue becomes even more complex with respect to any environmental carrying capacity. Who should consider and vote on the acceptability or otherwise of a project that brings environmental impacts? The environment itself may signify changes and species of flora and fauna may suffer from development but they do not have a vote! How will environmental acceptability be considered and voiced within the planning framework?

The above issues relate to all aspects of carrying capacity, perhaps with the exception of the acceptability of developments to tourists. Visitor satisfaction surveys are frequently undertaken by many destinations to monitor acceptability. Furthermore, if the carrying capacity in this respect is exceeded, tourists will vote with their cheque books and go elsewhere.

In spite of the problems involved in converting this theoretical definition of carrying capacity into an operational tool, it does fit in well with modern development strategies that increasingly incorporate attempts to impose some constraint on the ultimate level of development to prevent damaging impacts on the environment and society or to avoid the risk of over-dependence.

The dynamics of carrying capacity

The literature on carrying capacity, rather like the literature on tourism development planning, gives the impression that it is in some way static or absolute. The very word capacity makes one think of a specific level like filling the seats on a boat or an aircraft. Nothing could be further from the truth! Carrying capacity is an extremely fluid and dynamic concept. As with many human traits, exposure to stimuli brings with it acceptability. Socio-cultural tolerance levels change over time with gradual exposure to tourists. If, for example, a small island destination goes from 100 to 1 000 000 tourists in the space of a year it is likely that the socio-cultural, economic and environmental impacts will be devastating. Take the same destination and increase the volume of tourists by the same amount over a 50-year period and the discernible impact is likely to be far less. People become accustomed to change – it does not make the change any less but it does make it more acceptable. Economies too are better at adjusting to structural change, which takes place over a long time period, rather than dealing with rapid changes. Sufficient time will allow for the necessary linkages and support services to be brought into place and, in consequence, allow the destination to optimise its benefits from tourism. Even the environment, or at least the local population's concern for it, may be better able to cope if change comes slowly.

In effect the carrying capacity of today will not be the carrying capacity of tomorrow! In the 1950s few of the top tourist destinations in the world could have imagined the volume of tourists that they are playing host to today. This dynamic characteristic of carrying capacity, together with the difficulty in finding a universally acceptable definition has resulted in some bodies, such as the United States National Park Service, choosing to adopt an alternative terminology, that of 'Limits of Acceptable Change' (LAC), as their planning indicator.

Therefore, carrying capacity is a dynamic concept in the sense that the threshold levels that determine carrying capacity are likely to grow over time, providing that the development of tourism is sound. Unplanned rapid development could easily result in low tolerance levels and carrying capacities of much lower values.

Other factors influencing carrying capacity

In addition to the characteristics of the tourists and their hosts, there are a number of other factors that will influence the carrying capacity of a destination. It has already been noted that the speed of change is an important factor. The difference between the tourists and hosts is also an important consideration. It is not the absolute characteristics of either population group that is important, but the relative difference. This is one reason why domestic tourism is often, but not always, more acceptable than international tourism in terms of the socio-cultural impacts.

If the demographic profiles of tourists are similar to those of the host population, particularly in relation to age distribution, socio-economic grouping and religion, then the socio-cultural impact of increasing tourist numbers is likely to be relatively low. On the other hand, major differences in any of these factors can result in significant socio-cultural impacts even though the number of tourists in both scenarios is the same.

The fact that there are four broad groups of capacity indicators, economic, environmental, socio-cultural and tourist satisfaction levels gives rise to some difficulty in establishing exactly what the carrying capacity of a specific destination may be. It is likely that, for any given destination, the carrying capacity will be reached in just one of these areas before it is reached in the rest. Thus, a destination may find that tourism activity brings pressure to, say, the local ecosystem before it creates any significant threats to the social structure, the culture or the economy. This means that, regardless of the threshold limits in these latter areas, the carrying capacity for this destination is dictated by the vulnerability of the ecosystem. In order to move away from the qualitative to the quantitative approach for determining carrying capacity it is necessary to delineate the different areas of study (outlined overleaf) and examine the processes by which carrying capacity is determined and how it may change over time.

The process of determining carrying capacity

Figure 9.1 outlines the process by which carrying capacity is influenced and can be measured. The diagram shows the broad groups of factors that determine carrying capacity along with the different stages that can influence the magnitude and direction of the impacts and hence the carrying capacity. The different areas of the flow diagram are set out as follows.

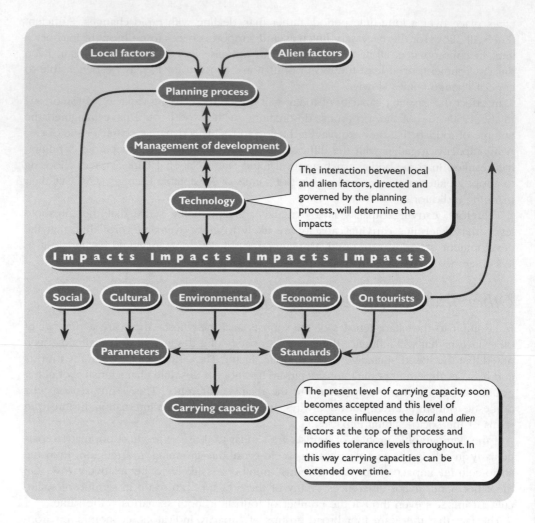

Local factors

There are many local factors that will influence the magnitude and direction of impacts but what is important, besides the nature of the local factors, is the relative difference between the local factors and the tourist counterparts and the speed of change. Looking at individual factors we can see how complex the issues are.

Social structure

The social structure of the destination is vital in determining the scale and nature of any impacts. For example, taking two extreme views, the social structures of London, New York and Sydney are more able to absorb and tolerate the presence of tourists than cities such as Apia in Western Samoa or Port Louis in Mauritius. The former can tolerate the presence of tourists without incurring any significant changes to their social structures because those changes have already occurred. They are larger in population and cosmopolitan in structure, making them more adaptable to change. The latter have relatively small populations, the extended family system is still largely intact (particularly in Apia) and they are not as cosmopolitan in structure. Therefore, some societies can accept large-volume tourism with little obvious effect while others cannot. In general, the smaller the local population, the more dramatic will be the social impact of tourism, particularly if that tourism is based upon large-volume tourist flows.

Cultural heritage

The cultural heritage of a destination is very important when attempting to determine the impact and carrying capacity. The more unusual the cultural background, the more attractive a destination may become to potential tourists. Ironically, the more unusual the cultural background, the more likely it is to be adversely affected by the presence of tourists. The end result is either the destruction of the cultural heritage or, more probably, the distortion of the local culture through staged authenticity, over-commercialisation of cultural features and traditions, such as dances and costumes, religious ceremonies, arts and crafts. The destination soon becomes in danger of becoming a caricature of itself!

Environment

The environment *will* be changed by the presence of tourists no matter how sympathetic they may be or how careful the tourism activity is planned. The environment can be either artificial or natural. In general the former is more resilient to tourism impacts than the latter. Environmental change is inevitable and will be more obvious and pronounced in those areas that are sparsely populated and not subject to frequent high-volume tourist visits. The more fragile and unique an environment, the more vulnerable it is to change from the presence of humans. It is important to remember that the environment is also changed by many factors, not just tourism, and it is often difficult to isolate those effects created by tourists from those created by other factors.

Economic structure

The economic structure will determine the benefits and costs associated with tourism activity. In general, the more developed and industrialised the economy, the more robust and adaptable it will be. As economies grow and diversify, so too do the skills of the workforce. This, together with a more refined capital system, allows such economies to respond and adapt to the changes brought by tourism. These countries will be able to secure the greatest benefits from tourism activity while incurring the minimum costs. In contrast, economies that are not sophisticated may find that rapid developments in tourism can distort the allocation of resources quite drastically and set up importation habits that may be difficult to break in the future.

Tourism development, particularly rapid development, tends to be resort-based and this may bring with it the economic problems associated with:

● migration from rural to urban areas; and

● the transfer of labour from traditional industries to tourism and its related industries.

Economies have to be mature to be able to adjust to these pressures.

Political structure

The political structure can affect the impacts of tourism and its carrying capacity in a number of ways. To begin with, political instability will deter tourists and therefore hinder tourism development. Some groups of tourists are more sensitive to political instability than others but few tourists are unaffected by the prospect of political instability. The political structure may also have direct influences upon tourism development if, in reflecting the ideals and beliefs of the population, it is decided that tourism development should be constrained or even discouraged. Some countries limit tourism development by restricting the number of visas issued within any given year (Bhutan, for example), whereas others may increase the costs of obtaining visas or make the acquisition of visas difficult, thereby restricting them to only the most determined. The political openness may well reflect the willingness of society to welcome tourism development and this may either raise or lower the carrying capacity thresholds.

Resources

The availability of local resources (labour, capital, land, etc.) is likely to have a major influence on the acceptability and desirability of tourism development, and even on the form that development takes. Where resources are scarce, competition for them will be high and the opportunity cost of using these resources for tourism will also be high. The local infrastructure is also part of the resource base. If tourism development means that the local infrastructure will be over-utilised then this will create a capacity constraint (at least in the short term) that may well become operative before any of the other carrying capacity constraints are approached. If the infrastructure is over-utilised because of tourism development then this may well breed resentment and hostility among the local population and then the social impact of tourism will create a carrying capacity constraint.

On a more positive note, tourism development may well result in an improved infrastructure, which will also be available to hosts as well as tourists and this may increase the carrying capacity level by enhancing the lives of the local community.

Alien factors

Tourist characteristics

Clearly, the characteristics of the tourists who visit any given destination are an important factor in determining the social and cultural impact of tourism on the host community. For instance, tourists who belong to the mass or charter groups are more likely to have a greater social and cultural impact than those who belong to the explorer, adventurer and ethnic tourist categories. The former tends to demand Western amenities and bring their culture with them without adapting to the local norms and customs. The latter tend to be far more sympathetic towards local customs and traditions and actively seek them out as part of their vacation experience. This, however, is not always the case. The important factor is the relative difference between tourists and hosts. The greater the difference between the host's and the tourist's social and cultural backgrounds, the greater the impact and consequent change. Tourist characteristics also include visitor expenditure patterns, mode of transport, structure and size of party, age, educational background, income and purpose of visit. All of these factors will influence the nature and magnitude of the impacts on the host community.

Carrying capacity is centred around tolerance levels:

- How tolerant the ecological system is to tourist intrusion and activity, as well as those activities created as a result of tourism activity.
- How tolerant the socio-cultural structure is to the introduction of foreign cultures, ideal and beliefs.
- How much tolerance there is within the economic structure.

However, carrying capacity is also about the tolerance levels of the tourists. A destination that is considered to be over-crowded by the tourists will have exceeded its carrying capacity and, in consequence, will find its tourist arrivals diminishing or the composition of tourists changing. The tolerance level of tourists introduces a further complication into

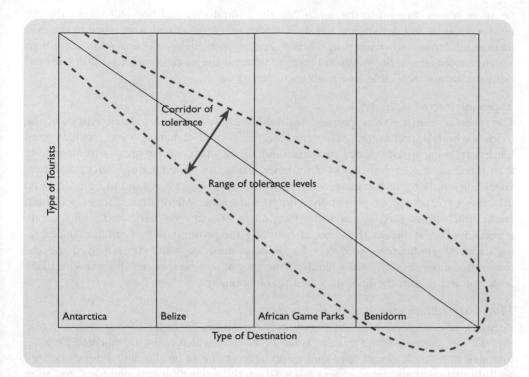

Figure 9.2: The relationships among tourists, destinations and tolerance level

the issue of determining carrying capacity. Different categories of tourists will display different levels of tolerance with respect to deviations from their expected experience.

Figure 9.2 demonstrates how tolerance levels associated with different types of tourists and within different types of resorts may change. The figure represents two planes. The horizontal plane depicts the nature and characteristics of the destination with a range moving from the fragile and vulnerable, such as Antarctica, through the vulnerable but less fragile areas, such as the Galapagos Islands, to the more organised and controlled but nevertheless vulnerable game parks, such as those found in Kenya, right through to the full blown totally dedicated destinations such as Hawaii and Benidorm in Spain.

The vertical plane represents the type of tourist and ranges from the explorer to the mass tourist as you move down the plane. The diagonal line running from the top left-hand corner through to the bottom right-hand corner demonstrates the 'fit' between tourist and destination. Thus, starting in the top right-hand corner we find that the explorer will seek out the fragile but exclusive destinations such as Antarctica. At the bottom left-hand corner, reading across the horizontal plane and down the vertical plane we find that the mass tourist will seek out the no-surprise destinations such as Benidorm. The range along the line, between these two polar extremes also shows the 'fit' between the characteristics of the tourist and the destination. The dotted lines that run alongside the central diagonal line represent the tolerance levels. By this we mean that each type of tourist will be associated with an average given level of tolerance with respect to how close a destination may match her or his expectations. Thus, the explorer may generally be regarded as being fairly intolerant of significant deviations from her or his expectations. If the destination does not live up to expectations he or she will quickly seek alternative destinations. At the other extreme, the mass tourist is generally more tolerant of deviations from the expected. Thus, the corridor of tolerance increases in size as we move away from the top left-hand corner. The tolerance levels of destinations can also be seen in this diagram in the sense that the central diagonal line still shows the 'fit' between tourist and destination, but the corridor of tolerance may also relate to the destination's tolerance to changes in tourism. Fragile destinations are unable to cope with significant changes in the volume of tourism whereas the more commercial purpose-built destinations are more able to absorb such deviations.

Types of tourist activity

The types of tourist activity pursued will be closely linked to the characteristics of the tourists who take part in them. However, the presence of certain activities, such as gambling, can bring specific social problems and stresses that are far greater in magnitude than those associated with the same number of tourists undertaking different activities. Gambling can bring with it increased risks to the host community (and to other tourists) in terms of exposure to prostitution, drugs and crime. All of these factors will help create much lower carrying capacities than might normally be associated with tourism. It need not be just the emotive cases of gambling and prostitution that can limit the carrying capacity. Destinations with very fragile ecosystems or with, say, rare bird species, may suffer more severely at the hands of the special interest groups who would actively seek out and disturb the habitats, albeit unintentionally.

Planning management and technology

Planning is concerned with the organisation of factors in order to manipulate future events. The management of tourism is the process by which plans are put into practice. Changes in technology will have direct and indirect effects on the difficulties associated with the planning and management tasks. Given the interaction between local and alien factors within the host environment, the planning and management process should aim to secure the maximum positive benefits (as dictated by the planning objectives) while incurring the minimum costs. Figure 9.1 shows that the planning, management and technology factors act as a funnel between the 'raw' interaction of the local and alien factors and the impact that this interaction has on the destination. The more successful the planning and management, the less will be the impacts and the greater will be the carrying capacity. The dynamic nature of this process is such that suitable developments combined with appropriate visitor flow management will 'naturally' select the required tourist market segments, while allowing the local factors the amount of time and space needed to adapt to the alien factors. The end result is a destination that can enjoy both growth and sustainability (growth + sustainability = development).

Impacts

The local and alien factors, manipulated by planning and the management of tourism development, will result in impacts on the social structure, culture, environment and economy, and upon other tourists. Impacts are the yardsticks of carrying capacity, but they are derived variables. The task to the planner and tourism management specialists is to ensure that the appropriate impacts occur.

Parameters

The impacts that occur reflect the nature and magnitude of change brought about by the interaction between tourists and hosts, given the management and planning that has been implemented. The parameters can be identified as the changes that take place to the local and alien factors as a result of different levels and types of interaction. They are *factual* in the sense that they are devoid of value judgements and simply relate tourist host interaction and tourist presence to changes in the social, cultural, environmental and economic factors.

Standards

The standards may be seen as acceptable limits applied to the parameters. They refer to the value judgements imposed by the host and tourist populations with respect to how much a variable may change without incurring irreversible or undesirable damage to the nature of tourism and the environment in which it takes place.

Carrying capacity

Carrying capacity is the dependent variable. It is not possible to over-emphasise the word variable because it is not a fixed value based on tourist presence. The dynamic nature of carrying capacity is based upon the changing tolerance levels of each of the determining factors as a result of both exposure and management.

The feedback over time, between carrying capacity and the local and alien factors, will be responsible for increasing/decreasing the magnitude of acceptable tourist presence. The carrying capacity will also feed back into the planning and management stages in order to inform and enhance the processes of visitor and destination management.

If the carrying capacity is exceeded, with respect to any of the impact areas, the tourism development process will be hindered and the development may be considered unsustainable. The damage created by exceeding the carrying capacity may be related to any of the impact areas or in terms of tourist satisfaction, but the end result will be the same. Either the destination will experience diminishing numbers as its tourism industry declines – tourists pursuing alternative destinations – or the mix of tourist arrivals may change, making it increasingly difficult for the destination to achieve its declared planning objectives.

The vulnerability of different destinations to tourist presence will be a major factor in setting the acceptable standards to be maintained during the management process. To illustrate this point the plight of World Heritage Sites can be examined. The very nature of World Heritage Sites means that they are not only finite but also irreplaceable and the successful management of such sites is vital. The World Heritage Convention requires that the international community cooperates to ensure that measures taken to protect and conserve these sites are effective. The management of these sites is almost always translated into access control. The management of Keoladeo National Park in India relies upon the access provided by the restricted number of trained guides or by bicycles and specified trails set out for the tourists. In other areas more arbitrary, but still restrictive, limits are set such as the 11 800 visitors per annum allowed to view the resident gorilla families. Alternative strategies can also be used, such as the spacing of tourist visits, or restrictions based on a specific aspect of a destination in order to manage its overall tourism development.

Measurement criteria

Carrying capacity is subject to multiple determination and as such, each of the separate components must be investigated. Tables 9.1 and 9.2 are provided to give some guidance to the variables that may be measured, the thresholds that may be encountered and the effects of over-exploitation.

Finally, the only practical way forward not only to determine a destination's carrying capacity but also to use this information to inform and guide the planning process, is to develop integrated impact-modelling tools. One such tool is shown as Case Study 9.2 and demonstrates the use of fully integrated impact software. This model was developed by

Table 9.1:
Variables and
thresholds

Impact on	Variable	Threshold(s)
Economic		
Investment	Investment by sector	Availability of funds
Labour	Employment by sector	Labour shortages/training
Dependency	Contribution to GNP	Economic control/imports
Price inflation	Inflation/tourist spend	Social costs/distribution
Income	Growth and distribution	Wage inflation/imports
Physical		
Access	Cost/ease/volume	Supply bottlenecks/hazards
Accommodation	Number/size/quality	Limits/overcrowding
Land	Proportion of land usage	Land price inflation
Transportation	Availability/cost	Limits/congestion/accidents
Infrastructure	Investment/quality	Limit of funds/health risks
Attractions	Number/size/type	Availability of land
Environmental		
Changes to environment	Species, populations	Extinction, declining pop.
Hazards	Fires, erosion, pollution	Increase in problem cases
Viability of wildlife	Urban encroachment	Land usage/species count
Socio-cultural		
Migration	Population movement	Income distribution/housing
Living standards	Consumption patterns	Inflation levels
Social values	Crime, drugs, health	Social disruption
Traditions	Attitudes towards tourism	Pseudo societies
Political		
Plans	Objectives met	Conflicts, miss targets
Resources	Expenditure/revenue	Budgetary constraints
Cooperation	Joint ventures	Availability of funds

Table 9.2: The
effects of the
scale of
developments on
impacts and
carrying capacity

Effect on	Large-scale concentrated	Small-scale dispersed
Accommodation		
Range of products	Greater diversity	Limited diversity
Price	Medium/expensive	Cheap/medium
Seasonality	Wider season	Vacation based – narrow
Ownership	Foreign	Local
Facilities		
Range	Greater diversity	Limited diversity
Finance	Support often required	Local funding
Usage	Overcrowding	Peak season demand
Sectoral support	High	Low
Transport		
Demand levels	Congestion during peaks	Limited availability
Supplier	Greater public supply	Reliance on private sector
Stimulating supply	Demands greater facilities	Little effect
Labour market		
Demand/Supply	High skills demand	Learning by doing
	Imported labour	Local labour
	Migration	Reliance on local labour force

Case Study 9.2 User Fiendly Inter-Active Planning Software – A Schematic Presentation

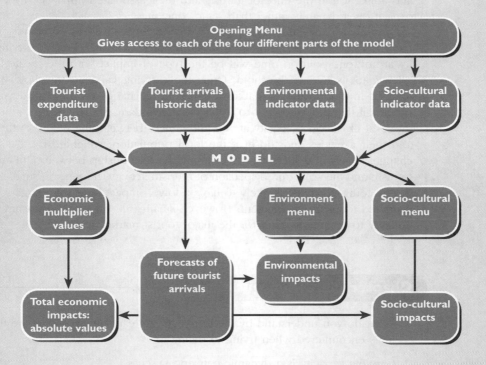

The above model encourages data collection with respect to planning variables. Once the empirical data are inputted they are subjected to the input-output methodology to obtain the economic and environmental direct, indirect and induced effects. The socio-cultural impacts are evaluated using ratios, e.g. host to guest ratios, penetration levels, etc. The results obtained from the model are generated in terms of multiplier values and absolute economic impact values (i.e. income, employment and import implications of a given level of tourist spending). The forecasts of arrivals are produced using an auto-regressive linear function. This type of model can be used to estimate the future likely impacts based upon current trends, or to test hypothetical changes to existing patterns of spending or arrivals.

staff at the International Centre for Tourism and Hospitality, Bournemouth University, and provides a valuable planning tool that demonstrates the interrelatedness between each of the types of impact while allowing these impacts to be examined from either forecasted future impacts or from those drawn as hypothetical case studies.

Conclusion

Carrying capacity can only be examined in a case-by-case situation because it is sensitive to location, the type of tourist activity, the difference in cultures between tourists and guests, the speed of tourism growth and the temporal ▷

> **Conclusion continued**
>
> dimension of development. Time is a great healer and it allows destinations to adapt and adjust to the presence of tourists and their associated impacts. Thus, carrying capacity is a dynamic rather than static concept.
>
> Carrying capacity thresholds may manifest themselves in economic, environmental, socio-cultural and political structures. The determination of carrying capacity at any one point in time will be the type of impact with the greatest change relative to its impact threshold. Once the carrying capacity threshold has been reached in one of these variables it will limit or change the tourism development process if that process is not to suffer long-term damage. The major influences on the level of carrying capacity are the differences between the nature of the tourists and their activities and those of the local population, weighted by the speed of change. Finally, it is important to examine the relationship between the impacts of tourism and the scale and dispersion of tourism activity. In general, small-scale dispersed tourism activity is likely to have a lower impact level than large-scale concentrated tourism development. However, small-scale dispersed tourism activity is unlikely to be able to cater for the major tourist market segments.

Chapter discussion questions

1. What do you understand by the term carrying capacity and what are the problems encountered when trying to define it?

2. Carrying capacity is a dynamic concept. Discuss.

3. What efforts can be made to extend the carrying capacity of a destination?

4. The carrying capacity of any given destination is influenced more by the speed of tourism development and the *relative* differences between tourists and hosts than it is by their *absolute* characteristics. Discuss.

Recommended further reading

- An Forbas Forbatha (1996) *Planning for Amenity and Tourism*, Bord Failte, Dublin.
- Butler, R. W. (1997) 'The concept of carrying capacity for tourism destinations', pp. 11–22 in *Tourism Development: Environmental and Community Issues*, Cooper, C. P. and Wanhill, S. R. C. (eds), Wiley, Chichester.
- Getz, D. (1983) 'Capacity to absorb tourism: concepts and implications for stategic planning', *Annals of Tourism Research*, **10**(2), 239–63.
- Johnson, P. and Thomas, B. (1994) 'The notion of capacity in tourism: a review of the issues', pp. 297–308 in *Progress in Tourism, Recreation and Hospitality Management*, Cooper, C. P. and Lockwood, A. (eds), Wiley, Chichester.

Bibliography

- Mathieson, A. and Wall, G. (1982) *Tourism: Economic, Physical and Social Impacts*, Longman, Harlow.

Chapter Ten

Tourism and development planning

Introduction

Any form of economic development requires careful planning if it is to be successful in achieving the implicit or explicit objectives that underlie the development. In this chapter we show that tourism development, because it is a multisector activity and because it brings with it the environmental, social and economic impacts discussed in Chapters 6–8, requires considerable planning if it is to be successful and sustainable. We also state that the development of tourism will not be optimal if it is left entirely in the hands of private sector entrepreneurs for they are primarily motivated by shorter-term *profit-and-loss* related objectives. But on the other hand, if tourism development is dominated by the public sector then it is unlikely to be developed at the optimal rate from the point of view of maximising economic benefits. We therefore point out in this chapter that tourism development planning requires careful cooperation and coordination of both the public and private sectors. We show that the emphasis of tourism development planning has moved away from the rigid 'grand design' **master plan** in favour of more flexible and reactive development plans. This change in approach is, in no small way, due to the recognition that development is not a finite concept. Development is infinite and takes place in an ever-changing environment. Therefore development plans should attempt to facilitate the desired objectives while taking into account the changing factors that influence not only the objectives but also the means of achieving them.

Chapter learning objectives

The objectives of this chapter are to ensure the reader:

- understands the importance of integrated tourism planning and development, development planning layers and the role of the community in this respect;
- is able to identify characteristics of the tourism product that have implications for tourism planning and development; and
- can outline the major steps involved in the tourism planning and development process.

Integrated planning and development

There are a variety of approaches that may be adopted when planning for the development of any industry or any economy. One can take a proactive stance and develop strategies to secure the desired development path. This approach requires deep and thorough understanding of not only the local economy and its structure, limitations and strengths, but also the probable effects of external factors, how they may impinge on the local development process and what form these external effects are likely to take. Alternatively, one can adopt the reactive stance of chaos theory. This approach is based upon the premise that there are too many variables, internally and externally, to be able to plan. These variables cannot be controlled nor can they be predicted with sufficient levels of accuracy. Therefore, it is better to develop reactive schemes in order to be in good order to meet the unexpected rather than to attempt a proactive but indeterminable development path. This latter approach has been likened to training policymakers on flight simulators so that their reactions develop in positive and enlightened ways. However, both proactive and reactive approaches can use such an analogy. Pilots are trained to fly to predetermined paths and schedules while, at the same time, they are trained to be able to react sensibly to unexpected events. The same may be said about tourism development planning. To rely purely on reactive policy solutions is to forsake the prospect of optimising tourism development.

A second issue that has given rise to much academic debate during the 1990s is the notion of sustainable development (see Chapters 5 and 21). Although much that has been said about sustainable development is sound from an academic viewpoint, it is neither innovative nor radical. The notion that we must look forward to future generations when we are planning to consume finite resources is commendable and such notions should also be transferred to all other production and consumption activities, not just tourism! Furthermore, the term *sustainable development* is a misnomer and has led to much confusion. Development has sometimes been confused with the concept of growth and it is *this* misunderstanding that has caused the increased volume of literature to be published proclaiming the call for sustainable development. In reality, development has to be sustainable to be classified as development at all, otherwise it is short-term growth. Most textbooks that attempt a definition of development include some statement about self-sustained growth. However, the allocation of finite resources to productive activities is not sustainable unless technological inventions and innovations can find alternative resources in the future. There is a danger in inhibiting specific forms of tourism activities in order to reduce the immediate impacts of tourism in the short term because such remedial actions may unleash far more devastating and less sustainable impacts in the future. Clearly, there is no simple answer to the sustainability debate. Only to state that development planning has *always* been concerned with sustainability issues and it is only 'bad' planning that has given so much impetus to these recent debates.

Tourism and development

If tourism is to be incorporated into a country's development plan it must be organised and developed according to a strategy constructed on sound foundations. These foundations should take account of the coordination of the tourism-related sectors, and the supply and demand for the tourism product. The process of development planning involves a wide cross-section of participants who may bring with them goals that are conflicting. Furthermore, different stakeholders may well bring with them incompatible perceptions about the industry and the development process itself. Before looking at the process of tourism development planning it is worth considering some of the advantages and disadvantages associated with selecting tourism as a catalyst for general development.

Tourism product characteristics

The tourism product is unique in terms of its range and diversity. Few products can compete with the wide variety of activities included under the tourism heading. Tourists can add to this uniqueness by bringing an extra dimension to the product. Furthermore, the tourism product must be consumed within the geographical boundaries of the destination. The producers of the tourism product, however, are not always confined to the local economy and may include foreign transport providers, tour operators, travel agents and information providers. As with any personal service, production and consumption occur simultaneously and, in the case of tourism, such production affects most other sectors (directly and indirectly) of the economy. As seen in Chapter 17, this simultaneity of production and consumption also creates specific social (and to some extent, environmental) impacts not normally associated with the production of other goods and services.

Tourism as a means of wealth redistribution

Tourism is widely recognised to be one of the fastest earners of foreign exchange and one of the most effective redistribution factors in international development. Although, in many respects, it has been disappointing as a vehicle to redress the global economic imbalance between North and South, it has provided a valuable source of foreign exchange to those smaller developing countries that find it difficult to compete in the tangible goods markets.

Domestic tourism is a very effective means of redistributing income between different areas within a national economy. This is because tourism tends to take place in the more sparsely populated scenic areas where there is little in the way of manufacturing industry. Therefore tourism provides the opportunity to create employment and income in areas with limited alternative sources. Thus, English residents head for Cornwall, the Peak District, Scotland and Wales for the domestic trips, the French leave Paris *en masse* in August and generally head south. The mass exodus of people out of the cities throughout Europe, the Americas and Australia during the main vacation periods is evidence of this domestic redistribution.

The literature on international tourism as a means of income redistribution is somewhat deceptive. Many of the articles written about tourism development tend to focus upon economically, environmentally and/or socially vulnerable destinations. This is because they provide a more visible stage on which to examine each of the consequences of tourism development. However, in reality, the vast bulk of international tourist movement takes place between industrialised countries. To support this viewpoint it can be noted that in 1996 international tourist arrivals to European countries came from other European countries and the Americas (84.7% and 6.8%, respectively). In terms of the North–South debate, tourists escape the industrialised countries to visit other industrialised countries and the South enjoys little in the way of a significant share of the wealth created by tourism. This is a fact that should be borne in mind when examining the global consequences of tourism development.

Tourism as a labour-intensive industry

Tourism, in common with most personal service industries, is labour-intensive. For developing countries with surplus labour and for industrialised countries with high levels of unemployment, tourism provides an effective means of generating employment opportunities. In general, at a time when the labour/capital ratio is moving strongly against labour in

Figure 10.1:
Typical hotel
employment
structure

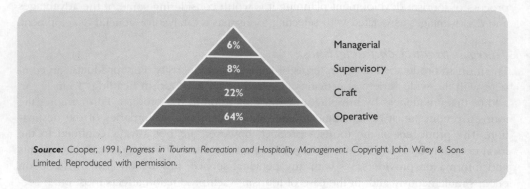

6%	Managerial
8%	Supervisory
22%	Craft
64%	Operative

Source: Cooper, 1991, *Progress in Tourism, Recreation and Hospitality Management.* Copyright John Wiley & Sons Limited. Reproduced with permission.

most production industries, the importance of the labour-absorbing qualities of tourism cannot be overlooked. However, in many countries there are labour shortages and it is not uncommon to find these countries importing labour to work in their tourism industries. Under such circumstances one might question whether these countries have a comparative advantage in tourism and whether or not their factors of production would be better employed in alternative industries.

Even in those situations where there is an abundance of labour it may be the case that there are other factors of production that suggest a development route other than through tourism. Where there are clear indications that the local destination would benefit from the employment created by tourism, this view should be tempered by the characteristics of the labour force generally associated with tourism-related establishments. The employment profile of large hotels, for example, tends to yield a relatively flat occupational pyramid such as that shown in Figure 10.1. This means that middle and senior management posts are relatively scarce compared with the high number of low-skill employees. Such an occupational pyramid results in a lack of career development and, consequently, a lack of staff motivation. A point also worthy of consideration is the predominance of females and young people employed in tourism-related establishments.

Attempts have been made to increase the height of the occupational pyramid by, for example, the introduction of departments and layers of middle management posts in luxury hotels. This, it was hoped, would provide a much-needed impetus to career prospects and motivation. However, recent experience suggests that there has been a reversal of this trend with 'de-layering' and the career development prospects in large hotels is not significantly different from that exhibited three decades ago. Thus, although tourism may provide a quick and ready means of increasing the number of employed people in the local economy, its contribution to long-term development may be questionable. To expand this argument further it is necessary to consider the secondary employment effects associated with tourism development and here one can find a much broader range of skill requirements and career development paths. Therefore, although the direct employment effects of tourism may be subject to some limiting characteristics, the indirect effects do not suffer in the same way.

Tourism and on-the-job training

The development of travel and hospitality skills in the local labour market is unlikely to make large demands on educational resources. The educational qualifications of those employed in the accommodation sector are heavily weighted in favour of those with only a rudimentary education. This is neither desirable from the point of view of the future of the industry nor in terms of the overall development of the destination. There is often an urgent need for training and education at all levels in both the private and

Level	Supplementary accommodation (%)	Activities (%)
University	1	3
Other higher education	4	5
Secondary		
Higher	30	45
Lower	34	40
No qualifications	31	7

Source: WTO (1980).

public sectors. However, industry often chooses to ignore this need and to enjoy the benefits of a cheap and plentiful labour market, and the public sector is often more concerned with the short-term goal of achieving employment opportunities rather than the development of a well-educated and qualified labour force. There is an unquestionable need for education and training in the tourism and hospitality industries and the reliance upon untrained labour with on-the-job training is responsible for many poor quality tourism products. These destinations fail to compete with high-quality tourism destinations that, in consequence, are able to charge higher prices and enjoy more buoyant demand for their products.

The poor quality and inadequate education and training related to the tourism and hospitality industries is an aspect that has been known for almost two decades, as Table 10.1 demonstrates. From a short-term growth point of view rather than as a development option, this educational profile has both positive and negative implications. On the positive side it means that the labour force for tourism growth can be mobilised relatively quickly. The training can be undertaken on the job, which means that units of labour can be brought in quickly from either the unemployed or, as is often the case in developing countries, from agriculture and fishing industries. On the negative side, the lack of educational qualifications found in tourism-related businesses means that the growth of tourism does not necessarily result in a more educated labour force – one of the factors perceived to be an important ingredient in the economic development process.

The structure of the tourism industry

One of the more notable features of the tourism industry is the proportion of SMEs. The nature of tourism as a personal service industry tends to make it attractive to single and family entrepreneurs. The proliferation of small businesses brings with it advantages and disadvantages. In the first instance it facilitates quick start-ups and flexible supply sources that can respond to fluctuations in demand. It is also an industry that, from the outside, does not appear technically daunting and thus encourages budding entrepreneurs to enter the industry. There are few barriers to entry, room for product differentiation and it can require little in the way of capital. However, these advantages can also be the source of the industry's worst problems in terms of:

- inadequate staff training;
- too high a debt/equity ratio leading to business failure; and
- inefficiency problems because of a failure to capitalise on economies of large-scale production.

Although the vast majority of business establishments in tourism may be considered to be SMEs, most of the output of the industry is attributable to the larger national and multinational corporations. Nevertheless there is certainly scope for a wide range of business structures within tourism from bed and breakfast units through to international hotel chains, from independent sightseeing flight operators to national airline giants. Each type of business has its own operating characteristics with a tendency for the smaller firms to be more labour-intensive and dependent upon local suppliers; to the larger companies that make extensive use of capital and bulk purchase from a global warehouse.

Protectionism

The simultaneity of production and consumption of tourism means that the tourists must travel to the destination to enjoy the product. This makes tourism unique as an export industry. The consumers of international tourism (the importing country) often fail to recognise their tourist spending overseas as an import and hence do not see it as a serious threat to the level of employment in their own countries. Thus, tourism tends to escape the danger of being singled out for protectionism or trade retaliation, except as part of a general macro-economic policy which restricts foreign exchange allowances to correct balance of payment problems. Having said that, it is often the existence of foreign exchange restrictions in many of the developing regions of the world that explains the relatively slow rates of growth in interregional tourism (as, for example, in South East Asia). Similarly, when countries are faced with currency crises (such as the UK in the 1960s and 1970s and currency crises in Malaysia in the 1990s) the government of the day imposes restrictions on the amount of currency that outbound tourists can convert.

Multitude of industries

Tourism is a composite industry product. That is, it is composed of the output of the travel, accommodation and food and beverage, retail, entertainment sectors plus many others. This means that its economic and development impacts are felt quite widely from the initial impact onwards. It also tends to suggest that tourism has strong linkages with many other sectors of the economy and it is the strength of these linkages that determine the value of the output, income and employment multipliers associated with tourist expenditure.

The variety of industries included under the umbrella of tourism means that there are a variety of employment opportunities generated by tourism activity. This may stimulate the labour market and the delivery of vocational training.

Price flexibility

Many developing countries are dependent upon the world market prices for primary agriculture produce for their foreign exchange receipts. That is, the prices of, say, cocoa, sugar, rice, etc., are determined in world commodity markets and are not within the control of the individual producing country. Tourism provides a source of foreign exchange that is subject to some degree of control by the host country. However, tourism is also highly price competitive.

Price competitive

The bulk of the tourism market, which is resort tourism, is extremely price sensitive and, consequently, internationally competitive. The effects of currency fluctuations on the number of international arrivals and the volume of tourist expenditure adequately demonstrate this fact. Although most mass tourism destinations claim a high degree of product differentiation, a brief examination of the major tour operators' brochures selling sun, sand and sea products will show that the major battleground is fought not on hotels, the quality of beaches or the sea, but the price of the package. Price competition is a fundamental feature of the budget tourism market for both destinations and operators.

The greater product differentiation that is either innate or can be engineered, the greater the monopolistic power and hence the greater freedom a destination has in setting its own price. Product differentiation can be based on natural factors ranging from broad aspects such as climate (Florida, Bermuda and Iceland as examples) to specific natural attractions (such as Victoria Falls, Great Barrier Reef and Grand Canyon). Differentiation can also be achieved through socio-cultural aspects, heritage and even in terms of the quality of the tourism product itself. Basically, it does not matter what aspect is used to differentiate the product providing there is sufficient demand for it.

Seasonality

A striking feature of tourism in many countries is the way in which the level of activity fluctuates throughout the year. This is not a characteristic unique to tourism – agriculture is also an industry used to seasonal fluctuations in activity – but the majority of industries are not subject to the degree of seasonality experienced by tourism establishments.

The seasonality of tourism is reflected in:

- employment (casual/seasonal staff);
- investment (low annual returns on capital);
- pricing policies (discounted off-season prices).

From an economics point of view, any business subject to seasonal fluctuations in demand for its output is faced with a dilemma. If it purchases sufficient resources to meet the peak load demand, then it will have to carry spare productive capacity for the remainder of the year. If it gauges its resources according to the average level of demand it will spend part of the year carrying spare capacity and be unable to meet the peak load demand level. Alternatively, it can take on variable resources (staff) to meet the peak load demand and then shed these variable factors of resources during the off-season. Although attractive from the point of view of the profit and loss account, this widely practised solution does nothing to improve employer/employee relations. Also there is an inherent waste in taking on staff each year on a temporary basis, investing in human resources (by training) and then losing that investment at the end of the main season.

In order to offset some of the costs associated with seasonality many hotels and operators offer holidays for off-season periods with heavily discounted prices. By offering lower prices it is possible to induce visitors to a destination at a time when they would otherwise not visit. However, there are limits to such discounting. First, the revenue that establishments receive during the off-season must *at least* cover the variable costs of production. If this is the case then, by opening in the off-season, they will be able to maintain their staff and, perhaps make some contribution to their fixed costs. Secondly, the discounting of off-season packages should not be so great as to damage the desirability of the main season product.

There are also destinations that do not suffer from seasonal variations and this provides them with a competitive advantage by allowing them to operate at a higher throughput of tourist activity across the year without suffering from as much socio-cultural and environmental impacts as their seasonal competitors.

Figure 10.2:
Fixed cost effects

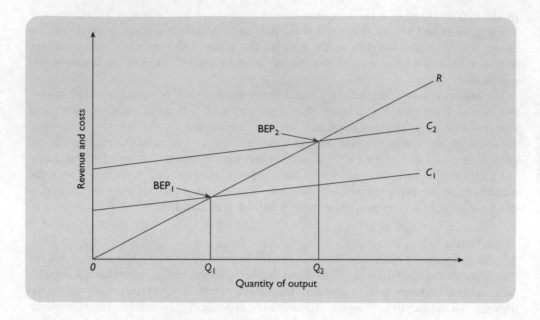

High operating leverage/fixed costs

Many of the tourism-related industries are subject to high levels of fixed costs. That is, there is a large capital element that must be committed before any output is produced. In industries subject to this type of cost structure (e.g. airlines and hotels) the volume of sales becomes the all-important factor. This aspect is shown in Figure 10.2, where the vertical axis measures revenue and costs, and the horizontal axis depicts the quantity of output produced during the time period under consideration. The break-even output for the non-tourism industry is represented by Q1 whereas Q2 shows the break-even output for the tourism industry. The cost curve C_1 relates to the cost function of a non-tourism industry and C_2 relates to the cost function of a typical tourism-related industry. We can see that both industries are subject to the same variable-cost structures (that is why the two cost functions run parallel to each other) but the tourism-related industry is subject to a higher fixed-cost element. The end result is that the break-even point for the tourism-related industry (BEP_2) is much higher than that for the non-tourism industry, thus the volume of output becomes all important for high fixed-cost industries. The break-even point refers to that level of revenue and output that will just cover the costs involved in producing the output.

The pre-occupation with volume displayed by industries that have high operating leverages can also influence the mind set of the national tourist organisations. Many tourist destinations base their tourism development plans on volume figures. Countries the world over tend to celebrate the fact that visitor numbers exceed some *magical* annual threshold and many countries still express the targets/objectives of their development plans in terms of bed spaces and tourist nights. However, the presence of tourists in itself is not the main objective of any of these destinations. The primary aims are economic and the indicators of performance and targets should be expressed in economic rather than volume figures and/or constrained by environmental or social indicator values.

Clearly, there is overwhelming evidence to support the view that there are a number of factors related to the tourism industry which make it an attractive development option. But some of these factors may make it less attractive if they are not controlled or alleviated by proper planning.

Development planning layers

Tourism development planning can take place at international, national and subnational levels.

International tourism planning

At the international level organisations such as the WTO, EU, OECD, Caribbean Tourism Organisation (CTO) and the Tourism Council for the South Pacific (TCSP) all undertake, albeit limited, forms of tourism planning. This level of planning is often weak in structure and lacks enforcement. It is generally provided in a guideline form in order to assist the member states.

National tourism planning

National tourism planning encapsulates the tourism development plans for a country as a whole but often includes specific objectives for particular subnational regions or types of areas within the national boundary. The plans manifest themselves in a variety of forms including:

- tourism policy;
- marketing strategies;
- taxation structure;
- incentive/grant schemes;
- legislation (e.g. employment, investment, repatriation of profits);
- infrastructure developments;
- external and internal transport systems and organisations;
- education/training and manpower programmes.

Regional/local tourism planning

Regional and local tourism planning deals with specific issues that affect a subnational area. It tends to be much more detailed and specific than its national counterpart and can vary quite significantly from area to area. For instance, there may be areas where tourism development is to be encouraged and others where specific types of tourism activity are actively discouraged. Such plans may relate to a state within a country, to a county, a city or even a local resort area.

However, there are constraints on how different regional plans can be from other regional plans or from the national plan. Certainly they should not detract from the overall aims and objectives of the national plan or those of another region. Ideally, the subnational plans should work in harmony with the national plan as far as local conditions will allow.

Plans at all levels should include consideration of how information is transferred to the consumer – the tourist. It should also be borne in mind that what you *do not* tell the tourist is often as vital as what you *do!* This is particularly true from the point of view of visitor management when attempts are made to direct the tourists towards some specific regions but away from others. Such information can be disseminated through a variety of media including the Internet which is becoming increasingly important as a tool for tourism development and marketing. However, traditionally the following media have been used:

- visitor orientation centres;
- tourist information centres;
- advertising brochures, maps, magazine articles and broadcasting;
- self-guided tours and trails;
- official guides;
- posters and displays.

The above can all be seen as a means to visitor awareness and can be used to support more formal programmes run by tourism officials.

The tourism development planning process

The concept of planning is concerned with organising some future events in order to achieve prespecified objectives. Integrated planning and development is a form of comprehensive planning: comprehensive because it integrates all forms of planning – economic, physical, social and cultural. Planning is not a static concept, it attempts to deploy the best strategy in a world of changing internal and external influences. Although planning, as a dynamic concept, can take a variety of forms, there is a consistent structure that can be applied to the process of planning. That structure and its sequence is set out in Figure 10.3.

Study recognition and preparation

The study recognition and preparation are really concerned with the recognition by the planning authorities (normally the government), the private industry and the local community that tourism is a desirable development option, together with some awareness of the constraints within which it must develop. The fact that it is recognised that a strategy is required is an important indication that the government and people are aware of the complexity of the tourism industry and its need for coordination.

Setting of objectives or goals for the strategy

In order to design a development plan successfully it is necessary to have a clear understanding of the objectives that are to be achieved by the development of tourism. A common mistake in tourism development planning is to lose sight of the reasons why tourism has been selected as a development option. If it is the case that tourism is seen as the most appropriate vehicle for generating foreign exchange and employment opportunities, these goals should be embedded in the development plan from the start. This helps to avoid the problems encountered when the objectives are set down in terms of visitor numbers or annual guest nights.

Some major objectives, commonly found in tourism development plans, are set out below:

- To develop a tourism sector that, in all respects and at all levels, is of high quality, though not necessarily of high cost.
- To encourage the use of tourism for both cultural and economic exchange.
- To distribute the economic benefits of tourism, both direct and indirect, as widely and to as many of the host community as feasible.
- To preserve cultural and natural resources as part of tourism development and facilitate this through architectural and landscape design which reflect local traditions.
- To appeal to a broad cross-section of international (and domestic) tourists through policies and programmes of site and facility development.

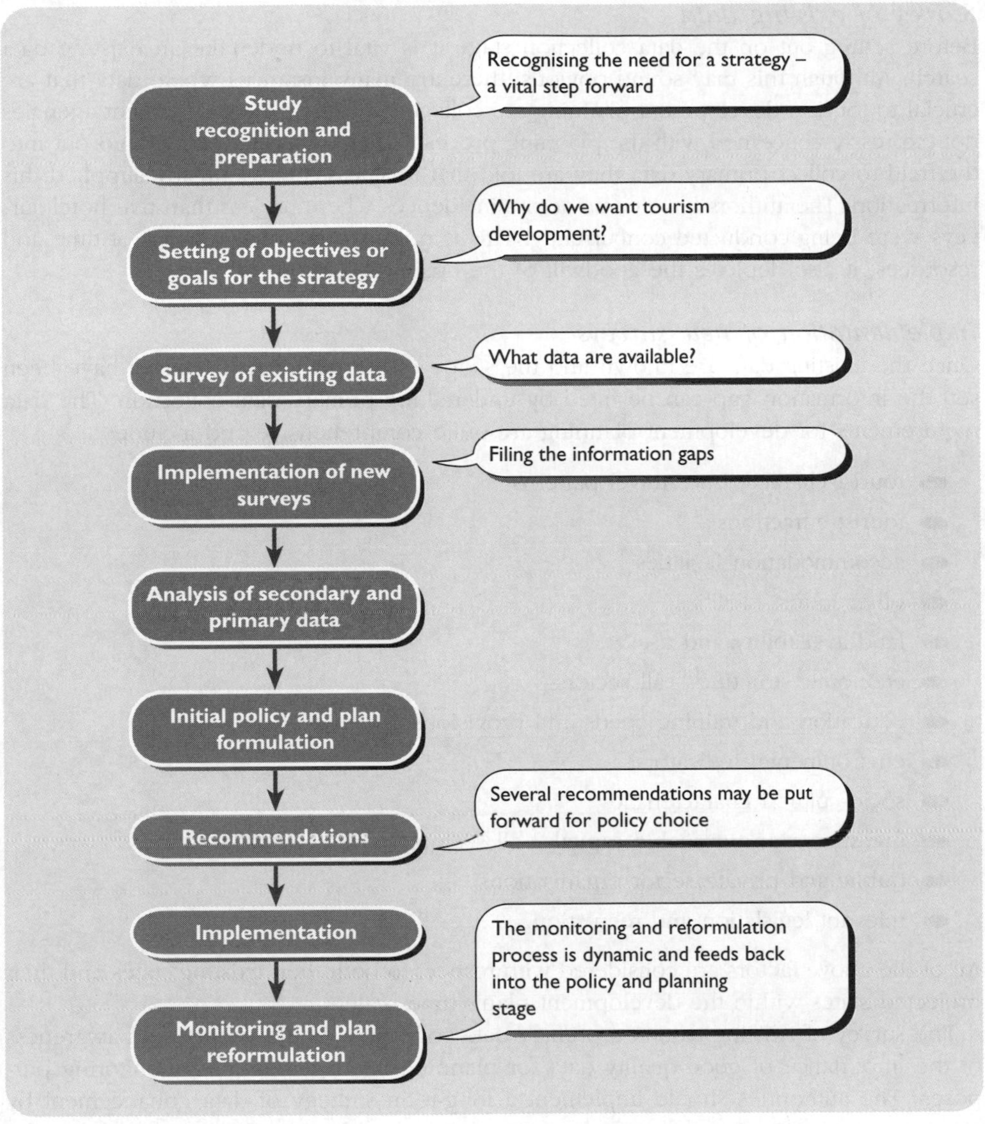

Figure 10.3:
The planning
process

Figure 10.3: The planning process

- **Study recognition and preparation** — Recognising the need for a strategy – a vital step forward
- **Setting of objectives or goals for the strategy** — Why do we want tourism development?
- **Survey of existing data** — What data are available?
- **Implementation of new surveys** — Filing the information gaps
- **Analysis of secondary and primary data**
- **Initial policy and plan formulation**
- **Recommendations** — Several recommendations may be put forward for policy choice
- **Implementation**
- **Monitoring and plan reformulation** — The monitoring and reformulation process is dynamic and feeds back into the policy and planning stage

- To maximise foreign exchange earnings to ensure a sound balance of payments.
- Attract high-spending 'up-market' tourists.
- Increase employment opportunities.
- Aid peripheral regions by raising incomes and employment, thus slowing down or halting emigration.

It is important that the objectives set out in the development plan are *clear, unambiguous, non-conflicting* and *achievable*. We can see from the above list of objectives that these examples are not specific in nature, thus it would be difficult to assess whether or not the objective had indeed been achieved. Also, some of the objectives may be conflicting, particularly those relating to the type of tourist to be attracted and the desired impact. Where the objectives are vague and/or conflicting, the tourism development plan is doomed to failure.

Survey of existing data

Before setting out on the data collection stage it is vital to undertake an existing data search. Although this may sound obvious, there are many instances where data that are crucial to tourism development planning are collected and held by government agencies not expressly concerned with the planning process. Thus, when researchers go out into the field to collect primary data they are told that businesses have already supplied this information. The authors have come across incidences where no less than five hotel surveys were being conducted concurrently! This is not only wasteful in terms of time and resources, it also depletes the goodwill of the business community.

Implementation of new surveys

Once the existing data are known and the scope of the planning objectives have been set, the information gap can be filled by undertaking primary data collection. The data requirements for development planning are quite comprehensive and include:

- tourist characteristics/travel patterns;
- tourist attractions;
- accommodation facilities;
- other tourist facilities;
- land availability and use;
- economic structure – all sectors;
- education and training needs and provisions;
- environmental indicators;
- socio-cultural characteristics;
- investment and available capital – all sectors;
- public and private sector organisations;
- relevant legislation and regulation.

All of the above factors are considered with respect to both their existing states and their projected states within the development plan's time scale.

The survey of existing data and primary data collection should generate an awareness of the importance of good-quality data for planning, management and monitoring purposes. The authorities should implement a long-term strategy of data enhancement by setting up a management information system that is flexible enough to accommodate the collection of new data when it becomes available and to encompass issues not necessarily identified within the current strategy.

Analyses

Once the objectives have been formulated, the analytical framework chosen will determine the precise sets of data to be collected. Once collected the data are analysed by considering a wide range of issues. The major issues to be considered generally fall into four subject areas:

1. **Asset evaluation**. This area of analysis examines the existing and potential stock of assets, the ways in which they can be developed and the probable constraints on that development. The asset evaluation should also include an appraisal of the infrastructure in order to determine whether or not further investment is required. The asset evaluation should begin with a broad approach looking at assets across

a wide range of sectors and their alternative uses. The evaluation could then be focused to concentrate on the tourism-related assets and how they should be best employed within that framework.

2. **Market analysis**. The market analysis is clearly a crucial component of a sound development plan. The market analysis undertaken during tourism development planning is sometimes too narrow in scope to be of optimum use. Initial issues that need to be addressed concern global, regional and country market trends by type of tourism activity. Another fundamental question is 'Why do tourists come to this destination?' Too many development plans of the past have relied upon the assumption of constant market share and this is not a valid assumption. To appraise the development plans, attempts must be made to determine whether or not the proposed developments are appropriate, the markets that are likely to be attracted by these developments and the price level or tariff structure that should be adopted. The market analysis must also incorporate a study of developments in competitive markets and/or in competitive modes of transport. Generally these issues will be tackled within a competitive and comparative advantage study that incorporates a SWOT analysis.

3. **Development planning**. A major issue to be studied under this heading is the time phasing of the development plan in order to ensure successful implementation. The possible sources of funding of the development are examined and the appropriate level of foreign funding (if any) is calculated. The analysis section encompasses all issues, such as the number of foreign employees, the marketing strategy to be adopted, investment incentives, organisational structures and training programmes.

4. **Impact analyses**. The impact analyses should be all-embracing, covering issues such as the probable effects that the development will have on the host community and the environment, the economic implications in terms of key indicators (employment, income, government revenue and foreign exchange flows) and the probable economic rates of return. Analyses should also examine the risks involved and the sensitivity of the results to changing assumptions. The integration of economic, environmental and socio-cultural impact analyses is a vital advancement to tourism planning tools which took place in the closing years of the twentieth century. The incorporation of a forecasting model, so that future economic, environmental and social impacts can be assessed, is equally crucial. Tourism researchers are constantly striving to develop enhanced planning tools for use in tourism development and models, such as those developed within the International Centre for Tourism and Hospitality Research, Bournemouth University, will play a major part in providing the framework for future tourism planning exercises.

The analyses set out above are of both a quantitative and qualitative nature and most of these issues must be faced before a move can be made towards formulating policy recommendations.

Policy and plan formulation

The results from the analyses of the survey data are unlikely to yield a unique solution and, instead, will tend to suggest a number of possibilities for development strategies. The process from here is one of formulating draft plans on the basis of each policy option derived from the analyses. The alternative plans are then evaluated in terms of their potential economic, physical and socio-cultural costs and benefits, together with any possible problem areas that may result from the implementation of each plan. The plans that achieve the most objectives while not exposing the destination to potentially serious problems are then selected and drawn up in full. Finally, a 'preferred' plan is drafted for policy consideration.

Recommendations

The preferred plan that has been selected on the basis of the analyses, having now been completed in detail, is submitted to the authorities by the planning team. This submission is sent to the authorities, together with recommendations concerning the optimum methods of developing tourism in the destination and, in so doing, achieving the plan's objectives. It is more than likely that the planning team will present the authorities with a selection of recommendations that all fulfil the requirements of the preferred plan. It is at this stage that feedback between the authorities and the development plan team is essential in order to focus attention on issues where attention is needed and to play down areas where it is not. During the process of these discussions the final development plan is formulated. Therefore, the recommendations stage should really be regarded as a period of dialogue between the planning team and the policy makers.

Implementation of the plan

The methods of implementing the development plan will have been considered throughout most stages of its construction. Thus, during the secondary data survey stage attention will have been paid to many aspects that relate to implementation – such as the existing legislative and regulatory frameworks. By the time that the implementation stage is reached, all of the necessary legislation and regulation controls will have been brought into effect. Furthermore, the methods used to facilitate public debate and discussions relating to the development will have been devised and enquiry and appeal mechanisms will be in place. During the implementation stage particular attention will need to be paid to the phasing of the plan and the critical path analyses will have highlighted areas that may be the cause of concern.

Monitoring and reformulation

Once the development plan has been implemented it must be closely monitored in order to detect any deviations that may occur from the projected path of development. Any such deviations, and there will probably be some, must be analysed in order to assess how they will affect the development plan and its objectives. Once this secondary analysis has been completed, the research team can report back to the authorities with recommendations as to how the plan and its policy recommendations should be modified in order to stay on target. External and internal factors may influence the performance of the strategy and it is important that the monitoring systems enable the research team to be fully informed about all relevant changes. Furthermore, even with the best-laid plans, unexpected events do occur and it is here that the re-active policy skills of the research team and policy makers come into play. For instance, there could be outbreaks of disease that are of international headline importance (the outbreak of the plague in India), terrorist activities (New York, London and Cairo) or political unrest (Sri Lanka) that cause the international flows of tourists to deviate from their expected path. Even positive developments in competing countries, such as the liberalisation of South Africa, can have unforeseen effects on other destinations. It is important that the research team is aware of how sensitive the strategy is to each of the conceivable variables and how best to react to such events. Even then the tourism plan is likely to face inconceivable events where the research team and policy makers will have to rely upon intuition!

The development plan team

The development plan team will need considerable expertise and experience in the formulation of such plans. In general, the team will consist of four groups of specialists, falling into the broad categories of technical services, marketing specialists, planners and economists. In more detail, the likely spread of specialist skills will include:

- market analysts;
- physical planners;
- economists;
- environmental scientists;
- infrastructure engineers;
- transport engineers;
- social scientists;
- draughtsmen and designers;
- legal experts.

The plan will be constructed over a period of time and this time can be broken down into five distinct phases.

1. **Identification and inventory of the existing situation**. This phase includes:
   (a) characteristics and structure of current consumer demand;
   (b) study of consumer choice;
   (c) current land use, land tenure and land-use control;
   (d) existing natural and artificial attractions;
   (e) ecosystem factors – particularly those considered to be vulnerable;
   (f) economic structures and the capacity thresholds of industries;
   (g) labour force skill mix and educational base, together with availability;
   (h) accommodation facilities;
   (i) tourist services facilities;
   (j) infrastructure facilities and their capacities;
   (k) transport facilities and their capacities;
   (l) graphic presentation of physical inventory.
   The above data will be used to establish the adequacy of existing structures and facilities, the classification and cost organisation of existing facilities (together with an index of standards currently achieved), and the economic impact of present tourism activity. This then leads on to the second phase.

2. **Forecasts for the future**. This phase will include forecasts of future demand and probable tourist movements and needs. This will be complemented by an analysis of the implications of these forecasts for future production levels of each relevant service and good, together with the infrastructural requirements. Anticipated standards of service will be examined and the economic forecasts of local repercussions will be estimated.

3. **Plan formulation**. The formulation of the plan will include proposed programmes of market organisation and promotion, comprehensive land use and control planning, detailed infrastructural plans and the economic, environmental and social evaluations associated with the proposed development plan. Again it is likely to include a graphic presentation of land use and infrastructure, together with a mapping of social impacts and the constraints imposed by the environmental considerations.

4. **Specific project development**. This phase will include an analysis of specific policies and projects for marketing, and tourism management. The physical planners and architects will draw up selections of alternative layouts relating to specific projects and alternative solutions to infrastructural development problems will be developed. Costs of the alternative projects and infrastructural schemes will be assessed, along with the economic analysis of the various possible investment projects. Once the specific projects have been selected from the various alternatives these will, again, be subject to graphic presentations. The local environmental issues will be assessed and methods of alleviating problems will be set out. Examples of environmental planning actions could be broadly based, such as the treatment of raw sewage and the maintenance of water quality, or highly specific, such as the planned periodic movements of footpaths to prevent serious erosion. Matters relating to visitor orientation programmes, visitor management and interpretation will all be considered and set out within this phase.

5. **Implementation**. The implementation programme will be set into motion with construction and supervision, technical and managerial assistance in tourism development projects, and financial analysis, and the recommended infrastructure investment programme will commence. The implementation stage will include the setting up of the continuing monitoring and re-evaluation activities to ensure that the strategy is performing optimally and so that adjustments can be made swiftly if the circumstances (internally or externally) change.

Tourism development planning: when it goes wrong!

A large number of tourism development plans are, to varying degrees, unsuccessful. Given the fact that such plans operate in an environment that is constantly changing because of forces acting outside the control of the authorities, often outside the geographical area of the destination, perhaps this is not surprising. However, many plans fail as a result of the development plans themselves. Discussions about this latter type of failure can be broken down into two categories: failure at the design stage and failure at the implementation stage.

Design stage plan failure

Many of the tourism development plans that fail do so because, at the design stage, they follow no more than the basic formulation of tourism development. Consider the basic tourism development plan in Figure 10.4. A plan of this structure will provide a general framework for state and municipal/local investments and will help to guide and evaluate the proposals of private developers. However, this type of plan structure lacks the analytical detail and scope necessary for a successful tourism development plan. Quite often this absence of analytical components is a reflection of the planning bodies who carry out the construction of the plan, bodies lacking in planning expertise and experience.

More importantly, the plan does not give a clear statement with respect to its objectives – objectives must be achievable, unambiguous and non-conflicting. The plan also fails to take into account the wider issues relating to environmental and social impacts because it is driven uniquely by its financial returns. One of the dangers of drawing up development plans in order to seek external funding is that the myopic view of financial profit and loss accounts may cause the planners to overlook some of the fundamental issues involved. This may well result in a plan that will fail financially as well as structurally.

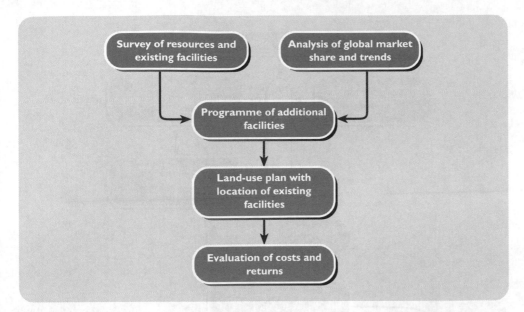

The development plan takes no consideration of the impact of tourism on the host community, the environment and the economy. The projects are only evaluated on a financial basis (profit and loss accounts) and take no account of social costs and benefits.

Too much emphasis is placed upon physical development, i.e. supply-led tourism development without proper consideration of returns to capital investments and effects on the market. The plan structure fails to make adequate market assessment. The global approach of examining tourist flows from the tourist-generating countries and projecting forward to future time periods under the assumption that all destinations will receive their fair share, fails to address the fundamental issue of *why people want to come to this particular destination*. Unless this issue is addressed future projections can be wildly off target.

Taking the above points into account, the basic development plan structure can be modified as in Figure 10.5.

Implementation stage plan failure

Problems encountered at the implementation stage are largely, but not exclusively, concerned with miscalculations regarding the use of land and the control of land usage. Tourism is, after all, an activity largely involved in real estate development. The type of land difficulties encountered during the implementation stage include the following:

● Those that actually undertake the development are sometimes more concerned with real estate speculation rather than the operation of tourist facilities. Thus, the motivation for development (particularly when incentives are on offer) may be more to do with capital gain than the tourism product. Such speculative development can lead to poorly designed facilities which are inefficient to operate, or facilities located in poor locations.

● Development often takes place on the basis of a high debt/equity ratio using land values as security for the loans. This may lead to financial failure when property sales and operating profits do not materialise.

● The planning authorities often under-estimate the difficulties that can be encountered when attempting to control the use of land. The only certain way of controlling land usage is by ownership.

Figure 10.5:
Modified basic
development plan

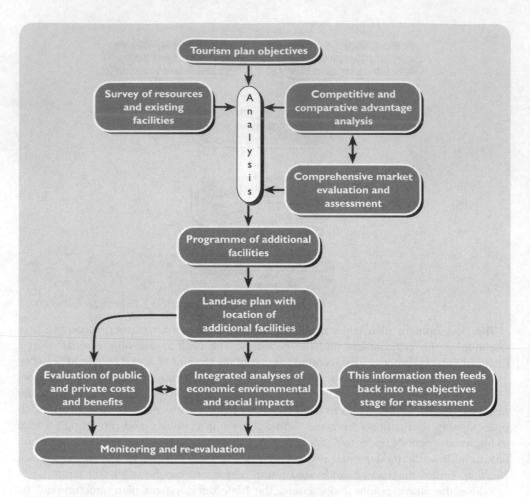

Failure to introduce the required planning legislation in time to implement the development plan or the lack of ability to enforce such legislation.

If the specific sites earmarked for development are 'leaked' prior to the implementation of the development plan, land speculation and price inflation may follow. This will alter the economic evaluations and may turn a viable project into a certain failure.

Other problems that may be encountered include the following:

Failure to coordinate intermediaries in the travel trade, private sector development and public sector provision. Such a lack of coordination can result in supply bottlenecks, affecting most aspects of the tourism product; damage the economic benefits associated with the tourism activity; adversely affect visitor satisfaction; and consequently cause the plan to miss its targets.

Poor communications and infrastructure.

Inadequate procedures to deal with public opposition and representations concerning the proposed development. A lack of such a mechanism can slow the development process down considerably and result in plan failure.

One of the most common scenarios from unsound tourism planning policies is over-exploitation – when the carrying capacity thresholds of a destination are exceeded. Such excesses tend to lead to a decline in the quality of the tourism product and, ultimately, to a decline in the 'quality' of tourists, i.e. tourists associated with greater undesirable impacts and lower spend. Under such circumstances the destination may find some or all of the following indicators:

- ecological imbalance through over-use of resources;
- outbreaks of diseases through infrastructural failure;
- congestion, queues and economic inefficiencies;
- deterioration of natural and artificial environment through over-use;
- resentment towards tourists;
- increases in criminal activities;
- destruction of host community's values.

Although some of the above problems can be alleviated, such as improving the infrastructure to reduce the health risks of water and sewage treatment failure, some of them cannot. The effects of over-exploitation can be minimised, however, by diverting pressures. For instance, ecological imbalances can be tackled by:

- appropriate visitor flow management;
- fencing-off areas subject to over-use;
- providing alternative routes and facilities for tourists to relieve others;
- dispersing tourists over wider or to different areas;
- zoning tourism-related activities;
- educating tourists and hosts to limit socio-cultural damage; and
- encouraging more positive local involvement in tourism activities.

One of the most well-tried techniques is that of access control – the volume or flow of tourists can be controlled economically through prices, or physically, through closures, limiting parking facilities, transport or issuing quotas.

There are, of course, dangers related to these remedial actions. For instance, dispersing tourists to other areas or to a wider area can sow the seeds for greater long-term problems if the source of the over-exploitation is not harnessed. Dispersing tourists temporally by extending the tourist season can reduce the time that some destinations need to recover from the industry's activities. Re-directing tourism flows may alleviate damaged areas in the short term, but only to replace them with newly damaged areas in the longer term. Zoning brings with it many limitations and problems, particularly in border areas. Therefore, when the remedial actions are implemented they should be seen as short-term alleviation methods until the true source of the problems can be tackled.

Finally the issue of quality should be embedded in all aspects of tourism development planning. The issue of quality is vital for successful tourism development and should manifest itself in the structure and nature of the plans, the educational institutions that train the management and labour force and the monitoring and evaluation of the tourism development process. There are destinations, such as Mauritius and some Indonesian resorts, that owe their competitive advantage to the 'quality' of their tourism product and use 'quality' as a means of product differentiation. However, when quality is the only factor leading to a competitive edge, then the development of the destination is vulnerable because quality is replicable by other destinations. This means that quality should be considered as a vital part of any tourism development strategy if the strategy is to achieve long-term success.

Conclusion

The successful development of tourism requires the construction of a development plan or strategy that is flexible and thorough. Flexibility is required in order to adjust and reformulate in response to internal and external changes. Thoroughness is required because of the complexity of the tourism industry and the economic, environmental and social consequences of its development. The issue of 'sustainability' is no more than sound planning because development requires that the path chosen is one that is in some way sustainable. Although the process of tourism development planning will be specific from destination to destination there are processes that need to be followed at national and subnational levels and these processes provide the framework for tourism development planning.

Finally, tourism development plan failure, when it occurs, is likely to be attributable to failures at either the design stage (inadequate planning structure) or the implementation stage. Both forms of failure are common but in many instances there are remedial actions that may be taken to alleviate some of the problems encountered by failure.

Chapter discussion questions

1. What are the major steps that need to be undertaken as part of the planning process?
2. Why do tourism development plans fail?
3. Is sustainable development a viable concept?
4. What are the characteristics of the tourism product that make planning such an important aspect of successful development?

Recommended further reading

● Gunn, C. (1994) *Tourism Planning*, Taylor and Francis, Philadelphia, PA.
● Inskeep, E. (1991) *Tourism Planning: An Integrated and Sustainable Development Approach*, Van Nostrand Reinhold, New York.
● Inskeep, E. and Kallenberger, M. (1992) *An Integrated Approach to Resort Development: Six Case Studies*, WTO, Madrid.
● Lawson, F. and Baud-Bovy, M. (1977) *Tourism and Recreation: A Handbook of Physical Planning*, CBI, Boston, MA.
● Pearce, D. (1989) *Tourism: A Community Approach* (2nd edn) Longman, Harlow.

Bibliography

● Ashworth, G. and Dietvorst, A. (1995) *Tourism and Spatial Transformations: Implications for Policy and Planning*, CAB, Oxford.
● Bodlender, J. and Gerty, M. (1992) *Guidelines on Tourism Investment*, WTO, Madrid.
● Bodlender, J. and Ward, T. (1982) *An Examination of Tourism Investment Incentives*, WTO, Madrid.

- Chopra, S. (1991) *Tourism and Development in India*, Ashish Publishers, New York.
- Cooper, C. (ed.) (1991) *Progress in Tourism, Recreation and Hospitality Management*, Belhaven, London.
- Cooper, C. and Wanhill, S. (1997) *Tourism Development: Environmental and Community Issues*, Wiley, New York.
- De Kadt, E. (1979) *Tourism, Passport to Development*, Oxford University Press, Oxford.
- Edgell, D. (1990) *International Tourism Policy*, Van Nostrand Reinhold, New York.
- Farrell, B. H. (1987) *Tourism and the Physical Environment*, Pergamon, Oxford.
- Getz, D. (1991) *Festivals, Special Events and Tourism*, Van Nostrand Reinhold, New York.
- Gunn, C. A. (1988) *Vacationscape, Designing Tourist Regions*, Van Nostrand Reinhold, New York.
- Gunn, C. (1994) *Tourism Planning*, Taylor and Francis, Washington, DC.
- Hall, C. M. (1992) *Hallmark Tourist Events, Impacts, Management, Planning*, Belhaven Press, London.
- Hall, C. M. (1994) *Tourism and Politics*, Wiley, New York.
- Hall, C. M. and Jenkins, J. M. (1994) *Tourism and Public Policy*, Routledge, London.
- Hawkins, D. E., Shafer, E. L. and Rovelstadt, J. M. (eds) (1980) *Tourism Planning and Development Issues*, George Washington University Press, Washington, DC.
- Inskeep, E. (1991) *Tourism Planning – An Integrated Planning and Development Approach*, Van Nostrand Reinhold, New York.
- Inskeep, E. (1993) *National and Regional Planning, Methodologies and Case Studies*, WTO/Routledge, Madrid/London.
- Inskeep, E. and Kallenberger, M. (1992) *An Integrated Approach to Resort Development*, WTO, Madrid.
- Jansen-Verbeke, M. (1998) *Leisure, Recreation and Tourism in Inner Cities*, Routledge, London.
- Johnson, P. and Thomas, B. (eds) (1992) *Perspectives on Tourism Policy*, Mansell, London.
- Kinniard, V. H. and Hall, D. R. (eds) (1994) *Tourism Development: The Gender Dimension*, Belhaven, London.
- Law, C. (1993) *Urban Tourism: Attracting Visitors to Large Cities*, Mansell, London.
- Laws, E. (1995) *Tourist Destination Management, Issues, Analysis and Policies*, Routledge, London.
- Lawson, F. (1995) *Hotels and Resorts: Planning, Design and Refurbishment*, Butterworth-Heinemann, Oxford.
- Lawson, F. R. and Baud-Bovy, M. (1989) *Tourism Recreation and Development – A Handbook of Physical Planning*, Longman, Harlow.
- Lickorish, L. J. (ed.) (1991) *Developing Tourism Destinations, Policies and Perspectives*, Longman, Harlow.
- Murphy, P. (1997) *Quality Management in Urban Tourism*, Wiley, New York.
- Page, S. (1994) *Urban Tourism*, Routledge, London.
- Pearce, D. (1989) *Tourist Development*, Longman, Harlow.
- Pearce, D. (1992) *Tourist Organisations*, Longman, Harlow.
- WTO (1980) *The Manila Declaration on World Tourism*, WTO, Madrid.

PART THREE

The tourism industry

Introduction

In Part 3, we turn our attention to the tourism industry and those governmental organisations that influence and support tourism demand and supply. We have adopted an analytical and evaluative approach to this section, identifying the main subsectors that, when combined, constitute the tourism industry. We have focused generally on providing insights into the operating characteristics, trends and issues that dominate the industry and, specifically, upon governmental organisations, intermediaries, transportation, attractions and accommodation. Although these do not represent an exhaustive range of enterprises in the tourism industry, they do illustrate the dominant characteristics of the industry and demonstrate key operational practices.

Leiper defined the tourism industry as 'the range of businesses and organisations involved in delivering the tourism product' and, in the light of his model of the tourism system (as discussed in detail in 'An introduction to tourism'), these businesses and organisations represent a key element. However, despite the unique nature of the tourism industry and the differing attributes of the individual sectors, there are common characteristics, trends and issues that are evident across the board:

● The low level of concentration in an industry where small businesses dominate despite the fact that a relatively few, large corporations have market prominence.

● The high ratio of fixed costs to variable costs which has considerable implications for financial stability and which dominates tactical and strategic operation.

● The high levels of customer contact, demanding staff to be highly trained in both operational aspects and customer care.

● The general lack of marketing and human resource management expertise remains a key constraint in all sectors of the tourism industry.

● The importance of location *vis-à-vis* access to markets.

● The perishable nature of the product for all sectors of the tourism industry demands investment in computer reservation and yield management systems.

● The lack of loyalty in consumer demand and in the distribution chain.

● The prevalence of seasonal and irrational demand patterns, involving enterprises in the use of promotional and pricing strategies.

● The belated adoption of environmental auditing and EIA techniques.

● The increasing degree of both vertical and horizontal integration throughout the industry.

● The fragmentation of the industry which, allied to its geographical dispersion, acts to discourage the formation of industry associations.

● The traditional outlook of service industries and, arguably, the so-called 'under management' of the tourism industry which means that the industry as a whole is vulnerable to ideas and takeovers from other industrial sectors.

● Conversely, the increasing professionalism of the industry.

These are issues and difficulties that dominate the tourism industry as a whole, irrespective of sector. Nevertheless, it is also possible to isolate the key sectors and attribute more detailed and precise characteristics to each; thus, we have divided this section into five chapters.

However, it is important that the reader understands the complex linkages and interrelationships that exist between the various individual sectors of the tourism industry and the mutual dependency of one sector on the next. To illustrate this, take a Mediterranean inclusive tour. The assembly of the tour, its distribution and the delivery of the product to the consumer involve just about every sector of the industry, but the relationships are revealing. The providers of accommodation to the tourist may well be operating on very tight costs owing to financial pressure from the tour operator, who is attempting to offer the tour at a low price to achieve a target load factor. Yet the travel agent that keeps the operator's brochure may be placing pressure on the operator for higher commission levels as the sales of that particular operator's products increase. In turn, the operator may have 'locked in' the agent to its own computer reservation system (CRS). All of this may contravene the relevant national tourism organisation's policy to position and market its country to up-market tourists in order to increase the financial yield per visitor. It is the objective of this section, therefore, to highlight these complex relationships and to explore the implications of these on tourism as a whole.

In Chapter 11, we concentrate on those government organisations that are crucial to tourism and discuss the role of governmental intervention in tourism. We consider the importance of public sector involvement in tourism and review its current, and changing, role: increasingly, the public sector is withdrawing from tourism and private sector organisations are being encouraged to step in. However, it is argued here that, while tourism must involve participation and funding by the private sector, there are many clear and powerful reasons why the public sector must remain involved:

● Many core tourist attractions – such as landscapes, culture and built heritage and architecture – are public goods and, to this end, public sector involvement is at worst desirable and at best, crucial.

● Many activities such as planning, research, resource allocation, management and regulation can be undertaken most effectively – and most impartially – by the public sector.

● The lack of expertise in the tourism industry in certain key areas (such as marketing), and the domination of small businesses with inadequate funds to promote themselves sufficiently, provides a compelling argument for continued involvement of the public sector.

We also use this chapter to demonstrate the global and local policy frameworks for tourism and to provide an overview of the likely administrative structure of a national tourist office (NTO). In addition, the impact of the public sector in respect of its demand and revenue management roles (marketing, promotion and information provision) and its supply and cost management roles (planning controls, building regulations, land-use decisions, market regulation, market research, and planning and investment incentives) are also considered in detail.

Chapter 12 introduces and reviews the role of intermediaries in the packaging and distribution of the tourism product. The distribution of the tourism product is unusual insofar as it is achieved, almost exclusively, by intermediaries, rendering the distribution channel extremely competitive and susceptible to fierce power struggles and damaging price wars. The structure of the distribution channel and the respective roles of intermediaries make the distribution of the tourism product very risky, particularly in light of the precarious economics of tour operation/wholesaling and the intense financial pressures that dominate their operation.

Chapter 13 concentrates on transportation for tourism and offers a thorough review of the issues which dominate this sector. Particular emphasis is placed on the changing competitive framework.

Chapter 14 focuses on the attractions segment of the tourism industry, incorporating natural and artificial attractions. Attractions are integral to the tourism product, often providing the primary motivation for tourist visits, yet they continue to receive a patchy and undisciplined coverage in the literature. We use this chapter to consider some of the possible visitor management techniques that may be implemented to address the adverse social, cultural and environmental impacts of tourism at both natural and artificial sites.

Chapter 15 is concerned with accommodation, perhaps the most visible and ubiquitous of all sectors of the tourism industry. The scope and size of the industry is explored and the relationship between this sub-sector and the complete tourism product is discussed. We also evaluate many of the key issues that are currently influencing the accommodation sector such as the potential of information technology, the new-found emphasis on environmental issues and the role and importance of quality and branding.

It is clear that, while the individual sectors of the tourism industry are interlinked and, to some extent, are mutually dependent upon each other, there is a potential for conflict within and between sectors. This may be attributed to the fact that each sector is working to its own agenda with a view to its own profit maximisation. One of the primary objectives of the public sector, therefore, is to temper over-ambitious individual providers and sectors and to provide a strategic approach to product development, distribution and marketing for the overall benefit of the destination. However, it may be argued that the intermediaries are perhaps the most powerful determinants of the ultimate success or failure of a destination in terms of revenue, market share and visitor numbers, since it is in the hands of the intermediaries that influence is exerted most directly on tourism demand.

In the next five chapters, we explore many of the key issues in respect of the above and provide the reader with a greater understanding and appreciation of the tourism industry, its core business and its operating practices.

Chapter Eleven

Government organisations

Introduction

Governments are involved with tourist organisations at both the international and national level. In the latter case they are normally the instigators for the establishment of a national tourist office, while in the former instance, they are partners along with other member states in such bodies as the WTO, the European Travel Commission (ETC), the Pacific Asia Travel Association (PATA) and so on. All these bodies can contribute to the formation of a country's tourism policy. In this chapter we look at the overall policy framework and consider the experience of different governments in order to illustrate the changes that occur in policy, noting the very many organisations that express an interest in tourism at the national level. As national tourist offices are commonly the executive agency for government policy, their administrative structure and functions are considered in some detail. The last part of the chapter examines intervention by the public sector in tourism. Particular consideration is given to the variety of instruments governments have at their disposal to manage the direction of tourism development in the interests of the host community.

Chapter learning objectives

The focus of this chapter is on the role of the public sector, in the shape of governmental organisations, in tourism. Specifically, upon completion, the reader will have:

- a knowledge of the key organisations globally with an interest in and influence upon tourism;
- an understanding of the key functions of NTOs and an insight into how such offices might be structured and how responsibilities are divided; and
- an overview of the role of the public sector and how governments may use their public sector organisations to manipulate demand for tourism and control supply of it.

Public policy framework

World-wide, the significance of tourism as a mechanism for economic development has meant that it is an investment opportunity that few governments can afford to ignore. Since the tourist industry does not control all those factors that make up the attractiveness of a destination and the impact on the host population can be considerable, it is necessary for the options concerning the development of tourism to be considered at the highest level of government and the appropriate public administrative framework put in place. As a rule the greater the importance of tourism to a country's economy the greater is the involvement of the public sector, to the point of having a government ministry with sole responsibility for tourism.

Beyond this, governments are involved in supporting a variety of multinational agencies. The official flag carrier for international tourism is the WTO: it is an operative rather than a deliberative body whose functions include helping members to maximise the benefits from tourism, identifying markets, assisting in tourism planning as an executing agency of the United Nations Development Programme (UNDP), providing statistical information, advising on the harmonisation of policies and practices, sponsoring education and training, and identifying funding sources. Elsewhere there are a number of other international bodies whose activities impinge upon tourism: these include the World Bank, the United Nations, the International Air Transport Association (IATA), the International Civil Aviation Organization (ICAO) and the OECD.

At a lower level, there are a variety of regional bodies such as the Organization of American States (OAS), PATA and the ETC (Case Study 11.1). Most of their efforts are devoted to promotion and marketing, though they do provide technical assistance. Funds for developing the tourist infrastructure in low-income countries may be obtained from regional development banks such as the Asian Development Bank in Manila, the European Bank for Reconstruction and Development in London (for Eastern Europe), or the Caribbean Development Bank in Barbados.

Looking at the structure in Europe, officially, tourism in the EU comes under Directorate General XXIII but the regional development work of Directorate General XVI also involves tourism projects as a means of overcoming regional disparities. With the adoption

Case Study 11.1 The European Travel Commission (ETC)

The European Travel Commission was established as a non-profit making body by the national tourist offices of European states in 1948; it has 21 member countries. The objectives of the Commission are:

- to foster international tourism cooperation in Europe;
- to exchange information on tourism development projects and marketing techniques;
- to undertake/commission appropriate travel research;
- to promote tourism in and to Europe, particularly from North America and Japan.

The work of the ETC is supported by the European Commission which sees tourism as an industry of great economic and social significance within the European Union, particularly for the peripheral and somewhat poorer regions of Europe which are inclined to be located on the boundaries of the Union. Although a wide variety of regional disparities exist across the EU, from early on it was realised that there is a distinct tendency for the poorest regions to be situated on the outer areas of the Union and for the most prosperous regions, with the benefit of market access, to be centrally located.

of the Single European Act (1987), there is a commitment by the EU to promote economic and social cohesion through actions to reduce regional disparities, and the Maastricht Treaty (1992) acknowledged, for the first time, the role of tourism in these actions. The resources for mitigating regional differences are drawn from the structural funds, which are made up of contributions from member states with the express purposes of: helping regions lagging behind, particularly rural areas; assisting the economic conversion of regions facing industrial decline; combating long-term unemployment; and dealing with the very special problems of some of the sparsely populated Nordic regions. Alongside public monies, commercial funding of tourism projects is obtainable from the European Investment Bank.

The direct role of the EU in tourism is seen as one of simplification, harmonisation and the easing of restrictions on trade. Specifically, strategy is developed around the following objectives:

- improving the quality of European tourism services;
- stimulating the demand for European tourism outside common borders;
- improving the business environment in which tourist enterprises operate; and
- to move forward tourism developments in a sustainable manner, in order to guarantee that the activity continues on a regular basis.

It is important that, in developing its strategy for tourism, the European Commission does not duplicate the work of other organisations. Ultimately, the differing nature of the tourist product within Europe leaves the Commission with little option but to assign the primary role of tourism policy to member states and proceed with tourism projects only in close partnership with national and regional bodies. The principle applied is that of subsidiarity, which argues for decisions to be made at the lowest level of authority so as to best meet local needs. Tourism policy is therefore, to a large degree, the responsibility of member states but the provision of research and statistics, facilitation in terms of easing frontier formalities and improvements to transport infrastructure, together with general image promotion in association with the ETC, appear to be the most favoured policies for the Commission.

All European countries have NTOs: some are part of government as in France or Spain, or in the Eastern Europe where the state apparatus has emerged in a new form, while others are established independently of government but are supported by central grants and other income generating activities, as in the UK (Case Study 11.2 and Figure 11.1). The case for public sector involvement in tourism rests on concepts of market failure, namely that those who argue for the market mechanism as the sole arbiter in the allocation of resources for tourism are ignoring the lessons of history and are grossly oversimplifying the complex and varied nature of the product. In an EU context, research among member states has indicated a number of sources of market failure that the respective governments are seeking to address:

- Developing tourism as a common good that collectively benefits many businesses, with the NTO acting as a broker between suppliers and potential visitors.
- Infant industry development as part of regional policy (including peripheral areas), where commercial viability requires public sector support through the provision of essential infrastructure and financial incentives.
- Improving the tourism product, via the implementation of measures such as training programmes for tourism workers.

Case Study 11.2 Structure of the tourist boards in Britain

With the exception of the Northern Ireland Tourist Board (NITB) which was established by statute in 1948, the promotion of tourism to and within the country was left in private hands until the passing of the Development of Tourism Act in 1969. This Act, which is the substantive legislation that still applies today, was in three parts:

- establishment of the British Tourist Authority (BTA), English Tourist (ETB), Scottish Tourist Board (STB) and Wales Tourist Board (WTB), and their powers; this part also included an assistance scheme (known as Section 4) for particular tourist projects;
- provision of a hotel development grants scheme (which was wound up in 1973);
- enabling legislation for the compulsory registration of accommodation.

The NITB was not covered by the Act since it was already established and responsible to the then Northern Ireland Parliament at Stormont. Many years on, the outcome of the Act for Britain is the structure shown in Figure 11.1, whereby the BTA and ETB report to the Department for Culture, Media and Sport (DCMS) and other boards to their respective offices of state. As the BTA has the major responsibility of marketing in Britain, links are maintained between the BTA and all other boards and their respective reporting authorities.

The vast scope of the tourist industry means that the statutory tourist board framework in the UK can only be regarded as the core of public sector involvement in tourism. The Departments of Trade and Industry, Transport, Environment, Education and Science, Health and Social Security, together with the Ministry of Agriculture, Fisheries and Food, and the Home Office all undertake activities that can impinge upon tourism. These may vary from road construction, management of historic sites and the development of water-based recreation on reservoirs and canals, through to urban cultural provision, tourism education, alcohol licensing and the provision of holidays for the socially disadvantaged. Furthermore, besides the departments of state, appointed government agencies and the local authorities who have the planning powers to implement tourism programmes on the ground, there is a whole host of national non-governmental organisations that have an interest in tourism.

Figure 11.1:
Statutory tourist board framework in Britain

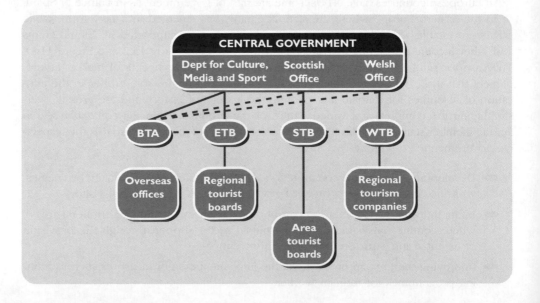

Case Study 11.3 The United States Travel and Tourism Administration (USTTA)

The rationale for government intervention in tourism is the concept of market failure, but this in itself is subject to political convictions as to the economic efficiency of the market for allocating resources, which may vary according to changes in the political power structure. Thus in early 1996, the US Government closed down USTTA, which had been set up in 1981 under the National Tourism Policy Act, and withdrew from representation at the WTO. Up until then, USTTA was supported by the Federal Government, although a major responsibility for tourism marketing and development still rested with the individual states. All NTOs normally have a statutory obligation to promote tourism in favour of the private tourist industry in the home country and in this respect USTTA was required:

- to stimulate travel to the US;
- to cooperate with local, state and foreign governments;
- to reduce barriers to travel;
- to encourage package tours, visitor services and the easing of travel formalities;
- to ensure coordination within the Department of Commerce;
- to collect and exchange tourism statistics;
- to represent the USA at the WTO.

Revising the federal role in 1996, the US Congress made it clear that the government would in future rely on private industry to market the United States as a destination, a function that previously was given to USTTA. In place of USTTA, a Tourism Industries office has been established within the Department of Commerce with the twin objectives of increasing the number of exporters by providing research and technical assistance to communities and businesses interested in tapping international markets, and coordinating tourism-related activities and policies within government itself.

By way of contrast, the US Congress took a much more market-orientated stance and closed down the United States Travel and Tourism Administration (USTTA) in 1996, some 15 years after its establishment (Case Study 11.3). Nevertheless, much of the tourist product in the USA is under federal control through the Department of the Interior, whose responsibilities include:

- preserving national scenic and historic areas;
- conserving, developing and utilising fish and wildlife resources;
- coordinating federal and state recreation programmes; and
- operating job corps conservation youth camps.

The Forest Service of the Department of Agriculture also takes an active role in promoting and sustaining the nation's landscape.

The US experience of changes in direction of tourism policy is not uncommon in other countries. In Britain, the 1969 Act was instigated by the recognition of tourism as an important earner of foreign exchange after the devaluation of 1967. Over the years since the Act's inception, the economic policy emphasis for tourism has shifted back and forth to the extent that there is little doubt that the frequent alterations in direction have been more of a handicap than a benefit to the development of public sector tourist organisations in Britain. There have been continual changes in tourism ministers followed by one tourism review after another, though all falling short of repealing the Act, but rather confining themselves to using funding as a means to curtail or expand the activities of the national boards. In 1985 the Trade and Industry Committee of the House of Commons summed up the Government's tourism policy thus:

> *The truth is that the Government cannot quite decide what its own role is. Along with general policy on industry, the present Government does not want to interfere with the development of the tourism industry in the private sector. Indeed, we were told that 'the Government see their own main role in relation to tourism as promoting a general economic climate favourable to the industry's development'. Given that the Government cannot control the most important climatic factor in this context – the weather – more specific strategies are needed. The Government minimises the appearance of involvement by reducing policy aims to statements of the obvious but maintains the fact of involvement in the tourist boards and the grants provided through them. The trouble is that this actual financial commitment is then left without there being any clear specific strategy to guide its use.*

On the question of financial commitment, the WTO has long used the rule that the minimum of 1% of a country's tourist receipts should be devoted to the NTO, but in Britain this has never been the case.

For political reasons there is always the temptation for governments to switch policy directions. This gives the impression of the dynamics of change, but can, in practice, generate chaos through conflicting objectives. It takes a long time to create tourist destinations and build up market positions. It is, therefore, rather simplistic to behave as if the factors influencing such developments can be turned on and off as with a tap. One of the principal difficulties is that tourism is a diverse and fragmented industry with many different economic agents acting in their own interests (often on the basis of imperfect information) which may not be to the long-term benefit of tourism as a whole. Uncoordinated market competition can, in these circumstances, produce cyclical growth patterns, with a consequent waste of resources. This places a premium on an overall planning body such as an NTO which is able to give a sense of direction by marketing the destination and acting as a distribution channel by drawing the attention of potential tourists and the travel trade to the products that the numerous suppliers in a country have to offer.

Administrative framework

There are considerable variations in the structure of public administration of tourism, which in turn depend on the size of the tourist industry and the importance the government attaches to the various reasons advanced for public sector involvement in tourism. A list of some of the most common arguments put forward for government participation is shown in Box 11.1. In most cases where tourism is a significant element of economic activity, so that a good deal of weight is allocated to the reasons presented in Box 11.1, it is common practice to have a Ministry of Tourism. This is particularly true of island economies, which often form some of the world's most attractive tourist destinations. The position of the NTO within this framework may be inside or outside the ministry. In the latter case, the NTO becomes a government agency or semi-governmental body. It usually has a separate constitution, enacted by law, and a board of directors appointed from outside government which, in theory, gives independence from the political system. However, the link is maintained through the NTO being the executive arm

Box 11.1 Reasons for government involvement in tourism

- Foreign exchange earnings and their importance for the balance of payments.
- Employment creation and the need to provide education and training.
- Large and fragmented industry requiring careful coordination of development and marketing.
- Maximise the net benefits to the host community.
- Spread the benefits and costs equitably.
- Building the image of the country as a tourist destination.
- Market regulation to protect consumers and prevent unfair competition.
- Provision of public goods and infrastructure as part of the tourist product.
- Protect tourism resources and the environment.
- Regulate aspects of social behaviour, for example, gambling.
- Monitor the level of tourism activity through statistical surveys.

of government policy as agreed by the ministry and public money providing the major source of funds for most NTOs. The reality is that few governments can resist giving specific policy directions for developments which are likely to influence election results in marginal areas.

Some NTOs, normally termed Convention and Visitor Bureau's (CVBs), are simply private associations whose constitution is determined by their membership, which may include government representation. Income is thus raised from a variety of sources and, like other business, the existence of these bureaux is dependent on the demand for their services in the market-place. In times of recession, such associations often have difficulty raising funds from the private sector to maintain their activities and need to have injections of public funds to continue with long-term projects.

Since the 1980s, the upsurge in market economics has seen more and more governments urging their NTOs to generate matching funds from the tourist industry. Methods to achieve this objective have included joint marketing initiatives and charging for a range of services, for example, market research reports and brokerage fees from arranging finance. However, the main obstacles to raising private sector revenue have always been the long-term and non-commercial nature of many of the tasks undertaken by NTOs. Added to this is the fact that when NTOs do embark on commercial activities they may be criticised by the private sector for unfair competition, because they are largely funded from taxation. Some countries, for example, many of the island tourist destinations such as Bermuda, have recognised these difficulties and have levied specific tourist taxes on the private sector to pay for the work of the NTO, although where such taxes are not separately set aside for tourism, it can also be argued that the tourist industry is just another source of tax revenue.

Structure of a national tourist office

A stylised organisational layout for an NTO, illustrating its principal divisions, is presented in Figure 11.2. This type of NTO is at 'arm's length' from the Ministry of Tourism by virtue of having its own chairman and board of directors. Where an NTO is a division

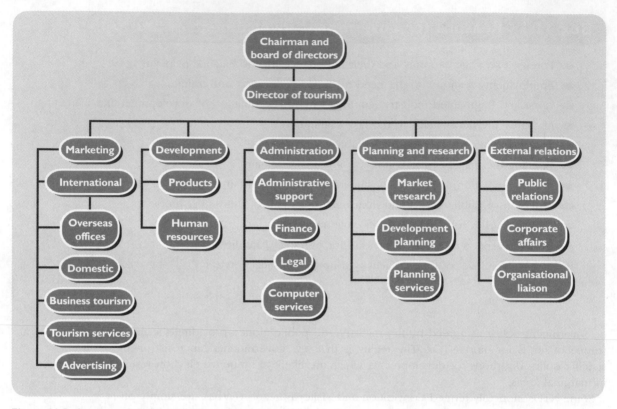

Figure 11.2: Structure of a national tourism organisation

of a ministry, which may have a wider portfolio of activities than just tourism, then it is usual for the director of tourism to report to the senior civil servant in the ministry rather than a board. Some NTOs only have marketing responsibilities and are designated as such, for example, the Singapore Tourist Promotion Board, which has overseas offices in 12 different countries. In these cases Figure 11.2 should not have a development division and research activity is likely to be included under the marketing division.

Clearly, the exact structure of an NTO will depend upon the objectives laid down for it by government and the tasks the organisation has to undertake in order to meet those same objectives. A specific example is shown in Box 11.2 which lists the objectives of the Wales Tourist Board (WTB).

To meet these objectives the WTB is organised into four functional areas: marketing; development; research and corporate planning; and finance and administration. It will be noticed that the word 'optimum' rather than 'maximum' is used as a description of the economic and social benefit. This is deliberate in the sense that trying to maximise the economic gain, particularly in the short-term, may not be in the long-term interests of the host community and could be at variance with the objective of protecting the natural and built environment. It is important that governments should not set NTOs objectives that may seriously conflict with each other. Too often governments talk of tourism quality yet measure the performance of the NTO in terms of numbers. Common examples of policy objectives which are most likely to be at variance with each other are:

● maximising foreign exchange earnings versus actions to encourage the regional dispersion of overseas visitors;

Box 11.2 Policy objectives of the Wales Tourist Board (WTB)

The Board seeks to develop and market tourism in ways which will yield the optimum economic and social benefit to the people of Wales. To meet this, the Board has the following specific policy objectives:

- To encourage the development of tourism facilities and amenities in Wales, with a view to enhancing the quality, market appeal and competitiveness of the product.
- To conduct a cost-effective and targeted programme of strategic marketing aimed at presenting Wales as an alternative destination for holiday and day visits through the year.
- To encourage the provision of tourist information, quality controls and other means of securing visitor satisfaction within Wales.
- To encourage education and training facilities for employees in tourism, and to promote the industry as an effective and proper source of employment.
- To inspire and work with all other organisations whose activities can help to develop and market tourism in Wales.
- To assist developers and operators within the tourism industry in Wales through advisory services.
- To encourage greater community involvement and indigenous enterprise in tourism, and to seek to integrate tourism development more closely with other forms of economic, community and social development.
- To undertake research and provide policy advice, with a view to assisting decision making within the industry and helping to monitor the performance of the industry and the Board.
- To sustain and promote the culture of Wales and the Welsh language.
- To safeguard the natural and built environment.

Source: WTB.

- attracting the high-spend tourist market versus policies to expand visitor numbers;
- maximising job creation through generating volume tourist flows versus conservation of the environment and heritage; and
- community tourism development versus mass tourism.

Marketing function of NTOs

Marketing is the principal responsibility of an NTO and therefore usually forms the largest functional area, especially when overseas offices are included. The marketing division formulates the NTO's marketing strategy and is given the task of producing the advertising campaign and publicity materials, and promoting sales through the media and the travel trade. The latter is achieved through the provision of 'familiarisation' visits to the destination, circulating a regular newsletter and press releases and attending a series of travel trade shows, of which the most significant are the International Travel Exchange, Berlin and the World Travel Market, London. Overseas offices are responsible for exercising the functions of the marketing division in a manner which takes particular account of the preferences of the travel trade and the potential visitors in the countries or areas where they are located. They also act as 'shop windows' where potential visitors may obtain information and brochures about the host country. Many governments do not actively promote domestic tourism and so their NTOs have this section absent from their structure.

Business tourism often merits its own section within an NTO because of its importance in terms of tourist expenditure and the different servicing requirements of meetings, exhibitions and incentive travel groups when compared with leisure tourism. Likewise, advertising is such a key activity that it may command its own specialist group to plan campaigns and deal with outside advertising agencies. Tourism services includes a multitude of tasks such as:

- operating a reservation system;
- handling tourist complaints;
- licensing and grading of hotels and other suppliers (which may include price controls);
- programming festivals, events and tours; and
- managing tourist facilities provided either solely or jointly by the NTO, for example, tourist information centres (TICs) or tourist beaches as in Cyprus.

Development function of NTOs

The development division can only have truly operational involvement if it is given funding to engage in projects with the private sector and implement training programmes and activities. If this is not the case then it can only take on a coordinating and strategic role. The former is achieved by acting as a 'one stop shop' for prospective developers through intermediation to obtain planning permission, licences and any financial assistance or incentives from the relevant authorities. In a strategic role the development division will acquire the planning functions that have been allocated to the planning and research division in Figure 11.2. The reason for the separation in Figure 11.2 rests on the fact that an operational development division is likely to be too heavily involved in day-to-day project management to be able to incorporate long-term development planning. The latter is a research activity and therefore best located in the unit equipped for this task. The planning services section is an important addendum to the role of an NTO in that it seeks to capitalise on the expertise of the organisation to provide advice and even undertake studies for the private sector and other public bodies, for example, drawing up tourism plans for local communities.

The remaining divisions shown in Figure 11.2 are, to a large extent, self-explanatory. Administration is responsible for the internal smooth running of the NTO and will normally adjudicate on legal matters in respect of tourism legislation, including, in some countries, carrying out prosecutions. External relations is a functional area of considerable significance because the NTO is frequently the representative of the government, both at home and overseas, and has to deal with a mass of enquiries from the public, the media and commercial operators, as well as taking an active stance in public relations to support the advertising and sales promotion administered by the marketing division. It is for the latter reason that external relations may be allocated to marketing, although the tasks given to the division are usually much broader than those required by marketing, as is the case in liaison activities with a variety of public bodies and voluntary associations who have an interest in tourism.

Impact of the public sector

In the light of public sector involvement with tourism, either directly through a ministry with responsibility for tourism and the NTO, or indirectly through, say, foreign policy, legal controls or the provision of infrastructure, the government has at its disposal a series of instruments which can be used to manage tourism flows to meet its policy objectives. The manner in which actions by governments influence tourism may be classified in two ways:

- demand and revenue management; and
- supply and cost management.

Demand and revenue management

There are primarily four policy instruments used by governments to manage demand:

- marketing and promotion;
- information provision;
- pricing; and
- controlling access.

Marketing and promotion

As has already been observed, marketing is the principal function of the NTO and the specific techniques are discussed in Part 4 of this book. It is sufficient here to point out that the key requirements for effective marketing are clear objectives, a thorough knowledge of markets and products, and the allocation of adequate resources. Typically, with many other calls on the government's budget, treasury officials are naturally parsimonious with regard to expenditure on marketing because of difficulties in measuring effectiveness. As a rule, the amounts spent by governments and other public organisations on destination promotion are only a fraction of what is spent in total by the private sector. One of the main reasons for this is that private enterprises are competing for market share *at the destination*, whereas governments are interested in expanding the total market *to the destination*.

Information provision

The ability of tourists to express their demands depends upon their awareness of the facilities available, particularly attractions which are a key component of leisure tourism. The evidence suggests that the creation of trails or tourist circuits will enhance the visitor experience as well as regulating tourist flows. The establishment of a network of TICs and tourist information points (TIPs) at transport terminals and prominent tourist spots will both help the visitor and assist in dispersion. It is often not appreciated that it is the poorly informed visitor who is likely to contribute to crowding and traffic congestion because of a lack of knowledge about where to go and what there is to see at the destination. Normally, visitors will first look for the main attractions and then move on to lesser attractions as their length of stay increases. Giving prominence to the variety of attractions available, restricting advertising and informing excursion operators of times when congestion can be avoided are examples of the way in which information management can be used to try to relieve pressure on sensitive tourist areas.

In some countries, NTOs use the provision of information to influence tourists' behaviour. This may come about through editing the information in the tour operator's brochure so that it does not generate unrealistic expectations about a destination and presents the tourist with an informed view of the culture of the host community. An alternative approach is a poster and leaflet campaign aimed directly at the tourist to explain the 'dos and don'ts' of acceptable behaviour; for example, several island resorts offering beach holidays produce leaflets on standards of dress and the unacceptability of wearing only swimsuits in shops, banks and so on.

Pricing

There are several ways in which the public sector may affect the price the tourist pays for staying at a destination. The direct influence arises out of state ownership, notably in the case of attractions. Many of the most important attractions at a destination fall within the public domain, an issue that is examined in some detail in Chapter 14, which is specifically about attractions. The trend in market-orientated economies is for governments to introduce charges for publicly owned attractions. Many of the world's airlines are owned by governments, though the trend is increasingly towards privatisation, and it is not uncommon in less developed countries to find state ownership of hotels and souvenir shops. Thus in some countries, the key elements making up holiday expenditure are directly affected by the public sector, to the point of reaching total control in the situation that existed in the former centrally planned economies of Eastern Europe.

Indirect influences come from economic directives such as foreign exchange restrictions, differential rates of sales tax, special duty free shops for tourists and price controls. Exchange restrictions are commonly employed in countries where foreign exchange is scarce and the tourist is usually compelled to change money at an overvalued exchange rate which serves to increase the real cost of the trip. Tourists are discouraged from changing money on the black market by threats of legal prosecution and severe penalties if caught. The case for price controls is advanced in terms of promoting the long-term growth of the tourist industry and preventing monopolistic exploitation of tourists through overcharging, a practice that can be damaging to the reputation of the destination.

The argument for price regulation is illustrated in Figure 11.3. Initially the destination is receiving V_1 visitors, paying an average package price of P_1 for their stay, with equilibrium being determined at the intersection of the demand schedule $D_1 D_1$ and the short-run supply curve $S_1 S_1$. Demand expands to $D_2 D_2$ which gives the opportunity for suppliers to raise prices to P_2, at the market equilibrium point B. This approach, characterised as

Figure 11.3:
Price controls

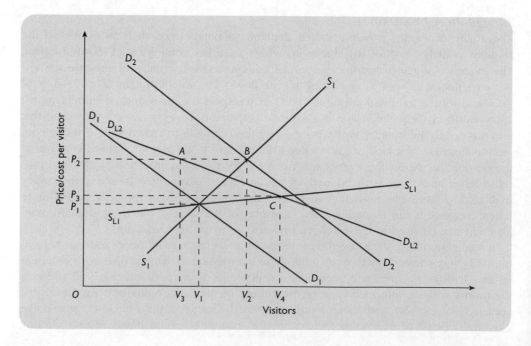

'making money while you can', can be counter-productive, because demand in the longer term is more sensitive (elastic) to price than in the short run, as illustrated by the slope of D_{L2}. The reasons for the latter lie in the number of competing destinations and the holiday price consciousness of travellers. By keeping price at P_2, existing suppliers will make excess profits at the expense of the destination's market share. Market equilibrium is achieved at A and visitor numbers fall back from V_2 to V_3. The country is perceived as 'pricing itself out of the market'.

There is no doubt that destinations are aware of their price competitiveness and some NTOs compile a tourist price index for their own country as well as others, in order to assess their relative market position. Where governments regulate prices, the objective is to set their level at, say, P_3 which is sufficient to encourage the long-run growth in supply as shown by S_{L1} and commensurate with market expansion to an equilibrium point such as C, giving a growth in visitor numbers to V_4. Producers, on the other hand, are prevented from making short-term excess profits.

Where price controls are enforced, they are normally a further stage in an overall market regulation package which commences with the registration and licensing of establishments. In the case of hotels this will include classification and possibly a quality grading system. Price regulation can be found in almost all instances where the government manages capacity and therefore restricts competition. World-wide, the most common example is the licensing and metering of taxis. Where competition exists then the argument put forward in Figure 11.3 hinges upon whether supply adjusts more quickly than demand. There are many examples of Mediterranean resorts where the growth of bed capacity has outstripped demand and so the problem for the authorities has been more an issue of controlling standards than prices, as well as trying to prevent ruinous competition among hoteliers. In market economics there is a basic ideology which is against regulating prices and where opportunities for suppliers to make excess profits in the short term do arise, control is often exercised informally through exhortation that it will not be in the long-term best interests of the destination. It is reasonable to assume that firms themselves will be aware of competition from other countries, though often they are under considerable short-term pressures to increase profitability.

Controlling access

Controlling access is a means of limiting visitor numbers or channelling visitor flows. At an international level, the easiest way for a country to limit demand is by restricting the number of visas issued. Prohibiting charter flights is a means by which several countries have conveyed an image of exclusiveness to the market and, in some instances, have protected the national air carrier. At the destination, controlling access is usually concerned with protecting popular cultural sites and natural resources. Thus visitor management techniques may be used to relieve congestion at peak times and planning legislation invoked to prohibit or control the development of tourist infrastructure (particularly accommodation) near or around natural sites. Visitor management techniques are explored in more detail in Chapter 14 and Major Case Study 2.

Supply and cost management

Government activity on the supply side is concerned with influencing the providers of tourist facilities and services, as opposed to demand management policies aimed at guiding the tourist's choice, controlling the costs of stay or stimulating/regulating visitor numbers. In the majority of countries, the development of tourism is regarded as a partnership between the private and public sectors. The extent of government involvement in this

Case Study 11.4 Fundo Nacional de Fomento al Turismo (FONATUR)

Tourism in Mexico began as a totally private sector activity. Its growth was limited in size (largely in the area of Acapulco), the product on offer was generally poor and developments were unplanned. To counteract this, the Government of Mexico, in 1974, created FONATUR for the purpose of developing resorts and funded the organisation from oil revenues and World Bank loans. Apart from trying to regulate development, the principal reasons for state involvement were:

- to realise potential demand by increasing the number of resorts;
- to generate foreign exchange;
- to create employment;
- for regional development, in particular moving the jobless from Mexico City to the new resorts and raising regional GDP.

FONATUR has developed and consolidated six regional resorts, attracting a wide range of international investors. The government gives FONATUR the development land it requires without charge, the resources to develop a master plan and the money to construct the necessary infrastructure, including hotel building. Once complete, the investment is sold to the private sector. The terms for private sector projects are generous: loans for up to 50% of the capital investment, over a period of 15 years. The 'flagship' project was Cancun on Mexico's Caribbean coast, but this is now mature and issues have arisen about spillover developments outside the original zone and adverse impacts on the environment.

Source: FONATUR.

partnership depends upon the prevailing economic, political and social policies of a country. Where the government envisages a particular direction for tourism growth or wishes to speed up the process, it may intervene extensively in the market-place by setting up a Tourist Development Corporation (TDC) and assigning it the responsibility for building resorts. A well-known example of this process was the building of new resorts in Languedoc–Roussillon, France, but many countries have instituted TDCs at one time or another, for example, Egypt, India, Malaysia, Mexico (Case Study 11.4), New Zealand and a number of African countries. In theory, once the resort has been built, the development corporation's function ceases and the assets are transferred to the private sector (at a price) and the local authority. This is the general trend in market-orientated economies, but in countries where there is a strong degree of central planning, the TDC often maintains an operational role in running hotels and tours.

The methods that are frequently used by governments to influence the supply side of the tourism industry are:

- land-use planning and control;
- building regulations;
- market regulation;
- market research and planning;
- taxation;
- ownership; and
- investment incentives.

Land-use planning and control

Control over land use is the most basic technique and arguably the one that has the greatest influence on the supply of tourist structures. All governments have a form of town and country planning legislation whereby permission is required to develop, extend or change the use of almost every piece of land. As a rule, the controls are designed to protect areas of high landscape and amenity value. Zoning of land and compulsory purchase are commonly used as a means of promoting tourism development. One of the key aspects of land control is that before any detailed site plans and future land requirements for tourism are published, the appropriate administrative organisation and legislation is in place in order to prevent speculation, land division or parcelling. Dealings or speculation in land prior to legislative control have been a common cause of failure in tourism master plans.

Building regulations

Building regulations are used to supplement land-use control and typically cover the size of buildings, height, shape, colour and car-parking arrangements. The latter is a matter which is not always given the attention it deserves in some resorts. To private sector operators, car-parks are often considered unproductive space and so there is a tendency to avoid having to provide them, leaving visitors little alternative than to park their cars in nearby streets. This may only serve to add to traffic congestion and the annoyance of local residents. In addition to structural regulations, many countries also have protective legislation governing cultural resources such as historic buildings, archaeological remains, religious monuments, conservation areas and even whole towns.

Market regulation

Governments pass legislation to regulate the market conduct of firms in matters of competitive practices and also to limit the degree of ownership in particular sectors of the industry to prevent the abuse of monopoly power. Governments may also regulate markets by imposing on suppliers obligations to consumers. This does not have to be legislation; it could be industry-enforced codes of conduct of the kind laid down as conditions for membership of national travel trade associations, though in Europe such codes have passed into the legislation of member states as a result of the EU Package Travel Directive (Chapter 12, Case Study 12.3).

One of the economic criteria dictating the optimal workings of markets is that consumers should have complete knowledge of the choices open to them. For if consumers do not have the right to safety, to be informed, to choose or of redress and firms are not behaving according to the accepted rules of conduct, then resources will be wasted, which may be seen to be inefficient. The economic aspects of a consumer policy are shown in Figure 11.4. As the level of protection increases, so wastage or compensation payments decline, while at the same time the costs of protection increase. The optimum amount of protection is where the two schedules intersect at point A, which defines level L on the axis below. This is the economic rationale: on social or political grounds the state may legislate to ensure nearly 100% protection. But the economic consequences of such an action could be to raise the supply price of the good or service to the point where the market is substantially diminished. At the consultation stage of the EU Package Travel Directive amendments were accepted to some of the proposals on the grounds that their compliance would significantly raise holiday prices.

Figure 11.4:
Economics of
consumer
protection

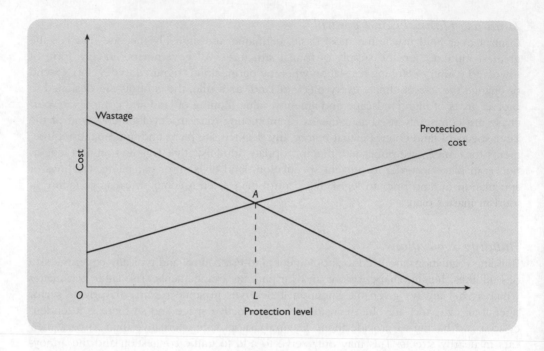

Market research and planning

The tourist industry usually expects the public sector to collect statistical information and carry out market surveys. For their own part, governments are interested in monitoring changes in the industry and carry out research to identify the social benefits and costs of tourism.

Taxation

There are two main reasons why governments levy specific taxes on the tourism sector. The first is the classic argument for a tourist tax, namely to allocate to the supply price the external costs imposed on the host community through providing public amenities for tourists. The second is for purposes of raising revenue; tourists are seen as part of the overall tax base and, from a political perspective, they are not voters in the desti-nation country. With the growth of tourism world-wide, there has been an escalation in the number of countries levying tourist taxes and in the rates of taxation, drawing the inference that governments principally see such taxes as a source of revenue. It is not unreasonable that the tourist industry should pay taxes, but the WTTC has argued that such payments should be made in accordance with the following guidelines:

- **Equity**: the fair and even-handed treatment of travel and tourism with respect to the other sectors of the economy.
- **Efficiency**: the development of tax policies that have a minimal effect on the demand for travel and tourism, unless specifically imposed for the purpose of reg-ulating tourist flows, to, say, environmentally sensitive areas (see Chapter 7).
- **Simplicity**: taxes should be simple to pay and administer, so as not to disrupt the operation of the travel and tourism system.

The most common forms of raising public income from tourism are airport departure taxes, ticket taxes and taxes on hotel occupancy. When it comes to raising revenue, casinos

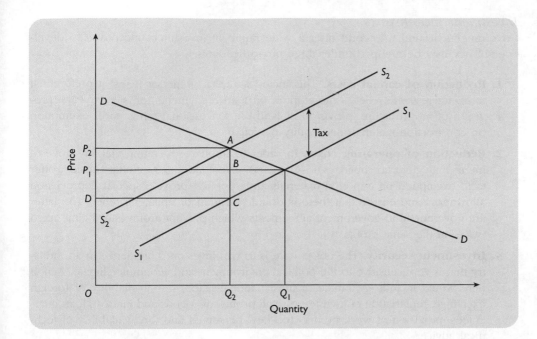

can be a very profitable source: governments have been known to take as much as 50% of the 'drop', which is the amount of money taken in from the tables.

Although a tourist tax may be paid by the guest at the hotel and collected from the hotelier, the incidence as to who bears the tax will depend on the responsiveness of demand and supply to a price change. In Figure 11.5, the imposition of a tax raises the supply price by moving the supply curve from S_1S_1 to S_2S_2, which in turn reduces the quantity of, say, room sales demanded from Q_1 to Q_2. However, the amount of tax income raised P_2ACD does not all fall on the tourists in the form of a higher price. Price rises from P_1 to P_2 only and the larger share of the incidence of the tax P_1BCD falls on the supplier in the form of reduced profits. Tourists contribute P_2ABP_1 of the tax revenue. The less sensitive tourists are to price, something that can be reflected in a much steeper demand schedule DD, the greater is the ability of suppliers to pass on the tax in the form of a higher price and therefore, the larger will be the share of the tax burden falling on the tourists.

Ownership

Mention has already been made of state ownership of attractions, natural amenities and some key revenue-earning activities such as hotels, modes of transport (especially airlines) and souvenir shops. It is possible to add to this list conference centres, exhibition halls, sports and leisure complexes (including casinos), and the provision of general infrastructure. The latter may include: banks; hospitals; public utilities (water and energy supplies); telecommunications road networks; transport terminals; and education and training establishments. The arguments for public ownership of these facilities rest on their importance as essential services for any economic development, the fact that outside investors would expect such provision and economies of scale in production. Traditionally, public infrastructure and transport networks have been regarded as natural monopolies; the minimum scale of production is such as to make it impossible for more than one firm to enjoy all the economies in the market, so that even if they were not publicly owned, these organisations would need to be publicly regulated.

Investment incentives

Governments around the world offer a wide range of investment incentives to developers. They may be grouped under three broad headings:

1. **Reduction of capital costs.** This includes capital grants or loans at preferential rates, interest rate relief, a moratorium on loan repayments for, say, *x* years, provision of infrastructure, provision of land on concessional terms, tariff exemption on construction materials and equity participation.

2. **Reduction of operating costs.** In order to improve operating viability governments may grant tax 'holidays' (5–10 years), give a labour or training subsidy, offer tariff exemption on imported materials and supplies, provide special depreciation allowances and ensure that there is double taxation or unilateral relief. The latter are government-to-government agreements which prevent an investor being taxed twice on the same profits.

3. **Investment security.** The object here is to win investors' confidence in an industry that is very sensitive to the political environment and economic climate. Action here would include guarantees against nationalisation, free availability of foreign exchange, repatriation of invested capital, profits, dividends and interest, loan guarantees, provision of work permits for 'key' personnel and the availability of technical advice.

The administration of grants or loans may be given to the NTO, a government-sponsored investment bank or the TDC. Tax matters will usually remain the responsibility of the treasury or the ministry in charge of finance. Less-developed countries are often able to attract low-cost investment funds from multinational aid agencies which they can use to augment their existing resources for the provision of development finance.

It may be taken that policies to ensure investment security are primary requirements for attracting tourism developers. The objective of financial incentives is to improve returns to capital so as to attract developers and investors. Where there is obvious market potential the government may only have to demonstrate its commitment to tourism by providing the necessary climate for investment security. Such a situation occurred in Bermuda during the early 1970s and so, in order to prevent over-exploitation of the tourism resources, the Bermuda government imposed a moratorium on large hotel building.

The impact of financial incentives on the amount of investment is illustrated in Figure 11.6. The schedule SS represents the supply of investible funds while D_1D is the scheduled of returns to capital employed. D_1D slopes downwards from left to right as more and more investment opportunities are taken up – the declining marginal efficiency of investment. In the initial situation, equilibrium is at A with the amount of investment being I_1 and the rate of return i_1.

Conditions of market failure imply that the community benefits from tourism investment are not entirely captured in the demand function D_1D. Optimal economic efficiency is where the demand function includes these external effects, as represented by D_2D. The government now implements a range of financial incentives that have the effect of raising the rate of return per unit of capital to i_2, moving the marginal efficiency of investment schedule to D_2D. The new return i_2 equals $(1 + s)i_1$, where s is the effective rate of subsidy. If the amount of investible funds available for tourism is limited at I_1, then the impact of incentives serves merely to raise the return to investors by raising the equilibrium point to B. The loss to the government treasury is the area $i_1 AB\, i_2$ which equals the gain to private investors.

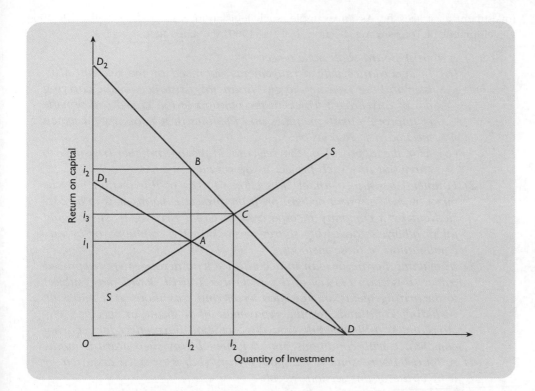

Figure 11.6:
Impact of financial incentives

There is no doubt that many countries have been forced by competitive pressures for foreign investment into situations that are similar to those above. Countries can become trapped in a bidding process to secure clients and as a result the variety of financial incentives multiplies together with an escalation of the rates of benefit, without evaluating their necessity or their true cost to the economy. Given that the supply of investment funds is responsive or elastic, the net effect of an incentives policy is to expand the amount of tourism projects to I_2 and the rate of return settles at i_3, the equilibrium point being C. The private opportunity cost of the investment funds is the area under the supply curve, $I_1\ AC\ I_2$, while the public willingness-to-pay for correcting for market failure is the area $I_1\ BC\ I_2$: subtracting the two areas gives a net gain represented by the area ABC.

It is important to note that there are frequent instances where it is gross uncertainty, as in times of recession, rather than limited potential that prevents the private sector investing. In such situations the principal role of government intervention is to act as a catalyst to give confidence to investors. Thus public funds are able to lever in private money by nature of the government's commitment to tourism and enable the market potential of an area to be realised.

In implementing a tourism investment policy the government has to decide to what extent incentives should be legislated as automatic entitlements, as against being discretionary awards. It has already been noted that automatic incentives may give too much money away, when what is required to ensure that the treasury receives maximum benefit from its funds is the application of the concept of 'additionality'. The latter seeks to provide financial support or the equivalent benefits in kind to the point where the developer will just proceed with the project.

The implication of additionality is an ideal situation where all incentives are discretionary and therefore offered selectively. The legislation would be fairly general, empowering the ministry responsible for tourism to offer loans, grants, tax exemptions and equity investment as it sees fit. As an example, such legislation is embodied in the UK 1969 Development of Tourism Act. Section 4 of the 1969 Act states that:

> 4. *(1) A Tourist Board shall have power –*
>   *(a) in accordance with arrangements approved by the relevant Minister and the Treasury, to give financial assistance for the carrying out of any project which in the opinion of the Board will provide or improve tourist amenities and facilities in the country for which the Board is responsible:*
>   *(b) with the approval of the relevant Minister and the Treasury, to carry out any such project as aforesaid.*
> *(2) Financial assistance under subsection (1) (a) of this section may be given by way of grant or loan or, if the project is being or is to be carried out by a company incorporated in Great Britain, by subscribing for or otherwise acquiring shares or stock in the company, or by any combination of those methods.*
> *(3) In making a grant or loan in accordance with arrangements approved under subsection (1) (a) of this section a Tourist Board may, subject to the arrangements, impose such terms and conditions as it thinks fit, including conditions for the repayment of a grant in specified circumstances; and Schedule 2 to this Act shall have effect for securing compliance with conditions subject to which any such grant is made.*
> *(4) A Tourist Board shall not dispose of any shares or stock acquired by it by virtue of this section except –*
>   *(a) after consultation with the company in which the shares or stock are held; and*
>   *(b) with the approval of the relevant Minister and the Treasury.*

The granting of incentives to prospective developers is in accordance with ministerial guidelines, which are regularly reviewed in response to the level of tourism activity.

To have only discretionary incentives, however, is a counsel of perfection. Competition for tourism investment frequently requires countries to legislate for automatic financial help in order to attract investors in the first instance. Some countries may legislate for all the incentives discussed here; others for a subset of them. Several countries have been guilty of copying incentive legislation without any real grasp of its meaning.

The appropriateness of the various financial incentives available depends on understanding the nature of the business risk and the probable returns to the tourist industry, as well as the ability of the country to afford them. Thus developing countries may find themselves in no position to offer grants or cheap loans, which highlights the importance of contributions from aid agencies. One of the main sources of business risk in tourist enterprises is the tendency to have a high ratio of capital charges in relation to operating expenses. It is for this reason that incentives to reduce capital costs are the preferred form of assistance when the viability of the business is being considered.

Intervention policy

The range of policy instruments available to governments is considerable and enables the public sector to exercise varying degrees of influence over the direction of tourism development. Around the globe governments have intervened to assist and regulate the private sector; this is because the complex nature of the tourist product makes it unlikely that private markets will satisfy all the tourism policy objectives of a country. As noted previously, the extent of public involvement depends on the economic philosophy of the government. The trend towards pure market-led economics in the 1980s led to a clawback of state involvement and the questioning of intervention as mechanisms more likely to lead to market distortions than market corrections. This was in total contrast to the concept of sustainable development which challenges the ability of private markets to improve the distribution of income and protect the environment.

The baseline scenario for sustainable development is the alleviation of absolute poverty and the replenishment of the resource stock so that at a minimum no one generation is worse off than any other. The spillover benefits of tourism are well known, and, more than any other industry, tourism deals with the use of natural and cultural resources. The lessons of the past indicate that it is unwise for governments to abandon their ability to influence the direction of tourism development. The current approach is not to reverse the market changes that have taken place, which would be difficult anyway, since the increasing globalisation of economic activity has reduced the power of national governments to control their destinies, but rather to move towards a more pragmatic approach to intervention and regulation, with an emphasis on international collaboration.

Conclusion

The role of governmental organisations in the influencing of tourism supply and the manipulation of tourism demand is critical in the shaping of the tourism system. We saw how governmental involvement may influence the demand for tourism in Part 1 of this book and, in this part, we demonstrate the function of public sector bodies in coordinating and funding the supply aspects of the tourism product. Thus, the role of governmental organisations continues to be a central one and one whose importance will not be diminished despite the threat of funding cuts in many regions of the world.

Chapter discussion questions

1. Taking a country of your choice, define the roles and functions of its national tourism office. How might an NTO exercise its responsibilities for marketing a country?

2. Why are world tourism organisations important for tourism and tourism development?

3. Compare and contrast the complementary and conflicting roles of the public and private sector in the coordination and funding of tourism.

4. Suggest some of the areas in Europe that might be classified as peripheral and the features that would make them attractive for tourism development.

5. Suggest some of the non-governmental organisations in your own country that have a significant influence on tourism policy.

6. The new approach in the USA is to treat tourism in the same manner as any other traded good or service and withdraw from direct action – is this correct? What are the principal features of tourism in the USA that seem to dictate a policy that runs counter to that of most other governments in the world?

Recommended further reading

- Akehurst, G., Bland, N. and Nevin, M. (1994) 'Successful tourism policies in the European Union', *Journal of Vacation Marketing*, **1**(1), 11–27.
- Charlton, C. and Essex, S. J. (1994) Public sector policies, pp. 45–59 in *Tourism Marketing and Management Handbook*, 2nd edn, Witt, S. and Moutinho, L. (eds), Prentice Hall, Hemel Hempstead.
- Joppe, M. (1994) Government controls on and support in tourism, pp. 60–69 in *Tourism Marketing and Management Handbook*, 2nd edn, Witt, S. and Moutinho, L. (eds), Prentice Hall, Hemel Hempstead.
- Middleton, V. T. C. (1994) *Marketing in Travel and Tourism*, 2nd edn, Butterworth-Heinemann, Oxford.
- Pearce, D. (1992) *Tourist Organizations*, Longman, Harlow.

Bibliography

- Akehurst, G., Bland, N. and Nevin, M. (1994) 'Successful tourism policies in the European Union', *Journal of Vacation Marketing*, **1**(1), 11–27.
- Barnard, C. (1989) 'Taxing international tourism', pp. 451–3 in *Tourism Marketing and Management Handbook*, Witt, S. and Moutinho, L. (eds), Prentice Hall, Hemel Hempstead.
- Charlton, C. and Essex, S. J. (1994) 'Public sector policies', pp. 45–59 in *Tourism Marketing and Management Handbook*, 2nd edn, Witt, S. and Moutinho, L. (eds), Prentice Hall, Hemel Hempstead.
- Heely, J. (1989) 'Role of national tourism organizations in the United Kingdom', pp. 369–74 in *Tourism Marketing and Management Handbook*, Witt, S. and Moutinho, L. (eds), Prentice Hall, Hemel Hempstead.
- House of Commons (1969) *Development of Tourism Act 1969*, HMSO, London.
- Holloway, J. C. (1994) *The Business of Tourism*, 4th edn, Addison Wesley Longman, Harlow.
- Joppe, M. (1994) 'Government controls on and support for tourism', pp. 60–64 in *Tourism Marketing and Management Handbook*, 2nd edn, Witt, S. and Moutinho, L. (eds), Prentice Hall, Hemel Hempstead.
- Lavery, P. and Van Doren, C. (1990) *Travel and Tourism: A North-American/European Perspective*, Elm Publications, Huntingdon.
- Middleton, V. T. C. (1994) *Marketing in Travel and Tourism*, 2nd edn, Butterworth-Heinemann, Oxford.
- Mill, R. C. and Morrison, A. M. (1992) *The Tourism System*, 2nd edn, Prentice Hall, Englewood Cliffs, NJ.
- Myers, J., Forsberg, P. and Holecek, D. (1997) 'A framework for monitoring global travel and tourism taxes: the WTTC Tax Barometer', *Tourism Economics*, **3**(1), 5–20.
- Pearce, D. (1992) *Tourist Organizations*, Longman, Harlow.
- Trade and Industry Committee (1985) *Tourism in the UK*, Vol. 1, Session 1985–1986, HMSO, London.
- Wanhill, S. R. C. (1994) 'Development and investment policy in tourism', pp. 242–5 in *Tourism Marketing and Management Handbook*, 2nd edn, Witt, S. and Moutinho, L. (eds), Prentice Hall, Hemel Hempstead.

Chapter Twelve

Intermediaries

Introduction

In this chapter we show that the principal role of intermediaries is to bring buyers and sellers together, either to create markets where they previously did not exist or to make existing markets work more efficiently and thereby expand market size. For travel and tourism, intermediation comes about through tour operators or wholesalers assembling the components of the tourist trip into a package and retailing the latter through travel agents, who deal directly with the public. However, as this chapter shows, this is not the only way by which the tourist product reaches the customer and we discuss several other distribution channels. Furthermore, the structure of intermediation is complicated by the fact that some retail agents and some of the principal suppliers, such as airlines, also act as tour wholesalers.

We examine the roles played by the travel agent and the tour operator consecutively, together with their respective economics of operation. We point out the differences between the North American and European travel trade systems, although our main emphasis is on the commonality of the underlying principles governing their activity. The conceptual aspects of tour operation are relatively straightforward but the implementation requires considerable organisation and planning, particularly in view of the time lags involved. We therefore discuss the main stages of tour operation in some detail. Finally, the factors making for market dominance are analysed.

Chapter learning objectives

The focus of the chapter is the packaging and distribution of the tourism product. By the end of this chapter, therefore, the reader will:

- be familiar with the operating characteristics of tour operators and travel agents;
- be able to identify the different roles and functions of tour operators and travel agents;
- have an understanding of the process of distribution; and
- be aware of the financial constraints on the operation of intermediaries and the difficulties these inflict.

The nature of intermediation

In all industries the task of intermediaries is to transform goods and services from a form that consumers do not want, to a product that they do want. For everyday household requirements, this is performed mainly through holding bulk supplies and breaking these down into amounts required by individuals, as well as bringing the goods to the market-place. In tourism the situation is somewhat different, for it is quite possible to buy the components of the tourism trip (accommodation, transport, excursions and entertainment) directly from producers. This dispenses with the need for a middleman. The fact that this does not happen in many cases is because the linkages (termed distribution channels) between the suppliers of tourism products and their potential customers are imperfect.

Given the above situation, we can see that it is possible for intermediaries to improve distribution channels and so to make markets by bringing buyers and sellers together. The bulk of this work falls upon the tour operator or wholesaler who packages the main components of the tourist trip into a single product and sells this at one price through retail travel agents or, particularly in North America, airline sales offices. By and large, the role of the retail travel agent has been to provide an outlet for the actual sales of tours, tickets and travel services, such as insurance or foreign exchange, to the public.

Benefits

By making markets, travel intermediaries bestow benefits on both producers, consumers and the destination. These benefits include the following:

● Producers are able to sell in bulk and so transfer risk to the tour operator, though wholesalers do attempt to cover themselves by including release clauses in agreements. These may vary from four or more weeks to seven days.

● Suppliers can reduce promotion costs by focusing on the travel trade, rather than consumer promotion which is much more expensive.

● By being able to purchase an inclusive tour, the traveller can avoid search and transaction costs in both time and money.

● Consumers gain from the specialist knowledge of the tour operator and the fact that the uncertainties of travel are minimised. For example, cruising and coach tours are attractive to senior citizens because the holiday starts the moment they board the ship or coach.

● The most significant gain for tourists is in lower prices, notably in the case of resorts dealing with large numbers of visitors as in the Mediterranean, Mexico and Hawaii. In such destinations wholesalers are able through their buying power to negotiate discounts of up to 60% off the normal tariff.

● Destinations, especially in developing countries where budgets are limited, may benefit considerably from the international marketing network of tour operators. However, it is naive to expect, as some countries do, that this should be a responsibility of these companies.

Structure

A schematic diagram of the structure of distribution channels is shown in Figure 12.1. Independent travellers put their own itinerary together. This they can do by purchasing the key components of accommodation and transport directly from suppliers, or from

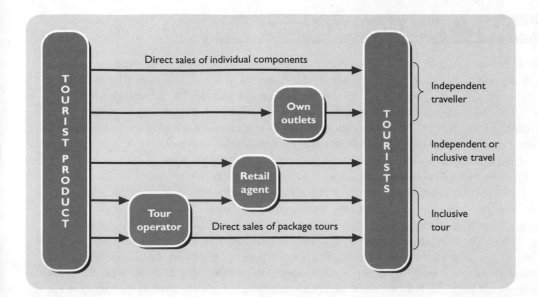

their own outlets, or via the retail travel agent. It is common in domestic tourism for consumers to purchase their trip requirements directly because they usually have good product knowledge and ready access to a telephone to make reservations. However, in order to boost the market for the domestic product in Britain, the national and regional tourist boards have produced commissionable brochures which they distribute in a number of ways: directly through the mail in response to inquiries or from a mailing list (termed direct response marketing), through TICs, or by persuading the travel trade to give the tourist boards' brochures rack space in their shops. These brochures simply give the public a portfolio of products to choose from, which avoids the tourist boards being classified as 'organisers' according to the EU Package Travel Directive.

It is not uncommon for airlines, bus and shipping companies to have their own outlets in large cities from which the public may purchase travel products directly. Airlines are particularly keen to secure their presence in the market by locating offices on flagship sites in capital cities. These serve both the trade and the public, and are especially important in cities such as Paris, Berlin, London or New York, where not only are there large numbers of business travellers, but also many overseas holidaymakers travelling independently. International hotel chains also use individual establishments (such as retail shops) for selling rooms in other properties belonging to the group. This has become increasingly easier with the continual development of more sophisticated CRSs.

The founding companies of today's travel trade, Thomas Cook and American Express (Case Study 12.1), are both travel agents and wholesalers, and so history is on the side of the retail agent that buys directly from producers. Through agency agreements (which, in the United States, are requirements set by what have been historically termed conferences representing the domestic and international airlines, shipping companies and railways), retailers sell the individual components of the trip, such as transport tickets, accommodation, and excursions, but they may also put together their own brand of tours, overbrand another tour operator's brochure or have a specialist wholesaler put together a brochure for them. Own branding is a practice that is much more common in North America than in Europe, as is the use of travel counsellors to assemble specially tailored packages for clients.

Case Study 12.1 The American Express Company

The American Express Company was established in the nineteenth century for the purpose of transporting cash and goods, including baggage, and all the financial obligations required to ensure the safe transfer of items given to their charge. In 1882 the company introduced the unforgeable postal money order, which removed the need for cash transactions, and in 1891 traveller's cheques were brought in, thus allowing tourists to cross borders without constantly exchanging cash. The system was also secure because of the double signature required and refunds were offered in case of loss.

The company expanded beyond its American origins so that by the turn of the century it had established travel offices in major European cities. As well as sales of railway and steamship tickets, a complete range of tours by rail, coach and private car were available before the advent of the First World War. After the war the company became agents for Cunard and went in to organising sea cruises. There was some interest in air travel, but this did not become significant until the growth of mass tourism in the 1950s. The company's financial services also increased with the growth in tourism, so that by the mid-1950s American Express traveller's cheques were available in the denominations of the major currencies of the world. A further boost to the market came in the 1970s with the relaxation of exchange controls, which allowed the company to sell traveller's cheques to the banking system, when previously they had been confined to travel agents.

Today, American Express offices are sophisticated travel centres, linked world-wide by computers. Not only do they sell holidays, but they also arrange business travel, offer passport and visa facilities, as well as dealing in a whole range of financial and personal matters. The latter include sales of traveller's cheques, buying and selling foreign exchange, money transfers and dealing with American Express cardholders' inquiries, offering a Helpline to cover emergencies and give travel assistance on a global basis.

Source: American Express.

As a rule, travel agents make the bulk of their money from selling inclusive tours and airline tickets. In Europe most inclusive tours are associated with foreign travel, whereas in North America domestic trips are the dominant source of inclusive tour sales. The importance of business travel has led to the growth of agencies, usually belonging to a chain, dealing solely with this aspect of tourism, to the extent of providing 'implants' in major corporations solely for the purpose of covering their travel needs.

The most common way of distributing foreign holiday travel in Europe is through inclusive tours packaged by tour operators and sold by travel agents. Some holiday packages are marketed directly to the public by wholesalers and at one stage it was thought that the electronic revolution through the establishment of global airline CRSs, such as Galileo, Sabre or Amadeus, with their attendant alliances with hotel companies, transport operators and activity providers, would lead more and more tours to be sold in this way, especially when there could be cost savings of 10% or more. However, this method of selling has failed to capture the public's attention and the percentage share of the market held by direct sell holidays is still small. It has also been put forward that the increasing sophistication of the travelling public, combined with the ease of making reservations, would lead to the demise of the package holiday. While it is true that more people are travelling independently, there is no evidence to support this view, for it still remains the case that operators can negotiate cheaper arrangements through their bulk purchasing power, and they are also able to respond to the public's demands by building in more options to their package offers. This is explored more fully in Chapter 20 which deals with information technology in tourism.

Integration

The term integration is an economic concept to describe formal linking arrangements between one organisation and another. Vertical integration is where the linking occurs along the production process, for example, when an airline establishes its own tour operating company, as in the case of British Airways or Lufthansa. The latter are examples of vertical integration forwards into the market-place, of which the most common in terms of intermediaries is where a tour wholesaler acquires through merger or purchase a retail travel chain. In Britain, the largest tour operator, Thomson Holidays, is part of the Thomson Travel Group. The latter not only has a chain of retail outlets, Lunn Poly, but also has its own airline, Britannia Airways. Of the other major operators in Britain, Airtours has its own airline, Airtours International, and retail chain, Going Places, while First Choice owns Air 2000 and has a strategic alliance (as opposed to control given by ownership) with Thomas Cook. Tour operators owning airlines provide an example of vertical integration backwards and this is also common among scheduled airlines who form alliances with (and even own) multinational hotel chains and surface transport companies to secure trading advantages over their rivals. One of the widest range of integrated activities may be found in the French conglomerate Groupe Accor. Originally known for its hotel operations, Groupe Accor's interests now include all aspects of tourism.

Looking at developments over time, it appears that the degree of vertical integration varies with the product life cycle. We illustrate this in Figure 12.2: at the early stage of development, as in the case of Thomas Cook, there is a high degree of vertical integration as there are few suppliers. But as demand expands so specialists develop to increase the efficiency of the distribution channel. Operators are bound together by their mutual interest in helping the market to grow. As the market matures, competitive pressures for market share force companies to seek the benefits of forming vertical links. These include:

Figure 12.2: Extent of forward vertical integration

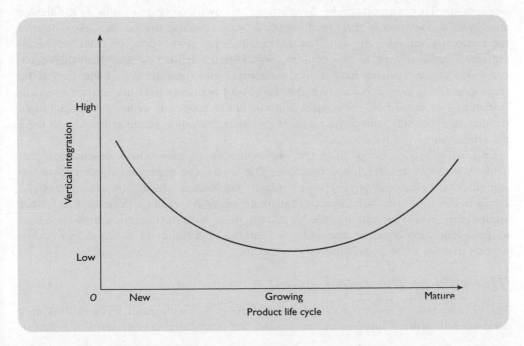

- economies of scale through the linking of complementary activities, investing in new technologies and improved management expertise in, say, foreign exchange transactions, forecasting and marketing;
- cutting out the middleman by being able to control costs and quality standards under the umbrella of one organisation;
- securing supplies and increasing buying power; and
- protecting market position by guaranteeing retail outlets on prime high street sites.

It is important to note that vertical integration forwards does not necessarily have to come about through ownership. Control may be exercised by franchising. This is a licensing agreement whereby the parent company grants another, usually smaller, firm the right to sell its products and use its brand name, but in return the firm should not sell the products of its competitors. In Germany, the package holiday business was developed by the major retail groups, such as Karstadt, Neckermann and Quelle in the 1960s. They already had the advantage of retail shops and mail order systems to distribute their products. Owing to stricter cartel laws, further expansion through vertical integration was difficult, so they developed market power through mutual shareholding agreements and a system of tied agency licensing, which gave them exclusive outlets for their products and protected their profit margins.

Another organisational aspect of the travel trade sector that should be considered is horizontal integration. This occurs when two tour operators or two travel agents amalgamate, either through merger or takeover. This strategy was very prevalent amongst retail travel chains in Britain during the 1980s and became known as the 'march of the multiples'. The reasons for this are similar to those for vertical integration but also include the spatial dimension of extending the geographical spread of outlets to ensure representation in all regions. Thomas Cook and Lunn Poly in Britain, and American Express and Ask Mr. Foster in the USA, are examples of major chains that have increased their geographical representation.

For the retailers, horizontal integration strengthens their buying power with regard to wholesalers. They support this by developing their own corporate identity in the design and style of operation of their branch outlets, so as to raise the public's awareness of the company. Naturally, the march of the multiples has drawn criticism from independent travel agents owing to loss of their market share. In Britain, as in North America, many small travel agencies have formed themselves into consortia to give themselves the same negotiating power as the multiples. Large tour operators have also grown by amalgamation, but instead of enforcing a uniform brand image, as in the case of multiple retailers, they usually maintain a range of products, including acquired brands, to meet the consumer's need for choice.

Criticism of major tour operators and wholesalers usually comes from destinations, particularly those in less-developed countries. The latter have expressed concern over the strength of the economic buying power of large wholesalers which allows them to obtain prices below those that would occur in markets where competition prevails. It is further argued that their specialist knowledge allows them to influence consumer choice in tourism-generating countries and so gives them the opportunity to switch sales to destinations that are more profitable to the company.

The role of the retail agent

The primary task of travel agents is to supply the public with travel services. This they do on behalf of their suppliers or 'principals', the latter being a trade term. A principal may be a tour operator or wholesaler, a hotel or a transport company. An agent may also offer travel-related services such as insurance or foreign exchange. For providing these services, the agent is rewarded by commission from the principals. Typically, commission amounts to 10% of the selling price, but this is normally 1 or 2% less for airline tickets, hotel bookings and rail travel. Insurance will usually generate commission of around 30% and car hire can, on occasions, make considerably more than the basic 10%. Sales of travellers cheques and currency will yield no more than about 2%. However, by dealing with preferred suppliers and achieving specified sales targets, agents can achieve 'overrides' which are extra commission amounting to about 2.5% of sales.

How a retail travel agency should set about discharging its primary function is a matter for discussion. Where an agent has no wholesaling function and therefore does not share in the risk of tour production by holding stock, it is suggested that the agent's main concern should be the choice of location to ensure ready availability of the principals' products in the market-place. The agent has access to a principal's stock through the reservation system and here efficiency is important. The customer expects instant confirmation and staff at the agency do not want to waste time with repeated telephone calls. Instant availability on a computer screen permits the staff to share the booking process with the customer to reinforce the buying decision. This approach to the role of the retailer likens the agent to a 'filling station' for travel: creating demand is the responsibility of the principals. If demand is given, then controlling costs is the best way for the agent to maintain profitability.

An alternative view argues that the acquisition of product knowledge and the assumption of the risks involved in assessing the extent and nature of demand is the job of the agent. The agent should thus take on the role of a travel counsellor to give the public impartial advice and seek to generate business in the local market area. Many countries have national associations for travel agents that also act as regulating bodies: the Association of British Travel Agents (ABTA) in Britain and the American Society of Travel Agents (ASTA) in the USA. The code of conduct of ABTA requires agents to take an active promotional role (Case Study 12.2).

It has already been noted that the counselling role has been far more prevalent in North America than in Europe. It appears that in Europe the tour operator's brochure, together with advertising and promotion, has held greater sway in destination choice. Thus, although there are many local exceptions, travel agents in Europe have tended to conform to the filling station model. The concept of impartial advice is also questionable in that while agents want to meet their client's needs, they are also mindful of the different rates of commission on offer and any bonuses, particularly in instances where they are owned by their principals. However, one of the features of the expansion of corporate chains has not only been their purchase of prime retail sites, but also their efforts to improve staff competencies and the provision of specialists, as well as providing better career prospects in a sector which is well known for relatively low pay.

Retail agency economics

Traditionally the retail travel trade has been characterised by ease of entry. This is because the retailer carries no stock and so capitalisation is relatively low. All that is required is a suitable shop front and the acquisition of agency agreements from tour operators to sell their products. It is then up to the marketing skill of the agent to establish the business within the locality. If the agent wishes to offer air transport services world-wide, which is essential for dealing with business travel, then it is necessary that the agent holds a licence from IATA. This requires a thorough investigation of the agency by IATA, particularly the qualifications and experience of the staff.

Case Study 12.2 Association of British Travel Agents (ABTA)

The Association was founded in 1950 to promote the interests of its members and to raise their prestige. In doing this, it has also come to represent the interests of consumers through developing procedures to safeguard against tour companies that suddenly go out of business and fail to meet their obligations to their customers. It now represents both travel agents and tour operators and, as a trade association, has an agreed Code of Conduct for its members, which, although not legally binding, does give ABTA the power to expel, fine or reprimand those members who fail to comply with its standards. The Association requires that the public should receive the best possible service from its members and that in matters of competition for business between them, the interests of the travelling public should predominate. There is a whole range of standards that members are expected to comply with including:

- advertising;
- brochure content and design;
- alterations to an agreed holiday;
- cancellations by the customer or by the provider;
- surcharges;
- travel taxes;
- overbooking;
- resort representation;
- handling complaints and arbitration.

ABTA has a continually evolving set of rules and regulations for membership. The most important milestones have been the implementation of financial bonding for new members (a financial guarantee from, say, a bank or an insurance company in the event of failure and payment into a reserve fund), laying down in its code of conduct the procedures for members to follow in their dealings with the public and the agreement that no ABTA tour operator would sell foreign inclusive holidays through non-ABTA agents and conversely. The latter has been the most contentious because it amounts to a restrictive practice in that nearly all British tour operators are members of ABTA, so it is extremely difficult for a retailer to trade without being a member of ABTA. This ruling has survived legal scrutiny in respect of unfair trading on the grounds that it operates in the public interest by giving assurance on quality for a product that is bought unseen. This was dropped with the advent of the 1990 EU Directive on Package Travel, which member states had to put into law by 1992 (Case Study 12.3) and much of ABTA's Code of Conduct was superseded by the force of law, as opposed to the voluntary agreement of the Association's members.

However, ABTA's remit is much wider than regulation, since as a trade association it:

- commissions research into the technological and business environment that is likely to affect its members;
- provides an information service to members;
- offers legal advice;
- undertakes training, validates courses and sets the standards for professional qualifications in travel and tourism;
- promotes the travel industry through public relations;
- acts as a spokesperson and lobbying body with respect to the British Government and the EU.

Source: ABTA *Members' Handbook.*

Item	Currency units
Sales	
Inclusive tours	530 000
Air tickets	330 000
Other transport tickets	49 000
Insurance	10 000
Car hire	3 000
Miscellaneous	78 000
Total	1 000 000
Revenue	
Commission	96 000
Other Income	5 000
Total	101 000
Costs	
Payroll expenses	46 500
Communications	12 000
Advertising	3 000
Energy	1 500
Administration	6 500
Repairs and maintenance	500
Accommodation expenses	12 500
Depreciation	2 500
Total	85 000
Net income	16 000

Source: trade information.

In the USA virtually all retailers are members of both IATA and the Airlines Reporting Corporation (ARC) which allows them to sell both international and domestic air tickets. This is because the major part of an agent's income in the USA is obtained from the sales of airline tickets. An ARC appointment is essential for retail agents in the USA and normally enables an agent to obtain other licences without difficulty. In Britain the extra cost of obtaining IATA membership tends to deter smaller agencies and leads them to specialise in selling inclusive package holidays which avoids the need for an IATA license.

A representative breakdown of the operating accounts of a medium to large travel agent is shown in Table 12.1. The example is drawn on European experience and is standardised to one million currency units of turnover. Table 12.1 gives an indication of the items that enter the operating account and shows that inclusive tours and air tickets are by far the most important sales items. The item for other transport tickets includes sales arising from acting as an agent for rail, shipping and coach companies. Miscellaneous includes independent bookings of hotels, theatres, etc., foreign exchange transactions and the sale of travel goods such as luggage, sports items, first aid kits and travel clothes.

The most important item of income to the agent is commission and since basic rates have not changed for decades, it will be appreciated that the ability of the agent to generate turnover is crucial, particularly for the independent retailer. The latter has been doubly squeezed: first, by fierce competition from the multiples and, second, from the fact that the relative cost of holidays has fallen in real terms while overheads have been generally increasing. Other income in the revenue statement includes interest earned on clients' deposit money. For accounting purposes this is a profit item which is only indirectly sales related. It could be excluded here and added into the net income statement afterwards.

The largest item of cost is remuneration to staff (including payments to directors or owners). The difficulty that independent agents have experienced in trying to expand turnover has tended to make them cost orientated in the operation of their businesses. Controlling costs, especially for the smaller agent, has been the short-term recipe for survival and this in turn has served to keep staff salaries low, which creates difficulties in both attracting experienced staff and retaining existing staff. The problem is often compounded by cutting advertising, training and investment in new technology. Administration costs include printing, stationery, insurance, bonding levy, legal and professional fees, bank charges, accounting and record-keeping, and any travel that may be incurred. Accommodation expenses refer to charges arising from occupation of the premises.

Although the independent retailer can compete with the multiple on the basis of the level of personal service, the argument for raising commission rates is a strong one. Ideally, the retailer is looking to wholesalers to provide a wide range of products that are regularly being upgraded, and that are capable of generating volume sales at high margins. The difficulty is that in a competitive environment higher commission rates may simply be countered by the multiples offering larger discounts.

The role of the tour operator/wholesaler

Since the dominant international leisure tourism flows are North–South to sun resorts, it is not surprising that much of the work of tour operators and wholesalers is bound up in providing single destination inclusive or package holidays. Multicentred holidays are more common on long-haul travel where the period of stay may extend to three weeks, and there is still a buoyant market for coach tours which were the main form of package holiday before the arrival of low-priced air travel in the 1950s. The first business to introduce the modern form of package holiday was the British company Horizon (later acquired by Thomson), when, in 1957, in order to circumvent exchange controls by paying the whole price in the country of origin, it marketed combined transport and accommodation arrangements to Corsica.

At its most fundamental, tour operating is a process of combining aircraft seats and beds in hotels (or other forms of accommodation), in a manner that will make the purchase price attractive to potential holidaymakers. As we noted earlier, tour wholesalers achieve this through bulk buying which generates economies of scale that can be passed on to the customer. The most essential link in this process is the tour operator's brochure which communicates the holiday product to the customer. The brochure must include within it:

- illustrations which provide a visual description of the destination and the holiday;
- copy, which is a written description of the holiday to help the customer match the type of product to his or her lifestyle; and
- price and departure panels which give the specifications of the holiday for different times of the season, duration of stay and the variety of departure points.

Large tour operators and wholesalers normally sell a wide portfolio of tours and therefore have a range of brochures. For instance, there will be separate brochures for summer sun and winter sun holidays, ski holidays, long-haul travel and short breaks. Popular destinations may have tour operators' brochures dealing solely with holidays to that country or region, for example, Greece, Florida or Turkey. Research has shown that the place to visit is often the first holiday decision made by some travellers. The brochure is designed to encourage customers to buy and is often the only information they might have concerning the resort until they arrive there. However, it cannot be a comprehensive travel guide. The number of pages is limited by considerations of cost and size, and operators try to put as much detail about accommodation and resorts as they can in the space available, but in so doing, they must also conform to the legal requirements of the consumer protection legislation that exists in the country where the brochure is marketed. Clearly, the contents of the brochure must be consistent with the brand image each operator is trying to convey, as they will each be competing for the customer's attention on travel agents' brochure racks.

Principal stages of tour operating/wholesaling

Although the conceptual principles of tour operating are easy to follow – linking transport and accommodation to produce a package that can be offered in a brochure – the practicalities of the tour-operating cycle require careful planning, preparation and coordination. For example, media advertising in support of the brochure must be booked well in advance, particularly if television is to be used. The process of brochure production is initiated early on in the cycle to ensure that printing deadlines are met. There is a myriad of tasks to be performed, not only by separate divisions within the tour company, but also by outside contractors. The task of coordinating all these activities usually falls upon the marketing department.

Because of the complexity of organising package trips, there are tour operators and wholesalers who do not put together their own programme. They simply contract the work out to a wholesaler and pass on the bookings as they come in. An example of this are organisations known as affinity groups. They range from travel clubs whose members may have ethnic ties with particular countries, to professional associations who may arrange to have their meetings in different parts of the world.

Figure 12.3 presents a stylised layout of an operating cycle for a large-scale summer programme selling one million or more holidays. From initial research to the commencement of sales, the period spans some 14 months and to first departures, 21 months. For winter programmes and short breaks, which are normally smaller in volume, the corresponding preparation periods are somewhat less. The example shown should not be taken as definitive since, by nature of the very many activities that are being performed and the differing objectives of tour companies, there will always be variances on timings; for example, spreading the season into April or curtailing it at the end of September or in mid-October.

Research
Key outcomes of research are the forecasts of overall market size and the changing patterns of holiday taking. These will assist in the selection of destinations, which in turn will be constrained by conditions of access, the extent of the tourist infrastructure and the political climate of the host country. In terms of destination choice, a specialist tour operator is able to respond far more quickly to changing market conditions than the volume or mass tour operator. The latter usually has long-term commitments to existing destinations which may include capital tied up in resorts. From destination choice, the research process will enable the operator to derive a market strategy, giving answers to the kind of decision model shown in Table 12.2.

Figure 12.3: Tour operating cycle of an abroad summer programme

ACTIVITY	Year 1					Year 2												Year 3									
	Aug.	S	O	N	D	Jan.	F	M	A	M	J	J	A	S	O	N	D	Jan.	F	M	A	M	J	J	A	S	O
Research																											
● Review market performance	X	X																									
● Forecast market trends		X																									
● Select and compare new and existing destinations			X	X																							
● Determine market strategy				X	X																						
Capacity planning																											
● Tour specifications						X																					
● Negotiate with and contract suppliers						X	X	X																			
Financial evaluation																											
● Determine exchange rates							X	X																			
● Estimate future selling prices							X	X																			
● Finalise tour prices									X																		
Marketing																											
● Brochure planning and production							X	X	X																		
● Brochure distribution and launch									X																		
● Media advertising and sales promotion										X	X	X	X	X													
● Market stimulation												X	X	X	X	X											
Administration																											
● Recruit reservation staff								X																			
● Establish reservation system									X																		
● Receive reservations by telephone and viewdata									X	X	X	X	X	X	X	X	X	X	X	X	X	X	X	X	X	X	X
● Tour accounting and documentation										X	X	X	X	X	X	X	X	X	X	X	X	X	X	X	X	X	X
● Recruit resort staff																X	X	X	X	X							
Tour management																											
● Customer care at resort											X	X	X	X									X	X	X	X	X
● Customer correspondence												X	X	X										X	X	X	X
● Payment of suppliers													X	X											X	X	X

Table 12.2:
Market strategy

	Products	
Markets	**Existing**	**New**
Existing	Market penetration	Product development
New	Market development	Diversification

Source: after Ansoff (1968).

Capacity planning

The market forecasts can be used to plan total capacity, which, together with the market strategy, will set tour specifications by type, destination and volume. Once the tour programme has been planned, negotiations for beds and aircraft or coach seats may take place. Bed contracts may take two forms: an allocation or a guarantee. An allocation operates on a sale or return basis with an appropriate release date. This type of contract is usually negotiated with medium-grade hotels and above, where opportunities for re-sale are generally easier. The risk is thus transferred from the tour operator/wholesaler to the hotelier. In turn the hotelier covers this risk by making contracts with several operators and quoting variable rates. With a guarantee, the wholesaler agrees to pay for the beds whether they are sold or not. Such a commitment naturally brings with it a cheaper rate than an allotment and is commonly applied to self-catering properties for the purpose of obtaining exclusive contracts.

Aircraft seats may be contracted in a variety of ways. The largest tour operators and wholesalers are likely to have their own airline and some airlines, particularly in the USA, also have tour wholesaling divisions or companies. In other circumstances, the tour operator may contract an aircraft for the whole season (a 'time charter'), for specified flights (a 'whole plane charter'), or purchase a block of seats on a scheduled service or a chartered airline (a 'part charter'). The use of scheduled services tends to be for specialist tours (which are often escorted) or tailor-made packages for customers. As scheduled flights are likely to work on a break-even 'load factor' of 60% or less, airlines are prepared to give good discounts for inclusive tour excursion fares.

Where an operator has contracted for a time charter, it is important to maximise the utilisation of the aircraft. The underlying principle is that charters should be operated back-to-back, namely that the plane should fly out with a new tour group and return with the previous group. Empty flights (known as 'empty legs') will arise at the beginning and end of the season, and these must be allowed for in the costing of seats. In summer the aircraft is likely to be used for three return trips or 'rotations' per day (two in winter) following the flight patterns shown in Figure 12.4. Aircraft may be used to rotate from one point of departure to a range of destinations or from a variety of departure points to one destination, or a combination of the two.

However, in the interests of protecting scheduled airlines from unfair competition through charters taking their normal traffic at peak times, aviation authorities have usually imposed operating restrictions on charter airlines. These may include the following:

● The trip must be an inclusive tour which implies the provision of accommodation as well as an airline seat.

● Airport terminals used by passengers must be the same on both the outward and return journeys.

Figure 12.4:
Time charter
aircraft flight
patterns:
(a) 'w' pattern;
(b) radial pattern

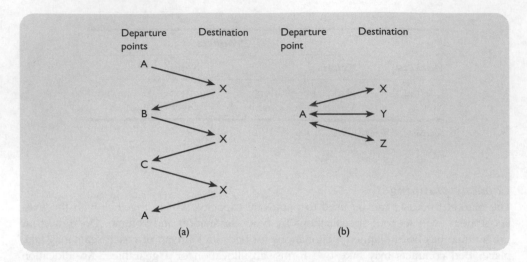

- The air ticket must be for a round trip and is neither transferable nor part usable in the sense that the holder may not use the return portion without having first travelled on the outbound flight.

Within the EU, competition policy dictates that such restrictions are no longer valid, for they are not appropriate to a policy of transport liberalisation or deregulation.

Financial evaluation

We can see from Figure 12.3 that tour operators and wholesalers have to finalise prices some eight months or more before the first tour departs. Apart from the usual hazards of forecasting so far in advance, there are several inherent risks that must be accounted for. These are:

- contracts with local suppliers are commonly made in the currency of the destination country;
- the currency for payment of airlines is usually US dollars;
- airlines maintain the right to raise prices in response to increases in aviation fuel costs; and
- alterations in dues, taxes or fees levied by governments.

Tour operators and wholesalers cover these risks (termed 'hedging') by trying to build in anticipated changes in exchange rates for the purposes of determining tour prices and then buying forward the foreign exchange required at an agreed rate in order to meet contractual obligations, and by bringing in surcharges at the point of final billing of customers. Because the latter have proved unpopular, operators have tried to avoid their negative impact by offering no-surcharge guarantees, limiting the amount of surcharge liability, or offering cancellation options. In this context, it is worth noting that surcharges are often regulated by consumer protection legislation, as in the EU Package Travel Directive (Case Study 12.3), which requires that latest date for price revisions (about a month before departure) must be included in the contract and that any significant alterations to the contract give the customer the right of cancellation without incurring penalties.

Marketing

Brochure production starts several months prior to the publication date with initial agreements about printing arrangements. It is usual for the layout of the brochure to be under-

Case Study 12.3 European Union Package Travel Directive

The issue of consumer protection in relation to the package holiday contract was first raised in the EU in 1982. Up until the Directive on Package Travel was adopted in 1990, all the then 12 member states had very different provisions for package holidays. The justification for the Directive lies in completion of the single market covering all of the Union, which requires the harmonisation of business practices. However, a European directive, as opposed to a regulation, allows member states to implement it in the best way they see fit and two years was given for the appropriate legislation on package travel to be enacted in each country. The Directive was in effect minimum harmonisation, as it allowed member states to adopt or retain more stringent conditions of consumer protection.

The Directive defined a package as a pre-arranged combination of at least two of the following:

- transport;
- accommodation;
- other significant tourist services.

The package has to be sold at an inclusive price and cover a period of more than 24 hours or include overnight accommodation.

Any tourist business involved in providing combinations of the above services in a pre-arranged form comes within the terms of the Directive, which, in effect, broadened the range of travel organisers who may be classified as a tour operator. In essence, the Directive required member states to give the force of law to what was already in the codes of conduct established by trade associations, but with three enhancements:

- The travel organiser (tour operator) is contractually liable for the proper performance of the elements of the package, whether provided directly by the organiser or other suppliers.
- Bonding of holidays was extended to all travel organisers offering arrangements that came within the definition of a package.
- Travel organisers and their agents are legally obliged to provide their customers with additional information on visa requirements, health formalities, transport stops and connections (and accommodation to be provided as necessary), local representation or an emergency telephone number, insurance and similar matters to ensure that the client is fully aware of the circumstances of the holiday purchase.

Source: EC Council Directive 90/314 on Package Travel, Package Holidays and Package Tours.

taken by a specialist design studio following the guidelines laid down by the tour operator's own staff. A variety of styles may be considered before the final choice is made. Particular attention is paid to the front cover to make sure that it conveys the right message to the target market segment and to ensure that it is likely to stand out on the travel agent's brochure racks. The draft final document is scrutinised for errors and corrected, with the pricing panels being left to the last possible moment before full production, to allow for any unforeseen economic changes.

It is important for the brochure to be launched well before the summer seasons starts because there is a section of the market that likes to book early in order to guarantee the destination and to take advantage of any promotional prices. The pattern of brochure distribution depends on the nature of the tours being offered and a trade-off between the costs of sending to all agents in order to maximise brochure exposure and limiting the number of outlets in the knowledge that the majority of the business will come from a minority of agents. Specialist wholesalers offering high-priced trips will restrict the number of retailers and in so doing convey the message of product exclusiveness to the customer. In any event, they are unlikely to be in a position to support a large network of travel agents. For cost-effective reasons even mass tour operators limit the number of agents they appoint and, as indicated previously, very large wholesalers often have their own retail travel chain to distribute their products.

Monitoring the progress of advertising and sales campaigns is achieved through booking patterns. Typically operators are looking for capacity utilisation factors of 85–90% in order to break-even. Past experience enables wholesalers to establish reference booking patterns so as to compare actual with predicted bookings. Tour operators/wholesalers reserve the right to cancel or 'consolidate' holidays, for example, merging flights or combining itineraries and switching accommodation, if the demand take-up is insufficient. This makes it relatively easy for operators to test new products in their brochures. However, on the supply side, merging charter flights is not normally feasible for a summer programme after January because of the cost of airline cancellation charges. Large operators benefit here by having their own airline.

On the demand side, consolidation is a common source of annoyance to customers and leaves the travel agent with unenviable task of advising his or her clients of the changes. Tour operators defend this practice on the grounds that if they where unable to use cancellation or consolidation to reduce over-capacity, then the average price of a holiday would rise. Underestimating demand is less of a difficulty because there is usually some flexibility in the system for procuring extra flights and accommodation. On the other hand, tour operators protect themselves against cancellation by their clients. Refunds are normally arranged on a sliding scale, so that the cancellation of a holiday six or seven weeks before departure may only result in a lost deposit, but after that the amount of the purchase price returned falls relatively sharply to zero for a cancellation only a day or so before departure.

Owing to the negative effects of consolidation on customers and the wider impacts this may have on public relations, tour operators and wholesalers prefer to use market stimulation techniques to boost sluggish booking patterns. Such tactical marketing (as opposed to strategic) methods will depend upon the time available and may vary from increasing advertising expenditure through special discounts for booking by a certain time, to substantial price cuts some six to four weeks before departure. Critical to obtaining last-minute sales is a network of retailers linked by viewdata into the operator's own computer reservation system so that price promotions may be quickly communicated to the travelling public. Consumers, in turn, have recognised the bargains on offer and these have, over the years, encouraged later booking.

Administration

Owing to the seasonal nature of tour operation, the extra staff required to run the reservation system and represent the operator/wholesaler overseas are recruited and trained when needed, with only a core being employed all year. Frequently the same staff come and work for the same operator every year, which reduces the need for training.

The reservation system holds the tour operator's stock of holidays and careful attention is paid to matching the information held by the system to that contained in the brochure. Normally, travel agents make direct bookings through computer terminals in their own offices, but many agents still have to make telephone bookings, either because they are dealing with small operators who do not have electronic systems in place or there is a need for clarification of the product on offer.

Tour management

Specialist tour operators are most likely to offer escorted tours whereby a tour manager accompanies holidaymakers throughout the whole of their journey in order to oversee arrangements. For the volume package tour market, the function of the operator's resort representative is to host the tour. This involves meeting the tourists when they arrive and ensuring that the transfer procedures to the places of accommodation go smoothly. The representative will be expected to spend some time at the resort before the start of the season checking facilities, noting any variations from the brochure and, with the authority of the company, requesting discrepancies to be put right. During the holiday, the representative is required to be available to guests at the various hotels to give advice and deal with the many problems that may arise, as well as supervising (and sometimes organising) social activities and excursions.

After the holiday the operator/wholesaler will receive customer correspondence that will include compliments, suggestions and complaints. Most correspondence can be dealt with by a standard letter and justified complaints may receive a small refund. For serious complaints, national travel associations may offer arbitration services which can reconcile disputes before steps are taken to instigate legal proceedings.

Tour operator economics

We have already considered many of the economic aspects of tour operation in our discussion of the benefits of intermediation and the way in which a tour programme is put together. Essentially the mass tour operator or wholesaler relies on the economies of scale generated by bulk purchase and this in turn allows individual packages to be competitively priced to the consumer on the basis of a high take-up rate of offers made.

Once the tour operator/wholesaler is committed to a programme, the financial risks are substantial, irrespective of tactical risk avoidance strategies such as late release clauses, surcharges and consolidation. This is because most of the costs of running the programme, if it is to run at all, are unavoidable and therefore fixed. The marginal or variable costs of selling an extra holiday are very small, which accounts for the large discounts on offer for 'late availability' trips that give the customer only a short period of notice (sometimes just a few days) before departure.

Leverage

The financial structure of tour operation is illustrated in Figure 12.5. R is the revenue line which increases with the level of capacity utilisation and C_1 the total cost line attributable to running the tour programme. It may be seen that C_1 cuts the revenue and costs axis some way above the point of origin. The latter is caused by the high level of fixed costs in relation to the variable costs of tour operation. The financial term for this is a 'high operating leverage'. By way of contrast, C_2 is a total cost line which has a low operating leverage: fixed costs are relatively small when compared to the steeply rising variable costs.

Consider a tour operator who is planning a break-even capacity utilisation level of O_2, but demand is such that O_3 holidays are sold. Clearly, O_3 is well above the break-even point (BEP) and so the operator makes substantial profits as shown by the difference between R and C_1. A firm that has a low operating leverage would not do so well, as can be seen from the difference between R and C_2. Conversely, if the tour operator did not manage to achieve targeted break-even sales and the realised utilisation was some way below the required level, say, O_1, the losses can be severe and may result in the collapse of the operator (Case Study 12.4). We show in Figure 12.5 that a firm with a low operating leverage would not be so badly affected.

Figure 12.5:
Financial
structure of tour
operation

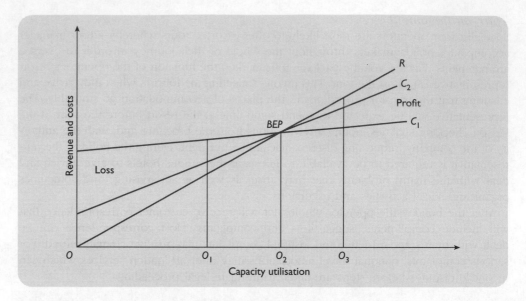

There is thus considerable financial risk associated with tour operation and this acts as a deterrent to entry. Specialist operators cover this risk by dealing with niche markets, and using scheduled airline services and high-grade hotels for which reservations may be readily cancelled if the minimum number of confirmed bookings for the tour are not met. The major tour operators address this financial risk by securing their market position through vertically integrating their operation both forwards and backwards. The tied agency scheme in Germany was particularly effective in allowing the large tour operators to profit from their market position. It is in the middle ground, among wholesalers who have neither their own chartered aircraft (and so must purchase a part charter) nor their own retail network, where the financial risk tends to be at its highest. These are the tour operators that are most likely to go out of business when demand falters. To safeguard the public from lost holidays or from being stranded abroad when a tour operator collapses, most governments have legislation dealing with bonding arrangements (Case Study 12.4), though the fund is not always sufficient to meet the losses or extra expenses incurred.

Sales mix

During the 1950s holiday tourism was largely centred around the traditional summer break at a coastal resort, but rising affluence, longer holiday periods and an increasing desire to travel have led to an expansion in the degree of market segmentation. Tour operators and wholesalers have responded to changing consumer preferences by diversifying their portfolio of products. This in turn has helped to spread risk and generate all-year business. Thus most major tour operators have winter and summer programmes.

Table 12.3 presents the sales mix that would be appropriate for a large European operator offering summer sun holidays to Mediterranean resorts. Most holiday movements in Europe are still towards beach destinations in summertime, though winter holidays have increased their market share in response to more frequent holiday-taking. Minimum rated packages are effectively the transport cost only, with nominal accommodation provision so as to comply with the legal definitions of an inclusive tour.

Pricing

The price of an inclusive holiday in a wholesaler's brochure will be bounded above by what the market will bear and below by the cost of providing the holiday. Thus customers

Case Study 12.4   International Leisure Group (ILG)

In 1991 ILG collapsed when it was the second largest tour operator in Britain. This is an ironic twist of fate, in that ILG was built up from a company called Intasun in the wake of the failure of the largest British tour operator, Clarkson's, in 1974, by taking over their supplier capacity and lost bookings. At the time, Clarkson's was carrying 750 000 holidays and had its own airline. The company had been involved in a price war for market share with the second largest tour operator, Thomson, since the mid-1960s, which had eroded profit margins and had recently been acquired by a conglomerate, Court Line, whose other travel interests included Horizon Holidays.

Court Line crashed at the height of the holiday season and with it Clarkson's, leaving customers with lost holidays and stranded overseas, without much financial recourse as the bonding and assets of the company were insufficient. The dramatic effects of this and the press stories that followed, were the most important factors in the extension of bonding through ABTA (Case Study 12.2) to protect holidaymakers against financial collapse. The reasons for the failure of Court Line lie in the economics of running a high-volume, low-margin travel business in the economic uncertainty caused by the oil crisis of 1973, which accelerated fuel costs and depressed consumer spending on items which could be considered a luxury, such as foreign holidays.

Taking advantage of the Court Line failure, Intasun grew rapidly during the second half of 1970s, when it then began to have difficulties in securing the number of aircraft seats it required, since many charter airlines were also tour operators in direct competition with the company. Therefore, the company began operating its own charter airline, Air Europe in 1979. In the early 1980s, the UK travel industry had many small operators with the major player being Thomson. Intasun took the decision to expand through price cutting, to be followed by Thomson. In the years 1983–87, Intasun doubled the volume carried and in 1985 changed its name to ILG, for by this time it had acquired interests in airlines, hotels and a range of holiday companies, the latter reflecting different markets segments, particularly by age groups. Intasun was known for only cheap sun holidays and the change of name was introduced to best reflect the diversity of their holiday offers.

The economic conditions surrounding the collapse of Intasun may be traced to the continual price war with Thomson to achieve market dominance, the ending of a boom period in the British economy in 1988 and the outbreak of the Gulf War in 1991. The specific circumstances may be found in the decision of the company in 1987 to buy out the public shareholders and once again become private, so that it was no longer subject to the movements of the stock market, and the decision to expand Air Europe into scheduled services. Both of these actions, but particularly the latter, substantially increased the debt burden on the company at a time when the cost of borrowing was rising. The company was thus increasing its fixed costs (see Figure 12.5) in the face of stagnating revenues, which lead to serious cash flow issues that could not be solved. Attempts to raise further loans and find buyers for the operation failed, and so ILG's £60 million bond was called in.

expect exclusive holidays to be relatively expensive and so price is used as an indicator of quality, which in turn gives the tour operator the opportunity of securing higher margins. The volume market for inclusive tours is sold competitively on price. Hence operators will consider a range offers, taking account of a number of factors, namely:

- seasonal effects – the range of variation between low and peak season prices is usually around 20 to 30%;

- exchange rate movements;

- competitors' prices and the degree of product differentiation;

- promotional pricing to encourage early booking and late availability discounts;

Table 12.3:
Sales structure
of a large tour
operator

Sales	Percentages
Summer inclusive tours	60
Winter inclusive tours	25
Minimum rated packages	10
Excursions and insurance	4
Interest on deposits	1
Total	100

Source: trade information.

Table 12.4:
Price structure
of a 14 night
inclusive tour

Item	Percentages
Price	100
Direct costs	
Accommodation	40
Air seat (including taxes)	36
Transfers, excursions, etc.	2
Agent's commission	10
Total	88
Gross margin	12
Indirect costs	
Payroll expenses	4
Marketing	3
Office expenses	2
Total	9
Net income	
Trading profit	3
Interest on deposits	1
Total	4

Source: trade information.

- market segmentation pricing, with special offers for senior citizens, young people and families with children below a certain age; and
- discounts for affinity group travel.

The price structure for a typical mass market inclusive tour undertaken within Europe is shown in Table 12.4. Competition keeps profit margins low, and so the emphasis is on volume sales and cost control to sustain net income. In these circumstances, the importance of hedging on foreign exchange is readily appreciated, because uncovered fluctuations in exchange rates may easily erode slender profit margins. This does not entirely remove the risk, for the tour operator/wholesaler still has to predict the amount of business going to each destination.

Air seats

For wholesalers who operate their own airlines or secure whole plane or time charters, an important element in determining the tour price is the costing of an air seat. This is calculated from the following formula:

$$s = \frac{dR}{(d-1)LN} + t$$

where, s = unit seat cost per round trip,
d = number of aircraft departures,
R = aircraft cost per rotation,
L = load factor,
N = number of seats per flight.
t = airport tax.

As an example, consider an aircraft of 250 seats contracted on a time charter for 30 departures. The rotation cost is calculated at 50 000 currency units, the load factor at 90% and airport tax is ascertained to be 5 currency units. By substitution into the above formula, the unit seat cost per return flight is:

$$s = \frac{30 \times 50\,000}{29 \times 0.9 \times 250} + 5$$

$$= 235$$

Note that the number of departures in the denominator of the equation is reduced by 1 to allow for empty legs.

Strategic positioning

History has shown that while there are no major constraints on entry into travel wholesaling, the mass holiday market in any country tends to be dominated by only a handful of companies. The tour operator/wholesaler has no monopoly over airline seats or hotel beds and product standards are easy to emulate. This being the case, the lessons of success indicate strategic market positions secured by a combination of the following factors:

● economies of scale through bulk purchase and volume distribution;
● low-cost distribution network together with national coverage;
● developing new products and markets, and adopting new technologies;
● competitive pricing;
● multibranding to attract different market segments; and
● product differentiation to avoid competing on price alone.

As with major retail stores and supermarket chains, volume throughput and national presence are critical to the success of a mass tour operator. This being the case, in a European context, it is unlikely that any wholesaler can compete effectively, particularly on price, in the mass-market segment with sales of under a million holidays. When account is taken of the organisation structure needed and bonding requirements of around 10% of turnover if belonging to a recognised trade association with its own reserve fund, but as much as 25% otherwise (EU Package Travel Directive), it will be appreciated that the costs of entry into the volume market do act as a considerable deterrent. However, once the volume market has been penetrated, the substantial fixed costs involved are easily transferable to rival operations, as illustrated by the collapse of the International Leisure Group (ILG) in 1991 (Case Study 12.4). The other major British tour operators simply took over ILG's capacity and this aspect tends to make the competition for market share intense, which, in turn, serves to bring down prices to the consumer.

The factors giving rise to a winning strategy are also the cause of a high degree of sales concentration in the tour operation industry, leaving small operators to create their own distinctive market share through specialised holidays. The economics of the industry are such that this situation is one that can only continue, for the large operators are prepared to defend their market position by diversifying their products, even into specialist areas, by multibranding to reach economic sales levels in particular markets quickly, by undertaking price wars and generally enforcing the success criteria outlined above.

Conclusion

We have used this chapter to review the way in which the individual elements of the tourism product may be packaged together for convenience and then distributed to the market efficiently. There are important variations in the way in which this procedure is executed in different regions of the world but, as a result of the predominant North–South flow in tourism, it is the northern countries of the world that have developed the most sophisticated network of distribution to satisfy the volume of market demand.

However, it is important to remember that the distribution of the tourism product is the aspect of the tourism system that has the most potential for change over the next few years as new technology permeates the market-place and direct access to the tourism product becomes more prevalent.

Chapter discussion questions

1. Review and discuss the respective roles of tour operators and travel agencies.

2. Compare and contrast differences in the distribution of the tourism product between Europe and the USA.

3. Identify potential threats to the continued dominance of tour operators and travel agencies and assess the likely impact of technological progress in respect of distribution.

4. What are the benefits and handicaps of vertical integration in the distribution channel in tourism?

5. Given the similarity of the holiday product on offer and the unpredictable nature of the market, is the volume tour operation business inherently unstable?

6. What are the likely advantages and disadvantages to the travel industry of the proposed introduction of a single currency in Europe?

7. Is it an impossible task for trade associations to represent fairly the rights of consumers, when their obligations are to their members?

8. How important is bonding in the travel industry? To what extent is it a restriction on new entry to the industry?

9. What events might occur that could disrupt a holiday, yet leave the travel organiser not liable for breach of contract?

10. Is the legal protection of the holiday traveller now excessive?

Recommended further reading

- Beaver, A. (1993) *Mind Your Own Travel Business*, Beaver Travel, Edgeware.
- Lavery, P. and Van Doren, C. (1990) *Travel and Tourism: A North American/European Perspective*, Elm Publications, Huntingdon.
- Laws, E. (1997) *Managing Packaged Tours*, International Thomson Business Press, London.
- Middleton, V. T. C. (1994) *Marketing in Travel and Tourism*, 2nd edn, Butterworth-Heinemann, Oxford.
- Yale, P. (1995) *The Business of Tour Operations*, Longman Scientific and Technical, Harlow.

Bibliography

- Anshoff, M. I. (1968) *Corporate Strategy*, Penguin, London.
- Beaver, A. (1993) *Mind Your Own Travel Business*, Beaver Travel, Edgeware.
- Garnham, R. (1996) 'Alliances and liaisons in tourism: concepts and implications', *Tourism Economics*, **2**(1), 61–77.
- Gilbert, D. C. (1990) 'Tourism product purchase systems', *The Service Industry Journal*, **10**(4), 664–79.
- Holloway, J. C. (1994) *The Business of Tourism*, 4th edn, Addison Wesley Longman, Harlow.
- Lavery, P. and Van Doren, C. (1990) *Travel and Tourism: A North American/European Perspective*, Elm Publications, Huntington.
- Laws, E. (1997) *Managing Packaged Tours*, International Thomson Business Press, London.
- Middleton, V. T. C. (1994) *Marketing in Travel and Tourism*, 2nd edn, Butterworth-Heinemann, Oxford.
- Mill, R. C. and Morrison, A. M. (1992) *The Tourism System*, 2nd edn, Prentice Hall, Englewood Cliffs, NJ.
- Renshaw, M. (1989) 'Tour operations', pp. 143–66 in *Travel and Tourism*, Callaghan, P. (ed), Business Education Publishers, Durham.
- Sheldon, P. J. (1994) 'Tour wholesaling', pp. 399–403 in *Tourism Marketing and Management Handbook*, 2nd edn, Witt, S. and Moutinho, L. (eds), Prentice Hall, Hemel Hempstead.
- Ward, J. (1991) *Tourism in Action: Ten Case Studies in Tourism*, Stanley Thornes, Cheltenham.
- Yale, P. (1995) *The Business of Tour Operations*, Longman Scientific and Technical, Harlow.

Chapter Thirteen

Transportation

Introduction

Tourism is about being elsewhere and, in consequence, the relationship between transportation and tourism development has traditionally been regarded as 'chicken and egg'. Adequate transportation infrastructure and access to generating markets is one of the most important prerequisites for the development of any destination. In most cases tourism has been developed in areas where extensive transportation networks were in place and the potential for further development was available. The fact that in most destinations world-wide, the traveller can find adequate hospitality and leisure facilities close to transportation terminals demonstrates this point.

On the other hand, tourism demand has stimulated the rapid development of transportation. As millions of tourists expect to be transported safely, quickly and comfortably to their destinations at a reasonable cost, the transportation industry has had to adjust in order to accommodate to this increased, and also more sophisticated, demand. In response, technology has allowed new forms of fleet to be produced rapidly, while there are also examples of a radical improvement in the quality of transport services for tourism in the past two decades.

In this chapter we provide a framework for the analysis of passenger transportation operations for tourism. We explore the modes and elements of transportation, examine issues such as regulation of transport and perform a competitive analysis for the major modes of transportation. Finally, the chapter illustrates the major future political and economic trends that are expected to influence tourist transportation as it enters the third millennium.

Chapter learning objectives

The primary objective of this chapter is to demonstrate the importance of transportation to the overall tourism product: transport is responsible not only for physically moving demand for tourism to supply regions, but also for transporting tourists once they arrive at the destination. With this in mind, on completion of this chapter, the reader will have:

- an understanding of the major modes of transportation for tourism and the competitive advantages and disadvantages of each;
- an appreciation of the influence of political developments on transportation for tourism;
- a knowledge of the purpose of regulation in transportation and some of the key developments; and
- an awareness of issues and future trends that will have an impact upon transportation for tourism.

Definitions and background

Transportation for tourism is an essential element of the tourist product in two ways: it is the means to reach the destination and it is necessary as a means of movement at the destination. Increasingly, as transport is viewed as part of leisure, the journey is at least as important as the destination itself. For some categories of visitor, the trip is therefore seen as an attraction in its own right and certainly part of the tourist experience. The view from the coach or the excitement of flying are both examples of the utility of travel. However, for the business traveller, transport may be seen as a necessary evil and is associated with a frictional element.

Transport as a component of the tourist product

If we interpret the tourist product, in its widest sense, as everything that the visitor consumes not only at the destination but also *en route* to and from the destination, then transport provides some key elements of the product. For example, as part of an air inclusive tour, transport provides a variable proportion of the total cost to the tour operator; for short-haul destinations, transport may represent up to 55% of the total cost, but for long-haul locations, the proportion may be greater. Once at the destination, independent visitors make use of taxis, rental cars, domestic air, rail, ferries and possibly scheduled coach services, whereas both packaged and independent visitors may purchase local tours which are often based on the coach as a means of transportation. We can use visitor expenditure figures to illustrate the importance of transport as an element of the product – transport at the destination can represent as much as 15% of international visitor expenditure within a large country such as Indonesia.

Increasingly, there are instances of transport, both within and between countries, becoming an attractive tourist product in its own right. Examples include:

- railway products – the Palace on Wheels (India), the Blue Train (South Africa), the Orient Express, and the Eastern & Oriental Express;
- air products – day trips on Concorde, nostalgic flights in vintage aircraft; and

Table 13.1: Mode of transport and visitor type with examples of product types

Visitor type	Road		Air		Sea/water		Railways
	Car	Coach	Scheduled	Charter	Ferry	Cruise	
Holiday – inclusive tour	Car hire Fly drive	Coach tour	Long haul City break Packages	Medium/short haul packages	Ferry package	World cruise	Orient Express
– independent	Touring private car	Scheduled coach	Backpackers Individual	Seat only to – villa – timeshare	Private car		Runabout fare
Business and conference	Company car	Executive coach	Fully flexible fare		Hovercraft		TGV
VFR	Private car	Scheduled service	Cheapest fare		Private car		Excursion fare
Other special and common interest, e.g. religion	Car hire Private car	Coach charter	Cheap or flexible fare	Group travel			Group fare
Same day visitors (excursion)	Private car	Scheduled excursion fare	Scheduled excursion fare	Special flights	Coach/car excursion	Local day cruise	Day excursion fare

- sea products – cruising, particularly themed cruising such as the Carnival Cruise Line products, and day trips by ferry in the Baltic Sea and across the English Channel.

Mode of transportation

The most obvious way of analysing transport is by mode to denote the manner in which transport takes place. There are four major modes of travelling:

- road;
- rail;
- water; and
- air.

Some of these modes may be further distinguished by transport *to* the destination as opposed to transport *at* the destination.

To a substantial extent, the choice of mode of transport by the visitor is related to purpose of travel. Table 13.1 provides a structure for the consideration of these relationships. In general, the visitor's choice of mode of transport is affected by:

- distance and time factors;
- status and comfort;
- safety and utility;
- comparative price of services offered;
- geographical position and isolation;
- range of services offered; and
- level of competition between services.

The relative importance of these major influences upon modal choice will vary from one visitor type to another. However visitor types are no longer as homogeneous as previously assumed; some inclusive tour passengers will elect to travel business class by scheduled air rather than by charter, for example.

Increasingly transport operators are attempting to identify segments of demand for whom specific categories of service will appeal; in Europe coaches now offer degrees of comfort and service unheard of in the 1970s while UK ferry companies have become expert in organising a range of centred, or varied itineraries for motorists holidaying overseas with their own car.

Road transport

Road transport is dominated by the motor car and coaches. Indeed, the car is almost the perfect tool for providing door-to-door flexibility, giving views of the landscape and a means of transporting recreational equipment. It even offers residential accommodation in the case of recreational vehicles (RVs), caravans and trailer tents. Hire cars almost exclusively serve visitors but it is difficult to estimate the proportion of total car miles on the roads of any one country which are tourist and excursionist related. Coaches which are chartered are, by definition, almost exclusively for visitor purposes, but again, scheduled services provide for commuters and shoppers as well as visitors.

Rail transport

The extent of provision of a mode and the use of it by visitors as opposed to other users depends on a variety of factors such as history, government involvement and financing,

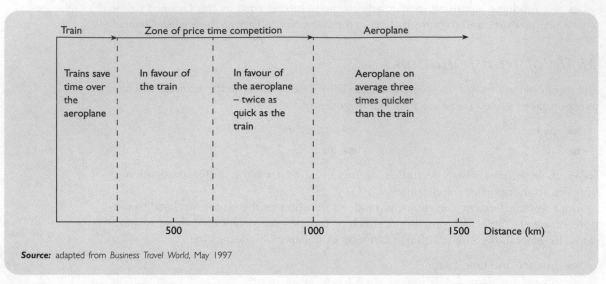

Train	Zone of price time competition			Aeroplane
Trains save time over the aeroplane	In favour of the train	In favour of the aeroplane – twice as quick as the train		Aeroplane on average three times quicker than the train

| | 500 | 1000 | 1500 | Distance (km) |

Source: adapted from *Business Travel World*, May 1997

Figure 13.1: Competition between the aeroplane and the high-speed train on international routes in Europe

topography and geography. Nowhere is this more relevant than with rail transport. In Europe for example an international network, often strongly supported and subsidised by most governments, offers specific services to visitors as well as commuters – car transportation and special tariffs for holiday run-abouts, are examples here.

Railways provide examples of the specific development of business visitor products, such as the Train de Grande Vitesse (TGV) in France and the Eurostar between France and Great Britain. For rail the main competition between modes is often based upon the time and distance comparison, city centre to city centre, compared with air. Beyond a certain distance, some visitors see rail as being too cumbersome and tiring and it is then that notions of adventurism and sightseeing take over as the attractions of the rail mode (Figure 13.1).

Air transport

The majority of travellers by *air* are by definition visitors; diplomats, crew and the other categories which are excluded for the purposes of tourist statistics make up the remainder. Air travel is attractive because of its speed and range and, increasingly for business visitors, it offers status as well as saving valuable work time when travelling on a long-haul basis. Where geographical isolation exists, such as with island communities, air is the dominant and often the only reasonably fast means of travel. Air transport comprises both scheduled and chartered categories and, in some parts of the world, air taxis. Charter transport by air emerged in the 1950s in Europe and North America, transporting holiday visitors from the colder northern climates to the southern sun destinations of the Mediterranean and Florida/the Caribbean respectively.

Sea transportation

In broad terms, we can divide water-borne transport into short sea ferry transport and ocean-going cruises. Other categories exist such as inland waterway craft and small pleasure craft, but assume less significance as a means of transport as they are more destination products in their own right. Cruising should also be thought of as a holiday product as much as a mode of transport. Ferry services, which include or exclude vehicles, can provide lifeline services to islands as well as a focus for visitors who normally are packaged holidaymakers, independent or same-day visitors. Hydrofoil and hovercraft tend to be faster than conventional forms of ship technology but, in general (unless for short-sea commuting such as between Hong Kong and Macau), business visitors tend to choose other modes of transport. Owing to the vagaries of the sea, visitors either like, accept or dislike this means of transport. Geographical factors tend to determine the provision of ferry transport leaving some destinations heavily dependent upon such links. Examples include:

- Aegean island hopping or travel to and from the Greek mainland; or
- channel crossings such as the English Channel, Irish Sea, the Cook Strait between the North and South islands of New Zealand, and the Baltic Sea.

Elements of transportation

We can identify four basic elements in any transportation system, namely:

- the way;
- the terminal;
- the carrying unit; and
- motive power.

These elements vary for each transportation mode and vehicle.

The way

The way is the medium of travel used by a transport mode. It may be purely artificial such as roads and railways; or natural, such as air or water. Roads, railways and inland waterways restrict vehicles to movement to a specific pattern, while air and sea allow flexibility. However, international regulations delineate both sea and air corridors and routes such that standard operating procedures are applied world-wide to limit the freedom of these ways. In considering transport modes, the availability of the way is very important in the case of roads, railways and inland waterways where substantial investment is needed to provide them. In the case of water and air, this is not an issue except for harbour access or air traffic control procedures.

The terminal

The terminal represents the second important element of a transport mode. Terminals give access to the way for the users, or act as an interchange between different types of way. The terminal is the furthest point to which the transport system extends – literally the end of the line. Probably the simplest terminal is parking for a private car, while the most complex one is an airport. In fact, most terminals are becoming integrated transportation points as they can act as interchanges where travellers can transfer between vehicles or modes. Switzerland has examples of integrated rail and air transport with rail termini further linked to the post-bus. Airports for example, can be used as transfer points between two aircraft, or other modes of travelling, such as the car or train. The design of terminals and the amenities they offer depend heavily upon the type of journey and transportation involved. Although we can observe a general tendency towards the development of integrated terminals, which cater for all the potential needs of the traveller, not all modes need to have sophisticated points as terminals; coaches for instance can and do operate from roadside locations.

The carrying unit

The carrying unit is the actual transportation media: the vehicle that facilitates the movement. Each 'way' demands a distinctive form of carrying unit; aircraft for the sky, ships for the sea, vehicles for roads, and train or tram for rails. The nature of carrying units has been influenced by numerous factors which include travel demand and technology employed, as well as the other elements of the mode, such as motive power. In the past few decades developments have occurred in the carrying units which are designed towards greater efficiency and consumer orientation. Flexibility is also important – vehicles increasingly need to be altered easily and quickly, in order to accommodate changing tourism demand. Executive style coaches with on-board services, airline-style reclining seats on trains and railway viewing cars are examples.

Motive power

Finally, and perhaps the most important, motive power is the key element in transportation development. Natural power of horse-drawn carriages and sailing vessels provided the initial energy for transportation. The exploration of steam power provided the opportunity for the radical introduction of steam ships and railways while the internal combustion engine stimulated the development of road and air transportation. Finally, jet propulsion enabled air transportation to be competitively priced and gave aircraft both speed and range. However, even in the 1990s a number of activity holidays such as cycling, pony trekking and sailing involve human-generated motive power as part of the recreational activities. Motive power is closely related to a number of issues such as the capacity and the type of the carrying unit, demand, and the desired speed and range of the vehicle. As costs of operation have been modified then increasingly the engine needs to be more fuel efficient and, for safety reasons, reliable.

The easiest way in which to demonstrate the role of the four basic elements is to consider the historical changes over time that have occurred. Except for being quieter because of continuous welded tracks, railways are little different from when first designed; railways, like airways, have become much busier and congested. Roadways have grown and universally the *autostrada* or motorway provides functional means of movement; however, the view from the road is less interesting than that from the observation dome of the tourist train.

Terminals, especially airports, have become not only design pieces in themselves but in some instances the centre of hub and spoke traffic which have grown to the size of a small town to deal with transit traffic (as at Changi Airport, Singapore). Also the shopping mall concept has been merged with the terminal as for instance at London Gatwick's North Terminal which now has been developed in a number of other airport locations world-wide. However the concept of complete intermodal transfer for baggage and people is not yet reality at all airport termini. Termini are still centres of congestion for passengers and pose difficulties for operators in terms of baggage retrieval and security.

The carrying unit in some instances differs little from previous decades but in the case of coaches and trains, comfort has been built into the design and operation. The last two decades have seen quieter but not necessarily faster aircraft being built; the latest Boeing 747-400 series has a longer range but takes about as many passengers as previous models. The 550-seater superjumbo has been talked about but has yet to emerge.

Table 13.2: The historical development of tourism: recent changes in transport

	1930s	1940s–1950s	1960s–1970s	1980s–1990s
Air	Civil aviation established Travel is expensive and limited	Propeller technology Travel still limited Basic terminals 400–480 km/h	Jet aircraft Boeing 707 Cheap fuel 800–950 km/h Charters take off	Wide-bodied jet 747 Extended range Fuel efficient No increases in speed except Concorde
Sea	Ocean liners and cruises Short sea ferry speed Less than 40 km/h	Little competition from air No increase in speed	Air overtakes sea on N. Atlantic Hovercraft and faster craft being developed	Fly–Cruise established Larger and more comfortable ferries Fast catamarans developed
Road	Cars 55 km/h Coaches develop	Cars 100 km/h	Cars used for domestic tourism Speed 115 km/h	Speed limits in USA Rise in car ownership rates Urban congestion Green fuel Improved coaches
Rail	Steam era Speed exceed cars	Railways at peak	Electrification Cuts in rail systems: some resorts isolated	High-speed networks develop in Europe Business products offered – memorabilia and steam

The emphasis has been on developing medium-sized jets such as the Boeing 767, the 777 and the various Airbuses. Efficiency of motive power may have changed for all modes of transport but speed of travel and size of fleet have stabilised in the last decade. The major changes are illustrated in Table 13.2.

The recent history of transport for tourism is characterised by changes in technology involving not only the jet age but more powerful and fuel-efficient engines for aircraft and automobiles. The use of more universal access to travel has led to a wider but increasingly more varied market; operators have responded with more differentiated products reflecting comfort and level of service for customers. Business class products by air, and executive style rail services, are examples here. The history of competition has been one where soon after the Second World War, an undifferentiated product was offered, whereas now speed, comfort and value for money are seen as bases for gaining or maintaining market share. However, in recent decades speed of travel has either stabilised or increased only in certain respects such as fast sea craft or high-speed rail services.

The development of fuel-efficient technology has been encouraged by the rising cost of fuel caused by three incidents:

1. In 1973–74, the Arab–Israeli War.

2. In 1978–79 the Iranian crisis.

3. In 1991 the Gulf War.

Air charter operators now need to use new fleet rather than, as in the early 1970s, second-hand older equipment. Indeed, airline operation illustrates the changing cost structure over time and this can be seen by considering fuel as a percentage of operating costs; in 1973 for international scheduled services, fuel accounted for 12% of total costs but rose beyond 25% by 1980. With the introduction of fuel-efficient aircraft during the ensuing decade, this item of variable cost was reduced; in 1989 fuel accounted for 14% of all costs and currently ranges between 10 and 20% of total costs.

A competitive analysis

We can see that modern passenger transportation is a very complex and competitive industry. This competition is expressed between the various modes and vehicles of transportation, between different companies and even between countries.

In this section we provide a competitive analysis of transportation modes, based on consumer behaviour variables. These variables have been identified as:

- safety;
- price/cost;
- time/speed;
- distance;
- convenience;
- departure and arrival times;
- reliability;
- availability;

- flexibility;
- service quality;
- comfort/luxury;
- incentives;
- ground services;
- terminal facilities and locations;
- status and prestige;
- enjoyment of trip.

Road transportation

For tourism the attractions of road transport are:

- the control of the route and the stops *en route*;
- the control of departure times;
- the ability to carry baggage and equipment easily;
- the ability to use the vehicle for accommodation;
- privacy;
- the freedom to use the automobile once the destination is reached; and
- the low perceived out-of-pocket expenses.

The car

Some nations tend to utilise a car much more than others for recreation and tourism, depending upon the transportation facilities and climate. Trips by car account for 90% of the pleasure/personal and business trips taken by Canadian and US residents and for almost 83% of the total passenger kilometres in Europe. Furthermore, travellers in the Continent of Europe, such as those from Germany, Italy, Austria, Switzerland and France, tend to use the motor car for holidaying in the southern Mediterranean and at home.

The coach

The hired coach has traditionally been employed by groups for transfers to and from terminals. In addition, sightseeing trips and tours are normally conducted by coaches. This mode is particularly useful for short and medium distance journeys. It has traditionally attracted the elderly and inexpensive markets and the stereotype is of the lower occupational or social groups and the over-50 market. Increasingly, local towns at the destination make use of the mini or microbus. Safaris in particular use the adapted microbus for sightseeing and game watching, such as in Kenya.

Public coaches operate regular scheduled services and may transfer passengers to remote areas where there is inadequate infrastructure for alternative transportation (the Mountain Goat minibus service in the English Lake District National Park is an example). Beyond a certain threshold distance, lack of comfort and the relatively slower speed compared with other modes has to be traded off against cheaper and more attractive pricing structures.

Railway transportation

Trains are perceived to be safe, inexpensive and offer the convenience of movement within the carrying unit. They may also travel through attractive scenery and are a relatively 'green' form of travel. The fact that railway terminals are often in the centre of the destination is an asset in comparison with, say, airports which are often located 20 or 30 kilometres away from the centre.

Not all trains are fast, and trains do depend on the 'way' (track) which makes them inflexible in routeing and overloads them with a very high fixed cost. Normally this cost is borne by the public sector. Although train operators try to emphasise the rest and relaxation of travel by train, rarely do they offer high-quality services throughout the network of a country. The luxury and comfort attributes are therefore limited to journeys between 200 to 500 kilometres between major cities; current projections in Europe suggest that the increase in speed of modern trains will increase this range to 1000 kilometres.

The most important reasons from travelling by train are:

- safety;
- the ability to look out of the train and see *en route*;
- the ability to move around the coach;
- arriving at the destination rested and relaxed;
- personal comfort;
- centrally located termini;
- environmentally friendly form of transport; and
- decongested routes.

The traditional market for the train has been regarded as the independent holiday visitor, particularly the VFR category; they may also attract a significant 'fear of flying' market. Although in the USA trains are considered a second-rate means of passenger transportation, in Western Europe trains hold a valuable market share of passenger traffic, primarily because of policies of protectionism and subsidy by the respective governments. However, the introduction of high-speed and intercity services, such as the TGV in France, has improved the level of service and comfort offered. Many new trains have good sleeping facilities and they are also able to carry automobiles. Moreover, the opening of the Channel Tunnel in 1993 has created rail demand from London to Paris and Brussels initially, and will affect other European cities later.

In addition there is a tendency to change the image and function of trains towards an environmentally friendly, traditional, stylish, relaxed, reliable and consumer-orientated form of transport. Consumers with entirely different lifestyles from the previous rail clientele have been identified; in Europe for tourism purposes, railway systems would seem to offer substantial competition for other modes in the future. In Britain, the development of a privatised system of railway transport has not had any noticeable impact upon transport for tourism – although there are fears that it leads to less integration of tourist product components owing to localised networks.

Sea transport

As far as the transportation of vehicles and merchandise is required on short sea crossings, ferries offer inexpensive, reliable and safe services. Ferry transportation is the only possibility in the case of remote and small islands which have no airport. This situation can be found in Greece, where there are only 15 airports to serve 95 inhabited islands. In this case, large ferries provide coastal shipping services linking the mainland ports and islands as well as the islands with each other. Furthermore, smaller regional ferries undertake transportation between the islands, especially during the summer peak period.

However, in many cases, air can be a viable alternative to sea transportation between larger islands and the mainland. The main advantage of ferry operators when compared with air transportation is price, combined with the fact that passengers can carry their own vehicles and use them at the destination. The popularity of motoring holidays and self drive packages as well as the introduction of roll on – roll off facilities which enables the ports to handle a much greater volume of vehicles demonstrates the increase of passenger demand for ferry services.

In Europe, the gradual liberalisation of air transportation, the decrease of air fares, the construction of the Channel Tunnel and the development of alternative modes of travel have forced the ferry companies to improve the luxury of their vessels considerably, to increase the cruising speed, to increase the size and to install leisure facilities – casinos, swimming pools, sports and shopping – and to offer a more consumer-orientated service.

Modern vessels, such as the wave-piercing catamaran, hydrofoils and the hovercraft have been introduced on some routes in recent decades. Their main aim is to offer a passenger-only service in a shorter crossing time than the traditional ferry service. Their speed is up to three times that of a conventional ferry, while they have a great manoeuvrability, fast turn-around in port and need minimum dock facilities. They therefore attract up-market tourists who appreciate the importance of their time and desire to reach the destination as soon as possible. However, these vessels are:

● much more expensive than the ferries;

● vulnerable in rough seas and strong winds; and

● noisy.

Also, as they offer coach type accommodation they are uncomfortable for long distance trips, because they prevent free movement on the decks.

Cruising is more of a leisure *product* than a *mode* of sea transportation. In this case the sea voyage, the entertainment and leisure facilities offered within the ship and the excursions at the ports are more important trip elements than the places visited – the cruise ship is the destination itself.

The decline in ocean liner shipping since the 1950s signified the development of the cruise industry as most shipping lines diversified into cruising. Increasingly, with the development of themed, special interest or hobby-type cruises the trip can be as short as one day or as long as several months.

The typical cruise passenger used to be older, wealthy and predominantly North American. However, the cruise market now caters for all types of needs, ages and purchasing abilities. Increasingly fly-cruises are offered as holiday products, combining the speed and efficiency of air transportation and the relaxing, romantic attributes of cruise ships. New types of products have emerged of the smaller cruise ship undertaking regional itineraries for instance, in South East Asia along the Malay Peninsula and around the islands of Indonesia.

Air transport

Travelling by air is probably the most important transportation innovation of the twentieth century. It has enabled the transportation of passengers in the shortest time and it has boosted the demand for long-haul trips. In fact no part of the world is now more than 24 hours flying time from any other part.

Air transportation has managed in the past few decades to gain a very significant share of the transportation market, especially for movements over 500 kilometres. As new aircraft, such as the Boeing 747-400 series, have come on line, the range for air travel has been extended to up to 15 000 kilometres for non-stop flights.

Scheduled airlines offer a safe, convenient, reliable, frequent and relatively consumer-orientated product; airlines attract business travellers, who appreciate its speed and flexibility between the various flights, especially on popular routes, as well as the leisure passengers who enjoy the ability to arrive at the destination quickly, and without spending time and money on route. Normally, ground services, and the terminal facilities are much more advanced and sophisticated than for any other mode and therefore the travelling experience is enhanced. The quality of services and the comforts offered on board have introduced new industry standards for the other modes of transport. Finally, airlines offer a number of incentives for their loyal customers through various 'frequent flyer' programmes. (See Major Case Study 5 (p. 492) which details relationship marketing in respect of airline schemes). However, air transportation is the most expensive mode of transportation, especially for the short-haul routes, say in Europe, where an economic cruising speed cannot be achieved.

Promotional fares try to offer cheaper prices by minimising the opportunities for alterations on the travel arrangements and by securing the passenger as early as possible. These fares include Advanced Purchase Excursion Fare (APEX); previously standby and other forms of Instant Purchase Fares (IPEX) were experimented with. Yield management enables the airlines to alter their fares in order to achieve maximum yield by taking account of potential demand and supply factors, historical data, time lost before the flight and current load factors. Thus appropriate prices are suggested for the current market environment in order to maximise the airline yield. Following on from developments in the USA, in Europe we have seen the emergence of low-cost, no-frills airlines, but frequencies and schedule times cannot compare with the established operators.

Charter flights are utilised widely to facilitate the movement of holidaymakers on package tours or even on so-called 'seat only' arrangements. Sometimes charter airlines belong to tour operators who attempt to integrate their operations vertically such as Britannia Airways and Thomson Holidays in the UK (see Chapter 12). Charter airlines offer *ad hoc* transportation services; they normally fly directly to the final destination and therefore passengers do not need to change aircraft at a hub. This can be achieved by:

● minimising the flexibility in altering flights;
● by flying at inconvenient and therefore not busy hours;
● reducing the space within the aircraft; and
● offering elementary luxuries and services.

The higher load factor achieved on charter services (of 90% or more) compared with scheduled services (which can be as low as 20%) is the final factor explaining the substantial difference in the unit cost of production and the price at which the product can be sold.

The bulk of air travel is orientated towards either business or leisure travellers. In the first case people travel for their economic activities and therefore their fares are paid by their employers. Maximum flexibility is required in order to be able to alter their travelling arrangements at short notice; as a result business travellers use only scheduled airlines. Services, terminals and aircraft have to be designed to facilitate the function of the busy business traveller. It is estimated that business travellers account for about 30% of all international air traffic.

Leisure travellers' share of air transportation has increased rapidly during the recent decades. Leisure travellers have much more time and they do not necessarily require very high-quality services. They are free to make their holiday arrangements well in advance and thus they do not need flexibility. However, unlike the business traveller they do pay their own fares an, therefore, they are price conscious. The development of specific leisure fares by scheduled airlines as well as the charter airlines in Europe, has catered for the needs of this market adequately. Overall it is estimated that around 15% of international tourism uses air transportation while 86% of the Europeans use planes for trips outside Europe. Growth in air travel is forecast to average 5.5% per year to 2000 and 5% per year from 2000 to 2010.

Political influences on transport for tourism

International tourist movements have always been affected by the activities of governments and transport for tourism has also been influenced by such factors. Barriers to communication, apart from distance, have been border controls, the need for visas or transit visas and customs control. For rail and road the boundary between nations is the place of border control, and for sea transport the land/sea interface or the port is the point of control; however, for air transport the airport termini, wherever located, is the processing point.

The concept of sovereignty of airspace versus the freedom of the high seas has always been a factor limiting and influencing provision of transport for tourism by air. Rail transport across and between nations, apart from gauge differences, has always been relatively smooth compared with quota regulations for coaches in transit or entering other countries. The motorist has been affected by the insurance requirements for a Green Card and international driving licences, but in Europe, with the introduction of the single market in 1993, such barriers and restraints are now disappearing.

Because of its very nature, transport for tourism by air has developed as a complex political issue and the key factors need to be highlighted. Airlines are important within the national economy for foreign exchange and for fare payments from foreign travellers. Generally airlines have been owned by the state, have been subsidised by governments and have been seen to be prestige elements flying the colours of the national flag. Scandinavian Airline System (SAS) and Air Afrique are exceptions to the rule that most countries possess their own national airline. Equally, the size of an airline is not necessarily related to the size of traffic potential of that country; the examples of KLM and Swissair illustrate this point.

The notion of the territory held by a nation or the sovereignty that it expresses over its colonies has been important for air transport; the concept of cabotage applies to transport within the boundary of a country and therefore permission to overfly the land of other countries and to pick up and set down passengers is not required from another nation. Countries that had colonies in the past not only developed route structures to service these points but also applied favourable pricing structures to benefit their residents and those of the colonies.

Transport for tourism operates within a competitive political and economic environment, especially in the international context, because it represents the means to transfer across borders and to cross other territories to reach the intended destination. This competitive environment is illustrated by the extent to which transport for tourism has been regulated and controlled by governments.

Regulation of competition

Since their inception, transport media have been subject to regulation by governments for safety and technical reasons. In addition, legal and economic forms of regulation have applied to specific transport modes. In many countries transport operation has been subject to legislation to protect so-called 'pioneer operators' who incur costs, set up routes and pick up points, but are then vulnerable to another operator moving in without those costs to recoup. This was the basis of coaching legislation in the UK in 1930 which was modified as recently as 1980 with the legislation for the deregulation of coaching. Railways tend to be national monopolies and to be state-owned and subsidised, except in Britain where the concept of privatisation has been applied to the railway system in the mid-1990s. Sea transport has tended to be less regulated than other modes of transport and the basis for this lies in the relative freedom of movement over water given to all vessels. However in the 1970s the British government was concerned with the apparent collusion over fares between rival ferry operators on the North Sea and the English Channel routes. In the 1990s, there is still concern over the possible anti-restrictive practices that might be operated by ferry providers in their competition with the Channel Tunnel operators.

Regulation policies

Policies on regulation have tended to focus on air transport to a greater degree than other modes; international air law is a factor that controls the extent to which national airlines may operate. In the United States the so-called anti-trust provisions have always existed to prevent the development of price fixing, cartels and collusion between competitors. In Europe under the Treaty of Rome, transport has been deemed to be subject to competition rules and the European Commission has outlawed agreements between pairs of national carriers who pool their capacity and revenues.

The need for regulation of transport has hinged on the relative ease of entry into operation of a service; the barriers to entry are relatively low compared with other industries. Given that the evils of cut-throat competition can lead to both the demise of a regular reliable schedule and lead to social disadvantages to travellers, regulation policies have specified procedures for entry into and exit from operation. The arguments for and against regulation are many, but basically in the short term, customers benefit from increased competition and efficiency through lower fares; but in the long term, they may suffer disadvantages from the lack of an organised and reliable schedule of services as competitors go out of business.

The Airline Deregulation Act 1978 was introduced in President Carter's era in the United States and lead to the development of an open skies policy. This Act is often cited as the extreme of what deregulation can do in practice. The Civil Aeronautics Board as a regulatory body devising policy was phased out. Its role had been to devise regulations on conditions of service such as frequency and capacity, on exit and entry into operation and on fares and prices. Such matters then became the subject of free competition within the US domestic environment. Up until the late 1970s the IATA was the *de facto* controlling body world-wide, being a trade association for airlines, though in reality it represented governments as well. However, ever since the famous Show Cause Order where IATA had to show good cause why it should be exempt from the provisions of US anti-trust provisions, this body has lost its stature and strength to implement fare structures to protect its high-cost airline members. IATA's influence varies from continent to continent and it is still strong in parts of Europe, Africa and Latin America.

Following the Chicago convention of 1944 where a truly multilateral agreement between countries was not reached, a series of bilateral arrangements between governments emerged. National governments approve and licence carriers and are nominated to fly between the home, country and an overseas destination; fares are fixed by reference to IATA conference machinery or between respective governments. Even in a truly deregulated environment fares are fixed by mutual agreement between partners or merely filed. The so-called 'five freedoms of movement' giving technical and traffic rights to airlines are still important for international movements. These are outlined in Figure 13.2. Subsequent to the Chicago Convention, sixth and seventh freedoms have been formulated.

Figure 13.2:
The five freedoms of the air as agreed at the Chicago Convention 1944

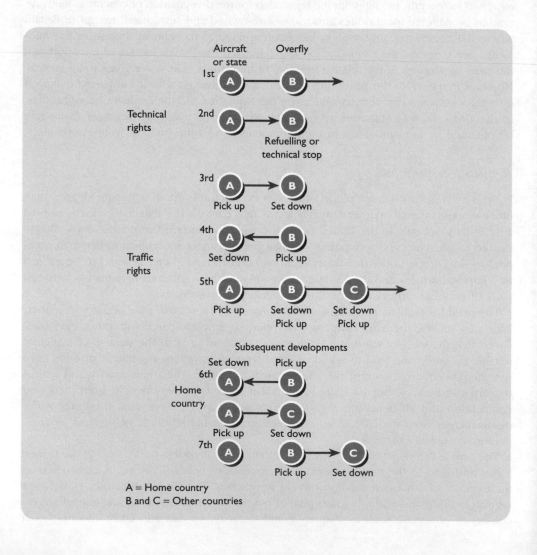

The extent to which US domestic policies have been translated to overseas situations has been limited. Within the USA, as a result of fierce competition, instability was initiated where a great number of air carriers entered the market and the fares reached their lowest levels. However, in the following years only a few carriers could survive and most of the small or weak airlines were absorbed or merged with the stronger ones. Unfortunately fares have increased while choice has been reduced.

European skies have been quite reluctant to open up to complete deregulation. This is partly because of the public sector's role in the airline industry as well as the social role of the carriers to maintain uneconomic routes in the peripheral areas purely for national and social reasons. After three directives from the European Commission, the development of true cabotage arrangements for Europe, where it is seen as one domestic territory, finally happened on 1 April 1997. Europe, though, is still dominated by state-controlled and owned airlines, some of whom have received substantial subsidies from the European Commission.

External environment and future trends

Currently passenger transportation is probably at its most competitive since its existence; alternative forms and modes of travelling develop strong competitive advantages and they attempt to attract the bulk of the passengers. Each mode has of course distinctive characteristics and attributes as well as strengths and weaknesses for each market segment. In this section we provide an analysis of the external environment and the future trends of passenger transportation.

Efficiency

Great pressure has been placed upon all transportation media to reduce their prices and offer a better quality of service. This has forced all companies to identify new methods of increasing their efficiency; in particular this has been applied in the airline world where modern techniques such as yield management, hub and spoke operations and modern distribution channels such as CRS have changed the way that business is operated.

Yield management maximises the airline's yield by suggesting the maximum prices which can be achieved for every available seat. It has been defined as the maximisation of revenue through optimum seat mix, competitive buy-up pricing strategies, accurate overbooking, high yield spill and spoilage controls and demand forecasting.

CRS has been used to control scheduled seats and fares in order to distribute products effectively and to maximise profits following the deregulation of air transportation in the USA. CRS enabled other efficiencies and competitive techniques (such as yield management and frequent flyer programmes) to be developed while becoming a source for strong competitive advantage and changing the balance of the airline world.

Development of hub and spoke systems increased the rationalisation of air transportation by using major airports as transit points. Short-haul flights (spokes) connect through a limited number of airports (hubs) and passengers are transferred to long-haul trips. This enabled the airlines to achieve higher load factors and keep prices down.

Air congestion is an emerging problem which will influence the airlines severely since the lack of terminal and air-corridor capacity is now becoming apparent. In 1988 and 1989, Europe's air traffic control systems were in severe crisis because of congestion. It is suggested that the intra-Europe traffic will double from 1990 to 2005 and by the year 2010 all but four of Europe's 27 leading airports will reach their capacity; the result would damage air transportation and stimulate people to switch to alternative modes.

A number of improvements are therefore required at airports and, more specifically, on the control procedures, the design and construction of the terminals and the inter-connectivity with other modes of travel. Furthermore the efficiency of airlines should increase by extending hub operations, reorganising the schedule, utilising larger aircraft and by achieving higher load factors.

Some see the solution being larger aircraft, such as the Airbus A3XX, offering 550 seats, but there remains uncertainty over passenger acceptance of such large aircraft and the ability of route structures and infrastructure (air traffic control, airports, etc.) to sustain and support such large loads.

Globalisation and integration

Globalisation is one of the major trends in the international tourism industry and involves a convergence in tastes, preferences and products. The global firm is one that capitalises on this trend and produces standardised products contributing to the homogenisation of the world tourism market. Essentially this means an increase in world-wide business between multinational corporations irrespective of the geographical location and can lead to the virtual firm as a transport operator. As a result, a great concentration can be observed in tourism and transportation; some suggest that by 2000, there will be 12 major global carriers dominating air transport.

In this way airlines, as they expand their services on a global basis, are forging strategic alliances because of:

- the maturity of domestic traffic;
- the competition for terminal space and slots;
- the need for extensive networks world-wide;
- the necessity for economies of scale in airline operation;
- the control of the new distribution channels (CRS); and
- the gradual deregulation in world transportation.

Many examples can illustrate the globalisation of airlines but perhaps the best is British Airways, which:

- in 1997 had franchise operators BA Regional, British Asia Airways, Bryman Airways and TAT;
- in 1992 bought a stake in US Air but decided to sell in 1996;
- had shares in Deutsche BA, Air Liberte and Quantas; and
- planned a transatlantic alliance with American Airlines.

Other schemes include the Star Alliance programme of Thai, Canadian, United, Lufthansa and SAS which will:

- integrate products and connecting services;
- offer common check-in and reservation services;
- share airport lounge services; and
- share marketing, communications and rewards services.

As far as vertical integration is concerned, transportation industry has always acknowledged that travellers need to use a combination of the various modes in order to complete their trip. Therefore, transportation companies are moving towards alternative modes which can be combined and offer integrated services. As a result, chauffeur services are offered by various airlines for their loyal and full-fare customers, while fly–drive programmes are very successful. Finally, the ambition of airlines such as Lufthansa to penetrate into rail transport, by offering private services primarily for their airline clients, demonstrates the point.

Conclusion

As tourism demand grows, transportation – and indeed transportation infrastructure – will become increasingly important. New technology in respect of every aspect of transportation will be influential, and the transport industry of the future will supply visitors with ticketless travel, smart card technology for payment, and also perhaps for visa and passport purposes in certain country groups.

However, the transport industry for tourism has many issues confronting it as numbers of visitors world-wide increase. All forms of transport pollute the environment and some will never be able to develop totally green policies. Airlines will still burn kerosene and create noise. Trains can be electrically operated, but ultimately rely on nuclear or fossil fuels. Coaches and cars burn fossil fuels and sea-borne craft likewise, except leisure craft, which are wind driven. As other suppliers of the elements of the tourist product develop more environmentally friendly policies and practices, operators must be seen as natural polluters in the foreseeable future.

Chapter discussion questions

1. Justify government regulation of transport for tourism.

2. Examine the extent to which the provision of transport and accommodation for tourism may be said to be interdependent.

3. The history and development of tourism is inextricably linked to advances in transport technology. Expand on this statement.

4. With reference to examples, comment on the importance of the role of transport in tourism development.

5. What do you consider to be the most influential factors in transport for tourism when considering future trends in tourism?

6. Discuss the view that transport for tourism is very much still a homogeneous product.

Recommended further reading

● Doganis, R. (1985) *Flying Off Course: The Economics of International Airlines*, George Allen and Unwin, London.
● Doganis, R. (1992) *The Airport Business*, Routledge, London.
● Hanlon, P. (1996) *Global Airlines*, Butterworth-Heinemann, Oxford.
● Page, S. (1994) *Transport for Tourism*, Routledge, London.

- Shaw, S. (1990) *Airline Marketing and Management*, 3rd edn, Pitman, London.
- Wheatcroft, S. (1988) 'European Air Transport in the 1990s', *Tourism Management*, **9**(3), 187–98.
- Wheatcroft, S. (1989) 'Present and future demand for transport', pp. 299–304 in *Tourism Marketing and Management Handbook*, Witt, C. and Moutinho, L. (eds), Prentice Hall, Hemel Hempstead.

Bibliography

- Beaver, A. (1996) 'Frequent flyer programmes: the beginning of the end', *Tourism Economics*, **2**(1), 43–60.
- British Airways (1996) *Annual Environmental Report*, London.
- Collison, F. and Boberg, K. (1987) 'Marketing of airline services in a deregulated environment', *Tourism Management*, **8**(3), 195–204.
- Doganis, R. (1985) *Flying Off Course: The Economics of International Airlines*, George Allen and Unwin, London.
- Doganis, R. (1992) *The Airport Business*, Routledge, London.
- Fitzroy, F. and Smith, I. (1995) 'The demand for rail transport in European countries', *Transport Policy*, **2**(3), 153–8.
- French, T. (1996) 'No frills airlines in Europe', *Travel & Tourism Analyst*, **3**, 4–19.
- French, T. (1996) 'World airport development plans and constraints', *Travel & Tourism Analyst*, **1**, 4–16.
- Gialoreto, L. (1988) *Strategic Airline Management*, Pitman, London.
- Hanlon, P. (1989) 'Hub operation and airline competition', *Tourism Management*, **10**(2), 111–24.
- Hanlon, P. (1996) *Global Airlines*, Butterworth-Heinemann, Oxford.
- Holloway, C. (1989) *The Business of Tourism*, 3rd edn, Pitman, London.
- Leontiades, J. (1986) 'Going global – global strategies versus national strategies', *Long Range Planning*, **19**(6), 96–104.
- Mill, R. and Morrison, A. (1985) *The Tourism System: An Introductory Text*, Prentice Hall, Englewood Cliffs, NJ.
- Page, S. (1994) *Transport for Tourism*, Routledge, London.
- Pattison, T. (1992) 'The future for the coach industry', *Insights*, **5** 1991/92, English Tourist Board, London.
- Peisley, T. (1992) *World Cruise Ship Industry in the 1990's*, Economist Publications Special Report No. 2104, London.
- Shaw, S. (1990) *Airline Marketing and Management*, 3rd edn, Pitman, London.
- Speakman, C. (1995) 'Britain's changing railways and the tourist package', *Insights*, **7**(5), 1995/6, English Tourist Board, London.
- Wheatcroft, S. (1988) 'European air transport in the 1990's', *Tourism Management*, **9**(3), 187–98.
- Wheatcroft, S. (1989) 'Present and future demand for transport', pp. 299–304 in *Tourism Marketing and Management Handbook*, Witt, C. and Moutinho, L. (eds), Prentice Hall, Hemel Hempstead.
- Wheatcroft, S. (1991) 'Airlines, tourism and the environment', *Tourism Management*, **12**(2), 119–24.
- Wheatcroft, S. and Lipman, G. (1990) *European Liberalisation and World Air Transport Towards a Transnational Industry*, Economist Publications, Special Report No. 2015, London.
- WTO (1994) *Aviation and Tourism Policies*, Routledge, London.

Chapter author: John Westlake

Chapter Fourteen

Attractions

Introduction

Tourist attractions may be grouped into those that are gifts of nature and those that are artificial. The former includes the landscape, climate, vegetation, forests and wildlife. The latter are principally the products of history and culture, but also include artificially created entertainment complexes such as theme parks. Attractions may be further subdivided into those that are site-specific, because of the location of facilities, and events that are periodic. Events may be used to complement site-specific attractions.

Many attractions, both natural and artificial, come within the domain of the public sector, while others are owned by voluntary organisations and the private commercial sector. In this chapter we look at some of the reasons for these different ownership patterns and examine the business consequences. We also consider problems of cost structure, pricing and seasonality to demonstrate the economic aspects of operating attractions.

Resource and visitor management techniques are discussed from the standpoint of alleviating crowding brought about by the continual rise in tourist numbers. This leads on to the issue of sustainable tourism development in which the object is to manage tourism growth in a manner that ensures that tourists do not destroy by pressure of numbers the very attractions they come to see. A related matter is the authenticity of the visitor experience: countries frequently stage events and aspects of site-specific attractions as a means of serving the tourist efficiently. This results in a loss of authenticity from the travel experience.

Chapter learning objectives

Attractions are an integral part of the tourism product and, in this chapter, we focus on providing the reader with:

- a review of possible classifications and an understanding of the various types of man-made and natural attractions that may be classified as tourist attractions;
- a discussion of the roles and responsibilities of the public and private sectors in respect of the development and management of tourist attractions;
- a consideration of all issues associated with resource management; and
- an analysis of environmental issues in respect of tourist attractions and an evaluation of strategies that have been developed with a view to alleviating environmental impacts of tourism at attractions.

Characteristics of attractions

We know that attractions provide the single most important reason for leisure tourism to a destination. Many of the components of the tourist trip – for example, transport and accommodation – are demands derived from the consumer's desire to enjoy what a destination has to offer in terms of 'things to see and do'. Thus a tourist attraction is a focus for recreational and, in part, educational activity undertaken by both day and stay visitors. This has been recognised, for example, by the international hotel chain Radisson, which has been encouraging its properties to forge partnerships with historic, heritage, cultural, artistic and theatrical organisations in their communities, through a programme entitled 'Radisson Partnering with the Arts', in order to add value to its product.

We may note also that it is a common feature of tourist attractions that they are shared with the host community. This in turn may give rise to conflict in popular destinations, where tourism is perceived to cause problems of crowding, traffic congestion, environmental damage and litter.

Classification

There are many different types of attractions, and a number of attempts have been made to classify them. Classification is possible along a number of different dimensions:

- ownership;
- capacity;
- market or catchment area;
- permanency;
- type.

Early attempts at classification were according to type, distinguishing between natural resources and artificial features or products. Artificial features were as follows:

- **Cultural** – religion, modern culture, museums, art galleries, architecture, archaeological sites.
- **Traditions** – folklore, animated culture, festivals.
- **Events** – sports activities and cultural events.

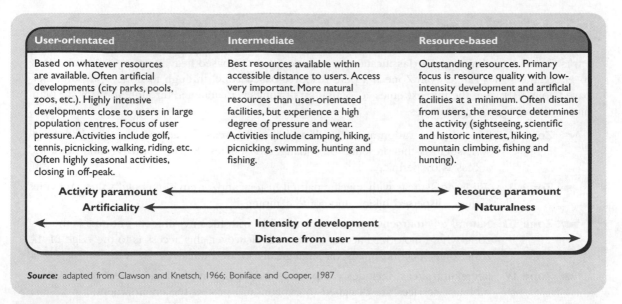

Source: adapted from Clawson and Knetsch, 1966; Boniface and Cooper, 1987

Figure 14.1: Clawson's classification of recreation resources

Natural resources included national parks, wildlife, viewpoints and outstanding natural phenomena such as the Grand Canyon in Colorado or the Niagara Falls in Ontario.

An alternative and more complex approach is that designed by Clawson and Knetsh (1966) and shown in Figure 14.1. In one diagram Clawson and Knetsh linked the classification of attractions in a spatial sense, according to their proximity to markets, to their level of uniqueness and to their intensity of use. Clawson's approach is flexible and best utilised as a way of thinking about attractions. For example, a major historic building is clearly a resource-based attraction, but it may extend its market by adding a user-orientated element, such as a small theme park or garden development, as has occurred with many of the stately homes and palaces in Britain and Continental Europe. Parks Canada has adopted a variant of Clawson's ideas to provide functional zones related to use in their parks (Case Study 14.1).

In this chapter, for purposes of analytical convenience, we have adopted the straightforward classification shown in Table 14.1. Here attractions are divided between natural resources, for example, country parks in Britain, lakes in Canada, mountains in Switzerland and the coast in Spain, and artificial products. The latter are most commonly the results of the history and culture of a country which leaves a legacy of historic monuments and buildings, but also includes specially created entertainment complexes such as theme parks, of which the most well known are the Walt Disney parks, originating in California, but now reproduced in Florida, Tokyo and near Paris (Case Study 14.4).

Going further, it will be appreciated that the basic classification may be subdivided again into attractions that are site-specific because of the physical location of facilities and therefore act as a destination, and attractions that are intangible and ephemeral because they are events. For events, it is what is happening at the time that is important, rather than the location. Thus some of the most spectacular events in the form of parades or carnivals take place in large cities, for example, the Lord Mayor's Show in London or the Calgary Stampede in Alberta, because cities provide access to a large market and have the economic base to support them.

Case Study 14.1   Functional zoning applied by Parks Canada

Parks Canada has developed a classification of its park resources based heavily upon Clawson's ideas. In effect, the zones range from Zone I, a pure resource-based zone, through to Zone V, a pure user-based zone. Between the two extremes, a continuum of zones is maintained through appropriate planning and management strategies.

● **Zone I** Special preservation areas: small and specific areas designated for a particular reason, such as the presence of endangered species. Entry is strictly controlled and access is by permit.

● **Zone II** Wilderness: areas with specific natural history and/or environmental value. Activities include dispersed hiking and some camping.

● **Zone III** Natural environments: access is compatible with the environment and this is the first zone where motorized access is allowed. However, this access is to the edge of the zone; entry beyond this is via strategically located trails.

● **Zone IV** Recreation areas: includes camp sites, boating, skiing and motorised access. Interpretative services are designed to explain and protect the environment.

● **Zone V** Park services: includes centralised visitor support services, park administration offices, etc., which are all located and designed to blend in with the surroundings. In some parks this zone is located outside the park boundary.

Source: adapted from Murphy (1985).

Table 14.1:
Classification of attractions

	Site	*Event*
Natural resources	Country parks	Festival of the countryside
Artificial	Historic monuments and buildings	Theatrical performance

Site and event attractions can be complementary activities as illustrated in Table 14.1. Staging a festival of the countryside can enhance the appeal of a country park, and similarly for the performance of a Shakespeare tragedy in the courtyard of an historic castle. Events are frequently used to raise the image of a destination, a factor that lies behind the very competitive bidding for mega-events such as the Olympics. They are also used to give animation to object-orientated attractions, such as museums, to encourage new and repeat visitors, particularly in the off-season.

The division between natural resources and artificial attractions is not always clear cut. Many natural attractions require considerable inputs of infrastructure and management in order to use them for tourism purposes. This is the case of water parks, ski resorts, safari parks, aquaria and many attractions based on nature. This infrastructure may also be put in place to protect the resource from environmental damage. In Britain, for example, as in many other countries, it is no longer possible to have open public access to many forests. Specific sites are designated for cars, caravans and camping, and there are colour coded trails for walkers.

Artificial attractions that are the legacy of history and culture also share with natural resources the fact that they cannot be reproduced without considerable expense and alterations to their authenticity, unlike attractions designed principally for entertainment. They therefore deserve greater protection and management input to guard against excessive use. Such attractions are commonly in the control of the state. A good example is Stonehenge which exhibits all the features of being resource-based and non-reproducible, so that for some time it has been threatened by too many visitors. Measures to resolve this have included the construction of a new visitor centre some distance from the monument and putting a cordon around the stones to prevent them being further defaced by touching and, in some instances, chipping of the stones by capricious visitors.

Natural resources

In the instance of natural features it is often the quality of the resource that provides the attraction and location becomes secondary. Their appeal is both national and international. Thus tourists come from all over the globe to enjoy the Himalayas in Nepal, the Grand Canyon in Colorado, the Blue Ridge Mountains of Virginia, the Lake District in Britain or the Ring of Kerry in Southern Ireland. Traditionally water-based resources, either coastlines or lakes, have always been the most important tourism resource and still are, but with more frequent holiday taking, the countryside and panoramic scenery have witnessed increasing usage. However, natural amenities are not only confined to the landscape but also include, for example, climate (which accounts for the dominant tourist flows being North–South to sun resorts), vegetation, forests and wildlife.

The most common aspect of natural resources is that they are generally fixed in supply and are able to provide only a limited amount of services in any given time period. But in many cases, the services provided by this fixed stock of natural amenities can be put to several different uses. Thus if it is proposed to increase the land available for tourism and recreation purposes, it may often be at the expense of other land users, say, industry. There is therefore a trade-off that must take place to ensure that the resource is used to the best advantage of society. This is demonstrated in Figure 14.2: the vertical axis represents the social net benefits (social benefits less social costs) of using a given area of land for tourism or industrial purposes. The schedule *TT* illustrates how these net benefits decline as more land is made available for tourism and similarly for

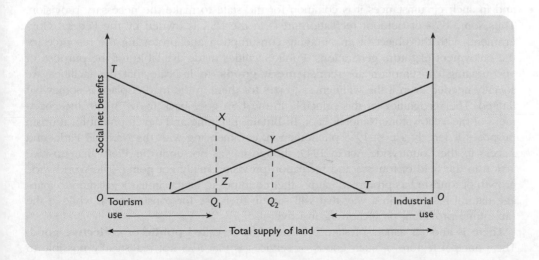

Figure 14.2: Optimal resource allocation

the schedule II which applies to industrial use. At Q_1 the social net benefit from the last portion of land devoted to industry is measured by the distance ZQ_1, while that for tourism use is given by XQ_1. Clearly, the net benefits obtainable from tourism use are much greater than those that can be gained from industrial use and so it will pay society to switch land from industrial designation to tourist use. The optimal point will be at Q_2 where the net social benefits from each use are equalised. By undertaking such a move, society increases social net benefits by the amount XYZ, for the total gain from tourism use is XQ_1Q_2Y but this must be offset by a loss to industry of ZQ_1Q_2Y.

The essence of land-use planning and the legislation that enforces it is to determine some optimal allocation in the manner shown by Figure 14.3. In this way land is zoned for a variety of uses, from tourism and recreation through to urban development, and when disputes occur as to use it is customary to hold some form of public inquiry in which the benefits and costs of alternative choices are evaluated to reach an appropriate decision. Most governments maintain strict planning controls on alternative uses of land, whether it is publicly or privately owned. Thus social considerations via the political process are the main driving force behind land allocation. In the case of privately owned land, social choice may be enforced through compulsory purchase by the state. In some cases the stark choice presented in Figure 14.2 is nullified in practice because multiple land use is possible. National parks in Britain, for example, include residential, farming, forestry, recreational activities and small-scale production within their boundaries.

Market failure and public provision

One of the problems concerning the provision of outdoor areas for leisure purposes on a large scale is that they are rarely commercially viable in terms of the investment costs and operating expenditure necessary to establish and maintain them. The reasons for this lie in their periodic use (weekends and holidays) and the political and administrative difficulties of establishing private markets in what are perceived by the public as gifts of nature. This suggests that if left to market forces the result is more likely to be under-provision of natural resources for leisure purposes rather than over-provision. Yet there are considerable social benefits to be enjoyed by the population from the availability of recreational amenities and in the control of land use to prevent unsightly development spoiling the beauty of the landscape.

Economists ascribe the term **market failure** to situations of the kind outlined above and in such circumstances it is common for the state to make the necessary provision. Thus some 85% of outdoor recreation areas in the USA is owned by the Federal Government, with the object of encouraging consumption and protecting the resource for the enjoyment of future generations. Public facilities made available for the purpose of encouraging consumption are termed **merit goods**, to indicate that the facilities are socially needed even if the willingness to pay for them in the market-place is somewhat limited. The recognition of this principle in the USA goes back to 1872 with the enactment of the Yellowstone National Park. In Britain, planning and development for tourism purposes is largely a post-1945 phenomenon, commencing with the National Parks and Access to the Countryside Act in 1949, though it was not until the 1960s that positive action in the field of tourism and recreation provision really got going. The world-wide growth of tourism has prompted many other countries to enact similar legislation to manage natural resources in a way that will sustain their use for consumption, while at the same time providing protection against over-use.

There is another aspect of state provision: the so-called **public** or **collective good**. The principal feature of such goods or services is that it is not realistically possible to exclude individuals from consumption once they have been made available. Private markets for these goods would quickly disintegrate because the optimal strategy for the individual consumer is to wait until someone else pays for the good and then to reap the benefits for nothing. Thus if the good or service is to be provided at all, it may be consumed by everyone without exception and normally without charge at the point of use. The natural environment is a typical example of a public good and the growing pressure of tourist development has created concern for the environment in a number of countries. The point of issue is that public goods form no part of the private costs facing the tourism developer and are therefore open to abuse through over-use. In response the state, in addition to enforcing collective provision out of taxation, regulates individual behaviour through legislation to preserve environmental amenity. For example, in Bermuda tourists are not allowed to hire cars, but only mopeds, while on the Greek island of Rhodes, vehicles are banned from the touristically attractive town of Lindos. Mauritius has a planning law that restricts buildings to a height no greater than the palm trees. In practice, this means hotels of only two storeys and thus permits adequate screening on the seaward side. Where legislation is considered impractical, or overly restrictive, then the approach is to try to change behaviour through educational awareness campaigns. Two examples of this are shown in Case Studies 14.2 and 14.3, which present national and local approaches to codes of conduct provided to visitors. The purpose of such codes is to disseminate information and persuade tourists that on their own volition they should avoid damage to the environment and adverse socio-cultural impacts. These codes do not apply only to visitors; there are also industry codes to educate staff and the business community in the recycling of materials and respect for the environment, as well as codes for the host community to help in understanding tourism and the benefits it brings, so as to encourage better relationships between hosts and guests.

Resource management

Given a fixed amount of natural resources for leisure purposes, it is only possible to alter the supply by adopting different use patterns. Critical to this is the generally accepted premise that tourists should not destroy through excessive use the natural features that they came to enjoy. This view is encapsulated in the concept of sustainable tourism development which argues that economic growth is only acceptable if it can maintain, at a minimum, the stock of tourist assets intact from one generation to another. Emphasis tends to be placed on the natural environment because it cannot be directly substituted for artificial facilities, and the danger of irreversible damage appears more likely. This danger is also present with artificial attractions such as historic artefacts, but here the concept is more subjective in that it has to do with authenticity; namely, at what point does repair and replacement of stone, say, on an historic monument owing to erosion and visitor damage, mean that it is no longer authentic? This is further complicated by the fact that perception seems to vary according to the nature of the historic artefact under consideration – whether it is glassware, tapestry, a sculpture or features of a building.

It has already been noted that the application of capital, labour and management to the natural environment is often necessary to render them suitable for tourist use, as in the case of a beach resource. This permits more intensive use of the beach provided that the necessary safeguards are put in place to prevent over-exploitation of the free availability of the resource in its role as a public good. One way of achieving this is to restrict accommodation provision to match the desired density of the population on the beach. A high-quality resort would aim at allocating 20 square metres per person, compared with 10 square metres per person for a budget resort. In other situations, the degree of

Case Study 14.2 The Himalayan Tourist Code

By following these simple guidelines, you can help preserve the unique environment and ancient cultures of the Himalayas.

Protect the natural environment

- Limit deforestation – make no open fires and discourage others from doing so on your behalf. Where water is heated by scarce firewood, use as little as possible. When possible choose accommodation that uses kerosene or fuel efficient wood stoves.

- Remove litter, burn or bury paper and carry out all non-degradable litter. Graffiti are permanent examples of environmental pollution.

- Keep local water clean and avoid using pollutants such as detergents in streams or springs. If no toilet facilities are available, make sure you are at least 30 metres away from water sources, and bury or cover wastes.

- Plants should be left to flourish in their natural environment – taking cuttings, seeds and roots is illegal in many parts of the Himalayas.

- Help your guides and porters to follow conservation measures.

- When taking photographs, respect privacy – ask permission and use restraint.

- Respect Holy places – preserve what you have come to see, never touch or remove religious objects. Shoes should be removed when visiting temples.

- Giving to children encourages begging. A donation to a project, health centre or school is a more constructive way to help.

- You will be accepted and welcomed if you follow local customs. Use only your right hand for eating and greeting. Do not share cutlery or cups, etc. It is polite to use both hands when giving or receiving gifts.

- Respect for local etiquette earns you respect – loose, light weight clothes are preferable to revealing shorts, skimpy tops and tight fitting action wear. Hand holding or kissing in public are disliked by local people.

- Observe standard food and bed charges but do not condone overcharging. Remember when you're shopping that the bargains you buy may only be possible because of low income to others.

- Visitors who value local traditions encourage local pride and maintain local cultures, please help local people gain a realistic view of life in Western Countries.

Source: Tourism Concern in consultation with the Annapurna Conservation Area Project.

inaccessibility may be used to control visitor numbers. This is illustrated in Figure 14.3 which demonstrates the inverse relationship between visitor numbers and difficulties of access and is also indicated in Clawson's classification (Figure 14.1). The latter may be due to time, distance or restrictions imposed by the managing authority. For example, with natural attractions which draw visitors both at the national and international level it is common for the authorities to implement 'park and ride' schemes so as to control the flow of cars in the area. Another popular strategy is the use of 'honey pots', whereby a variety of attractions, shops, restaurants and accommodation are clustered around one or two viewpoints to create a complex capable of absorbing a high population density.

Case Study 14.3   Yorkshire Dales Visitor Code

- Enjoy the countryside, by respecting its lifestyles, work and customs.
- Support local skills, services and produce.
- Wherever you go keep to public routes.
- Use gates and stiles to cross dry-stone walls, fences and hedges.
- Leave all gates as you find them, open or closed.
- Avoid trampling meadow grass by staying in single file through meadows in summer.
- Protect wild animals, trees and other plants. In particular, leave wild flowers for others to enjoy, and avoid disturbing birds and other animals.
- Keep your dog under close control, preferably on a lead.
- Leave livestock and farm machinery alone. Be aware of farmyard dangers.
- Take your litter home.
- Guard against risk of fire.
- Help to keep rivers, streams and lakes clean.
- Whenever possible use public transport.
- Take special care on narrow roads.
- Park thoughtfully. Where available use car parks.
- Respect other people's peace and quiet.
- Show consideration for those who use the countryside in other legitimate ways.

Source: Yorkshire Dales National Park.

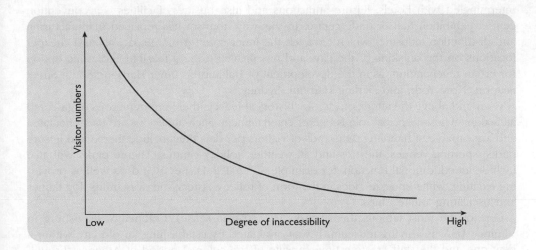

Figure 14.3: Visitor access function

The honey pot concept augments natural attractions with artificial, user-orientated attractions capable of drawing visitors away from the rest of the natural resource area. It is well known, for example, that the demand for domestic tourism and recreation facilities arises, in the main, from urban areas but that pressures on attractions and rural areas generally decrease with distance from city centres. Hence greater opportunities for protection and management of natural sanctuaries for wildlife and vegetation can be found by locating them in areas remote from urban environments. As the city centre is approached so there is a need to provide purpose-built facilities to cope with day excursions and weekend trips. Depending on the climate and country these will include seaside or lakeside resorts, mountain resorts, health centres, spas, and themed and nature parks. Within the city boundary there will be a requirement for town parks, and sport and leisure complexes. Thus as the volume of leisure demand increases so the need to augment natural attractions with artificial facilities arises. In this respect, capital cities such as London, Paris, Sydney and New York have always been great magnets for tourists because of their historical and cultural resources. For these same reasons cities everywhere are becoming tourist destinations in their own right rather than just places where people live and work. Today's better-educated traveller is looking for experiences that combine educational interest and entertainment, with the result that cultural tourism is expanding world-wide and with it the growth in urban tourism.

Artificial attractions

Many artificial attractions are products of history and culture. The range of museums and art galleries in the world's top tourist destinations is usually extensive and many are subject-specific, for example, the National Portrait Gallery in London or Chicago's Museum of Science and Industry. Added to this are numerous historic buildings which include castles, palaces, churches, houses and even completely walled medieval towns such as Carcassonne in France, as well as a variety of early industrial sites which are capable of satisfying the public's interest in bygone times.

Where old industrial buildings, disused market halls, railway stations and docks are located close to urban centres, it has been quite common to convert them into tourist zones which serve both visitors and residents alike. Since shopping is an important tourist activity, the focus has been on speciality shopping – as in Covent Garden, London – intermingled with hotels, leisure attractions and also business facilities – a convention centre, exhibition hall or trade centre. In this way, tourism has replaced manufacturing and distribution industries which have left the inner core for more spacious and cheaper locations on the outskirts of the city, and has proved to be a feasible economic option for urban regeneration, as in the development of Baltimore's Inner Harbour, South Street Seaport, New York, and Darling Harbour, Sydney.

Over and above the attractions left by historical legacy, there are numerous engineered attractions whose principal role is one of entertainment. Such attractions are user-orientated and are capable of handling thousands of visitors per day: they include theme and leisure parks, sporting venues, theatres and all-weather holiday centres. Theme parks will also include an educational function, for example, EPCOT in Disney World, as well as providing exciting 'white knuckle' rides in the form of roller coasters, runaway trains, log flames and oscillating 'pirate' ships.

One of the most famous theme parks (in the true sense), Colonial Williamsburg in Virginia, USA, is a living museum. It was originated by establishing an old city within a new one and the staff create a time capsule of the colonial period of America through role play and using the technology of the day. Its success has drawn in a range of partners to propagate the cultural richness of the State of Virginia. A similar re-creation has taken place at Beamish in the North of England. The museum has been positioned at a time just before the First World War and staff demonstrate the technology and converse with visitors in the way of life of that period. As far as possible the houses, shops, transport system, goods and artefacts are genuine articles of the time that have been brought to the site from all parts of the UK. In this manner, Beamish and Colonial Williamsburg have crossed the boundary between a theme park and a museum. In so doing they have captured the public's imagination by allowing participation. The public is now attuned to experiencing the sights and sounds of the era being witnessed, which gives opportunities for using technology creatively to enhance the visitor experience. We know that ultimately it is the visitor experience that is the marketed output of tourist attractions.

To this extent, static attractions and object-orientated museums, unless they are national collections, no longer appeal to visitors as they once did. The quest for improving the attraction experience forces theme and leisure park operators to install more complicated rides and challenging entertainment as the public seeks to increase the skill content of their consumption. Similarly historic properties, museums and gardens change their displays and feature special exhibitions/events to maintain interest. Some attractions are fortunate enough to be able to tie themselves to regular events aimed at an enthusiast market, for example automobile rallies, for which demand is more or less continual.

Economic aspects

As with natural resources, a great many artificial tourist attractions, because of their historical legacy, are not commercially owned. They are owned by central government, in the case of national collections, quasi-public bodies which are at an 'arm's length' from the government, local government and voluntary bodies in the form of charitable trusts. One of the most well-known examples of the latter in Britain is the National Trust, which maintains a wide range of historic properties, parks and woodlands, and is an institutional model that has been copied elsewhere. Acquisition has normally been via bequests from previous owners together with a substantial endowment. As in the case of many other non-profit organisations, the National Trust receives its income from admission charges, shops, catering, membership subscriptions, grants and donations, sponsorship, events and services rendered, for example, lecture programmes.

Public ownership

Publicly owned attractions may receive all or a substantial part of their funds from general taxation either directly or via grant-in-aid for quasi-public bodies. They are thus provided in the manner of a merit good and in so doing impose a degree of coercion on everyone, as individuals are not free to adjust the amounts that are made available. This is shown by Figure 14.4: the schedule SS is the quantity of, say, museum services supplied to each person as a result of public provision. The distance $0t$ represents the amount of income foregone per person in terms of tax and A the demand curve of individual A and similarly for B. At a tax cost $0t$, A demands only Q_A museum services while B demands Q_B. Clearly, the supply of services exceeds A's demand by XY, but falls below B's demand by YZ. It follows therefore that public provision is likely to generate political debate and lobbying as individuals try to alter the amounts produced to suit their own requirements. In market orientated economies the trend has been towards charging for national museums in order to cut public expenditure, though there is still resistance among certain sections of the community, including museum managers, who feel that museums have a public obligation requirement. As a consequence, only voluntary admission donations have been introduced in some instances, with a recommended minimum contribution, while other museums have simply refused to charge for admission, but the trend is one of introducing user charges.

Figure 14.4:
Public provision

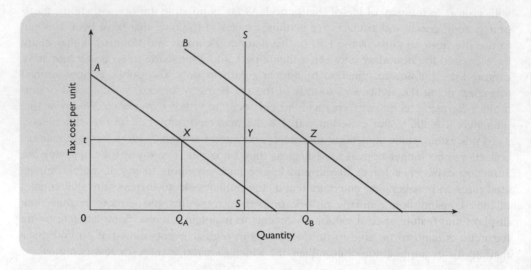

It is evident from the above discussion that the classification of goods and services into public and private provision is by no means clear cut. It is up to society to decide upon the dividing line through the political process. Nevertheless, governments do have to make everyday decisions on which projects to promote. This is particularly true of tourist attractions because they are frequently sponsored by local authorities and voluntary organisations who look to central government for grant assistance. To aid decision making, economists have devised the analytical framework of cost–benefit analysis which takes a wider and longer look at project decisions. The diversity of tourism expenditure is such that the most feasible method of assessing government support is to look at the impact that spending by visitors to the attraction has a local income and employment via the multiplier process. Implicit in this process is the requirement that the normal financial checks will be undertaken to ascertain whether the project is able to sustain itself operationally: if not, then it will need permanent subsidy if it is to proceed.

Voluntary organisations

Many museums and events have arisen out of the collections or interests of a group of enthusiasts who come together to provide for themselves and others collective goods and services which are unlikely to have any widespread commercial appeal (market failure) and are equally unlikely to be of sufficient importance to attract central provision by the state. Mention has already been made of the National Trust in Britain; an events example is the Sealed Knot society which undertakes re-enactment battles of the English Civil War (1642–51). Similarly, there are several military history associations in the USA that undertake re-enactments of events that took place in the American Civil War (1861–65). These organisations are in effect clubs, and because they normally have non-profit aims, they are entitled to claim the status of charities for tax purposes. However, in contrast to the public sector, they are not able to raise funds from taxation and so in the long run must cover their costs out of income. Yet, unlike the private commercial sector, their income is not made up principally of admission charges and visitor spending inside the attraction. Membership fees, gifts and bequests often take on a far greater significance in the income statement. As a consequence, recruiting new members to share the collective visitor experience is a priority task for these organisations. On the cost side, voluntary societies benefit from the fact that much of the labour input and some of the materials are provided free of charge.

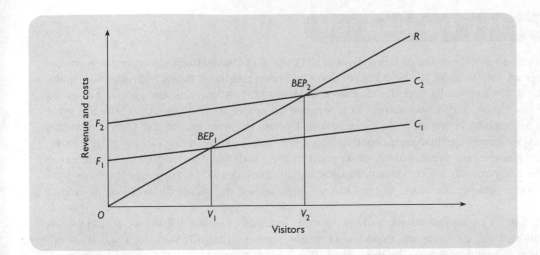

Commercial sector

For the commercial attractions the rules of market economics apply. They are required to make profits so as to contribute a return on the capital invested. In theory this return, at a minimum, should be equal to the current cost of raising money for investment purposes, and for new or 'venture' projects considerably more. In situations where attractions are owned by multiproduct firms or conglomerates, the ability of the facility to contribute to the cash flow of the overall business is often given a higher priority than return on capital. Production industries frequently have long lead times between incurring costs and receiving revenues. In these circumstances, the ownership of subsidiaries capable of generating ready cash inflows into the organisation on a daily and weekly basis can contribute greatly to total financial stability.

The principal economic concern of most commercial attractions are the same ones that face many other tourist enterprises, namely their cost structure and the seasonal nature of demand. Furthermore, for user-orientated attractions, fashions and tastes also play a considerable part. As noted earlier, theme park owners have to add new rides and replace old ones long before they are physically worn out simply to maintain attendances. Historic properties and museums can fall back on the intrinsic value of their buildings and collections, but even here presentation and interpretation have become more important.

Costs

Typically the cost structure of tourist attractions is made up of a high level of fixed, and therefore unavoidable, costs in relation to the operational or variable costs of running the enterprise. The main component of the fixed costs is the capital investment required to establish the attraction in the first place and capital additions from new development. The economic consequence of having a high level of fixed costs is to raise the break-even point in terms of sales or visitor numbers as shown in Figure 14.5. The revenue line from sales to visitors over a given time period is represented by R. The lines C_1 and C_2 are total cost schedules according to different visitor numbers: the slope of these cost schedules is determined by the variable costs incurred per visitor (marginal costs) and where they cut the revenue and costs axis determines the level of fixed costs. It may easily be seen that with overall fixed costs of F_1 the break-even point (BEP$_1$) which is at the intersection of R and C_1, is achieved at V_1 level of visitors. If fixed costs are set at F_2, then the number of visitors needed to break-even rises substantially to V_2, which

Case Study 14.4   Disneyland Paris

With the successful opening of Tokyo Disneyland in 1983, the Walt Disney Corporation began research-ing into European sites in 1984. By 1985 site selection had been narrowed down to France and Spain, and the contract was eventually signed with France in March 1987. At the time the project was called the Euro Disney Resort and it was set up as a separate company (Euro Disneyland SCA), in what amounted to a franchise operation from the American Disney. Payment was in the form of royalties from generated revenues, a management contract and a 49% shareholding in Euro Disney. The remain-ing 51% of the shares were put to public subscription in 1989 and raised around US$1 000 million in capital for the company. In effect, Disney was shifting the project risk to European investors who would have no recourse to the assets of the Disney Corporation if the planned development did not materialise.

In the USA, Disney outperforms by far any of its rivals in terms of visitor attendance and in its first year of operation, 1992, the company expected 11 million visitors to Euro Disney, as it was then, ris-ing to 21 million in two theme parks by the end of 1996. Such forecasts required a great leap in imag-ination, since other European theme parks at that time were drawing around 1.5–2.5 million admissions and there was some scepticism about whether the targets could be achieved. In the event, the 1992 attendance figures at around 6 million, although impressive by previous standards, were well short of the target and only reached 12 million in one park for 1996. This drew the complex into a spiral of cumulative losses for the intervening years. Poor financial performance had a dramatic effect on share values, which plummeted to a fraction of their 1992 peak, with the accompanying loss of the investors' confidence and that of the media in the product.

Many factors have been put forward to explain the misfortunes of the complex, but the principal causes appear to have been:

- prices were perceived high by European standards;

- additional spend within the park was much less than expected and relatively few were pre-pared to stay in the adjoining hotel accommodation;

- the opening coincided with rising recession in Europe generally, which depressed tourism demand;

- the location near Paris suffers from poor weather for part of the year and so demand exhibits seasonal fluctuations, unlike the Florida and Californian sites;

- there were cultural differences which generated tensions for both staff and customers: Europeans insisted on eating at midday rather than 'grazing' throughout their visit, as Amer-icans have grown accustomed to do, while French visitors were particularly dismayed by the no alcohol rule.

Since 1994, there has been a financial restructuring of Euro Disney, bringing in new investors, with moral pressure being put on American Disney to accept some responsibility and inject further cap-ital. Moreover, the brand image, 'Euro Disney', was found to be much weaker than expected and so the park has been re-launched as Disneyland Paris, with a new management team that is working much more closely to European traditions in tourism. Even so, there is still a considerable way to go to retrieve the situation and the capital markets are still looking at the complex as a speculative invest-ment because of the outstanding debt, but it is difficult to suppose that the park will not survive, given the 'flagship' nature of such a project.

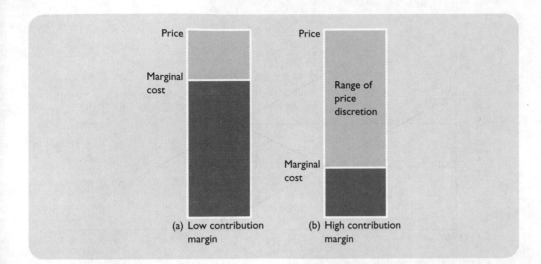

Figure 14.6:
Market
orientation

increases the amount of risk in the successful running of the operation. This also has an impact on location, because for user-orientated attractions population catchment areas in terms of ease of access to the site are of prime importance. The greater the visitor numbers required in order for an attraction project to break-even, the fewer are the number of acceptable locations. Hence the Disney Corporation, for example, undertook considerable research before deciding on a site close to Paris at Marne la Vallée for its European venture, though subsequent performance has provided a salutary lesson for the theme park industry (Case Study 14.4). It follows from this that government initiatives to stimulate the development of tourist attractions largely hinge, for their success, on the amount of assistance that can be given to help with the capital costs of starting up the project. This assistance may be in the form of cash grants, subsidised ('soft') loans, shared ownership, the provision of benefits-in-kind such as land, infrastructure and access routes or a combination of any of these. For example, the site for Disneyland Paris was obtained at 1971 agricultural prices, in spite of the fact that it had already been zoned for urban development. As a rule, cash grants are perceived by the commercial sector as the most effective form of financial help.

Pricing policy

The effects of having high fixed costs also spills over into pricing policy. The difference between the price charged for admission to an attraction and the variable or marginal cost of providing the visitor experience for the customer is the contribution margin per customer towards paying the fixed costs and meeting targets on profitability. As shown in Figure 14.6, where the contribution margin desired is low because fixed costs are low, the marginal cost of supplying an additional unit is relatively high and so provides a good guide to setting the price level. This is known as cost-orientated pricing. On the other hand, where there are high fixed costs, the admission charge has to be set considerably above the marginal cost of provision, in order to ensure a high contribution margin to meet the financial costs of servicing the investment that has been sunk into the attraction. In this instance, the marginal cost of provision is no longer a good guide to pricing and the enterprise is forced to take a market-orientated stance in its pricing policy. The difference between the admissions price and marginal cost is the range of

Figure 14.7:
Seasonal demand

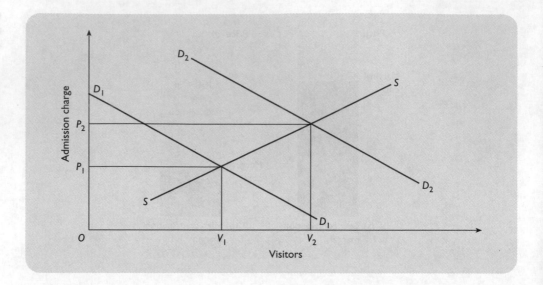

price discretion that the organisation has, for it must cover its operating costs in the short run, but may take a longer-term perspective in terms of how it might cover its fixed costs. By seeking out a range of different market segments with a variety of different prices, including discounts for volume sales and long-term contracts, the commercial attraction operator will try to optimise the yield on the site's assets. This is termed 'yield management' and the operator's ability to improve the yield will be constrained by the economic climate surrounding the firm, which will include the customers' perceptions of value for money ('what the market will bear'), personal income levels, particularly amounts for discretionary (non-essential) spending, and the degree of competition.

Seasonality

Seasonality becomes an issue in tourist attractions because the product, the visitor experience, cannot be stored. This being the case, it is peak demand that determines capacity and user-orientated attractions are frequently designed to a standard based on a fixed number of days per annum when capacity is likely to be reached or exceeded. This implies that at most times of the year the attraction has too much capacity. The level of investment is therefore more than what would be required if the product was storable. In turn, seasonality can affect pricing policy as presented in Figure 14.7. SS is the supply schedule representing the incremental cost of expanding visitor numbers. D_2D_2 is the demand for the visitor experience in the main season, while D_1D_1 is the off-season demand. Market clearing requires a policy of seasonal price differentiation, charging P_2 in the main season and P_1 in the off-season. However, in practice many attraction managers are opposed to seasonal pricing, because, they argue, it simply reacts on customers' perceived value for money. Visitors feel that they are being overcharged because they are unable to come in the off-season. To counter this perception problem, attraction operators tend to narrow seasonal price ranges and offer additional product benefits, in the form of free entrance to different parts of the site, to those visitors coming when the attraction is not busy.

Another method of smoothing the difference in prices is to charge a two-part tariff. Instead of the major contribution to fixed costs being borne by main season visitors, the admission price is made up of a fixed charge to meet the requirement to cover fixed costs in the long term and a variable charge depending on the level of usage. While most attractions pay attention to segmented pricing techniques for groups, senior citizens, children and schools, the dictates of yield management do require operators to address the seasonal and spatial limitations of demand in their pricing policy.

Visitor management

Price has often been used as a method of regulating demand and enforcing exclusivity as in luxury resorts such as Malibu and Monaco, or in luxury hotels, for example the Savoy and Dorchester in London. To be able to use price to limit the number of visitors requires that consumption should be excludable – only those who pay can benefit from the visitor experience. But this is frequently deemed undesirable in the case of natural resources or the historical and cultural artefacts of a country, either because they are public goods, so that it is not practical to exclude consumption, or because they are merit goods whereby it is to the benefit of society that consumption should be encouraged. Even commercial attractions would have difficulty in using price as the sole regulator of visitor numbers. In any one year such attractions have a variety of peaks and troughs which would therefore entail a whole range of different prices. In Western economies, the public does not respond well to wildly fluctuating prices and so all attractions resort to some non-price methods to manage visitor flows.

Box 14.1 presents a list of possible actions to manage visitors at busy times and thereby avoid congestion and improve the visitor experience. These start with marketing and information provision and go through to techniques that can influence the visitor's behaviour on the site. Some attractions have adopted deliberate demarketing at peak times, but where they are nationally or internationally known this is only of limited effectiveness. First-time visitors to capital cities nearly always want to see the principal landmarks: the Empire State Building in New York, Buckingham Palace in London, and the Eiffel Tower in Paris. The first step at any site is to deal with car and bus traffic, if only to prevent congestion building up and blocking main roads. Once on-site, visitors can be channelled using internal transport systems, for example land trains, where distances involve a considerable amount of walking. For theme parks, queue management is often necessary for popular attractions and rides, so that excessive waiting does not detract from the visitor's enjoyment. This may be achieved by ensuring that the queue line passes through a stimulating environment, with the ability to view the attraction as the latter is approached, by providing entertainers and by using markers to indicate the length of time people will have to wait at different stages of the queue.

Authenticity issues

It is the concern of social researchers that tourists should be given a genuine appreciation of the destination they are visiting. In too many cases, it is argued, tourists are given the impression that the destination is some idyllic fantasy world, and that they are fooled into this by attractions, particularly events, that are staged and may have little relevance to the culture of the country. Thus the tourists do not see the real landscape and way of life of the host community. This implies a loss of authenticity in the visitor experience. Of course some tourists do not want an authentic experience: the purpose of going to leisure or theme parks to participate on the rides is for entertainment and excitement.

The ideal situation is considered to be where both the host community and the visitor see the experience as authentic. However, given mass tourism flows, it is virtually impossible to meet the curiosity of visitors without staging events and certain aspects of

Box 14.1 Visitor management techniques

Marketing and information provision

- Withdrawing promotion at peak times and informing local radio stations and TICs when the attraction is nearing capacity.
- Encouraging visitors to come out of season.
- Promoting alternative attractions and ensuring that TICs make visitors aware of the full range of attractions available.
- Targeting specific market segments only.

Influencing on-site behaviour

- Visitor orientation centres.
- Signposts, information points and marked routes.
- Only permit guiding in groups.
- Use of guides, actors in role play and audio cassette tours to channel visitor movements.
- Temporary closure, restricted access using rope barriers, one-way systems and dispersal to less sensitive areas.
- Timed ticketing and advanced booking systems.
- Queue management systems and queue entertainment.
- Zoning areas or time scheduling for different activities.
- Managing car-parks to direct visitors to alternative location on the site.
- Installing on-site transport systems.

historic attractions. Many historic properties in Britain stage period tableaux to give visitors an impression of what living was like at those times. The visitor knows that they are staged, yet at the same time every effort is made to give the most authentic representation possible, even including the reproduction of smells, as in the Jorvik Centre in York which places visitors in a 'time' car to travel around the re-creation of a Viking village. Authenticity becomes questionable when the destination tries to conceal the staging of an event by giving visitors the impression that what they are seeing is real, when in fact it may be an artificially created event or belong to a time gone by and have no place in the current life of the community. Historic and cultural staging presents the visitor with the salient features of a community's heritage and reduces the need for encroaching on the private space of the host population. It may also generate pride and interest among the local community who have previously taken these aspects for granted.

Environment

The concern for the tourism environment, be it natural or artificial, is linked with the notion of sustainable development. Rarely in history has any society willingly absorbed the imposition of a variety of outside cultures upon it, yet, in the interests of generating

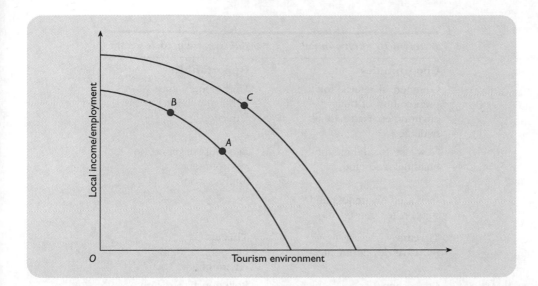

local economic activity and employment, this is precisely what host communities are expected to do with regard to the development of tourism. The situation is depicted in Figure 14.8. Suppose the local economy is positioned at A and the desire is to increase employment. The adverse consequence is where such a policy can only be accomplished by a move from A to B which trades off employment against environmental quality. The concept of sustainable tourism development argues that economic growth and environmental quality are not mutually exclusive events. By changes in technology to improve the use of resources, controlling waste and managing visitor flows to prevent damage to non-renewable tourism resources, it is possible to reach a position such as C in Figure 14.8.

Going 'green' can build a platform for long-term growth by offering a better tourist product, saving resources and raise the public's perception of the tourism industry. Sustainable development thus offers a way to escape the 'limits to growth' syndrome illustrated by a move from A to B. But, care of the environment is more than just preservation or protection: some of the key principles that should govern environmental policy for the implementation of any tourism development plan are:

- recognition of a two-way relationship between tourism and the environment, yielding possibilities of conservation through tourism;
- visitor management to reduce pressure;
- environmental improvement for the benefit of residents and visitors;
- sensitive development that respects and, if possible, enhances the environment;
- responsible operation through ecologically sound practice in tourism businesses and the means of travel.

The significant feature that should be communicated to the various agencies in tourism is the existence of a two-way relationship between tourism and the environment, as illustrated in Table 14.2. The tendency in the discussion of the impacts of tourism has been to give weight to the negative aspects of tourism on the environment rather than the positive opportunities that are available.

Tourism to environment	*Environment to tourism*
Opportunities	**Opportunities**
Commercial returns for preservation of built environment and natural heritage.	Fine scenery and heritage as visitor attractions.
New use for redundant buildings and land.	Eco-tourism based on environmental appreciation.
Increased awareness and support for conservation.	
Threats	**Threats**
Intrusive development.	Off-putting, drab environments.
Congestion.	Pollution hazards on beaches, in water, and in rural and urban areas.
Disturbance and physical damage.	Intrusive developments by other industries.
Pollution and resource consumption.	

Regulation or market solutions?

The question posed is how should the mechanism for sustainable development work? In market-orientated economies the policy preference is for solutions based on the principle that the 'polluter' should pay, thus prices should reflect not only the economic costs of provision but also the social costs. The different approaches to the impact of visitors on the tourism environment are shown in Figure 14.9. *DD* is the demand schedule and at low rates of tourist consumption, say, V_1, the social cost per unit (*SC*) is equal to the economic cost (*EC*) of usage. Thus up to V_1 current consumption does not interfere with future consumption or damage the resource. If only current demand is considered then the resource would be used to a level V_2 with visitor expenditure settling at point *B*. This results in resource depletion to the extent that *SC* is as high as point *A*. The market solution is to drive consumption back to V_3 by imposing a tourist tax *CE* on usage to compensate for the renewal cost of the resource.

The difficulty with market solutions is that, as discussed elsewhere, many natural attractions have public good properties whereby consumption is non-excludable and there is an element of public resistance to charging for a nation's heritage which is presumed to belong to all, although some museums and galleries do discriminate between domestic and foreign visitors, through having, say, a local residents' 'privilege' card. In such situations there is little choice other than to control visitor flows by influencing behaviour and/or to follow a programme of continual repair and maintenance. The significant aspect of many environmental matters is that the sheer number of agents involved in tourism,

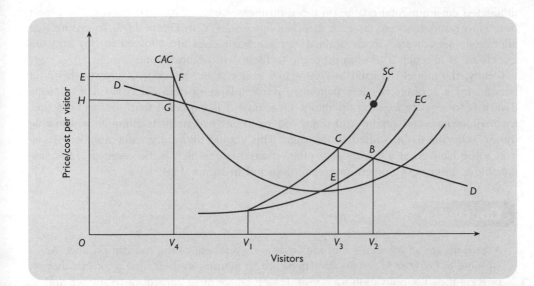

Figure 14.9:
Control versus
market solutions

both public and private, with very different objectives and performance measures, make it virtually impossible to achieve concerted action other than through a regulating agency that has the force of law, which leaves little scope for market economics. The British experience, for example, has been that rarely have visitors or tourist businesses been charged directly for the social and environmental costs generated by their actions. The money is paid indirectly through general taxation and most of the burden of coping with congestion, litter and visitor management falls on the public sector, particularly local authorities. To this extent the government tries to take account of the influx of visitors in its support grant for local provision of public services. This is not to say that the 'polluter pays principle' through the application of 'green' taxes may not be appropriate in certain circumstances. Thus the Australian authorities raise a specific charge on visitors to the Great Barrier Reef, a popular destination that is under considerable environmental pressure.

The pure conservation solution requires that demand is driven back to V_1 by simply limiting the number of visitors, so that no social costs are incurred whatsoever and any social benefits that may be gained by expanding demand to V_3 are ignored. Such a position contrasts strongly with the ideas expressed in Table 14.2. A more extreme situation, one in which society becomes over-zealous in its actions, is depicted by V_4 in Figure 14.9. *CAC* represents the combined average cost curve of the tourism plant in the community. If demand is forced back to V_4 it may be seen that this plant is no longer viable, for the average cost of supply (point F) is greater than the average visitor spend (point G), and so in order to survive in the longer term the tourism enterprises have to be subsidised by an amount *EFGH*. One of the paradoxes of tourism is that those who do not see that their income is directly dependent on the tourism industry are frequently opposed to it, yet closing down the tourism plant reverses the multiplier process. Quite soon local businesses and employment are affected, and the economic rationale for the community may be impaired, which can affect the very jobs of those who are opposed to tourism development.

Regulation and market solutions to manage the tourism environment are not necessarily mutually exclusive. A compromise is to assign quotas at the conservation level V_1 to tourist enterprises, but at the same time allowing market forces to work by levying a graduated environmental charge on those businesses exceeding their quotas. The object here is to position society as near as possible to point C in Figure 14.9. To ensure that allocations are adjusted in an optimal manner, businesses are allowed to buy and sell quotas so as to reach a level appropriate to their own organisation.

Clearly, the model depicted in Figure 14.9 is not static. In times of growth this is of benefit, for it is politically less painful to refuse planning permission for new projects than it is to regulate existing operators. Over time it is expected that new technologies for maintenance and repair, and improved visitor management techniques will enable the SC schedule to be shifted to the right. This should allow a greater number of visitors to be handled at a lower cost to the environment, which is the essence of the sustainable tourism development argument depicted in Figure 14.8.

Conclusion

Attractions are an integral – and important – component of the tourism product. As we note in Chapter 5, certain attractions are so alluring in their own right that they provide the sole motivation for a visit. However, for most attractions to survive and flourish, other elements of the tourism product must also be on offer at a destination, at a complementary level, quality and price, to support the attraction and to provide the tourist with the necessary supporting infrastructure and superstructure.

As an area of investigation and study, tourist attractions are becoming increasingly important. Their contribution to the overall tourism product has been recognised and, as new technology-based innovations have been applied in this domain, the profile of many tourist attractions has risen dramatically.

Attractions remain the focal point for new visitor management and control techniques which aim to alleviate the pressure of large numbers of tourists and to ensure natural resources are protected and sustained.

While there remains a debate about the effectiveness of these strategies, there exists also discord as to who should be responsible for investing in the development and maintenance of resources which are enjoyed by many groups, including the local community. The role of the public sector versus the private sector in attraction investment and management has become an important issue as both strive to balance the oft-conflicting needs of user groups and to enhance the quality of the attraction experience for all.

Chapter discussion questions

1. Review the roles and responsibilities of public and private sector bodies in the provision and maintenance of tourist attractions in a country, area or region with which you are familiar.

2. Evaluate the implications on other aspects of the tourism system such as tourism demand as a result of the mix of attractions present at a given destination.

3. Assess the effectiveness of visitor management techniques employed at a tourist attraction known to you.

Chapter discussion questions continued

4. What are the basic similarities between the local code for visitors in Case Study 14.3 and the national code shown in Case Study 14.2?

5. Typically, codes of conduct are aimed at tourists, but should they not apply equally to the travel trade?

6. What are the principal factors that should be taken into account when zoning areas for tourist use?

7. Drawing on local information, how does zoning areas for different uses affect land prices?

8. At what stage in the holiday process should tourists be informed of local customs and any restrictions that they may impose on holiday behaviour?

9. Consider why it is that tourists often resort to 'behaviour inversions' when on holiday, i.e. exhibiting behaviour patterns that would normally be taboo in their own country?

10. What role can 'flagship projects' such as Disneyland Paris play in tourism?

Recommended further reading

● Durlacher, D. (1994) 'Theme parks', pp. 14–18 in *Tourism Marketing and Management Handbook*, 2nd edn, Witt, S. and Moutinho, L. (eds), Prentice Hall, Hemel Hempstead.

● Getz, D. E. (1991) *Festivals, Special Events and Tourism*, Van Nostrand Reinhold, New York.

● Middleton, V. T. C. (1994) *Marketing in Travel and Tourism*, 2nd edn, Butterworth-Heinemann, Oxford.

● Mill, R. C. and Morrison, A. M. (1992) *The Tourism System*, 2nd edn, Prentice Hall, Englewood Cliffs, NJ.

● Prentice, R. (1994) 'Heritage: a key sector of the "new" tourism', pp. 309–24 in *Progress in Tourism, Recreation and Hospitality Management*, Vol. 5, Cooper, C. P. and Lockwood, A. (eds), Wiley, Chichester.

● Swarbrooke, J. (1995) *The Development and Management of Tourist Attractions*, Butterworth-Heinemann, Oxford.

Bibliography

● Boniface, B. and Cooper, C. (1987) *The Geography of Travel and Tourism*, Heinemann, London.

● Clawson, M. and Knetsch, J. (1966) *The Economics of Outdoor Recreation*, Johns Hopkins, University Press, Baltimore, MD.

● Corze, J. C. (1989) 'Theme and leisure parks', pp. 459–62 in *Tourism Marketing and Management Handbook*, Witt, S. and Moutinho, L. (eds), Prentice Hall, Hemel Hempstead.

● Durlacher, D. (1994) 'Theme parks', pp. 14–18 in *Tourism Marketing and Management Handbook*, 2nd edn, Witt, S. and Moutinho, L. (eds), Prentice Hall, Hemel Hempstead.

● Getz, D. E. (1991) *Festivals, Special Events and Tourism*, Van Nostrand Reinhold, New York.

● Holloway, J. C. (1994) *The Business of Tourism*, 4th edn, Longman, Harlow.

- Hughes, H. L. (1989) 'Entertainment', pp. 127–30 in *Tourism Marketing and Management Handbook*, Witt, S. and Moutinho, L. (eds), Prentice Hall, Hemel Hempstead.
- Mason, P. and Mowforth, M. (1996) 'Codes of conduct in tourism', *Progress in Tourism and Hospitality Research*, **1**(2), 151–67.
- Middleton, V. T. C. (1994) *Marketing in Travel and Tourism*, 2nd edn, Butterworth-Heinemann, Oxford.
- Mill, R. C. and Morrison, A. M. (1992) *The Tourism System*, 2nd edn, Prentice Hall, Englewood Cliffs, NJ.
- Murphy, P. E. (1985) *Tourism: A Community Approach*, Methuen, London.
- Prentice, R. (1994) 'Heritage: a key sector of the "new" tourism', pp. 309–24 in *Progress in Tourism, Recreation and Hospitality Management*, Vol. 5, Cooper, C. P. and Lockwood, A. (eds), Wiley, Chichester.
- Richards, G. (1994) 'Cultural tourism in Europe', pp. 99–115 in *Progress in Tourism, Recreation and Hospitality Management*, Vol. 5, Cooper, C. P. and Lockwood, A. (eds), Wiley, Chichester.
- Stevens, T. R. (1991) 'Visitor attractions: their management and contribution to tourism', pp. 106–113 in *Progress in Tourism, Recreation and Hospitality Management*, Vol. 3, Cooper, C. P. (ed.), Belhaven Press, London.
- Swarbrooke, J. (1995) *The Development and Management of Tourist Attractions*, Butterworth-Heinemann, Oxford.
- Wheeller, B. (1992) 'Is progressive tourism appropriate?', *Tourism Management*, **13**(1), 104–5.
- Wheeller, B. (1994) 'Ecotourism: a ruse by any other name', pp. 3–11 in *Progress in Tourism, Recreation and Hospitality Management*, Vol. 6, Cooper, C. P. and Lockwood, A. (eds), Wiley, Chichester.

Chapter Fifteen

Accommodation

Introduction

Accommodation or lodging is, by a long way, the largest and most ubiquitous subsector within the tourism economy. With few exceptions, tourists require a location where they can rest and revive during their travels through, or stay within, a tourism destination. We can therefore see that accommodation is an important support facility in Leiper's destination region and, with few exceptions, commercial accommodation facilities are found wherever tourists venture. Of course, there is great diversity in the size, type and organisation of this accommodation. This diversity ranges from:

- accommodation that provides for one or two guests in simple, home style, to 'bedroom factories' with capacity to cater for up to 5000 guests;

- accommodation in a very basic, functional form, or in extreme luxury and opulence.

- ownership can be private and informal, or accommodation may be provided within units operated by major multinational organisations.

In short, accommodation is characterised by extreme heterogeneity and any attempt to generalise about the sector must take this into account.

In this chapter, we are primarily concerned with those establishments and organisations that provide places of rest and revival on a commercial and organised basis. We therefore give rather less consideration to lodging in the VFR sector where accommodation is, usually, within the normal home of those being visited. Although VFR is in many countries the most important tourist motivation, its value to the commercial accommodation sector is generally more limited.

This chapter, therefore, is mainly concerned with

- fully or partially serviced accommodation such as hotels, motels, rhyokan (a Japanese-style lodging house), aparthotels, guesthouses, bed and breakfasts, and farmhouses;

- self-catering accommodation such as apartments, country cottages, gites, campus accommodation, camping and static caravan sites, and timeshare;

- ■■ accommodation support facilities where provision is made for campers, cara-vanners and trailer owners who bring their own accommodation with them, in other words mobile sites; and

- ■■ accommodation within mobile transportation such as cruise ships, ferries, trains and airliners.

These accommodation types vary in their importance and contribution to both domestic and international tourism. There are also close links between accommodation providers and other sectors within tourism where the cross-sectoral characteristics of tourism organisations are increasing with integration in the tourism industry. For example, hotels have always been major providers of food service but this role has, as we shall see, changed significantly in recent years. Hotels are also, however, major providers of leisure, sporting and entertainment facilities as well as business and conference services. Likewise, accommodation's relationship with transportation is one of long standing but it is one that is increasing in its sophistication and complexity, as transport providers recognise that accommodation can be an attraction to guests in its own right and not just a necessary service to be provided *en route*.

Chapter learning objectives

During this chapter, we will focus on the accommodation sector and some of the issues that currently influence it. The learning objectives for this chapter, therefore, may be defined as:

- ■■ identifying and assessing the scope of the hospitality industry;

- ■■ understanding the structure of the accommodation sector, the role of brands and the different ownership models that predominate;

- ■■ assimilating the sector's historical development and the effect of this on today's operation; and

- ■■ discussing some of the key issues that dominate the sector today and that will influence its future development.

Accommodation and the tourism product

In the context of the tourism sector in general, accommodation rarely has a place or rationale in its own right. It is rare for a tourist to select to stay in a hotel or other form of accommodation for its own sake. Rather, the choice is made because the accommodation provides a support service for the wider motivation which has brought the visitor to the destination, whether for business or leisure purposes. It is arguable that some resort hotels may fall outside this generalisation in that guests may choose to stay at Greenbriars or Gleneagles because of the accommodation experience that such hotels provide but, generally, this motivation will be coupled with the desire to avail of a wider tourism product within the resort or locality.

Accommodation is a necessary component in the development of tourism within any destination that seeks to serve visitors other than day trippers. The quality and range of accommodation available will both reflect and influence the range of visitors to a location. As such, achieving the appropriate balance of accommodation to meet the destination's strategic tourism development objectives can be a challenge. It is arguable, for example, that the inability of traditional destinations such as the Isle of Man to create new market opportunities in the wake of the decline of its traditional visitor base (family holidays) was directly linked to its old and inflexible accommodation stock. We can identify situations where accommodation is seen as part of the overall tourism infrastructure without which tourists will not visit the location. It therefore also assists in attracting wider investment in the tourism product at the locality. For example, the province of Newfoundland, in Canada, built four hotels in strategic locations as part of its tourism development strategy in the early 1980s. Accommodation can also feature as an element in wider economic development strategies. Similarly, the town of Akueryi, in Iceland, built and operates a hotel at a deficit because it is seen as an essential support facility for wider economic development, particularly in the fisheries sector. Accommodation, therefore, has an integral but varied role as part of the wider tourism product.

Accommodation also plays an important role in the overall economic contribution which tourism makes at a local and national level. It is difficult to generalise about the proportion of total tourist expenditure that is allocated to accommodation because this varies greatly according to the market, accommodation type and nature of product purchased. As a very general rule, perhaps 33% of total trip expenditure is allocated to this sector. This figure decreases in the case of fully inclusive packages to, say, the Mediterranean resorts where intermediaries negotiate low-cost bulk purchases of apartment or hotel rooms. By contrast, the proportion may be considerably higher in the case of domestic tourism where transportation costs are, generally, lower than is the case with international travel. Accommodation may be sold as a 'loss leader' to promote expenditure on other components of the tourism product. Off-season 'offers' are frequently promoted whereby hotel rooms are provided 'free' on condition that guests purchase a specified minimum in terms of food and beverage. This strategy recognises important dimensions of the accommodation sector:

- demand is highly volatile and fluctuates on a seasonal and weekly basis; and
- accommodation can act as the catalyst for a range of additional sales opportunities within complex tourism and hospitality businesses – traditionally, casino hotels have discounted accommodation in anticipation of generating considerable profits from customers at the gaming table while golfing hotels may seek to generate profits from green fees rather than room revenues.

Indeed, accommodation pricing in general is a complex and, sometimes, controversial area. Rack room rates (those formally published as the price of the room) are rarely achieved and extensive discounting for group bookings, advance reservations and corporate contracts are widespread. Fixed pricing is only successful and commonplace within the budget hotel sector. Yield, measured against potential, rarely runs at much more than 60% in the mid- to upper-market levels of the hotel industry and yield management systems are in place, within most large companies, in order to maximise achieved rates while optimising occupancy potential. Managing contracts in order to maximise yield is also an important strategy for accommodation units with the objective of replacing low yield groups or aircrew business with higher yield business or fully inclusive tour (FIT) guests.

Defining the accommodation sector

Hotels

Hotels are undoubtedly the most significant and visible subsector within accommodation or lodging. Although a highly varied collection of properties in most countries, hotels are the tourism subsector that provides the greatest total employment in global terms and probably accounts for the highest level of receipts. The traditional view of a hotel was an establishment providing accommodation as well as food and beverage services to short-stay guests on a paying basis. This view has influenced most attempts to define hotels. But, as we shall see later in this chapter, this is a somewhat inadequate description in view of the growth of ancillary activities commonly associated with the hotel sector (leisure, business, etc.) and the withdrawal of many hotel companies from the operation of food and beverage services entirely.

In most countries of the world, hotel businesses are dominated by small, family-owned operations, which have developed hand-in-hand with the tourism sector often earlier in the twentieth century and, in particular, since 1945. Thus, the typical hotel business is represented by 30-bedroom seafront establishments in resorts, country house hotels or the wide range of city properties. This small business sector has, in many parts of the world, declined in importance in recent years, faced with the challenge of branded multiple operators offering a range of products from budget to luxury. The cost of re-investment in order to meet changing consumer demand combined with the marketing and operational challenges posed by technology have forced many hotels of this kind out of business. Those that do survive successfully in the contemporary tourism industry do so because they have recognised the importance of niche marketing by tailoring their products and services to meet the specific niche requirements of identified market groups. An important survival strategy for small, independent hotels is membership of a marketing consortium representing similar operations at a national or international level. Best Western and Golden Tulip are two of the best known international consortia while Scotland's Best represents a similar approach but within a niche geographical market.

The group or chain component of the hotel subsector accounts for between 5% and 10% of the property stock in most European countries but this figure is much higher in South East Asia and in North America. In terms of the bedroom inventory of most countries, the percentage penetration of groups/chains is rather greater:

- up to 30% of the total in the UK; and
- over 50% in the USA.

This reflects the fact that hotels that are part of multiples tend to be considerably larger (and generally more recently built) than independents. The almost universal trend in the hotel subsector is for multiples to gain market share from independent operators within expanding markets.

Ownership and management of hotels reflect the growing complexity of business formats within the private sector generally. There are three major operating models with various combinations:.

1. Hotel companies may *own and operate* the hotels which operate under their name or they may have a part equity stake in the property.

2. Alternatively, the hotel may be operated and owned by a *franchise partner* – this is a rapidly growing business format, especially within the budget market. Franchises may be operated at an individual property level or as part of a master franchise arrangement whereby a company owns or operates a large number of properties, typically at a national or regional level, under the umbrella of an established brand or brands. Hospitality Franchise Systems (HFS) is an American company that operates master franchises on behalf of a number of established brands but manages these franchises, in large part, through individual local franchisees and owners. HFS is, thus, frequently referred to as the world's largest hotel company although its actual ownership is minimal.

3. Finally, the hotel company may *manage the property on behalf of an owner* – this is a common format at the top end of the international market, to be found in the portfolios of major companies such as Hilton, Hyatt, Inter-Continental and Marriott.

Case Study 15.1 represents the company CDL, which is involved in the hotel industry in a variety of business formats but is primarily a company that seeks to own, in part or in full, the hotels with which it is involved.

Case Study 15.1 CDL Hotels

CDL Hotels is one of the fastest and most aggressively growing international hotel companies at the present time. With headquarters in Singapore and quoted on the Hong Kong Stock Exchange, CDL represents one of a growing number of Asian companies investing in the international accommodation sector.

CDL is a majority owned subsidiary of Hong Leng Investment Holding Pte Ltd, a Singapore investment company with primary interests in land (real estate) and its development through the construction of diverse property types – commercial and residential. It is evident that much of CDL's growth strategy, especially in its earlier days, was driven by the real estate culture of its parent company and this, as we shall see, has led to some difficulties in the branding and marketing of its hotel portfolio.

CDL, as a hotel company, grew out of hotel purchases, initially in Singapore, in 1970. These purchases, the best known of which is the Orchard Hotel, were very much property-driven and, at that time, there was only limited vision of operating the hotel properties as a coherent and cohesive group. Indeed, two of the Singapore hotels were purchased while operated, under management, by internationally recognised brands, Novotel and Dai-Ichi. CDL expanded rapidly from its Singapore base during the late 1980s and early 1990s, with regional acquisitions (or partnership acquisitions) in Malaysia, Hong Kong, the Philippines, Taiwan and, subsequently, Australia and New Zealand where the chain operating the Choice franchise was purchased. Two hotels were purchased in New York, three in London and, in 1995, the Copthorne chain of hotels, consisting of 16 hotels in the UK, France and Germany, was acquired from Aer Lingus. In 1997, the Britannia Hotel, in London, was purchased after a number of years of operation under the Intercontinental flag. CDL is regularly associated with hotel properties placed on the market by their owners in key business and leisure locations and is certainly willing to acquire additional properties if the right is perceived to be appropriate.

CDL's acquisition policy has, in the main, been opportunistic, driven by the chance to purchase property at an attractive price. As a consequence, the group's hotel portfolio is eclectic, includes close to 60 hotels and is operated through a number of mechanisms. It includes properties managed by other operators (notably, the Millennium Hilton in New York; and the Grand Hyatt in Taipei); franchises from other major international hospitality companies (such as the Novotels in Penang and Singapore; and the Choice hotels in New Zealand); as well as a large number of properties owned and operated by the company directly. In the context, one of the most significant acquisitions, was that of the Copthorne group. This provided the group with a ready-branded and coherent group of hotels within a discrete geographical area (the UK, Germany and France) and has formed the nucleus of attempts to create a clear branding strategy.

CDL moved towards creating a focused image for their hotel portfolio by the establishment of Millennium Hotel and Resorts in December 1994 with the intention to use the Millennium name (taken from the New York hotel) as the unifying label for all the hotels. For legal reasons, this was not possible with respect to the company's 'home' Singapore hotels. Branding of CDL hotels was announced in early 1997 at three levels, reflecting demand from different market segments as well as the diverse product standards and specifications within the company's hotel portfolio. The announced brands are:

▷

- **Grand Millennium Hotels**, the company's luxury range of hotels, exhibiting weak branding characteristics and representing collection of major, international luxury hotels aimed at the discerning leisure and premium business traveller;
- **Millennium Hotels**, the company's mainstream hotels, located in major cities and catering for the four-star plus business and leisure market.
- **Millennium Copthorne Hotels**, based upon the existing Copthorne portfolio of three to four-star business hotels located in major and secondary cities in Europe.

The re-branding has, initially, focused on CDL hotels in Europe and North America, following the separate floatation of Millennium and Copthorne Hotels Ltd on the London Stock exchange, with CDL as 55% majority owner of the European and American subsidiary. It was also possible as a result of major investment and refurbishment in existing hotels, particularly those located in London to a standard where coherent branding was possible. Brand extension to the Pacific Rim region is likely when the situation on operating arrangements and naming rights have been clarified.

CDL represents an interesting international accommodation sector company case study because its growth strategy has created a diverse portfolio of hotels in four continents. Diversity is reflected in different type, size and standards of product and service within the group. It also features in the operating and management arrangements which CDL has chosen to employ in order to achieve maximum return on investment – full and part equity ownership; self-management in its own name; external management under a recognised international brand name; and franchising of existing products. This complexity represents a future, within the accommodation sector, which is very different from the rather more traditional and simple ownership and management models employed by other major hotel companies.

A major influence on the publicly quoted hotel sector in recent years has been that of increasingly focused performance demands placed upon operators by stock market investors. In the past, especially in Europe, average return on investment within the hotel sector was considerably below that achieved in other industrial and service sectors. This reflects in part the small business structure of hotel companies as well as perceptions of an operating culture which set hotels apart from other businesses – one where the focus was on hospitality rather than profitability. The view was that the two were, in some way, incompatible. This perception lost its primacy in North America some time before influencing the European industry. The success of many Asian companies in combining the two objectives of profitable service and excellence has led to change in Europe as well. Companies such as Accor, Granada and Whitbread, each owners and operators of a portfolio of different hotel brands, now operate to profit criteria designed to satisfy 'City' interests as their first priority. In this context, Le Meridien's Welcome Charter (included in Case Study 15.3) demonstrates that hospitality and profitability *can* be entirely compatible objectives within the accommodation sector.

Guesthouses, bed and breakfasts, farmhouse accommodation, inns

This subsector brings together a number of different types of operation with the common characteristics of offering accommodation plus some food and beverage (often just breakfast) in a small, family-style environment. Such properties may provide many similar facilities to smaller hotels although the category also includes simple and limited operations where guests may share facilities and, indeed, meals with their hosts.

Internationally there are significant contrasts in the operation of this subsector:

- In the UK, bed and breakfast and guesthouses enterprises are not significantly different, although the former require fewer controls or licences in order to operate. Indeed, it is a subsector where many operators take guests on a seasonal or sporadic basis and, as a result, can offer a flexible accommodation resource to a city or locality, available for use as and when required but without large fixed costs, particularly in terms of labour.

- Bed and breakfast enterprises in the USA, however, tend to be rather more sophisticated in their approach and comprehensive in their services. In European terms, they resemble inns or small hotels and are frequently members of national or regional marketing consortia.

- In Canada, inns are similar and can be grouped together on a themed or regional basis for marketing purposes. The Heritage Inns of Atlantic Canada is one example and membership depends upon a number of criteria, of which one is age – all properties must have been built before 1930. Some Canadian inns offer very sophisticated facilities. One example is the Spruce Pine Acres Country Inn in Port au Port, Newfoundland, which is a modern, purpose-built facility with just six bedrooms but its services also include a licensed dining room, a well-equipped meeting room and a business centre with Internet access.

Farmhouse accommodation is a central component in the growing international agritourism movement. Not only has this become a major feature of tourism development in a number of countries such as Ireland and New Zealand, but it is also a component in the development plans of countries in Eastern Europe and Asia.

Accommodation is, generally, similar to that afforded by bed and breakfast operations but the context is different. Provision is usually within a working farm environment and guests may be able to participate in various aspects of the agricultural working routine as part of their stay. Marketing of farmhouse accommodation includes consortia operating at a national and/or international level.

Small, independent operators across this subsector face significant challenges from the growing budget hotel sector, especially in Europe. In physical product terms, there may be considerable similarities between the two in terms of their bedrooms – indeed, budget properties may well exceed the competition in this respect. For example, the growth of the budget sector has forced the generally unregulated family-style sector in the UK to up-grade facilities or to cease operating. As a result, many such operations now provide en-suite bathrooms, multi-channel television and tea and coffee-making facilities.

Self-catering accommodation – apartments, cottages, gites, etc.

Self-catering accommodation is an important and varied component of the lodging sector within tourism. Essentially, what such properties have in common is a combination of accommodation with additional recreational areas and the facility to prepare food on a personal basis. Apartments form a major element within the accommodation available in many Mediterranean resorts but the sector also includes:

- individual cottages and gites – frequently adapted from normal residential use; and

- purpose-built cottage colonies developed and marketed as a distinct brand – for example, Rent an Irish Cottage, established in 1968 by Shannon Development (a public sector body) but subsequently sold off to private interests in the early 1990s.

Self-catering holiday accommodation may be rented as part of a vacation package, through an agency or independently direct from the owner. Alternatively, holiday accommodation ownership is a major component in the tourism industries of some countries and specific destinations. This is so much so in some places that in the off-season, communities can be just a fraction of those at peak periods. In some countries, ownership of a country or beach cottage is commonplace and not confined to the wealthy – this is certainly true of Norway and its seaside or mountain *hutte*. Where holiday homes are not purpose-built, but purchased within the normal housing market, they can create considerable distortion to the local property market and resentment within local communities who may see prices rise and young people unable to buy into the local housing market. North and west Wales are examples of areas where holiday homes have been a sensitive political issue in the past. The issues were reviewed and discussed in more detail in Chapter 6 which dealt with the economic impacts of tourism.

It is quite common for local residents' homes to form the accommodation for self-catering vacations. This may be through a number of mechanisms:

● House-swap schemes by which a family from, say, Sweden, exchanges homes for a month with counterparts (often in the same professional or work area) from Canada; the exchange may include use of vehicles and responsibility for pets as well as accommodation.

● Major events can also prompt local residents to vacate their homes in favour of visitors on a pay basis – SW19 in London experiences much of this during Wimbledon tennis fortnight as does the village of Silverstone during the British Formula 1 Grand Prix weekend.

Campus accommodation

Campus accommodation includes facilities that are used both within and outside the tourism sector. For much of the time, most campus accommodation is used on a semi-permanent basis by students, as many readers of this book will know. However, increasingly, universities and colleges seek to utilise a resource that is under-used during major periods of the year when students are on vacation. Accommodation is, therefore, widely used not only for conference and meetings purposes, but also as a leisure location, especially by campuses close to scenic or vacation areas. In addition, some campuses include permanent hotel-style facilities, designed for short-term visitors such as those attending executive development modules in business schools. Generally, the trend is towards up-grading of facilities in campus accommodation so that its use for non-student lets is competitive with other accommodation providers. The marketing of campus facilities is also now professional – in Scotland, an umbrella organisation, the Scottish Universities Accommodation Consortium, is responsible for supporting this aspect.

Time-share

Time-share is a form of period-constrained (i.e. one or two weeks a year) self-catering, holiday home ownership which provides additional benefits to owners in the form of possible access to other similar properties in resorts throughout the world. Many time-share properties also provide a range of additional services and facilities, including food service and sports/recreation so that they have much in common with resort hotels. Pressure-selling of time-share has gained the sector a bad reputation in some countries.

Youth accommodation

Youth travel is an important, growing and little researched sector of the tourism market. The extent of such travel and the specific facilities designed to meet its needs vary greatly between countries. Young people tend to utilise accommodation at the low cost end of the market – bed and breakfasts, youth hostels such as those run by the Youth Hostel Association (YHA), Young Men's Christian Association (YMCA) and Young Women's Christian Association (YWCA) and their local equivalents as well as camp sites. Books such as *Cheap Sleeps Europe* (K. Wood, 1997) and *Eastern Europe on a Shoestring* (1997) provide information and listings of establishments that would, otherwise, find it difficult to market their services.

Specialist accommodation providers to the youth market, such as youth hostels in many countries, YMCA/YWCAs and backpacker hostels in Australia, have moved from offering simple, frequently dormitory-style accommodation, to providing greater comfort, a more sophisticated product and more comprehensive services. In some cases, there is little to distinguish these providers from equivalently priced hotel products – the YMCA in Hong Kong is a good example. These trends reflect changing youth market demand, expectations and travel experience together with the increasing affluence of young people in many countries.

Camping and caravan sites

An important component in the domestic and international tourism of many countries is that where visitors bring their own accommodation to the destination in the form of tents, caravans or trailers. The accommodation levels provided on these sites has improved greatly from the camping experience of earlier generations but is still restricted in terms of space and privacy. An important provider, within tourism, is the subsector offering sites for campers or caravaners. Such sites may be basic fields with few if any utilities provided or sophisticated resort locations including a range of comfort services as well as leisure, food service and retail options.

Some sites offer permanently sited tents or caravans and tourists travel to the locations for a one- or two-week stay. Companies, such as Eurocamp, package these site holidays in Mediterranean locations for north European clients on very much the same basis as hotel or apartment-based fully inclusive packages. Permanent caravan sites include vehicles for short-term let, as well as those owned by visitors who may use the accommodation on a regular basis throughout the season.

Medical facility accommodation

This area is not normally seen as part of the tourism industry although facilities in hospitals, especially private institutions, are close to the best available within tourism accommodation. However, some specialist medical facilities also offer quality accommodation to relatives and friends. This may be true of premium children's hospitals, for example.

Nursing homes and other long-stay facilities for the elderly, likewise, are not normally associated with tourism. However, this market has attracted increasing attention from hotel companies such as Accor and Marriott who have developed a long-stay product for the seniors market which is a hybrid of a luxury hotel and a nursing home, offering medical as well as leisure facilities within the one establishment.

In Eastern Europe, countries such as Romania have spa tourism where resorts offer integrated medical treatment and hotel accommodation at all levels from the very basic to the very luxurious.

Cruise liners and ferries

Long-distance passenger liners were, of course, the main form of transport for those wishing to travel trans-Atlantic or otherwise intercontinental in the era that preceded the development of wide-bodied jets. Such liners provided functional accommodation to all but first-class passengers, designed as a necessary facility and ancillary to the prime purpose of transport. Likewise, ferries provided functional but limited accommodation services.

The growth of cruising from European and North American ports in the 1960s grew as an alternative use for the now-redundant liners and little attempt was made to alter the form of accommodation or the attendant facilities provided. Accommodation management also retained a marine and functional ethos. The building of dedicated cruise ships has changed the focus of on-board services from one where the main purpose was on transport to an environment where the cruise itself became equally important to the destinations visited. The popularity of the 'cruise to nowhere' concept in South-East Asia testifies to this. Modern cruise ships have more in common with all-inclusive resorts than with traditional marine transport. From an accommodation perspective, they are designed to offer comfort, facilities and service comparable to that of equivalent resort hotels. Indeed, the terminology used and the culture is that of hotel services.

Ferries, too, have changed in a similar way, particularly those offering longer services between, for example, the UK and Scandinavia or Spain. This was explored in more detail in Chapter 13, Transportation.

Trains and aircraft

Although luxuriously appointed accommodation as part of train travel has a long history, the more common model was that akin to seaborne comfort. The natural constraints of space, which railways impose on sleeping accommodation, are difficult to overcome and, as a result, most overnight sleeper facilities remain basic and functional. However, there has been a revival of luxury, on-train accommodation, spearheaded by companies such as Orient Express in Europe and between Singapore and Bangkok, as well as by a number of operators in India, Australia and South Africa. These trains, either modernised versions of old rollingstock or purpose-built, provide hotel comforts to the maximum permitted by space constraints.

Aircraft are faced with similar space constraints in providing sleeping accommodation for regular fare-paying passengers. A number of first-class products make claims to provide bed-like comfort for long-haul travellers. However, by comparison with their hotel equivalents, even the best of these products is akin to dormitory-style accommodation with a lack of real space or individual privacy.

Visiting friends and relatives

While outside the commercial accommodation sector, VFR tourists generally, but not exclusively, utilise facilities within the homes of their family or friends. As a result, their economic contribution to a community or region may be limited but, none the less, VFR constitutes a major element within the tourism industries of many countries, especially domestic tourism. In many developed countries, as family ties continue to weaken, it is likely that the VFR option may be used by fewer and fewer people. Where the return home is to a society that is markedly different from that where the tourists originate (for example, Afro- or Irish-American visitors to their roots), it is quite likely that commercial accommodation providers will be used for VFR visits although payment may well be by the host family rather than the visitors.

Sectoral overlap

The accommodation sector may or may not exist in organisational isolation from other sectors of the tourism economy. In other words, there are operations that provide accommodation facilities and nothing else to their customers – some budget hotel products, self-catering cottages and campsites are examples of businesses where there may be minimal horizontal integration with other activities in tourism. By contrast, there are operations where accommodation is just one of a range of integrated tourism services provided by the one organisation. All-inclusive resorts and cruise ships, offering a wide range of entertainment, leisure, retail and food service facilities in addition to accommodation, provide good examples. The problem, from a definitional point of view, is that terms in the accommodation area, are used very loosely so that the word 'hotel' may be employed to describe a small, family-owned bed and breakfast establishment, a budget hotel, a luxury country house property or an integrated resort such as Gleneagles in Scotland. As a result, official definitions are rarely of much value and are mainly used in order to regulate or grade the sector.

An important trend, in the hotel sector, is the disaggregation of accommodation from other aspects of hotel services, particularly in the moderate and economy sectors of the market-place. The customer may not always be aware of this disaggregation because it frequently represents a business rather than a service arrangement. Hallam and Baum (1996) discuss the growing trend towards out-sourcing food and beverage services within hotels, to either individual operators or to branded chain restaurants, allowing some hotel companies to concentrate on high-yield, low-cost accommodation provision while ensuring that their customers have access to appropriate food service opportunities. Other concepts such as Embassy All-Suites, in the USA, and Travelodge in the budget sector in the UK, have been designed as almost exclusively accommodation providers, encouraging guests to make use of external food service, leisure and entertainment facilities. This disaggregation process appears to represent a growing trend in the tourism industry at one end of the market. At the other end, increasingly sophisticated integrated all-inclusive resort provision points in the opposite direction.

Box 15.1 Accommodation: an historical perspective

Accommodation has been a travel requirement since the first trading, missionary and pilgrimage routes were established in Asia and Europe in pre-Christian times. The basis of such accommodation was, generally, non-paying with travellers provided with a roof and sustenance as part of religious obligation or in the hope that similar hospitality might be offered to the host in the future. Possibly the first reference to commercial accommodation provision in Europe comes from thirteenth-century Florence but an identifiable commercial accommodation sector cannot really be identified until the late eighteenth century when coaching inns in Britain developed in response to organised ▷

Box 15.1 continued

stagecoach travel and the first large hotels were opened in France and the USA. The dawn of the railway era stimulated hotel development in many countries of Europe and elsewhere and the railway companies were among the main promoters of hotel building, proximate or integral to main termini in cities such as New York, London or Edinburgh. In many respects, these were the first hotel multiples or chains with which we are familiar today.

The latter half of the nineteenth century also saw increased travel stimulate the development of some of the great luxury hotels of the major capital cities of the world, many of which continue to set standards of luxury for the industry today. Hotels such as the Waldorf Astoria in New York; the Savoy, Dorchester and Claridges in London, and the Ritz in Paris all date from this era. Raffles in Singapore and the Taj Mahal in Bombay, while somewhat different in the motivation for their establishment, also date from the same period and represent a tradition of European-style accommodation or hotel-keeping which provided the dominant model until superseded by the American approach in the late 1940s and early 1950s. At the other end of the luxury scale, the growth of popular and accessible tourism options in most industrialised countries stimulated the development of low-cost seaside accommodation in resorts such as Deauville, Douglas, Blackpool and Atlantic City.

The post-1945 period saw the development of the American model of accommodation management and operations. Dominated, in its early days, by concepts of standardisation, risk avoidance and the application of Fordian principles of mass production, the American model is one that has spawned most of the major hotel corporations which increasingly dominate the international accommodation sector: Hilton, Hyatt, Holiday Inn, Sheraton, Inter-Continental all have their origins in this concept of the hotel, although not all the companies in question are American-owned today.

The American influence on the contemporary accommodation or lodging sector has been profound and it is arguable that this source continues to dominate new ideas, products and systems. The European concept of professional hospitality has been very important, especially in translating service from the *mine host* environment of the small hospitality business into larger organisations in all parts of the world. Similarly, the more recent influence of Asian service cannot be underestimated. The American contribution has been to apply successive industrial models to the accommodation sector and thus create the foundations of an industrial sector from what was a loose amalgam of small business enterprises. While the American influence has been most noticeable within the hotel sector, the impact has been felt in other subsectors such as bed and breakfast and cruise liners. The American influence has been wide-ranging and we will only address a selection of examples here.

● The mass mobility of millions of Americans, previewed in the 1930s and a true reality in the post-1945 era created roadside demand for value and informal accommodation which led to the motel concept, the forerunner of today's chain budget or economy lodge. With minimum service, these largely family-run operations were opened along all main highways in the country and established a new form of accessible and low-cost accommodation available to a segment of the population which, previously, had been unable to afford conventional hotels. The heyday of the motel was the 1940s and 1950s before they were overtaken by the chain or franchise alternatives of the major lodging companies. However, the old style, independent motel is still to be found in more remote parts of the USA – a journey along Highway I through Maine and to the Canadian border is one past a large number of such businesses to which few changes or compromises to modernity have been made since their opening some 50 years ago.

● The creation of the standardised chain offering common services, prices and reducing the risk in accommodation choice for the frequent traveller is commonly attributed to Kemmons Wilson and the foundation of the Holiday Inn chain. Nickson (1997) expands on this story: ▷

Box 15.1 continued

Kemmons Wilson developed the idea for Holiday Inns (the first one opened in 1952) after the experience of what he called 'the most miserable vacation of my life' (Lee, 1985 [cited in Nichson, 1997]). This was the result of the unpredictable quality and prices of motels which Wilson had experienced. As a result of this, Holiday Inn was based and developed on the notion of concept standardization, to ensure operational control and guest consistency. (p. 126)

- Wilson also introduced franchising into the accommodation sector on a large scale for the first time, thus facilitating rapid growth for his concept and, at the same time, applying strict operating standards and consistency to a previously unregulated area of the tourism industry.

- Holiday Inn was one example of the growth of hotel chains or groups, some standardised and some not, which became an important feature of the American lodging industry – household names such as Hilton, Hyatt, Inter-Continental, Marriott and Sheraton all have their origins from this period when multiple hotel operations were unusual elsewhere in the world and, where they existed, rarely operated under the banner of a common brand name.

- The strength of the emerging American hotel chains, coupled with US-led commercial and travel growth, created the first major wave of internationalisation in the accommodation sector. Nickson (1997) talks about this:

internationalisation process which drew heavily on the certainties offered to the American hotel chains in their home country. Thus as these firms begin to serve markets outside of their home country, they did so in a resolutely American way.

It is arguable that the major impact of this early internationalisation in the hotel sector, was to create models and set standards which newer, non-American entrants into this market have adopted and enhanced, without ever losing the key flavour of their origins. Nickson argues that recent dilution of American ownership in the international hotel sector represents a shift of influence to Asia and Europe in terms of the sector's culture. Given the strength of early American influence on what we know today as the international hotel, this argument is, at least, open to debate.

- Finally, in this context, the American lodging model has given respectability to minimalism in terms of service and services within the accommodation sector. American lodging, from motels onwards, have increasingly accepted the business benefits of the separation of food service from accommodation in operational and ownership terms (Hallam and Baum, 1996) or, indeed, its total elimination which is commonplace in the modern budget or economy property.

The accommodation sector, today, is moving from traditions that were predominantly national to a more international stage, although the truly global accommodation brand, in the sense of Coca Cola or Kellogg's, remains some way off. Companies are, increasingly, looking to investment that is international in focus so as to create brand awareness on a larger scale, to the benefit of domestic businesses and those in the countries of investment. American companies are developing elsewhere because of perceived saturation in the market-place at home where reinvestment in tired mid-market, franchised properties is of greater need than the creation of additional capacity. European and Asian companies see the opportunity to bring the distinctive flavour of their brands (for example, Novotel and Mandarin Oriental) to new markets. Competition in the accommodation sector, therefore, increasingly exists at an international level but is complemented by strengthening and up-grading of many independent or small chain operators at a local level.

Quality issues and grading in the accommodation sector

In common with all areas of tourism, the accommodation sector in any one location is a product of local and global forces representing historical, political, economic, socio-cultural and technological factors. The interplay of these environmental determinants is the main cause of the sector's heterogeneity.

Comparison, therefore, becomes difficult between subsectors within accommodation and between operations in different countries and regions of the world. There are few meaningful frameworks or criteria that can compare the physical product attributes and ambience of, for example, Ashford Castle in the west of Ireland with its focus on the traditional in the style of the landed aristocracy and the ultra-modernity of the Ritz Carlton, Millenia, Singapore, situated in the heart of that urbanised city state. Both offer excellence within their own location and context but their physical product is completely different. Where comparison may be ventured is in terms of service quality but this dimension presents numerous problems of, in particular, subjective assessment.

Quality comparisons are attempted through various accommodation grading and classification schemes. These, generally, operate on a national or regional basis within countries and may be run by either public (e.g. tourist board) or private sector (e.g. the Automobile Association (AA) or the American Automobile Association (AAA)) organisations. Attempts to introduce trans-national systems within, for example, the EU, have failed largely because of diversity within the industry of each country.

Accommodation classification or grading may be applied to all subsectors but is predominantly used with respect to hotels, guest houses, farmhouse accommodation, bed and breakfast establishments and campsites. There is a difference in focus and purpose between classification and grading:

- **Classification** may be defined as 'the assignment of hotels to a categorical rating according to type of property, facilities, and amenities offered' (Gee, 1994). This is the traditional focus of most schemes.

- **Grading** in contrast emphasises quality dimensions. In practice, most national or commercially operated schemes concentrate on classification with quality perceived to be an *add-on* which does not impact upon the star rating of an establishment.

The purposes of accommodation classification are varied. They include:

- *standardisation* – to establish a system of uniform service and product quality that helps to create an orderly travel market distribution system for buyers and sellers;

- *marketing* – to advise travellers on the range and types of accommodation available within a destination as a means of promoting the destination and encouraging healthy competition in the market-place;

- *consumer protection* – to ensure that accommodation meets minimum standards of accommodation, facilities, and service within classification and grade definitions;

- *revenue generation* – to provide revenue from licensing, the sale of guide books and so forth;

- *control* – to provide a system for controlling general industry quality; and

- *investment incentive* – to give operators incentive to up-grade their facilities and services in order to meet grading/classification criteria.

Accommodation classification, however, is not without problems. One of these relates to the subjectivity of judgement involved in assessing many key aspects of both the tangible and intangible elements of the accommodation experience such as personal service or the quality of products. As a consequence, many classification schemes concentrate, primarily, on the physical and quantifiable attributes of operations determining level of grade on the basis of features such as

- room size;
- room facilities, especially whether en-suite or not; and
- availability of services – laundry, room-service, 24-hour reception.

However, this is commonly done without any attempt to assess the quality of such provision or the consistency of its delivery. Other problems with classification schemes include:

- political pressures to offer classification and grading towards the top end of the spectrum to most hotels, thus creating a top-heavy structure;
- the cost of administering and operating a comprehensive classification assessment scheme, especially where subjective, intangible dimensions are to be included;
- industry objections to state-imposed, compulsory schemes; and
- the tendency of classification schemes to encourage standardisation rather than individual excellence within hotels.

Case Study 15.2 is an extract from the research study undertaken prior to implementing changes to the Scottish Tourist Board's (STB) scheme. Within this scheme, star grading (one to four stars) is based exclusively upon assessment of quality and will provide the headline information for consumer choice and information. Information on facilities will be provided in directories and similar publications. Thus, a small establishment, excelling in its service but limited in the range of facilities available for guests, could be graded as five star while a large, international property with a full range of product attributes (leisure, business) could be graded as three star on the basis of the quality of its service and products.

Quality and quality assessment are rooted in the culture and context of the country in which they are located. As a result, a five-star or deluxe hotel in South East Asia will be significantly different from a property which purports equivalence in Turkey or the UK. At best (and even this is debatable), classification can provide a guide to national standards. Even this is not always the case. In Spain, for example, the level of tax which a hotel pays is related to its grade, with five-star properties paying more than twice the amount of four-star hotels. As a consequence, there are few five-star hotels in Spain and a clustering of four-star properties covering a wide range of standards. Hotels such as Sofitel, Intercontinental and Crowne Plaza are classified as four star when, elsewhere in Europe, these hotel brands would attract higher levels. Indeed, neighbouring Sofitel and Novotel properties in Madrid are both classified as four star, making a mockery of parent company Accor's branding intentions where they are clearly differentiated.

Probably the major difficulty faced by hotel classification schemes in Europe and North America is how to include the growing number of budget or economy hotels within schemes without creating unworkable ambiguities. The modern budget or economy hotel room contains a comprehensive range of simple but comfortable furnishings and facilities in a spacious, clean and modern environment. The comfort to be found in such rooms is primarily related to the physical product and is, generally, offered with minimum levels of service. One effect of the growth within this sector has been to create

Case Study 15.2 Scotland's Commended Hotels

Scotland's Commended Hotels (SCH) is best described as an association of individually owned and managed country and town house hotels, ranging within the four to five star quality range. The hotels pride themselves on the individuality of their products and services, with a particular emphasis on quality ambience and personal attention to guest needs. The consortium came into being in 1990 when the British Tourist Authority discontinued its development promotion of distinctive regional and product collections.

SCH is a cooperative, organised on a membership basis with a democratic, participative structure, operating to an elected Board of Directors. The focus of the organisation is on achieving consensus in its strategies and operations and thus ensuring that its members have shared market positions and stated values. The main purpose of SCH is to market the products and services of its membership within the domestic and international market-place; to promote cooperation and guest referral; and to obtain purchasing advantage, on behalf of members, through volume arrangements.

SCH has 66 full members, who represent 1159 bedrooms, an average property size of 17.5 bedrooms. Membership criteria include the requirement that hotels

- are independently owned and managed;
- have high standards of food and beverage;
- are graded as a minimum of 4 Crown Highly Commended within the STB's Grading Scheme;
- have a maximum of 40 bedrooms;
- are individual and original in character; and
- that members are actively committed to SCH and participate in the activities of the consortium, particularly through brochure display and referral.

The strengths of SCH can be summarised as follows:

- association of top, independently owned hotels all having the same stated values;
- in comparison to the identified competitor organisations, it is a low-cost consortium to join;
- variety of hotel types, which are individual, personally managed and not standardised;
- comprehensive geographic spread, good range of prices, with quality products at each price level;
- strong market proposition of collectively good products;
- members directly involved in selling the products;
- STB support of the only cohesive consortium that represents the Scottish hotel product.

(With thanks to Dr Alison Morrison, The Scottish Hotel School.)

very real problems for hotel classification systems which find it difficult to accommodate physical comfort with the absence of services available to the guest.

The AA in the UK have created a special category to cater for budget accommodation, called 'lodges', as did the STB as early as 1993. The STB (1996) states

> *The introduction of this category [lodges] acknowledges the popularity and growing provision of purpose built bedroom accommodation designed primarily to provide convenient overnight accommodation for short stay visitors. Many establishments of this nature do not provide meals or offer lounge facilities and are unlikely to meet the requirements of a normal Crown classification.*

These establishments will usually have 100% of bedrooms en suite and have restaurant or dining facilities nearby.

Budget hotels, in Europe, are a response to changing customer needs and expectations and their importance can be dated from the mid-1980s. Prior to their development, the consumer in search of low-cost accommodation would have patronised one of the large number of small, independent hotels, guesthouses or bed and breakfast establishments, generally at the unclassified, one- or two-star level, to be found in all Western European countries. Products and services were very varied – just the problem faced by Kemmons Wilson in the USA some 30 years previously. The option of quality, low-cost and modern accommodation in the form of budget hotels, branded under names such as Formule 1, Travelodge, Travel Inn and Campanile, has moved a significant volume of demand away from traditional operators and resulted in both widespread up-grading of facilities and business failure in this sector.

As a consequence, the overall quality of bedroom accommodation in the lower-priced segments of the Western European lodging industry has improved significantly over the past two decades. The quality gap between this sector of the market, measured in physical product terms, and that provided by mid- to upper-sector hotels (three to five stars) has decreased greatly as a result and, with the growing impact of low-cost technology, this is a gap that is likely to further narrow. It is a reasonable expectation that, just as en-suite facilities, hot beverage equipment, international direct dialling (IDD) telephones and satellite television services are virtually the norm throughout much of the accommodation range, additional benefits (fax, Internet) will become available to properties at all levels and simultaneously.

The challenge for higher priced and graded accommodation providers, therefore, is to ensure clear market differentiation between their offering and that of the budget sector. However, as up to 50% of the custom of budget hotels in the UK is from the business market, this suggests that, at present, they are not particularly successful in doing so. The key differentiation that they are able to offer, given that physical attributes no longer provide such clear water, is that of service in its widest sense. There is considerable evidence that there is an accommodation market that is able and willing to pay considerably more for the benefits that attentive, individualised and problem-solving service provides. Balmer and Baum (1993) provide a theoretical explanation for this, based on the work of Herzberg.

Accommodation organisations place increasing emphasis on their ability to respond positively to the service demands of their customers and companies such as Ritz Carlton and Marriott have established international reputations for their focus on service. Case Study 15.3 is taken from Le Meridien's Welcome Charter, designed to provide new staff with an induction into the group's service quality standards.

The accommodation sector and environmental issues

The accommodation sector is not one that we generally think of as evoking images of pollution and environmental degradation. However, the structure of the sector, with operational units widely dispersed in some of the most fragile natural environments as well as within ancient and historic cities, means that its environmental impact can be very significant at both macro and micro levels. Indeed, visitors' fascination with the most fragile natural, historic and cultural environments may create demand for accommodation in locations that, otherwise, would be totally off the beaten track.

The accommodation sector's impact, in environmental terms, is varied and complex. The key areas include the following.

Case Study 15.3 Le Meridien

This case study contain an extract from Le Meridien/Forte Grand's *Welcome Charter Manual* which contains guidelines for all departments within the company's hotels. The Charter is the outcome of guest survey conducted within 20 hotels and 5000 members of the chain's 'Carte Noire' loyalty programme. In this case, we include the section entitled 'Welcome basics' which is applied to all departments of the hotel.

Welcome Basics

Mission statement

To be the Number One for quality and consistency in the international up-market hotel business.

Brand positioning

An international brand of hotels of four-star level and above, which serves business and leisure guests, and is European in character, French in origin and integrated with local culture.

We will deliver superior profitability by recognising that our guests are the most important people in our business and our employees are our most important resource. Suppliers will be treated as partners.

Respect for oneself and for guests

Performance Criteria

Appearance

- Uniforms must be impeccable and complete at all times (including polished shoes).
- Badges must be worn at all times.
- A neat appearance is essential:
  - neat, conventional hairstyle
  - tasteful, subtle makeup
  - discreet jewelry
- Immaculate hygiene at all times.

Language

- A warm, but never familiar approach.
- Direct, but not arrogant or vulgar.
- Distinct, precise diction.
- Controlled physical gestures.
- Greet the guest in the local language if appropriate but converse with them in the language that suits them best.

Posture

- Maintain dignified poise in every situation.

Case Study 15.3 continued

Caring for guests

Performance Criteria

The smile

- The most universal of all languages.
- Understood by everyone and the starting point for all welcome actions.

Consideration

- Know how to recognise and anticipate the expectations of our guests.
- All times, show courtesy and willingness to please.

Listen

- Know how to listen to a guest in order to assimilate both requests and complaints accurately.
- Never argue with a guest.

Be available

- Know how to stop doing something in order immediately to satisfy a request from a guest.
- Do not let guests repeat the same request to several departments. Do it for them.

Professionalism

Performance Criteria

Responsibility

- Always keep a cool head – whatever the circumstances.
- Know how to reassure guests.
- Remain vigilant to constantly ensure guest safety.

Efficiency

- Respond quickly and ensure that guest requests are always followed through.

Offer a choice

- Always find and propose alternatives to guests to avoid ever being unable to satisfy them.

Reliability

- Always honour a promise made to a guest.

Provide information

- Keep informed in order to be able to keep guests informed.
- Always inform guests if unforeseen circumstances arise which may cause problems.

Nurture a team spirit

- Make a positive contribution to the hotel's overall friendly atmosphere.
- Always support each other since guests notice this.

Source: with thanks to Le Meridien

Water use

Tourists are high consumers of water and many major tourist destinations are located in areas of potential or actual water shortage. Much of the water that visitors use during their time is within accommodation units – for baths, showers, in the swimming pool, laundry, maintaining green and attractive garden areas and sports facilities such as golf courses. Generally, tourists are less likely to visit destinations or stay in accommodation where there are restrictions on the use of water or where its quality is substandard. However, the long-term impact of unregulated water use by tourists can be very significant. In parts of southern Spain for example, the permanent lowering of the water table affects other economic activities, notably agriculture. Likewise, rice farmers in Phuket, Thailand have had restrictions placed on their cropping seasons in order to preserve water for tourists. Sectors of the accommodation industry have responded to the pressures of a finite water supply and also the increasing tendency to charge businesses for consumption by activating varied water conservation measures. Towel reuse opportunities are in place in many hotels, whereby guests are asked to indicate which of their towels require laundering and which can be reused. Some hotels, such as the Holiday Inn in Phuket, has its own water treatment plant which permits sufficient treatment of waste water to allow for its use in the hotel's gardens and leisure facilities.

The Hotel Nikko's implementation of Hong Kong's 'A Guide to Energy and Water Conservation in Hotels' is an example of a practical hotel response to water and energy conservation opportunities which stresses both the environmental and businesses benefits of this approach. Case Study 15.4 includes the Guide's key practical recommendations.

Case Study 15.4 Hotel Nikko, Hong Kong

This case study contains an extract from a report entitled *A Guide to Energy and Water Conservation in Hotel* published by the Hong Kong Polytechnic University in collaboration with the Hotel Nikko, Hong Kong, in 1996. Two parts of the Guide are included – Part 1 which relates to management and Part 2 which is intended for departmental staff.

Part I: Determination by hotel management

Awareness: Hotel management should be aware of the importance and significance of energy and water conservation in terms of financial incentive and environmental benefits. A reduction in energy and water cost can make a useful contribution to the total cost effectiveness of hotel operation, making the hotel more competitive. Perhaps more important it helps to minimise the damage to our precious environment caused by excessive usage of energy, in order to leave a better and greener world to future generations.

Determination: The first step to energy and water conservation is the determination of hotel management. If senior management in a hotel has no interest in cost cutting or environmental issues, then it is almost impossible for any energy or water conservation programme to succeed.

Maintain service quality: It is important for the management to understand that any energy- or water-saving measures taken should in no way affect the quality of service and or the quality of the hotel's indoor environment, to standards appropriate to the class of the hotel. For example, if guests are not satisfied with the shower system (e.g. restricted water flow, insufficient hot water or inadequate temperature) after the implementation of a conservation measure, then it is obviously unacceptable. Energy and water conservation for any hotel is sensible only when the expected quality of service, hospitality and convenience are maintained. Energy- and water-saving measures should seek to reduce wastage and to improve operating efficiency. ▷

Case Study 15.4 continued

Consumption: Room occupancy in a hotel may be a seasonal variable, and so too is energy consumption. Energy used for cooking, water heating, etc., depends on occupancy. As the weather in Hong Kong is hot and humid in summer, the electricity consumption for air conditioning and ventilation is seasonal, obviously being much higher in summer. Typically, annual electricity use for air conditioning may account for over 50% of total electricity used in a hotel. The second largest electricity user is lighting systems which, in contrast to air conditioning systems, has a fairly constant energy consumption throughout a year. Electricity consumed for lighting is normally in the range of 25–35% of total electricity consumption in a hotel. The greatest electricity-saving potential most probably resides in these two areas. Large water consumers in a hotel include the laundry, kitchens and guest rooms. This is where water conservation potential should be explored.

Good housekeeping: Much can be done to conserve energy and water through 'good housekeeping'. This approach does not require major capital investment and specialist knowledge, but significant reductions in energy and water consumption, and thereby, operational cost can be obtained. Up to 10% reduction in energy and water consumption are achievable.

Good housekeeping means reducing wastage of water and energy when they are not required, or where they are oversupplied. For example, lights and air conditioning being switched off when a room is not in use; turning on water taps in kitchens only when needed; turning off equipment such as coffee machines when not in use. The key to successful good housekeeping is engendering self-motivation in the staff responsible for operating and maintaining equipment in the laundry, kitchens, guest floors and other areas.

Senior management should try its best to encourage and educate staff about the merits of saving energy and water through individual good housekeeping practices. The ultimate aim is that every staff member in the hotel is aware of the importance of energy and water conservation and is an active participant. The message that energy and water saving through good housekeeping is everyone's responsibility should be clearly communicated to all hotel staff.

Checklist: A checklist of good housekeeping practices can be found in the second part of this guide. It is by no means exhaustive and hotel management, and section or department heads, might design their own list, appropriate to the work nature in their respective sections.

Motivating staff: Some staff may perceive that these practices would bring 'inconvenience' or cause 'additional work' for them. For instance kitchen staff tend to leave water taps on when they are busy with other work, but for good housekeeping a tap should only be turned on when it is needed. Only when the staff understand what they are doing can they be self-motivated to take action without any complaints or unwillingness. Some forms of energy and water saving award to individuals or departments and competition among departments might be worthwhile to stimulate staff's morale and to promote the practices. Suggestions from staff on ways to save energy and water, and to improve efficiency should be encouraged and carefully considered. These should be implemented whenever feasible.

Engineering staff: Engineering staff in a hotel are at the front line of water and energy conservation, as they are responsible for operating and maintaining services and systems that are energy- and water-intensive. Therefore, their attitudes, skills and actions can have significant impact on water and energy consumption. These staff should receive adequate education and training to raise their awareness of energy and water conservation, and to update their job skills. Such investment helps ▷

improve the efficiency of building services equipment through better operations and maintenance. Appropriate resources and funding should be allocated for this purpose.

Equipment: Senior management should be aware that no matter what class of hotel, there are likely to be serious deficiencies in the equipment that services the hotel. Equipment is often oversized or lacks proper control function. Instrumentation which tells the operator how well equipment is performing is also likely to be inadequate. Imagine assessing the fuel consumption of a motor car without a reasonably accurate fuel gauge, or its speed without a speedometer!

Involve guests: Requesting hotel guests to participate in the energy saving and environmental protection initiatives can prove fruitful. This might include a campaign of 'reused towels' by displaying a tent-card inside guest room requesting guests to indicate whether some unused towers can be reused, thus reducing the laundry load and saving water and energy.

Energy manager: Like any other kinds of management, energy and water consumption management is an important part of management work in a hotel. The top-down management ethos that ensures quality of personnel services in leading hotels can be applied to energy and water conservation. A senior member of management can be assigned as the 'energy manager', to monitor energy and water use in the hotel, supporting initiatives to reduce consumption. This manager, preferably having some technical knowledge, works together with engineering staff to make technically and economically sound decisions on energy and water conservation.

Going further: Identifying energy and water saving potential beyond good housekeeping practices, for example, optimising central air conditioning plant performance needs technical expertise. This would normally require investment in outside advice, and on measuring and monitoring equipment. In this case justification on best investment return should be sought.

And further: Energy and water conservation programmes in a hotel can be internally financed by allocating all or part of annual savings, depending on scale and nature of these programmes. However, financial assistance from external sources may be available for various water and energy conservation initiatives. Cooperation with an educational institute with expertise in water and energy conservation to carry out a well-planned programme may prove fruitful, with relatively low cost.

Part II: Good Housekeeping Practices Checklist

This checklist is intended for all staff working in a hotel to guide them in their routine work in good housekeeping practices which minimise energy and water wastage.

Kitchens:
- Turn off or turn down kitchen equipment, in particular gas cookers, when not in use.
- Minimise the opening of doors of cold store and freezers.
- Turn on a water tap only when needed and never let water run continuously.
- Adjust water flow rate and water temperature to suit different kitchen use and for cleaning. ▷

- Turn off ventilation and lights when no one is in a kitchen, or turn off local ventilation and lighting if the local area is not in use.
- Operate dishwashers at or near their full load to minimise the number of operations.
- Keep kitchens clean at all times to reduce the amount of water used.
- Clean daily and check frequently all kitchen equipment for highest possible efficiency.
- Follow the operating instructions of kitchen equipment manufactures.
- Kitchen doors adjacent to dining areas should normally be kept closed to prevent excessive kitchen exhaust make-up air drawn from the dining areas (this needs to be done in consultation with engineering department to check whether the exhaust make-up is via dining area).

Laundry:
- Turn off lights and ventilation or air conditioning when the laundry is not in use.
- Run full loads in washing machines to minimise number of operations. Weigh loads if necessary.
- Ensure that water temperature and amount of water are in accordance with the specification by washing machine manufacturer.

Guest rooms:
- When a room is not occupied, ensure that drapes and/or blinds are closed.
- Housekeeping supervisors, in consultation with engineering staff, should ensure that temperature and fan speed settings for room thermostats are correctly adjusted.
- Report and leaking taps, running toilets and similar faults and ensure all room windows are closed.
- For guest rooms without automatic access control system, ensure that all power and lighting is off in unoccupied room as soon as guests have checked out.

Main entrance:
- Ensure that the main entrance door is normally closed to avoid air filtration.

Source: with thanks to Hotel Nikko, Hong Kong

Energy use

Reducing energy use, whether for heating in a winter climate or air-conditioning in hot climates, has clear environmental as well as financial savings to the business concerned. The Hong Kong Guide identifies practical routes to energy conservation within all departments of hotels. Computer technology permits the more effective control of energy, whether heat, air-conditioning or light and it is possible, for example, to close down rooms, corridors or whole blocks automatically if vacated by guests.

Recycling

Re-use of paper products from reception and administrative areas, replacement of individual shampoo sachets in bathrooms with dispensers and the avoidance of disposable tableware are examples of how the accommodation sector can recycle items normally bound for disposal.

Waste disposal

Accommodation operations, especially large hotels, create large amounts of liquid and solid waste which requires sensitive disposal. In some situations, especially small island locations such as the Maldives, disposal is a major problem and solid waste may need to be shipped off island for disposal. In some countries, hotels quite freely dispose of liquid waste directly into the sea or rivers. This can be seriously damaging to health and the environment.

Fragile nature

Hotels and other accommodation units, located within fragile natural environments (such as safari lodges) pose major threats to the fauna and flora of such locations. Such environments need to be managed with appropriate sensitivity so that guests are not disappointed in their experience but, at the same time, their presence does not destroy the very resource they have come to experience.

The critical concern here is one of the education of both employees within accommodation units and of their guests in the importance of environmental sensitivity and responsibility. The accommodation sector's role, in environmental and conservation terms, is not entirely negative. The contribution to the conservation and, indeed, enhancement of historic houses and castles in many parts of the world, adapted for hotel use, cannot be ignored for these are properties which may otherwise not have found another suitable use without conversion to accommodation facilities.

Information technology and the accommodation sector

In common with all other areas of services and, indeed, most areas of tourism, the accommodation sector is increasingly influenced by developments in the information and communications technology field (see Chapter 20 for a full review of information technology in the hotel industry). In many respects, technology has permitted the creation of highly labour efficient and quality product budget or economy units by centralising all non-customer contact functions (reservations, marketing, finance) and allowing the property to concentrate on the delivery of a limited but consistent product. Technology impacts both at the unit level, within accommodation, and in terms of macro marketing and financial aspects:

- **Unit level.** Technology is the key to the efficient management of resources at unit level – energy, stock, human and financial. The training implications, for effective use of technology in the small accommodation business, is an issue that is not widely recognised.

- **Macro level.** The significant development at this level is the increasing dominance of global distribution system (GDS) as the lead method of securing market share and marketing advantage for major accommodation brands. At the same time, cost of participation within GDS means that small companies and independent operators may be excluded from this technology-driven avenue of reaching key customers unless they are able to establish sufficient market presence through participation in an established consortium such as Best Western.

Human resources and the accommodation sector

Service-intensive businesses within accommodation are also labour-intensive and are always likely to remain so. This is despite considerable improvements in:

- productivity through use of technology;
- training;
- systems efficiency; and
- management effectiveness.

There are few significant labour-saving initiatives that can drastically reduce the level of employment in say, housekeeping. By contrast, the budget or economy sector is able to provide a quality product without significant service levels through minimising the level of staffing employed.

In spite of significant changes to the use and productivity of labour within the sector, accommodation remains an area that provides employment opportunity for a wide range of skills and aptitudes, reflecting not only the diversity of businesses that operate under the accommodation umbrella but also the variety of tasks that working in the sector demands. In many communities, accommodation businesses contribute socially by providing employment opportunities for people who would find it difficult to work in other sectors of the economy. Accommodation also provides relatively easy access to employment for new immigrants (legal and illegal) as well as those entering the labour market for the first time (school-leavers, students). These positive dimensions must be counterbalanced by recognition of perceived and actual problems with respect to work conditions, pay and general industry image issues, especially in developed countries. These issues and their wider human resource implications are addressed in detail elsewhere (Baum, 1995; R. C. Wood, 1997).

Conclusion

In this chapter, we have addressed the largest and, arguably, the most important subsector within tourism at a domestic and international level. The purpose of the chapter has been to demonstrate the position of accommodation within the wider tourism sector and to show how its diversity meets the requirements of virtually all tourism market groups. The origins of the accommodation sector are considered and the dominant influence of the US model of commercial hospitality discussed. Issues such as standardisation, the management of standards and the accommodation sector's environmental responsibilities are addressed.

Accommodation is a rapidly changing sector within tourism and, as a consequence, it is an area where many businesses are casualties in the face of competition from new products and service/product standards. It is unlikely that the pace of change will slow in the foreseeable future.

Chapter discussion questions

1. In what ways has the accommodation sector changed since 1945 and what effect has this had on the wider tourism industry?

2. Account for the diversity in the accommodation sector between different countries and regions.

3. Given its diversity, how can the accommodation sector provide meaningful comparisons of quality?

4. Review and discuss the key issues facing the accommodation sector and their likely impact in the future.

5. What are the benefits, to the small independent hotel, of participation in a marketing consortium such as Scotland's Commended Hotels?

6. What practical problems might occur with the cooperative model used by SCH?

7. What benefits and difficulties might the consumer face in using SCH properties?

Recommended further reading

● Gee, C. Y. (1994) *International Hotels Development and Management*, Educational Institute of the American Hotel and Motel Association, East Lansing.
● Jones, P. (ed.) (1996) *Introduction to Hospitality Operations*, Cassell, London.
● Vallen, J. J. and Vallen, G. K. (1991) *Check-in Check-out* (4th edn), Wm C. Brown, Dubuque, IA.

Bibliography

● Balmer, S. and Baum, T. (1993) 'Applying Herzberg's hygiene factors to the changing accommodation environment: the application of motivational theory to the field of guest satisfaction', *International Journal of Contemporary Hospitality Management*, **5**(2), 32–5.
● Baum, T. (1995) *Managing Human Resources in the European Tourism and Hospitality Industry: A Strategic Approach*, London: Chapman and Hall.
● *Eastern Europe on a Shoestring*, 4th edn (1997) Lonely Planet, Hawthorn, Vic.
● Gee, C. (1994) *International Hotels. Development and Management*, Educational Institute of the American Hotel and Motel Association, East Lansing.
● Hallam, G. and Baum, T. (1996) 'Contracting out food and beverage operations in hotels: a comparative study of practice in North America and the United Kingdom', *International Journal of Hospitality Management*, **15**(1), 41–50.
● Nickson, D. (1997), 'Continuity or change in the international hotel industry', pp. 213–28 in *Hospitality, Tourism and Leisure Management: Issues in Strategy and Culture* Foley, M., Lennon, J. and Maxwell G. (eds), London, Cassell.
● STB (1996) *Quality Assurance*, Inverness: Scottish Tourist Board.
● Wood, K. (1997) *Cheap Sleeps Europe*, 6th edn, Ebury Press, London.
● Wood, R. C. (1997) *Working in Hotels and Catering*, 2nd edn, Thomson International Press, London.

Chapter author: Professor Tom Baum

Marketing for tourism

Introduction

The tourism market is maturing and, despite the fact that overall demand rates are continuing to rise, growth rates are predicted to slow over the next couple of decades. Thus, the role of marketing will become increasingly important for tourism organisations, operating in both public and private sectors, as they continue to strive to protect and improve their market share.

The process of marketing and its management provides companies and organisations with the tools to communicate with target markets. It is a complex area that, as this section highlights, requires expertise and experience for success. In this section, we provide a comprehensive evaluation of all aspects of the management of tourism marketing including the strategies and tools that may be applied to deliver the tourism product effectively and efficiently to satisfy the tourism consumer.

In Chapter 16, we begin by looking at the historical development of marketing in general and how its roots have influenced the application of marketing theory to the tourism product in particular. While marketing in its purest form has been in existence for centuries, the relative youth of mass production techniques and mass consumption demand have meant that marketing, in its current, more sophisticated guise, has evolved relatively rapidly in the last 50 years.

In Chapter 17, we introduce and discuss the characteristics of the service product such as intangibility, perishability and inseparability which, it is argued, differentiate the tourism product from others. In addition, we outline other characteristics centred around the notion of risk which also distinguish the tourism product from manufactured goods. To combat the risk brought about by the characteristics of the product, the concept of quality – and its management – has become a prevailing force in tourism marketing: the lack of control over the service process, which is essentially an unpredictable human encounter, has become a prime target for the application of quality techniques to standardise the delivery of the product. We present key models in respect of the service delivery system appropriate to the tourism industry and outline some of the criticisms which have been levelled at tourism marketing.

Chapter 18, Marketing planning, is concerned with the introduction of tactical and strategic marketing planning procedures in respect of the tourism product. We define marketing planning and emphasise its role and application to the diverse sectors which, when amalgamated, form the tourism industry. We review the benefits and purposes of marketing planning, consider the structure of a marketing plan and explore the implications of neglecting tourism marketing planning.

The final chapter in this part, Chapter 19, relates to the marketing mix. This is a key strategic tool which is integral to the effective manipulation of the tourism product and the successful implementation of marketing planning procedures. However, the fundamental starting point for the creation of a successful marketing mix strategy is the definition of target markets since this will dictate the direction of the elements of the marketing mix and provide a focus for all marketing mix decisions and activity.

Thus, Part 4 presents a complete approach to the marketing of tourism, together with a comprehensive review of key issues and considerations. However, the application of marketing management techniques in the tourism industry, it has been suggested, is hampered by a number of factors that are inherent in the nature of tourism itself:

● Firstly, it has been suggested that while the tourism product is sufficiently distinctive to demand a unique marketing approach, the result of this has been that marketing strategies, tools and techniques in tourism are less evolved and advanced than in other (manufacturing) industries.

● Secondly, the relative immaturity of the diverse tourism industry has also impaired the development of marketing procedures designed specifically to take into account the unique characteristics of the product.

- Thirdly, the predominant practice in tourism is developing managers from grass roots. The implications of this are, that while they may be good generalists, few have the marketing training and expertise necessary to maximise marketing potential.

- Fourthly, many enterprises in tourism are small operations which have neither the expertise, nor the resources, to devote to a fully fledged marketing management approach.

- Finally, the late development and application of technology in tourism has also handicapped the tourism industry, especially in relation to product formulation and distribution.

While some of these criticisms are accurate, some do not take into account more recent changes in the tourism industry. Although it is important that the unique nature of the tourism product is recognised by marketers, there is now a body of knowledge and battery of techniques for marketing in the service industries and these are outlined in Chapter 19. The tourism industry does, however, create its own handicaps to effective marketing:

- Data relating to the market and to the actions of competitors are scarce.

- A short-term outlook prevails, denying a structured and strategic marketing planning approach.

- Managers in tourism tend to have risen through the ranks and to be generalists. The organisation of the industry thus works against the development of specialists in marketing, and indeed some managers neither respect nor value marketing-related skills.

In addition, it is important to make the point that the tourism industry is subject to governmental regulation of its activities, and consumer protection is well developed in tourism. These factors may be instrumental in restricting the marketing options of a tourism company.

Public sector organisations in tourism are also somewhat handicapped in adopting a true marketing orientation. It is, for example, not uncommon to find visitor and convention bureaux with the following problems:

- They may be hidebound by government personnel operating guidelines in terms of working hours and remuneration of staff.

- They may possess insufficient resources to build a presence in the marketplace, particularly in respect of the international arena.

- They may lack marketing expertise.

- They may have to be even-handed in their support of products and enterprises at the destination.

- They may have little or no control over the quality of the product they are marketing.

- They may be being driven by 12-monthly budgeting cycles which preclude the long-term planning framework essential to enhance and improve the tourism product.

This section clearly emphasises the interlinkages that characterise the tourism industry. For example, the nature of tourism demand is inextricably linked to marketing of the product and the manipulation of the marketing mix to attract pre-identified demand segments. Likewise, marketing is also linked to the supply of tourism at the destination being marketed: it is crucial, if the destination is to sustain its market share, that the range and quality of the attractions and facilities on offer live up to those communicated to target market(s) via the marketing process.

Marketing is, therefore, an important tool in an industry where loyalty in both the distribution chain and to the company is low; indeed, many companies have promotional campaigns targeted at other sectors of the industry (such as retail travel agents) as well as the consumer to encourage more loyalty in the distribution chain. Similarly, governmental organisations often find it more cost-effective to market to intermediaries and carriers rather than to potential travellers.

While marketing remains an under-utilised tool for many organisations and companies in the tourism industry, we would contend that improving training and education among the tourism workforce, coupled with the realities of increasingly intense competition, are encouraging a new emphasis on marketing management and a greater marketing orientation within the industry.

Chapter Sixteen

Marketing for tourism – the historical roots

Introduction

In this chapter we introduce the evolution and concept of marketing as it applies to tourism. We demonstrate that tourism marketing has emerged as a result of business and social changes which have occurred throughout the twentieth century as a reaction to the conditions that impinge on business operations. However, while we are able to identify different business philosophies that have influenced the adoption of a marketing orientation and the application of the marketing concept, understanding of marketing lies in the way marketing management functions in attempting to create and maximise consumer satisfactions.

Chapter learning objectives

This chapter provides a comprehensive introduction to marketing as it relates to the tourism industry. By the end of this chapter, therefore, the reader will:

- understand the concept of marketing, what it is and how it has developed into its current form;
- be able to differentiate between selling and marketing;
- recognise that companies may have different business philosophies and be able to identify the implications of these differences for marketing; and
- appreciate the components that, when combined, will result in a true marketing orientation.

What is marketing?

Tourism can be traced back for centuries but because the elements of the product and conditions of the market-place have changed so enormously in the last few decades, there has been a corresponding requirement for a change in business methods. This has led to the adoption and use of tourism marketing. We have all experienced 'marketing' in some form and as it affects us all in different ways, everyone has their own idea of what marketing is. We are all involved in, or influenced by, marketing in one way or another. It will not have been long since you last saw a promotion for either an airline, hotel group, holiday, leisure centre or overseas country.

We are continually bombarded with advertising and sales material. Each day the post-man delivers yet another letter containing one type of offer or another. There are thousands of advertisements on television and radio stations and all shops have numerous promotional messages. We are surrounded by invasive messages and communication which have been paid for by marketing budgets. However, this is a very narrow interpretation of the activity of marketing and, as we shall see, marketing is far more than the promotion of a product. This forms only *one* aspect of marketing.

It is often stated that we live in an era of marketing, but what does this actually mean? One possible method of understanding marketing is to treat it as the development of ideas. If this is the case all we have to do is to trace what has been written of marketing in the past. Unfortunately, this is not possible because while historical accounts show that trade has always existed, the term 'marketing' was only used as a noun in the first part of this century. In addition there is also no equivalent for this word in other languages. In France, for example, the term *'le marketing'* has been adopted. Thus, marketing as defined and described in this chapter is a relatively new phenomenon. The use of the word marketing in the early stages of the twentieth century was associated with a number of actions that were loosely related to the activity of achieving a sale. Therefore marketing as we know it today is a recent development.

One way of attempting to answer a question 'what is marketing?' is to examine accepted definitions. Although it is in fact very easy to describe what is meant by the term marketing, it is far more difficult to describe the practice of marketing. This is because a central tenet of marketing is the body of underlying concepts that form the general guide for organisational and managerial thinking, planning and action. Consequently, for a comprehensive understanding of marketing it is necessary to master the underlying concepts.

The evolution of marketing

Marketing has evolved against a background of economic and business pressures. These pressures have required an increased focus on the adoption of a series of managerial measures based upon satisfying consumer needs. The key to the importance of marketing within tourism has been the level of economic growth throughout the twentieth century which has led to subsequent improvements in living standards, an enlargement of the population, and increases in discretionary time. Such changes led Disney management in 1955 to launch the Disneyland theme park concept and McDonald's to open its first fast-food restaurant.

In a short period of time the tourism industry has become one of the most important industries in the world in economic terms. Occurring simultaneously with this growth has been the continuing concentration of the tourism industry into fewer and larger organisations. Such organisations need to reduce the widening gulf between managers of the business and the consumer which is developing as a result of a lack of first-hand knowledge of the consumer's tastes and needs.

Where marketing has been adopted, the emphasis is on developing a full understanding of the dynamics of consumer behaviour (see Chapter 3). We should be aware that those organisations that use marketing are not limited to commercial companies. Marketing techniques are being used by tourist boards, museums and charities organising free or subsidised holidays for the elderly or handicapped. However, within the market-place, it is those organisations that have adapted most successfully to contemporary changes by directing management resources to obtaining research on market and consumer trends, and by also improving channels of distribution and communication campaigns, that are the strongest.

The nature of the tourism industry is one where custom and tradition have been particularly strong. The interpersonal service delivery aspects of the industry have created styles of interaction where the service provider remains distanced from the act of service provision. As with many other industries in the service sector, this has preserved the customary, well-established ways of doing business.

The need for change has been forced upon the industry because of the changes that have occurred in relation to consumer and market forces. Modern tourism marketing has emerged as a business reaction to changes in the social and economic environment, with the most successful companies or tourist bodies having demonstrated a keen sense of providing the right organisation structure and product offering for the consumer or visitor. This relies as much upon an approach or attitude to business or the market, as it does to specific management expertise. Marketing is therefore initially a philosophy that relies on the art and science of different managerial approaches.

The development of marketing is fashioned as the outcome of social and business pressures. The most widely accepted account of the development of marketing is that proposed by Keith (1981) who discerned an evolution of production, to sales, and finally to marketing in the Pillsbury company in the USA. In 1960 Keith (1981) argued that the growing recognition of consumer orientation 'will have far reaching implications for business, achieving a virtual revolution in economic thinking'. He inferred that, in the late 1950s, consumer orientation was only just beginning to be accepted as a business concept. A survey of the literature reveals an account of the history of marketing and modern business practice as having developed in three distinct stages (Gilbert and Bailey, 1990):

1. **The production era.** This occurred when there was a belief that, if products were priced cheaply enough, they would be bought. Therefore it was important to supply products to the market-place with the emphasis on consistently reducing costs. The focus of management was on increasing efficiency of production which involved an *inward, product-orientated* emphasis rather than an outward, market-orientated emphasis. The overriding objective for management was the development of a standardised product which could be offered at the lowest price to the market.

2. **The sales era.** This is an evolutionary phase where companies attempted *to sell the products they had formulated.* This led to a search for more effective means of selling. As competition increased, companies realised they could not survive without knowing more about different markets and improving their sales techniques. Therefore they attempted to influence demand and tailor it *to meet their supply* through simple sales techniques.

3. **The marketing era.** This era is characterised by a reversal of the preceding philosophy as organisations started to provide the products they could sell, *rather* than trying to sell what they had produced or formulated. Organisations adopted a consumer-led approach and concentrated on improving the marketing mix. This era was effectively a recognition that *meeting customer needs* and *providing consumer satisfaction* were the most *effective basis* for planning and that an organisation has to be outward looking to be successful.

There are continuing arguments as to the dates of the above eras, and indeed whether they can be treated as discrete periods at all. For our purposes, in the majority of texts, the marketing era is identified to have been established from the 1950s onward. For a full discussion see Gilbert and Bailey (1990) or Baker (1996). The important factors that have ushered in the marketing era during the twentieth century are as follows:

- The increases in demand were at a lower rate than the rises in productivity. In tourism, this culminated in an oversupply of accommodation in specific locations, and of aircraft seats on important routes and too many inefficient companies in the market-place. The increase in competition and the risks associated with the tourism market-place led to more reliance on the use of marketing. The business system can be viewed as an organism that is concerned with survival and proliferation. Following this argument, when a business system is threatened it will take functional steps to improve the situation. As marketing can provide for tactical change and modification of the system, in times of risk where there is oversupply and market saturation, marketing assumes a much more important role.

- The consumer was becoming more affluent and therefore it was possible to develop products that could be sold using a range of non-price attributes. This required the development of methods designed to create or change consumer attitudes and beliefs.

- The distance between the tourism product provider and tourist has been continually increasing. This led to a need for marketing research related to the gathering of information on market trends, evaluating levels of satisfaction and understanding consumer behaviour.

- As society developed, the mass market splintered into a number of submarkets, while at the same time the mass market became increasingly difficult to reach. This was due to the increase in specialist media and the potential for a whole range of alternative leisure pursuits. The changes required improved expertise in the segmentation of markets and the provision of different marketing mix strategies which would maximise demand for individual segments.

Definitions and concepts of marketing

No definition of marketing can ever disregard the importance of Philip Kotler. He has established himself as the most widely referenced proponent of general marketing theory. Kotler (1996) defines marketing as: 'a social and managerial process by which individuals and groups obtain what they need and want through creating and exchanging products and value with others'. Kotler argues the definition is built on the main concepts of wants, needs, demands, satisfactions and marketing and marketers because they are central to the study of marketing.

In 1984 the British Chartered Institute of Marketing defined marketing as: 'the management process responsible for identifying, anticipating and satisfying customers' requirements profitably'.

An examination of both definitions reveals significant core similarities. On comparison it is found that both stress marketing as a management process. Such approaches provide a concept as one where the process is established by way of a marketing channel connecting the (tourism) organisation with its market. This is based upon management to convert customer purchasing power into effective demand. In addition the British Chartered Institute clarifies the management responsibility to be one of assessment of consumer demand through the identification and anticipation of customer requirements. This denotes the importance of research and analysis as part of this process.

One important difference is that Kotler's definition is more appropriate to non-profit organisations where there is free entrance or a subsidisation toward the cost of a service. It is also more fitting when facilitators of tourism such as tourist boards are considered.

However, the most important aspect and one that should be at the heart of any definition of marketing, is the emphasis placed on the consumer's needs as the origin of all of the organisation's effort. The marketing concept has been expressed in many succinct ways from the: 'Have it your way' from Burger King, to 'You're the boss' of United Airlines. This is the basis of the modern marketing concept whereby the principal means of success is based not only on identifying different consumer needs but also on delivering a tourist product whose experiences provide sets of satisfactions that are preferable to those of the competitors. In addition these satisfactions have to be delivered with attention to their cost effectiveness, since marketing has to be evaluated on the basis of its efficiency of expenditure.

We have seen how the definitions of marketing lead to the marketing concept, whereby the consumer is the driving force for all business activities. Prior to the introduction and discussion about the notion of the marketing concept, we will spend some time differentiating the principles and activities associated with marketing and selling.

The differences between marketing and selling

By now it should be obvious to the reader that marketing and selling are not the same. Levitt (1960) described the differences as follows:

> *Selling focuses on the need of the seller; marketing on the needs of the buyer. Selling is preoccupied with the seller's need to convert his product into cash; marketing with the idea of satisfying the needs of the customer by means of the product and the whole cluster of things associated with creating, delivering and finally consuming it. (p. 45)*

Drucker (1973) points out:

> *Selling and marketing are antithetical rather than synonymous or even complementary. There will always, one can assume, be a need for some selling, but the aim of marketing is to make selling superfluous. (p. 64)*

The contrast between the sales and marketing approach highlights the importance of marketing planning and analysis related to customers and the market-place.

The sales concept focuses on products and uses selling and promotion to achieve profits through sales volume. The underlying weakness is that the sales concept does not necessarily satisfy the consumer and may only culminate in short-term, rather than long-term, company success. The marketing concept focuses on customer needs and utilises integrated marketing to achieve profits through customer satisfaction (Figure 16.1).

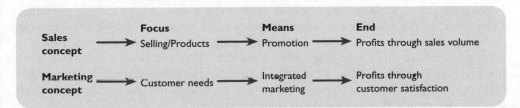

	Focus	**Means**	**End**
Sales concept	Selling/Products	Promotion	Profits through sales volume
Marketing concept	Customer needs	Integrated marketing	Profits through customer satisfaction

Figure 16.1: The sales and marketing concepts compared

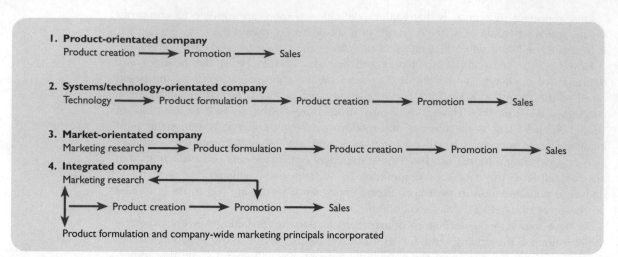

Figure 16.2: Four possible business philosophies

Different business philosophies

As we have seen, marketing is a business philosophy that places the consumer, and his or her needs, at the forefront of all activities. For example, it is known that business travellers want frequent and reliable transport systems with sensible timings of departure and arrival. They favour priority check-in and check-out facilities and efficient, good-quality staff. Business travellers need to feel they can make their trips and have their meetings without any worry of delay or discomfort. A knowledge of business travellers' needs occurs only when someone takes care to identify those needs.

While it is important to recognise the importance of structuring any organisation so that its focus is upon the customer, a number of alternative philosophies can be identified (see Figure 16.2). Each of these philosophies acts as a guiding orientation and system of approaching the market, and while a product-led company may be less effective, it is still possible to identify such companies within the tourism sector.

It is important to understand the initial starting place within the chains of the individual systems in Figure 16.2, since this is the first stage in the sequence of events which clearly demonstrates the focus of the organisation's approach to effecting exchange relationships. Examples (1) and (2) can be ineffective because of problems encountered in having the wrong product for the market, and as a consequence, having to waste more resources on promotion and selling in order to achieve a sale. In these examples it is normal to find that organisations believe their products are acceptable, and that all that is required for sales to occur is the identification of prime markets and methods of selling. Such an approach to the market-place by destination, hotel or airline marketing department is characterised by an emphasis on pictures of empty bedrooms, government buildings or the exterior of an aircraft. An emphasis on the product rather than the benefits the consumer is seeking is still at the heart of a great deal of today's marketing. Quite often tourist promotional literature is devoid of scenes of tourists enjoying rest, enjoyment or good service. A product-focused philosophy is acceptable when there is shortage or boom times, which are characterised by little competition. However, both the first two philosophies provide for inward-looking management which concentrates on improvement within the company, rather than on outward-looking management which concentrates on the consumer and emerging tourist needs.

Examples (3) and (4) in Figure 16.2 offer the ideal approach to organising business in the modern tourism market-place. They are driven by research that creates an understanding of the consumer, the business and the market-place. Research will be both secondary and primary. Information has to be collected from within and outside the company in order to establish a clear picture of the marketing environment. The integrated approach provides a sequence of events that commences with an understanding of the consumer, the competitors, the types of product that the company is capable of providing and a system that sensitises the whole organisation to a marketing orientation. The integrated system helps to ensure that methods of improving the satisfaction levels of the consumer are incorporated into each department's objectives.

Within the final two examples of company philosophy, it can be seen that the feedback process allows the marketing department to develop products as well as different forms of promotion that are right for the consumer. This establishes a more effective means of ensuring products are successful and that marketing budgets are used efficiently.

The tourism industry is spending vast sums of money on developing new attractions, improving products, building hotels and investing in technology. The only way for the risk level to be kept to a minimum is through the adoption of a marketing philosophy that provides products related to the needs of consumers.

However, all companies operate in a fiercely competitive environment that impinges upon the flexibility of management and company action. Marketing starts with the consumer and the market. This reflects the sovereignty of the consumer in the process. Such an approach has to be the correct strategy because it is the consumer who ultimately supports, through personal expenditure, tomorrow's tourism market-place.

Marketing orientation

The dynamic nature of business activity has led to many different sales and marketing opportunities in the tourism industry. The industry has thrown off many of its traditional attitudes toward the customer. This has come about through the realisation of the importance of a marketing orientation. As such, five main areas can be identified:

1. **It is a management orientation or philosophy.** The focus of the organisation's effort is placed on the consumer, and this then leads to an integrated structure and decision-making process within the organisation. There is the recognition that the conduct of the organisation's business must revolve around the long-term interests of the customers it serves. This is an outward-looking orientation which requires responsive action in relation to external events.

2. **It encourages exchange transactions.** These involve the attitudes and decisions of consumers in relation to the willingness to buy from producers or distributors. Marketers have to develop innovative methods to encourage exchange to take place. Creativity and the willingness to accept change are essential aspects of management thinking.

   There is the need to ensure the service offers value for money which may mean there is a requirement for creating a range of benefits over time. This has led to loyalty schemes and what is known as 'relationship marketing' (RM). Relationship marketing is an approach whereby marketers attempt to retain the customer over longer periods of time through club or loyalty programmes such as airline frequent flyer programmes. This is based upon the organisation becoming more involved with the customer as part of relationship marketing as opposed to the idea of concentrating on only a single sale or transaction (Table 16.1).

Transaction marketing	Relationship marketing
Short-term orientation: sale as end result	Long-term orientation: the sale is only the beginning
'Me' orientated	'We' orientated
Focus on achieving a sale	Focus on retention and repeat sales
Emphasis on persuasion to buy	Stress on creating positive relationships
Need to win, manipulation	Providing trust and service
Stress of conflict of achieving a transaction	Partnership and cooperation to minimise defection and provide longer-term relationships (with customers or strategic alliances, joint ventures, vendor partnering, etc.)
Anonymous customer won by conquest in a carefully planned event	Individual profile of customer known so that a continuing process can emerge

As part of the analogy, the RM process is available to advance relationships to higher levels of loyalty until a status is achieved whereby the customer is not only loyal but also champions the company, the employees and service to others. RM should not be confused with brand loyalty based upon simple commitment to the product, as RM is a far more complex and wider alliance and association (see Gilbert, 1996, for a full discussion of relationship marketing and airlines).

The rationale for RM is that it makes business sense to focus on long-term financial benefits that can accrue once a customer has been won for the first time. This is because it has been estimated to be five to ten more times more expensive to recruit a new customer than to retain an existing one. Therefore there is importance placed upon the retention of a customer with commercial consideration of the lifetime value of customers based upon quantity of repeat purchases. Such an approach enables the costs of acquisition and conversion of the prospect to be set against the revenues earned over the longer term. In an effective scheme sales and profits improve in direct proportion to the length of the relationship.

3. **It involves long- and short-term planning.** This concerns strategic planning and tactical activity. The long-term success of an organisation requires the efficient use of resources and assets, while tactical action will be required to keep plans on course.

4. **It requires efficient, cost-effective methods.** Marketing's principal concern within any organisation has to be the delivery of maximum satisfaction and value to the customer at acceptable or minimum cost to the company, so as to ensure long-term profit. However, in many organisations, the dilemma is that management is judged by short-term success in relation to sales and profit performance.

5. **It requires the development of an integrated company environment.** The organisation's efforts and structure must be matched with the needs of the target customers. Everybody working for the organisation must participate in a total corporate, marketing environment with each division maximising the satisfaction level of consumers. Integration is not just a smile or politeness. Barriers to serving the customer have to be destroyed. The onus is on the organisation to provide organisational structures which are responsive and will undergo change to suit customer needs. Such an environment has to be based upon a culture of adaptation of each and every company department in line with customer and market requirements.

Conclusion

We have demonstrated that the concept of marketing and its practical application have evolved as a result of changing business and social conditions that have emerged throughout the twentieth century. In the course of this chapter, we have identified different business philosophies that currently exist, the basis of the marketing concept and the benefits of a marketing orientation to the tourism industry.

Chapter discussion questions

1. Taking several organisations of your choice with which you are familiar, identify their business philosophies and judge the degrees of their market orientation.

2. Identify the differences between selling and marketing using examples associated with the tourism industry.

3. Review current trends in marketing in the tourism industry.

Recommended further reading

- Baker, M. (1996) *Marketing, An Introductory Text*, Macmillan Press, London.
- Gilbert, D. C. and Bailey, N. (1990) 'The development of marketing – a compendium of historical approaches', *Quarterly Review of Marketing*, **15**(2), 6–13.
- Kotler, P. and Armstrong, G. (1996) *Principles of Marketing*, Prentice Hall, Englewood Cliffs, NJ.
- Middleton, V. (1994) *Marketing in Travel and Tourism*, Butterworth-Heinemann, Oxford.

Bibliography

- Baker, M. (1996) *Marketing, An Introductory Text*, Macmillan Press, London.
- Chartered Institute of Marketing (1984) Cookham, Berkshire.
- Drucker, P. (1973) *Management Tasks, Responsibilities, Practices*, Harper and Row, New York.
- Gilbert, D. C. and Bailey, N. (1990) 'The development of marketing – a compendium of historical approaches', *Quarterly Review of Marketing*, **15**(2), 6–13.

● Gilbert, D. C. (1996) 'Relationship marketing and airline loyalty schemes', *Tourism Management*, **17**(8), 575–82.
● Keith, R. J. (1981) 'The Marketing Revolution', pp. 44–9 in *Marketing Classics*, 4th edn, Enis, B. M. and Cox K. K. (eds), Allyn and Bacon, London.
● Kotler, P. and Armstrong, G. (1996) *Principles of Marketing*, Prentice Hall, Englewood Cliffs, NJ.
● Levitt, T. (1960) 'Marketing myopia', *Harvard Business Review*, July/August, 45–56.

Chapter Seventeen

Marketing management for tourism

Introduction

In this chapter we show that the marketing management of tourism cannot ignore the primary characteristics that set tourism apart from other products. Tourism, as a specialised service product, creates a number of important considerations which need to be fully understood if a tourism enterprise or organisation is to maximise its potential and be successful. The management of tourism cannot be divorced from the management of service and quality. In addition, the need to undertake the tasks of research, analysis, product formulation, recommending price policies, promotion and distribution are of paramount significance for those involved in tourism marketing management.

We demonstrate that a great deal of management involves decisions based upon judgement, information and experience. All these areas rely on an understanding of the characteristics and issues that apply specifically to the market conditions for a product. When marketing any one of the different tourism products we find in the market-place, there are a number of tasks and characteristics of which we need to be aware. In this chapter we stress that the first factor that managers of tourism have to understand is the service management aspects related to the purchase of the tourism product.

Chapter learning objectives

The objective of this chapter is to furnish the reader with a comprehensive understanding of all aspects of marketing management for tourism. After reading this chapter the reader should:

- appreciate the importance of the characteristics of the service product and the implications of these differentiating characteristics for the approach an organisation might adopt for its marketing effort;
- recognise that the purchase of tourism products is associated with the need for quality management and the reduction of perceived risk;
- understand the importance of quality management in the tourism industry and the methods that may be employed to establish an integrated approach; and
- be familiar with the key criticisms targeted at tourism marketing and the problems of properly utilising tourism marketing techniques.

The service product

With tourism, hospitality and leisure products we are dealing with a service product that has specific characteristics that set the product apart from the more general goods sold in the market-place. An understanding of the complexity of the service product concept is an essential prerequisite for successful marketing. This is because the emphasis is increasingly placed on the service provider to develop a deeper understanding of the linkages that correspond to consumer benefits sought and the nature of the service delivery system itself.

A starting point is an examination of the dimensions of the service product concept. Products can be placed along a continuum of services and goods, with most products being a combination of the two. A pure service would be consultancy or teaching whereas a pure good would be a can of beans or clothing. Some products will have more of a service content than others, and if they are able to be placed to the left-hand side of the continuum shown in Figure 17.1, they may be termed service products.

Figure 17.1: Services and goods continuum

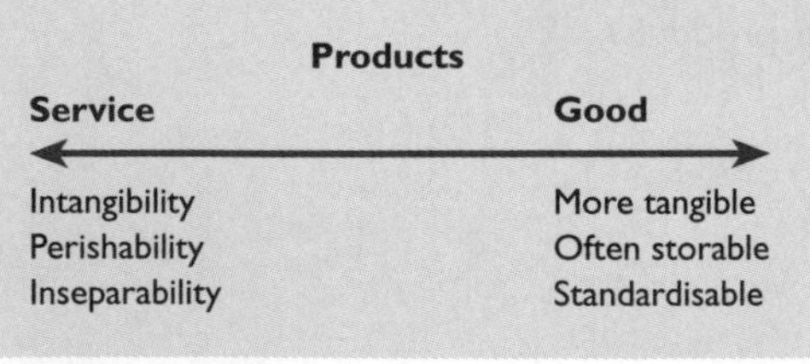
Products
Service
Good
Intangibility
Perishability
Inseparability
More tangible
Often storable
Standardisable

The characteristics of the service product

Intangibility

The service product is intangible which means it cannot be easily evaluated or demonstrated in advance of its purchase. For example, a travel agent cannot allow the testing or sampling of the tourism product. On the other hand, an automobile or computer game can be tested prior to purchase, and clothing can be tried on. Much of the selling of tourism and hospitality is related to the promise of safe and timely delivery of the individual by transport companies, or comfort and good service by accommodation companies. Only a ticket or a voucher is exchanged at the time of purchase. Greater difficulty is therefore faced by the marketers of tourism and hospitality products. Because of fixed time and space constraints they cannot easily demonstrate the benefits of the products they are selling. The problem for the tourism service marketer is overcome by the production of a range of printed literature, videos or other means of providing clues as to the type of product on offer in an attempt to increase tangibility. In addition, there is a need to ensure marketing provides clear and well-managed branding of accommodation, transport and distribution organisations. This positions the brand name more tangibly in the mind of the consumer.

Perishability

This means that service products such as tourism, unlike goods, cannot be stored for a sale on a future occasion. For example, a hotel bed or an airline seat unsold or a convention centre left empty is revenue that can never be recouped. This leads to the high-risk nature of the tourism industry. Marketers in the tourism and hospitality sector have to devise complex pricing and promotion policies in an attempt to sell 'off-season' periods and create greater synchronisation of staffing levels and supply with demand patterns. Weak demand is not the only problem as the sector is characterised by hotels, airlines, attractions, museums, galleries, etc., all of which have fixed capacity with a maximum upper-level demand constraint. In peak periods the industry often has difficulty in coping with demand and therefore charges premium prices or uses queuing as a control mechanism, but in the low periods there is a need for greater marketing activity. The reaction to perishability is for marketers to try to smooth out demand curves by careful use of the marketing mix, for example, cheaper tickets for matinee shows. There is also a concentration on the use of computerised reservation systems in order to forecast the need for tactical action if demand is believed to be below expected levels.

Inseparability

Service products are often referred to as being inseparable which means the product is often consumed and produced simultaneously. Because there is less opportunity to pre-check a tourism or hospitality product, it can vary in the standard of its service delivery. This is sometimes characterised by authors as **heterogeneity**. The tourism sector offers an amalgam of services which make up the delivery of the product. This occurs in a fragmented system where different organisations may have responsibility for the level of service delivery. Even for a single service such as air travel there will be the travel agent, airport checking-in agent and staff, airline staff, catering company, baggage handling staff, cabin cleaning staff; all of whom provide the single continuous flight experience. Variance occurs because of the inseparable nature of the product's delivery when the customer is part of the production system. The simultaneous process of production and consumption can lead to situations where it is difficult to ensure the overall satisfaction of consumers. For example, peak loads of demand cannot always be forecast and may create dissatisfaction and secondary problems. There is also the potential problem of having sets or types of clients with conflicting needs which may result in disharmony. Whether on the aircraft, in the hotel, or in the restaurant there could be the clash of social values, noisiness, drunkenness, high spirits or a child crying. Staff may also have had personal problems or be feeling ill or tired, and this can affect their level of commitment to their performance of giving good service or resolving problems.

As the nature of the tourism service product is largely one of interpersonal relation-ships, where the performance level of staff is directly related to the satisfaction and over-all experience of the consumer, there is a need for quality assurance programmes. Staff are emotional and changeable and if a high content of the product is based upon inter-personal relationships between 'strangers', as guest and service provider, it is important to ensure standardised service levels are adhered to. Quality assurance is important as a basis of planning for competitive advantage and controlling the standards of staff inter-actions. To reduce the problems that can be associated with inseparability there is a need for investment in company training programmes for all service staff.

Tourism products and risk

Tourism products are important in relation to the type of marketing they require. Tourism has developed rapidly over the past few decades, led by a marketing thrust which has created diversity of supply, focused on important consumer segments and stimulated high levels of demand. Within this development marketing has often concentrated more on improving the product than on understanding the consumer, and the complexity of his or her decision processes.

A major aspect of consumer behaviour, linked to the purchase of tourism products, is the notion of risk. Tourism products involve a complex decision-making process because the purchase is of relatively high risk and high involvement. Throughout the popula-tion the threshold at which an individual perceives the following risks differs by age, income and experience.

Economic risk

Economic risk is associated with the decision for potential tourists as to whether the product offer is of good value or not. All consumers face economic or financial risk when they purchase tourism products that they are not sure will deliver desired benefits. Tourism involves the purchase of an expensive product that cannot easily be seen or sampled prior to consumption. This type of risk is heightened for those with low levels of disposable income, for whom the purchase represents a major expenditure.

Physical risk

Some overseas destinations may be perceived to be dangerous owing to disease or crime, and some transport companies such as ferry or airline operators are thought to be safer than others. Some people fear flying no matter what airline they fly with, while others may reduce the perception of physical risks by selecting certain 'safer' airlines.

Performance risk

The quality of different destinations or unknown hotel brands cannot be assessed in advance. This type of risk is associated with feelings that the product may not deliver the desired benefits. It is rarely possible for those who have had a bad holiday to make up for it by attempting to have another better holiday in the same year. Most consumers do not have the additional money or holiday entitlement to make good the holiday that went wrong. This heightens their awareness of the risk factors involved. One important performance risk for UK travellers is weather. The risk of poor weather while holiday-ing in the UK is one reason why many people travel abroad.

Psychological risk

Status can be lost through visiting the wrong country or travelling with a company that has a poor image. This risk occurs when the potential customer feels the purchase may not reflect the self-image he or she wishes to portray.

From a marketing point of view, these risks have to be minimised through product and promotion strategies. Creating and delivering information in brochures and leaflets which helps to convince the potential traveller of the reliability of the company will lessen the perception of risk. By acquiring information the consumer builds up mental pictures and attitudes that create the expectation of positive benefits from the travel or destination experience.

It is also important for the quality of the product to be controlled especially in relation to the process of service delivery.

Planning the service encounter

If we examine a systems perspective that identifies the linkage between the consumer's needs and the service delivery, we can be more aware of the management principles associated with service products. This can also be utilised in the establishment of benchmark points against which the service can be positioned.

A well-positioned service enables the organisation to achieve the following two important objectives.

- to differentiate its position so as to distinguish itself from competitors; and
- to deliver superior service to that accepted as the norm.

The above allow the organisation to plan and build competitive advantage by establishing leadership principles of service standards and delivery. Once the standards are established there should be a policy to communicate and reinforce the service provision philosophy at every possible opportunity: meetings, training and internal marketing programmes, induction programmes and appraisal systems. The human resource function needs to be organised so as to ensure the different levels in the following figure are always clearly understood and reinforced through organisational culture and reward. Without good internal organisational procedures and relationships it is unlikely that even the most well conceived of quality programmes will be successful.

The levels shown in Figure 17.2 illustrate the linkages for designing a successful service delivery process. For the model to be successful there is the need for the implementation process to consider the need for the following:

- Leadership and commitment by senior management with clear goals and a policy on quality being established. There is also the need to release the appropriate resources to create changes and achieve the required results.
- All changes and objectives to be defined by the customer. All the definitions of quality delivery and standards have to be delineated in all of the dimensions of the service delivery with reference to customers' needs.
- The orientation of the organisation to change to adopt a process and systems approach to match or exceed customer expectations. This relies on a workable quality audit system which applies measurement and inspection to ensure defects are corrected and the system delivers optimum quality results.
- Effective human resource management to motivate, educate, train and educate staff to understand the concepts of quality. Teamwork values with champions of quality product delivery are a prerequisite for competitive advantage.

Figure 17.2:
Planning the
service
encounter

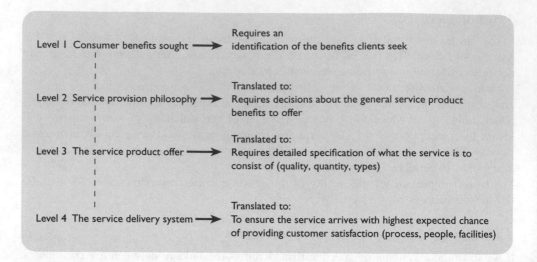

An assessment to be made of the added value and benefit of any change rather than there being a simple cost-cutting and price-leadership strategy. The long-term benefits of any change need to the focus of service encounter decision making.

- Quality audits and control to ensure the service meets or exceeds customer expectations.

It is crucial that an organisation creates its own quality management culture and does not simply attempt to clone a system used by a competitor. A successful service encounter approach requires honest two-way communication between management and staff which will build confidence in the implementation process. This means staff have to be allowed to own up to weaknesses and problems of poor quality in a supportive atmosphere where the organisation attempts to learn from weaknesses rather than to punish staff. Such methods create teamwork, confidence and commitment. However, there is also the need for competence to deliver the changes. This may require further training and seminars for staff and follow-up sessions. The recognition that there is a need to treat other members of staff as internal customers will assist the transition to a **total quality management** (TQM) system.

It is obvious that organisations have customers from within as well as without. With this in mind, if employees visualise the relationships between each other based upon supplier and customer links as a quality chain, then the question is always, 'am I meeting the full requirements of my role?' For example, the secretary is a supplier to the boss with the need to provide timely error-free work in order to aid him or her as supplier to his or her internal customer, who may be a director. An organisation, therefore, is a web of internal suppliers and customers. Such chains are easily weakened or broken by faulty equipment or people. The important issue is that an internal quality chain failure will ultimately have some effect on the external customer.

Quality management

We cannot adequately describe the management of tourism without touching on the importance of the growing emphasis on quality management. There are four main reasons that may account for the growing relevance of quality management:

1. Organisations need to find ways of creating differential advantage by having better service levels than their competitors.

2. The increased level of consumerism and the greater media attention on quality has meant organisations have to be more responsive to quality issues. Consumers are far more aware of their rights and are less likely to suffer quietly from the results of poor quality.

3. There has been a growing sophistication of consumer markets with the non-price factors of image, product positioning and service delivery strategies becoming more important.

4. More recently technology is one of the new applications to quality enhancement. Technology can aid service by providing higher levels of convenience, e.g. automatic vending or ticketing machines or up-to-date information for products and services.

It is important for the quality of the product to be controlled, especially in relation to the process of service delivery. This is because relative quality between service providers or retailers has implications for market share and profitability. Quality is therefore one of the key components that contribute to a successful strategy. Quality has emerged as a major competitive component of a service organisation's strategy.

However, when we examine the employment of the term 'quality', there is almost a super-abundance of the use of this word in relation to the way management operates. There is a crusade for quality management and improvement within industry world-wide and the campaign for improved quality was rooted in the manufacturing industry prior to the expansion into the service industry. However, many individuals in the industry are still unaware of the theoretical grounding of quality management.

What are the key terms for quality?

There are several key concepts related to quality. Quality is the totality of relationships between service providers (functional aspects) and the features of the product (technical aspects) which are related to the delivery of satisfaction. It is therefore important to create systems of **quality control** which are checks and monitoring to ensure measurement of service delivery is taking place. To this end **TQM** is a holistic organisational approach which systematically attempts to enhance customer satisfaction by focusing on continuous improvements without incurring unacceptable cost increases. These improvements are part of an unending quest for excellence in all aspects of quality service delivery. Therefore, TQM has to form the values and mind set for all employees, which leads to quality being an integrated element of corporate culture. For success, quality must be the concern of all employees and the culture, therefore, should not be based upon a departmental or technical understanding of quality. Instead, the notion of quality must be disseminated to employees throughout the organisational structure and implemented as a systematic process extending throughout the organisation. The focus of any change in quality must be based upon external customer expectations and not internal organisational ideas.

TQM is managed by **quality assurance** arrangements whereby a system is instituted to allocate responsibility for planned and systematic activities that will ensure the product will provide the right levels of satisfaction to all concerned. A service guarantee system can provide more quality control and data capture in an organisation.

This facilitates a better understanding of potential for improvement by capturing information on what is going wrong. Following this the information gathered on what goes wrong allows for a reaction in improvement of service. Some companies are now guaranteeing their service or paying out compensation with schemes such as flight delay insurance. A good service guarantee is identified as unconditional, easy to understand and communicate, meaningful, and easy to invoke and to obtain recompense. But there is a need not:

- to promise something your customers already expect;
- to shroud a guarantee in so many conditions that it is meaningless; or
- to offer a guarantee so mild that it is never invoked.

A guarantee can set clear standards and allow the company personnel to be clear about what the organisation stands for. If customers can complain easily, there is the benefit of collecting data on common problems that subsequently need to be addressed and eradicated. This is because a guarantee system forces the focus on why the failure occurred and what needs to be done about it to improve service quality. Moreover, a guarantee adds credibility and weight to the marketing effort of the organisation. It allows for the emphasis of the guarantee which also provides a reduction in the perception of risk associated with purchase and may lead to higher levels of customer loyalty.

As a measure of whether the quality delivery complies to the planned delivery of the service a **quality audit** needs to take place to judge the effectiveness of the total service delivery arrangements. For a system to be audited correctly there is a need for a method of creating unbiased feedback. While a range of aspects of quality can be assessed, a number of categories exist. These may include the following, which are based upon various research that attempted to establish categories of service quality determinants:

- **Tangibles.** This will include physical evidence of the service: such as physical aspects of airline cabin, hotel bedrooms and facilities or material the customer can see, touch, use, etc., such as equipment, merchandise, personnel
  - physical facilities
  - appearance of personnel
  - tools or equipment used to provide the service
  - physical representation of the service, e.g. airline loyalty card
  - other customers in the service facility

- **Reliability.** This involves consistency of performance and dependability. It means the company should perform the service right the *first time*. It also means the firm honours its promises: the ability to trust employees with the responsibility to deliver service consistently and accurately which meets policy standards
  - accuracy in charging
  - keeping the correct records
  - performing the service at designated time, e.g. accurate to opening hour promise

- **Responsiveness.** This refers to the willingness or readiness of employees to provide service: the reaction and willingness to help customers and give timely service
  - mailing a transaction slip immediately
  - calling a customer back quickly after a query
  - giving prompt service (e.g. arranging a change of itinerary)

- **Competence.** This concerns knowledge and courtesy of employees: the assurance that employees will have the knowledge, skills and courtesy to create trust and confidence in the customer base.

Internal inspection	Auditing
● Statistical process control based upon quality failure information and objective measures	● Internal auditors of quality
	● External bodies
● Visual inspections to check against standards and consistency	● Consultants, regular users, non-user surveys and feedback
● Management by walking about	● Cross-department audits
● Quality control group feedback	● Mystery shoppers
● Inspection of competitors' offer and assessment of own company offer	● Content analysis of complaint and praise letters and documented problems
	● Free telephone line feedback

- knowledge and skill of the contact personnel
- explaining the service itself
- the reputation of the organisation
- personal characteristics of the contact personnel
- confidentiality, financial and personal security

● **Empathy.** This relates to the individualised attention to customers: the caring, individual concern and attention for others and their emotions
- recognising regular customers
- learning the customer specific requirements
- providing individualised (customised service)

The elements that could be assessed in the above could also include: availability of items the customer demands; after-sales service and contact; the way telephone orders and queries are handled; the reliability and safety of the items being sold; availability of sales literature and brochures; the number and type of items that can be demonstrated; technical knowledge of staff; the way an employee deals with a complaint, etc.

Table 17.1 indicates some of the ways that quality can be assessed. It is important to realise that whatever system is used to audit quality at the end of the day, that which is not measured cannot be controlled.

Is quality a cost or a long-term benefit?

Although there are benefits for firms adopting TQM approaches it is found that some organisations embarking upon service quality programmes perceive them to be costly; to need a lot of management time; to create difficulty in measuring the intangible benefits; and to be difficult to implement. Given the nature of tourism as a people-based industry with employee performance and interaction being of paramount importance, then we are dealing with a human medium where errors are inevitable. There is therefore a need to judge the benefit of increased usage and repeat business in relation to the loss of custom. The moment of truth or impact on the bottom line of any organisation is therefore the judgement by customers of the quality of its service. Figure 17.3 is based upon Hart *et al.* (1990) who argue for the linkages of service encounters as creating a self-reinforcing mechanism. It indicates the relationship between the customer on the left

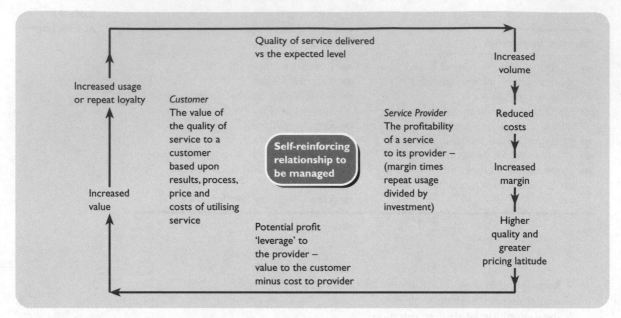

Figure 17.3: Self-reinforcing system of service encounters

and the service provider to the right. This overcomes the notion that improvement in quality is associated with increased costs. The model indicates that in the long-term true quality improvement leads to an improved trading position.

The above proposition that a continuous improvement in service is not a cost but an investment in a customer who will return more profit in the long term is becoming more widely supported. The premise is based upon research which indicates the cost of acquiring a new customer is five times as high as retaining an existing customer through providing quality service. Such argument is based upon non-traditional accounting practices which stress: satisfied customers will be willing to pay higher prices owing to the service quality they have experienced and liked; there is a free advertising benefit due to the positive word of mouth recommendation; there is a different cost in acquiring new customers as opposed to retaining existing customers over longer time periods. Thus, in general, following the ideas of relationship marketing, it is suggested that to keep a customer over the long term provides important savings. On a cost–benefit basis good service quality is thought to increase revenue and reduce long-term costs.

Given that the cost of finding a new customer is far greater than that of retaining an existing one, there is growing emphasis on customer retention and relationship marketing as discussed in Chapter 16 and Major Case Study 5. Long-term revenue can be enhanced by service recovery strategies. These include the following:

● **Watching for sign language.** Allowing those customers who are reticent or mute when it comes to complaints to break their silence. Organisations need the opportunity to prove their commitment to the customer through service quality measures. However, the silent customer who is not satisfied will escape company notice but may tell many acquaintances of the problem. Some organisations provide free telephone lines for complainants or employee training to enable staff to test for the weak signals of a customer's dissatisfaction. Many organisations empower staff to provide remedial action if they suspect poor service has been experienced. Alternatively service may be tested with the use of mystery customers or staff listening to customers' reactions to the service provision.

- **Preplanning.** There is the need to analyse the service delivery process so as to anticipate those aspects of service that may exceed the tolerance level of customers. Times of peak demand or low levels of staffing may affect the judgement of the customer as to the overall level of service quality delivery.

- **Training.** As service is an interpersonal performance activity then the provision of communication and customer relation skills will enhance the ability of staff to deal with the most difficult of situations. Perhaps, more importantly, training will allow staff to feel confident in the service encounter transaction and allow them to deal professionally with all situations.

- **Empowerment.** A great deal of staff service delivery goes unsupervised. The front-line staff therefore need to react quickly to service problem situations without the input of supervisors. A staff member who provides some extra means of satisfying a customer may allay a more difficult or serious situation. A long wait to be seated in a restaurant may be acknowledged by a reduction in the bill or free coffee. Empowerment provides an obligation to act, the trust in front line staff to act and not just the focus on blame for a poor service encounter.

Good service recovery procedures allow a customer to refocus on the satisfactions received from the service delivery process rather than to question why corrective action was not taken. A problem tests the system and if a customer complaint is dealt with appropriately, the customer is likely to become more loyal.

We can classify the different approaches to quality management into two categories: the product-attribute approach and the consumer-orientated approach (Gilbert and Joshi, 1992).

The product-attribute approach

The product-attribute approach is based upon trying to match the product's conformance to standardised requirements which have been set by reference to what organisational managers think the failure point to be. Product-attribute approaches rely on trying to control the organisation's products using an internal product perspective. This relies on an inward-looking product-led approach.

The consumer-orientated approach

It is therefore more appropriate to adopt a consumer-orientated approach which recognises the holistic process of service delivery has to be controlled by taking into consideration the expectations and attitudes of tourism and hospitality clients. If the starting point for management is the understanding of how quality is judged by clients then the perception processes of this judgement, as to whether a service is good or bad, can be managed. Gronroos is a leading author who has clarified this concept.

The Gronroos model

Gronroos (1982) developed a model to explain what he called the 'missing service quality concept'. The model shown in Figure 17.4 focuses mainly on the construct of image, which represents the point at which a gap can occur between expected service and

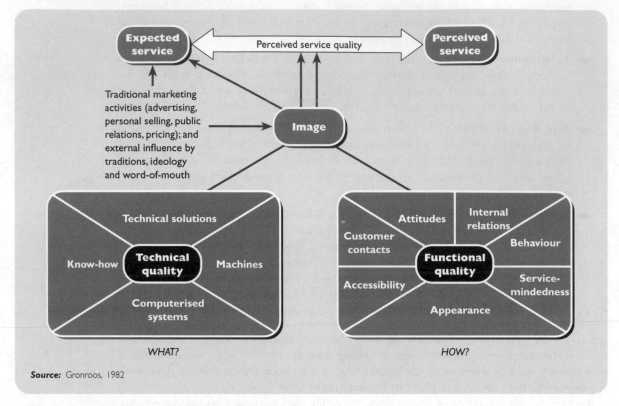

Figure 17.4: Managing the perceived service quality

perceived service. Gronroos makes us more aware of the ways image is created from the aggregation of different aspects of technical and functional variables. By following his model of different inputs, we are alerted to the fact that we should not reduce quality to a simplistic description, but should try to understand the full range of inputs. This is because to speak just of quality gives the manager no indication of what aspects of the product should be controlled.

Gronroos argued that the function and range of resources and activities include what customers are looking for, what they are evaluating, how service quality is perceived and in what way service quality is influenced. He defined the 'perceived quality' of the service as dependent on two variables. These are 'experienced service' and 'perceived service' which collectively provide the outcome of the evaluation.

As part of his analysis, Gronroos distinguished between 'technical quality' and 'functional quality' as the components of the service image delivery:

- Technical quality refers to what the customer is actually receiving from the service. This is capable of objective measurement, as with tangible goods.

- Functional quality refers to how the technical elements of the service are transferred. We know that a customer in a restaurant will not only evaluate the quality of the food consumed but also the way in which it was delivered (the style, manner and appearance of the staff, or the ambience of the place itself). Figure 17.4 shows that the attitudes, behaviour and general service-mindedness of personnel can be influenced by management.

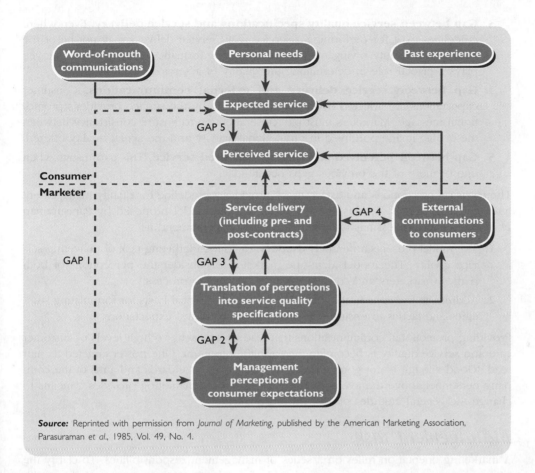

Figure 17.5:
Service quality
model

Source: Reprinted with permission from *Journal of Marketing*, published by the American Marketing Association, Parasuraman *et al.*, 1985, Vol. 49, No. 1.

The Parasuraman, Zeithaml and Berry model

Parasuraman, Zeithaml and Berry (1985) also developed a model of service quality which claimed the consumer evaluates the quality of a service experience as the outcome of the difference (gap) between expected and perceived service (Figure 17.5). The model highlighted the main requirements for a service provider delivering the expected service quality. From the model we can identify five gaps that may lead to unsuccessful service delivery.

By understanding the flow of this model we believe it is possible to provide greater management control over tourist service relationships. This should lead to an improved realisation of the key points of influence on the satisfactions of the consumer.

1. **Gap between consumer expectation and management perception.** This may result from a lack of understanding of what consumers expect from a service. An extensive study by Nightingale (1983) confirms this disparity, by revealing that what providers perceive as being important to consumers is often different from what consumers themselves actually expect.

2. **Gap between management perception and service quality specification.** This gap results when there is a discrepancy between what management perceives to be consumer expectations and the actual service quality specifications established. Management might not set quality standards or very clear ones, or they may be clear but unrealistic. Alternatively, the standards might be clear and realistic, but management may quite simply not be committed to enforcing them.

3. **Gap between service quality specifications and service delivery.** Even where guidelines exist for performing a service well, service delivery may not be of the appropriate quality owing to poor employee performance. Indeed the employee plays a pivotal role in determining the quality of a service.

4. **Gap between service delivery and external communications.** Consumer expectations are affected by the promises made by the service provider's promotional message. Marketers must pay close attention to ensure consistency between the quality image portrayed in promotional activity and the actual quality offered.

5. **Gap between perceived service and delivered service.** This gap results when one or more of the previous gaps occur.

The focus on perceptions and expectations provides a guideline for quality management intervention strategies. To this end on examining the model proposed by Parasuraman *et al.*, we believe that it has two main strengths to recommend it:

1. The model presents an entirely dyadic view to the marketing task of delivering service quality. The model alerts the marketer to consider the perceptions of both parties (marketers and consumers) in the exchange process.

2. Addressing the gaps in the model can serve as a logical basis for formulating strategies and tactics to ensure consistent experiences and expectations.

Providing promotional communications that lead staff to achieve high levels of customer care and service quality is becoming increasingly important. One poster targeted to staff read, 'Good enough is not good enough' which sets the standards and aims of the company personnel above the average. This type of inward marketing provides a means to change the general attitudes of staff toward quality.

Management tasks

A marketing orientation relies on a series of management responsibilities. To clarify the situation, marketing can be seen to provide for a business-to-customer interface with responsibility for specific management tasks. These tasks are more clearly explained in Chapter 19 on the marketing mix. However, it should be quite clear that tourism organisations without a proper commitment to a marketing orientation have little likelihood of effectively executing the marketing function.

The marketing function can therefore be treated as a system which is designed to be an interface with the customer. This system is outlined in Table 17.2 and Figure 17.6.

Table 17.2:
The business-to-customer interface

Task	Marketing function
1. Identifying the customers' needs for a service-based, tourism product	Marketing research
2. Analysing marketing opportunities	Analysis and selection of target markets (segments)
3. Translating needs into products	Product planning and formulation
4. Determining the product's value to the customer at different seasonal periods	Pricing policy
5. Making the product available	Distribution
6. Informing and motivating the customer	Promotion (communicating, selling and advertising)

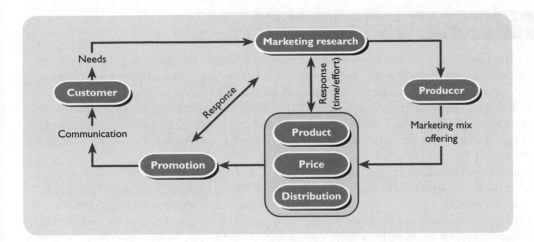

The adoption of a marketing orientation

The tourist industry, owing to the high service-based content of the product, has been characterised by a history of custom and tradition. There has been a lack of vision in the industry which has meant the demise of many organisations throughout the past 20 years. The airline sector has probably been the most at risk. An acknowledgement of the degree of competition between airlines brought about the tourism industry's earliest transformation to a marketing orientation (see Case Studies 17.1 and 17.2).

From the previous description of marketing the examples presented, you should now be aware that tourism marketing involves a number of special characteristics:

● Marketing is a philosophy with the overriding value that the decision-making process of any organisation has to be led by the consumers' needs, the market-place and the company's assets and resources.

● Successful marketing requires a special organisation structure that believes in integrating the principles of consumer orientation throughout the organisation.

● Marketing requires innovative methods of thinking and planning so that new ideas are generated to take advantage of opportunities or to improve existing methods of marketing.

However, it is important to remember that while the use of marketing is expanding, as a practice, it is not without its critics.

Criticisms of the marketing concept

As we move into the twenty-first century, there is a growing concern for protection of the environment and the adoption of business policies that will enable to the earth's resources to be sustained. The new values emerging are placing pressure on the underlying concepts of marketing. This is creating a great deal of debate regarding the ethical standpoint of marketing. Some of the most significant criticisms are considered in this section.

Case Study 17.1   The British Airways Experience

British Airways (BA) offers an example of success due to the adoption of a marketing orientation for the organisation. In the late 1970s BA suffered from a considerable personnel surplus and a growth rate that was too slow. The management at the time adopted a price reduction strategy to achieve growth, but this did not produce the desired results. The problems for BA were identified as poor management and structure. There were also external pressures as the company became caught up in the OPEC oil crisis which culminated in a doubling of the price of kerosene and a damping of world trade. The growth that BA had expected was not realised.

The change at BA commenced with the key appointment of Colin Marshall whose previous success at Avis had been built on an understanding of the importance of service and marketing. One day in 1983, 60 of the senior managers were dispensed with and the organisation set about changing the workforce philosophy to one of believing in customer care. The company achieved one of the largest and fastest turnarounds from loss to profit by a large commercial concern. The success is credited to the company's re-launch on the basis of its marketing orientation. The organisation reported (*Marketing*, May 1985), that, 'until reorganisation British Airways had not been truly marketing led. Even though it had a marketing department, it had been operations led. The key change was to ensure operations delivered what the marketing department requested due to an identification of consumer needs.' It was explained that the overall success could be attributed to three main thrusts: satisfying customer requirements; becoming more people orientated; and the creation of overall long-term strategies.

The company introduced a number of customer service programmes in order to manage a change in the company culture after privatisation (**Searching for the Edge** is planned for 1998):

- **Putting People First.** The programme which was introduced in 1984 reorientated the staff attitude to providing customer-focused service.

- **A Day in the Life.** Enabled bridges to be built as the scheme provided a greater understanding of the importance of the work carried out in different company departments.

- **To be the Best.** Focused on the different ways in which organisational performance could be improved to make it more competitive.

- **Winning for Customer.** A series of one-day programmes which brought groups of staff together to consider different case studies and what would be the best strategy to adopt in order to provide for service recovery.

This is not to say that BA always got it right as in 1983 the company lost a great deal of market share of their domestic market to British Midland. BA had identified that the business market was influenced by the technical aspects of punctuality, access to business centres and courtesy. However, because it did not serve an adequate, satisfying meal, the consumer discriminated against the company. BA was forced to develop the super shuttle concept which included a free breakfast. BA set up voluntary customer service teams within which staff discussed the results of consumer surveys in order to provide advice and recommendations for improving the service. These suggestions were then taken to management workshops where the team leaders proposed different courses of action. The outcomes were then formalised into changes in staff training and appraisal procedures. The whole process meant BA was able to set up benchmark performance measures related to waiting times, service delivery problems, complaint letters and other key indicators in order to monitor and react to any service shortfall. The airline was then able to go from strength to strength with increases in productivity per employee, turnover and profit.

▷

Case Study 17.1 continued

The success of the changes meant that by 1993 the company was in a position to take almost a quarter stake (24.6%) in US Air to form an alliance which allowed it to gain a foothold in the profitable US domestic air market-place. This strengthened BA's operating routes from Europe across the Atlantic and into the USA. Such growth strategies were part of the 1992 plans which culminated in alliances with Deutsche BA (49% stake), Qantas (25% stake), The French airline TAT (49.9% stake). In addition BA acquired Dan-Air.

Case Study 17.2 The SAS Experience

The Scandinavian Airline System (SAS) is another example of a company which recovered its position through properly planned market-orientated leadership. SAS was losing money when in 1980, Jan Carlzon took over as its new president. Carlzon introduced a consumer orientation into the organisation, which led to an emphasis on research, improvements of service and new values which provided the organisation with a new direction. The repositioning of the company involved sending 10 000 front-line staff on an SAS course entitled 'The human factor' in order to improve service to the business traveller. Carlzon also ensured his managers would create the right environment for staff to take responsibility for improvements in service. The changes produced an improved reputation for SAS which contributed to its gradual recovery. The impact of Carlzon's vision and leadership, in redefining the focus of the organisation onto the satisfaction of the consumer, led to a series of changes which, at the time, culminated in higher profits.

It might seem a simple change to listen to customers and provide what they say they want. But if we examine the marketing of the most important piece of leisure equipment of today – the television – this is not occurring. If you want to own or rent a TV, or have one repaired, companies are notorious in their inflexibility of working hours. They often work to their own delivery and work schedules. This leads to consumers having to wait in after taking time off work, cancelling social arrangements, or reorganising the children's travel to or from school. In 1989 Radio Rentals finally recognised the advantage of offering to install or repair televisions and a range of other equipment at a time when it was convenient to the consumer. This could include various times at weekends or evenings. As installations only take minutes, and because repairs are more often than not the replacement of a complete circuit board or parts, the cost of time to the company was not excessive. On the other hand, the company was able to build customer loyalty and stabilise the number of accounts it held.

Disregard of the environment and non-consumers

The marketing concept can lead to a tunnel vision, focusing on the potential consumers of the product and not the wider society. Other groups, such as the host population of a country, can be adversely affected by insensitive tourism marketing policies. In addition, pollution and damage as by-products of tourism activities are environmental and social costs carried by the whole of society and not simply the organisation's consumers. Tour operators/wholesalers have continuously developed new areas, expanded successful resorts and created promotional campaigns without due regard to the cost of impacts on the area and local population (see Part 2). Another type of marketing pollution is the over-abundance of different types of promotional material, which makes a home or overseas destination less attractive. There are roadside poster sites, advertisements on taxi cabs, messages painted on buildings, and leaflets given away and then discarded, all of which create invasive pollution. There is a trend to produce advertisements that aim to shock, and there are others that offend, such as the 'Beaver Espana' Club 18–30 poster or advertisements for sex-talk telephone numbers. The overall effect of these trends is to lead the general public to mistrust marketing.

Over-emphasis on profitable products

The marketing concept dictates that products can only be offered to the market-place when they are profitable. This has culminated in the axing of bus and train transport routes and the disregard of low-spending individuals. Where a want exists and the marketing opportunity cannot deliver the required profit return, then the product is seldom developed. The market-based system is guided by self-interest and profit motivation. Therefore, consumer preferences are only accounted for if there is an ability to pay. These values are represented by a lack of concern for those who cannot afford a holiday, or for the supply of amenities to cater for those who are disadvantaged or handicapped. Facilities for blind, infirm and handicapped people are of low priority in resort and accommodation planning.

Invasion of privacy

The power of IT allows organisations to capture a complete range of personal information for use in targeting direct mail campaigns. The more recent use of database and micro-marketing places the emphasis on using mailing lists with or without the consent of individuals. As organisations begin to spend more on research there is also the problem of a greater use of telephone, and high street interviews. And research is not confined to the business world as there is an increasing amount of research and projects carried out in schools and colleges. A consequence of the amount of interview requests is the growing refusal by many members of the public to take part in any form of research.

Waste of resources on tourism marketing

Marketing is perceived as wasteful owing to the high amounts of money spent on promoting products. The money given to tourism promotion is often associated with enticing consumers to buy products that they may not want. It is believed the most disadvantaged tourist consumers are the ones most likely to be influenced by high expenditure on tourism marketing. The levels of marketing expenditure are quite often blamed for changing consumer attitudes and bringing about a materialistic society where status is derived from the number and type of destinations we visit, or leisure and activities we undertake, rather than how good we are as caring members of society.

A societal marketing approach

It has been argued that the pressures affecting the image of marketing need to be more carefully considered. This has culminated in the movement toward a societal concept of marketing which stresses the enhancement of the needs of society as well as the consumer. We believe that this is an academic exercise as definitions have to evolve out of business practice rather than from academic debate. Some organisations such as brewers and distillers are creating campaigns to warn people of the excesses of drinking, but it is questionable whether they are worried as much about the customer as about the legislation that could affect their operations.

While some organisations may pay lip service to a societal concept for PR purposes, in a competitive situation many of the problems related to tourism, and its marketing, will continue. It is also important to recognise that consumers are now better educated and are competent to select products that are not creating undue problems to society. Moreover, if organisations or their products do create problems, there are articulate pressure groups and government legislation available for consumer and environmental protection.

Conclusion

The tourism product is predominately a service product with the main characteristics of intangibility, perishability and inseparability. The tourism purchase involves complex decisions related to perceptions of risk and the expectation of high levels of quality. As such there is a need for a deeper understanding of the process of TQM and consumer's expectation of service delivery standards.

Chapter discussion questions

1. Define the differences between the service product and other, more general goods, and review the implications for tourism and hospitality services.

2. What strategies are used by the tourism industry to alleviate the perception of risk in the purchase of the tourism product?

3. Taking a tourism company or organisation with which you are familiar, consider the methods and techniques utilised to encourage an integrated and successful approach to quality management.

Recommended further reading

- Gilbert, D. C., and Joshi, I. (1992) 'Quality management and the tourism and hospitality industry', pp. 149–68 in *Progress in Tourism, Recreation and Hospitality Management* Vol. 4, Cooper, C. and Lockwood, A. (eds), Belhaven Press, London.
- Gronroos, C. (1982) *Strategic Management and Marketing in the Service Sector*, Swedish School of Economics and Business Administration, Helsinki.
- Middleton, V. (1994), *Marketing in Travel and Tourism*, Butterworth-Heinemann, Oxford.
- Parasuraman, A., Zeithaml, V. A. and Berry, L. L. (1985) 'A conceptual model of service quality and its implications for future research', *Journal of Marketing*, **49**(4), 41–50.

Bibliography

- Dann, G. M. S. (1981) 'Tourist motivation: an appraisal', *Annals of Tourism Research*, **8**(2), 187–219.
- Gilbert, D. C. (1989) 'Tourism marketing – its emergence and establishment', pp. 77–90 in *Progress in Tourism, Recreation and Hospitality Management*, Vol. 1, Cooper, C. (ed.), Belhaven Press, London.

- Gilbert, D. C. (1991) 'An examination of the consumer behaviour process related to tourism', pp. 78–105 in *Progress in Tourism, Recreation and Hospitality Management*, Vol. 3, Cooper, C. (ed.), Belhaven Press, London.
- Gilbert, D. C. (1992) A study of the factors of consumer behaviour related to overseas holidays from the UK, unpublished PhD thesis, University of Surrey, Guildford.
- Gilbert, D. C. and Joshi, I. (1992) 'Quality management and the tourism and hospitality industry', pp. 149–68 in *Progress in Tourism, Recreation and Hospitality Management*, Vol. 4, Cooper, C. and Lockwood, A. (eds), Belhaven Press, London.
- Gronroos, C. (1982) *Strategic Management and Marketing in the Service Sector*, Swedish School of Economics and Business Administration, Helsinki.
- Hart, C. W. L., Heskett, J. L. and Sasser, W. E. (1990), 'The profitable part of service recovery', *Harvard Business Review*, July/August, 148–56.
- Nightingale, M. (1983) Determination and control of quality standards in hospitality services, MPhil. thesis, University of Surrey.
- Parasuraman, A., Zeithaml, V. A. and Berry, L. L. (1985) 'A conceptual model of service quality and its implications for future research', *Journal of Marketing*, **49**(4), 41–50.

Chapter Eighteen

Marketing planning

Introduction

In this chapter, we outline an approach to marketing planning in tourism and suggest that the marketing plan represents a structured guide to action. As such, it acts as a systematic method of data collection, objective setting and logical analysis of the most appropriate direction for an organisation, retailer or product. If a marketing plan is to be accepted by all concerned then the compilation of the plan has to involve all levels of personnel. This is because marketing plans require organisation-wide commitment if they are to be successful.

The plan must reflect the dynamic nature of the market-place, and as such the plan needs to be thought of as a loose-leaf binder rather than as a tablet of stone. This means the plan acts as a working document which can be updated or modified to take into account new opportunities, challenges or unanticipated problem situations.

Chapter learning objectives

Marketing planning is crucial to organisational survival in an environment that is unpredictable and volatile. In this chapter, therefore, we consider all aspects of marketing planning to ensure that, by the end of the chapter, the reader is able:

- to recognise the importance of marketing planning in respect of tourism and the implications of inefficient planning procedures;
- to understand the purposes of marketing planning in protecting the organisation and enhancing its market position;
- to appreciate the key stages of marketing planning and thus be in a better position to develop and implement a marketing plan successfully; and
- to identify the structure and content of an effective marketing plan.

What is marketing planning?

We all need to plan if we are to make a success of our lives. Very few Olympic medallists could be successful without a planned programme of training and events leading up to their Olympic finals and achievements. Whether it is for examinations, sports events, going on holiday or organising a party, the use of planning leads to a greater certainty that the event will be a success. Without the right approach, and a sensible plan, any other courses of action have seldom been considered and, consequently, there is the likelihood that individuals, companies or organisations may not function to their maximum potential.

Planning is the most important activity of marketing management. It should provide a common structure and focus for all of the organisation's management activities. It is therefore essential for us to understand planning in its context as the key function of management.

The tourism sector provides a combination of different products and activities, which range from the small taxi firm and guest house to the largest airline or hotel group. The concepts of change and survival are as important to the small business as they are to a destination, major international hotel chain or airline. The fact that change will occur, and with increasing speed, is the most predictable aspect of contemporary business life. It would therefore seem sensible to become familiar with the underlying trends and forces of change that impinge on tourism business activities. This enables the management of change towards desired objectives rather than being driven blindly before the tide of market forces.

The long-term survival of any organisation is dependent on how well the business relates to its environment. This relies on devising forward plans of where an organisation, destination or product would be best placed for the future. Some of the key points relating to marketing planning may be identified:

- The plan requires control over the changes that have to be made.
- It needs to allow for the exploitation of any short-term advantages and improvement on weaknesses.
- It has to promote the use of analysis, reason and evaluation as an integral part of planning procedure.

A lack of marketing planning will result in a wide range of possible consequences. For a destination, this could involve one or more of the following:

- failure to take advantage of potential growth markets and new marketing opportunities;
- lack of maintenance of demand from a spread of markets and erosion of market share due to the actions of competitors;
- demand problems in low-season periods;
- low level of awareness of the destination's product offering;
- poor image of the destination;
- lack of support for cooperative marketing initiatives;
- poor or inadequate tourism information services;
- decline in quality levels below acceptable limits;
- difficulty in attracting intermediaries to market or package holidays;
- disillusionment and lack of motivation of tourism service employees.

Thus, the implementation of marketing planning procedures can be instrumental in alleviating many of the difficulties which tourism organisations may face. This is reflected in Case Study 18.1 which focuses on Disneyland, Paris, and some of the weaknesses in the marketing planning procedures in respect of this venture.

However, although planning cannot guarantee success it can make the organisation less vulnerable to market forces and unpredictable events. Perhaps the demise of Laker Airways, Braniff Airways, Courtline and ILG could have been avoided if more attention had been given to planning activities by their respective managements, especially

Case Study 18.1 Disneyland Paris

Disneyland Paris, formerly Euro Disney, became a large embarrassment to the Walt Disney Corporation after it plunged into the red shortly after its opening in France in 1992. The cost of the theme park, at US$4.4 billion for the development of a 5000 acre site, represented the largest single piece of construction in Europe's history apart from the Channel Tunnel project linking England and France.

Cumulative losses at the end of 1993 exceeded US$1 billion with an estimated continuing loss of US$1.6 million a day. The loss is all the more significant when it is revealed that Euro Disney had achieved target attendance objectives of 11 million 'guests' in slightly over one year of operation. The situation did not improve in 1994 when Euro Disney reported a loss for the year to the end of September of US$317 million and attendance was 10% down on levels achieved in 1993. Share prices fell from a peak of FFr68 just before the park opened to only FFr6 in October 1994.

The main problem for Euro Disney can be found to lie with the planning assumptions and forecasts which did not reflect the European economy or the willingness of consumers to pay high entrance fees. There was also a mistaken belief in a flatter seasonal demand curve, which characterises demand in the USA, as a result of mid-semester or off-peak visits by parents with their children. As a result, the levels and patterns of demand never reached those anticipated by planners.

An additional problem is related to the homogeneity of European markets. Disney planners in the USA initially treated Europe as a single country, underestimating the inherent differences between the existing markets in respect of demand and importing marketing methods which had succeeded in America but which did not successfully transplant to the European context. Consequently, the American parent company was forced to accept that tourists' habits vary a great deal throughout the European context and that its prices were too high for French visitors.

As an integral part of the financial subsidisation for the development of the park, the plan had assumed that well-appointed, high-priced hotels and other property could be constructed and then sold on to entrepreneurs for considerable profits. Disney planners did not want to be faced with either the land-use problems they had experienced in the USA where extra land has had to be purchased for expansion, or the financial limitations imposed in Tokyo where Japanese investors take huge profits and Disney only earns 10% of gross earning on rides and 5% on food and beverage. Consequently, the planners were concerned with attempting to maximise profit opportunities from the outset.

Disney planners overlooked the worsening economic conditions prevailing in Europe in the early 1990s which led to a severe slump in the property market for accommodation. Euro Disney had embarked on a vast property development – including hotels, shops, offices and residential housing – ignoring the severe handicap this posed of potentially unrealistic financial obligations to its American parent. The hotels were not sold as originally planned and, in addition, currency devaluation in Great Britain and Italy further depressed purchasing power, driving down demand for foreign travel.

Other planning problems materialised. The design of the hotel' restaurants, for example, did not take into consideration the different tastes of the guests and were often too small, because of the belief that few Europeans would eat a full breakfast. Consequently, long waiting times and ▷

queuing problems ensued, culminating in guest dissatisfaction and complaints. The park's outlets were designed for snacking but the pattern was, that at one o'clock, there was a major demand for a reasonably substantial meal. Moreover, Disney outlets were restricted by a 'no alcohol' policy which meant the French custom of taking wine with a meal was not permissible.

The problems were further compounded by pre-opening reports by Disney that employees would comply with the written Disney code of dress which consisted, for women, of short fingernails, appropriate undergarments and strict policies on hairstyles. The global code was considered an insult by the French people who believed it attacked the underlying principles in French culture of individualism and privacy. Thus, unforeseen cultural issues emerged with newspapers, such as *Le Figaro*, stating: 'Euro Disney is the very symbol of the process by which people's cultural standards are lowered and money becomes all-conquering'.

French intellectuals accused Disney of stifling the imagination of young people, of turning children into consumers, even of creating a 'cultural Chernobyl'. In addition, Disney characters were attacked as likely to pollute the nation's culture. Euro Disney's image was further damaged by PR blunders by senior Disney officials who dismissed the criticism as fatuous. Nevertheless, concessions were made: emphasis was placed on European fairy tale characters such as Snow White and Pinocchio rather than Bambi and Dumbo. Also, in order to echo French culture, the turret which the company's 'imagineers' built was modelled not on Neuschwanstein, the Bavarian castle reconstructed at Disney's other theme parks, but on a drawing from a fifteenth-century French manuscript.

Recent changes

Following the embarrassment of heavy losses and low levels of demand in 1993 and 1994, Disney brought in French senior management who orchestrated key developments at Euro Disney. The theme park was renamed Disneyland, Paris and in 1994 a complete product reassessment and reduction programme was implemented. The number of souvenir lines was cut in half from 30 000 and restaurant menu items were also reduced from 5400 to 2000.

Marketing strategies were re-appraised and advertising messages modified. The advertising is now designed to make parents and grandparents sympathetic to their children's emotional pleasure while emphasising the adventure element for adults. Potential customers are targeted with special offers during off-peak winter months, a strategy which evolved in response to market research activity which demonstrated that levels of repeat visits were high. In addition, it was discovered that each visitor recommends the park to an average of 18 other potential visitors.

Pricing policies were also adjusted to offer reduced entrance admission charges in the evening, for example. Job flexibility arrangements, customer care programmes and other efficiency drives were also instigated, leading to the first ever surplus for Disneyland Paris at the end of 1995. Hotel occupancy has risen steadily from 55% in 1993 to 68% in 1995, compared with an average of roughly 60% for hotels in and around the Paris area. Other developments have led to improved profitability via the reduction of operating costs per visitor by almost 20%.

The new situation is linked closely to the restructuring of the park's interest payments and fees in 1994 which provided a suspension on payments of interest and royalties as well as financial charges. However, the terms of this agreement state that interest and royalties must eventually be resumed and, after 1999, management and incentive fees will again become payable.

Therefore, it is crucial that financial and marketing planning are implemented professionally if the park is to maintain its profitability and prosper in the European market-place. This is especially important given increasing competition from newly established theme parks such as Port Aventura in Spain.

in relation to cash flow, fixed cost and expansion attributes. The early no-frills, price advantage of Sir Freddie Laker's operation or the image of Braniff with Gucci-designed uniforms, and the cheap price policy of ILG provided excellent market positions for the products, yet the weakness of financial planning played a major part in each company's downfall.

Organisations or destinations that rely on *ad hoc* initiatives or fail to manage their future will find their future has been managed for them. Each organisation will adopt a different approach to the task of planning based upon the way senior executives see the purpose of marketing plans. The values of any organisation fall along a continuum which begins at *wait and see*, moves through the next set of values to *prepare and predict* and finally ends with organisations that want to *make it happen*. An organisation will benefit more from a future that is made to happen because of the clear direction provided for the workforce and other company resources.

The marketing environment of the organisation

Each and every organisation has to operate within a market environment. This environment is made up of different levels of influence that will affect the opportunities and marketing decisions that need to be made. The historical conditions affecting competition and rivalry in company markets, the values of stakeholder groups and the political, economic, social and technological changes of the wider environment, all affect the likely performance of the organisation and its brands.

The organisational setting, or environment of operation, is related to the four levels identified in Table 18.1. It should be noted that the influences and pressures of the different levels shown are only taken into account by those organisations following a market-led business philosophy.

Level 1	**The organisation**	Marketing subfunctions need to be well organised and integrated with other organisational functions. Marketing has to communicate the needs of the market environment as described in levels 2–4.
Level 2	**Company markets**	Identification of domestic and international consumer markets for products/services, or industrial, intermediary or institutional markets. The degree of rivalry and competitive activity will affect market activity choice.
Level 3	**Organisational stakeholders**	Interest groups will affect the context of decision making, e.g. shareholders, competitors, customers, employees, unions government, suppliers, debtors, local community or banks, all of whom may have conflicting values.
Level 4	**The wider environment**	STEP: social technological economic political. Interrelations of the different forces and changes in the above are powerful market environment determinants.

Table 18.1: Four levels of marketing environment affecting the organisation

The purpose of the marketing plan

The marketing plan is normally a short-term plan that will direct the organisation from one to three years. Typically, a five-year plan will be a strategic plan which is more general and less detailed than a marketing plan.

The strategic plan will concern itself more with external environmental influences and opportunities and less with the detail of the organisation's marketing activities. Strategic plans are normally either medium or long term, and marketing plans are short or medium term.

The marketing plan and its compilation is able to provide a number of benefits for an organisation. The creation of a marketing plan will result in a wide range of management benefits as well as the following:

- **Provide clear direction to the marketing operation based upon a systematic, written approach to planning and action.** The planning system allows a written mission statement and set of objectives to be established, both of which can be transmitted to the workforce. This provides a sense of leadership and allows the workforce to feel their own efforts are essential to the achievement of desired results.

- **Coordinate the resources of the organisation.** This eliminates confusion and misunderstanding in order to achieve maximum cooperation. Tasks and responsibilities can be set which clarify the direction and objectives of the organisation. To ensure there is a united effort, recommendations have to be presented in such a way that they can be fully understood at all organisational levels. The plan then acts as a master guide which will underpin all endeavour and decision making. The plan should lead to greater employee cohesion and make everyone feel part of a team in which each individual believes he or she can make a valuable contribution.

- **Set targets against which progress can be measured.** Quantified targets for volume or revenue provide the focus for individual, departmental or company performance. Some organisations will set targets at achievable levels whereas others will set artificially high targets to encourage enhanced employee effort. The targets, once set, act as the benchmark against which all marketing programmes are monitored.

- **Minimise risk through analysis of the internal and external environment.** The planning procedure allows managers to identify areas of strength and weakness so that the first can be exploited and the second surmounted. Additionally, threats and opportunities can be assessed.

- **Examine the various ways of targeting to different market segments.** This allows for different marketing mix strategies to be appraised prior to their implementation. As such estimates can be made of the likely impacts in relation to sales and revenue targets to the marketing budget.

- **Provide a record of the organisation's marketing policies and plans.** This allows managers to check what has been attempted in the past and to evaluate the effectiveness of previous programmes. It also provides continuity and a source of reference for new managers joining the organisation.

- **Think about the long-term business objectives so that the organisation plans to be in the best position to achieve its future aims.** This allows management to develop continuity of thought and action from one year to the next.

We know that organisational objectives should be based upon relevant market-centred opportunities. It is the responsibility of tourism marketers to identify these opportunities and to devise a system of planning that may lead to their exploitation.

Successful planning

Most textbooks suggest planning is simply the following of a series of simple steps. However, the true art of planning is to understand both the human aspects and procedural necessities involved. A poor planning experience may be a function of one or more of the following factors:

- **Lack of senior management support.** A lack of support, from the Chief Executive and other senior people, is a major problem and one that is difficult to resolve.

- **Inappropriate planning procedures.** The system of planning which is adopted may not suit the organisation. Within the organisation there is often the separation of different planning functions from each other, leading to a lack of integration. Therefore, the system often has to be designed to match the organisation and to achieve harmony between groups.

- **Poor planning and management.** The system of planning is often blamed when the weakness is actually poor planning and management. Sometimes there is confusion over available data or even planning terms. The requirement is for a plan to be compiled which clarifies times and responsibilities for different actions and meetings which will lead to the appropriate information and people being utilised.

- **Unpredictable external events.** Unexpected environmental changes may create adverse affects on the organisation's performance. Planning is then often blamed for not having incorporated such a scenario. The 1990/91 Gulf crisis is a classic example.

- **Organisational and managerial acceptance.** The values of the management team will imply different acceptance levels of the plan and ultimately determine its success or failure. There is often hostility toward plans because people feel they have not been involved in the planning process. This often occurs when the planning is left solely to a planner, or it becomes a once-a-year ritual.

- **Level of detail.** Problems occur when there is an overabundance of information which has to be filtered for its relevance. Too much detail in the early stages can produce 'paralysis analysis'.

It is distressing that those travel companies that have recognised the need for a more structured approach to planning, and subsequently adopted the formalised procedures found in the literature, seldom enjoy the advantages claimed when embarking on planning. In fact, it is often planning itself which is brought into disrepute when it fails to bring about the desired changes within an organisation.

The problems faced in marketing planning have led to a growing body of literature which indicates organisations should do what they are good at, rather than embarking upon higher-level planning exercises. We believe this is a retrograde step because organisations should attempt to take the most logical direction and not be hampered by internal failings of the human resource aspects of implementation, lack of planning expertise or disregard of the involvement of others in the planning process. An understanding of the social aspects of the organisation is a prerequisite for successful planning.

It is necessary for those involved in planning to recognise the need for involvement of all departments in the organisation in the formulation of the plan. This means that personnel are more likely to be motivated toward its successful implementation. Moreover, key personnel bring valuable knowledge and expertise to marketing plan formulation. It is also important to understand that most accomplishments in service industries, such as tourism, are made through people. The control of schedules, budgets, monitoring performance or corrective decisions can take place only through the medium of people. Each employee, who has responsibility, requires clear objectives against which he or she can judge if any necessary tactical action needs to be carried out.

It is important to ensure plans are not prepared within the vacuum of one department or by a marketing team that believes it is an élite. Structured management meetings can offer a setting where deliberation, responsibility and authority are shared and taken by all. This precludes dogmatic assertions about the particular methods of preparing and organising marketing planning.

The marketing planning system offers a structured approach to organising and coordinating the efforts and activities of those involved in deciding on the future of an organisation. However, there is no one right system for any particular tourism organisation, since organisations differ in size and diversity of operations, the values of the senior management and the expertise of those involved in the planning exercise.

Structure of the marketing plan

The construction of the marketing plan is characterised by a range of headings developed by different theorists. Some authors offer a list of sections with the first headed 'SWOT issues' or 'situational analysis', the second headed 'statement of objectives and goals' or 'setting objectives', the third is 'strategy' or 'marketing programming' and the last is 'monitoring' or 'control'. We prefer to use different stages which are more easily understood by managers and students. The stages are:

1. What is it we want?
2. Where are we now?
3. Where do we want to go?

4. How do we get there?
5. Where did we get to?

These are represented in Figure 18.1. In reading the structure of the marketing planning model it is important to realise the system is not always the linear progression it appears. Quite often the process needs to involve an interplay between the various stages with the flexibility to move backwards as well as forwards. We should also understand that refinement of the plan takes place as understanding of the interconnections improves. We should not presume that perfection will be achieved until a number of drafts have been completed.

Linked to the simplistic stages above, the model of marketing planning can be described as involving:

1. Ensuring the humanistic consideration for successful planning.
2. Corporate mission and goals.
3. External and internal audit.
4. Business situation analysis.
5. Creating the objectives.
6. Providing an effective marketing mix strategy.
7. Monitoring the plan.

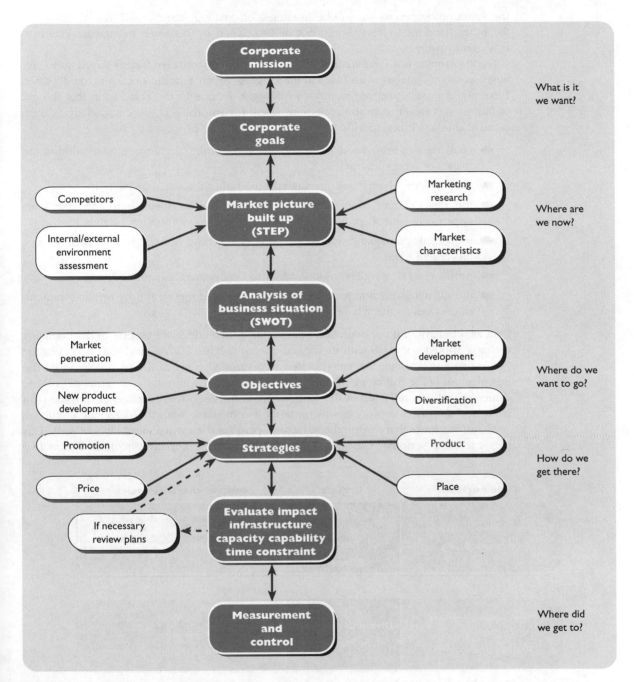

Figure 18.1: A model of marketing planning

The humanistic consideration for successful planning

The involvement of different departments will help reduce resistance to future changes or tasks. Continuous concern about the human aspects of planning can provide a greater possibility of the plan's success. The planner or planning team should be aware that they are only a technical service to a wider team. However we have to be careful not to make the system too open as we will be in danger of creating anarchy and loss of focus. On the other hand the system should not be too closed as this leads to increased bureaucracy and apathy.

Good planning is a combination of qualitative and quantitative factors based upon creative, as well as analytical and logical thinking. As Albert Einstein once remarked, 'When I examined myself, and my methods of thought, I came to the conclusion that the gift of fantasy has meant more to me than my talent for absorbing positive knowledge'. Thus, creative thinkers bring specific benefits to the planning process by enabling:

- challenges to norms and assumptions and the ability to question what others automatically accept as true;
- the focus on chance and the unexpected rather than safe answers;
- the development of new ways of altering familiar ideas into unconventional approaches and so provide new ideas and means of thinking of situations;
- individuals to make associations and so combine seemingly unrelated events, topics and ideas;
- product, service and promotion ideas to be updated and revised; and
- the planning function to retain its excitement and innovation by bringing humanistic values to the whole process.

One vital behavioural consideration of any plan which affects all aspects of the company is that it should not clash with the organisational culture. Such a clash can be overcome by ensuring staff values are incorporated into various stages of the planning cycle. The involvement of the full range of staff leads to a situation where the organisational culture values of staff are reflected in the 'bottom up' comments. This helps to ensure the plan is created as part of a process which makes it compatible with the corporate culture.

Again, we stress that organisations have to plan for the involvement level of staff. This needs to be as seriously considered as planning for the company's markets. Figure 18.2

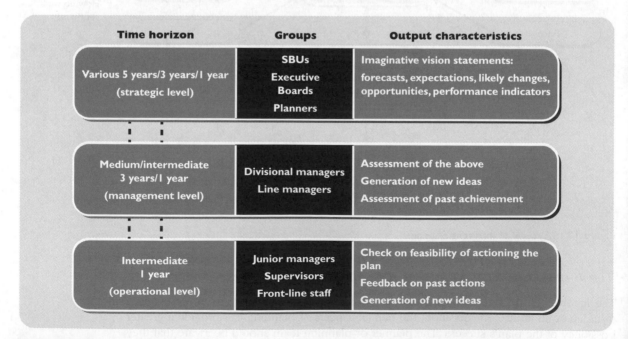

Figure 18.2: Involvement levels for marketing planning

provides one approach in dealing with the need to have marketing planning involvement at all levels.

One other important aspect of influence when including a cross-section of people in planning is their ability to hinder or help the plan. Within any company or organisation, managers' competence to plan will be based upon how busy they are, their preoccupation with other business matters, their career goals, their experience and their ability to think analytically. These attributes are linked to other managers' values and the cultural climate within the organisation, which may be more or less responsive to change and adaptation through adherence to the planning system.

A plan when completed should be read by far more people than actually do read it. This is often due to the lack of time by busy executives and the complexity of the plan. To overcome the problem all plans require the addition of a good management summary, written in clear, concise language, which will ensure the dominant points and themes are communicated. The summary should concentrate on objectives, main target markets, opportunities and threats, key strategies and timings.

Corporate mission and goals

It is important to understand what is expected of the plan from the long-term goals set at corporate level. The goals may be based upon the values and objectives of the key shareholders, board directors or senior managers. In some situations goals are set only after the establishment and evaluation of the marketing programmes. This is a parochial, programme-led method of planning, where management does not attempt to meet higher-level corporate goals within the planning process because managers are more prepared to settle for what they believe will work. An organisation with this approach will not investigate as broad a range of strategies as the organisation that is driven to ensure consistency with the overall corporate strategy and goals.

The most effective form of planning creates a balance between corporate direction and ensuring different levels of employee involvement (see Figure 18.2). If goals are dictated to employees, there is very little sense of ownership of the plan and a corresponding lack of motivation. Goals can be set in a functional, top-down approach or as a negotiation of goals through the combination of bottom-up and top-down processes.

The mission statement is a guide for employees to know what the purpose of the organisation is. The mission statement acts as a confirmation of what business the organisation is in from a consumer viewpoint. It then represents the overriding goal of the organisation. In the 1991/92 British Tourist Authority marketing plan the mission statement is: 'to strengthen the performance of Britain's tourist industry in international markets by encouraging the improvement and provision of tourist amenities and facilities in Britain'.

External and internal audit

It is necessary to gather enough relevant information about the external and internal organisational environment to be able to construct a business and market picture of current and future pressure and trends. One important part of marketing planning is knowing what to analyse. Executives have to be careful that they do not have too limited a view of the environment. Having checklists of necessary information is one way to prevent organisations scanning the environment based upon what they intend to do, rather than in relation to what they could or should do.

Box 18.1 STEP and market environment

- **Social**: demographics, holiday/leisure time entitlement, values (consumerism), lifestyle, male/female role changes, delay of first child, education, workforce changes.
- **Technological**: innovations, new systems (reservations, yield management) home technology, electronic fund transfer.
- **Economic**: inflation, unemployment, fuel costs, exchange rates, average salaries (plus see market environment list below).
- **Political**: taxation, duty, regulation, tourism policies, constraints on local authorities.

Box 18.2 Other environmental factors

- **Total market**: size, growth, trends, value, industry structure, identify the competitors, barriers to entry, extent of under- or over-capacity of supply, marketing methods.
- **Companies**: level of investment, takeovers, promotional expenditure, redundancies, revenue, profits.
- **Product development**: trends, new product types, service enhancements, competitiveness of other companies' products.
- **Price**: levels, range, terms, practices.
- **Distribution**: patterns, trade structure, policies.
- **Promotion**: expenditure, types, communication messages, brand strengths, effectiveness of own current promotion methods.

The information collected should, at the very least, form the basis of a STEP investigation. STEP analysis is an examination of the social, technological, economic and political changes that may affect the market, the organisation and ultimately the plan. Information gathering is part of an internal and external audit which should collect a range of information, as detailed in Box 18.1. In addition to incorporating these factors in the marketing plan, it is also necessary to take into account the factors outlined in Box 18.2. This information should be gathered on the basis of how it affects the organisation, especially in relation to its key competitors.

Business situation analysis

Once sufficient information has been collected, there is the need to carry out an analysis of the business situation and this is best done by identifying the major strengths, weaknesses, opportunities and threats facing an organisation. This is the so-called 'SWOT analysis'. There is also the need to check the results of the SWOT analysis against information provided from STEP analysis.

The systematic analysis carried out at this stage provides the formulation of a number of assumptions about the past performance, future conditions, product opportunities, resources and service priorities which all lead to the possibility of a range of strategic options for an organisation in the tourism sector.

At this stage of planning, it is possible to circulate the assumptions and forecasts to different company divisions. These should be offered as a range of alternatives. For example, if you have assumed the market will grow at x% and this will create $£Y$ with a specific strategy, then it is also wise to create alternative scenarios. You should estimate sales at lower and higher rates than expected so that the impact on profits can be assessed. For example a rate of growth of $x + 2$% may create a profit of $1.3 \times £Y$, or alternatively $x - 2$% gives $0.5 \times £Y$. Managers can then involve their team in discussions about the relevance of the material created from the foregoing environmental scanning stage.

Creating the objectives

Objectives are a combination of what is expected of the organisation by its shareholders or directors, and an evaluation of the options emerging out of the first stages of the planning process. The objectives should emerge as the most logical course of action for the organisation to embark upon given the detailed analysis in the preceding stages.

We also have to ensure the objectives are not only related to volume of sales and financial objectives, but also involve broader marketing objectives. One danger in planning is that large organisations often set financial objectives in terms of growth rate in earnings per share, return on equity or investment and so on, and ignore marketing objectives such as the selection of specific segments as target markets and the improvement of products, brand image or consumer awareness. Objectives should also include the expected market share achievements because this performance may only be realistic if certain budgets are made available.

Objectives need to be a balance of the aspirational and realistic so that the organisation attempts to improve its market position within acceptable risk limits. The basic criteria for setting objectives based upon the SMART acronym is that they need to be:

- **Specific** by being focused on the results required;
- **Measurable** for each objective set;
- **Achievable** set against trends and market position constraints and assessed fully;
- **Realistic** given resource constraints of time and money, etc.; and set against
- **Time limits** of when the objective(s) should be reached.

The objective stage inputs of Figure 18.1 are based upon growth strategies whereby a company is attempting to expand. Organisations will normally want to attack the market share of others by penetrating the market to increase their own share of the market. This takes place in the current markets and is normally based upon a more aggressive use of the marketing mix. The organisation may attempt to increase existing customer usage rates or attract competitors' customers. For example, Visa used promotional techniques in an attempt to get their cardholders to use their card while on holiday in preference to competitors' cards. Larger organisations or companies will try to increase sales through market development by attempting to sell current products in new markets. This may involve the addition of new locations such as McDonald's outlet openings to compete at airports, at tourist attractions and even within office buildings. Market development may also be based upon convincing the customer to find new uses for existing products. Larger organisations or companies will try to develop markets by selling the benefits of, say, self catering holidays to those who take hotel holidays. Organisations may also develop their markets by expanding internationally such as Holiday Inn and the Accor group.

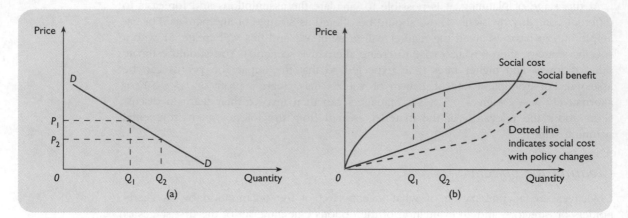

Figure 18.3: Tourism demand problems

Objectives may also include **new product development** or **diversification**. The Eurostar channel tunnel service is a new product development which required intensive product research and development. Tour operators/wholesalers develop new destinations and airlines embark upon new air routes. Diversification has occurred where companies such as Virgin developed a new business from its retail base into an airline operation. Hotel organisations have developed contract catering operations and vice versa. There has also been the diversification of airlines into the hotel business.

Providing an effective marketing mix strategy

The success of the plan relies on creating the right marketing mix strategies for achieving the objectives (see Chapter 19 for a clear explanation of the different aspects of the marketing mix). The use of the marketing mix involves balancing the elements of the marketing mix to achieve the highest expected probability of meeting the plan's objectives. However, mix strategies have to be checked to ensure they are acceptable. For example, if the strategy is for expansion of a destination, an impact or environmental analysis should be considered. Figure 18.3 shows a situation where there is no extra benefit in expanding tourist numbers, since the costs increase at the same rate as the benefits. Note that Q_1 and Q_2 are in exactly the same position in both parts (a) and (b) of Figure 18.3.

Figure 18.3(a) shows the relationship between demand and price for a tourism destination. If price is reduced from P_1 to P_2 then the resultant demand for the area increases from Q_1 to Q_2. Tourism destinations can reduce the average price of visits through government policies such as allowing more charter arrivals or reducing tourist taxes. If the positions of Figure 18.3(a) are examined against the social cost and benefit curves of Figure 18.3(b) it will be seen that position Q_2 is no better than position Q_1 as the social costs have increased at a rate that cancels out the increase in social benefits. The result is that the destination is no better off socially from an increase in arrivals and may have to check other criteria before it agrees to expansion policies.

Market segmentation

Emanating out of the SWOT analysis will be the objective to target specific submarkets or what are known as **segments**. Market segmentation is the process of dividing the

Characteristic	Typical classification
Geographic	Region of world, Country, Area of country Urban, Suburban, Rural areas City, Town, Zip code or Type of house.
Demographic	By age group, Family life cycle, ethnic group. Socio-economic classification of household based upon A, B, C1, C2, DE classifications.
Psychographic	Lifestyle. Personality Type – introvert, extrovert, high/low ego drive, independent, group worker.
Usership	Non-user, Current user, Past user, Potential user, Heavy user, Medium user, Light user
Kind of purchase	Special occasion (honeymoon, anniversary), Annual holiday trip, Business travel, Method of Purchase (agent, direct, etc.)
Attitudes	Towards product area, Towards brand, Towards usership and use situations
Benefits sought	Status, Convenience, Luxury, Economy, etc.

total perceived market into subsets, in each of which the potential customers have characteristics in common, which lead to similar demand needs for a product or service. The marketeer has to decide upon the coverage of the target market. This can be any one of a selection from a broad mass market, a selective market segment strategy or aiming at two or more multiple segments. Mass tourism operators selling undifferentiated European and long-haul destinations will target a very broad subset of consumers. This is because their success lies in offering a wide range of popular countries at value for money prices. In contrast, a specialist tour operator/wholesaler can attempt to identify a new segment or adopt an upmarket or downmarket position. A current lifestyle change is towards being healthier. The medical profession and a number of magazines and newspapers have changed attitudes to both leisure pursuits and eating habits. Both of these will have repercussions on the provision of leisure centres in hotels and resorts, activity holiday supply, spa and health products as well as be an opportunity for new product development.

The identification and selection of segments will require judgement based on the analysis of different data. The purpose of segmentation is to select a segment (target market) with the best potential on a range of criteria. The objective set is then to create product benefits, features and promotional messages which will appeal to the needs of the selected segment(s). A number of characteristics are examined when deciding upon target groups (see Chapter 2 on consumer behaviour for further discussion of some of these characteristics) as shown in Table 18.2.

In order for segmentation to be successful there is a need to apply intellectual rigour to the segmentation procedure. When a target group is identified it is prudent to use a checklist to ensure the segment offers a viable opportunity for the organisation:

● **Is the segment measurable?** Progress at various stages of the marketing activity needs to be measured. As changes occur these also have to be measurable.

Box 18.3 British Tourist Authority's lifestyle segmentation for American visitors to Britain

● **First time visitor**: stays in London and visits traditional and well-known attractions and sights around London, e.g. Windsor.

● **The traditionalist**: divide, time between London and more established regional locations such as Oxford, Cambridge, Chester, utilising trains and occasionally B&B accommodation. The type seeks an enriching vacation.

● **The explorer**: wants to know the country better. Stays outside London and utilises cities as a base for further touring of areas such as Wales and Scotland.

● **The Britophile**: has a lot of knowledge about Britain, returns on a regular basis, stays in upmarket accommodation and may have friends or relatives in Britain.

Source: British Tourist Authority Annual Report, 1994.

● **Is the segment accessible?** The segment requires that individual buyers can easily be contacted through promotional messages as well be accessible to purchase.

● **Is the segment substantial?** The segment must be large enough to provide a viable level of business.

● **Is the segment sustainable?** The choice of segment has to take into account whether the demand will last. Fashion and 'lifestyle' market segments are prone to change and demise.

● **Is the segment actionable?** Are there any impediments in putting together a marketing mix so that the target market can be reached with a clear product positioning, and message which will fit the needs, aspirational ideals and behaviour of the segment?

● **Is the segment defendable?** Can the target market be defended against competitor activity if they also target, and will rivalry cause any viability problems?

Segmentation leads to positioning of the service or product offer so that it is right for the target audience. This is reliant on adherence to the initial objectives and results in the final choice of the marketing mix. An example of market segmentation may be found in Box 18.3. Once the segments have emerged from the consideration process the objectives need to be reconsidered. If it is found that there are no problems with the objectives, and the plan is to be adopted, there has to be some assessment of whether the objectives can be achieved within specific time constraints. Competitors may be able to develop more quickly or the organisation may find it too difficult to change in a short period of time. The ability to change is often related to the availability of resources. It is necessary to question whether the resources available are sufficient to achieve the objectives (budgets, personnel, technology, existing hotels, aircraft or built facilities). If, after evaluation, it is decided the strategy is unacceptable, there is a need to review and revise the plan's objectives.

Agreeing the marketing mix strategy has to be linked to laying down task-related programmes which allocate budgets and create responsibilities and timings for the plan's implementation. There is always a need to link planning with budgeting which will allow for the adoption and execution of an effective marketing mix strategy to achieve the objectives of the plan.

Monitoring the plan

There should be a means of monitoring the achievements of the plan so that tactical action can be taken either to get the plan back on course or to take advantage of new opportunities. There is therefore the need for the provision of assessment and measurement methods that will monitor progress towards the achievement of the plan's overall objectives. There is also the need to know what deviations from the initial objectives are acceptable. This will allow for the review and amendment of the plan on a continuous basis.

The tourism and hospitality industry has invested in reservation systems that allow a continuous flow of financial and booking pattern data. This has enabled the modelling of different performance indicators. These can include forecasts of probable load factors or occupancy levels as well as assessment of the effectiveness of regional or national sales promotion, price changes and sales representative campaigns. More recently the airline and hotel sectors are applying these systems to yield management systems as a means to monitor demand and maximise the revenue from consumers.

Conclusion

Marketing planning is probably the most important activity for any tourism organisation. The long-term survival of organisations is related to the way that an organisation understands how to assess its environment, set sensible objectives and choose logical strategies for achieving success. The conditions for enjoying the advantages from planning are based upon the need to understand the human aspects of the process as well as the formalised procedures of a structured approach.

Chapter discussion questions

1. Explore the reasons why a marketing plan might fail and suggest strategies to reduce the likelihood of failure.

2. What are the most important purposes of a marketing plan in tourism?

3. Taking a tourism-related organisation of your choice, develop a marketing plan based on the content of this chapter.

Recommended further reading

- Kotler, P., Bowen, S. and Makens, J. (1996) *Marketing for Hospitality and Tourism*, Prentice Hall, Englewood Cliffs, NJ.
- Kotler, P. (1994) *Marketing Management – Analysis Planning and Control*, 8th edn or later, Prentice Hall, Englewood Cliffs, NJ.
- McDonald, M. (1989) *Marketing Plans*, Heinemann, Oxford.

Bibliography

- Kotler, P. (1994) *Marketing Management – Analysis Planning and Control*, 8th edn or later, Prentice Hall, Englewood Cliffs, NJ.
- McArdle, J. (1989) 'Product branding – the way forward', *Tourism Management*, **10**, 201.
- McDonald, M. (1989) *Marketing Plans*, Heinemann, Oxford.
- Ries, A. and Trout, J. (1981) *Positioning: The Battle for Your Mind*, McGraw-Hill, London.

Chapter Nineteen

Marketing mix

Introduction

Anyone who purchases a tourism product has probably been influenced by a promotional campaign, assessed the product offer, considered whether he or she is willing to pay the pay the price, and finally thought about how easy it would be to buy it. Each of these aspects of purchase are carefully planned by tourism marketers in an attempt to convince potential tourists to buy their products. They are the basic ingredients of the marketing mix, the aspect of marketing that we consider in detail in this chapter.

In actual fact a great deal of this book could have been written on the marketing mix, as it involves a whole range of different topic areas. Each of the areas that make up the marketing mix involves a complex set of management decisions which have to take into account both the individual mix strategy as well as the combined effect of the whole mix on the target market groups. This chapter will therefore provide some of the most important considerations for the planning of the marketing mix.

Chapter learning objectives

The marketing mix offers management a set of tools that may be manipulated to meet specific objectives and attract predefined target markets. The marketing mix is the focus of this chapter and, by the end of this chapter, readers will be able:

- to identify the elements that make up the marketing mix and understand how this may be applied to a tourism product;

- to recognise that the manipulation of the marketing mix generally, and the promotion and pricing in particular, will be beneficial in meeting specific predetermined objectives;

- to appreciate that distribution and product formulation are linked to, and influenced by, technological and structural changes in the tourism industry; and

- to understand the centrality of the concept of the target market to the marketing mix.

Figure 19.1:
The marketing mix

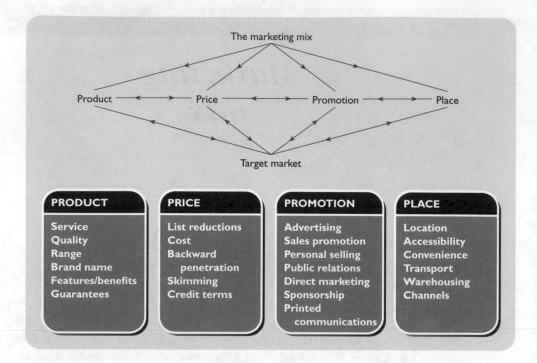

<What is the marketing mix?>

What is the marketing mix?

It is customary to accept that the marketing mix (Figure 19.1) is within the control of management and refers to decisions made in relation to the four Ps. These may be defined as:

- product;
- price;
- promotion; and
- place (distribution).

There are, however, alternative approaches where authors stress the need for an expansion of these four. This is an interesting development because the four Ps were conceived by McCarthy (1978) as an abridged version of a much wider range of what were termed 'marketing ingredients'. McCarthy based his four Ps upon a whole range of marketing ingredients offered much earlier by Borden (1965). We will discuss this later in this chapter.

Kotler and Armstrong (1996) indicate that the marketing mix is one of the key concepts in modern marketing theory. He defines the marketing mix as 'the set of marketing tools that work together to affect the marketplace'.

Target market

The fundamental starting point for the creation of a successful marketing mix strategy is to ensure the target market is clearly defined. Although the target market is not part of the marketing mix, its role in dictating the different ways the mix is used makes it indistinguishable from the concept and of paramount importance. The target market is the focus for all marketing mix activity.

Box 19.1 Benefits of targeting

Targeting facilitates the following:

● A fuller understanding of the unique characteristics and needs of the group to be satisfied. The target market acts as a reference point for marketing decisions, especially as to how the marketing mix should be planned. This should lead to greater effectiveness for the mix which in turn provides for the success of the programme.

● A better understanding of a company's competitors because it is possible to detect those who have made a similar selection of target markets. If an organisation does not clarify the markets it wishes to target, it may treat every other organisation in its sector as an equal competitor. If main competitors are identified their marketing efforts can be more closely followed.

● An improvement in understanding the changes and developments in the needs of the target market. Awareness is heightened due to the focus upon the target group's actions, and reactions to slightly different forms of the marketing mix.

The market for a product is made up of actual and potential consumers. This total available group of consumers will be analysed and a decision will made as to segments or subgroups to be targeted. The segments would probably have been identified as part of the marketing planning process (see Chapter 18 for an explanation of choosing segments) and would have emerged or been specified at the time of the setting of objectives. The specification of the target market has a number of important benefits which are discussed in Box 19.1.

As we have seen with the section on segmentation in Chapter 18, target markets can be based upon a number of factors such as:

● socio-economic groups;
● geographic location;
● age;
● sex;
● income levels;
● visitor type;
● benefits sought; and
● purchase behaviour and attitudes for both the international and domestic business, holiday visitor and recreationalist.

The target market acts as the focus for tailoring the mix so that target customers will judge the overall product to be superior to that of the competition. Segmentation and target marketing are central to efficient and effective marketing activity because they are instrumental in ensuring the marketing mix strategy is tailored to meet the specific needs of different customer groups.

Product

The effectiveness of planning the marketing mix depends as much on the ability to select the right target market as on the skill in devising a product which will generate high levels of satisfaction. Club Mediterranee is treated as having a singular product, yet it has more than 80 different holiday villages in over 30 countries, as well as boats and cruise ships, small 'villa' hotels and an escorted tour business.

Decisions regarding product formulation, therefore, involve the careful consideration of several important factors as considered below.

Service

This is concerned with creating the level of services to be offered. For a hotel, a tour operator/wholesaler, a restaurant or an airline, this poses the questions of how much of the service should the client be expected to perform and how much should be provided by staff? For example, self-service of food or the personal carrying of hand luggage is now thought of as acceptable and, at times, desirable by clients. Likewise, tea- and coffee-making facilities in hotel bedrooms where the guest helps him/herself is now seen to be integral to the accommodation product offering, especially if the provision of room service is limited to certain hours. Service provision for air travellers now satisfies communication needs, with some airlines offering an improved business product with in-flight telephone, telex or access to a personal computer. These developments are indicative of the relentless quest for cost-effective improvements to the service content of the tourism product.

Quality

Quality involves deciding on quality standards for the product and implementing a method of assurance on the performance level of staff and facilities. The management of quality is becoming an increasingly important management function (as discussed in Chapter 17) since it is crucial to create a good reputation for the quality of the product and service offered. This encourages a positive image for the company or organisation and a reputation for good quality is a major advantage in reducing the perception of risk in the minds of consumers. Tourism service providers are more likely to be successful if they can be depended upon to deliver higher-quality service levels than their competitors. Success through quality is often associated with the outcome of the relationship between a customer's prior expectations of service delivery and the perception of the actual service. With this in mind, Swissair aims for at least 96% of its passengers to rate the quality of its service as good or superior, otherwise it will take remedial action.

Range

It is necessary to decide how different individual products will fit into the overall range of the organisation's products offered to the market-place. A tour operator/wholesaler has to decide whether to include five-star or two-star hotels in their range of offering, or whether they should operate to traditional or newly emerging destinations. More recently the cruise market has expanded and many tour operators/wholesalers have altered their product range to include cruise ships to accommodate the resurgence of demand.

Tourism enterprises have to decide on the range of offers and how each product fits into the product mix. Such decisions will produce change over time, as is illuminated by some of the milestones in the development of Thomas Cook shown in Box 19.2.

Box 19.2 Example of the historical changes to the product range for Thomas Cook

1841	First excursion from Leicester to Loughborough
1845	Trip to Liverpool and excursions to Wales
1846	First tours to Scotland
1851	Trips for 165 000 people to the Great Exhibition
1855	First continental tours
1863	Tours organised to Switzerland
1866	First tours to North America
1869	First tours to the Holy Land
1872	Pioneers of round-the-world tours
1874	Traveller's cheques introduced
1902	First winter sports brochures and motor car tours
1919	The company advertises air tours
1927	First air charter, New York to Chicago for Dempsey fight
1939	First package tour to South of France
1972	Thomas Cook becomes part of the Midland Bank Group
1981	Agreement to launch Euro traveller's cheques
1988	Cessation of operation in the short-haul market
1989	Reinvestment in retail outlets to upgrade them
1989	Direct sales operation set up
1992	Thomas Cook sold by Midland Bank to Westdeutsche Landesbank (WestLB) and the LTU Group
1992	21.6% shareholding aquired from Owners Abroad in order to form an alliance (now First Choice)
1994	Thomas Cook corporate travel business and USA franchised travel offices sold to American Express
1994	Travel Kiosks set up to sell direct by the use of advanced technology.

Brand name

A brand name that is well known and associated with high satisfaction levels provides an improved image and added value to a product. This can also lead to consumers insisting on the product by brand name and, as a consequence of extreme brand loyalty, being less price sensitive.

Brands, and ranges of brands, may fall into a number of different categories:

● **Family brands.** This is where each of the company's products adopts the same brand name. Examples include many of the leading hotel companies which have a family name, such as Holiday Inn with its branded chains designed to attract different market segments.

● **Individual brands.** Alternatively, products offered by the same company may be branded very differently. For example, a tour operator can have individual brand names within its businesses, with its long-haul, medium and budget-priced product offerings, each having individual brand names unrelated to the others.

● **Own-brand and own-label brands.** Finally, organisations can have own-brand as well as own-label products. For example, Thomas Cook Holidays has its own brand selling long-haul holidays through a number of brochures. In addition, it has own-label brands which are offered via an alliance with First Choice Holidays.

This allows a synergy between the quality of other tour providers and the retail strength of Thomas Cook. As such, the Thomas Cook brand name can be strengthened.

There are strengths and weaknesses associated with each strategy. The individual brand name approach, for example, allows a company to search for the most appropriate brand name. Its weakness is that the promotional budget for each brand has to be sufficiently large to support that brand. With family brands there is a spin-off effect for each of the brands from the expenditure on any one brand. Conversely, if one of the family brands obtains poor publicity, because of association, there will be damage to the other brands. For family branding careful attention has to given to the quality control of the products. One other benefit of family branding is that each product brand performance (PBF) can be measured against the overall family brand performance (FBF). When FBF is divided by PBF and shows an increase over time, without good reason, it may mean that the product brand needs modification, revitalisation or a detailed review.

With individual branding an organisation is able to position brands and products at the cheaper (bottom) end of the market without the brand damaging the image of the rest of the company's brands. In addition, if there is bad publicity for one of the company's brands then the other company brands do not necessarily suffer.

Features and benefits

We know that consumers buy products for the benefits they are expected to deliver. It therefore makes sense to incorporate different features into the product that will help to differentiate it from the comparable product offered by competitors. Adding in the right features creates a higher probability that a purchase will occur. These features may be split into two basic categories:

Reduced risk

Tourism is normally associated with the risk of delayed flights, exchange rate fluctuations on little snow on skiing holidays. The potential risk of flight delay or inadequate snow cover on ski slopes can be insured against by the operator who passes on only a small premium to its clients in the price of the trip. Contract agreement to hotel rates, the early buying forward of currency or advance purchase of aircraft fuel will allow a company to offer the guarantee of no increase in a quoted price.

Value-added benefits

By complementing the basic product with special benefits that add value, the product is made more appealing to the consumer. Arranging a contract with car-parks near to airports in off-season periods can allow a company to offer the car-parking service free to its clients. The cost is passed on to each client as a fraction of the true cost of the service because the arrangement allows the car-park to acquire business at a difficult time. Features such as free car hire, pick up at the airport, fast check outs, study bedrooms and free tickets to tourism attractions or the theatre are all added benefits that can be planned into the product offer.

Price

The pricing policy selected for a tourism product is often directly related to the performance of its future demand. Setting the right price is also crucial to the profitability of the tourism enterprise. We believe that, of all the marketing mix, pricing decisions are the hardest to make. This is because prices for tourism products have to take into

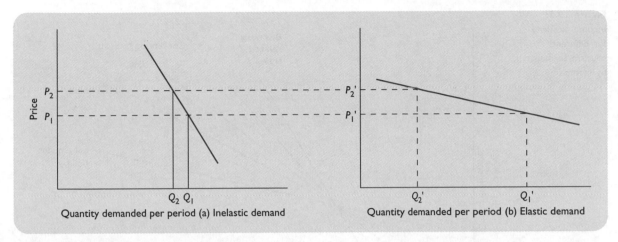

Figure 19.2: Price elasticity of demand

account the complexity created by seasonality of demand and the inherent perishability of the product. Also within tourism there are major differences in segments such as business travellers and those taking a vacation. The relative elasticities of demand for these segments are dissimilar and price sensitivity is affected by different factors.

Figure 19.2 shows demand curves that indicate different market reactions to price change, i.e. where demand is highly responsive (or price elastic) and where demand is not price responsive (or price inelastic). Tourism industry products related to vacations are associated with an elastic demand curve, where a small increase in price creates a large fall in demand. Leisure travel is price elastic because of the following:

● The ratio of tourism prices to income is normally high. This is the case not only for overseas travel but also for leisure centres, cinemas and attractions, especially in times of recession. However, the different types of tourism demand from business travel to deciding on a secondary holiday will be associated with different elasticities. These may be as shown in Figure 19.3.

● The consumer can choose a substitute or forgo the purchase if the overall value is considered to be unacceptable.

● It is relatively easy to judge the offer of alternative brands and products, and therefore easy to switch demand to cheaper alternatives. Although price may be an indicator of quality, the consumer is able to choose between several offers, by referring, for example, to the type of aircraft they may fly on or the star rating or brand of accommodation.

The setting of price cannot be solely concerned with the consumer. Care and attention have to be given to both the reaction of the consumer, as well as that of the competition. Owing to the high-risk nature of the tourism industry, a price advantage which takes market share from a competitor will often provoke a hostile re-pricing reaction. If Company A, in Figure 19.4(a), attempts to increase its market share by price cutting, it will need to take market share from Companies B and C. This is a situation in which C and B are likely to react by cutting their own prices. The outcome is that the market shares remain similar and can, as in the second example, lead the market to grow in volume, as in Figure 19.4(b), although not necessarily in overall revenue. The long-term result is that the market remains extremely unstable because smaller margins are being applied. In this situation an organisation has to ensure it has a high volume of business

Figure 19.3:
Income elasticity
for different
tourism segments
by income

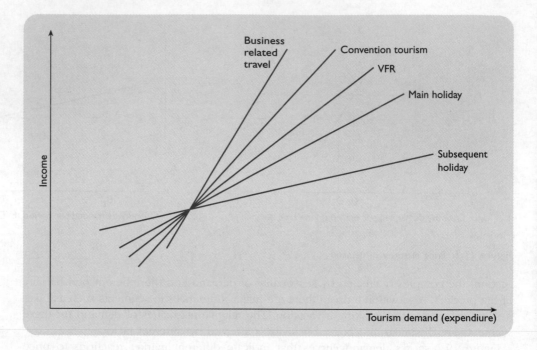

Figure 19.4: Price cutting

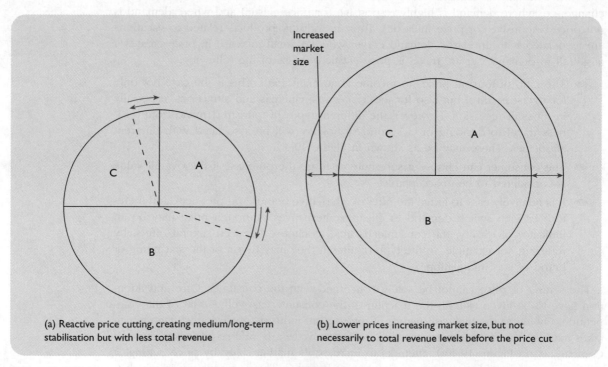

(a) Reactive price cutting, creating medium/long-term
stabilisation but with less total revenue

(b) Lower prices increasing market size, but not
necessarily to total revenue levels before the price cut

Box 19.3   Influences on pricing in the tourism industry

● The perishable nature of the product, which is unable to be stored until a future occasion, leads to various forms of last-minute tactical pricing.

● The high price elasticity of demand exhibited by holiday and leisure markets places emphasis on setting prices at the right levels.

● The volatility of the market due to short-run fluctuations in international costs, exchange rates, oil prices and political events requires sophisticated forward planning.

● Many companies are reliant on high volumes to break even and will forgo short-run profit in order to create acceptable load factor or occupancy levels.

● Cost control is an important part of pricing policy. Many tourism enterprises have high fixed costs and price near to break-even positions. This can make them vulnerable to financial collapse or takeover if costs are not controlled.

● Some regions and countries have price controls for airline travel and hotel accommodation.

● Seasonal demand leads to peak and low-season periods, which require demand management pricing to cope with the short-run capacity problems.

● Price is associated with the psychological aspects of both quality and status. It is therefore always important to gauge the way prices or their change will be perceived by the different target segments.

● Cash flow is high due to much of the payment for tourism products being made in advance of consumption. Many tourism companies make profit on the investment of this money.

in order to exceed its break-even point. Price-cutting policies have been a feature of the tour operating business in the UK and the dynamics of the theory above helps us understand what has led to the collapse of a whole range of different companies. Box 19.3 shows the various influences on pricing in the tourism industry.

Pricing policy has to consider the above and therefore the scope of choice is remarkably wide. The choice will probably be one or a combination of the following.

Cost-orientated pricing

Cost-orientated pricing refers to setting prices on the basis of an understanding of their costs.

Cost-plus pricing

Cost-plus pricing sets prices in relation to either marginal costs or total costs including overheads. A percentage mark-up is then normally applied to reach the final price.

This form of pricing is often used for the retail outlets of tourist attractions. Its weakness as a method of pricing for tourism is that it does not take into consideration demand for the product, what prices the market-place will bear and it is not based upon the price levels of the competitors. Knowing the cost breakdown of the product is crucial and it is often important to have calculated the operating price of a hotel bedroom or a sector flight airline seat. This allows the marketer to know what the effect of any tactical price reduction will be.

Rate of return

Rate of return pricing provides an organisation with an agreed rate of return on its investment. Whereas the cost-plus method concentrates on the costs associated with the running of the business, the rate of return method concentrates on the profits generated in relation to the capital invested. This approach is not appropriate for tourism enterprises as it ignores the need to link the pricing policy to the creation of a sales volume which is large enough to cover overheads and remains consistent over time.

To use either cost-plus or rate of return methods of pricing is generally not appropriate for tourism products that have to survive in a highly competitive market-place.

Demand-orientated pricing

Demand-orientated pricing takes into consideration the factors of demand rather than the level of costs in order to set the price. A conference centre, for example, may charge one price for admission to a rock concert and only half that price for admission to a classical concert.

Discrimination pricing

This is sometimes called flexible pricing and is often used in tourism where products are sold at two or more different prices. Quite often students and older people are charged lower prices at attractions, or events, than other segments. Discrimination pricing is often time-related, with cheaper drink charges in 'happy hour' periods or cheaper meal prices in the early evening prior to high-demand periods. For price discrimination to be successful it is necessary to be able to identify those segments that, without the price differentials, would be unable to purchase the product.

To obtain a high flow of business, a hotel will have to discount for customers who offer significant volume. This means that, while business travellers may benefit from corporate rates, those on vacation may be staying on tour operator/wholesaler rates.

Discrimination can also be based upon increasing the price of products that have higher potential demand. For example, if rooms in a hotel are all the same but some have good scenic views of the countryside or sea, then those rooms could be sold for a higher price.

Backward pricing

This is a market-based method of pricing that focuses on what the consumer is willing to pay. The price is worked backwards. First, an acceptable margin is agreed upon. Next, the costs are closely monitored so that the estimated final price is deemed to be acceptable to the target segment. The objective is to set a price that matches consumer preference. If necessary an adjustment is made to the quality of the product offer or service to meet the cost-led needs of this technique.

Tour operators/wholesalers selling on a price-led basis will often contract hotels one or two blocks back from the sea front, if this lowers the room rates making up the final price. Other methods include lowering the flight content of a holiday price by organising cheaper night flights which may also save on the first night's accommodation cost. To be successful with this method of pricing it is important to understand the psychological effects of creating products that may appeal to the price conscious. However, the holiday may not give satisfaction if the holiday experience and company are considered to be of poor quality.

Market penetration pricing

Market penetration pricing is adopted when an organisation wants to establish itself quickly in a market. Prices are set below those of the competition in order to create high growth for the company's products. Tour operators/wholesalers, when setting up an operation to a new destination, will use market penetration pricing for that destination in the first couple of years and then, once that destination becomes better established, will slowly increase the prices.

Skimming pricing

This method is utilised when there is a shortage of supply of the product and where demand will not be dampened by charging a premium price. Luxury villas with pools, set in good locations, are normally priced with higher margins than other accommodation products because of their shortage. Market skimming policies can only occur where there is a healthy demand for the tourism product on offer.

Whatever pricing policy is adopted, an organisation has to take into consideration the potential tourist's perceptual assessment. In deciding to buy a product, a consumer has to be willing to give up something in order to enjoy the satisfactions and benefits the product will deliver. This concept is more complex than it seems. The majority of tourists are looking for value when they buy product. Value can be treated as a function of quality and price, i.e.

$$\text{value} = \frac{\text{quality}}{\text{price}}$$

If a consumer believes the quality of a product is good, he or she will be willing to make greater sacrifices in order to purchase that product. That is how first-class travel can still continue to be successful on different forms of transport such as trains, aircraft and cruise ships.

If prices change then this can affect the consumer's quality perception. A price reduction can be associated with a belief that the company is in financial trouble, that it will have to cut service and quality, or that the prices are falling and if they wait, will come down even more. The value of the product is thought to have decreased because quality is seen to have fallen by a greater ratio than prices. The following shows the perception that the new value is only at half the level of its former position:

$$\text{value} = \frac{\text{quality}}{\text{price}}$$

then if

$$V = \frac{Q/2x}{P/x}$$

then

$$1/2 \ V = \frac{Q}{P}$$

Alternatively, a price increase may be interpreted as the way the organisation is going to pay to improve the quality and service of the product. However, some consumers may

Figure 19.5:
Pricing policy
considerations

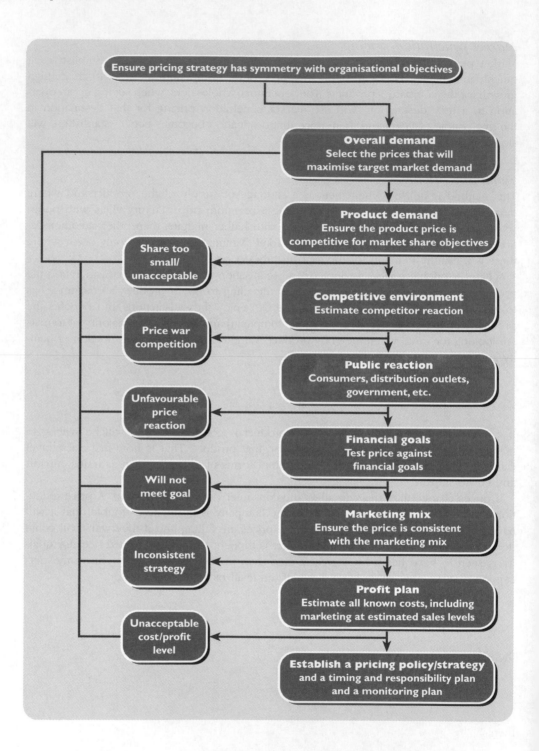

simply think that the company is being greedy and that quality has not improved. This means the consumer judges the value to have fallen.

To ensure the maximum chance of success for the pricing policy adopted, there is a need to check each stage of the procedure as in Figure 19.5. This figure identifies the important considerations required for the successful evolution of a pricing policy.

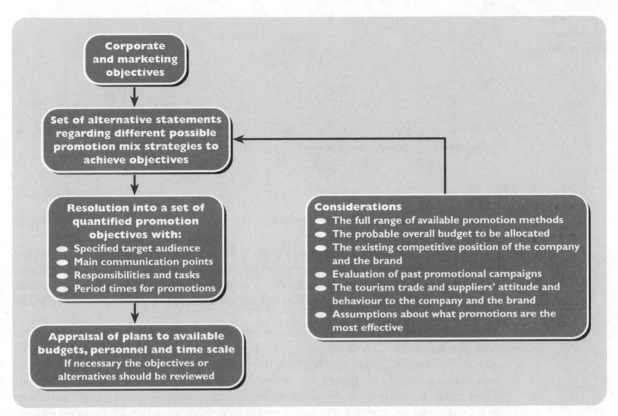

Figure 19.6: Development of promotional objectives

Promotion

Promotion is the descriptive term for the mix of communication activities that tourism organisations, or tourist boards, carry out in order to influence those publics on whom their sales depend. The important groups, which need to be influenced, are not simply the target market group of current, and potential customers. There is the need also to influence trade contacts such as retail agents and suppliers, as well as opinion formers such as journalists and travel writers. Even local, national and international politicians and important professional groups may need to be influenced.

Setting objectives

A range of promotional methods can be employed by the tourism marketer, so it is important to define what the promotion has to achieve. It is necessary to define the marketing objectives clearly so that the most effective types of promotion can be utilised. Figure 19.6 explains how promotional objectives can be developed.

Communication effects

There is always the need to plan to achieve the most effective response from the target market. An important part of the promotional effort is the building of brand and product

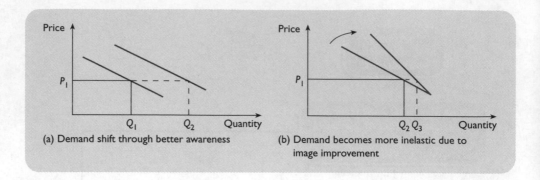

(a) Demand shift through better awareness

(b) Demand becomes more inelastic due to image improvement

awareness. Sometimes it will take a long time for the consumer to know about the brand and the type of products on offer.

A promotion campaign should aim to provide for knowledge of the product, to ensure the consumer will feel favourably towards the product, and build up preference for it. Any campaign has to sell the benefits that a customer would be seeking in a credible way so that the potential customer feels conviction and is more likely than not to make a purchase.

Figure 19.7 shows how a promotional campaign should aim to create awareness through information. The development of a positive image for a product creates a more price-elastic demand curve, which means the product is more resilient to price rises and does not have to rely on having low prices. In Figure 19.7(a) P_1Q_1 is existing demand before a campaign has been developed to create more awareness in the target audience. At P_1Q_2 demand has increased because, owing to a promotional effect, more people are aware of the company, the product and the benefits it can deliver. At P_1Q_3 in Figure 19.7(b) the campaign has improved the image of the organisation or destination so that more status is derived in travelling with the brand or to a destination. This changes the shape of the demand whereby it becomes more inelastic.

Advertising and sales promotion are the most widely used forms of promotion. Because of the intrusive characteristic of these forms of promotion, most consumers relate ideas of marketing to the use of advertising or sales promotion. The other major forms include public relations and personal selling.

Advertising

Advertising is any paid form of non-personal communication through the media which details a product that has an identified sponsor. The media may include travel guides, newspapers, magazines, radio, television, direct mail and billboards.

Advertising is used to achieve a whole range of objectives which may include changing attitudes or building image, as well as achieving sales. Advertising is often described as 'above-the-line' promotion with all other forms of promotion being termed 'below-the-line'.

Sales promotion

Sales promotion involves any activity that offers an incentive to induce a desired result from potential customers, trade intermediaries or the sales force. Sales promotion campaigns will add value to the product because the incentives will ordinarily not accompany the product. For example, free wine or free accommodation offers are frequently used in sales promotion campaigns for hotel restaurants which need improved demand at certain periods. Most incentives are planned to be short term in nature.

An integral part of sales promotion is the aspect of merchandising. Merchandising includes materials used in travel agents or in-house locations to stimulate sales. For a hotel, these would include tent cards which may attempt to sell cocktails or deserts, menus, in room material, posters and displays. Merchandising is important as a means of creating impulse purchase or reminding the consumer of what is on offer.

Sales promotion is often used in combination with other promotional tools in order to supplement the overall effort. However, it has to be remembered that it is sometimes difficult to terminate or change special promotions without causing adverse affects. Airline frequent flyer loyalty programmes are an example of this. Also a sales promotion (or series of promotions) has to take account of the likely effect it may have on the image of the brand or outlet. For example, there may be an unanticipated surge of negative perception which may occur due to association with banal and frivolous promotions.

Personal selling

Personal selling is an attempt to gain benefit through face-to-face or telephone contact between the seller's representative and those people with whom the seller wants to communicate. This type of selling may be based upon a non-profit-making tourist attraction as well as the conference manager of a large hotel.

A number of employees in travel agents or retail related to tourism are often viewed as order *takers* but they could possibly be order *procurers*. The intent of personal selling is:

- to obtain a sale – often customers enter the retail outlet after acquiring information and the salesperson needs to persuade potential customers to purchase;
- to stimulate sales of 'impulse buy' purchases by bringing attention to extra requirements such as travel insurance, car hire, excursions and airport transfers; or
- to complete a successful transaction with the customer utilising a range of sales skills. This will leave the customer satisfied and well informed about the detail of the transaction.

The benefit of personal selling is that a salesperson can adapt the communication of benefits to be gained to the specific needs of the customer. The feedback process of listening to the customer's needs allows the salesperson to be flexible in his or her approach. This is made easier in a selling situation because the personal contact produces heightened awareness and attention by the customer. However, the sales functions of retailers have to be carefully handled because staff who lack empathy will be judged as 'pushy'.

Public relations

Public relations is non-personal communication that changes opinion or achieves coverage in a mass medium and that is not paid for by the source. The coverage could include space given to a press release or favourable editorial comment. PR is important not only in obtaining editorial coverage, but also in suppressing potential bad coverage. An organisation that has good links with the media is more likely to have the opportunity to stop or moderate news that could be damaging to their organisation prior to its release.

The major benefit of PR is that it can provide and enhance an organisation's image. This is very important for service-based organisations which are reliant on a more tangible positive image in order to be successful. PR is a highly credible form of communication as people like to read 'news stories' and will believe them to be less biased than information provided in advertisements. However, editorial decisions over what is communicated will produce control over the message, its timing, placement and coverage.

Other promotional activity

There is a growing use of **sponsorship** and **direct marketing**. These do not comfortably fit into the other four promotion categories. Sponsorship is the material or financial support of a specific activity, normally but not exclusively sport or the arts, which does not form part of the sponsor organisation's normal business. Direct marketing is used extensively by direct-sell tour operators/wholesalers such as Saga Holidays and Portland. The main method is direct mail, which is postal communication by an identified sponsor. This is being expanded into database marketing based upon relationship marketing practices.

In addition, because tourism is an intangible product, a great deal of promotion includes the production of printed communications such as brochures or sales leaflets. The design, compilation and printing of tourism brochures is one of the most important of promotion functions. Printed communications are often costly. In fact the printing and distribution costs of brochures constitute the largest part of most marketing budgets within the tourism industry. This is a necessary expenditure as the brochure or leaflet is the major sales tool for tour operators/wholesalers and tourism organisations.

Characteristics of each promotional technique

Each of the above promotional elements has the capacity to achieve a different promotional objective. While personal selling has high potency for achieving communication objectives, only a relatively small number of people can be contacted. Therefore advertising is a more effective method of reaching a high number of people at relatively low unit cost. Public relations is more credible than advertising but organisations lack the control they have over advertising messages which may also be repeated on a regular basis. Thus, when it is difficult to raise advertising budgets, public relations is a lower-cost alternative, but it is difficult to control the timing and consistency of PR coverage. Sales promotion, such as leaflet drops that offer price discounts, may produce an initial trial for a product, such as the purchase of a leisure break in a hotel, but this type of promotion can only be used over a short-term period.

Each element of the promotions mix has its own strengths and weaknesses. While this may include the factors of cost, ability to target different groups and control, there are other important considerations. Figure 19.8 indicates the relative strengths of each of the four forms of promotion. They are compared on the basis of the level of awareness of the communication, its comprehension as well as whether it can build conviction and succeed in creating action.

Place (distribution)

The special characteristics of the tourism product have led to specific forms of distribution. The tourism product is one where no transfer of ownership takes place and service is simply rented or consumed. However, prior to consumption, the tourism product

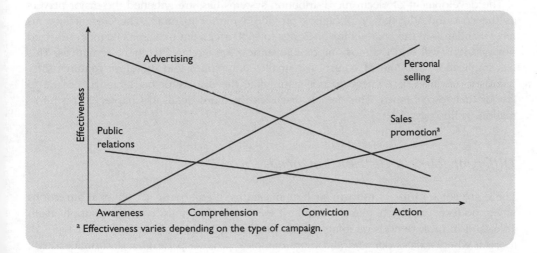

Figure 19.8:
Effectiveness of
different
promotion
methods

ᵃ Effectiveness varies depending on the type of campaign.

has to be both available and accessible. This requires a distribution system. A distribution system is the channel used to gain access, or means by which a tourism supplier gains access, to the potential buyers of the product.

The following aspects of tourism distribution should be noted:

- There is no actual product being distributed. There are only clues given through persuasive communication about the product.

- Tourism normally involves the episode of a purchase act related to decisions over travel to a destination, the stay and return. As such the nature of travel distribution is related to entering into the production as well as consumption of the product. Therefore the method of selling and environment within which the purchase is made becomes part of the overall tourism experience.

- Major amounts of money are allocated by the industry to the production and printing of literature as well as to its delivery direct to the customer or to the retail travel agent. Brochures are produced in high quantity, and often the distribution cost involves an amount for warehousing and the planned despatch of packs of brochures through different modes of transport.

- Distribution of overseas holidays in the UK is dominated by travel agents who sell a homogeneous set of choices. These agents have a vast amount of power and control over the companies that sell the products (principals). Agents decide on the brochures to display on their racks and the companies they will recommend to consumers.

There is continuing development of CRSs or GDSs. These offer an agent instant access to airline bookings as well as the major hotel, car hire and cruise lines. Such systems allow agents to tailor holidays to suit individual client requirements and this may lead to increases in direct bookings. The CRSs are led by developments from the principal airlines, with Galileo dominating the UK and being strong in both Europe and the USA, Amadeus being predominately strong in Europe, Sabre dominating in the USA, mainly because of its 100% ownership by American Airlines and, finally, Worldspan which is of less significance than the others.

The development of electronic distribution systems has strengthened the major players as the cost and adoption implications provide a barrier to entry. The current systems have standardised the channel for bookings to such an extent that small or medium-sized organisations will find it almost impossible to develop agency channel alternatives. This has implications for loss of control for smaller companies and therefore requires safeguards to ensure CRS owners do not manipulate the display or bookings procedure to favour their own brands. This area is discussed in more detail in Chapter 20 on information technology.

Different tourism distribution needs

There are some forms of tourism such as museums, theme parks or physical attractions where no form of prior booking is required as there is almost always excess supply available, and in peak periods queuing is the method of allocation. There are other types of tourism where excess demand and more complex product packaging and financial risk create the need for sophisticated advance booking systems. The booking system enables the organisation to spread demand as the consumer can often be convinced to arrive or travel at a different time.

In order for a tourism organisation to sell in advance of consumption and to have a record of the reservation, the company has to sell its available capacity through an inventory system. Whether it is a small guest house or large hotel, a farmhouse or cruise ship, some method of allocating capacity and creating reservations, without creating overbooking is important. The timing of these bookings may range from minutes prior to departure for an aircraft or a reserved place on a train service to several years for a major conference. For these reasons, the use of CRS is common in tourism. These systems combine the memory capacity of computers (to update and store information constantly) with the communication facility of telecommunications, which rapidly inform travel agents of the current capacity remaining. Such systems can then be programmed to maximise the 'yield' of the capacity as it is sold to the customer.

The next consideration is related to the location of the business. A well-located hotel, theatre or attraction will be able to pick up passing demand. In this case the consumers will find the product easily and there may be less need for a separate distribution channel. This is because the product is easily available for purchase.

In an increasingly competitive world, however, it has been necessary for most organisations to consider different forms of direct distribution. Companies are able to sell direct either from their place of location, or through direct marketing methods. Many hotels organise weekend break programmes to improve the weekend occupancy levels. These weekend packages are often promoted directly in newspapers and booked directly with the hotel. Thomas Cook set up Thomas Cook Direct in 1989 to offer the flexibility for individuals to phone their agency from home or work in order to receive information or make credit card bookings. The success can be gauged from the fact that by 1994, the service employed 150 staff. A more recent introduction by the company is that of the 'Travel Kiosk' in 1994 which is a self-service system utilising electronic images and sound to promote different products. The system also has the facility for the terminal to take a credit card for a sale and provide a printed receipt and booking confirmation.

The problem for direct selling by tour operators/wholesalers is how to sell last minute availability without the benefit of retail outlets. This is alleviated by the large organisations as they are able to switch some aspects of the product, such as the flight component, to their other brands selling through travel agents.

Case Study 19.1 Reasons for the use of retail travel agents

● **Easy accessibility:**
- To a range and choice of brochures.
- To product components of visas, traveller's cheques, insurance, etc.
- To booking outlets in every main town and city.
- To an alternative agent as well as products and brands.

● **Convenience:**
- For obtaining independent information and advice.
- For making the purchase and payment for the holiday.
- For making complaints and being represented by a third party if things go wrong.

● **Habit:**
- People can get into a pattern of behaviour which becomes habit forming. Only a major campaign by direct mail from direct-sell tour operators/wholesalers could change this habit.

● **Security/risk:**
- Consumers feel more secure when dealing with a reputable operator or agent.

● **Environment/atmosphere:**
- Travel agents offer an environment that is part of the holiday experience. The travel agency environment is the perfect setting for personal selling methods which are a powerful means of generating bookings.

● **Economic:**
- Because travel agents compete on price or added value, and tour operators/wholesalers have the smallest of margins, there is little difference in the price between travel agent's products and those available through direct-sell channels.

Source: based on Gilbert (1990).

Consumers and distribution

There has been a resistance among consumers to buy overseas holidays direct which seems surprising when there is a tradition of purchasing a domestic holiday direct. There is little doubt that for many the convenience of using an agent, for an overseas holiday, is an important element in the buying process. This is because a travel agent may offer greater opportunities for one-stop shopping which allows the choice between competing tour operators/wholesalers, parallel purchase of insurance, car hire, rail travel to the airport, traveller's cheques and so on. Case Study 19.1 describes a number of benefits related to travel agents showing why more travellers have not booked direct (Gilbert, 1990).

The marketing mix revisited: are the four Ps sufficient?

The adaptation of the marketing mix by authors such as Booms and Bitner (1981) has been based upon arguments that stress the original marketing mix is more appropriate to manufacturing rather than service companies. For example, Booms and Bitner added three extra Ps (see Figure 19.9):

Product	Price	Place	Promotion	People	Physical evidence	Process
Range	Level	Location	Advertising	Personnel:	Environment:	Policies
Quality	Discounts:	Accessibility	Personal selling	Training	Furnishings	Procedures
Level	Allowances	Distribution	Sales promotion	Discretion	Colour	Mechanisation
Brand name	Commissions	channels	Publicity	Commitment	Layout	Employee
Service line	Payment terms	Distribution	Public relations	Incentives	Noise level	discretion
Warranty	Customer's	coverage		Appearance	Facilitating	Customer
After-sales	perceived			Interpersonal	goods	involvement
service	value			behaviour	Tangible clues	Customer
	Quality/price			Attitudes		direction
	Differentiation			Other customers:		Flow of
				Behaviour		activities
				Degree of		
				involvement		
				Customer/		
				customer		
				contact		

Source: Reprinted by permission of the American Marketing Association from Booms and Bitner, 1981

Figure 19.9: The marketing mix for services

- people;
- physical evidence; and
- process.

Authors such as Booms and Bitner argue the marketing mix of four Ps is not comprehensive enough for the tourism and hospitality industry. The major difference is said to be the intangible element of human behaviour where quality and its control is of paramount importance.

We believe that there is a need for more research into the industry and its marketing before the four Ps require revision. For the present it is believed the four Ps offer an adequate framework into which the differences can be incorporated. The main task of marketers in tourism and hospitality is to understand the characteristics of the products they plan, control and manage. This will ensure that managers will attempt to control the aspects of the marketing mix which have most bearing on the satisfaction level of consumers. We provided the basis of this assessment in Chapter 17 on marketing management.

While it is obvious that there are differences between manufactured and service products, the framework of the four Ps is sufficient for planning purposes as physical evidence, people or process are part of the category of product or its implementation. The four categories do not presuppose the relegation of service product considerations to secondary importance. On the contrary, the four categories should ensure that within product formulation, greater focus will be placed on the integration of all the different service management considerations.

It should be apparent that marketing mix decisions must be geared to achieving the objectives of the company or organisation, and should be linked to acceptability throughout the organisation. While marketing departments often lead in setting the marketing mix strategy, they should not ignore input from others and should be sensitive to views on whether the strategy will be workable from an operational standpoint.

The marketing mix offers the range and spread of alternative strategies by which a marketer can influence demand. However, while the available range is very similar for all tourism marketers, the choice is not. For example, an NTO will not normally be involved in developing products or setting prices. The process of mix formulation and balancing is quite often unique to each organisation.

For an organisation to be successful with its marketing mix, it has to develop a differential advantage which will distinguish the organisation's product offering(s) from that of the competition. Only when an organisation has built an advantage will it find that customers seek it out, in which case it is easier to create higher profits. The advantage may be based upon quality, image, or product concept. Center Parcs in the UK has developed an advantage and the results can be seen in the high year-round demand for its product.

Destination marketing

Destinations rely on tourism as a major tool in the creation of economic development and support for the indigenous population. Destinations can be local, regional or even national: we can speak of America, California or San Francisco with each, and all, capable of being a destination.

The marketing of destinations is complex as we are dealing not only with the tangible inventory of physical attributes such as the natural geography, built environment and attractions, accommodation and transport facilities but also intangible social and

Case Study 19.2 The marketing of destinations

The marketing of destinations is a relatively new departure for many localities, particularly at the regional and local level. At these levels the lead agency tends to be the public sector and this in turn, has a number of implications for the marketing process which are rooted in the inability of the public sector to control the product. In addition, there is an issue here in terms of whether we should transform places where people live work and play into *products*. We are only beginning to understand how to translate generic marketing approaches to destinations. There are some key areas to consider here:

- The images of the destination which the marketing campaigns wish to communicate should take into account the views and sensitivities of local people.

- Public sector agencies have to be *even-handed* in their support for businesses at the destination – it is difficult politically for them to *back winners*.

- The public sector controls neither the business plans of private sector companies at the destination, nor the quality of service delivery.

- Tourist destinations often lack several key strategic business units and their limited resource base means that they are unable to redress this balance in their *portfolio*.

- Public sector marketing organisations seldom *close* a sale, rather they are instrumental in attracting the consumer to the *point of sale* – usually a private sector company. It is therefore difficult to evaluate the effectiveness of destination marketing.

- Finally, the critical issue of resources is a constant problem for public sector marketing budgets, especially for activities which may be perceived as dispensable – such as market research – but which in reality are crucial to success in the tourism market-place.

cultural factors. Although the destination is often the focus for all the marketing effort, it does not follow that there will be a local, regional or national agency that will take responsibility for its marketing (see Case Study 19.2). It is also often the case that where there is an organisation charged with destination marketing, its responsibility is based upon a fairly narrow set of powers and limited resources. Traditionally the public sector has been involved in destination marketing through NTOs, regional boards such as DMOs or local authorities, but increasingly, a trend is emerging where marketing agencies or conference and visitor bureau are established for cities. Such agencies are often funded by a mix of both private and public means.

The traditional role of many of these approaches has been elementary. The emphasis has been confined to promotional strategies which aim to improve the destination image or to produce more positive 'mental concepts' in relation to both potential as well as actual tourists. This is often related to the selection of desirable market segments that are targeted through the use of advertising, direct mail, print or PR campaigns (as discussed earlier in this chapter). There is further emphasis on providing information at the destination through information posters or tourist information centres.

Destinations need to identify those product attributes that will appeal to different tourist segments and then to ensure that the promotional campaign delivers a cohesive message. There is also the need to produce a distinctive identity or 'brand' which forms the basis of the 'positioning' of a destination area, providing it with a personality and differentiating it from competitors.

De Chernatony and McDonald (1992) describe the necessary attributes of a successful brand and these may also be applied to tourism destinations:

> *A successful brand is an identifiable product, service, person or place augmented in such a way that the buyer, or user, perceives relevant, unique added values which match their needs most closely. Its success results from being able to sustain these added values against competitors.*

Such results may be achieved through the theming of an area by linking it to a famous personality who may have lived in the area such as a painter (Constable), a writer or poet (Hemingway or Wordsworth), a TV series or film, an historical era (Pompeii) or seasonal beauty (New England in the autumn). There are many other themes than these, but all need to be developed with a creative flair for the tastes of the potential visitor as well as the acceptability of the theme to the media.

The involvement of tourist boards at the national and regional level is often one of facilitation. Facilitation is made up of a series of assistance schemes which support the constituent service sectors of the tourist industry forming the accommodation, transport and attraction provision of a country, region or locality. This may take the form of a set of objectives related to:

- the development of specific tourism areas or products;
- the targeting of specific segments from generating areas;
- the level of expenditure available;
- a range of promotional activities (PR, advertising, exhibitions, literature production); or
- the need for cooperative private initiatives or expenditure.

The industry is diverse and fragmented, comprising many small companies which require help in many areas such as:

- the collection and use of research data;
- the organisation of trade exhibitions and shows;
- representation through overseas offices;
- the production of trade manuals, catalogues and brochures (which can have space bought by smaller companies);
- the development of global reservation systems which can provide local information on a global basis; and
- research.

The facilitation process can help create an overall brand image of a destination through the total activity which takes place. However, the marketing, through all forms of promotion, will create a specific brand image. This is beneficial if a strong brand image is created.

An area that has a strong brand image is able:

- to achieve better margins and higher prices than commodity positioned brands;
- to differentiate itself more easily from competitors;
- to provide a sense of added value and so more easily entice customers to purchase;
- to act as a sign and enticement to the potential traveller; which implies fulfilment of expectations;
- to build repeat visits and loyalty; and
- to improve the strength of its position as a status area rather than as a commodity.

A destination has an image of place associated with it. This can be based upon differences related to what is normal in both a tourist-generating area and in the culture of the destination. The differences may be real or imagined. Promotion of a destination is based on an image selected by the tourism marketer and communicated to the generating markets, often providing stereotypical images of an exotic, carefree host culture. In reality this may mask a whole set of socio-cultural realities of what life is like for the average inhabitant of a destination.

The power to portray selective images of place relies on factors such as whether a tourist is a first-time visitor or a repeat visitor and also on the amount of information the tourist has gleaned from television, films, books or friends. A destination, once branded and having communicated a distinctive image, is in a far stronger position to influence demand if problems arise of price increases, excess demand and crowding or unfavourable currency exchange rates.

The Spanish Tourist Board, faced with the loss of a strong Spanish image for its resort areas, embarked upon an exercise to reposition and re-brand the country. The history, culture, traditions and inland areas had been under-promoted and weakly communicated. The new campaign from 1992 emphasised the 'Spanishness' of the country within a campaign which stressed, 'Spain – Passion for life'. The painter, Miro, was commissioned to create a logo that would reflect the fundamental spirit of Spain. He created a vibrant logo reflecting the national flag colours of yellow and red and this was used on all communication messages.

Consumers' concept of 'self-image'

When consumers choose among brands, they rationally consider practical issues about the relative functional capabilities of all the brands on offer. At the same time, they evaluate different brand personalities, forming a view about the brand that most closely represents the image with which they wish to be associated.

Applying this to tourism, it is possible to suggest that when competing destinations are perceived as being equal and similar in terms of their physical capabilities, the brand that comes closest to enhancing the consumer's self-concept is more likely to be chosen. Consumers look to brands not only for what they can do, but also for the message they communicate about the purchaser to peer groups. Trips to the south of France, for example, are not chosen just for their functional excellence, but also because they make an important statement about the traveller.

According to de Chernatony and McDonald (1992), the symbolic nature of brands increases the attraction for consumers as they:

- help set social scenes and enable people to mix with each other more easily;
- enable consumers to convey messages about themselves;
- provide a basis for better understanding of the way people act; and
- help consumers say something to themselves.

In effect, consumers are transmitting subtle messages to others by purchasing and displaying the use of particular brands in the hope that their reference groups decode the messages in a positive and acceptable way. Consumers hold what is called their own 'self-image' and buy brands that conform to that image. Consumers, therefore, could be said to admit brands and their 'personalities' into their social circle, in much the same way as consumers enjoy having like-minded people around them. When friends or colleagues admire a holiday destination choice, the traveller feels pleased that the destination brand reinforces his or her self-image and may therefore repeat the purchase.

The economic and social situation in which consumers find themselves will dictate, to some extent, the type of image they wish to project. Through anticipating and subsequently evaluating the people that they will meet at a particular event or destination, consumers then seek brands to reflect the situational self-image that they wish to display.

In addition, many consumers will also select a brand with which they are familiar and which, it has been proved, is capable of providing satisfaction and quality. A recognised destination will thus often be selected over an unknown destination: 'People will often buy a familiar brand because they are comfortable with the familiar' (Aaker, 1991). The awareness factor is also particularly important. The establishment of a strong brand image makes it more likely that the destination will be remembered and evaluated against other brands. A weak destination brand usually has little chance of entering any assessment and consequently will not be as successful.

Conclusion

The marketing mix cannot be effective without a full understanding of the target market and the needs of each of the segments. The marketing mix is formulated and implemented to satisfy the target market. We take the marketing mix to be made up of the four Ps of product, price, promotion and place (distribution), but there are alternative approaches where authors argue for an expansion owing to the service characteristics of tourism and hospitality products. However, the additional ingredients may be included in the headings associated with the four Ps and, as long as the characteristics of the tourism and hospitality product are emphasised, there is little benefit in predating McCarthy's simplification of 1978.

Chapter discussion questions

1. Identify the elements of the marketing mix and explain how the marketing of services might differ from the marketing of goods.

2. Consider the role and importance of the target market and its implications for the manipulation of the various elements of the marketing mix.

3. How is new technology affecting product formulation and distribution of the tourism product?

4. Discuss the most appropriate method for setting the price of a tourism product.

Recommended further reading

- Gilbert, D. C. (1990) *Strategic Marketing Planning for National Tourism*, **1**(90), 18–27.
- Kotler, P. and Armstrong, G. (1996) *Principles of Marketing*, Prentice Hall, Englewood Cliffs, NJ.
- Middleton, V. (1994) *Marketing in Travel and Tourism*, Butterworth-Heinemann, Oxford.

Bibliography

- Aaker, D. A. (1991) *Managing Brand Equity: Capitalising on the Value of a Brand Name*, The Free Press, New York.
- Aaker, D. A. and Biel, A. L. (1993) *Brand Equity and Advertising*, Lawrence Erlbaum Associates.
- Booms, B. H. and Bitner, M. J. (1981) 'Marketing strategies and organization structures for service firms', pp. 47–51 in *Marketing of Services*, Donnelly, J. and George, W. R. (eds), American Marketing Association, Chicago, IL.
- Borden, N. H. (1965) 'The concept of the marketing mix', pp. 386–97 *Science in Marketing*, Schwartz, G. Wiley, Chichester.
- de Chernatony, L. and Daniels, K. (1994) 'Developing a more effective brand positioning', *Journal of Brand Management*, **1**(6), 373–9.
- de Chernatony, L. and McDonald, M. H. B. (1992) *Creating Powerful Brands*, Butterworth-Heinemann, Oxford.
- de Chernatony, L. and McWilliam, G. (1989) 'The varying nature of brands as assets', *International Journal of Advertising*, **8**, 339–49.
- Gilbert, D. C. (1990) 'European product purchase methods and systems', *The Service Industries Journal*, **10**(4), 664–79.
- Hankinson, G. and Cowking, P. (1993), *Branding in Action: Cases and Strategies for Profitable Brand Management*, McGraw-Hill, London.
- Kotler, P. and Armstrong, G. (1996) *Principles of Marketing*, Prentice Hall, Englewood Cliffs, NJ.
- Kotler, P. (1991) *Marketing Management*, 7th edn, Prentice Hall, Hemel Hempstead.
- Kotler, P. and Armstrong, G. (1996) *Principles of Marketing*, Prentice Hall, Englewood Cliffs, NJ.
- McArdle, J. (1989) 'Product branding – the way forward', *Tourism Management*, **10**, 201.
- McCarthy, E. J. (1978) *Basic Marketing: A Managerial Approach*, 6th edn, Irwin, Homewood, IL.

The future of tourism

Introduction

A contemporary textbook, such as this one, would not be complete without an appraisal of some of the probable developments that will influence the future direction of tourism. While we have already reviewed many of the key trends in tourism demand, supply, marketing and distribution during the course of previous chapters, this section seeks to integrate themes that have already been addressed separately.

Future trends in tourism demand

The tourism system generally, and tourism demand in particular, have, historically, been susceptible to external influences and events which have demonstrated not only the vulnerability of tourism in the short term, but also its resilience in the long term. Although tourism demand has often dramatically fallen as a result of an unexpected political, economic or social event, looking back we can see that levels of demand are unaffected as the time perspective lengthens. Indeed, the overall trend for tourism demand remains upwards. This is not the case, however, for individual tourism destinations that have been subject to changes in tastes and fashion. Nevertheless, the unpredictability of external variables such as war, recession, natural or human disasters and fluctuations in exchange rates, result in severe difficulties for forecasters of volumes and patterns of demand for tourism. Consequently, statistical predictions of tourism growth rates must always be reviewed and interpreted with caution.

Despite these difficulties, however, there remain a number of key trends in respect of future tourism demand. Firstly, it will continue to grow on a global scale and current predictions estimate that by the year 2020 there will be 1.6 billion international tourist arrivals. It is anticipated that both domestic and international travel will continue to experience large growth rates and that while demand for tourism will almost certainly be heavily concentrated in Europe and North America, continued economic growth in the EAP region will result in these emergent nations becoming major generators and receivers of tourism activity. This development may be attributed to the major determinants of demand in these areas: an increase in disposable income, paid holiday entitlement and levels of education, all of which have historically stimulated demand for tourism. Other regions too, are also becoming major players on the global scene. For example, political developments in Eastern Europe have unlocked the region to tourism in respect of both demand and supply and stimulated investment in tourism training and education, infrastructure and superstructure.

Tourism demand, therefore, will continue to be influenced by economic and political changes globally. Likewise, demographic and social trends prevalent in populations around the world will also be significant features in the future direction of tourism demand. In particular, they are driving the continued trends towards shorter trips taken more frequently, an increased emphasis on home-based leisure and the emergence of the 'new tourist', all of which have an impact on the supply of tourism.

Future trends in the supply of tourism

Although it is almost impossible to identify a starting point for the tourism system, destinations must respond to demand trends if they are to continue to meet the needs of their markets and to maintain or extend their product life cycles. Thus, successful destinations are becoming more adept at researching their markets and implementing procedures to develop appropriate products to ensure market satisfaction.

Increasingly, destinations are recognising the need to plan and manage their resources to protect and enhance their products, both artificial and natural, for future generations. The growth of so-called 'sustainable tourism' has occurred as a response to the embracing of the 'green conscience' by the mainstream population. Destinations are necessarily having to become more concerned about implementing planning procedures that ensure protection of a resource while simultaneously attracting a volume of tourists that will bring economic benefits without compromising the socio-cultural and environmental fabric of the host community.

This balancing act between the stakeholders and interest groups has become a key theme in tourism. Destinations are becoming obliged to introduce strategies for minimising the negative impacts of tourism activity while simultaneously emphasising and maximising the positive effects. Many of these strategies have been criticised for doing little more than playing into the hands of the tourism industry but, arguably, they remain a step forward and crucial to destination management as we approach the next millennium. These developments have gone hand in hand with the move towards community-based and integrated planning philosophies which are now more visible in respect of tourism. Linked to this aspect is the trend towards enhanced public and private sector cooperation. In the Western World, lack of public sector funding and a withdrawal of governmental support has necessitated a move towards alliances and collaboration. Building bridges with the local community and local businesses to educate and involve has become a core function for many public sector tourism offices and this is a development which will become even more perceptible – and necessary – in the future. In addition, many tourism destinations that are established and outdated are having to come to terms with diversification and improvement. For many, the negative impacts of tourism have all but destroyed the natural resources but it is possible to identify areas which have, through innovative developmental, planning and management techniques, reversed the trend and successfully relaunched the destination.

Future transportation trends

As demand for tourism continues to grow, transportation networks around the world, particularly the airline network, will also be expanded at rapid rate in order to accommodate this growth. This trend is likely to have a number of serious implications. Firstly, many key areas around the world are already experiencing severe congestion with outdated air traffic control technology, inadequate infrastructure, restrictions on gate and slot availability at key airports and severe land-use conflicts. Local opposition to enhanced facilities in many developed regions of the world is also hampering attempts by authorities to overcome the aforementioned problems and issues. Noise, atmospheric emissions, waste and congestion remain serious threats to the continued expansion of international tourism. Despite legislation and technological advancements – the key two-pronged strategy to deal with these problems – the predicted increase in traffic and capacity looks set to transcend the limited relief that these strategies offer.

Globalisation and strategic alliances are other key trends that predominate in the airline industry. Increasingly, a small number of large, profitable airlines, are setting their sights beyond their immediate national boundaries; beyond even their continental boundaries. These airlines are seeking to develop a truly global product and service by linking up with other partners and providers to offer a world-wide route network.

Other modes of transport are also subject to key trends which will affect future operation and direction. Specifically, surface transport is becoming faster and more efficient and may even begin to compete with air transport on certain short- and medium-haul routes. In addition, surface transport in the form of cruising is becoming a popular alternative once again as a result of innovative new product development and creative marketing strategies which have successfully attracted new market segments, most notably younger travellers.

For all transportation one of the major influences looks set to be continued deregulation, which, it is argued, will encourage market forces to maximise consumer benefits. In the EU, at least, this is occurring within a protective framework to ensure that genuine benefits are derived. This is in contrast to the experience of the USA, where the deregulation of the airline industry has led to a concentration of power among a few airlines and serious concerns over cost-cutting operators to the detriment of the customer.

All of these trends are influenced by technology, particularly in the areas of marketing and distribution where the driving force of change is derived, in the main, from the influence of new technology and its application to tourism. New information technologies will continue to have a dramatic impact on all aspects of the travel and tourism industry, affecting its business and production procedures, product design philosophy, marketing methods, promotion and distribution strategies and pricing policies.

While intermediaries continue to rule the distribution channel in many countries, the potential for direct contact between supplier and customer is enormous. There are arguments that this may ultimately lead to disintermediation as both supplier and user realise the benefits, particularly the cost advantages, of communication, marketing and selling on a one-to-one basis.

Future marketing trends in tourism

The tourism market is maturing and while the overall levels of tourism demand are predicted to rise, growth rates in tourism markets will slow. Thus, the role of marketing, which facilitates communication between an organisation and its customer to encourage purchase, will become increasingly important as organisations seek to maintain and improve market share.

The major trends in marketing are embodied in the concept of the 4Ps (discussed in detail in Chapter 19): product, price, promotion and place (or distribution). The role – and potential – of technology in each of these areas is phenomenal, but it is in the spheres of distribution and product formulation that technological development will probably be the most influential. While tourism remains a composite product, new technology allows individual products to be more easily packaged together and presented to the consumer as a seamless entity. Thus, as a result of new technology, the sector is being encouraged to review and update all aspects of its marketing, promotion and distribution strategies.

Coupled with the growing volume of tourism demand is the fact that tourists have generally become more sophisticated in their demand requirements. Success in an increasingly competitive market-place, therefore, is determined by the ability of an organisation or company to offer tailor-made products, the details of which are instantly available. Tourism marketing, therefore, is continuing to be influenced by the development of new technology which is now permeating all aspects of product formulation and distribution.

Overview

We can see that all aspects of the tourism system will experience change. Since the system is essentially a dynamic one, it must be assumed that change in any area will inevitably change the equilibrium in all others. However, despite our guesses, the direction of that change remains elusive and although the key trends outlined above act as a guide, the future of tourism which will unfold in the next few years will be as exciting and unpredictable as ever.

Chapter Twenty

Information technology

Introduction

It has been said that information technologies (ITs) have been responsible for instigating a second industrial revolution. This revolution has had a major impact upon the competitiveness of tourism enterprises and destinations around the world: indeed this is only to be expected given the fact that the tourism industry is dependent upon both the efficient dissemination of information and effective product distribution. In this chapter we therefore aim to chart the main developments of information technology (IT) over the last 25 years of the twentieth century and to demonstrate the strategic implications of new technologies for all aspects of the tourism industry. In addition, we explain the various types of technology-based systems and show how they fit together in the production, distribution and delivery of tourism products.

Chapter learning objectives

The purpose of this chapter is to acquaint the reader with all aspects of ITs as they relate to tourism and the objectives, therefore, are:

- to provide an understanding of the concept of ITs, the different types of ITs and the development of ITs to the mid-1990s;
- to highlight the potential value of ITs for key elements of the marketing mix and their probable impact on this area in the future;
- to assess the format and roles of ITs in all sectors of the tourism industry and to discuss relevant problems and issues; and
- to identify the likely future development of ITs and their implications for tourism.

Defining information technologies

Poon (1993) defines ITs as

> *the collective term given to the most recent developments in the mode (electronic) and the mechanisms (computers and communications technologies) used for the acquisition, processing, analysis, storage, retrieval, dissemination, and application of information.*

In other words, ITs assimilate the knowledge of a society in respect of a wide range of industrial, mechanical, practical and business processes and can be thought of as a synthesis of electronics, computing and telecommunications technologies which enable the processing and flow of information within and between organisations. ITs are systems of integrated hardware, software and humanware, such as:

- computers;
- Videotext;
- teletext;
- telephones, fax, telex;
- management information systems;
- tele-conferencing;
- modems;
- multimedia, kiosks;
- computer networks;
- the Internet, Intranet, Extranet;
- satellites; and
- wireless communication systems.

The impact of information technologies on organisational structure

The development of ITs has inevitably had a major effect on the operation, structure and strategy of tourism organisations throughout the world. With new technology, communication and operational costs are reduced and flexibility, interactivity, efficiency, productivity and competitiveness are enhanced. The competitiveness of both enterprises and destinations is being redefined as they maximise the utilisation, development and application of these technologies.

ITs have been responsible for leading the shift from product-orientated tourism organisations, to more flexible and responsive market-orientated tourism operations, where success depends on sensing and responding to rapidly changing customer needs. Porter (1985) argues that ITs can contribute to the value chain of products and services, by either improving their cost position or product differentiation. We can see that the significance of this is a reshaping of competitiveness and the consequent strategic implications for organisational prosperity.

Of course, ITs are not a panacea for poor organisational performance, but they have provided unprecedented and unforeseen opportunities for those service providers who have instigated a redesign of systems to integrate new technologies fully. For example, they have enabled the development of networks that are used to enhance multilevel integration in the tourism industry. We can identify three basic types of networks:

1. **Internet** facilitates the interactivity of the enterprise and individuals with the entire range of external world through multimedia representations.

2. **Intranets** are closed, secured or 'firewalled' networks within organisations, which harness the needs of internal business users, by using a single controlled, user-friendly interface to demonstrate all company data.

2. **Extranets** utilise the same principle with external computer networks to enhance the interactivity and transparency between organisations and trusted partners. This works by linking and sharing data and processes to format a low cost and user-friendly electronic commerce arrangement, similar to the electronic data interchange (EDI) which was attempted in the previous ITs eras.

Implementing ITs

While ITs have a beneficial effect on organisational performance, the successful development and implementation of new systems to achieve sustainable competitive advantage has certain requirements to ensure success. These include:

- a need for long-term planning and strategic frameworks;
- the need for rational IT management and development of hardware and software;
- the need to re-engineer business processes;
- top management commitment and vision; and
- the need for training throughout the hierarchy.

Simply using ITs as a stand-alone initiative is inadequate; rather, business processes re-engineering argues that traditional hierarchical organisational structures will be unable to accommodate new ITs successfully. To exploit the benefits of ITs now available, corporations need to redesign their processes, structures, distribution channel strategies and management control systems to convert business functions to business processes.

Tourism and information technologies

Accompanying the technological revolution of the 1990s are many new opportunities and challenges for the tourism industry. Since tourism is a complex, global industry, information is its life-blood and technology has become fundamental to the ability of the industry to operate effectively and competitively. As Poon (1993) argues: 'A whole system of information technologies is being rapidly diffused throughout the tourism industry and no player will escape information technologies impacts'.

IT and the tourism product

We have seen that the tourism product differs from durable consumer goods in many aspects (as discussed in detail in Chapter 17). Specifically, tourism services are intangible: they cannot be physically displayed or inspected by potential customers at the point of sale prior to purchasing. Tourism products are normally bought before the time of use and away from the place of consumption, and therefore rely almost exclusively upon representations and descriptions provided by the travel trade and other intermediaries. Timely and accurate information, appropriate to consumers' needs, is often the key to successful satisfaction of tourists. ITs are therefore pivotal for tourism demand as few other activities require the generation, gathering, processing, application and communication of information for operations. In other words, the very nature of tourism means that the implications of technology are far-reaching.

Implications for tourism

The development of new ITs looks set to continue to influence the tourism industry profoundly. With new technology, enterprises and consumers alike should benefit from more

Table 20.1:
Estimated share
of travel agency
locations world-
wide for main
global
distribution
systems

	Market Share (%)	*Locations*
Amadeus	27	35 493
Galileo	24	32 326
Sabre	21	28 112
Worldspan	11	15 327
Others (Axess, Infini, Abacus, Gets, etc.)	17	23 090

Source: CRS Update, 23 November 1995.

efficient cooperation between individual providers of the tourism composite to ensure the seamless presentation of tourism products. ITs have had a dramatic impact on the travel industry, forcing the sector to reappraise the way in which it organises its business and production procedures, the methods it uses to market, promote and distribute its product, and the role played by training and development in respect of educating its workforce.

The growth of Global Distribution Systems in tourism

The computerised networks and electronic distribution systems developed in the 1970s led to dramatic structural changes within the tourism industry. A CRS is essentially a database that enables a tourism organisation to manage its inventory and improve accessibility to information within and between its partners. Airlines pioneered the CRS technology in the 1980s, by expanding geographical coverage and integrating horizontally and vertically to embrace the entire range of intermediaries and principals. Individual product suppliers became aware that systems integration, and the subsequent creation of a 'shop window' that allowed products to be displayed and purchased anywhere in the world, would be a crucial determining factor in the competitiveness and profitability of operations. As a result, the vast, new all-encompassing GDSs matured from their original development as airline CRSs.

Four systems, all connected to the major principals and offering similar services, dominated the global market from an early stage, as illustrated in Table 20.1. It is clear that GDSs are one of the major drivers of information technologies in tourism, as well as being the backbone of the tourism industry. According to many commentators, GDSs are the single most important facilitator of the globalisation of ITs (Truitt, Teye and Farris, 1991; Sheldon, 1993; WTO, 1995).

The Internet and the World Wide Web

Developments in GDSs were complemented by the introduction and expansion in the mid-1990s of the Internet and the World Wide Web (WWW). This development facilitated an unprecedented opportunity for distribution of multimedia information and interactivity between principals and consumers. This is especially so given the WWW's interlinking structure which enables the provision and packaging of themed information, products and services. Hitherto, however, the information available on the Internet is chaotic and loosely structured, mainly due to its immaturity and the lack of any type of standardisation.

Although there are no accurate numbers on the users of the WWW, nor indeed of the number of web sites, the pace of development demonstrates that the Internet is restructuring the lives of people and business processes world-wide. It has introduced new practices such as home-shopping, tele-entertainment, tele-working, tele-learning, tele-medicine and tele-banking. Eventually it is anticipated that the electronic/interactive/ intelligent/virtual home and enterprise will emerge. This will be accompanied by an entire range of communications with the external world and will support all the functions of everyday personal and professional life through interactive computer networks.

Tourism and the World Wide Web

In respect of tourism providers, the World Wide Web (WWW) provides an infrastructure for the global distribution and inexpensive delivery of tourism-related multimedia information. It also empowers the consumer through the provision of tailor-made products which meet their individual needs, so bridging the gap between the consumer and destination/supply in a flexible and interactive way.

The Internet can also strengthen the marketing and communication functions of remote, peripheral and insular destinations, as well as small and medium-sized tourism enterprises, by enabling direct communication with prospective customers. Hence the Internet provides unprecedented and affordable opportunities for the global representation and marketing for both large and small tourism suppliers.

It is anticipated that eventually GDSs will take advantage of the openness of the WWW and develop suitable interfaces for consumers and the industry. Sabre has already launched Travelocity (http://www.travelocity.com), an electronic travel agency, while other GDSs have announced similar actions or cooperations with travel providers on the Internet. These include Worldspan with Expedia (http://expedia.msn.com/) and Amadeus with the Internet Travel Network (ITN; http://www.itn.net).

In addition, the Internet provides unique opportunities for multimedia presentations: it can transform uninspiring, text-based screens of GDSs into interactive electronic brochures. This is particularly significant when GDSs aim to distribute less standardised products, such as hotel rooms and destination facilities. Distributed multimedia technologies and media-rich presentations, therefore, in combination with the reservation capabilities of GDSs, would provide a powerful selling tool for the industry. As a result, GDSs are expected to exploit the Internet in order to offer innovative interfaces for direct communication with consumers and support the emerging future trend to home travel-shopping.

As Hawkins (1996) suggests:

> business and organisations worldwide are realising that marketing on the WWW is multi-dimensional content-marketing that requires the following paradigm shifts: from traditional advertising to interactive marketing; and from developing and managing one way information flows to computer-mediated empowerment of users, consumers, and entrepreneurs who will be engaged in electronic commerce in the information age. (p. 6)

Issues and problems

For the full commercial potential of electronic commerce to be exploited by the tourism industry and its consumers we can identify several issues which must be resolved:

- increase security of transmissions;
- ensure credibility and accountability of information;
- secure intellectual property and copyright issues;
- enhance bandwidth and reduce speed limitations;
- reduce user confusion and dissatisfaction;
- provide adequately trained specialists;
- develop equal access for smaller and larger partners;
- establish pricing structures for distribution of information and reservations; and
- enhance the standardisation of information and reservation procedures.

Information technologies and tourism demand

As the volume of tourism demand has grown world-wide and the demands of tourists have become increasingly sophisticated, a new reliance on electronic media by consumers, suppliers and intermediaries has emerged. In an ever-more competitive marketplace, success for tourism enterprises will depend upon their ability to identify customer needs and to offer tailor-made products to satisfy those requirements instantly.

ITs enable travellers to access reliable and accurate information and undertake reservations in a fraction of the time, cost and inconvenience required by conventional methods. Thus, they improve service quality and contribute to a higher tourist satisfaction. Despite some bias and inaccuracies, GDSs and the Internet provide access to transparent and easy to compare information on destinations, holiday packages, travel, lodging and leisure services, as well as real-time prices and availability.

Increasingly consumers utilise commercial and non-commercial Internet sites for planning, searching, reserving, purchasing and amending tourism products. Experienced travellers are empowered by ITs and use information and booking systems to improve personal efficiency. Organisations that are not currently related to the tourism industry (such as Expedia/Microsoft) have seized the emergent opportunity to satisfy tourism demand by utilising IT tools, and may gradually resume a leading intermediation role (Williams, 1993, p. 201; Schertler *et al.*, 1995, p. 49).

Information technologies and tourism supply

On the tourism supply side, the impacts of ITs are evident in the production, marketing, operational and distribution functions of both the private and public sectors. The development of computerised systems, especially in the first two IT eras identified in Box 20.1, allowed tourism enterprises to handle inventory more efficiently and to perform business functions more effectively and productively.

The ability of tourism enterprises to communicate efficiently with remote branches, destinations, principals and agencies has also resulted in more effective operational control. Ultimately, this has enabled them to expand activities, while reducing costs and increasing competitiveness. Both operational (e.g. schedule planning, pricing, inventory handling and reservations) and support (e.g. payroll, accounting, marketing) functions have been improved considerably through ITs.

Distribution of the tourism product

ITs have pivotal implications for tourism distribution: essentially, they enable the amalgamation of independently produced elements into seamless complete products that constitute the tourist experience. As distribution is one of the few elements of the marketing

Box 20.1   The evolution of information technologies

Four main eras can be identified in the development of information technologies.

- In the first era, the 'data processing era', the main objective was to improve operational efficiency by automating information-based processes. This era began in the 1960s and it was characterised by the use of mainframes and mini-computers.

- The second era, the 'management information systems (MIS)' era, produced information technologies designed to increase managerial effectiveness by satisfying the organisational information requirements. Commencing in the 1970s, these systems utilised local processing procedures linked to information resources. At this time, information technologies were used primarily to address the needs of internal management, emphasising administrative and clerical functions.

- In the early 1980s 'strategic information systems (SIS)' aimed to improve competitiveness by changing the nature or conduct of business. Integrated information technologies networks were introduced in pursuit of competitive advantage to achieve organisational strategic objectives, to enhance performance, to coordinate activities across functional and business unit lines and to facilitate interactions with external entities.

- The early 1990s saw the emergence of a fourth, and more profound, era. The 'network era', where intra- and inter-organisational networking has proliferated via the use of local and wide area networks. Enhancements in information technology capabilities, decreasing equipment size and associated costs, together with improved reliability and interconnectivity of terminals and applications, have made information technologies an affordable and essential tool for organisations. Consequently, economies and enterprises, regardless of size, product and geographical coverage, have experienced a major business processes re-engineering which has transformed their ability to operate and compete in the emerging global market-place (Peppard, 1993; Robson, 1994; Tapscott, 1996).

mix that can still be manipulated to assist enterprises in improving competitiveness and profitability, ITs are instrumental in achieving advantage in the market-place in many cases. This may be by product differentiation, cost advantage or further efficiencies in the production and distribution processes.

ITs, therefore, have transformed distribution of the tourism product to form an electronic market-place where access to information is instantly achievable. Principals and consumers continue to experience unprecedented interactivity. Furthermore, the dramatic ongoing development of the Internet has resulted in the re-engineering of the entire production and distribution process for tourism products. As a consequence of this technological explosion, the packaging of tourism is becoming much more individualistic, leading inevitably to a certain degree of channel disintermediation; a process that will offer new opportunities and threats to all tourism partners.

A conceptual synthesis of information technologies in tourism

A conceptual synthesis of the emergent ITs as they relate to tourism is provided in Figure 20.1. This illustrates the paradigm shift and business processes re-engineering which will effectively shape the tourism industry into the next millennium. Figure 20.1 demonstrates the reliance of both tourism demand and tourism supply on new ITs. It also emphasises the role of ITs in facilitating inter- and intra-organisational communication

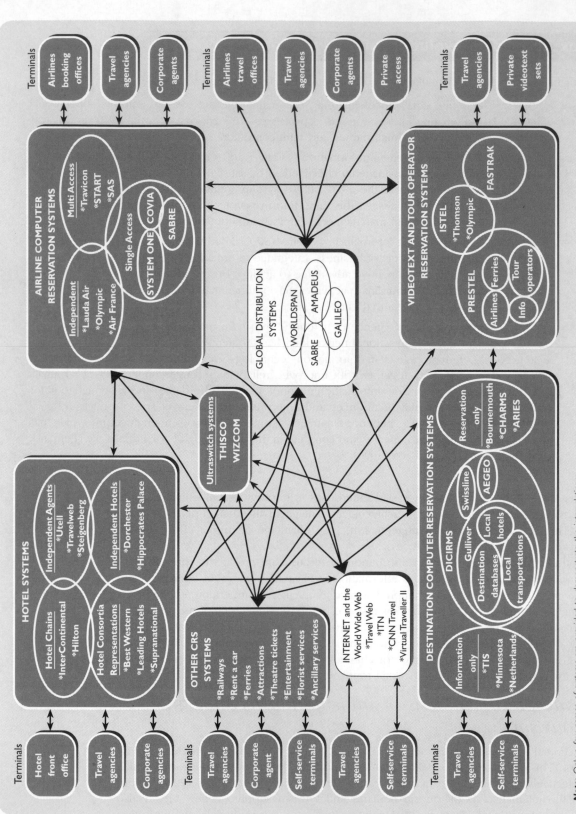

Figure 20.1: Conceptual synthesis of the emergent information technologies in tourism

Note: Only a few names of systems are provided to demonstrate the interrelations.

and the way in which new ITs may be integrated at multiple levels into an organisation's communication and technological processes.

Information technologies and airlines

Airlines have been largely responsible for spearheading the development of ITs as an inexpensive and accurate way of handling vast quantities of data and inventory. More recently, the growth of air traffic, coupled with air transportation deregulation, has stimulated the expansion of CRSs into Global Distribution Systems (GDSs). An indication of airline ownership and involvement in the main global distribution systems is presented in Figure 20.2.

As prices, schedules and routes have been liberated in the USA in the last few years, CRSs offered airlines extensive flexibility extending to all aspects of demand and supply management. CRSs also allowed airlines to compete more effectively by adapting schedules and fares to match availability with demand, by coordinating complex hub-and-spoke networks and by controlling complicated pricing systems to maximise their yield.

Furthermore, CRSs introduced three major financial benefits vendor airlines:

1. A wide distribution network.
2. Revenues generated from services to third parties.
3. Incremental benefits through directional selling to the parent carrier.

Other IT benefits and implications for airlines

The remote printing of travel documents, sale settlements between airlines and travel agencies, and the partnership marketing through frequent flyer programmes have all been invaluable benefits supported by emerging information technologies. CRSs have re-engineered the entire marketing and distribution processes of airlines and essentially, they have become strategic business units (SBUs) in their own right owing to their ability to generate income and to boost airlines' sales at the expense of competitors. The main benefits of CRSs may be defined as:

● enhancing interactivity; and building relationships with customers and partners;

● providing on-line reservations and electronic ticketing;

● facilitating yield management

● using last-minute electronic auctions;

● instigating disintermediation and redesigning agency commission schemes; and

● maximising the productivity of the new electronic distribution media.

Issues and problems

There are important issues in respect of new mega-CRS distribution networks which need attention. Firstly, the cost of distribution, though reduced, remains expensive and many airlines find these costs difficult to fund and control. This is particularly true for small, newly established, developing world airlines and regional carriers which cannot afford GDS fees and lack in-house technology facilities and expertise. In addition, vendor airlines with CRS influence are in a position to bias CRS screens to give higher display priority to their flights in preference to competitors. Again, it is the new, weaker airlines that are most seriously affected by this strategy (Buhalis, 1996).

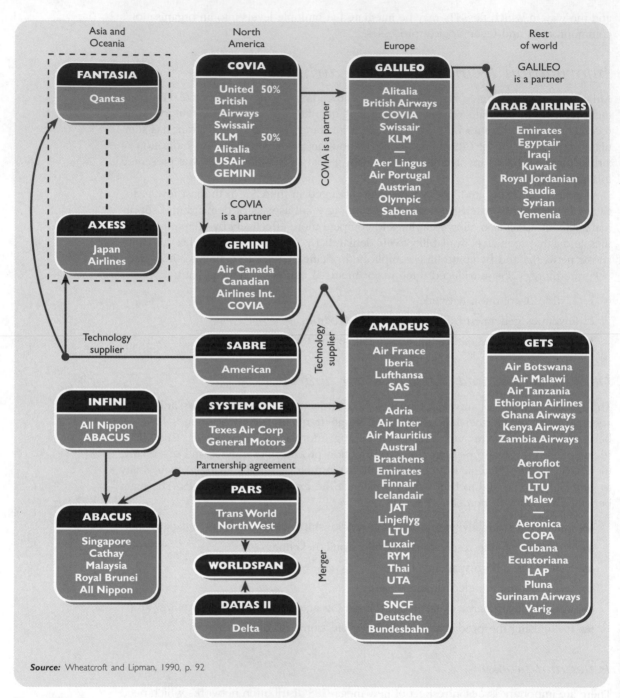

Figure 20.2: Interrelations of airline Computer Reservation Systems

Information technologies and hotels

Although central reservation offices (CROs) introduced central reservations in the 1970s, it was not until the expansion of airline CRSs and recent IT developments that hotels fully integrated their systems.

Hotels utilise information technologies for some of the following reasons:

● to interface with external GDSs;

● to maximise profitability by maximising revenues and minimising costs;

● to improve operational and financial efficiency;

● to assist in the control of all aspects of business;

● to facilitate yield management and inventory control;

● to reduce labour and training costs;

● to enable rapid response to customer and management requests;

● to provide customers and the travel trade with access to accurate information on availability; and

● to offer easy, efficient, inexpensive and reliable ways of making and confirming reservations.

In addition, in-house management systems (see Case Study 20.1) such as property management systems (PMSs) may also exist with the following objectives:

● to coordinate the front office, sales, planning and operational functions by administrating reservations and managing the hotel inventory;

● to integrate and unify the 'back' and 'front' of house management; and

● to improve general administration functions such as accounting, budgeting and finance, marketing research and planning, forecasting and yield management, payroll, personnel and purchasing (O'Connor, 1995).

Case Study 20.1   Hotel Property Management Systems: Fidelio

Fidelio was founded in 1987 in Munich and it has subsequently emerged as one of the leading and most innovative international systems integrator for the hospitality industries. It has irrevocably altered the way hotels utilise Information technologies, both operationally and strategically, by developing software that integrates both ongoing technological developments with changing organisational business environments.

Fidelio allows hotels, restaurants, cruise ships and catering and conference operations of any size to computerise operations following a complete analysis of a business's unique requirements to produce tailor-made software. For example, different hotel chains and managers need location information to accommodate the dissimilar legal requirements, accounting systems, tax reporting and guest statistics of countries in which they operate. Fidelio aims to meet these challenges and satisfies demand for every type of information requested, while simultaneously maintaining industry-wide standards which enable comparisons at a corporate level.

Fidelio incorporates the following functions:

● **Front office function.** This enables the management of functions such as reservations and registration data, guest histories, room itinerary management, pricing and yield management, billing, group management, night auditing, maintenance and concierge activities. It also facilitates the production of operational and management reports.

● **Food and beverage management system.** This function assists in revenue and cost budget management, stock control, return on investment analysis for each menu, kitchen control and bar management and control. A point-of-sales system integrates all revenue points with the central database facilitating accounting and cashiering functions.

▷

Case Study 20.1 continued

- **Sales and marketing programme.** This supports an hotel's entire sales and marketing functions, such as group event management and reservations, account management, activity management, contract generation and associated follow-up activities.

- **Miscellaneous support services.** In addition to information technologies primary functions, Fidelio offers additional services such as word processing, mail management, calendars and daily schedule organisation. The system interfaces with most telephone, point-of-sales, door locking, minibar, energy management, voice mail, video and paging networks, enabling a multi-level integration of all hotel processes.

These functions are delivered through the development of a local area network which coordinates all processes and enables hotel departments to share a data-rich and constantly up-dated database.

More recently, Fidelio has moved into the American hospitality market where there exists huge scope for large units and chains requiring comprehensive computerised systems. To maximise information technologies potential in this respect, Fidelio has become fully owned by Beltsville, Maryland, USA, which is one of the leading manufacturers of point-of-sale systems for the restaurant and hospitality industry. The company has now become the largest supplier of total IT solutions for the restaurant and hospitality industry world-wide. The alliance will provide an important platform for the free exchange of knowledge between two leading edge companies, supporting the further development of expertise and new products in this market.

Source: Fidelio Corporate Communications.

Interfacing with other systems

The development of the Internet has reduced capital and operational costs in respect of hotel operation. For example, the cost per individual booking can be reduced from US $10–15 for voice-based reservations to US $7.50–3.50 for reservations through GDSs or to US $0.25 through the WWW (Beaver, 1995). However, the level of untapped potential may be illustrated by the fact that although electronic bookings between 1981 and 1993 grew by 7750%, only 28% of these global reservations were booked electronically (Buhalis, 1996).

In addition, by utilising ITs and the Internet for distribution and marketing functions, further financial benefits may be derived from the diminished need to print, store, administrate and post promotional material and brochures without any associated reduction in the quality of information disseminated.

While most major hotel chains operate their own CRSs, the emergence of the Internet has raised issues with regard to the interconnectivity with other GDSs and the Internet information itself. As a result, 'switch' companies, such as The Hotel Industry Switch Company (THISCO) and WIZCOM have emerged to provide an interface between the various systems and to enable a certain degree of transparency. This reduces both set-up and reservation costs, while facilitating reservations through several distribution channels.

Issues and problems

As most hotels are small and medium-sized, independent, seasonal and family run, many lack the expertise and/or capital to utilise ITs fully. This is due to:

- lack of capital for purchasing hardware and software;
- insufficient marketing prowess;

- inadequate technological training and understanding;
- small size with no economies of scale; and
- the unwillingness of proprietors to lose control over their property.

Hence, small hotels are placed at a disadvantage by lack of presence in the electronic market-place. In addition, they fail to capitalise on the benefits that may be derived from emergent IT opportunities such as cost reduction and/or competitive enhancement.

One possible strategy to overcome this problem is the establishment of destination-based collaboration ventures which encourages small firms to pool resources together in order to share development and operation costs to the benefit of all by providing direct access to target markets at an affordable price (Buhalis, 1994).

Information technologies and tour operators

Leisure travellers frequently purchase travel packages consisting of individual elements pre-booked by tour operators. Tour operators distribute these assembled products through brochures displayed in travel agencies. Hence, in northern European countries, where tour operators dominate the leisure market, airline and hotel CRSs are rarely utilised for leisure travel. However, while GDSs have historically concentrated on business travel they are increasingly providing access to more leisure-based products.

In the early 1980s, tour operators realised the benefits of ITs in organising, promoting, distributing and coordinating packages. Thomson's Open-line Programme (TOP) was the first real-time computer-based central reservation office introduced in 1976. It offered direct communication with travel agencies in 1982, and announced that reservations for Thomson Holidays would only be accepted through TOP in 1986. This move was a critical turning point in respect of the communication processes between tour operators and travel agencies. Gradually, all major tour operators developed or acquired databases and established electronic links with travel agencies, aiming to reduce information handling costs and increase the speed of information transfer and retrieval. This was instrumental in improving productivity and capacity management while simultaneously enhancing services to agencies and consumers. Additionally, tour operators also utilised CRSs for market intelligence, for inventory management, as well as for monitoring booking progress and productivity of travel agencies.

Recent IT developments

Recent IT developments offer new opportunities for tour operators. For example, several tour operators distribute electronic brochures and booking forms through the WWW directly to consumers. This approach provides a number of important benefits to tour operators:

- It enables them to concentrate on niche markets by offering customised packages.
- It allows them to update brochures regularly.
- It saves the 10–20% commission usually made payable to other intermediaries in the distribution chain (e.g. travel agencies).
- It significantly reduces the costs of incentives, bonuses and educational trips for travel agencies.
- It saves the cost for developing, printing, storing and distributing conventional brochures which is estimated to be approximately £20 per booking (Buhalis, 1995).

However, research illustrates that tour operators are reluctant to focus primarily on product distribution via new ITs (Buhalis, 1995). Few realise the major transformation occurring within the market-place of the 1990s, while the majority continue to regard ITs exclusively as a support tool for current operations without understanding the IT roles in cost reduction and distribution innovation. As ITs will determine the future competitiveness of the industry, distribution channel leadership and power of tour operators may well be challenged if other channel members or newcomers utilise ITs effectively to package and distribute either unique or cheaper tourism products. Although a partial disintermediation seems inevitable, there will always be sufficient market share for tour operators who can add value to the tourism product and deliver competitive holiday packages (Kärcher, 1997).

Information technologies and travel agencies

ITs have become irreplaceable tools for travel agencies: they provide instantaneous information, complete reservation facilities (including the construction of complicated itineraries) and they support the intermediation between consumers and principals.

In addition, the introduction of ITs has resulted in organisational improvements through the integration of 'back office' functions (e.g. accounting and personnel) and 'front office' functions (e.g. customer records, itinerary construction, ticketing and communication with suppliers). All travel agencies use ITs for financial and operational control as well as for market research and strategic planning but multiple travel agencies, in particular, experience benefits by achieving better coordination and control between their remote branches and headquarters.

Most travel agencies operate a selection of reservation systems, mainly through Videotext networks and/or GDSs. These systems allow agencies to access information and make reservations on scheduled airlines, hotel chains, car rentals and a variety of ancillary services. The type of agency and clientele will determine the types of ITs utilised. Typically business travel agencies are more GDS-dependent, while leisure agencies and holiday shops tend to use a higher proportion of Videotext systems.

Table 20.2 illustrates GDS penetration in travel agencies around the world and Table 20.3 demonstrates the main GDSs market shares in European agencies. It can be observed that GDSs are more successful in the countries of their airline owners.

Leisure market

The vast majority of British leisure travel agencies, as well as a great number of agencies around the world, utilise Videotext networks to access tour operator and other reservation systems, such as ferry operators, railways and insurance companies.

Videotext systems have a number of benefits:

● they are relatively inexpensive to purchase and operate;
● they require little training and expertise; and
● they are fairly reliable.

Table 20.2:
Percentage of travel agencies using a GDS in 1992

Heavy users ◄--► Low users							
Korea	98%	Japan	85%	Singapore	56%	Malaysia	32%
USA	96%	Italy	85%	Spain	53%	Philippines	32%
Australia	91%	Hong Kong	65%	Taiwan	50%	United Kingdom	23%
France	85%	Scandinavia	61%	Germany	48%	Greece	16%

Source: adapted from Emmer et al. (1993), p. 81, and McGuffie (1994), p. 57.

Table 20.3: Penetration and market shares of GDSs in European travel agencies

	Germany	France	Spain	Denmark	UK	Italy	Netherlands	Belgium	Portugal	Greece[a]	Ireland[a]	Luxembourg[a]	Total
Agencies													
Amadeus	11 000	3 150	2 291	188	20	0	0	100	11	0	0	0	16 760
Galileo	200	124	101	22	2 185	2 384	403	158	350	84	47	0	6 058
Sabre	600	358	91	21	624	518	79	96	1	178	17	13	2 596
Worldspan	300	150	100	90	500	180	200	150	160	120	30	0	1 980
Total outlets	12 100	3 782	2 583	321	3 329	3 082	682	504	522	382	94	13	27 394
Terminals													
Amadeus	23 000	7 200	3 661	1 275	60	0	0	388	11	0	0	0	35 595
Galileo	400	250	111	115	9 421	5 267	2 100	438	554	88	211	0	18 955
Sabre	1 300	774	167	77	2 251	960	167	280	1	224	45	26	6 272
Worldspan	1 000	700	110	180	950	280	600	500	200	150	40	0	4 710
Total terminals	25 700	8 924	4 049	1 647	12 682	6 507	2 867	1 606	766	462	296	26	65 532
Terminals per outlet[a]	2.12	2.36	1.57	5.13	3.81	2.11	4.20	3.18	1.46	1.21	3.15	2.00	2.39

[a] Terminals per outlet = total terminals/total outlets. As travel agencies might operate more than one GDS, the 'terminals per outlet' ratio is provided only for comparison reasons between countries.

Source: adapted from Smith and Jenner (1994), p. 62, and Hyde (1992), pp. 26–7.

Case Study 20.2 Internet provider: Internet Travel Network (ITN)

The development of the Internet provides unprecedented opportunities for the tourism industry to promote and distribute ITs product globally via multimedia interfaces. As on-line spending for travel services is predicted to reach US$3 billion by the year 2000 (ITN Publicity Information), it is inevitable that a number of new providers emerge to take advantage of the opportunities.

In 1995, the Internet Travel Network (http://www.itn.net) was founded and revolutionised the industry by launching the first World Wide Web based air travel reservation interface. Later it added car and hotel modules followed by booking systems with corporate compliant policy filters. In addition, users can access up-to-date information on 22 000 destinations world-wide and view an extensive calendar of events for over 200 cities. It is also possible to search travel information, destination reviews and download on-line maps, photos and videos.

ITN's goal is to utilise the Internet to make travel planning as simple and effective as possible for both leisure and business travellers via the introduction of fast and efficient booking facilities. It utilises a strategic alliance with System One to access the Amadeus Central System, which allows on-line links to a great variety of principals globally. About 1.5 million users have registered in approximately 18 months and although the majority of the users hitherto have searched the system for suitable products prior to making reservations, they have largely reverted to conventional travel agencies for booking. However, on-line reservations are increasing with consumers collecting tickets and other documents from ITN's local partners.

Eventually, it is anticipated that ticketless travel booked on-line will become more widespread as public acceptance grows. It is predicted that the consumer will use booking references in the place of tickets for travel and the role of the travel agency, therefore, is becoming less certain. Without adding significant value to the tourism experience, the intermediation role of travel agencies may be challenged, especially by technologically adept frequent travellers who are familiar with those systems and procedures that expedite the booking process.

However, there are disadvantages to these systems:

- they are slow;
- there is a need for agents to retype basic data for each individual database searched;
- the systems fail to integrate with back office functions;
- they cannot interface with multimedia applications; and
- they are unable to take advantage of the emergent ITs.

Agency threats

Despite the improvements in ITs, most travel agencies have not yet managed to take full advantage of new technology. This may be attributed to a number of factors:

- Travel agencies are often deficient in IT expertise and understanding.
- They operate on low profit margins which hampers investment in new technology.
- They focus more fully on human interaction with consumers at the expense of ITs.

Combined, these factors result in low level of IT integration, implying that agencies lack access to new ITs and are provided with inadequate information to support strategic

Case Study 20.3 Destination Management System: Ireland

Destination Management Systems enable regions to promote and distribute product offerings through a centralised facility which is often coordinated by the public sector. In 1990, the Irish Tourist Board, in conjunction with the Northern Irish Tourist Board, pioneered the Gulliver project. Gulliver enables the electronic distribution of tourism products through the provision of on-line information and reservation facilities and is designed to assist in the management of Ireland's fledgling tourism industry which, in 1995, brought 4.2 million tourists to Ireland and generated IR£1.5 billion in foreign earnings or 6.4% of the gross domestic product (GDP).

Significantly, Gulliver primarily addresses the needs of the small and medium-sized enterprises which dominate the tourism industry in Ireland. It aims to give them access and opportunities which are on a par with those afforded to larger counterparts already represented in the emerging electronic market-place.

Gulliver was predominantly funded by the following sources:

- European Union Development Grants (IR£2.9m);
- Bord Failte (IR£2.6m);
- International Fund for Ireland Development Grants (IR£1.6m); and
- The Northern Ireland Tourism Board (IR£1.5m).

Structure

There exist three key elements that constitute the Gulliver system.

- **Gulliver central system.** This acts as the central processor and purveyor of data. It facilitates the distribution of tourism products from the supplier to the customer by providing a flow of accurate information.
- **Gulliver's supply side.** This element of the system incorporates details of all principals at the destination.
- **Gulliver's demand side.** This element of Gulliver supports distribution channels used to disseminate information such as TICs and national, regional and local tourism boards. In addition, this element of this system deals the interface between Gulliver and CRSs and Videotext networks.

While the original system was designed to provide information on-line, the high levels of central computing required to handle peak demand proved financially untenable. Consequently, Gulliver re-engineered ITs design to take advantage of the multimedia technologies emerging and divided information technologies data into static (e.g. descriptions, photos, history) and dynamic (e.g. availability, rates, schedules) categories. 'Static' data are now stored locally on PCs at key demand points, while users searching for 'dynamic' data link directly to the central system. Confirmation for available products takes about eight seconds and principals receive reservations either electronically or via fax machines. This distribution approach means that both central procession requirements and communication costs are minimised.

In December 1996 Gulliver was launched on the WWW (http://www.ireland.travel.ie) providing access to the most comprehensive, interactive, multimedia brochure about Irish tourism. Future plans include the expansion of the distribution network to all Bord Failte offices overseas and through kiosks at the destination. The major threat to Gulliver is the restructuring and downsizing of Bord Failte, a public sector body which has been experienced budget cuts. Without a new private sector partner, therefore, who is willing and able to fund these additional resources, continued expansion of Gulliver is unlikely.

Source: Adapted from O'Connor and Rafferty (1997).

and operational decision-making processes. This factor alone is a major threat for travel agencies who are becoming increasingly threatened by disintermediation. This threat is further exacerbated by other forces which are currently undermining the role of the travel agent such as:

- consumers are increasingly searching out information on the Internet and making their own reservations on-line;
- principals are aiming to control distribution costs by communicating directly with consumers and by developing 'relationship marketing' (as discussed in Chapter 16);
- most travel agencies have limited expertise as they employ inadequately trained personnel with little experience;
- new players (such as Microsoft's Expedia and ITN) are emerging and targeting consumers by taking advantage of the new ITs; and
- location is becoming less significant as specialised electronic travel agents using intelligent, well-trained agents are able to identify the best available options for the needs of their customers and issue electronic tickets collectable at the airport.

Therefore, the future of travel agencies will depend on their ability to adapt and utilise ITs to their fullest potential. Agencies that act as booking offices for tourism products will probably face the most significant difficulties. In contrast, knowledgeable and innovative agencies, utilising the entire range of technologies to provide suitable integrated tourism solutions, will successfully add value to the tourist experience.

Information technologies and destinations

Destinations are amalgams of individual elements, facilities and services which, when combined, make up the total tourism product. As demonstrated in Part 2 of this book, destinations need to satisfy the differing needs of all principal stakeholders, including the indigenous people of the region.

The role of destination management systems

Although ITs were never regarded as instruments for the development and management of destinations, increasingly destination management organisations (DMOs) use ITs in order to facilitate the tourist experience before, during and after a visit. In addition, these destination management systems (DMSs) are used to coordinate the activities of all partners involved in the production and delivery of the destination's tourism product.

More advanced DMSs provide interactive demonstrations of local amenities and facilities, and enable consumers to build their own itinerary based on their interests, requirements and constraints (see Case Study 20.2).

In addition, DMSs may be utilised to facilitate the management of DMOs, as well as the coordination of local suppliers at the destination level (Case Study 20.3). DMSs are particularly significant for small and medium tourism enterprises which lack the capital and expertise to undertake a comprehensive marketing strategy and rely on destination authorities for the promotion and coordination of their products. Thus, not only do DMSs provide information, accept reservations for local enterprises and coordinate facilities, but they promote tourism policy, control operational functions, increase the expenditure of tourists and boost the multiplier effects in the local economy.

Despite the fact that studies on destination-orientated CRSs have been traced back to as early as 1968 (Archdale et al., 1992), it was not until the early 1990s that the destination management system (DMS) concept emerged. Even at this stage, most DMSs were mere facilitators of the conventional activities of tourist boards, such as information dissemination or local bookings. However, in their most advanced form, DICIRMSs (or destination integrated computer information reservation management systems) can rationalise destination management and marketing by supporting promotion, distribution and operation, while also offering innovative tools for strategic management, product differentiation and amelioration of tourism impacts by better balancing the needs and expectations of tourists and locals.

Conclusion

A wide range of ITs are currently in use in the tourism industry. Table 20.4 (pages 442–3) demonstrates several tourism enterprises which take advantage of the Internet. However, while there are undoubtedly enormous benefits that may be reaped by organisations assimilating new technologies, such as increased competitiveness and profitability, it is crucial that ITs are accompanied by a pervasive re-engineering of business processes.

For tourism, where timely and accurate information is a crucial prerequisite for success, the implications of new ITs are far-reaching and perhaps, as yet, largely incomprehensible for the majority of consumers and suppliers as we head towards the next millennium.

Chapter discussion questions

1. Consider the major prerequisites for tourism enterprises wishing to take advantage of emergent ITs. Identify possible factors that can be instrumental in the success and failure of such systems.

2. What do you think might be the major opportunities and threats for small and medium-sized tourism enterprises in respect of ITs?

3. Review the way in which ITs may facilitate disintermediation of the tourism distribution channel. Think of some examples of innovative product distribution.

Recommended further reading

● Buhalis, D., Tjoa, A. M. and Jafari, J. (1998) *Information and Communication Technologies in Tourism*, Springer-Verlag, Wien–New York.
● Inkpen, G. (1998) *Information Technology for Travel and Tourism*, 2nd edn, Longman, London.
● Kärcher, K. (1997) *Reinventing the Package Holiday Business: New Information and Communication Technologies*, Deutscher Universitäts Verlag, Wiesbaden.
● O'Connor, P. (1995) *Using Computers in Hospitality*, Cassell, London.
● Sheldon, P. (1994) 'Information technology and computer systems', pp. 126–30 in *Tourism Marketing and Management Handbook*, 2nd edn, Witt, S. and Moutinho, L. (eds), Prentice Hall, Hemel Hempstead.

Table 20.4: Representation of tourism enterprises on the Internet

Airlines	Uniform Resource Locator	Hotels	Uniform Resource Locator
Aer Lingus	www.aerlingus.ie/	Best Western	www.travelweb.com/best.html
Aeroflot	www.seanet.com/Bazar/Aeroflot/Aeroflot.html	Choice Hotels	www.hotelchoice.com
Air Canada	www.aircanada.ca/	Consort Hotels	www.u-net.com/hotelnet/
Air France	www.airfrance.fr/	Embassy Suites	www.promus.com/embassy.html
Air UK	www.airuk.co.uk	Flag International	www.hilink.com.au/flag/flaghome.html
American Airlines	www.amrcorp.com/aa_home/aa_home.htm	Forte & Le Meridien	www.forte-hotels.com
Austrian Airlines	www.aua.co.at/aua/	Forte Travelodge	www.fortetravelodge/com/index.html
British Airways	www.british-airways.com/bans/checkin.htm	Grand Heritage	www.grandheritage.com/
British Midland	www.iflybritishmidland.com	Hilton Hotels Corporation	www.secapl.com/secapl/edgar.html
Canadian Airlines	www.CdnAir.ca:80/	Holiday Inn Worldwide	www.holiday-inn.com/
Cathay Pacific	www.cathay-usa.com	Hong Kong Hotels	www.hk.super.net/~rlowe/bizhk/comp/hotel
Continental Airlines	www.flycontinental.com	Hyatt Hotels & Resorts	www.travelweb.com/hyatt.html
Delta Airlines	www.com-stock.com/dave/delta.htm	Inter-Continental	www.interconti.com/
Emirates	www.onu.edu/~mparham/uae/emirates/emirates	Kempinski hotels	www.travelwiz.com/HOTELS/KEMPINSKI/index
Finnair	www.inteactive.line.com/finland/finair.home.html	Leading Hotels of the World	www.interactive.line.com/lead/
Iberia Airlines	www.civeng.carleton.ca/SiSpain/travelli/iberia/menu	Mandarin Oriental	www.travelweb.com/this-co/mandor/common/manres.html
Icelandair	www.arctic.is/Transport/Icelandair/Icelandair.html	Marriott International	www.marriott.com
Indonesian Airlines	www.emp.pdx.edu/htliono/trans.html	Millennium and Copthorne	www.ibmpcug.co.uk/~ecs/copthorn.html
Japan Airlines	www.spin.ad.jp/jal/home-e.html	Novotel	www.novotel.com/welcome/
KLM	www.ib.com:8080/business/klm/klm.html	Pan Pacific Hotels and Resorts	www.panpac.com/hotels
Lauda Air	www.lauraair.com/engl/indexe.htm	Radisson Hotels	www2.pcy.mci.net/marketplace/radisson/
LOT Polich Airlines	www.poland.net/lot	Red Lion Hotels	www.teleport.com/~peekra/RLhome.html
Lufthansa	www.lufthansa.co.uk	Relais & Chateaux	www.calvacom.fr/relais/accueil.html
Malaysia Airlines	www.sino.net/asean/malaysia.html#travwtc	Luxury Hotels of the World	www.slh.com/slh/
Mexicana	www.mexicana.com	Virgin Ultimate	www.virgin.com/ultimate/ultimate.html
Northwest Airlines	www.winternet.com/~tela/nwa-info.html	Westin Hotels and Resorts	www.westin.com/

Qantas Airways — www.anzac.com/qantas/qantas.com
Saudia Airlines — www.ee.wpi.edu/~zakharia/saudi-communications
Singapore Airlines — www.technet.sg/InfoWEB/communications/industry
South African Airlines — www.saa.co.za/saa/
Southwest Airlines — www.iflyswa.com/
United Airlines — www.ual.com/
Virgin Atlantic Airways — www.fly.virgin.com

Travel information

GNN Travel Center — gnn.com/gnn/meta/travel/
Dr Memory's Favorites — www.access.digex.net/~drmemory/cyber_travel.htm
Travel Weekly Online — www.traveler.net/two
Rough Guides — www.hotwired.com/rough/
Lonely Planet — lonelyplanet.com/
Moon Travel handbook — www.moon.com
Fodor — www.fodors.com/
Trav. & Tech. Network — www/ten-io.com
Around the world in 80 — www.coolsite.com/arworld.html

Internet reservation services

Expedia — expedia.msn.com/
Travelocity — www.travelocity.com
Internet Travel Network — www.itn.net/

Car rental

Hertz — www.travelweb.com
Alamo — www.freeways.com/
Eurodollar — www.eurodollar.co.uk/

Hotel directories

Hotel Net — www.demon.co.uk/hotel-net/
Travel Web — www.travelweb.com/
Worldwide Hotel Directory — www.travind.com/hotels/
First Option Hotel — www.expotel.co.uk/expotel
London Hotels Discount — www.demon.co.uk/hotel-net/lhdr.from.html
AMTRAK — www.amtrak.com/

Rail travel

Australian Timetables — brother.cc.monash.edu.au/ccstaff2/che/bromage/www/tt/index.html
Deutsche Bahn AG — www.bahn.de/index_e.html
European Rail Information — www.eurorail.html
Eurostar — oworld.avonibp.co.uk/eurostar/eurostar.html
Rail Timetables — www-cse.ucsd.edu/users/bowdicge/railroad/rail-gopher.html
Rail Server — rail.rz.unikarlsruhe.de/retail/english.html
Railway Schedules — www.wku.edu/~campbjw/schedule.html

Tourism Organisations

World Tourism Organisation — www.world-tourism.org/
Tourism Research Source — www.geocities.com/ResearchTriangle/9481/Tourism.htm
World Tourism Travel Council — www.wttc.org
ABTA — www.abtanet.com

Destinations

Ireland — www.Ireland.travel.ie
Scotland — www.scotland.net
Spain — www/ozemail.com.au/~spain
Singapore On-Line — www.travel.com.sg/sog
Japan — www.jnto.go.jp

● Sheldon, P. (1997) *Tourism Information Technology*, Cab International, Oxford.
● Truitt, L., Teye, V. and Farris, M. (1991) 'The role of computer reservation systems: international implications for the tourism industry', *Tourism Management*, **12**(1), 21–36.
● Vlitos-Rowe, I. (1995) *The Impact of Technology on the Travel Industry*, Financial Times Management Reports, London.
● WTO (1995) *Global Distribution Systems in the Tourism Industry*, World Tourism Organization, Madrid.

Bibliography

● Archdale, G. (1993) 'Computer reservation systems and public tourist offices', *Tourism Management*, **14**(1), 3–14.
● Archdale, G., Stanton, R. and Jones, G. (1992) *Destination Databases: Issues and Priorities*, Pacific Asia Travel Association, San Francisco, CA.
● Beaver, A. (1992) 'Hotel CRS – an overview', *Tourism Management*, **13**(1), 15–21.
● Beaver, A. (1995) 'Lack of CRS accessibility may be strangling small hoteliers, the lifeblood of European tourism', *Tourism Economics*, **1**(4), 341–55.
● Bennett, M. (1993) 'Information technology and travel agency: a customer service perspective', *Tourism Management*, **14**(4), 259–66.
● Braham, B. (1988) *Computer Systems in the Hotel and Catering Industry*, Cassell, London.
● Buhalis, D. (1993) 'Regional integrated computer information reservation management systems as a strategic tool for the small and medium tourism enterprises', *Tourism Management*, **14**(5), 366–78.
● Buhalis, D. (1994) 'Information and telecommunications technologies as a strategic tool for small and medium tourism enterprises in the contemporary business environment', pp. 254–75 in *Tourism–The State of the Art: The Strathclyde Symposium*, Seaton, A. *et al.* (eds), J. Wiley and Sons, Chichester.
● Buhalis, D. (1995) 'The impact of information telecommunication technologies on tourism distribution channels: implications for the small and medium sized tourism enterprises' strategic management and marketing', University of Surrey PhD Thesis, Department of Management Studies, Guildford.
● Buhalis, D. (1996) 'Technology transfer for African tourism', *Tourism Management*, **17**(8), 619–20.
● Buhalis, D. (1997) 'Information technologies as a strategic tool for economic, cultural and environmental benefits enhancement of tourism at destination regions', *Progress in Tourism and Hospitality Research*, **3**(1), 71–93.
● Chervenak, L. (1993) 'Hotel technology at the start of the millennium', *Hospitality Research Journal*, **17**(1), 113–20.
● Emmer, R., Tauck, C., Wilkinson, S. and Moore, R. (1993) 'Marketing hotels using Global Distribution Systems', *The Cornell Hotel Restaurant Administration Quarterly*, **34**(6), 80–9.
● Feeny, D. (1988) 'Creating and sustaining competitive advantage with IT', pp. 98–117 in *Information Management: The Strategic Dimension*, Earl, M. (ed.), Clarendon Press, Oxford.
● Feldman, J. (1988) 'CRS and fair airline competition', *Travel and Tourism Analyst*, **2**, 5–22.
● Go, F. (1992) 'The role of computerised reservation systems in the hospitality industry', *Tourism Management*, **13**(1), 22–6.
● Go, F. and Welch, P. (1991) *Competitive Strategies for the International Hotel Industry*, Special report, no.1180, The Economist Intelligence Unit, London.
● Hammer, M. and Champy, J. (1993) *Reengineering the Corporation: A Manifesto for Business Revolution*, Nicholas Brealey, London.

● Hawkins, D. (1996) 'The information technology paradigm shift: Implications for tourism in the 21st century', Paper presented at the International Scientific Conference on Tourism in the 21st Century, Suez Canal University, Sharl El-Sheikh, 24–26 September.

● Hawkins, D., Leventhal, M. and Oden, W. (1996) 'The virtual tourism environment: Utilisation of information technology to enhance strategic travel marketing', *Progress in Tourism and Hospitality Research*, **2**(3&4), 223–39.

● Hewson, D. (1996) 'To the seaside via cyberspace', *The Sunday Times*, 26 May, p. 10.

● Hopper, L. (1990) 'Rattling SABRE – new ways to compete on information', *Harvard Business Review*, **68**(3), 118–25.

● Hyde, J. (1992) 'Amadeus builds its defence against its advancing CRS competitors', *Travel Trade Gazette*, **2020** (10 Sept.), 25–7.

● Inkpen, G. (1998) *Information Technology for Travel and Tourism*, 2nd edn, Longman, London.

● Karcher, K. (1996) 'Re-engineering the package holiday business', in pp. 221–33 *Information and Communication Technologies in Tourism*, Conference proceedings ENTER'96, Klein, S. *et al.* (eds), Springer-Verlag, Vienna.

● McGuffie, J. (1994) 'CRS development in the hotel sector', *Travel and Tourism Analyst*, **2**, 53–68.

● Mutch, A. (1995) 'Destination information and the World Wide Web', *Insights*, September, D.5–9.

● O'Connor, P. (1995) *Using Computers in Hospitality*, Cassell, London.

● O'Connor, P. and Rafferty, J. (1997) 'Gulliver – distributing Irish tourism electronically', *Electronic Markets*, **7**(2), 40–45.

● Peacock, M. (1995) *Information Technology in Hospitality*, Cassell, London.

● Peppard, J. (ed.) (1993) *IT Strategy for Business*, Pitman, London.

● Poon, A. (1993) *Tourism, Technology and Competitive Strategies*, CAB International, Oxford.

● Porter, M. (1985) 'Technology and competitive advantage', *The Journal of Business Strategy*, Winter, 60–70.

● Robson, W. (1994) *Strategic Management and Information Systems: An Integrated Approach*, Pitman, London.

● Schertler, W., Maier, M. and Rohte, S. (1995) 'The end user acceptance of new information and communication technologies in tourism', pp. 46–52 in *Information and Communication Technologies in Tourism*, Conference proceedings ENTER'95, Schertler, W. *et al.* (eds), Springer-Verlag, Vienna.

● Sheldon, P. (1993) 'Destination information systems', *Annals of Tourism Research*, **20**(4), 633–49.

● Sheldon, P. (1994) 'Information technology and computer systems', pp. 126–30 in *Tourism Marketing and Management Handbook*, 2nd edn, Witt, S. and Moutinho, L. (eds), Prentice Hall, Hemel Hempstead.

● Smith, C. and Jenner, P. (1994) 'Travel agents in Europe', *Travel and Tourism Analyst*, **3**, 57–71.

● Tapscott, D. (1996) *The Digital Economy: Promise and Peril in the Age of Networked Intelligence*, McGraw Hill, New York.

● Tapscott, D. and Caston, A. (1993) *Paradigm Shift: The New Promise of Information Technology*, McGraw Hill, New York.

● Truitt, L., Teye, V. and Farris, M. (1991) 'The role of computer reservation systems: international implications for the tourism industry', *Tourism Management*, **12**(1), 21–36.

● Vlitos-Rowe, I. (1995) *The Impact of Technology on the Travel Industry*, Financial Times Management Reports, London.

● Wardell, D. (1987), 'Airline reservation systems in the USA: CRS agency dealerships and the gold handcuff', *Travel and Tourism Analyst*, **1**(January), 45–56.

- Wheatcroft, S. and Lipman, G. (1990) *European Liberalisation and World Air Transport: Towards a Transnational Industry*, Special Report, No.2015, Economist Intelligence Unit, London.
- Williams, P. (1993) 'Information technology and tourism: a dependent factor for future survival', pp. 200–205 in *World Travel and Tourism Review: Indicators, Trends and Issues*, **3**, Ritchie, B. *et al.* (eds), CAB International, Oxford.
- WTO (1995) *Global Distribution Systems in the Tourism Industry*, World Tourism Organization, Madrid.

Chapter author: Dr Dimitrios Buhalis

Chapter Twenty-one

The future of tourism

Introduction

Although the history of tourism may be traced back many thousands of years to the Ancient Greeks and the Romans, it is only relatively recently, with the advent of mass tourism, that international activity has become so prevalent in the developed world. The rapid expansion of leisure travel from the 1960s onwards, precipitated by transportation developments, continues to influence all aspects of the tourism system today but it is the future of tourism to which we now turn our attention.

Predicted demographic, political and technological developments outside the control of the tourism industry, coupled with the effect of tourism-specific variables such as creative packaging, consumer tastes and transportation developments, will continue to influence all aspects of the tourism system. Demand for tourism, supply of tourism at the destination, marketing, distribution and transportation are all dynamic and changes in one of these variables will inevitably encroach on all of the others. Simultaneously, other crucial issues will evolve, such as human resource considerations, and these too, in combination with the above, will be instrumental in determining the future direction of tourism.

As tourism approaches and enters a new millennium, futurists have produced many predictions and visions of the way that the sector will develop. However, despite these many forecasts we have based this chapter upon two key reliable sources: firstly, the results of the George Washington University Tourism Policy Forum and, secondly, the WTO's global tourism forecasting exercise. These sources agree that the one feature that will distinguish the future of tourism from the *old tourism* is the fact that not only will rapid change be evident, but that it will be accepted as inevitable and therefore tourism organisations will need *to manage change*. In this chapter we identify the variables that are the driving force of this change. We can see that, in certain decades there are predominant drivers of change. For example, in the mid-nineteenth century and the early decades of the twentieth century, transport developments were critical influences upon tourism. However, in the 1980s and 1990s it is both technological developments and the maturing of the tourism market-place that have come to the fore. This suggests that some of these variables are already evident, while others are still emerging.

Chapter learning objectives

During the course of this book, for the sake of simplicity and study, we have systematically separated the many complicated interrelated elements and issues which, when combined, make up the sum total of tourism. The purpose of this chapter is to re-integrate these individual components and to draw together the various strands and themes which have been introduced and discussed in the preceding pages.

Thus, this chapter:

▮▮ will encourage the reader to view tourism as a dynamic system which is subject to constant influence from both exogenous and tourism-related variables;

▮▮ will ensure readers are able to identify the key variables influencing the growth and development of tourism and understand the probable influence that changes in one variable will have upon others in the tourism system; and

▮▮ will provide a focus for individual chapters in the book, demonstrating to the reader the likely scenario in respect of the future of tourism.

The pace of change

WTO forecasts suggest that tourism will continue to grow beyond the year 2000 – on average at about 3 or 4% annually, suggesting that international tourism will double between 1990 and 2010. This means that by the year 2000 around 660 million international tourism arrivals will be experienced and a billion international arrivals will be reached by 2010. Demand for domestic tourism will expand at a slower rate and some countries will have reached demand-side ceilings of capacity and available leisure time which will constrain further growth, while on the supply-side, problems of terrorism and disease may also discourage tourism growth in some areas. The distribution of tourism by the early years of the next millennium will therefore differ in some respects from the position in the 1990s. In particular the countries of the EAP region will become important as both Taiwan and Korea become major generators of tourists not only within but also outside the region. By the year 2000 the EAP region will rival Europe and North America in its significance for tourism. None the less, other regions will also be significant players in tourism in the next millennium. The WTO forecasts that strong destinations will include the Caribbean, North Africa and South Asia, while major generators of outbound tourism will include Central and South America, Asia, as well as Africa and the Middle East.

The drivers of change

The pace of change in tourism markets is clearly set to continue. The response of the tourism sector to these levels of growth will determine the degree of success and acceptability of tourism in the future. An important part of the management process is the understanding of the drivers of change and determining the appropriate response. In this chapter we identify two types of influence:

● Firstly, there are a number of influences that are outside the control of tourism itself and yet will have an impact upon its development. These can be termed **exogenous variables**.

- Secondly, the changing nature of the tourism system itself is also driving change internally within the sector. These influences can be termed **tourism-related variables**.

In reality, most of these trends and variables are interlinked and are combining to accelerate the pace of change. For example, while there is no doubt that the social and economic trends that we identify will continue to encourage the growth of tourism, the nature of the market will also change with consequent implications for the management of destinations and products. For instance, the trend to more frequent, yet shorter trips will demand more leisure facilities close to generating markets, especially artificial 'enclave' resorts (such as Center Parcs in Europe) and resources (artificial ski slopes in Japan for example).

The new consumer of tourism is knowledgeable, discerning, seeks quality and participation and, in the developed world, is increasingly drawn from an older age group. Motivations for travel are moving away from passive sunlust towards educational and curiosity motives. At the same time, travel will be facilitated by flexible working practices and early retirement. This increasingly knowledgeable and sophisticated new tourist can now be catered for by a tourism industry that is firmly embracing the marketing concept, facilitated by technological developments such as the Internet, GDS and database marketing. The momentum of change away from passive mass tourism and towards more tailor-made, individual consumption of active tourism is set to accelerate. At the same time, shifts in the economic and political maps of the world will be reflected in a new politics of tourism and changed tourism flows as new generators of both domestic and international tourists, and new destinations, emerge. There is no doubt that these new destinations will need to be better planned and managed, and show more concern and respect for their environment and host community, than did their earlier counterparts. Indeed, all tourism visioning exercises suggest that everyone involved in tourism will have to take increased responsibility for social and environmental issues. But none of this will be possible without a well-trained tourism workforce. We therefore conclude the chapter with an examination of future trends and issues in human resource management in the tourism industry.

We can see that, as a result of these drivers, change in tourism has become inevitable, just as we have come to accept tourism growth as inevitable. This means that, not only will more tourists be seeking authentic experiences in new destinations, but also most places will be seeking to take advantage of these heightened levels of demand to boost income and employment. This is the case for most regions of the world, even the ones that have not been traditionally regarded as potential destinations – urban centres, remote and hostile regions, or industrial sites, for example. All of this means that it will be much more difficult for destinations to be successful. In particular, those destinations and enterprises in the decline stage of the life cycle will find it much more difficult to survive and may have to manage and even de-market their tourism, in order to mitigate negative impacts.

In 'An introduction to tourism' we introduced Leiper's tourism system as a way of thinking about tourism. It is possible to recast this model to take into account the ideas and issues involved in the future of tourism and to act as a framework for this chapter (Figure 21.1).

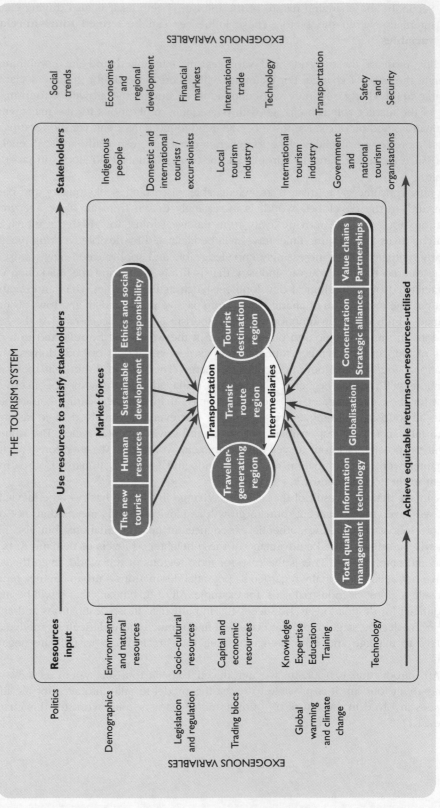

Figure 21.1: A framework for tourism trends analysis: exogenous variables

Exogenous variables

Demographic and social trends

Future demographic and social trends will be critical in shaping tourism demand to the year 2000 and beyond. Demographic trends such as ageing populations in the major generating countries, allied to the declining numbers of young people as the post-1945 baby bulge works through the decades are particularly important. Demographics are inextricably entangled with the social trends that are leading to later marriage, couples deferring having children, increased numbers of single and childless-couple households, and the enhanced role of women in travel activity. Interwoven with these trends are the changing values of the population which impact upon consumer behaviour, in particular the adoption of family values and the search for safety and security, all wrapped into cocooning behaviour where the home becomes the basis for leisure activities. In the developing world a burgeoning workforce will lead to immigration to the developed world and the growth of knowledge and interest in other countries will see a convergence of lifestyles across the world. With increased media attention and levels of education, these trends will give people more time, resources and inclination to travel. This will be encouraged by the growth and spread of discretionary incomes and the liberalisation of trade on an international scale.

Political developments

In the late 1980s and early 1990s, we saw a redrafting of the political map of the world and this has a number of continuing implications for tourism. The emergence of market economies in Eastern Europe has led to an increased demand to travel from the populations of those countries, and also to the development of destinations and products in the region. Business and specialist leisure travel, particularly cultural tourism, has grown as travel restrictions have been eased, infrastructure improved and attitudes to service changed. Indeed, so successful has been the opening up of tourism in the region that Hungary, Poland, the Czech Republic and the Russian Federation have moved into the top 20 international destinations in the mid-1990s. However, not only are some of these destinations suffering from tourism pressure – Prague, Lake Balaton – but international tourism is pricing out domestic demand in some countries. In other parts of the world too, new destinations such as South Africa are developing as they become politically acceptable, or emerge from conflict – as in Vietnam and the Lebanon.

At the same time, the creation of trading blocs throughout the world is facilitating tourism. Such blocs include the North American Free Trade Agreement (NAFTA), the ASEAN and the EU. Membership of these blocs is dynamic – the EU, for example, has joined with the European Free Trade Association (EFTA) countries to form the European Economic Area (EEA). These countries are likely to be joined by other new entrants such as some of the former Eastern European countries in the medium term.

Yet, the spread of democracy and the liberalisation of trade is complemented by a contradictory trend – the rise of regionalism and a search for local identity. Of course, this may lead to conflict (as in the regions of ex-Yugoslavia), but elsewhere the trend is less sinister with the emergence of **city states** as major tourist destinations whether it be as cultural centres (such as Dublin) or for hosting major events, such as the 2000 Olympics in Sydney. These developments are changing the politics of tourism. There is a trend for national administrations to withdraw from the support and funding of tourism and to pass on responsibility to the regional level or to the private sector. In the mid-1990s, the USA for example dismantled its national tourism administration,

Case Study 21.1   Space tourism

Although space tourism can be thought of as an activity in the distant future, it is estimated that by 2020 space technology will be applied to intercontinental travel. Already companies are taking bookings for space trips.

Taking Leiper's system again, it is clear that space tourism should include not only the market for the product and the means of transport, but also the destination. For space tourism, the destination may indeed include the Moon, but it can also be thought of as present-day theme parks on earth – such as the Kennedy Space Centre at Cape Canaveral, Florida, or simulated rides such as the Star Wars rides at the Disney theme parks. Other earth-based simulations of weightlessness, or driving Moon buggies could also come under the label of space tourism. In the future, options will not only include the ability to travel to destinations in space, but also activities such as orbital flight, or the ability to stay in space-based hotels or space stations.

while parts of Scandinavia have sanctioned the private sector to deal with tourism promotion.

Transportation developments

Historically, change in tourism has been closely linked to transport innovations. In the future, the influence of transport will be diluted by the emergence of new drivers of change. None the less, the influence of transport should not be underestimated. Tourism remains dependent upon transport technology and the consequent improvements in efficiency, range and safety of travel – even to the extent of tourism in space (see Case Study 21.1). Equally, tourism may also be constrained by transportation in the future as old systems fail to accommodate increased levels of demand. The inadequate capacity of the American and European air traffic control systems are cases in point here, as are the many examples of inadequate airport capacity and aircraft noise restrictions which constrain tourism volume. We can also see a change in the management and approach of transport enterprises with an emphasis on both marketing and the building of strategic alliances to gain market share. There is no doubt that transport innovations and tourism development do go hand-in-hand. To quote Boniface and Cooper (1994):

> In the [future] intercontinental airline operations will be characterised by the use of larger aircraft and more non-stop, very long flights – aided by the development of Concorde's hypersonic successor. The increased emphasis on hub and spoke operations, where airlines realign schedules at their hub and time schedules on the spokes so they connect at the hub will also continue. This gives the hub airline a potentially strong competitive position and leads to a system of 'fortress' hubs keeping out newcomers. These airports will need well co-ordinated flights, a prime geographical location, and good terminal facilities.
>
> Although it is generally accepted that total deregulation of the international airline industry is not practical, the trend towards deregulation will continue. . . . In the US, deregulation has led to domination by a small number of larger airlines – a trend which is emerging in other sectors of the tourism industry.
>
> Forecasts of international transport . . . predict that technological developments, increased airline efficiency and labour productivity savings will offset

any rises in aviation fuel prices and thus, in real terms, fares will continue to fall. This will support the continued trend towards long haul travel. However, if energy costs do rise significantly, then a shift towards surface transport and shorter journey lengths can be expected.

Despite the focus of much writing on air transport, most tourism journeys are by car. Whilst the use of the car for inter-city travel has declined in the USA there seems little prospect for use of the car to decline in Europe [and other parts of the world] where the market is nowhere near reaching saturation. Continued . . . developments of car technology to make driving more comfortable and environmentally acceptable; and improved fuel efficiency will all make motoring cheaper and more attractive. (pp. 241–2)

At the same time, we believe that by the year 2000 and beyond there will be a gradual modal switch away from air to surface transport. Not only is there a fear that the new investment required to equip airlines with new aircraft will not be forthcoming, but also the competition from surface transport is sharpening. This will be characterised by improved rail services and rail-based tourism products, the realisation of the environmental advantages of rail and continued technological developments in the area of high-speed train networks.

Other trends and influences

We can identify a range of other variables which also impinge upon the future of tourism. These include long-term factors such as global warming and the erosion of the ozone layer. On the supply-side, there is no doubt that the raising of the Earth's temperature and the consequent rise in sea level will affect tourism. Much of tourism investment is found in locations fringing the coast, and vital tourism resources such as the flora and fauna of destinations will be irrevocably altered by global warming. On the demand-side, fear of skin cancer and eye cataracts may reduce the demand for products such as beach tourism which, in turn will impact upon destination and product development. Tourists' behaviour too, is a threat to tourism as the spread of AIDS may render some otherwise attractive destinations no-go areas while increasingly vociferous campaigns against sex tourism may also alter tourism flows and motivations. Elsewhere, disease in some parts of the world and decreasing levels of safety will constrain the uninhibited expansion of tourism. At the macro-level, these factors are largely outside the control of tourism and their consequences may be severe, yet at the micro-level, the tourism industry will increasingly manage issues such as safety and security at the destination.

Finally, technological innovations such as virtual reality (VR) may one day replace the authentic travel experience all together. By simply strapping on a body suit and plugging into the virtual reality programme you could be transported to the sights, sounds and sensations of, say, the Caribbean. The tourist can experience the destination but without any risk of skin cancer, AIDS, or the other side effects of travel; while for the destination, negative impacts are removed – but so are the positive effects of income, jobs and regional development. The debate as to the real impact of VR is still ongoing:

- *Proponents* say that, as cocooning behaviour increasingly places the home as a central and secure base for leisure activities, VR may depress demand for the real thing.

- *Opponents* contend that VR will simply whet the appetite for more travel through enhanced exposure to, and awareness of, the product.

Tourism-related variables

The new tourist

Many tourism futurists (such as Poon) have suggested that the maturing of the tourism market is creating a new tourist who can be characterised as experienced, sophisticated and demanding. This means that the traditional annual family holiday mostly spent in a beach resort may be gradually superseded by multi-interest travel and a range of creative and innovative travel experiences (such as activity, adventure, learning and nature-based tourism). These trends will see the relative importance of conventional packaged tours decline in favour of independently organised tourism, or at least a more bespoke form of tourism.

To an extent, the new sophisticated traveller has emerged as a result of experience. Tourists from the major generating regions of the world have become frequent travellers, are linguistically and technologically skilled and can function in multicultural and demanding environments overseas. Add to this media and Internet exposure of tourism destinations and the reduction of perceived distance to reach such places and the stage is set for a reappraisal of holiday formulae. Education too has played a part, together with enhanced communications, and has led to more sophisticated requirements from holidaymakers who are now looking for new experiences combined with rewarding activities to fill their leisure time and satisfy their cultural, intellectual and sporting interests. Here, the emergence of the knowledge-based society is significant for tourism as travel products are merged with education and entertainment. This creates **info-tainment** or **edu-tainment** at destinations and specifically at commercial attractions through interpretation and education programmes.

Of course, the sophistication of the customer will have an impact upon product development throughout the industry; not only will there be an increased requirement for high standards of product design, efficiency and safety, but also the tourist will be more critical of the product and have the experience to compare offerings. At the same time, as the new tourist is conscious of value for money rather than simply price, other elements of the marketing mix will become important. In particular, this will mean that quality will remain a key attribute in tourism product development and customer convenience in all its forms will be demanded by the new travellers, a trend fuelled by consumer legislation in tourism.

Every tourist is different, bringing a unique blend of experiences, motivations and desires. Tourism is increasingly following the trend of other industries towards customising. Here technology enables products to be tailored to meet individual tastes. The old tourism products did not adopt this approach. Instead they were general and unspecialised with very similar characteristics traded as commodities rather than services under the mass tourism philosophy. This philosophy said that tourism products should appeal to all tastes and be sold at a low price in order to attract as wide a range of customers as possible.

Much of the above discussion points to the need for effective segmentation of the tourism market. Traditionally, tourism marketers have been using geographic and demographic criteria in order to describe their markets, but psychographics and behavioural criteria will be increasingly used in order:

● to provide detailed customer profiles;

● to identify motivations, needs and determinants; and

● to offer an appropriate marketing mix and service delivery strategy.

Technology, globalisation and concentration

As the tourism market matures, heightened competition will force enterprises both to identify and to utilise modern methods of management. These methods will allow the sector to minimise operational costs and maximise output, while at the same time creating competitive advantage through differentiation throughout the tourism industry. This is achieved by

- efficiency and productivity which deliver **cost** advantage; and
- differentiation and positioning which deliver **value** advantage.

In Chapter 20 we identified technology as a major facilitator in this respect. At the micro-level, technology will wire the entire enterprise and enable effective and quick management. Integrated property management systems in hotels for example can perform a range of functions, while at the macro-level IT will allow diagonal integration in the tourism industry by facilitating the production, distribution and delivery of an integrated tourist product and wrapping the entire variety of tourism products within technology platforms such as GDS or the Internet.

The widespread use of technology in the tourism industry will enable tourist enterprises to improve their profitability. Yield management is used by hotels and airlines to manipulate demand effectively. This is done by identifying the most appropriate price for the product at a particular moment by assessing the demand and supply for the requested period, the timing of the request, as well as by taking the historic pattern of sales. The system suggests a price that maximises the yield of an airline seat or bed for the sale in question. In addition, technology enables tourism enterprises to have a closer relationship with their customers and reward loyalty. Database marketing allows personalised treatment and the launch of initiatives such as frequent flyer schemes by airlines (see Major Case Study 5). Hotels also create guest history databases, reward frequent stayers and store information relating to guest requests and preferences which can be utilised in forging alliances with other providers.

The need for efficiency in the international tourism market has accelerated the emergence of multinational corporations which provide tourism services in various countries. Globalisation is one of the major trends in the international tourism industry. It is based on convergence in world tastes and product preferences which results in globally standardised products and is facilitated by the technological innovations of systems such as GDS. Of course it is only the larger, international companies who can take advantage of these trends. Indeed, globalisation goes hand-in-hand with increased concentration in the tourism industry as major companies gain market share and market influence. At the same time we are seeing the concentration of capital in the hands of a few major players in the tourism sector; a trend that also drives tourism towards the performance indicators and business practices demanded by the finance industry. The pace of concentration being generated by both horizontal and vertical integration is such that for medium-sized companies in tourism the days ahead may be difficult. Quite simply for a tourism enterprise there are many advantages to increased size in a multinational market:

- economies of scale;
- ability to resource high-profile promotional campaigns;
- brand name benefits through standardisation and quality control;
- ability to spread the risk among various markets;
- implementation of advanced marketing techniques on an international basis;

- utilisation of technology (especially GDS and the Internet);
- optimisation of capacity/inventory usage and reduction of seasonality problems;
- access to the international labour market;
- advantages over other members of the distribution channel;
- improved political influence;
- managers who have more time to manage; and
- market prominence and stronger branding.

However, a particular problem associated with this trend is that most of the larger corporations do not have a relationship with a specific destination. Some commentators feel that they will therefore be less sensitive to the impact of their operations on the host environments, economies and communities. In addition, small and medium-sized tourism enterprises and local destinations fear the **neo-colonial relationship** which can emerge from dealing with large companies. To complement these global players a new breed of successful, smaller, niched, operators are emerging as influential in the future of tourism. Their competitive advantages include:

- a differentiated product which does not compete on price;
- a high level of personalised service;
- a high level of product knowledge;
- quality/price ratio;
- a deregulated market-place reducing the barriers to entry; and
- a synergistic relationship with the destination.

We can use two examples to illustrate how these three trends of technology, globalisation and concentration are converging to impact upon tourism:

1. **The accommodation/lodging sector.** In the hotel sector companies have recognised the changing characteristics and demands of the consumer and responded accordingly by developing hospitality products that:

    (a) are increasingly research-based to understand individual customer needs;

    (b) are quality controlled;

    (c) are flexible and convenient;

    (d) are good value, particularly the accommodation/lodging element;

    (e) provide for segmented service occasions at the point of consumption; and

    (f) are technology driven from management systems to **smart** hotel rooms.

    Interestingly too, it is in the accommodation sector that we can see a clear polarisation between global and niche players.

2. **GDS and the Internet.** GDS and the Internet are a good example of the convergence of these trends of technology, globalisation, concentration and a focus on the new tourist. Both GDS and the Internet have already caused major structural changes within the tourism industry, and combined with a more knowledgeable tourist market, they will facilitate the emergence of a growing number of independent travellers and the gradual bypassing of intermediaries in the tourism distribution chain. This is because suppliers will be able to target their products more closely to meet the desires of their customer segments – and display them effectively through new media development and home-based access to visual,

interactive travel information. This will also allow the consumer to access products directly through the Internet. The alliance of global distribution systems with Internet suppliers will provide a one-stop reservation facility for the entire range of tourist products. This trend is expected to dominate the future development of the Internet as it evolves to offer an organisational platform for the distribution of the integrated tourist product. There are, however, possible constraints upon the capacity of these systems which include satellite availability and future government regulation of the Internet.

Sustainable tourism development

While many bemoan the fact that the tourism sector is not recognised by governments and the media, it is to be regretted that when such recognition does emerge, it sees tourism as a despoiler of environments, exploiter of indigenous peoples and a sector focused on the short-term profit imperative. This view of tourism became potent with the rise of environmentalism and green consciousness in the mid to late 1980s which culminated with the Rio Earth Summit conference in 1992. In part, these trends are a reflection of the growing maturity of both the tourist as consumer and the tourism industry itself. Mass tourism began with short-term perspectives as the industry and public agencies attempted to handle growing demand. In the 1980s and 1990s growth rates slowed and consumers have questioned some of the excesses of tourism development. In response, longer planning horizons are being considered and alternative forms of tourism advocated. As we have seen throughout this book, sustainable tourism development has become the organising concept for all aspects of tourism and there is no reason to see a dilution of this trend. Archer and Cooper (1994) speak of:

> the belated discovery of the relevance of the sustainable development concept to tourism. As with many service industries, some of the most important ideas and innovations come from outside the industry or the subject area. The concept of sustainable development has a long pedigree in the field of resource management and, at last, is becoming an acceptable term in tourism. The Brundtland Report puts it simply as 'meeting the needs of the present without compromising the ability of future generations to meet their own needs' (World Commission on Environment and Development, 1987). The concept of sustainability is central to the reassessment of tourism's role in society. It demands a long-term view of economic activity, questions the imperative of continued economic growth, and ensures that consumption of tourism does not exceed the ability of a host destination to provide for future tourists. In other words, it represents a trade-off between present and future needs. In the past, sustainability has been a low priority compared with the short-term drive for profitability and growth but, with pressure growing for a more responsible tourism industry, it is difficult to see how such short-term views on consumption can continue long into the 1990s. Indeed, destination 'regulations' are being developed in some areas and already, the band-wagon for sustainable development and responsible consumption is rolling. Public agencies are issuing guidelines for acceptable development; tourism consumer groups are growing in number and influence and guides to responsible tourism are available.
> (p. 87)

We can see that the central issue here is the gradual shift from short-term to longer-term thinking and planning in tourism. It is no longer acceptable for the industry to exploit and use up destinations and then move on; indeed we are already seeing the results of this in the demise of some of the mass tourism resorts built in the 1960s and 1970s – Acapulco in Mexico is an example here. The concepts of the tourism area life cycle and strategic planning provide a much needed long-term perspective in this respect. Consumers will place pressure upon the industry and destination managers to behave in a responsible manner; if they do not then their destination may be shunned as *environmentally unacceptable* to visit. Destinations are responding to these demands in a variety of ways. Resource-based destinations are adopting sophisticated planning, management and interpretive techniques to provide both a welcome and a rich experience for the tourist while at the same time ensuring protection of the resource itself. It is felt that once tourists understand why a destination is significant they will want to protect it. Good planning and management of the destination lies at the heart of providing the new tourist with a high-quality experience and it may be that tourists will have to accept increasingly restricted viewing times at popular sites, higher prices and even replicas of the real thing.

The industry itself is also anxious to demonstrate that it is both responsible and acting to curb some of the excesses of past development. Here, a number of initiatives are notable:

- The WTTC represents the tourism industry and has been active in researching the impacts of tourism. It has introduced an environmental awareness programme, *Green Globe*.
- The PATA has launched an environmental membership and endorsement scheme, *Green Leaf*.
- *Green Suitcase* sets out environmental quality standards for resorts, accommodation and travel agents in Europe, developed by Okologischer Tourismus in Europe.
- Companies have initiated awards, such as *Tourism for Tomorrow* by British Airways.

Of course, there is an element of self-preservation here as green products will become increasingly popular and a sector that is seen to be responsible will not attract regulation by government. It also raises the issue of the *ethical* consumption and development of tourism, where organisations recognise their long-term responsibilities and their relationship with a variety of stakeholders. This is becoming evident in the brochures of tour operator/wholesalers where the consumer is urged to **respect**, **re-use**, **recycle** *and* **rescue** consumption.

Careers, human resources and training

Many of you reading this book will be looking towards the tourism industry for a career. Indeed, the challenges facing the tourism industry will only be met successfully by a well-educated, well-trained, bright, energetic, multilingual and entrepreneurial workforce who understand the nature of tourism and have a professional training. A high quality of professional human resources in tourism will allow enterprises to gain a competitive edge and deliver added value with their service. Tourism is a high-touch, high-tech, high-involvement industry where it is the people that make the difference. Yet, in a number of countries, an acute shortage of trained manpower may prejudice the growth of tourism.

There is no doubt that the tourism industry is under pressure. Changing markets, industry restructuring and more competitive domestic and international markets are placing great burdens on their expertise. The ability to succeed, and the future performance of tourism and related activities will depend largely upon the skills, qualities and knowledge that managers will be able to bring to their business.

In the past, tourism has been characterised by a lack of sophistication in human resource policies and practices, imposed by outmoded styles of human resource management and approaches to operational circumstances. This leaves tourism vulnerable to ideas, takeovers and domination by management practices found in other economic sectors. Indeed, practices that are commonplace in other service industries – comprehensive induction, regular appraisal, effective employee communications – are underdeveloped in many tourism and leisure businesses. Educators and trainers have a role to play here by facilitating innovation, encouraging empowerment, motivating the workforce and, in partnership with industry, working to overcome the specific problems of tourism.

A high-quality tourism workforce can only be achieved through high standards of tourism education and training. Tourism education and training involves the communication of knowledge, concepts and techniques that are specific to the field of tourism. Traditionally, the domain of tourism education has been the encouragement of analytical thinking and the understanding of conceptual issues in order to contribute to the professional and intellectual development of a person. Tourism training, on the other hand, is more concerned with delivering practical knowledge, skills and techniques.

Tourism training has a long pedigree and emerged as the tourism industry grew both in size and complexity. Initially, training was linked to the operations of intermediaries, particularly in areas such as ticketing, or in the various craft operations for hospitality. In the developing world much of tourism training is still confined to these areas but in the developed world, tourism training has expanded to embrace many functions as the industry becomes more professional and demands higher standards of its practitioners. Tourism education is a much more recent activity. Apart from a handful of institutions, most tourism education courses are a product of the 1980s and 1990s. This is because it is only in recent years that governments have recognised the value of tourism to their economies and in particular linked manpower planning and education/training for tourism with competitiveness and productivity.

The benefits of both education and training for tourism should be clear:

- They ensure a high quality of service is provided to the consumer.
- For the industry as a whole they add value, raise the quality of personnel and infuse a sense of professionalism and ownership.
- They also help to define the industry and point out the underlying similarities of the many differing sectors (transport, hospitality, attractions, etc.).
- Those working in the industry also understand the interrelationships of the sectors and begin to perceive business opportunities.
- Training, in particular, delivers skills and practical knowledge which boosts the performance and productivity of personnel across the industry, and the linking of education and training with manpower planning allows a closer gearing of the needs of the sector with the output of hotel and tourism schools.
- They help to retain staff, provide a career path for employees and overall, achieve a better use of human resources in the tourism industry.
- They ensure that a destination's tourism product is delivered by local people and not by imported labour.

In the future, tourism education and training must be responsive to the changing needs of the sector and here, we can identify three key trends:

1. **Deepening within the subject area.** We are seeing an evolution of tourism education and training that recognises the need for a broad-based education system.

In the past, the weight of provision tended to be confined to hospitality elements. The inclusion of tourism and travel into these programmes will ensure that not only will the accommodation sector be well managed, but also that the country's attractions, transportation and ground handling will be professionally organised with high standards of service, destination management and guiding.

2. **Broadening to other subject areas.** A second trend is the shifting balance between tourism and hospitality course content and core management and business areas such as finance or marketing. In the future, the tourism manager will need to be knowledgeable in say, generic marketing approaches, but will also have to be able to apply that expertise within a tourism or hospitality context.

3. **Development of quality standards.** A third trend is the involvement of international bodies such as the WTO to integrate quality standards into tourism education and training.

Emergent patterns

Poon (1989), a leading commentator on future trends in tourism, predicts the demise of the old tourism and the emergence of a new tourism (Figure 21.2). She sees the key trends leading to this new tourism as:

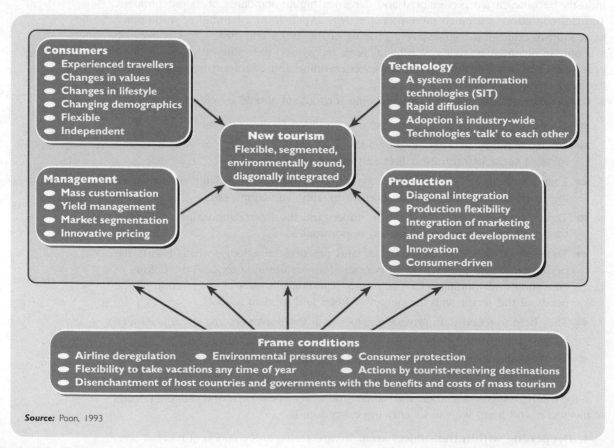

Source: Poon, 1993

Figure 21.2: Poon's new tourism

*the diffusion of a system of new information technologies in the tourism indus-
try; deregulation of the airline industry and financial services; the negative
impact of mass tourism on host countries; the movement away from sun-lust
to sun-plus tourism; environmental pressures; technology; competition; and
changing consumer tastes. . . . (p. 92)*

In other words the future of tourism will be one of flexible, segmented, customised and
diagonally integrated tourism rather than the mass, rigid, standardised and packaged
tourism of the 1970s. Here, the WTO has provided a useful set of strategic signals to
guide the sector into the twenty-first century (see Case Study 21.2).

Case Study 21.2 Strategic signals for the twenty-first century

The WTO has presented two subsets of strategic signals to guide countries in their planning and development of tourism into the next century.

Planning and marketing

- Establish (and adhere closely to) a system of planning that is comprehensive, integrated, continuing and flexible. Base this on accurate and up-to-date information on market trends including the strategies, developments and performance of competitor countries and private sector
tourism operators (international and national).

- Establish realistic tourist market *targets* for a decade ahead and develop strategies and programmes to achieve these, i.e. marketing, infrastructure/amenity/facility development, personnel
education and training.

- Create new and diversified travel products and services, based on the unique natural and cultural features, attributes and resources of individual countries.

- Incorporate the local communities both in the planning and operation of tourism.

- Develop a partnership of close communication and cooperation between administrators/regu-
lators and operators.

- Create value, by avoiding excessive tax burdens on tourism and by controlling avoidable price
inflation in the sector.

- Invest environmentally by controlling harmful developments and practices, and encouraging
those which conserve or protect.

- Eliminate amateurism at all levels through well-designed education and training programmes,
and the implementation of a sound system of professional standards.

Information technology

- Embrace technology to facilitate tourist movements.

- Explore and exploit to the full all IT possibilities in the distribution and marketing of tourism
products and services (through computer reservations systems, electronic destination databases,
etc.).

Use computer technology to collect, analyse and present a wider range of tourism statistics, both first
level/direct and second level/indirect, thereby facilitating a clearer picture and better understanding
of the performance and potential of tourist markets.

Conclusion

This chapter has attempted to draw together the many disparate trends that influence the future of tourism. It has also, in a sense, acted to draw together the threads of this book as a whole. The message is clear. Tourism will only be an acceptable and successful industry in the future if a well-trained and professional workforce is in place and able to implement the very best practice in managing tourism. This book has brought together these practices and wrapped them around a state of the art commentary on tourism, its principles and practice. Of course, any book written in the mid-1990s will be tested in a number of ways because it faces the dynamic nature of the modern world. However, we have tried to provide general principles and practices rather than specifics which will date. We offer you the challenges of tourism management and believe it will become clearer if you follow the frameworks and approaches that we have provided.

Chapter discussion questions

1. Consider the implications of the emergence of the new tourism for all aspects of the tourism system.

2. Identify key trends in tourism which may affect its future development.

3. Is the future of tourism a secure one?

Recommended further reading

- International Hotel Association (1994) *Events Shaping the Future and Their Impact Upon the Multinational Hotel Industry*, IHA, Paris.
- Poon, A. (1993) *Tourism, Technology and Competitive Strategies*, CAB, Oxford.
- WTO (1994) *Global Tourism Forecasts to the Year 2000 and Beyond*, WTO, Madrid.

Bibliography

- Archer, B. H. and Cooper, C. (1994) 'The positive and negative impacts of tourism' pp. 73–91 in *Global Tourism. The Next Decade*, Theobold, W. (ed.), Butterworth-Heinemann, Oxford.
- Boniface, B. and Cooper, C. (1994) *The Geography of Travel and Tourism*, Butterworth-Heinemann, Oxford.
- International Hotel Association (1994) *Events Shaping the Future and Their Impact Upon the Multinational Hotel Industry*, IHA, Paris.
- Leiper, N. (1990) *Tourism Systems*, Massey University Department of Management Systems Occasional Paper 2, Auckland, New Zealand.
- Poon, A. (1989) 'Competitive strategies for a new tourism,' pp. 91–102 in *Progress in Tourism, Recreation and Hospitality Management*, Vol. 1, Cooper, C. (ed.), Belhaven, London.

- Poon, A. (1993) *Tourism, Technology and Competitive Strategies*, CAB, Oxford.
- Ritchie, J. R. B. (1992) 'New horizons, new realities: perspectives of the tourism educator,' pp. 257–263, in *World Travel and Tourism Review*, Ritchie, J. R. B. and Hawkins, D. (eds), CAB, Oxford.
- WCED (1987) *Our Common Future*, Oxford University Press, New York.
- WTO (1994) *Global Tourism Forecasts to the Year 2000 and Beyond*, WTO, Madrid.
- WTTC (1995) *Agenda 21 for the Travel and Tourism Industry*, WTTC, London.

Major Case Studies

Introduction

The dynamics of the tourism system are complex and although we have compartmentalised the study of tourism into its constituent parts for manageability, such division is actually wholly artificial. All aspects of the system are interlinked in reality and each will exert mutual influence on the other. It is, therefore, impossible to evaluate and explain fully one element without considering its influence upon the others.

The objective of Part 6, which incorporates six major case studies, is to reintegrate the individual sectors of demand, supply, industry and marketing to demonstrate the domino effect that occurs when one part of the tourism system changes. The case studies we have selected are designed to illustrate the dynamism of tourism under the following headings:

- Major Case Study 1 – Tourism destinations in decline
- Major Case Study 2 – Visitor management

- Major Case Study 3 – Tourism planning in Eastern Europe
- Major Case Study 4 – Tourism project assistance
- Major Case Study 5 – Relationship marketing
- Major Case Study 6 – Information technology

Major Case Study 1 – Tourism destinations in decline

Although tourism, in its purest form, has been an activity for many hundreds of years, the advent of mass tourism is a much more recent phenomenon. Destinations developed rapidly in many areas of the world, the Spanish Costas being a prime example, to meet the needs of large numbers of tourists concentrated spatially and temporally. However, many of these mass tourism destinations have entered what may be termed the decline stages of their life cycles. They have become unpopular and unfashionable as a result of unplanned and uncontrolled development accompanied subsequently by environmental destruction. As tastes have changed, tourists have moved on to new areas where they may enjoy a less degraded experience.

Unfortunately, for those destinations that have been subject to abandonment, the impacts of desertion are significant. Unlike products in other markets, tourism products, i.e. resorts and destinations, cannot be easily withdrawn from the market-place or simply manipulated by adding new features or updating existing ones. The development of new attractions, facilities and amenities have long lead times and the human and economic implications of withdrawal from tourism reduce the viability of this option.

The first of our major case studies, therefore, demonstrates the interactivity of the tourism system by focusing on tourism policy and planning, the marketing implications of product redevelopment, and the roles of both public and private sectors.

Major Case Study 2 – Visitor management

As the less discernible impacts of tourism activity have become apparent, they have provided the impetus for destinations to evolve new strategies and techniques aimed at protecting the resource from over-use and damage while providing the tourist with an appropriate experience. At a general level, these pressures have fuelled the debate that centres on the need for sustainable development to ensure preservation for the enjoyment of future generation. At specific site level, these pressures have encouraged the introduction of new techniques for visitor management which aim to maximise preservation of the attraction while optimising visitor satisfaction.

The second major case study focuses on these techniques and the crucial role they are increasingly playing in the management of important sites and resources. We use this case study to review the principles behind visitor management and its benefits for all stakeholders and tourists. A framework for approaching visitor management is discussed and we conclude this chapter by reviewing pertinent issues.

Major Case Study 3 – Tourism planning in Eastern Europe

Major Case Study 3 details tourism planning in Eastern Europe and demonstrates how Western tourism expertise and knowledge may be transferred to other countries and regions, in this case to Szolnok County in Hungary.

We use this case study to show that tourism planning and development may best be implemented in a controlled and systematic manner to protect the environment and culture of the indigenous population. The case study provides a comprehensive analysis of the tourism planning process, a review of all pertinent facts and a discussion of the key issues involved.

Major Case Study 4 – Tourism project assistance

The fourth of the Major Case Studies focuses on the system that exists within the EU for tourism projects. Specifically, we turn our attention to the schemes that make monetary assistance available for tourism investment and development and the criteria that must be met prior to the receipt of such monies. The existence of these initiatives at a high level on a pan-European basis are designed to encourage and support certain types of tourism development which meet stringent criteria.

Major Case Study 5 – Relationship marketing

The fifth Major Case Study demonstrates the evolution of what is called 'relationship marketing' as it relates to the phenomenon of airline loyalty schemes. Relationship marketing has characterised the aviation industry in recent years as a response to destabilised operating conditions brought about by external events such as wars and economic recession. These have resulted in falling load factors for airlines and the industry has reacted by implementing discounted fare structures and promotional strategies. Although these strategies have increased load factors they have simultaneously adversely affected profitability, leading airlines to investigate the advantages of marketing activities which encourage customer loyalty and long-term commitment through the use of a reward system.

Since it is estimated to be considerably more expensive to attract a customer than to retain one, relationship marketing has become a key strategy for virtually all major airlines in America and Europe. These programmes are also expanding in Asia and the Far East where carriers are reluctantly being drawn into these schemes despite initial resistance.

We use this case study to review the historical development of airline loyalty schemes, the objectives they are designed to meet and the benefits they supposedly derive. In addition, we consider the problems associated with frequent flyer schemes and raise pertinent discussion points for readers to contemplate.

Major Case Study 6 – Information technology

The four major GDSs are Galileo, Sabre, Amadeus and Worldspan. In this case study, we focus on Amadeus, one of the key global players accounting for an estimated 27% of all travel agency locations world-wide (Buhalis, 1996). Amadeus was established in 1987 and developed as a response to the introduction of sophisticated CRSs in the USA and impending deregulation in Europe which presented opportunities for new, more effective, methods of distribution.

The implications of these new systems continue to be far-reaching. The distribution of the tourism product, in particular, has been revolutionised by systems such as Amadeus and the marketing benefits. In this case, study, therefore, we outline the range of products and the benefits of mass distribution which links demand for tourism instantaneously with the supply of the tourism product. We consider the possible future strategies of these global systems and likely future developments.

Overview

Thus, Part 6 is a crucial and valuable addition to this textbook and it fulfils a number of very important objectives:

- It encourages readers to consider the totality of the tourism system after having studied its individual elements in the textbook.
- It demonstrates contemporary issues from all aspects of tourism.
- It draws the individual strands explored throughout the textbook together.
- It offers readers the opportunity to explore real-life scenarios which are detailed, comprehensive and contemporary.

Reference

- Buhalis, D. (1996) 'Technology transfer for African tourism', *Tourism Management*, **17**(8), 619–20.

Destinations
in decline

Case Study objectives

▬ To provide an understanding of the issues facing destinations in decline.

▬ To expand on the concept of the tourism area life cycle.

▬ To discuss possible strategies which may be implemented to alleviate the problems in declining destinations.

Introduction

Much of the writing and research on tourism has examined the positive aspects of growth and development. Rather less popular has been work examining the decline stages of the tourism area life cycle (TALC) (see Chapter 5). Yet these stages of the life cycle are becoming an increasing reality for many countries and regions as mass international tourism matures. After all many mass tourism destinations have a long pedigree. For example, the Spanish Costas date back to the 1960s while many British and northern European resorts can be traced to the eighteenth and nineteenth centuries.

Setting the scene

The problem is a simple one – destinations, with age, lose their appeal to the market as tastes and preferences alter and resorts are left stranded in a time warp identifiable by their physical facilities, architectural styles and layout. However, while the *problem* may be simple, the *solution* is difficult – the tourism sector in these resorts is left with a dilemma: whether to pull out of tourism all together and become a retirement centre, dormitory town or health centre, or whether to readjust their marketing plans and development strategies to *re-launch*, or *rejuvenate* the resort. This case study examines the options for such resorts in the later stages of the TALC.

The problem

Resorts or destinations in decline tend to have a number of factors in common:

- a demoralised tourism industry;
- a low-spending, downmarket clientele of both staying and day visitors;
- a high percentage of repeat clients;
- environmental problems;
- high seasonal unemployment in the off-peak;
- a poor competitive position;
- acute seasonality; and
- shortage of market research.

Clearly, some of these problems are internal to the resort and can be addressed, while others are outside their control. Turning around such a situation is difficult and it is here that the analogy between the TALC and product life cycles begins to break down. Product life cycles in the decline stage signal to the marketing manager that the production line should be terminated or the product withdrawn from production. For resorts, this is problematic – tourism is often interwoven in the fabric of the town, supporting jobs, retailing, entertainment and other facilities. It is impossible simply to switch tourism off. Resorts are therefore faced with the dilemma of how to seek new markets and redevelop their product offering to compete effectively with contemporary destinations.

Strategies

An idealised planning framework for the development of strategies for destinations in decline is outlined as Figure CS1.1. The approach is taken from classic strategic management as adopted in companies and corporations. But it is here that, again, the analogy of treating the resort as a product breaks down. In companies there are clear reporting lines, and decisions are made on a hierarchical basis. Yet for resorts, there are no such reporting lines. Indeed, the whole process will be fraught with political difficulty from day one as each one from a mosaic of interest groups demands a say in the process. Such a political process demands a thorough grasp of the local political situation and the role of power brokers and interest groups, and involves a skilful process of conflict resolution and reconciliation. Any one who has lived in a resort or on a small island will have first-hand knowledge of the complexity and high profile of such politics. As if this was not difficult enough, the process is unlikely to be informed by adequate research or quantitative data in most cases. Again this contrasts with the model of strategic planning in a company where the SWOT analysis would be assembled from a raft of good quality data.

However, there is evidence from many parts of the world that these problems can be overcome and a successful re-launch achieved. Equally, there is now sufficient documentation of these approaches being undertaken that it is possible to classify the strategies. Diamond (1988) for example has suggested a grouping of four possible approaches:

1. **Turnaround.** Here the resort invests in a major effort literally to *turnaround* the problem by investment, planning and promotion. This approach is resource-intensive, demanding a public sector lead and backing from both the industry and residential population.

2. **Sustainable growth.** This approach is less drastic than the turnaround strategy and relies on gradual replenishment of declining markets by seeking out new areas of market potential. However, the original, though reducing, markets are still nurtured and maintained. This is more of a marketing-led approach with lower levels of investment and development in physical plant required.

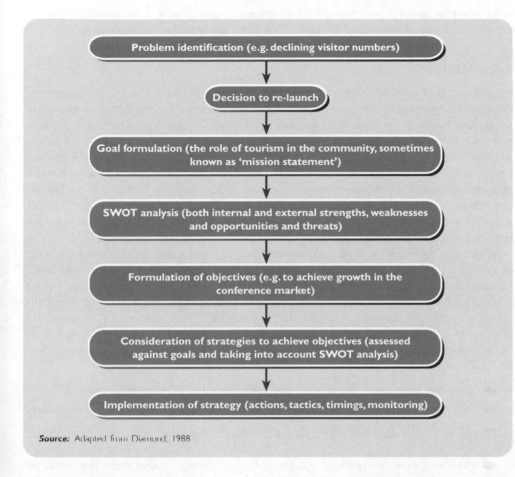

Figure CS1.1:
Stages of
strategic planning
for destinations
in decline

3. Incremental growth. Here new markets and product development is phased over a number of years through test marketing and development projects. Examples here would include development of, say, nature-based tourism in the hinterland of a resort or development of sports tourism with upgrading of existing facilities.

4. Selective tourism. Again this strategy relies upon accurate identification of new growth markets and the aggressive promotion of the resort to these markets and development of facilities to serve them. In other words, market segments are targeted that capitalise on the resort's strengths or particular character. Examples here would include the redevelopment of spa tourism in parts of Eastern Europe, or in the old spa towns of England and Wales.

The decision as to the most appropriate strategy for each resort is dependent upon a variety of interrelated factors:

- the competitive position of the resort;
- the existing market;
- the stage in the life cycle;
- available investment and public funds;
- political and community support; and
- attitude of the tourism industry.

None the less, lessons from completed strategies suggest that it is the political will and the driving force of individual *champions* of these projects that guarantees success.

Discussion

Consideration of destinations in decline is unfashionable in tourism. It implies failure and does not fit comfortably with the hype about growth that we are used to reading of contemporary tourism. Yet declining destinations are a real problem which will become increasingly evident as the mass tourism destinations of the 1960s and 1970s fail to satisfy the vacation aspirations of the new tourists of the next millennium – the list is a long one and includes Acapulco, Hawaii, the Spanish Costas, the Italian Riviera, Pattaya, many resorts on the northeastern seaboard of the USA and resorts on the coasts of northern Europe. As case studies, these resorts draw together all aspects of tourism – demand, supply, the role of the public sector, community and industry participation, and of course both tourism marketing and planning.

As tourism becomes more professional and adopts sustainable practices at each stage of the life cycle, then the economic, architectural and social future of such resorts will be more assured. From an academic point of view the examples are useful as they point out the contrasts between mainstream business applications – such as the product life cycle and strategic planning and their application in tourism. Indeed, it suggests that tourism as an activity and application is sufficiently different in its implementation of these concepts that new approaches are required. The case also points up a number of key questions:

- Does the analogy of the product life cycle and the TALC work in practice?
- Does the TALC provide practical and operational assistance for such destinations?
- What are the considerations of a strategic planning exercise in destinations in decline?
- How important are political considerations in turning around these destinations?
- Do large mass tourism resorts represent a more sustainable approach in their high capacity to absorb visitation, than more fashionable low-density developments?
- And finally, try to visit a resort that could be identified as in decline. Walk the streets and the promenade and observe the types of facilities on offer, the prices in the accommodation, food and beverage outlets and shops, and try to categorise the market segments that you see. How would you begin to tackle the problem of redeveloping this particular resort and can you see any evidence that the process is already underway?

Bibliography

- Butler, R. W. (1980) 'The concept of a tourist area cycle of evolution. Implications for management of resources', *Canadian Geographer,* **24**, 5–12.
- Cooper, C. P. (1990) 'Resorts in decline – the management response', *Tourism Management,* **11**(1), 63–7.
- Diamond, N. (1988) 'A strategy for cold water resorts in the year 2000', unpublished MSc thesis, University of Surrey, UK.

Visitor management

Case Study objectives

■ To identify the prerequisites necessary for the successful implementation of visitor management techniques and the objectives they should seek to meet.

■ To demonstrate the role and importance of visitor management techniques in sustainable tourism activity.

■ To discuss key criteria in the approach to visitor management.

Introduction

Tourism in the next millennium will demand not only that the visitor receives a satisfying and high-quality experience but also that the destination is sustainable. These twin objectives of tourism in the future will be difficult to achieve, particularly if we do not utilise innovative and effective techniques. One such approach is the application of visitor management techniques to tourism. Visitor management is a true tool of the new tourism as it ensures that the increasingly experienced and discerning new tourist does indeed receive a high-quality experience, while also sustaining the destination for future use.

Setting the scene

Visitor management is an approach that was developed in natural areas, particularly national parks and sensitive natural reserves, where there was a need to manage visitation. Here, the real innovation of visitor management approaches is their focus on *positive* planning and provision rather than *negative* restrictions and prohibition. In so doing, visitor management provides a true focus on the visitor, and recognises that each visitor is different, bringing to a destination or site, their own prejudices, needs, preferences and ignorances. After all, a group of teenage friends visiting a theme park will be seeking very different benefits from, say, a family group.

The objectives of visitor management are therefore transparent and straightforward. On the part of the visitor, it:

- enhances the visit experience;
- increases the chances of repeat visitation;
- encourages higher spending; and
- induces greater sympathy for the cause of say wildlife conservation, or historic preservation, at a site.

At the same time, visitor management provides a flow of benefits to the site or destination:

- It allows visits to be spread in both space and time.
- It encourages a longer length of stay (or dwell time).
- It reduces the environmental impact of visitation through effective management.
- There is increasing evidence that visitor management, and particularly interpretation techniques, foster a sense of civic pride and sense of ownership amongst the host community.

Visitor management should be integrated into the management of every site and destination but it is still viewed as an approach that can be *added in* at the end. In one sense this recognises the lack of exposure to the technique on behalf of tourism planners and consultants. Visitor management is very much a practitioner-based approach with few manuals of good practice or well-documented case studies of its positive effects. And yet there a number of leading attractions companies – such as the Disney Corporation – who are very skilled at the art.

Figure CS2.1 shows the outline approach that may be adopted for visitor management of a site, destination or region. For a museum, for example, the critical unit will be the rooms housing the displays and the pathways between – the technique will ensure visitors move freely between each room and get the best out of the experience. However, for a theme park it will be the themed areas and their links that form the unit of analysis, while for a region the approach will be based on sub-areas and resorts.

Figure CS2.1:
A model of visitor management

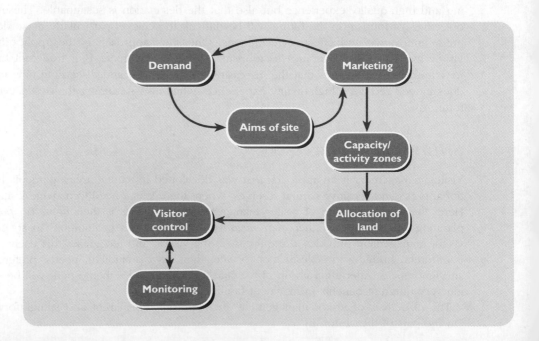

Approaching visitor management

Objectives

Determination of objectives is critical for the successful management of any site. The simple decision to be taken is *why are we opening this place to visitors?* Of course, the obvious answer may be an economic one of profit or return on investment. Other reasons, however, are also possible. These include educational reasons (for a wildlife reserve, say) or propaganda (as in show sites in socialist republics). The visitor management process demands that we are very clear on these objectives since they drive the whole process.

Demand and marketing

A second key variable is demand – the profile and numbers of visitors attracted to the site. It is important that marketing communicates clearly the objectives of the site to ensure that appropriate types of visitor are attracted. The most common management problems occur when the wrong type of visitor is attracted to a site. If these problems do arise, then it is the role of marketing constantly to adjust the visitor profile to the objectives of the site. This can be done in subtle ways such as through the choice of merchandising in the shops, the type and price of food and beverage in the cafes, or communication strategies adopted in the marketing campaign. A key consideration here is the determination of approaches for resource-based and user-based sites (see Chapter 14).

Capacity and activity zones

At this stage of the visitor management process, decisions are taken as to the intensity of visitation at each part of the site, and also the type of activity to be scheduled there. For green field sites the planner has a relatively free hand, but for sites such as museums or historic houses than it is probable that the use of rooms and displays will be fixed. Nonetheless there are two important principles involved at this stage:

1. **Determination of capacity.** Here planners have to determine the volume of visitors that can be sustained in each part of the site. This is done using the concepts of:
   - (a) **annual physical capacity** (APC) which is the number of users that can be sustained in one year; and
   - (b) **sustained physical capacity** (SPC) which is the maximum number of visitors that can be accommodated at any one point in time without a deterioration in the condition of the site.

   The calculation is then:

   APC = SPC × number of periods open

   This is a useful approach as it allows planners to build-in seasonality effects. The key question is then: *do you manage a site for its peak capacity, or to a percentage of that capacity?* A detailed consideration of capacity was given in Chapter 5.

2. **Avoidance of conflicting uses in the same area.** For example, the use of motorised vehicles or trail bikes where children are likely to congregate, or allowing motorboats and bathing in the same area of water are both examples of conflicting uses and should be avoided. Matrices of compatible and conflicting activities can easily be drawn up.

Hard management	Soft management
Negative signing	Interpretation/information
Fencing	Marketing
Charging	Landscaping and planting
Zoning	Signing
Security staff	Location of facilities

Visitor control

Once a decision has been made for the site to open, it is then important to ensure that visitors are managed in such a way as to ensure capacity levels in each area are not exceeded, and therefore that the quality of experience is maintained. Influencing visitor movement and behaviour is a subtle science and can be seen as selection from a range of options along a continuum from hard management to soft management.

Hard visitor management can be problematic as it suggests a breakdown in the planning process. Here neither manager nor visitor is satisfied as both recognise the severity of the measures adopted, however, there are occasions where hard management is inevitable. Guarding valuable sites for example, or where there is potential danger to visitors, are cases in point here. Soft management on the other hand is perhaps the most effective form of visitor management. The visitor is influenced without knowing it and the manager is effective because the site is running smoothly. There are many well-known examples of soft management:

- In theme parks where one area is over capacity and another is under capacity, managers assemble a cast of their characters playing in a band and walk them through the busy area. Visitors all follow and are led into the under-used area – perfect and unobtrusive visitor control!
- At sites where there are 'pinch points', i.e. areas where too many visitors congregate in small areas preventing an even flow around the site, it is common to provide a taped commentary of the object or display in question. Once the tape loop is complete and begins again, visitors naturally move on to the next display.

Table CS2.1 provides a range of examples of both hard and soft management approaches.

Monitoring

There is no point in developing sophisticated visitor management approaches without a means of monitoring their success. There is a variety of options here:

- a formal questionnaire with the visitor to elicit their level of enjoyment;
- the more cost-effective debrief of site staff on a regular basis to check all is well; or
- many of the larger theme parks have constant monitoring through electronic eyes, turnstiles, etc.

Discussion

There is much to be said for the technique of visitor management as a contemporary tool to deliver many of the benefits sought by both visitor and destination alike. From the point of view of this text it neatly ties together the nature of the destination, elements of the *new demand* and approaches to both planning and marketing at the destination level.

However the technique could be seen as controversial and does raise a number of important questions:

- Are we becoming too scientific and organised in our development of tourist attractions and thereby losing some of the magic?

- Are techniques such as interpretation taking away the spontaneity and moment of discovery if everything is labelled and sanitised?

- Are we simply becoming too slick in the marketing, merchandising and management of attractions?

- Are some places just too 'busy' with information, sign boards and hi-tech interpretive equipment?

- Do these approaches sanitise sensitive issues such as war or social inequality in the past?

- Who decides on the information to be given or displayed to the visitor and is this 'gatekeeper' role one we can safely entrust to planners and interpreters, or should the local community be more involved?

- Finally, this is an approach which is being increasingly adopted in sites around the world. Take a tourist site with which you are familiar – such as a theme park or museum – and revisit it with the eyes of a visitor manager. Take each of the stages of visitor management outlined above and analyse the site accordingly. And finally, make your own evaluation – does the site work in terms of visitor movement and rhythms, is the experience enhanced and did you enjoy it?

Bibliography

- Cooper, C. P. (1991) 'The technique of interpretation', pp. 224–230 in *Managing Tourism*, Medlik, S. (ed.) Butterworth-Heinemann, Oxford.
- English Heritage (1988) *Visitors Welcome*, HMSO, London.
- Grant, M. (1994) 'Visitor management', *Insights* **A41–A46**, ETB, London.
- Harrison, R. (1994) *A Manual of Heritage Management*, Butterworth-Heinemann, Oxford.

Tourism planning in Eastern Europe

Case Study objectives

- To provide a real-life example of knowledge and expertise transfer to a county in Hungary.
- To demonstrate the tourism planning process as it relates to a developing destination in Hungary.
- To discuss the issues and implications thereof.

Introduction

Tourism in Eastern Europe has been the subject of considerable change since the political events of 1988/89 propelled the region towards a market economy. Tourism is seen to be central to the process of change as it cuts across a variety of economic sectors and primarily comprises small and medium-sized enterprises (SMEs). This case study provides an account of one of the first attempts to implement Western tourism expertise and knowledge transfer within a county in Hungary.

Tourism in Eastern Europe

Between 1945 and the late 1980s the countries of Eastern Europe could be said to form a political and economic region, sharply differentiated from those on the Western side of the 'Iron Curtain' border. As a result, both the demand and supply of tourism has acquired a special identity, mainly for political reasons, since 1945 (Boniface and Cooper, 1994). The adoption of Communism as the political and economic model has had a profound effect on tourism in the region. Following the political events of the late 1980s, the countries of Eastern Europe are moving from a centralised to a market economy, and from a totalitarian, one party system towards a pluralist democracy. However, this transition has presented a new set of issues which Hall (1991, 1992) groups into five categories:

- economic restructuring/fiscal constraints;
- tourism administration;
- regulation of travel;

- environmental image; and
- tourism infrastructure.

Tourism in Hungary

Hungary is a relatively small, land-locked country in central Europe, distinguished from its neighbours by the Magyar language and history. In many respects Hungary is at the vanguard of the changes identified above. The country was always more liberal than many of its neighbours and yet, historically, Hungary has a potentially large tourism market because of its cultural ties with other central European countries and its easy access to the markets of Austria, Germany and Italy. Hungary easily outperforms its neighbours when it comes to staying visitors. There are many reasons for Hungary's success but the key lies in the process of political and economic reform which has followed a gradual but steady path for the past 20 years, making Hungary the most *westernised* country in the former Eastern Europe. Hungary has recognised the advantages that tourism can bring as a:

- hard currency earner;
- agent of social change;
- symbol of new freedoms;
- method of upgrading of local infrastructure;
- complement to other business sectors as conference and business tourism is put into place.

The growth of tourism in Hungary has been based on the selling of two outstanding tourist destinations – Budapest and Lake Balaton. The Hungarian tourist authorities and planners have long been concerned with increasing the regional distribution of tourism in order to spread benefits, and more recently, the pressure on Lake Balaton has raised issues about the longer-term health of the lake. Similarly, tourist developments so far have tended to concentrate in the western part of Hungary and the potential of the eastern part has yet to be exploited. In this respect, a tourism plan was commissioned for the eastern county of Szolnok (Figure CS3.1).

Planning for tourism in Szolnok

Southeast of Budapest lies the county of Szolnok. Tourism in Szolnok County is seen as a development option that will provide a source of income and employment that can be widely dispersed throughout the county and assist in the further development of an entrepreneurial culture to enhance the transitional process of market economy development.

The sparsely populated characteristics of the county, together with its agricultural base and sensitive environmental features, require that tourism be developed in a controlled and systematic manner if its development is not to herald serious environmental and social damage. The future development of tourism in the county must use and exploit the natural resources of the region while acknowledging the fragility of such natural resources. Therefore, a tourism plan should be based upon a development scenario which operates in harmony with the local environment.

The plan aimed:

- to increase the per capita spend of tourists visiting the county;
- to increase the number of foreign tourists visiting the county; and
- to increase the length of the local tourism season to maximise the use of facilities.

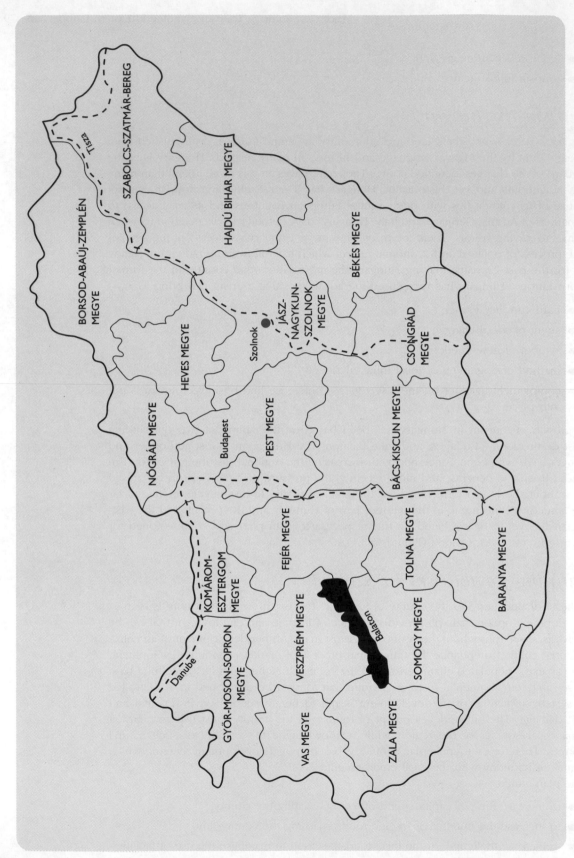

Figure CS3.I: The location of Szolnok in Hungary

Although the design of the strategy plan was a major exercise in itself, much more difficult and telling for the future of tourism in the region was the acceptance and implementation of the plan by local public authorities and entrepreneurs.

Elements of the tourism plan

A survey of tourism in Szolnok

To inform the tourism strategy, a major survey of the tourist resources and market for Szolnok County was carried out. The purpose of the survey was to identify existing tourist resources, survey the potential for new tourism development in the county and to assess the problems and issues that tourism development would both encounter and need to overcome. The survey findings can be summarised as follows.

Szolnok County strengths:

- transport and road links – generally efficient;
- relatively unspoilt environment;
- good river and lake facilities;
- Szolnok city as a main location;
- distinctive cultural heritage;
- natural friendliness towards strangers; and
- good value for money.

Szolnok County weaknesses:

- relatively flat countryside;
- lack of quality accommodation in all product positions of the market;
- need for tourist industry training;
- general lack of interest in tourism development;
- plant and facilities need upgrading;
- absence of tourism marketing;
- absence of international menu offerings;
- lack of information in foreign languages;
- lack of all-weather facilities and family attractions; and
- short season and length of stay.

Phased development of the tourism plan for Szolnok

Phase 1: immediate action

- Improve quality of existing facilities:
    - adopt hotel grading system and monitor sector;
    - adopt approval system of accommodation/catering facilities;
    - set up two visitor orientation centres (VOCs);
    - set up six TICs;
    - improve information provision; and
    - create a single identity of tourist industry.

- Improve utilisation of existing facilities:
  - adopt new marketing approach;
  - develop existing attractions;
  - create a strong image;
  - improve interpretation;
  - regulate tourism flows; and
  - exploit heritage, culture and nature more fully.
- Improve economic benefits from tourism:
  - develop new opportunities for tourism spending;
  - target high-spending West European tourists;
  - capitalise on local resources; and
  - coordinate development.
- Improve performance of existing entrepreneurs:
  - create a tourism forum;
  - implement seminars on entrepreneurial skills;
  - publish regular tourism newsletter; and
  - appoint tourism advisory panel.
- Create environment for future tourism planning:
  - implement tourism statistical database;
  - implement public awareness programme;
  - appoint County Board of Tourism; and
  - zone county for tourism activities.

Phase 2: immediate to medium-term action

- Develop Szolnok Town as tourist centre.
- Increase accommodation stock.
- Create new restaurants/cafes in tourist areas.
- Develop new tourism activities.
- Build on existing cultural/heritage attractions.
- Encourage the development of closer linkages between the various sectors of the county to maximise economic benefits.

Phase 3: medium- to long-term action

- Widen tourist base – conference and business.
- Develop upmarket tourist facilities.
- Widen marketing activities.
- Establish strong links with national and international tourist organisations.
- Adopt a fully international CRS.
- Continue to develop monitoring/regulation and research into tourism activities.
- Develop new five-yearly tourism development plans.

Implementation

The major issues facing the implementation programme were:

- to motivate an enthusiastic entrepreneurial population to see tourism as an industry that can generate significant income and employment opportunities;
- to demonstrate the need for managing and controlling visitor flows through the setting up of TICs and VOCs;
- to *westernise* the concepts of marketing and good business practice; and
- to demonstrate how the abundant culture and heritage of such a region can be exploited without demeaning the participants or diminishing their pride in their national identity.

Conclusion

The plan and its implementation highlights many of the problems facing the future development and reorientation of tourism in East European states. From an economics point of view they are faced with the paradoxical situation that development on a scale that will attract significant numbers of high-spending visitors requires investment of a level that simply is not available. It is possible to circumvent this problem by bringing in foreign investment and know-how in order to create the tourism superstructure, but in so doing they run the risk of diminishing the positive economic benefits associated with tourism development as a result of repatriated income. Clearly, there is a need for foreign involvement in a number of instances where the capital requirements are high, but these should be undertaken as joint ventures wherever possible and the main aspects of the tourism industry should evolve at a rate that is commensurate with local levels of investment, where the social and environmental impacts can be monitored and contained and where there is significant learning by doing.

The result of the plan and its implementation is a county that is now poised to break through into wider tourist markets, armed with promotional material of high-quality tourist information and maps, together with a broad spectrum of tourist products and a network of commercial and organisational links that will enable it to capitalise on the potential market for visitors from within and to Eastern Europe.

Bibliography

- Boniface, B. and Cooper, C. (1994) *The Geography of Travel and Tourism*, Butterworth-Heinemann, Oxford.
- Hall, D. R. (ed.) (1991) *Tourism and Economic Development in Eastern Europe and the Soviet Union*, Belhaven, London.
- Hall, D. R. (1992) 'The challenge of international tourism in Eastern Europe', *Tourism Management*, **13**(1), 41–4.

Tourism project assistance from the European Union

Case Study objectives

■ To provide an understanding of the framework for the allocation of structural funds by the European Union.

■ To illustrate the range of criteria against which proposals are judged and funds allocated.

■ To offer an overview of the system in action.

Introduction

Above the investment support offered separately by the governments of the EU, there is the pan-European programme of regional aid made available to member states through the Union's structural funds. The objectives are to improve economic convergence; that is to eliminate major disparities of wealth, and ensure a better spread of economic activities throughout the territories located within the boundaries of the Union. Project assistance from the Union is given under four structural funds:

1. The European Regional Development Fund (ERDF), which is focused mainly on productive investment, infrastructure and SME development in less favoured regions, and is the principal vehicle for regional support.

2. The European Social Fund (ESF), which has the task of promoting jobs through vocational training and employment assistance.

3. The European Agricultural Guidance and Guarantee Fund Guidance Section (EAGGF), which promotes the adjustment of agricultural businesses and rural development measures.

4. The Financial Instrument for Fisheries Guidance (FIFG), which was established in 1993 to promote structural measures in that sector.

The European Commission recognises that the funds make a major contribution to the development of tourism in the EU and in so doing, progress the objectives of economic and social cohesion as defined in Article 130a, Treaty of the European Union (the

Maastricht Treaty), 1992. In essence, the Commission's policy for using tourism as an instrument of regional economic development is one of taking advantage of the many positive aspects of the industry, namely:

- the continuing growth in tourism world-wide;
- disadvantaged regions often have a comparative advantage in natural tourism resources;
- tourism attracts spending from outside the regions;
- tourism has important spillover benefits (multiplier effects) elsewhere in the regional economy; and
- job creation within a relatively short period of time is an important aspect of tourism development.

Background

Prior to 1988, there was no coherent system for the disbursement of the structural funds, which resulted in the dissipation of funds over many areas, thus reducing their effectiveness. Therefore, in 1988, a new regulation on the uses of the funds was adopted in preparation for the first planning period 1989–93, with lesser changes for the next interval from 1994–99. The changes were based on three fundamental principles:

1. Transforming structural policy into an instrument with real economic impact by concentration on priority objectives.
2. Using a multi-annual programming approach for expenditure planning to assure member states of the stability and predictability of EU support.
3. Implementing a partnership with all the parties actively participating in structural policy, especially the regional authorities.

From 1989 onwards, member states were required to coordinate, for the first time, the use of the funds and draw together all forms of Union support, including lending by the European Investment Bank (EIB) and the European Coal and Steel Community (ECSC). This also allowed the EU to adopt a greater degree of control on the use of the funds within the sphere of integrated regional development plans put forward by member states.

In the 1989–93 planning term, priorities were determined through community support frameworks (CSFs) and agreed by the Commission, working in close association with member states and the competent regional or local authority designated by them, from which a series of programmes were derived. This is now most appropriate for regions coming within the scope of the structural funds for the first time. The alternative is for the member state to submit single programming documents (SPDs) which combine priorities and programmes from the outset and become operational as soon as they have the Commission's approval. SPDs have been the most common method of submitting development programmes in the 1994–99 planning period, since most of the eligible regions have already established a track record during the 1989–93 phase of the structural funds. In contrast to the investment incentives discussed in Chapter 11, which may be applied in a piece-wise manner, project promoters are only eligible for assistance from the structural funds if their schemes are included in a CSF or SPD and meet one of the Community objectives shown in Table CS4.1.

Objective	Aim
Objective 1	The economic adjustment of regions whose development is lagging behind.
Objective 2	The economic conversion of declining industrial areas.
Objective 3	Combating long-term unemployment, integrating young people and those threatened with exclusion from the labour market, into working life.
Objective 4	The adaptation of workers to changes in industry and systems of production through measures to prevent unemployment.
Objective 5a	Adapting the structures in the sectors of agriculture and fisheries in line with reform of the common agricultural policy.
Objective 5b	The economic diversification of fragile rural areas.
Objective 6	Meeting the special problems of the very thinly populated regions of the Nordic countries.

Funding policy

The ERDF is the principal instrument for regional intervention and the sums available dwarf the other three structural funds. The method of subvention from the funds is grant aid that is conditional to the project and requires matching funding from the project promoter. The limit rate of grant is normally 50%, but can be up to 55% in the case of projects of particular importance to the development of the region or areas in which they are located. The majority of projects no longer receive support at the limit rate. For tourism investment, grants are unlikely to be in excess of 45% of the investment cost and may usually be less.

Tourism projects tend to be public sector led and the principal aspects that should be addressed when bidding for European assistance are:

- the use of the project should be 50% non-local;
- the project should result in an increase in overnight stays;
- the project should result in an increase in employment opportunities;
- the economic position of the project within the local area should be examined;
- the project should form part of a tourism strategy for the local area. Thus the project should sit within a CSF/SPD, which is the regional strategy approved by the member state and the Community; and
- national/regional tourist organisation support will give weight to the application.

Evaluation

Member states are given considerable flexibility as to how they present a proposal, which is consistent with the principle of *subsidiarity* outlined in Chapter 11. What follows is therefore representative of the criteria that are employed in evaluating a project proposal, namely:

- the project should be feasible in that the scheme has the capacity to generate revenues above operating costs so that it can support its own running arrangements;
- viability is assured after financial assistance in order that the project can service the capital investment costs out of its operating surplus;
- the need for structural funds support should be proven;
- displacement of visitors from other tourism businesses within the area of the CSF/SPD, or from any other European-assisted area, should be minimised; and
- multiplier effects in terms of job creation should be examined.

In practice, local income and employment generation, measured in full-time equivalent (FTE) jobs are the most significant factors affecting project acceptability, since the primary use of structural funds is to correct for regional imbalances. We may note that tourism and hospitality projects are usually well suited to European funding requirements because they are labour using and commonly have a high operating leverage; that is, a relatively low level of operating costs but a high level of fixed costs caused by prior capital spending. Once the financing of the capital has been adequately taken care of, the project usually runs into surplus after three years and can maintain itself thereafter.

Impact assessment

In Table CS4.2 we present data that have been drawn from case study material on attractions, to show how the employment effects of a tourism project may be measured. The workings of Table CS4.2 are along the following lines: using visitor expenditure surveys, the total expected on-site and off-site spending arising from the project is estimated, in European Currency Units, at ECU4 472 000.

Item	On-site expenditure (ECU)	Off-site expenditure (ECU)
Visitor markets		
Stay	394 000	2 307 000
Day	440 000	393 000
Local residents	683 000	255 000
Total	1 517 000	2 955 000
Visitor additionality		
Stay	Not applicable	15%
Day	Not applicable	90%
Local residents	Not applicable	100%
Displacement		
Stay	0%	0%
Day	30%	30%
Local residents	100%	100%
FTE multipliers per ECU10 000		
Direct	0.0995	0.0816
Indirect	0.0535	0.0508
Induced	0.0077	0.0077
Total	**0.1607**	**0.1401**

Table CS4.2: Assessing the impact of a tourist attraction

It is at this point that the concept of **visitor additionality** is invoked: clearly, on-site expenditure by visitors is attributable absolutely to the attraction as the customers have demonstrated their preferences through their willingness to pay, but this is not the case with off-site spending. The extent to which off-site spending may be attributed to the attraction depends on the importance of the attraction in the customer's decision to visit the location. This can only be ascertained by surveying visitors and asking about their motivations for coming to the destination.

Suppose that surveys have shown that only 15% of staying visitors are likely to come to the destination because of the existence of the attraction. But, as is to be expected, a much higher percentage is recorded for day visitors and local residents, because they normally make a specific decision to go to a place, an event or an attraction. Using the visitor additionality factors in Table CS4.2 to account for attributable off-site expenditure, the gross expenditure benefits (B) from the attraction are:

$$B = \text{ECU1 517 000} + (0.15 \times \text{ECU2 307 000}) + (0.9 \times \text{ECU393 000})$$
$$+ (1.0 \times \text{ECU255 000})$$
$$= \text{ECU2 471 750}$$

It is anticipated that the attraction will create 21.5 FTE jobs directly on-site, and so the required additions to this number will be the expected indirect and induced employment generated from on-site spending. Using the appropriate FTE multipliers shown in Table CS4.2 and calculated as a decimal fraction of a given amount of tourist expenditure, this figure comes to

$$(0.0535 + 0.0077) \times \text{ECU1 517 000/ECU10 000} = 9.3 \text{ FTE jobs}$$

Off-site jobs amount to

$$0.1401 \times \text{ECU954 750/ECU10 000} = 13.4 \text{ FTE jobs}$$

Hence, the gross employment generated (E), in terms of FTEs, is expected to be:

$$E = 21.5 \text{ FTEs} + 9.3 \text{ FTEs} + 13.4 \text{ FTEs}$$
$$= 44.2 \text{ FTEs}$$

So far the analysis has only measured gross FTEs likely to be generated by the attraction. The net figures have to account for what is termed **displacement**, which is factored into Table CS4.2. Displacement has to do with the extent to which an attraction may capture tourist spending from competitors in the local area. It is estimated that 0% of staying visitors will be taken from competitors; the attraction is providing more to 'see and do' at the destination and the tourists' budgets have sufficient margin of flexibility. For day visitors, it is probable that 30% will be displaced from other attractions, while for local residents a conservative assumption is made that all expenditure will be displaced from elsewhere in the local economy. The latter assumption is overly pessimistic in practice, for household budgets are not that inflexible.

Weighting the displacement factors in Table CS4.2 by the different categories of visitor spending gives an overall displacement value of 0.4758. Thus, the net employment (N) that can be expected to result from the attraction is:

$$N = 44.2 - 0.4758 \times 44.2$$
$$= 23.2 \text{ FTEs}$$

It is this number of FTEs that should be used to evaluate the project's worth in public policy decision making when applications for European support or comparisons with alternative projects are being are being made.

Project monitoring

Once the bundle of projects within a CSF/SPD has been agreed upon for assistance, the principle of subsidiarity devolves the monitoring function to the local level through programme monitoring committees. The latter are made up of representatives from central and local government, public agencies and any other interested parties, and they will be responsible for all projects within a CSF/SPD. For every project, targets are set at the approval stage and returns must be submitted quarterly, showing the progress of each scheme against its targets.

It is a member state's responsibility to make site visits and evaluate project performance: these tasks usually fall to the government department responsible for administering the CSF/SPD that contains the project. Member states have the responsibility to ensure that European funds are correctly spent and yield good value for money in terms of the project evaluation criteria. This responsibility is regulated by the European Court of Auditors, who have powers of examination and verification to establish that projects are:

- eligible for European funds as specified;
- managed in accordance with European Commission's rules with regard to technical and financial controls; and
- claiming grant against justifiable expenditure.

The above verifications are undertaken by making one or two visits every year and subjecting a group of preselected projects to detailed checking.

Conclusion

Since about 1975, the entry of the EU into regional policy, in order to create a greater convergence between the economies of the Union, has ended members states' monopoly of regional policy within their borders. Inside the Union, there is a distinct tendency for the poorest regions to be situated on the geographical periphery and the more prosperous regions, with the benefit of market access, to be centrally located. With the adoption of the Single European Act (1987), with the intention to create one market in Europe and a single currency, there is a commitment by the EU to promote economic and social cohesion through actions to reduce regional disparities and the Maastricht Treaty (1992) acknowledged, for the first time, the role of tourism in these actions.

The resources for mitigating regional differences are drawn from the structural funds, which have been increased, in real terms, from about ECU85 billion (1994 prices) in the 1989–93 programme to around ECU150 billion for the 1994–99 planning period. The funds have specific objectives, as shown in Table CS4.1, and support for tourism development particularly manifests itself in the Objective 1 regions, which already have an established tourist industry; also, in Objective 2 regions, where tourism has contributed to the diversification of economic activities in areas of industrial decline, and in Objective 5b regions, with the growth of rural and community-based tourism. Tourism programmes are set to gain considerably from the funds over the 1994–99 period. In support of this, the case study discusses the principles of structural assistance and the methodology for project evaluation, with particular emphasis on job creation, though we should be mindful of the clear intention of the European Commission to move forward with tourism developments in a sustainable manner, in order to guarantee that the activity continues on a regular basis.

Conclusion continued

The division of intervention in the tourist industry between member states and the EU is always likely to remain contentious, but given the diversity of the tourist product, the Union has to work in close partnership with national and regional authorities. At the political level, this issue has been technically put to one side by Article 3b of the Maastricht Treaty which states that

the Community shall take action, in accordance with the principle of subsidiarity, only if and in so far as the objectives of the proposed action cannot be sufficiently achieved by the Member States and can therefore, by reason of the scale or effects of the proposed action, be better achieved by the Community.

Questions

1. Why is the EU concerned about regional inequalities?

2. How important is tourism in the EU in respect of its contribution to the GDP of member states and employment in the Union?

3. What are the strengths and weaknesses of positioning tourism projects within an overall strategy to guide their use as opposed to opportunistic development?

4. Which of the objectives in Table CS4.1 match closely with tourism development?

5. The nature of grant aid from the EU has been described as conditional matching funding. Other forms of grant mechanisms are lump-sum payments, which may be tied to specific projects (conditional) or just given to the overall program (unconditional). What are the relative merits of these different systems?

6. How would you go about preparing a local area tourism strategy?

7. With reference to Chapter 6, what are the concepts that lie behind the measurement of direct, indirect and induced income and employment multipliers?

8. The capital investment for the attraction project illustrated in Table CS4.2 is ECU1 200 000. The European Commission decides to grant aid the scheme at 25% of the capital cost. What is the grant cost per direct FTE job created onsite, for the gross employment generated and net jobs created by the project?

9. Suppose the EU has a rule limiting grant support to ECU12 000 per net job created. How much would the project now receive in grant aid as a percentage of the capital cost?

Bibliography

● Commission of the European Communities (1991) *Guide to the Reform of the Community's Structural Funds*, Office for Official Publications of the European Communities, Luxembourg.

- Commission of the European Community (1994) *Guide to the Community Initiatives*, Office for Official Publications of the European Communities, Luxembourg.
- Commission of the European Communities (1995) *The Role of the Union in the Field of Tourism*, COM (95), 97 final, Brussels.
- Commission of the European Communities (1996) *Structural Funds and Cohesion Fund 1994–99*, Office for Official Publications of the European Communities, Luxembourg.
- Lowyck, E. and Wanhill, S. (1992) 'Regional development and tourism within the European Community', pp. 227–44 in *Progress in Tourism, Recreation and Hospitality Management*, Cooper, C. and Lockwood, A. (eds), Belhaven Press, London.
- Wanhill, S. (1994) 'Appraising tourism projects', pp. 120–35 in *Tourism: The State of the Art*, Seaton, A. V. *et al.* (eds), Wiley, Chichester.
- Wanhill, S. (1994) 'Evaluating the worth of investment incentives for tourism development', *Journal of Travel Research*, **33**(2), 33–9.
- Wanhill, S. (1997) 'Peripheral area tourism: a European perspective', *Progress in Tourism and Hospitality Research*, **3**(1), 47–70.

Relationship marketing

Case Study objectives

■ To introduce and discuss the concept of relationship marketing in the tourism industry, using the specific example of frequent flyer programmes.

■ To familiarise the reader with the format and approach to frequent flyer programmes and their intended objectives and benefits.

■ To identify key issues in respect of frequent flyer programmes and their impact on the future development of such schemes.

Introduction

The aviation industry has, over recent years, been affected by global unrest, political instability and deteriorating economic conditions. The Western airline industry has recently lost the benefit of political support as a result of deregulation in the USA and liberalisation in Europe. The outcome has been that airlines throughout the world have struggled to develop marketing strategies that maintain market share and maximise revenue. The overwhelming response of airlines has been to use discounted fare structures and promotional strategies to entice passengers, filling aircraft but adversely affecting profitability. In order to address these issues, airlines are increasingly adopting the concept of relationship marketing (RM) schemes which aim to bond the customer with the brand through specific loyalty programmes.

Airline loyalty schemes: competitive strategies

Fewer airlines now exist than in the 1980s with many of the larger carriers needing to enhance revenue from higher yield target segments such as business travellers. In order to communicate with this desirable market segment, airlines have turned to increasingly sophisticated sales promotion techniques and one of the most innovative of these is the frequent flyer programme (FFP). FFPs are schemes targeted to the high mileage traveller and providing rewards for the frequency of usage of the airline and distance travelled, thus building brand preference.

The growing trend is for airlines to seek as many strategic improvements as possible for their operation. This is brought about in three ways:

1. **Partnerships.** These may be links between airlines through equity or cooperation arrangements. Examples include KLM and Air UK, British Airways and TAT, Swissair and Sabena. Sometimes the links are forged as part of a longer-term strategy to provide for hub, or even global, domination. This limits rivalry and therefore price competition. It may also lead to the sharing of CRSs and shared costs for CRS and frequent flyer development programmes.

2. **Efficiencies through scope and scale.** Some airlines have sought out efficiencies and savings wherever possible, introducing more cost-effective operations. Examples include Lufthansa Express and Condor owned by Lufthansa, or Iberia and Viva Air. The totality of the volumes of passengers carried by all the brands, in terms of scale, can lead to larger budgets being made available for travel agent incentives or FFPs. This provides for specific competitive advantage.

3. **Overhead efficiencies.** Cost saving through the reduction of staff and the selling off of peripheral services, such as catering, to increase procurement power and to improve flexibility in purchasing for the non-core functions.

Relationship marketing

Marketing is evolving from a focus on the single transaction to becoming increasingly concerned with the development and maintenance of mutually satisfying long-term relationships with customers. The most successful RM campaigns allow for competitive advantage and enduring relationships with customers which are hard to duplicate. This is based upon the company becoming 'relationship-driven' rather than 'transaction-driven' as described in Table CS5.1.

There is a recognition of the long-term value of a customer in recent literature. Gronroos (1990), for example, argues all marketing strategies lie on a continuum ranging from transactional to relational marketing where relationship marketing can be judged in terms of measures of customer retention rather than market share. The focus, therefore, is on the need for a relationship to be developed:

Table CS5.1:
The differences between transaction marketing and relationship marketing

Transaction marketing	Relationship marketing
● Short-term orientation on the sale as the end result	● Long-term orientation. The sale is only the beginning
● 'Me' orientated	● 'We' orientated
● Focus on achieving a specific sale	● Focus on retention and repeat sales
● Emphasis on persuasion to buy	● Stress on creating positive relationships
● Need to win, manipulation	● Providing trust and service
● Stress of conflict of achieving a transaction	● Partnership and cooperation to minimise defection and provide longer-term relationships (with customers or strategic alliances, joint ventures, vendor partnering, etc.)
● Anonymous customer won by conquest in a carefully planned event	● Individual profile of customer known so that a continuing process can emerge

> *Marketing is to establish, maintain and enhance relationships with customers and other partners, at a profit, so that the objectives of the parties involved are met. This is achieved by a mutual exchange and fulfilment of promises.*

This definition can be seen as an attempt to integrate both the transactional and the relational qualities of marketing.

The rationale for RM is that it makes business sense to focus on long-term financial benefits which can accrue once a customer has been won for the first time since it has been estimated that it is five to ten more times more expensive to recruit a new customer than to retain an existing one (e.g. Rosenberg and Czepiel, 1984).

Frequent flyer programmes

A frequent flyer programme (FFP) is a club concept with passenger rewards for loyalty. Enrolment is typically completed through the filling in of a short application form which will capture details of the address for the promotional material and accumulated credit statements to be forwarded at regular intervals. The airlines automatically follow the individual's booking patterns through the use of their CRS as members have simply to present their membership cards, when checking in for a flight, for the data to be captured.

The impact of deregulation of the US air transport sector in 1979 produced such a shake out of the industry that it became essential to create cost-effective marketing promotions to persuade air travellers to remain loyal and provide consistency of demand. Historically, in the evolution of airline marketing, FFPs are a direct link to Southwest Airline's 1970's scheme of giving 'sweetheart stamps' for bookings which would allow the business traveller to collect benefits in order to take a partner on a free flight.

The development of relationship programmes is closely linked to the evolution of global computer reservation systems and the ability afforded by these systems to capture sophisticated consumer data. American Airlines utilised the Sabre system's sales history data in order to reveal the travel patterns of its passengers. The sales team identified the telephone numbers of those passengers who had flown more than twice in a six-month period. Once identified they were recruited to the 'Very Important Travellers Club'. It did not take the sales team long to recognise the importance the passengers gave to free air travel miles. American Airlines' AAdvantage programme, initiated in May 1981, became the industry standard to be copied as part of globalised market promotion practices centring around the frequent traveller concept. American had no early worry that it could be copied owing to its belief that with such an extensive route system it could sustain a competitive advantage. However, within a short space of time the emulators were offering superior benefits to American which forced the airline to alter its programme to match that of the competition.

The success of the early FFPs provided the basis for their retention and development. By the end of 1986, 24 out of 27 US carriers had devised similar programmes. Since their introduction, they have grown rapidly into the largest promotional weapon of the major carriers. For example, American Airlines has 22 million club members. Once adopted, a 'club' basis for the flyer programme is developed which relies on the targeting of the right market for increases in member recruitment. The database developed for and from such clubs offers an abundance of information on travel patterns for which special promotional offers can be constructed.

Through time, several modifications to the original FFP idea of providing free travel have occurred for US airlines (and increasingly their overseas imitators) to create new means by which their members could generate additional mileage credits, often from non-travel sources. An article by Mason and Barker (1996) has identified some of the companies participating in providing extra benefits. Among the most popular of the schemes creating more added value and benefit have been:

- non-airline travel services such as those offered by car rental companies, tour operators and hotel chains;
- airline-affiliated credit card purchases (i.e. mileage credits according to the volume of purchases processed through a particular card);
- long-distance telephone calls through particular US telephone companies; and
- additionally, in some cases, credits for buying stocks and bonds through particular US brokerage houses.

Expansion of FFPs outside the USA

Foreign carriers, having recognised the need to develop FFPs, were considerably slower than their US counterparts in integrating frequent traveller programmes into their operations. In the 1980s this was in part due to their underdeveloped computer reservation systems technology virtually a prerequisite for the movement and management of complex frequent flyer travel arrangements, mileage awards and other benefits. Development was rapid in light of the prospect of losing valuable high-yield traffic to US competitors and by the 1990s most European carriers, led by BA, developed a variety of FFPs to oppose this threat. BA was compelled to launch *Lattitudes* in April 1991 because of rising competition (*Travel Trade Gazette*).

FFPs are also expanding in Asia and the Far East. It is quite clear, however, that Far East carriers are being drawn into the FFP culture with considerable reluctance. This reflects partly their relatively protected status, partly the buoyancy of their regional economy and partly a dislike of having the FFPs imposed on them by aggressive, revenue-hungry competitors from the USA and Europe. Verchere reported that Asia/Pacific carriers had to enter the FFP arena following the launch of the Qantas scheme which itself was an attempt to counteract US airlines operating trans-Pacific routes.

As with all promotions there is a need for innovation to compete against the consumer fatigue factor of the scheme. Virgin Atlantic are offering action weekends and even a holiday on Richard Branson's private island in the Caribbean. Whatever offers the airlines provide, the secret is for them to create biased behavioural responses expressed through time. Thus reward motivators act as a bias on decision-making and may replace existing brand loyalty. The resultant demand can be characterised as a specific form of preference buying behaviour which involves repeat commitment owing to the way rewards need to be built up over time. Given that an individual has a vested interest in gaining further credits for flights while the company pays for the flight costs, it is obvious there will be less price sensitivity of travel cost or the likelihood of defection to other airline schemes.

The approach to loyalty schemes

RM requires the effective acquisition and retention of customers for the building of a more efficient operation and ultimately stronger competitive position. Acquisition is based upon the historical approach to marketing with the targeting of prospects through the media and distribution outlets. Virgin utilises direct mail as it offers corporate as well as individual membership, American Airlines places emphasis on acquisition at the reservations and departure desk stage and Northwest on the introduction of new members

Stage	*Objective/strategy*	*Typical mechanism*
1. Identify	Compile information on what an individual purchases or may want. Create a profile of the customer.	Measure reaction to different offers. Accounts records. Incentive questionnaire to collect data.
2. Improve	Improve aspects of the service that are not meeting or exceeding the expectations of customer's TQM.	Collect attitudes to the services or loyalty programmes. Contact lapsed, inactive customers.
3. Inform	Increase the knowledge of customers about the airline and the loyalty scheme to enhance brand loyalty.	Newsletters. Bulletins regarding new products/services/offers/benefits. Lists and locations of key agents.
4. Tempt	Persuade customers to try new service, product or sector; or purchase more through personalised contact.	Special offer leaflet. Trial vouchers. Extension of benefits (e.g. use of business lounge at airport). Up sell/cross sell. Renewals of membership.
5. Retain	Develop loyalty building schemes aimed at retaining and reinforcing the link with customers. Check: ● acquisition costs, ● attrition curves, ● lifetime values, ● profit potential.	Members' magazines. Events and invitations. Membership cards. Reward schemes. Enhanced payment schemes.

by existing members. In addition, American Airlines target large companies in London who carry out business in America. Individuals are approached privately and offered enhanced gold card status to join the AAdvantage scheme.

Retention marketing may be a better term than relationship marketing as this places the emphasis on the strategies that are adopted to retain customers. The approach is to achieve acquisition through current marketing methods to acquire customers from prospects. However, the difference is that there is then the requirement for effective retention or relationship marketing approaches (see Table CS5.2). Retention requires the steps of:

1. **identify** more about customer through database analysis;
2. **improve** and make the product/service more attractive (at check in AAdvantage members are identified by a star against their name. Gold and Platinum members are identified as requiring VIP treatment);
3. **inform** to build customer's knowledge of the company;
4. **tempt** customers to purchase more regularly, try different products, etc. (this is often achieved through creating different levels of membership – member, gold, platinum, based upon revenue miles flown);

5. **retain** the customer by developing different forms of loyalty schemes; and

6. as a system this should lead to increased customer value to deliver higher profits and enable the company to make increased investment in further acquisition of new members. The foregoing can be viewed as an increasing spiral which places the company in a stronger and stronger position.

It is important to review the above approach within four critical financial measures:

1. **Customer acquisition and break-even costs.** It is important to estimate the allowable cost that will be employed to acquire a customer.

2. **Attrition curves.** It is important to analyse the attrition of customers over time. There is a need to collect periodic figures to analyse any losses being suffered in order to check on natural attrition (death, relocation) as opposed to substantive reduction. The problem with airline loyalty schemes is that members may be inactive because they have joined other schemes rather than left the scheme.

3. **Lifetime values.** There is a need to identify the lifetime value of the customer so as to calculate the costs and benefits of different acquisition and retention strategies. As loyalty scheme members often belong to several schemes it is easy for cross-comparison research to be carried out.

4. **Profit potential.** Based upon the above, the profit potential of different loyalty programmes or new sector and product launches are critical as a guide to future business planning.

The relationship marketing problems of FFPs

Relationship marketing in the form of FFPs can be ruined if there is no due concern for the alienation of third parties and the overall cost and efficiency of expanding customer loyalty. The current dilemmas associated with airline RM schemes may be identified as follows:

- There is a growing hostility to the programmes by companies that fund business travel and are unable to control their travel policies effectively as a result of employee distortion of company guidelines. The changing 'corporate travel market' requires airlines to recognise the implications related to the shift from the traveller-driven to that of a purchasing-manager-driven environment. There is a need to direct relationship marketing to the corporate buyer and company rather than the individual business traveller. This is because of the growing importance and power of the procurement professional in devising rigid travel policies (Gilbert, 1993).

- Airlines have failed to recognise the heavy liability of unredeemed miles. This has placed a huge onus on re-planning the rules and conditions of FFPs. While most airline publicity extols the virtues of the FFP concept, there is the question of whether they actually enhance or erode yields. As a result of a fear of loss, ineligibility rules are now imposed on certain dates and sectors, often for periods of several weeks at a time, and the deadlines by which points must be redeemed have been shortened. In addition there is more careful management utilising CRS yield programmes that limit the volume of FFP liability on specific flights. Major US airlines have also reacted by raising the qualification for internal US flights from 20 000 to 25 000 miles flown and some have cut the bonus miles available for business and first class travel.

● Questions must also be raised about potential competitive advantage of FFPs if all airlines offer similar rewards. It may be argued that the cost of retaining existing, or winning new customers, may actually increase as a consequence.

The base of frequent traveller programmes has become so general and led to such a build up of rewards that such schemes are affecting profitability and effectiveness as well as adding pressure for constant product innovation and improvement. The schemes are here to stay as the evidence to date indicates that once FFPs are established, it is extremely difficult, if not impossible, for airlines to discontinue them. This is not a problem as long as the airlines adopt a sophisticated relationship marketing approach.

● Governments may introduce taxation on FFPs as a means of acquiring revenue benefits. In Europe, for example, some EU officials are already indicating that they believe it is necessary to ensure such personal benefits accrued by business travellers on frequent flier schemes are taxed. There may also be tighter control of FFPs to re-establish a fairer market for smaller airlines or new entrants to the market-place. It has been found that restrictive marketing practices associated increasingly with CRS and frequent flyer offers make it more difficult for airlines to compete effectively in each other's markets. The reason for FFPs to be considered as potentially anti-competitive is mainly because they favour larger airlines at the expense of smaller carriers.

Conclusion

The situation in the USA over the past decade is one where the growth of frequent flyer benefits has provided progressively less and less return owing to the number of similar programmes. The future may, therefore, herald an emphasis on retention through quality and improved relationship marketing programmes.

It is clear that airline relationship marketing strategies differ between geographic areas. The American emphasis is on increasing frequency of use whereas in Europe there was a necessary reaction to compete and devise loyalty programmes. The successful airlines will be those who are willing to build an improved approach to airline customers based upon three key elements of micro-marketing:

1. Greater emphasis on the database information held so as to slice and apportion it to provide improved aspects of individual or group service delivery.

2. The essence of relationship marketing needs to be the provision of differentiated communication and services. These have to be customised based upon the researched characteristics of potential and current customers.

3. The need to track and monitor each member of FFPs to ensure there is an assessment of the lifetime value and retention history of the individual.

This case study is based upon an edited article published by D. Gilbert (1996) 'Relationship marketing and airline loyalty schemes', *Tourism Management*, **17**(8), 575–82.

Questions

1. What type of promotion is a frequent flyer loyalty scheme?

2. Can you think of any other similar schemes utilised by other sectors such as retailers, etc.?

3. Identify the major characteristics of a loyalty scheme which is likely to succeed and some of the potential dangers associated with the development and implementation of such schemes.

4. Do you think the relationship marketing approach will become more popular within the wider tourism industry? Give the developments and arguments to support your views.

5. Is competitive advantage eroded if all providers offer similar schemes?

6. Do FFPs necessarily overcome inadequacies in other aspects of the product such as service, inferior route networks, etc.?

Bibliography

● Churchill, D. (1993) 'War in the air', *Sunday Times*, 14 November, p. 8.
● Evans, J. R. and Laskin, R. L. (1994) 'The relationship marketing process: A conceptualisation and application', *Industrial Marketing Management*, **23**(5), 439–52.
● Gilbert, D. (1993) *Study of the Formulation, Control and Implementation of Travel Management Policy*, Thomas Cook Research Centre Report, University of Surrey.
● Gronroos, C. (1990) 'Relationship approach to the marketing function in service contexts: the marketing and organization behavior interface', *Journal of Business Research*, **20**(1), 3–12.
● Mason, G. and Barker, N. (1996) 'Buy now fly later: an investigation of airline frequent flyer programmes', *Tourism Management*, **17**(3), 219–32.
● Mowlana, H. and Smith, G. (1993) 'Tourism in a global context: the case of frequent traveller programs', *Journal of Travel Research*, Winter, 20–26.
● O'Brien, K. (1992) 'European business travel in the 1990s', *Economist Intelligence Unit, Travel and Tourism Analyst*, **1**, 77–89.
● Rosenberg, L. J. and Czepiel, J. A. (1984) 'A marketing approach to customer retention', *Journal of Consumer Marketing*, **1**, 45–51.
● *Travel Trade Gazette* (1992) BA to go it alone with US frequent flyer Plan', 13 February, p. 1.
● Verchere, I. (1993) 'Frequent flyer programmes' *Economist Intelligence Unit, Travel and Tourism Analyst*, **3**, 5–19.

Information technology

Case Study objectives

▬ To provide an analysis of the development and operation of Amadeus, one of the four major GDSs.

▬ To illustrate the type and range of products provided by Amadeus to its customers.

▬ To consider the future development strategies of GDS.

Introduction

Amadeus Global Travel Distribution is a neutral and global computerised distribution and reservation system for the travel industry. It was founded in 1987 and began operating in January 1992. Although European national carriers had developed their own reservation systems which served respective national markets, other factors emerged that made further cooperative technological advancement a necessity:

● The sophistication of CRS in the USA, and the planned expansion of these systems in the 1980s, was seen as a threat to the European aviation industry and served to highlight the need for a comparative, independent system in Europe.

● The imminence of air transport deregulation in Europe made it imperative to create a distribution system able to serve the European and global market.

Thus, Amadeus (and its rival Galileo) emerged as a European response to the American global systems already in place. It had the following objectives:

● To replace existing airline reservation systems in the markets of its owner and partner airlines with a system that would provide a totally neutral distribution system with leading-edge technology.

● To increase the efficiency of airline bookings, dramatically.

● To give equally comprehensive access to car rental and hotel services to create a truly global system.

Ownership of Amadeus

Amadeus's main shareholders are listed below:

- Air France (29%);
- Lufthansa (29%); and
- Iberia (29%);
- Continental Airlines (13%)

In addition, 36 national marketing companies belonging to partner airlines are closely involved in the management and promotion of the system in 115 countries. With over 1 000 employees, Amadeus is organised as a holding company based in Madrid, with three subsidiaries:

- Development (Sophia Antipolis);
- Marketing (Madrid/Sophia Antipolis); and
- Operations (Munich).

In 1995 Amadeus acquired System One, a 100% subsidiary of Continental Airlines and expanded rapidly into the American market.

Goals and objectives of Amadeus

To meet the requirements of the European travel market, the Amadeus CRS is designed as a powerful international complement to the existing national distribution networks. Amadeus has four primary goals:

1. To offer travel service providers (airlines, railways, hotels, car rental firms, tour operators, ferry and cruise lines) a broad-based, efficient distribution network which gives access to the largest travel agency client base in Europe.

2. To offer Amadeus subscribers (travel agencies) a range of products, booking facilities, and support services. This increases their competitiveness allowing local requirements to be met and by integrating their front and back office needs.

3. To offer airlines a neutral display of availability and the possibility of using Amadeus in their sales offices.

4. To provide global service through technical links and alliances with other systems, in order to enable principals to distribute their products globally and also to enable travellers to purchase all types of travel services anywhere and at any time.

The Amadeus product

Amadeus Central System

The Amadeus Central System located in Munich is connected to the world via its own reliable high-speed communication network (Amanet). The Central System and Amanet operate 24 hours a day, 365 days a year. The central system offers all the products and booking facilities required by travel agencies, specifically:

- immediate guaranteed confirmation of airline, car hire and hotel reservations;
- integrated intelligent passenger name records (PNRs) which store all customers' travel data and integrate them with customer profiles stored by agency databases;
- providing on-line information on destinations, principals, airports, formalities, ski and sport events;

- offering on-line training for users; and
- utilising customised procedures to save time.

Products are grouped into:

- Amadeus Air;
- Amadeus Cars;
- Amadeus Hotels; and
- Amadeus Services.

Amadeus Air

In 1996, Amadeus Air incorporated the schedules of 730 airlines, and displayed neutral availability and provided reservations for 432 airlines, giving the choice of thousands of city pairs and millions of routes and connections representing almost all scheduled flights world-wide.

Booking details are transmitted to airlines which update availability and acknowledge the reservation simultaneously by sending a record locator number to Amadeus and agencies. The Amadeus Fare Quote system provides prices automatically for complex itineraries by incorporating the cost and restrictions for all segments and components. Negotiated fares between distribution channel partners can be incorporated into the fare quotation and ticketing process. Amadeus also provides access to live displays of aircraft seat maps and enables agencies to reserve a specific seat number.

Amadeus Cars

Amadeus Cars provides access to 55 global car rental companies and enables the display of information on availability and pricing. Car companies are often displayed according to location and/or terminals of other modes of transportation, such as airports, train stations and ports. Last car availability enables transparency between the fleet stock of car companies and travel agencies. Reservations are confirmed instantly and incorporated in travellers' PNRs, and vouchers are printed automatically.

Amadeus Hotels

Similarly, Amadeus Hotels provides accurate information on 30 000 hotel properties world-wide, covering hundreds of hotel chains. Location, last room availability, hotel features and rates are all shown. Access to major hotel chains gives up-to-date booking information so that agencies can check availability and receive immediate guaranteed confirmation. Amadeus also offers the facility to access and sell special or promotional rates negotiated by travel agencies or the clients themselves. The display and processing of these rates is guaranteed secure: when a reservation is made, the negotiated or special code rate is noted and the rate automatically confirmed by the hotel, along with the booking. Amadeus hotels are also linked to the hotel switches THISCO and WIZ-COM systems, achieving a higher transparency with hotel and other tourism-related CRS.

Amadeus Leisure

Amadeus Leisure enables UK travel agencies to network with AT&T Istel and use Video-text links with tour operators and leisure travel suppliers. This provides an opportunity for travel agencies to use the same computer terminals and network for both leisure and business travel, covering the entire range of products.

Amadeus Service

Amadeus Service groups all the value-added functions and information features which ease the reservation process and provide support for the use of system and products. Central profiles enable agents to secure and access travel-related data for private and corporate clients. Menu-driven and user-friendly displays include all possible information needed for a booking (traveller itinerary, contacts, history, payments, documents) and they are integrated with PNRs for future reference. Changes in clients' travel plans *en route* are easy to handle because all travel agencies connected to Amadeus have the option to authorise specified agencies using Amadeus to share central profiles.

Amadeus Information System

The Amadeus Information System gives extensive and accurate information on travel products and destinations in a number of languages. In order to integrate the front and back office, Amadeus offers the Amadeus Pro Package, a PC/Windows-based travel agency management system that provides an interactive and integrated management and control system.

The benefits of Amadeus

Several benefits are introduced by Amadeus for all its stakeholders:

- time-saving through the provision of single-screen access to all travel, client and agency information that travellers need;
- improvement in service by delivering up-to-date information around the clock in real-time;
- an increase in productivity by making on-screen information easy to find and understand;
- improved economy by maximising efficiency through a stable system performance and rapid response times;
- improved control by integrating intelligent applications that cover the entire travel agency business processes; and
- increased profitability by offering identifying opportunities, cross-selling of products and providing clients with more travel services.

Future strategy

To retain and/or increase market share, Amadeus has outlined a number of future strategies to increase the coverage and range of principals represented on the network. These include the improvement of technology, the extension of services, the enhancement of interactivity between front and back office and a continued emphasis on providing top-quality service to travel agencies and other clients.

The company plans to achieve these objectives by reinforcing and extending Amadeus's market position through three parallel and complementary steps:

1. Expansion through partnership.
2. Expansion using its own resources.
3. Cooperation with other major CRSs.

The main competitive advantage of Amadeus remains its structure which incorporates expertise provided by national marketing companies. This provides a unique local knowledge as well as a constant flow of information which may be utilised to improve the Amadeus product offering. In addition, Amadeus aims to continue to build on its relationship with partners and clients. The company's vision remains: it aims to be the leading GDS in terms of customer satisfaction, product superiority and profitability.

Conclusion

Amadeus is seeking to increase its market-share around the world, especially in areas where shareholders have strong commercial interests. Achieving greater penetration in more travel agencies is absolutely vital for the future of the system and therefore a range of add-ons are already provided in order to offer an integrated solution package to its subscribers. This range will be extended in the future.

Although Internet developments remain low-profile (as they imply a certain degree of disintermediation and can create confrontation with travel agencies), Amadeus and all the other GDSs are looking to the emergent technologies to identify new opportunities – specifically, to reach out and contact the consumer directly.

Despite the fact that the GDS industry remains very volatile and expansion historically has been through mergers and acquisitions, Amadeus and its main competitors (Galileo, Sable and Worldspan) retain a strong position. This position will probably be consolidated despite fierce competition as major players capitalise on their strength to expand globally by serving niche markets Constant innovation and change, however, will characterise the market-place, and the development and implementation of leading-edge technology will be critical for these systems to meet the requirements of the marketplace and ensure future prosperity.

Source: compiled through Amadeus Corporate Communication material.

Questions

1. What do you think might be the disadvantages and drawbacks of the concentration of power amongst the four major GDSs?

2. Who is likely to benefit from the current structure of the GDSs and which groups or regions might suffer as a result of the concentration of ownership?

3. Do you think it likely that GDSs will be circumvented by the advent of new, direct technology (such as the Internet and WWW) and will their power and influence be diluted as a result?

4. How might the further development of GDSs and technology impinge on other aspects of the tourism system, e.g. marketing, demand, supply?

5. Are there any other forms of innovative product distribution or other trends in distribution that might threaten the continued dominance of GDSs?

6. Do you think the future development strategies of Amadeus are appropriate and will they be successful?

A compendium
of tourism
sources

This compendium of tourism sources provides a comprehensive listing of the major academic literature devoted to tourism in printed form. In addition to this list there are also materials in other media such as:

- Software
- World Wide Web
- Television
- Radio
- Film
- Video

- Newspaper
- Trade press
- Promotional materials
- Consultant reports
- Government reports
- Guide books.

This list is testament to the interest that tourism generates and also provides a rich resource for tourism researchers, writers and students to use in their work.

General texts

Bull, A., *The Economics of Travel and Tourism*, Longman, 1995

Burkhart, A. J. and Medlik, S., *Tourism, Past, Present and Future*, Heinemann, 1991

Callaghan, P. (ed.), *Travel and Tourism*, Business Educational Publishers, 1989

Coltman, M., *Introduction to Travel and Tourism*, Van Nostrand Reinhold, 1989

Foster, D., *Travel and Tourism Management*, Macmillan, 1985

Fridgen, J., *Dimensions of Tourism*, AH&MA, 1991

Gee, C. Y., Choy, D. J. L. and Makens, J. C., *The Travel Industry*, Van Nostrand Reinhold, 1989

Gee, C. Y. and Fayos, Sola E. (eds), *International Tourism: A Global Perspective*, WTO, 1997

Holloway, C., *The Business of Tourism*, Addison Wesley Longman, 1994

Howell, D. W., *Passport: An Introduction to the Travel and Tourism Industry*, South Western, 1993

Hudman, L. E., *Tourism: A Shrinking World*, Wiley, 1980

Leiper, N., *The Tourism System*, Massey University Press, 1990

Likorish, L. and Jenkins, C. L., *An Introduction to Tourism*, Butterworth-Heinemann, 1997

Lundberg, D. E., *The Tourist Business*, Van Nostrand Reinhold, 1975

Lundberg, D. E., Stavenga, M. H. and Krishanmoorthy, M., *Tourism Economics*, Wiley, 1995

McIntosh, R., Goeldner, C. and Ritchie, J. R. B., *Tourism: Principles, Practices, Philosophies*, Wiley, 1995

Medlik, S., *Managing Tourism*, Butterworth-Heinemann, 1995

Mill, R. C., *Tourism. The International Business*, Prentice Hall, 1990

Mill, R. C. and Morrison, A., *The Tourism System: An Introductory Text*, Prentice Hall, 1992

Poon, A., *Tourism, Technology and Competitive Strategies* CAB, 1993

Ryan, C., *Recreational Tourism: A Social Science Perspective*, Routledge, 1991

Sharpley, R., *Tourism Tourists and Society*, Elm, 1994

Shaw, G. and Williams, A., *Critical Issues in Tourism*, Blackwell, 1994

Theobald, W. F., *Global Tourism: The Next Decade*, Butterworth-Heinemann, 1994

Tribe, J., *The Economics of Leisure and Tourism: Environments, Markets and Impacts*, Butterworth-Heinemann, 1995

Vellas, F. and Becherel, L., *International Tourism*, Macmillan, 1995

Wahab, S., *Tourism Management*, Tourism International Press, 1993

Ward, J., *Tourism in Action*, Stanley Thornes, 1991

Witt, S., Brooke, M. Z. and Buckley, P. J., *The Management of International Tourism*, Unwin Hyman, 1995

Geographical and regional studies

Barke, M., Towner, J. and Newton, M. T. (eds), *Tourism in Spain: Critical Issues*, CAB, 1996

Boniface, B. and Cooper, C., *The Geography of Travel and Tourism*, Butterworth-Heinemann, 1994

Burton, R., *Travel Geography*, Addison Wesley Longman, 1991

Conlin, M. V. and Baum, T., *Island Tourism*, Wiley, 1995

Davidson, R., *Tourism in Europe*, Addison Wesley Longman, 1992

Drakakis-Smith, G. and Lockhart, D., *Island Tourism: Trends and Prospects*, Pinter, 1997

Farrell, B. H., *Hawaii, the Legend that Sells*, University Of Hawaii Press, 1982

Gayle, D. J., *Tourism Marketing and Management in the Caribbean*, Routledge, 1993

Hall, C. M. and Johnston, M., *Polar Tourism*, Wiley, 1995

Hall, D., *Tourism and Economic Development in Eastern Europe and the Soviet Union*, Belhaven, 1991

Harrison, D., *Tourism and Less Developed Countries*, Wiley, 1994

Herbote, B., *World Tourism Directory: Part 1 Europe; Part 2 The Americas; Part 3 Africa, Middle East, Asia and Oceania.* Saur/Reed Travel and WTO, 1995

Hernmann, E., Hitchcock, M. J., King, V. T. and Parnwell, M. (eds), *Tourism in South East Asia*, Routledge, 1992

Hitchcock, M., *Tourism in South East Asia*, Routledge, 1993

Hudman, L. E., *Geography of Travel and Tourism*, Delmar, 1990

Jackson, I., *An Introduction to Tourism in Australia*, Hospitality Press, 1989

Lavery, P. (ed.), *Recreational Geography*, David and Charles, 1971

Lea, J., *Tourism and Development in the Third World*, Routledge, 1988

Montanaria, A. and Williams, A., *European Tourism: Regions, Spaces and Restructuring*, Wiley, 1995

Pearce, D., *Tourism Today. A Geographical Analysis*, Longman, 1995

Pompl, W. and Lavery, P. (eds), *Tourism in Europe: Structures and Developments*, CAB, 1993

Quinn, B., World Travel Guide CD-ROM (Windows), Columbus Press, 1997

Quinn, B., *World Travel Guide*, Columbus Press, 1997

Richter, L. K., *The Politics of Tourism in Asia*, University of Hawaii Press, 1989

Shaw, G. and Williams, A. M., *Critical Issues in Tourism: A Geographical Perspective*, Blackwell, 1994

Sinclair, T. and Stabler, M. (eds), *The Tourism Industry: An International Analysis*, CAB, 1991

Taylor, M., *World Travel Atlas*, Columbus Press, 1997

Williams, A. M. and Shaw, G. J. (eds), *Tourism and Economic Development: Western European Experiences*, Belhaven Press, 1991

Historical perspectives

Brendon, P., *Thomas Cook. 150 Years of Popular Tourism*, Secker, 1990

Pimlott, J. A. R., *The Englishman's Holiday*, Faber and Faber, 1947

Soane, J., *Fashionable Resort Regions, Their Evolution and Transformation*, CAB, 1993

Swinglehurst, E., *Cooks Tours, the Story of Popular Travel*, Blandford Press, 1982

Towner, J., *An Historical Geography of Recreation and Tourism*, Belhaven, 1994

Turner, L. and Ash, J., *The Golden Hordes, International Tourism and the Pleasure Periphery*, Constable, 1975

Research

Baron, R., *Travel and Tourism Data, a Comprehensive Research Handbook*, Euromonitor, 1989

Butler, R. W. and Pearce, D. G. (eds), *Tourism Research*, Routledge, 1993

Frechtling, D., *Practical Tourism Forecasting*, Butterworth-Heinemann, 1996

Pearce, D. and Butler, R. (eds), *Tourism Research, Critiques and Challenges*, Routledge, 1993

Pearce, P. L., *The Ulysses Factor, Evaluating Visitors in Tourist Settings*, Springer Verlag, 1988

Poynter, J. M., *How to Research and Write a Thesis in Hospitality and Tourism*, Wiley, 1993

Ritchie, J. R. B. and Goeldner, C. R., *Travel, Tourism and Hospitality Research. A Handbook for Managers and Researchers*, Wiley, 1994

Ryan, C., *Researching Tourist Satisfaction, Issues, Concepts and Problems*, Routledge, 1995

Smith, S., *Recreation Geography*, Longman, 1983

Smith, S., *Tourism Analysis: A Handbook*, Addison Wesley Longman, 1994

Veal, A., *Research Methods for Leisure and Tourism*, Longman, 1992

Witt, S. and Witt, C., *Modelling and Forecasting Demand in Tourism*, Academic Press, 1991

Leisure and recreation

Ashworth, G., *Recreation and Tourism*, Bell and Hyman, 1984

Borrett, N., *Leisure and Tourism Services*, Macmillan, 1991

Dumazedier, J., *Towards a Society of Leisure*, Free Press, 1967

Glyptis, S., *Leisure and the Environment*, Wiley, 1993

Graefe, A. and Parker, S. (eds), *Recreation and Leisure, An Introductory Handbook*, Venture Publishing, 1987

Henry, I. (ed.), *Management and Planning in the Leisure Industries*, Macmillan, 1990

Iso-Ahola, S. E., *The Social Psychology of Leisure and Recreation*, W. C. Brown, 1980

Jubenville, A., Twight, D. W. and Becker, R. H., *Outdoor Recreation Management Theory and Applications*, Venture Publishing, 1987

Kelly, J. R., *Leisure*, Prentice Hall, 1990

Maccannell, D., *The Tourist, a New Theory of the Leisure Class*, Macmillan, 1976

Mercer, D., *In Pursuit of Leisure*, Sorret, 1980

Patmore, J. A., *Land and Leisure*, Penguin, 1972

Patmore, J. A., *Recreation and Resources*, Blackwell, 1983

Pigram, J., *Outdoor Recreation and Resource Management*, Croom Helm, 1993

Stowkowski, P. A., *Leisure in Society, a Network Structural Perspective*, Mansell, 1994

Development, planning and policy

Ashworth, G. and Dietvorst, A., *Tourism and Spatial Transformations: Implications for Policy and Planning*, CAB, 1995

Bodlender, J. and Gerty, M., *Guidelines on Tourism Investment*, WTO, 1992

Bodlender, J. and Ward, T., *An Examination of Tourism Investment Incentives*, WTO, 1982

Chopra, S., *Tourism and Development in India*, Ashish Publishers, 1991

Cooper, C. and Wanhill, S., *Tourism Development: Environmental and Community Issues*, Wiley, 1997

De Kadt, E., *Tourism, Passport to Development*, Oxford University Press, 1979

Edgell, D., *International Tourism Policy*, Van Nostrand Reinhold, 1990

Farrell, B. H., *Tourism and the Physical Environment*, Pergamon, 1987

Gearing, S. E., Swart, W. W. and Var, T. (eds), *Planning for Tourism Development*, Praeger, 1976

Gee, C. Y., *Resort Development and Management*, AH&MA, 1988

Getz, D., *Festivals, Special Events and Tourism*, Van Nostrand Reinhold, 1991

Gunn, C. A., *Vacationscape, Designing Tourist Regions*, Van Nostrand Reinhold, 1988

Gunn, C., *Tourism Planning*, Taylor and Francis, 1994

Hall, C. M., *Hallmark Tourist Events, Impacts, Management, Planning*, Belhaven Press, 1992

Hall, C. M., *Tourism and Politics*, Wiley, 1994

Hall, C. M. and Jenkins, J. M., *Tourism and Public Policy*, Routledge, 1994

Hawkins, D. E., Shafer, E. L. and Rovelstadt, J. M. (eds), *Tourism Planning and Development Issues*, George Washington University Press, 1980

Inskeep, E., *Tourism Planning – An Integrated Planning and Development Approach*, Van Nostrand Reinhold, 1991

Inskeep, E., *National and Regional Planning, Methodologies and Case Studies*, WTO/ Routledge, 1993

Inskeep, E. and Kallenberger, M., *An Integrated Approach to Resort Development*, WTO, 1992

Jansen-Verbeke, M., *Leisure, Recreation and Tourism in Inner Cities*, Routledge, 1988

Johnson, P. and Thomas, B. (eds), *Perspectives on Tourism Policy*, Mansell, 1992

Kinniard, V. H. and Hall, D. R. (eds), *Tourism Development: The Gender Dimension*, Belhaven, 1994

Law, C., *Urban Tourism: Attracting Visitors to Large Cities*, Mansell, 1993

Laws, E., *Tourist Destination Management, Issues, Analysis and Policies*, Routledge, 1995

Lawson, F., *Hotels and Resorts: Planning, Design and Refurbishment*, Butterworth-Heinemann, 1995

Lawson, F. R. and Baud-Bovy, M., *Tourism Recreation and Development – A Handbook of Physical Planning*, Longman, 1989

Lickorish, L. J. (ed.), *Developing Tourism Destinations, Policies and Perspectives*, Longman, 1991

Murphy, P., *Quality Management in Urban Tourism*, Wiley, 1997

Page, S., *Urban Tourism*, Routledge, 1994

Pearce, D., *Tourist Development*, Longman, 1989

Pearce, D., *Tourist Organisations*, Longman, 1992

Powers, T., *Appraising International Tourism Projects*, Inter-American Development Bank, 1974

Uzzell, D. (ed.), *Heritage Interpretation* (2 volumes), Belhaven Press, 1989

Ward, T. and Dillon, M., *Guidelines to Hotel and Leisure Project Financing*, WTO, 1991

Impacts and sustainability

Boissevain, J., *Coping With Tourists: European Reaction to Mass Tourism*, Berghahn Books, 1996

Boo, E., *Ecotourism: The Potentials and Pitfalls*, World Wildlife Fund, 1990

Bramwell, W. and Lane, B. (eds), *Rural Tourism and Sustainable Rural Development*, Channel View Publications, 1993

Bramwell, W., Henry, I., Jackson, G., Prat, A., Richards, G. and Van Der Straaten, J., *Sustainable Tourism Management: Principles and Practice*, Tilburg University Press, 1996

Briassoulis, H, and Van Der Straaten, J. (eds), *Tourism and the Environment: Regional, Economic and Policy Issues*, Kluwer, 1993

Briguglio, L. (ed.), *Sustainable Tourism*, Cassell, 1995

Burns, P. M. and Holden, A., *Tourism, a New Perspective*, Prentice Hall, 1995

Butler, R. and Hinch, T., *Tourism and Indigenous Peoples*, International Thomson Business Press, 1996

Clift, S. and Page, S. (eds), *Health Issues in Tourism Management*, Routledge, 1996

Coccosis, H. and Nijcamp, P., *Sustainable Tourism Development*, Avebury-Gower, 1995

Craig-Smith, S., *Learning to Live With Tourism*, Addison Wesley Longman, 1994

Croall, J., *Preserve or Destroy: Tourism and the Environment*, Calousie Gulbenkian/Tourism Concern, 1995

Eber, S. (ed.), *Beyond the Green Horizon: Principles of Sustainable Tourism*, Tourism Concern, 1995

Edington, J. M. and Edington, M. A., *Ecology, Recreation and Tourism*, Cambridge University Press, 1990

Forsyth, T., *Sustainable Tourism: Moving from Theory to Practice*, World Wide Fund for Nature/Tourism Concern, 1996

Glasson, J., Godfrey, K. and Goodey, B., *Towards Visitor Impact Management: Visitor Impacts, Carrying Capacity and Management Responses in Europe's Historic Towns and Cities*, Avebury, 1995

Harris, R. and Leiper, N., *Sustainable Tourism – An Australian Perspective*, Butterworth-Heinemann, 1995

Harrison, L. and Husbands, W., *Practising Responsible Tourism*, Wiley, 1996

Hunter, C. and Green, H., *Tourism and Environment: A Sustainable Relationship?* Routledge, 1995

Jenner, P. and Smith, C., *Tourism Industry and the Environment*, EIU, 1995

Krippendorf, J., *The Holiday Makers – Understanding the Impact of Leisure and Travel*, Heinemann, 1987

Lowman, G. and Cater, E., *Ecotourism*, Wiley, 1994

Maccannell, D., *Empty Meeting Grounds*, Routledge, 1992

Mason, P. and Mowforth, M., *Codes of Conduct in Tourism*, Occasional Papers In Geography, University of Plymouth, 1995

Mathieson, A. and Wall, G., *Tourism: Economic, Physical and Social Impacts*, Longman, 1989

Murphy, P. E., *Tourism, a Community Approach*, Methuen, 1991

OECD, *Case Studies of the Impact of Tourism on the Environment*, OECD, 1981

Pearce, D., and Butler, R. (eds), *Change in Tourism: People, Places, Processes*, Routledge, 1995

Pizam, A. and Mansfield, Y., *Tourism, Crime and International Security Issues*, Wiley, 1996

Price, M., *People and Tourism in Fragile Environments*, Wiley, 1996

Shackley, M., *Wildlife Tourism*, Thomson International Business Press, 1996

Smith, V. L. and Eadington, W. R. (eds), *Tourism Alternatives: Potential Problems in the Development of Tourism*, University of Pennsylvania Press, 1995

WTO, *Sustainable Tourism Development: Lessons for Local Planners*, WTO, 1993

Ziffer, K., *Ecotourism: The Uneasy Alliance*, Ernst and Young, 1989

Socio-cultural and heritage perspectives

Ashworth, G. J. and Tunbridge, J. E., *The Tourist – Historic City*, Belhaven, 1990

Boniface, P. and Fowler, P., *Heritage and Tourism in the Global Village*, Routledge, 1993

Dann, G. S., *The Language of Tourism*, CAB, 1997

Fladmark, M., *Cultural Tourism*, Dunhead, 1995

Harrison, R. (ed.), *Manual of Heritage Management*, Butterworth-Heinemann, 1994

Herbert, D. (ed.), *Heritage Sites, Strategies for Marketing and Development*, Gower, 1992

Nash, D., *The Anthropology of Tourism*, Pergamon, 1996

Pearce, P. L., *The Social Psychology of Tourist Behaviour*, Pergamon, 1982

Richards, G., *Cultural Tourism in Europe*, CAB, 1996

Robinson, M. (ed.), *Culture as the Tourist Product*, Business Education Publishers, 1996

Ross, G. F., *The Psychology of Tourism*, Hospitality Press, 1996

Ryan, C. (ed.), *The Tourist Experience. A New Introduction*, Cassell, 1997

Selwyn, T., *The Tourist Image: Myths and Myth Making in Tourism*, Wiley, 1996

Smith, V. L., *Hosts and Guests*, University of Pennsylvania Press, 1989

Urry, J., *The Tourist Gaze*, Sage Publications, 1990

Weiler, B. and Hall, C. M., *Special Interest Tourism*, Wiley, 1992

The industry

Adams, D., *Management Accounting for the Hospitality Industry*, Cassell, 1995

Andrew, W. P. and Schmidgall, R. S., *Financial Management for the Hospitality Industry*, AH&MA, 1993

Angelo, R. M. and Vladimir, A. N., *Hospitality Today*, AH&MA, 1994

Astroff, M. T., *Convention Sales and Services*, Waterbury Press, 1991

Atkinson, H. and Jarvis, R., *Business Accounting for Hospitality and Tourism*, Thomson Business Press, 1995

Beaver, A., *Mind Your Own Travel Business, a Manual of Retail Travel Practice* (3 volumes), Beaver Travel Publishers, 1993

Davidson, R., *Business Travel*, Addison Wesley Longman, 1994

Fay, B., *Essentials of Tour Management*, Prentice Hall, 1992

Foster, D., *Business of Travel Agency Operations*, McGraw Hill, 1991

Gee, C., *Resort Development and Management*. AH&MA, 1988

Go, F. and Pine, R., *Globalisation Strategy in the Hotel Industry*, International Thomson Business Press, 1995

Gregory, A., *A Travel Agent: Dealer in Dreams*, Prentice Hall, 1993

Grover, R., *The Disney Touch*, Business One, 1991

Harris, P., *Accounting and Finance in the International Hospitality Industry*, Butterworth-Heinemann, 1997

Hodgson, A. (ed.), *The Travel and Tourism Industries, Strategies for the Future*, Pergamon, 1987

Jones, P., *Introduction to Hospitality Operations*, Cassell, 1995

Jones, P. and Pizam, A. (eds), *The International Hospitality Industry: Organizational and Operational Issues*, Addison Wesley Longman, 1993

Knowles, T., *Hospitality Management: An Introduction*, Addison Wesley Longman, 1992

Knowles, T., *Corporate Strategy for Hospitality*, Addison Wesley Longman, 1996

Lattin, G. W., *The Lodging and Food Service Industry*, AH&MA, 1993

Laws, E., *Managing Packaged Tourism: Relationships, Responsibilities, and Service Quality in the Inclusive Holiday Industry*, International Thomson Business Press, 1997

Lockwood, A. and Jones, P., *The Management of Hotel Operations*, Cassell, 1988

Lundberg, D. E., *The Tourism Business*, Van Nostrand Reinhold, 1990

Mills, P., *Quality in the Leisure Industry*, Longman, 1992

Owen, C., *Accounting for Hospitality, Tourism and Leisure*, Addison Wesley Longman, 1994

Powers, T., *Introduction to the Hospitality Industry*, Wiley, 1995

Powers, T., *Introduction to Management in the Hospitality Industry*, Wiley, 1995

Poynter, M., *Tour Design and Management*, Prentice Hall, 1993

Renshaw, M., *The Travel Agent*, Business Education Publishers, 1992

Rogers, H. and Slinn, J., *Tourism: Management of Facilities*, M & E Handbooks, 1993

Swarbrooke, J., *The Development and Management of Visitor Attractions*, Butterworth-Heinemann, 1995

Syrart, G., *Manual of Travel Agent Practice*, Butterworth-Heinemann, 1995

Teare, R. and Boer, A., *Strategic Hospitality Management*, Cassell, 1991

Teare, R. and Olsen, M., *International Hospitality Management*, Addison Wesley Longman, 1992

Teare, R., Adams, D. and Messenger, S. (eds), *Managing Projects in Hospitality Organisations*, Cassell, 1992

Venison, P., *Managing Hotels*, Butterworth-Heinemann, 1983

Watt, D., *Leisure and Events Management and Organisation Manual*, Longman, 1992

Yale, P., *The Business of Tour Operations*, Addison Wesley Longman, 1995

WTTC, *Travel and Tourism: A New Economic Perspective*, World Travel & Tourism Council, 1993

Legal perspectives

Appleton, A., *Cases and Materials on Tourism Law*, Elm Publications, 1992

Bowen, A., *The Implementation of the European Directive on Package Travel*, Addison Wesley Longman, 1994

Corke, J., *Tourism Law*, Elm Publications, 1988

Downes, D. and Paton, A. *Travel Agency Law*, Addison Wesley Longman, 1993

Pannett, A., *Principles of Hotel and Catering Law*, Cassell, 1992

Poustie, M., Geddes, N., Stewart, W. and Ross, J., *Hospitality and Tourism Law*, Thomson Business Press, 1996

Human resource management/education and training

Baum, T., *Manpower in Tourism*, Butterworth, 1991

Baum, T., *Human Resources in International Tourism*, Butterworth-Heinemann, 1993

Baum, T., *Human Resources Management for the European Tourism and Hospitality*, Butterworth-Heinemann, 1994

Cooper, C., Shepherd, R. and Westlake, J., *Educate the Educators: A Manual of Tourism and Hospitality Education*, WTO, 1996

Hall, D. and Kinnaird, V., *Tourism: A Gender Analysis*, Wiley, 1994

Lockwood, A. and Jones, P., *People and the Hotel and Catering Industry*, Cassell, 1993

Mullins, L., *Hospitality Management: A Human Resources Approach*, Addison Wesley Longman, 1995

Nelson, H. H. (ed.), *Tourism and Social Science*, Pergamon, 1991

Riley, M., *Human Resource Management: A Guide to Personnel Management in the Hotel and Catering Industries*, Butterworth Heinemann, 1996

Wood, R., *Organisational Behaviour for Hospitality Management*, Butterworth-Heinemann, 1994

Woods, R. H., *Managing Hospitality Human Resources*, AH&MA, 1992

Transportation

Ashford, N., *Airport Operations*, Addison Wesley Longman, 1991

Blackshaw, C., *Aviation Law and Regulation*, Addison Wesley Longman, 1992

Cole, S., *Applied Transport Economics*, Kogan Page, 1987

Doganis, R. D., *Flying Off Course – The Economics of International Airlines*, George Allen & Unwin, 1985

Doganis, R., *The Airport Business*, Routledge, 1992

Gialloreto, L., *Strategic Airline Management*, Addison Wesley Longman, 1988

Graham, B., *Geography and Air Transport*, Wiley, 1995

Hanion, P., *Global Airlines: Competition in a Transnational Industry*, Butterworth-Heinemann, 1995

Miller, J. C. and Sawers, P., *The Technical Development of Modern Aviation*, Routledge, 1988

Page, S., *Transport for Tourism*, Routledge, 1994

Shaw, S., *Airline Marketing and Management*, Addison Wesley Longman, 1987

Wheatcroft, S., *Aviation and Tourism Policies: Balancing the Benefits*, Routledge/WTO, 1994

Wheatcroft, S. and Lipman, G., *European Liberalisation and World Air Transport: Towards a Transnational Policy*, Economist Intelligence Unit, Special Report, No. 2015, 1990

Marketing

Abbey, J. R., *Hospitality Sales and Advertising*, AH&MaA, 1993

Ashworth, G. and Goodall, B. (eds), *Marketing Tourism Places*, Routledge, 1990

Buttle, F., *Hotel and Food Service Marketing*, Holt, 1986

Crotts, J. C. and Van Raaij, W. F. (eds), *Economic Psychology of Travel and Tourism*, Haworth Press, 1995

Czepiel, J. A., Soloman, M. R. and Surprenant, C. F. (eds), *The Service Encounter*, Lexington Books, 1985

Foster, D., *Sales and Marketing for the Travel Professional*, McGraw Hill, 1991

French, Y., *PR in Leisure and Tourism*, Addison Wesley Longman, 1994

Gold, J. and Ward, S., *Place Promotion: The Use of PR to Sell Places*, Belhaven, 1993

Goodall, B. and Ashworth, G. (eds), *Marketing in the Tourism Industry: The Promotion of Destination Regions*, Croom Helm, 1988

Heath, E. and Wall, G., *Marketing Tourism Destinations: A Strategic Planning Approach*, Wiley, 1992

Hollins, G. and Hollins, B., *Total Design, Managing the Design Process in the Service Sector*, Addison Wesley Longman, 1991

Holloway, J. C. and Robinson, C., *Marketing for Tourism*, Longman, 1995

Horner, S. and Swarbrooke, J., *Marketing Tourism Leisure and Hospitality in Europe*, International Thomson Business Press, 1996

Jefferson, A. and Lickorish, L., *Marketing Tourism*, Longman, 1988

Johnson, P. and Thomas, B. (eds), *Choice and Demand in Tourism*, Mansell, 1992

Jung, G. P., *A Practical Guide to Selling Travel*, Prentice Hall, 1993

King, B., *Tourism Marketing in Australia*, Hospitality Press, 1989

Kotler, P., Haider, D. H. and Rein, L., *Marketing Places*, The Free Press, 1993

Kotler, P., Bowen, S. and Makens, S., *Marketing for Hospitality and Tourism*, Prentice Hall, 1996

Laws, E., *Tourism Marketing, Service and Quality Management Perspectives*, Stanley Thornes, 1991

Lovelock, C. H., *Managing Services Marketing Operations and Human Resources*, Prentice Hall, 1992

Masternbroek, W. (ed.), *Managing for Quality in the Service Sector*, Blackwell Business, 1991

Mckenna, R., *Relationship Marketing, Successful Strategies for the Age of the Customer*, Addison Wesley Longman, 1991

Middleton, V. T. C., *Marketing in Travel and Tourism*, Butterworth-Heinemann, 1995

Morrison, A. M., *Hospitality and Travel Marketing*, Delmar, 1989

Moutinho, L., *Consumer Behaviour in Tourism*, MCB University Press, 1987

Payne, A., *The Essence of Services Marketing*, Prentice Hall, 1993

Seaton, A. and Bennett, M., *Marketing Tourism Products: Concepts, Issues and Cases*, International Thomson Business Press, 1996

Teare, R., Olsen, M. D. and Gummesson, E. (eds), *Service Quality in Hospitality Organisations*, Cassell, 1995

Uysal, M. and Fesenmaier, D. R. (eds), *Communication and Channel Systems in Tourism Marketing*, Haworth Press, 1993

Wahab, S., Crampon, L. J. and Rothfield, L. M., *Tourism Marketing*, Tourism International Press, 1976

Information technology

Braham, B., *Computer Systems in the Hotel and Catering Industry*, Cassell, 1988

Inkpen, G., *Information Technology for Travel and Tourism*, Addison Wesley Longman, 1994

Klien, S., Schmid, B., Tjoa, A. and Werther, H. (eds), *Information and Communication Technologies in Tourism*, Springer-Verlag, 1996

Moutinho, L., Rita, P. and Curry, B., *Expert Systems in Tourism Marketing*, Routledge, 1996

O'Connor, J., *Using Computers in Hospitality*, Cassell, 1995

Peacock, M., *Information Technology in Hospitality*, Cassell, 1995

Dictionaries, yearbooks and encyclopaedias

Cooper, C. and Lockwood, A. (eds) (annual), *Progress in Tourism, Recreation and Hospitality Management*, Volumes 1–6, Belhaven

Khan, M., Olsen, M. and Var, T., *Encyclopedia of Hospitality and Tourism*, Van Nostrand Reinhold, 1993

Medlik, S., *Dictionary of Transport, Travel and Hospitality*, Butterworth-Heinemann, 1993

Ritchie, J. R. B. and Hawkins, D. (eds) (annual), *World Travel and Tourism Review*, Volumes 1–3, CAB

Seaton, A., Wood, R., Dieke, P. and Jenkins, C. (eds), *Tourism – The State of the Art: the Strathclyde Symposium*, Wiley, 1994

Witt, S. F. and Mountinho, L. (eds), *Tourism Marketing and Management Handbook*, 2nd edn, Prentice Hall, 1994

Witt, S. F. and Mountinho, L. (eds), *Tourism Marketing and Management Handbook. Student Edition*, Prentice Hall, 1995

Abstracts

Articles in Tourism (Monthly), Universities of Bournemouth, Oxford Brookes and Surrey

International Tourism and Hospitality Data Base CD-Rom, The Guide to Industry and Academic Resources, Wiley

Leisure, Recreation and Tourism Abstracts (Quarterly), CAB

The Travel and Tourism Index, Brigham Young University Hawaii Campus, USA

Statistical sources

OECD, *Tourism Policy and International Tourism in OECD Member Countries*, OECD (annual)

WTO, *Compendium of Tourism Statistics*, WTO (annual)

Tourism journals

Annals of Tourism Research
Asia Pacific Journal of Tourism Research
Current Issues in Tourism
Festival Management and Event Tourism
International Tourism Reports
Journal of Air Transport Management
Journal of Air Transport Geography
Journal of Sustainable Tourism
Journal of Tourism Studies
Journal of Travel and Tourism Marketing
Journal of Travel Research

Journal of Vacation Marketing
Progress in Tourism and Hospitality Research
Service Industries Journal
The Tourist Review
Tourism Analysis
Tourism, Culture and Communication
Tourism Economics
Tourism Management
Tourism Recreation Research
Travel and Tourism Analyst

Hospitality journals

Australian Journal of Hospitality Management
Cornell Hotel and Restaurant Administration Quarterly
FIU Hospitality Review
Hospitality and Tourism Educator
International Journal of Contemporary Hospitality Management
International Journal of Hospitality and Tourism Technology
International Journal of Hospitality Management
International Journal of Service Industry Management
Journal of Hospitality and Leisure Marketing
Journal of Hospitality and Tourism Research

Leisure journals

Journal of Applied Recreation Research
Journal of Leisure Research
Journal of Park and Recreation Administration
Journal of Sports Tourism
Leisure Futures
Leisure Sciences
Leisure Studies
Managing Leisure
Mintel Leisure Intelligence Journal
Society and Leisure
Visions in Leisure and Business
World Leisure and Recreation Association Journal

Index